Theoretical Research Programs: Studies in the Growth of Theory

Contributors

Joseph Berger
Bruce Bueno de Mesquita
Elizabeth G. Cohen
Karen S. Cook
Thomas J. Fararo
Rebecca Ford
Louis N. Gray
David R. Heise
Guillermina Jasso
Edward J. Lawler
Neil J. MacKinnon
Barry Markovsky
Linda D. Molm
John Skvoretz
Jonathan H. Turner
David G. Wagner
Henry A. Walker
David Willer
Toshio Yamagishi
Morris Zelditch, Jr.

THEORETICAL
RESEARCH
PROGRAMS

Studies in the Growth of Theory

EDITED BY

Joseph Berger and Morris Zelditch, Jr.

STANFORD UNIVERSITY PRESS
STANFORD, CALIFORNIA
1993

Stanford University Press
Stanford, California

© 1993 by the Board of Trustees of the
Leland Stanford Junior University

Printed in the United States of America

CIP data are at the end of the book

TO OUR CHILDREN

Adam David Berger, Rachel Leah Berger, and Gideon Olen Berger
Miriam Leah Zelditch and Steven Morris Zelditch

Contents

Contributors

Joseph Berger (Ph.D., Harvard University) is Professor of Sociology and Senior Fellow (By Courtesy) at the Hoover Institution. He was Chairman of the Department of Sociology at Stanford University from 1976 to 1983 and 1985 to 1989. He is the recipient of the 1991 Cooley-Mead Award. His current research interests are status processes and expectation states, reward expectations and distributive justice, and problems in the development of cumulative theory in sociology. He has coauthored and coedited many publications, including *Expectation States Theory: A Theoretical Research Program*; *Status Characteristics and Social Interaction*; *Status, Rewards, and Influence: How Expectations Organize Behavior*; *Types of Formalization in Small Groups Research*; and *Sociological Theories in Progress*, Volumes I, II, and III.

Bruce Bueno de Mesquita is Senior Fellow at the Hoover Institution, Stanford University, and Professor of Political Science at the University of Rochester. He received his Ph.D. in Political Science from the University of Michigan in 1971. His research interests include the causes and consequences of international conflict, applications of game theory to policy analysis and political forecasting, and the investigation of democratic politics. He has recently completed *War and Reason* (with David Lalman), published by Yale University Press in 1992.

Elizabeth G. Cohen is Professor of Education and Sociology, Stanford University. She received her Ph.D. in Sociology from Harvard's Department of Social Relations in 1958. Her research interests include the organization of teaching, the social structure of classrooms, and the treatment of status inequalities in desegregated and multilingual classrooms. She serves as Director of the Program for Complex Instruction.

KAREN S. COOK is Professor of Sociology and Chair of the Department at the University of Washington. She is the former editor of *Social Psychology Quarterly*. Her recent work includes *Social Exchange Theory* (1987), *The Future of Sociology* (edited with Borgatta, 1988) and *The Limits of Rationality* (edited with Levi, 1990). She is involved in research on social exchange, networks, trust, and social justice.

THOMAS J. FARARO is Professor of Sociology at the University of Pittsburgh. His primary research interests concern the formalization and unification of theoretical frameworks in sociology. His published work includes *Mathematical Sociology* (Wiley, 1973) and *The Meaning of General Theoretical Sociology: Tradition and Formalization* (Cambridge, 1989).

REBECCA FORD received her Ph.D. in Sociology from the University of Iowa in 1988, and is currently Assistant Professor of Sociology at the University of Florida. Her interests are social psychology, theory, group processes, and gender. She is engaged in research on how power differences affect the tactical behavior of lower power actors in a conflict. Her work has appeared in the *American Sociological Review* and *Social Psychology Quarterly*.

LOUIS N. GRAY is Professor of Sociology at Washington State University. His primary research interests concern the mathematical structure of choice and decision processes in individual and interactive settings and the implications of these processes for behavioral power relations involving external feedback. His work has appeared primarily in *Social Psychology Quarterly*, *Social Forces*, and *Small Group Research*.

DAVID R. HEISE received his doctorate from the University of Chicago in 1964, and he currently is Rudy Professor of Sociology at Indiana University. Aside from his research on social interaction, he has published a book on causal analysis, and he is a past editor of *Sociological Methodology* and of *Sociological Methods and Research*.

GUILLERMINA JASSO is Professor of Sociology at New York University. Research interests include general sociological theory (mathematically expressed) and methods for both theoretical and empirical analysis, as well as topics in inequality, distributive justice, sexuality, and international migration. Recent work includes "Self-Interest, Distributive Justice, and the Income Distribution: A Theoretical Fragment Based on St. Anselm's Postulate" (*Social Justice Research*, 1989); *The New Chosen People: Immigrants in the United States*, with M. R. Rosenzweig (Russell

Sage, 1990); "Methods for the Theoretical and Empirical Analysis of Comparison Processes" (*Sociological Methodology*, 1990); and "Choice and Emotion in Comparison Theory" (*Rationality and Society*, 1993).

EDWARD J. LAWLER is Duane C. Spriestersbach Professor of Liberal Arts and a member of the Department of Sociology at the University of Iowa. His current research includes analyses of power in dyadic bargaining and in larger social exchange networks. He is working on a theory that explains the emergence of ritual behavior in social exchange. He is editor of the series *Advances in Group Processes* (JAI Press), and coauthor (with Samuel B. Bacharach) of *Power and Politics in Organizations* (1980) and *Bargaining: Power, Tactics, and Outcomes* (1981).

NEIL J. MACKINNON received his doctorate from the University of Illinois in 1970 and currently is Professor in the Department of Sociology and Anthropology at the University of Guelph in Ontario, Canada. He has done extensive empirical research on affect control theory with Canadian respondents, and in a forthcoming book he relates affect control theory to classical symbolic interactionism. He additionally has done research on status attainment and on norms.

BARRY MARKOVSKY is Associate Professor of Sociology at the University of Iowa. He received his Ph.D. in 1983 from Stanford University. His research has included theoretical and empirical work on issues of justice, power, and status in groups, using survey, laboratory, and computer simulation techniques. His current research focuses on interactions between individual decision strategies and larger relational patterns in social exchange networks, and their consequences for variations in social outcomes and network structure.

LINDA D. MOLM is Professor of Sociology at the University of Arizona. She received her Ph.D. in Sociology from the University of North Carolina in 1976. Her primary research interest is the experimental analysis of theories of social exchange and power. She is currently investigating how risk in nonnegotiated exchange affects the link between structure and action for both reward–based and coercive forms of power.

JOHN SKVORETZ is Professor of Sociology and Chair of the Department at the University of South Carolina. He received his Ph.D. in Sociology from the University of Pittsburgh in 1976. His research interests center around the mathematical study of social structures. He is currently working on formal models of exchange and power in network and on the biased net theory of social structures and intergroup relations.

JONATHAN H. TURNER is Professor of Sociology at the University of California at Riverside. He received his Ph.D. from Cornell University in 1968. His primary research interests revolve around developing general explanatory theory, although he has done work in several substantive fields, including stratification, race and ethnic relations, social institutions, sociology of law, sociobiology, and American social structure. He is author of eighteen books, plus three edited volumes, and numerous articles in professional sociology and anthropology journals. He is currently writing a three-volume work entitled "A General Theory of Social Organization."

DAVID G. WAGNER is Associate Professor of Sociology at the State University of New York at Albany. He has published extensively in theory and social psychology. His work on theory and theory growth includes two books, *The Growth of Sociological Theories* and *Postmodernism and Social Theory* (edited with Steven Seidman). He has also published theory and research in the expectation states program concerned with the reduction of status inequality (especially with respect to gender), preferences for reward allocation, and the social control of status deviance. He is currently testing implications of the relation between task and reward expectations and completing a book that further develops his ideas about theory generation, analysis, and growth.

HENRY A. WALKER is Professor of Sociology at Cornell University. He received the Ph.D. in Sociology from Stanford University in 1979. His published work includes studies of the legitimacy of status structures, race and family structure, and the use of scope statements in formal theories. His current work focuses on gender differences in task organization, the status attainments of black Americans, and the testing and reformulation of theories of legitimacy.

DAVID WILLER is Professor and Director of the Laboratory for Sociological Research, University of South Carolina. He received his Ph.D. in Sociology from Purdue University in 1964. His research has included the development of theoretic methods and the historical study of power structures. Currently, his research focuses on a program developing elementary theory and experimentally testing its predictions.

TOSHIO YAMAGISHI is Professor of Social Psychology at Hokkaido University, Sapporo, Japan, and an Abe Fellow. He has published theoretical,

experimental, and simulation work on social dilemmas, equity, and social exchange networks both in English and Japanese. His book, *Social
Dilemmas*, has been published in Japanese. His recent research interests
are on cross-cultural comparison of the structure and the role of interpersonal trust, prisoner's dilemma networks, evolution of social norms,
and social exchange networks.

Morris Zelditch, Jr. (Ph.D., Harvard University) is Professor of Sociology at Stanford University and Chairman of the Department of Sociology at Stanford from 1964 to 1968 and 1989 to the present. He was
editor of the *American Sociological Review* from 1975 to 1978. He has co-
authored and coedited many publications, including *Status, Rewards, and
Influence: How Expectations Organize Behavior*; *Status Characteristics and Expectation States*; *Types of Formalization in Small Groups Research*; and *Sociological Theories in Progress*, Volumes I, II, and III. He is currently writing
a book with Henry A. Walker on the politics of redistributive agendas.

PART I

Introduction

Orienting Strategies and Theory Growth

Joseph Berger and Morris Zelditch, Jr.

Introduction

The papers in the present volume describe the growth of a number of theories of group process.* Each chapter is concerned with one system of interrelated theories, together with the relevant theoretical and applied research, of one such process. Wagner and Berger (1985) have called this kind of theoretical structure a *theoretical research program*. In Wagner and Berger's analysis, the chief significance of theoretical research programs is that they undergo progressive change. Criteria exist that permit one to decide whether such change is or is not an advance, hence such programs grow. The purpose of the present, introductory chapter is to ask how we are to understand this growth.

In the first instance, this chapter further refines the analysis of growth given in Wagner and Berger (1985). Wagner and Berger's analysis had two broad features. First, it distinguished three levels of theoretical activity. One level is the *unit theory*, consisting of a set of interrelated concepts and principles that are abstract and general and which as a set possess empirical import. A unit theory describes a specific empirical social process. At quite a different level is the *orienting strategy*, a metatheoretical structure consisting of a system of interrelated concepts, goals, standards, presuppositions, and directives that, though most of the elements are nonempirical, may nevertheless guide the construction of empirical theories. The third level is the theoretical research program, made up of interrelated unit theories and relevant theoretical and applied research. The theoretical research program is Wagner and Berger's unit for the analysis of growth because it has more context for assessment of growth than unit theories, more empirical content than orienting strategies.

*We gratefully acknowledge research support to Joseph Berger from the Hoover Institution, Stanford University.

A second broad feature of Wagner and Berger's analysis is its multi-dimensional approach to the analysis of theoretical research programs. Wagner and Berger analyze growth in terms of the relations among theories in these programs. They identify five such relations—elaboration, proliferation, confrontation among variants and among (more distant) rivals, and integration. Because there is more than one relation between the theories in theoretical research programs, there is more than one pattern of growth to analyze. Hence, Wagner and Berger emphasize a more multidimensional approach. In the present volume a considerable number of examples are offered of the diversity of patterns of growth of theory. A close study of these examples makes it possible to further refine and elaborate Wagner and Berger's analysis. Thus, the first question we want to address in the present chapter is, What is the nature of growth, in terms of inter-theory relations in programs?

In addition, this chapter examines further the analysis of the role of orienting strategies in growth given in Wagner and Berger. Wagner and Berger argue that orienting strategies do play a role in growth—they guide the selection of problems, they provide tools for formulating them and for formulating solutions to them, they provide the criteria by which the worth of a solution to a problem is assessed. But this analysis is relatively simple and undifferentiated, and it is assumed that strategies themselves do not grow or grow only very slowly. Two papers since Wagner and Berger (1985) have elaborated on this initial analysis, Berger, Wagner, and Zelditch (1989, 1992). First, these papers differentiate among the diverse elements of which orienting strategies are made up, ranging from broad orienting aims and ultimate ontologies and epistemologies and conceptions of the actor, action, and order, to very specific and concrete substantive and methodological directives for constructing and evaluating theories, which they call *working strategies*. While aims, fundamental metamethodological positions, and very general substantive foundations may change only slowly (if at all), and may play only a very general role in growth of theory, working strategies may play a very specific, differentiated role in the growth of theory and may themselves change and grow.

A number of the papers in the present volume deal with the role of metatheoretical structures in the growth of theory. In some this is explicit: Fararo and Skvoretz think explicitly about what a theory is and what kind of theories grow; Lawler and Ford make the role of meta-theory in growth a major theme of their paper; Willer and Markovsky begin their analysis with a metatheoretical introduction; Wagner and Berger end with one; and in MacKinnon and Heise the first six principles of their program are understood to be metatheoretical. In other papers metatheory is implicit, as in Turner's analysis of sensitizing concepts, but it is nevertheless central to the paper. A close study of these examples makes it possible to say some new things about the role of orienting strategies in growth, extending the analysis beyond our previous discussions of this question. Thus, the second question we want to address in this chapter is, What is the role of orienting strategies in the growth of theoretical research programs?

The Nature of Growth in Theoretical Research Programs

Wagner and Berger (1985) argue that whatever else theoretical research programs are they are sets of interrelated theories with relevant bodies of theoretical and applied research. They propose describing these inter-theory relations in terms of the ideas of elaboration, proliferation, variation, competition, and integration. What do these relations mean?

Elaboration

We say of two theories, T_1 and T_2, that T_2 is an *elaboration* of T_1 if T_2 is more comprehensive *or* has greater analytic power *or* has greater empirical grounding than T_1, provided that T_1 and T_2 share the same family of concepts and principles and that they are addressed to the same general explanatory domains.

T_2 may become more comprehensive than T_1 by an expansion of the scope conditions of T_1 and/or by an expansion of the explanatory domain dealt with by T_1. Both types of growth are to be found in the papers in this volume. For example, as Jasso describes her program in this volume, her early formulations dealt with situations involving "quantity-goods" while subsequent formulations were expanded to include situations involving "quality-goods" and "bads"; as described by Cook, Molm, and Yamagishi, Molm initially dealt with situations involving control of positive outcomes but then dealt with situations involving the control of both positive and negative outcomes; and, as described by MacKinnon and Heise, Heise's actor-behavior-object settings are extended by Smith-Lovin in later formulations to actor-behavior-object-situation settings. In all such cases the scope conditions of the later theory include those of the earlier theory, and more.

Similarly, we see examples in these papers of growth by expansion of explanatory domains. The original explanatory focus of the status theory in Wagner and Berger (this volume) is the development and organization of "power and prestige orders." Subsequently, this is expanded to cover processes of legitimation and delegitimation and also to cover processes involved in the formation of reward expectations in status situations.

Also, as Bueno de Mesquita describes it, his initial concern was explaining the single policy choice of a nation to join or not join an ongoing war, and his more recent formulations deal with a wider variety of policy choices including some involving domestic considerations.

Increases in the analytic power of the theories in a program are most often realized through formalization of the theory and through model building. Almost all the papers in this volume document this role of formalization in theory growth. Fararo and Skvoretz, in particular, stress the importance of the choice of a particular formal system in theory building, and in fact we see a variety of such systems being employed including signed graph structures, stochastic processes, and game-theoretic systems. We also see examples of the modeling of specific situations as, for instance, in the work, described by Wagner and Berger, of Fisek, Berger, and Norman on status processes in open interaction settings, and in the work, described by Cook, Molm, and Yamagishi, of Molm on dynamic models of power use. Such models increase the analytic power of the theory by providing highly precise information about the process under study for a specific set of scope conditions.

In the case of almost every research program in this volume later theories are more empirically grounded than earlier ones. By this we mean that there are more empirical consequences and/or that there is a better fit between theory and data in later theories than in earlier theories. In large part this is due to the fact that the development of these programs through successive formulations has been shaped by considerations of how much more we can say empirically and how we can improve the empirical adequacy of our theories.

Elaboration is a basic form of growth in research programs and is driven by a *combination* of goals. These include theoretical—expanding the explanatory domain of a theory and enlarging its scope of application; analytical—formalizing a theoretical structure and developing models; and empirical—increasing the empirical consequences of a theory and its corroboration. It is important to recognize, however, as Heckathorn (1984) has argued, that it is not always possible to realize each of these goals at the same time in a given elaboration. For example, in increasing the analytic power of a theory it may be necessary to restrict its scope, as in the case of constructing situation-specific models of evaluation processes described by Wagner and Berger (this volume), and in constructing the power use models as described by Cook, Molm, and Yamagishi (this volume). While it is possible, therefore, for an elaborant to replace an earlier theory upon which it is built, it is also possible that this does not occur, with the earlier theory continuing as a component in the program.

Proliferation

We say of two theories, T_1 and T_2, that T_2 is a *proliferation* of T_1 if T_2 enlarges the range of application of the ideas and principles in T_1 to social phenomena beyond the original domain or the original set of problems (within a domain) addressed by T_1. Through proliferation, concepts and theoretical principles from T_1 are carried over to T_2, often with significant modifications. In addition, new and auxiliary concepts and principles are introduced to deal with the specific issues of the new domain and the new set of problems. Thus while sharing major concepts and principles, proliferants will also differ in the concepts and principles that they employ. Unlike the situation where T_2 is an elaboration of T_1 and where T_2 may be used to predict what T_1 predicts and more, in the case where T_2 is a proliferant of T_1, T_2 may make few if any specific predictions about the problems dealt with by T_1. In this sense the status characteristics and the distributive justice theories described by Wagner and Berger (this volume) are proliferants. In this sense, also, constructing a theory of how status characteristics emerge, or of how legitimation originates in a structure, or of how social identities acquire sentiments to begin with, involves constructing proliferants, respectively, in Wagner and Berger's status program, Walker and Zelditch's legitimation program, and MacKinnon and Heise's affect control program.

Proliferants may evolve in different ways—one theory spinning off from a second, or two or more theories differentiating from some common formulation with each developing as a distinct branch in the program. The latter case is clearly seen, for example, in the emergence of the power dependence and punitive power branches in the Lawler and Ford program on bargaining processes, and in the emergence of the exchange network and the behavioral-structural branches in the power dependence program by Cook, Molm, and Yamagishi. In each case what links the proliferants and the branches they generate within a program are common concepts and principles and what distinguishes them are additional concepts and principles introduced to deal with the distinct problems and domains they each address.

Proliferants represent "theoretical leaps" in the growth of a program. By these theoretical leaps existing concepts and principles in combination with new and "auxiliary" concepts and principles are used to extend the range of the program in terms of scope and domain.

Variants

We say that two theories, T_1 and T_2, are *variants* of each other if they employ concepts and principles from the same family of concepts and principles and if they are addressed to similar explanatory problems. Variant theories are closely related and often apply to similar if not identical scope conditions. They differ, however, in that they make use of one or more different mechanisms to describe how the relevant process operates. The balancing and combining theories of status-organizing processes designed by Wagner and Berger are clear examples of variant theories: they address the same explanatory phenomena, they have similar scope conditions, and they employ similar concepts and principles. They differ only in the concepts and principles that describe how multiple items of status information are processed.

Variants are often constructed by theorists in an effort to get more precise knowledge of how a process works. This strategy involves constructing theories so that, for specified conditions, they generate conflicting predictions. Since the theories are conceptually similar, empirical research can provide information that is specifically relevant to the mechanisms on which they differ.

Lawler and Ford describe an almost classic example of this strategy in use. Versions of conflict spiral and conflict deterrence theory are formulated in terms of similar concepts and theoretical principles. At the same time each also describes a different mechanism by which the process works. The theories are formulated so that they can be pitted against each other.

The outcome of research on variant theories may be that one theory replaces the other or an integration is formulated that describes the conditions under which each holds. In either case there is an advance in theoretical knowledge.

Thus variants contribute to theory growth by providing precise knowledge on alternative conceptions of a specific process that can be formulated within a single family of concepts and principles.

Competitors

We say two theories T_1 and T_2 are competitors if their structures involve different concepts and theoretical principles and if at some point they address the same explanatory problems.

Competitors may differ in fundamental ways, focusing on different behaviors, different explanatory factors, and being addressed to distinct explanatory phenomena. However, if for some particular explanatory problems they confront each other with conflicting predictions, their relations to each other can be important to theory growth. As MacKinnon and Heise argue, they may each set standards for the other, they may each be a source of ideas that can be expressed within the theory of the other, and it is also possible that research on overlapping problems that supports one formulation may also provide support for the second formulation.

Conflicts between competitors normally are more difficult to resolve than those between variants, and competitors can exist side by side for long periods of time. This is due not only to their differences in conceptual structure but also to the fact that they often address disparate problems in addition to those they have in common. Nevertheless, resolutions can occur. For specific explanatory problems one theory may come to dominate the second—e.g., cognitive behavioral theory over psychoanalytic theory for major sexual dysfunctions—and it is also possible that concepts and principles from each theory are expressed within some third formulation.

Thus competitors contribute to growth of theory by providing knowledge on alternative conceptions of some specific process or of some specific set of theoretical problems, where these conceptions are drawn from different families of concepts and principles.

Integration

Integration is a relation between three theories, T_1, T_2, and T_3, where T_3 consolidates many of the ideas found in T_1 and T_2 in a single formulation usually suggesting interrelationships between these ideas (cf. Wagner and Berger 1985).

We can distinguish different types of integration. To begin with there are integrations of variants and integrations of proliferants. In the case of variants a common mode of relating the theories to each other is through *conditionalization*, which involves specifying conditions under which the process described by each variant operates. We find just this type of consolidation in Lawler and Ford's integration of conflict spiral and conflict deterrence theories. In the case of proliferants, a common mode of consolidating the ideas from each theory is to describe the *interrelation* of the different processes conceptualized by these theories. We see this in the theory of the formation of reward expectations described by Wagner and Berger which deals with the simultaneous emergence and reciprocal effects of reward and performance expectations on each other.

We also distinguish integration of competitors and, following the analysis of Fararo and Skvoretz, what we may call the integration of "independents," where the theories differ in their basic conceptual structures. In the former case, the two theories compete on common explanatory problems, as balance and exchange theories of distributive justice do, but they may also have disparate explanatory domains. In the latter

case, the explanatory problems of the theories are fully distinct, and they
do not compete on common problems. Since competitors and independents employ concepts and principles from different conceptual families,
a major task in the integration of such theories is to express ideas and
principles from the two different theories in the common language of
still a third theory. Just this type of rendering of ideas from two independent theories is involved in Fararo and Skvoretz's use of the theory of
biased nets to integrate Granovetter's (1973) theory of weak ties and
Blau's (1977) theory of differentiation (Fararo and Skvoretz 1987).

In integrating competitors or independents, ideas from the original
theories may be combined into new concepts and principles that appear in neither of the original formulations. Jasso's justice evaluation
function, which is based on ideas from the equity and status value
conceptions of distributive justice, in fact is found in neither of these
theories. It is also possible that processes described in T_1 and T_2 which
are initially unrelated are interrelated in T_3, as is the case in Fararo and
Skvoretz's integration of Granovetter's and Blau's theories. Finally, it
is also possible that processes described in T_1 and T_2 are conditionalized
in T_3. This is what occurs in Bueno de Mesquita's integration of balance of power theories and preponderance of power theories, where
he stipulates conditions under which the arguments from each of these
theories hold.

Integrations represent major steps in theory growth in that T_3 is
normally more comprehensive *or* is more empirically grounded *or* has
greater analytic power than T_1 and T_2. Integrations, however, as Laudan
(1977) has argued, may also entail losses. Ideas and principles in T_1 and
T_2 may not be captured in T_3. For example, in Jasso's integration of the
exchange and status value theories of distributive justice, principles on
the "spread of status value" that are within the latter theory are not
represented. (In this connection see also Wagner and Berger's discussion
of Fisek, Berger, and Norman's integration of the power and prestige
theory and the status characteristics theory, where arguments from the
power and prestige theory are not represented in the integration.) The
fact that theories may not be fully replaced in a program highlights
the importance of treating the program as a whole as the unit of analysis
in understanding theory growth.

The Role of Orienting Strategies

In elaborating on Wagner and Berger's (1985) analysis of the role of
orienting strategies in theory growth, we address three questions. First,
what more can we say about the role of orienting strategies than that

they provide the problems, solutions, and criteria that guide growth? Second, do orienting strategies themselves grow? On the one hand, because they are nonempirical structures, a strong case could be made that orienting strategies do not grow or grow only very slowly. On the other hand, Berger, Wagner, and Zelditch (1989, 1992) argue that at least some elements of orienting strategies grow as a consequence of the experience of using strategies in the construction of theories. We would therefore like to see if the orienting strategies that guide the programs in this volume show any evidence of growth and change. Third, do orienting strategies precede or follow theory building? On the one hand, one could argue that, because they are prerequisite to theory construction, orienting strategies precede theory building and theory growth (cf. Alexander 1982). On the other, Ritzer (1990) has argued that metatheory follows, is in fact an after-the-fact analysis of, theory building and theory growth.

Answering these three questions is complicated by the fact that orienting strategies are made up of diverse elements (Berger, Wagner, and Zelditch 1992). Wagner and Berger (1985), like a good deal of the literature on metatheory, treated strategies as all of a piece, as if they were coherent wholes. But strategies in fact consist of a variety of different kinds of elements. These include broad aims of inquiry, such as reliable, general, instrumental knowledge; broad, abstract metamethodological foundations, like epistemologies and equally broad, abstract substantive foundations, like the nature of action, the actor, and order; but also quite specific, concrete methodological directives, such as Fararo and Skvoretz's argument for modeling over axiomatic theory, and equally specific, concrete substantive directives, such as the situationalism of Wagner and Berger's "state-organizing processes." These diverse elements differ not only in nature and function but also in stability. While the broader, more abstract elements such as aims, basic metamethodological positions, and basic substantive positions seem to be very stable, the more specific, concrete directives, substantive and methodological working strategies, are more frequently rethought, more often change, and even grow. Because of the diversity of the elements of which an orienting strategy is made up, the most useful approach to them is to differentiate various elements of a strategy, fixing on a particular element as the unit of reference in discussing the properties of strategies.

In the present volume, specific and concrete substantive and methodological strategies are more often addressed than broad, abstract, ultimate aims and foundations. It is the more specific, concrete directives, which might be termed *working strategies*, that are more immediately involved in guiding the construction of theories. In fact, none of these papers attempt to debate issues of ontology or epistemology and all take pretty much the same aims of inquiry for granted. There is some discussion of moderately abstract metamethodological positions, but the working strategy is the level of metatheoretical analysis that most consistently attracts attention in the papers in this volume. This dictates the organization of our discussion of the role of orienting strategies in theory growth. Like the papers in this volume, ours will mostly address the role of working strategies in growth, whether working strategies themselves evolve, and whether working strategies precede or follow theory construction. But a last section will attempt to discover what might also be said about the relation of other elements of orienting strategies to growth of theory.

Working Strategies and Theory Growth

Working strategies are made up of sufficiently specific concepts and directives that they provide theorists with specific and concrete guides for theory building. A working strategy may be a single idea or a set of ideas. This set may be loosely or tightly integrated. Methodological working strategies deal with "how to" problems: how to construct a theory, how to formulate an explanation, how to assess theories; substantive working strategies deal with "about what" problems: what kinds of concepts to use, what kinds of principles to formulate, and what theoretical questions to ask and answer.

Lawler and Ford's argument that power should be conceptualized in nonzero-sum terms, is, in our sense, a substantive working strategy. Willer and Markovsky's ideas on theoretical principles, representational systems, and laws are parts of a methodological working strategy which has evolved out of the work of Toulmin (1953).

The state-organizing process described by Wagner and Berger requires a theorist employing the strategy to specify what concrete elements of the larger social framework enter into any particular situation of action. Specific theories constructed by this strategy may, in fact do, have different social frameworks. The "status characteristic" is such an element in the theory of status characteristics and expectation states, the "referential structure" is such an element in the theory of distributive justice. But each of the many different expectation states theories has one or more of such elements. Similarly, each theory provides some answer to the working strategy's specific question of what activates the social process with which the theory is concerned, though the activating conditions differ from theory to theory. Playing a similar role is the almost algorithm-like actor-behavior-other-setting pattern of affect control theory (MacKinnon and Heise, this volume). It requires any affect control theory to specify the identity of an actor from whose perspective the situation is defined, the behaviors associated with that identity in a specific setting relative to a specific other, as well as the identity of the other and the setting. The strategy directs the theorist to formulate each of these elements in terms of the affect associated with the cognitions that define them. But because it is a generalizing strategy, it directs the theorist to formulate these affects in terms of cross-culturally invariant underlying dimensions (evaluation, potency, and activity) that abstract from the unique features of affective responses. Hence, the great importance to this strategy of dictionaries, constructed for each particular culture, that generate evaluation-potency-activity profiles of roles, behaviors, and settings.

That working strategies guide theory construction confers a certain continuity on the growth of theoretical research programs. Thus, programs will have not only some concepts and propositions but also metatheoretical directives in common. But working strategies also play a more active role in growth of theory. Not only do they direct the construction of the unit theories of the program, they also guide the relations that emerge between theories. They do this in part because of the role they play in formulating problems and in part because of the role they play in assessing solutions. Thus, a significant development in the Bacharach-Lawler program (Lawler and Ford, this volume) was the distinction between absolute and relative power that emerged from a (rather subtle) anomaly in the results of their earliest tests of power dependence theory. This anomaly had to do with differences in the importance of own and other's alternatives in choosing power tactics in bargaining. As Lawler and Ford point out, however, the distinction between absolute and relative power was there in power dependence theory to begin with. The anomaly seems at one and the same time to have been noticed because the theory provides concepts that sensitize one to it while leading, once noticed, to the explicit use of the distinction in the formulation of subsequent problems and solutions by the program.

A second, perhaps more familiar, way that working strategies guide growth is through the criteria that a working strategy offers for assessing solutions. Thus, Bueno de Mesquita tells us that his first theory of internation conflict was not sufficiently precise; the form of his utility functions was *ad hoc* where he wanted them to be informed by theory; he felt they could be made more general; and he felt that he could improve the fit of the model to the data. The drive for greater precision, theoretical power, generality, and fit continued to guide the growth of his program, leading eventually to a conception of a continuous process formulated interactively. Substantive working strategies sometimes play a similar, criterion-like role in guiding growth. Thus, Gray's commitment to the group as an entity, in what looks like an otherwise unusually psychologistic theory for a sociologist, led him to develop theories in which odds ratios of events permitted formulation of structures, displacing an earlier theory in which probabilities of events at the individual level were predicted.

A somewhat different example of the role of substantive directives is found in MacKinnon and Heise, who describe efforts to synthesize many competing but related theories in order to fill out missing elements of their own theory. The selection of the kinds of theories to which they paid attention is guided by their working strategy. What appears to the investigator as likely to be a "useful" source of ideas is determined by the similarity of variants, even competitors, in terms of the ideas of the working strategy that guides the program.

Working strategies are sufficiently specific and concrete that they are sometimes mistaken for theories. Thus, Merton in "Manifest and Latent Functions" (1968 [1949]) treated the "paradigm of functionalism" as a theory rather than a strategy. He attempted to transform such "postulates" as "functional unity," "universal functionalism," and "indispensability" into variables capable of empirical measurement, though in fact they remained nonempirical directives for how to formulate the idea of a social system, its boundaries, and the factors relevant to its "survival."

The concepts and directives which are part of every working strategy, whether functionalist or any other, do play a role in observation. This role is often referred to as "sensitizing" (Blumer 1969), and Turner devotes considerable attention in his paper in this volume to developing such sensitizing schemes. But, while working strategies are important factors in growth (and Lawler and Ford argue that the more explicit the strategy, the richer the growth), the working strategy does not grow if it does not produce theories. Merton's paradigm has been evidently difficult to realize. For example, it has proved difficult to develop a theory within which one could determine the positive, negative, and net functions of a structure. But theoretical growth depends on using strategies to formulate theories. Thus, despite Alexander's "neofunctionalism,"* Merton's paradigm of functionalism does not seem to have grown at all unless one takes its abandonment as a kind of growth. One might suspect

* Alexander's revival of functionalism (reviewed in Alexander and Colomy 1990) seems to grow not from Merton's paradigm, but rather from critiques of various features of the Parsonian attempt to integrate all of sociology around a hybrid of functionalism and the theory of action.

that in fact failure to distinguish a strategy from a theory actually inhibits growth.

Do Working Strategies Grow?

There seem to be good reasons, at least at first sight, to think that working strategies may guide growth but they do not themselves grow. No matter how concrete and specific, they are metatheoretical structures. They are made up of nonempirical elements like concepts, values, presuppositions, and directives. Why should they grow? But there are a number of examples in the present volume of changing working strategies. The conception of a state-organizing process (Wagner and Berger, this volume) evolved gradually over a period of years out of the experience of formulating a succession of specific expectation states theories. The experience in part led to increasing explicitness of the strategy that lay behind the theories. But it also led to abstraction from particular earlier theories of more general and abstract concepts that were then employed to formulate later theories. For example, the importance of the social framework defining the initial conditions of a situation of action emerged out of reflection on the concepts of a status characteristic and a referential structure in two of the early theories of the program. The more generalized role of social frameworks was not at first formulated as an explicit directive of the strategy. The same increasing applications and abstraction from earlier theories in the program are found in the chapter by Lawler and Ford. On the other hand, in the case of MacKinnon and Heise, empirical anomalies and gaps in the theory motivated a search for, and adoption of, concepts from other strategies, such as Fararo and Skvoretz's concept of a "production function" (1984). The production function became not merely an element in one of the theories of the program but a component of the working strategy behind construction of its other theories.

It is not that working strategies are in any sense directly tested by the theoretical research of a program. They are, in fact, as nonempirical as metatheoretical structures are generally held to be. But the theories that employ them are testable, and the fertility and fruitfulness of strategies can be indirectly assessed by the successes and failures of the theories that they generate. Theories are assessed by criteria such as empirical corroboration, analytic power, comprehensiveness of scope, precision, and instrumental value (in applications). Working strategies are assessed by the extent to which the theories to which they lead satisfy these criteria. A change in a working strategy, or a change from one working strategy to another, can be said to be "growth" to the extent that the theories constructed with the reformulated strategy or the newer strategy satisfy more of these criteria or satisfy them better. Thus, working strategies can be, and in fact are, evaluated by the people who use them by constructing theories and comparing their value as solutions relative to some problem or set of problems, including applied problems as in Cohen (this volume). The kind of religious commitment that theorists are sometimes supposed to have to their orienting strategies (Kuhn 1970; Lakatos 1968, 1970) does not seem to extend to their attitudes toward working strategies. And in Turner (this volume) one in fact sees a continual orientation to examination and reexamination of a working strategy.*

Does the Working Strategy Precede or Follow Theory and Research?

This is a question that arises in the first instance from the role of metatheory in theory construction and growth. Working strategies provide the tools employed by theorists in formulating and reformulating theories. This implies that a working strategy is a prerequisite of theory construction or, equivalently, that there is no presuppositionless theory. But suppose that some metatheoretical questions are unanswered? Certainly there is plenty of evidence that theorists rethink metatheoretical issues all the time, as in this volume Fararo and Skvoretz are rethinking metamethodological questions, and Turner is rethinking substantive foundations. Yet what we have said about the growth of working strategies implies that, absent theory, they do not change or that, if they do change, such change cannot be described as growth because assessment of growth depends on comparing the success of the theories to which different strategies lead.

But the dilemma implied in the question is spurious. The fact that working strategies can change and evolve on grounds of reason and evidence implies that, like theories, they can be "provisional." Therefore, one can begin with a provisional working strategy, use it to construct one or more theories, use the criteria that one employs for assessing theories to decide how precise, well corroborated, comprehensive, powerful, and instrumental they are; then one can employ the outcome of such theory-assessments to assess, indirectly, the utility of the working strategy. This, together with the number of problems the working strategy has demonstrated it can address, constitutes a basis for reformulating the strategy so that it grows reciprocally (or "reflexively," as Berger, Wagner, and Zelditch [1989] put it) as its theoretical research program grows.

---

*It is worth emphasizing, perhaps more than we do here, that success and failure are relative to a given set of problems. Among other things, this implies that there is probably no one working strategy for all sociological problems and no reason to attempt to construct any such strategy.

Thus, the question of which comes first, strategy or theory, does not require an "either/or" answer.

The Relation of Other Elements of Orienting Strategy to Theory Growth

The papers in this volume have less to say about aims, or basic substantive and metamethodological positions, than they do about substantive or methodological working strategies. It is evident that they share many of the same aims and very broad metamethodological positions, though this is less true of substantive foundations. But they tend to take ultimate foundation questions for granted and therefore hardly mention them. In fact, the most notable thing about this "higher" level of orienting strategies is that the same foundations are consistent with a large number of different substantive and methodological working strategies. But this in itself offers some insight into the relations among the elements of an orienting strategy.

Clearly, there is no unique relation between a given set of aims, basic substantive positions, and basic metamethodological positions and the substantive and methodological working strategies that "derive" from them. The relation is not deductive, it is a one-to-many relation. In this volume, though the aims and metamethodology are more or less shared, there are several different methodological working strategies and almost as many substantive working strategies as there are programs. The same aims, etc., are compatible with many working strategies.

"Compatibility" is a relation that only very loosely integrates the parts of an orienting strategy. (Indeed, Laudan [1984] argues that it is a mistake to think of such strategies as coherent at all.) But a one : many relation, even though it admits many alternatives consistent with the same position, does exclude some things. There are many methodological working strategies that are inconsistent with the aims and positions shared by the papers in this volume, and clearly do not and would not appear in it. For example, Maines and Molseed (1986) have stretched post-positivism to its outer limits, arguing that testability itself is problematic, since what constitutes a test depends on one's orienting strategy. Testability is problematic because evidence is constructed by theory. Theory, in turn, is itself constructed by values and faith. Furthermore, implicit in the argument is the assumption that values are themselves determined by the observer's social position. A subjectivism this radical, implying that all fact is relative, is incompatible with the basic epistemological position of any of the papers in this volume. All of them share the presupposition that knowledge gained by use of the rules and methods of scientific procedure is objective in the sense that, collectively and institutionally if not

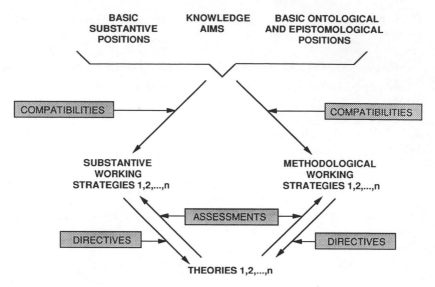

Fig. 1. Elements in an orienting strategy.

individually, it is independent of the social position of individual scientists. Nor is a subjectivism as radical as Maines and Molseed's compatible with aims such as reliable, general, instrumental knowledge or an ontology such as a world independent of the observer. One could not simultaneously hold these aims, believe in these metamethodological positions, yet develop a radically relativistic working strategy.

Figure 1 depicts the relations we have described between those elements of an orienting strategy that we have considered in this chapter. (There are of course other important elements that we have not considered.) On the first level we have basic substantive positions, basic ontological and epistemological positions, and knowledge aims embodied in a particular orienting strategy. On the second level are the substantive and methodological working strategies. Elements on the first and second levels are connected by relations of compatibility and incompatibility. On the third level we have specific theories that are constructed. The elements of the second and third levels are connected by directives and assessments. Substantive and methodological working strategies provide directives that are used in the construction of specific theories. The assessment of the relative success, failure, or realizability of specific theories feeds back to produce changes on the level of working strategies.

The papers in the present volume are not on orienting strategies, although as we have argued they make extensive use of methodological and working strategies. The papers are about theoretical research programs which consist of unit theories that are interrelated by growth relations of the type we have described. Each of the unit theories in these programs is itself abstract and general and has empirical reference. These theoretical research programs represent long-sustained, cumulative research, in some cases for twenty, even thirty, years. Insofar as we understand growth, each shows sustained growth. Our purpose in presenting these papers is in part didactic: we think study of these papers suggests what theoretical growth in sociology is about and how to achieve it. But our primary purpose is scientific. These papers are intended to contribute to the further growth of sociological theory.

PART II

Theoretical Research Programs:
Status, Affect, and Social Interaction

Status Characteristics Theory: The Growth of a Program

David G. Wagner and Joseph Berger

Status differences organize much of social interaction. When wives defer to their husbands' job opportunities or when workers' salaries and wages are based on seniority, status-organizing processes are involved. When juries select accountants over electricians as forepersons or when black youths are encouraged to focus on athletics as a means of educational advancement, status-organizing processes are involved. In all these cases beliefs about actors' social characteristics become the basis for the evaluation of performances, the allocation of rewards, and the attainment of power and prestige positions.

A major theme of the theoretical research program on expectation states has been the development of accounts of just how and under what conditions status organizes interaction. An entire branch of the program—status characteristics theory—has been devoted to this effort. The expectation states program, as with other theoretical research programs, consists of a set of interrelated theories, bodies of empirical research, and research on applications and interventions. Such programs share a core set of essential ideas about the variety of phenomena they investigate. Branches of programs use some of these core ideas to investigate a specific phenomenon—status-organizing processes, in the case of status characteristics theory. Note that a branch of a program can be considered a special kind of program in its own right, one whose core ideas are more limited in their focus of application than those of the "parent" program.

Our purpose is to review what we have learned about status-organizing processes through status characteristics theory.* First, we re-

*Morris Zelditch, Jr., and R. Owen Harris provided extensive critical commentary on earlier versions of this review. Their assistance has been invaluable. We also gratefully acknowledge the research support provided by the Hoover Institution to Joseph Berger.

view some of the background of this work in the larger program and in research on particular status characteristics. We then consider in turn each of the three formulations of status characteristics theory (referred to as the *initial formulation*, the *revised formulation*, and the *graph-theoretical formulation*). We discuss the structure of each formulation and indicate the advances achieved as each succeeding formulation has been developed. As these formulations have emerged, other collateral developments have occurred. These have included proliferations of the core ideas to deal with related issues (e.g., distributive justice, the development of self-other expectations) and applications of the core ideas to practical social problems. A section devoted to these developments follows our consideration of the major formulations. We then consider extensions of the core ideas in the status program to deal with specific issues that have arisen within the established domain of explanation of the status formulations. Here we discuss work on reward expectations, the evolution of status expectations across interaction situations, status cues, the legitimation of power and prestige hierarchies, and work integrating concepts and principles about the emergence and maintenance of power and prestige hierarchies (the original concern of the expectation states program) with those in the status characteristics formulations. We next examine the overall structure of the status characteristics program, focusing on its development and growth. In the concluding section, we discuss some of the work in new areas of inquiry that is currently in progress.

Background

Power and Prestige Theory

Status characteristics theory is rooted in earlier work in the expectation states program on the formation and maintenance of hierarchies of power and prestige in task groups. The earlier work—power and prestige theory (also referred to as *behavior-expectation theory*)—focused originally on informal problem-solving groups like those investigated by Bales and his associates in the early 1950's. (See especially Bales 1950, 1953; Bales et al. 1951; Bales and Slater 1955; Heinecke and Bales 1953.) Bales had shown that in groups whose actors were initially similar in status (and strangers to one another) there quickly evolved inequalities in interaction. These inequalities included differences in opportunities to contribute to the group's problem solving, actual participation in solving the problem, communicated evaluations of these contributions, and influence over the group's decisions. Moreover, these inequalities were highly intercorrelated, forming a single hierarchy of observable power and prestige differences in the group. Once such a hierarchy emerged, it tended to be stable.

Power and prestige theories treat these phenomena as a function of an underlying structure of expectations for future task performance that emerges from the interaction of the group's members. Since all these inequalities are seen as functions of the same underlying expectation states, the high intercorrelation among the inequalities is accounted for. Once these expectations emerge, they determine the course of future interaction in the group, which operates to reinforce the existing structure of expectations. Thus, given that the initial conditions of interaction are unchanged, the structure of expectations and the observable power and prestige will be stable. Although these processes occur under a wide variety of conditions, they seem most likely to occur in situations where actors who are initially similar in status work together collectively on a valued task. (See Berger 1958, 1960; and Berger and Conner 1969, for theory and research concerning the basic character of this argument.)

A series of related mathematical models were constructed that focused on abstracting the specific process by which expectations emerge from evaluations of specific performances (i.e., unit evaluations). These models (see Berger and Snell 1961; Conner 1966; Berger, Conner, and McKeown 1969; Fararo 1973) suggest that the necessity of resolving disagreements in these task groups requires actors to evaluate their own and others' performances and to accept or reject influence from others on that basis. As a consequence, at each stage of the process (i.e., with respect to each decision made) there is a specifiable probability that the actor will come to develop an expectation state for each actor (i.e., an anticipation for the quality of an actor's future contributions) that is consistent with the preponderance of evaluations for the contributions of each actor. Further, once generated, these states remain differentiated for the course of the interaction unless other structural factors intervene, e.g., new members or new information is introduced or the task force changes.

Later work on power and prestige has modeled the emergence of expectations for more complex interaction situations. Thus, for example, Fisek (1968, 1974) constructed a Markov chain model that shows how differences in rates of participation can generate underlying expectation states that determine stable power and prestige hierarchies. Drawing on this and other related work, Berger and Conner (1974) then showed how inequalities with respect to any one aspect of the group's interaction, not just the evaluation of individual units of performance, may spread to other components in generating a hierarchy. More recently, Fararo and Skvoretz (1986) have developed an extension of Fisek's expectation states model to deal with the emergence of hierarchies from interaction in situations involving any number of actors of different types.

What all these models have in common is that they describe processes by which behaviors determine expectation states and expectations determine behaviors. In terms of their structure, they are all finite state, discrete time Markov chain models, with self-other expectations being the states of the chain and with different types of behavior being probabilistic functions of these states. Thus all these models capture in a rigorous manner the key idea that observable power and prestige behaviors are determined by an underlying structure and that inferences about the unobservable states in the structure are made on the basis of behaviors which lead to their formation and which also are determined by them.

In a series of related studies, Foschi (1970, 1971, 1972; Foschi and Foschi 1976, 1979) considers how objective evaluations from external sources may help to generate and to overcome established expectation states. Using Bayesian models, she shows that the relative frequency of different evaluations of specific performances (i.e., unit evaluations) determines the structure of expectations established. Consequently, the establishment of expectations depends on achieving a threshold value of consistent evaluations. Moreover, changing those expectations depends on the number and extremity of evaluations that contradict the established expectations.

Research on Particular Status Characteristics

The Bales research (and power and prestige theory) primarily concerns task situations in which actors are similar with respect to concrete status distinctions like race or gender that may be significant in society at large. But what if actors are not similar? Status characteristics theory draws heavily on the research on this issue. Although it is consistent with the Bales research, this research is also different.

Basically, external status distinctions become the bases for internal ones in that status inequalities significant in the larger society remain so in the task situation. They are present as soon as the group is formed and serve as the basis for the distribution of power and prestige in the group. Furthermore, the same effects occur whether or not the status distinction bears any association with the group's task. Thus, for example, Torrance (1954), in a study of Air Force bomber crews, found that Air Force rank determined influence over decisions on a variety of group tasks, even when rank had nothing to do with the task performed.

Perhaps equally important, the results do not seem to depend on which concrete social distinctions are present. For example, Strodtbeck, James, and Hawkins (1958) showed that both gender and occupation determined the selection of a foreman and the rates of participation and influence in mock juries. Investigations of group situations involving other status distinctions have all shown the same results. (See, for example, Caudill 1958; Hurwitz, Zander, and Hymovitch 1960; Leik 1963. For a review of this research and how it relates to status characteristics theory, see Cohen, Berger, and Zelditch 1972.)

In summary, then, the research on particular status characteristics shows that external status distinctions determine the distribution of power and prestige in task groups whether or not these distinctions are explicitly related to the group task. This abstractly stated empirical generalization provides the focus for the first formulation of status characteristics theory.

The Initial Formulation

Scope

In the development of our accounts of status-organizing processes, the strategy has been to understand the simplest situations first, and then to gradually introduce complexities as our understanding grew. Thus, the first formulation of status characteristics theory (Berger, Cohen, and Zelditch 1966; updated, and with a report of empirical results, in Berger, Cohen, and Zelditch 1972) was intentionally quite limited in scope. It considered how status organizes interaction only in a constrained class of situations involving two actors who are working collectively on a valued task, and who differ with respect to only a single diffuse status distinction.

Core Ideas

This initial formulation of status characteristics theory incorporated several important ideas from the power and prestige branch of the program. In particular, it absorbed the concepts of an expectation state and of an observable hierarchy of power and prestige behaviors, and the assumption that expectations both determine and are determined by these power and prestige behaviors. The major difference of course is that power and prestige theories consider how expectations emerge in the course of the group's interaction, whereas status characteristics theory focuses on how initial status differences become the basis of expectations in the immediate situation.

Such status differences are characterized in terms of the possession of different states of a *diffuse status characteristic*. We say that a characteristic is a diffuse status characteristic if it involves two or more states that are differentially valued; and associated with each state are distinct sets of specific expectation states, each itself evaluated; and associated with each state is a similarly evaluated general expectation state.* Gender, race, ethnicity, educational attainment, occupation, and physical attractiveness each may be a diffuse status characteristic when these features are present for a particular actor in the social situation.

Four core principles account for how such diffuse status information is organized into expectations and translated into task behavior. First is *activation* (later called *salience*): What status information is available for processing by actors in these situations? That is, under what circumstances does the actor come to attribute to self and other the generalized capacities and specific abilities associated with each state of a diffuse status characteristic? This proposition argues that any diffuse status information that discriminates between the actors in the situation or that is believed to be task-relevant will be activated. Thus, activation occurs if actors possess different states of the same diffuse status characteristic, as would be the case, for example, in mixed gender or biracial groups; or if the characteristic is culturally associated with the group's task, as might be true, for example, with gender-type tasks.

The second principle concerns establishing the relevance of salient status information to performance of the task. The *burden of proof* principle argues that status information that is salient will become relevant to the task unless its inapplicability is believed or demonstrated. The burden of proof is demonstrating that the status information should not be considered relevant, rather than the other way around. The information will be assumed task-relevant unless there is specific information to the contrary. Consequently, status characteristics and status advantages will be applied, as a matter of normal interaction, to every new task and every new situation.

Given relevance, then, actors *assign expectations* for performance at the task to self and other based on the relevant status information. The

---

*Thus, an actor who believes that to be male is better than to be female and that men are generally more capable at tasks than women or more rational, and so on, than women is treating gender as a diffuse status characteristic. Note that the differentiating elements of a diffuse status characteristic are based on attributions made by the actor. These attributions need not have objective validity. More likely, they represent beliefs and values in cultural systems that the actor is exposed to. Consequently, whether or not a particular characteristic constitutes a diffuse status difference is a factual issue (i.e., whether actors in a particular group at a particular time make the relevant distinctions), not a theoretical one.

actor with a status advantage is expected to perform more capably at the task than the actor with a status disadvantage. Concepts are then introduced from the power and prestige theory to explain how the assigned expectations govern behavior. According to the *basic expectation* assumption, the observed power and prestige behaviors (i.e., opportunities to initiate action, actual performance outputs, communicated evaluations of units of performance, and influence) are direct functions of the difference in self and other expectations. For example, an actor for whom expectations are relatively high in comparison to a second actor will initiate more interaction and exercise greater influence than the second actor.

Linking these four principles together, we see that the existence of a single diffuse status characteristic which discriminates between the actors in a task situation is sufficient to generate a differentiated power and prestige order, provided that the status differences are not dissociated from the task. Specifically, the theory predicts that individuals will be ordered in their power and prestige positions by their initial status differences. This ordering (as opposed to the specification of numerical values) does not depend on whether or not the status characteristic is initially task-relevant. It also does not depend on how much status information there is in the situation, provided that all the information that is present is consistent.

Testing

Two experimental tests of the initial formulation provided direct support for its principles. The first study (reported in Berger, Cohen, and Zelditch 1972) was performed at an Air Force base with Air Force rank serving as the diffuse status difference. This study demonstrated clearly that the same power and prestige ordering emerges regardless of the amount of information available to define the situation. The higher-status actor is deferred to more frequently than the low-status actor when the situation is *maximally structured* (i.e., when the discriminating characteristic is activated and individuals possess performance capacities that are relevant to the task and consistent with the states of the status characteristic they possess). But it is also the case, as predicted, that the higher-status actor defers more frequently than the lower-status actor when the situation is *minimally structured* (i.e., when actors simply possess the states of the status characteristic that discriminates between them). In the second study, Moore (1968), using reputed college attainment as the status difference, showed that influence behavior was directly related to the status difference regardless of whether the status states were initially defined as relevant to the task or not. Thus this study provided support, in particular, for the operation of the burden of proof process.

Several additional studies refined and extended the initial formulation. For example, Berger, Fisek, and Freese (1976) and Freese (1970) considered the contribution of *specific status characteristics* (i.e., those that involve the ability to perform specifically defined tasks) to the status–organizing process. The first of these two studies suggested that the information about a specific status is used in establishing task expectations if it is either directly or indirectly related (through some other status element) to the group task. The second study suggested that two specific characteristics could be involved in establishing expectations on the specific task even when they are not directly related to the task, provided that they are related in a consistent manner to each other (i.e., have consistent performance implications).

Still another study (Berger and Fisek 1970; extended in Berger, Fisek, and Crosbie 1970) concerned multi-characteristic status situations (i.e., situations in which actors possess states of two or more characteristics). Consistent situations (i.e., ones in which actors possess only similarly evaluated states of characteristics) seem unproblematic. But what happens when the situation is inconsistent (i.e., actors possess differently evaluated states of two or more characteristics)? Berger, Fisek, and Crosbie, investigating only the case in which two specific characteristics are initially defined as relevant to the task and are inconsistent, found evidence suggesting that actors combine the information from multiple independent statuses to form expectations that are in some sense an "average" of the inconsistent status definitions. Parcel and Cook (1977) later replicated this study in a situation in which characteristics are not initially defined as relevant to the task. This study also yielded results that suggested a combining process.

The Revised Formulation

Scope

The primary focus in elaborating the status characteristics theory was to expand its scope so that it could deal with multi-characteristic status situations. What are the implications for the power and prestige hierarchy when there is more than one status characteristic possessed by actors and they are consistently evaluated? What are the implications when they are inconsistently evaluated?

The revised theory also describes the operation of specific status characteristics. Basically, it argues that if such characteristics are not initially relevant to the task, they will become relevant, through a burden of proof process, provided that they have become salient. Once these characteristics are task-relevant, they will be processed further, along with the other status elements that have become task-relevant. Thus the scope of the revised theory covers multi-characteristic status situations, involving any number of diffuse or specific status characteristics and in which the actors are oriented to a valued collective task.

Added Core Ideas

The revised formulation assumed, as before, that status information that is either task-relevant or discriminating becomes salient in the situation. With respect to information that equates actors, however, the revised theory argues that such information becomes salient if it is specifically believed to be task-relevant. Thus, for example, race is *not* predicted to be salient when black group members work together on a task unless race is believed to be relevant to the task they are performing.

When multiple status characteristics that are inconsistent do become salient, status organization may occur in either of two basic ways. Actors may eliminate some of the salient information and define their expectations and behavior on the basis of a limited subset of the information available. Most eliminating arguments (also referred to as balancing arguments) assume that actors make use of only a consistent subset of available status information. Behavioral expectations should therefore be uniformly high or uniformly low, depending on which consistent subset is used to define the situation.

Elimination is the kind of assumption that has often been made by those who have investigated status inconsistency. In Lenski's (1966) status crystalization theory, for example, inconsistencies are assumed to create tension and anxiety. Actors can reduce the tension by eliminating (e.g., ignoring or hiding) inconsistent statuses. If they cannot reduce the inconsistency, then they may become isolated and be prone to various types of coping behaviors (e.g., political radicalism). The kind of elimination most often assumed is based on a maximization principle, by which actors prefer status definitions that reflect positively on them. Thus, when confronted with inconsistent definitions, they are most likely to eliminate negative status information, maximizing the positive.

An equally plausible alternative argument for processing inconsistent status information is that actors combine all salient status information in arriving at expectations. Combining arguments assume that actors use all the information that is available to them, provided that it is salient. As a consequence, inconsistency in the implications of the salient status differences should serve to moderate expectations.

In part because of evidence from the studies refining and extending the initial formulation, the revised formulation adopts the combining assumption. It assumes that each salient status characteristic in the situation comes to be related to task performance through a *path of task relevance*. Each path defines an expectancy for task performance; in effect, it represents the task significance for that characteristic. Paths with positive task significance (i.e., ones that connect the actor to performing better at the task) are combined with paths with negative task significance (i.e., ones that connect the actor to doing worse at the task) to form *aggregated expectation states*. The actor's *expectation advantage* (or disadvantage) relative to another actor, then, is equal to the aggregated expectation for self minus the aggregated expectation for the other. Finally, the basic expectation assumption dictates that the distribution of power and prestige behaviors in the group is a direct probabilistic function of expectation advantage. If the expectation advantage is large, the power and prestige hierarchy will be strongly differentiated; if the expectation advantage is relatively small, so too will be the differentiation in the power and prestige hierarchy. The revised formulation thus makes it possible to order status situations in relation to the degree of differentiation in task behaviors that they imply.

Testing the Revised Formulation

As noted, several of the studies that extended the initial formulation were used to develop key arguments in the revised formulation. Other studies served to test some of the ordering predictions of the revised formulation.

The results in most of the studies were consistent with the ordering predictions of the revised formulation. An experiment by Kervin (1972), designed to test a variant to the revised formulation, provided a test of some of the assumptions common to both theories. Kervin demonstrated that the number, length, and consistency of the paths of task relevance linking actors with task outcomes all directly affect the degree of differentiation in power and prestige that results.* That is, the shorter a path (i.e., the stronger the link between a differentiating characteristic and a task outcome), the greater the differentiating effect; the greater the num-

*Publication dates can be misleading. The first version of the revised theory was presented at a meeting of the West Coast Small Groups Conference (Berger and Fisek 1969). A version of the theory quite similar to that which was eventually published already existed by the time this experiment was conducted.

ber of characteristics linked by paths of equal length to the same task outcome, the greater the differentiating effect; the more consistent the allocation of these characteristics to self and other, the greater the differentiating effect.

In a second study, Wagner and Berger (1974, 1982) determined that paths of relevance operated in a similar way but with opposite effect when they linked inconsistent as against consistent status elements. Thus, if possession of a high status implies low task ability, the effect on subsequent expectations is opposite to what it is when it implies the possession of high task ability.

In a third study, Webster and Berger (1975) investigated equating characteristics (i.e., statuses that do not differentiate actors). Their results showed that equating status information that is not initially defined as relevant to task performance does not become salient and was not combined with other status information to form expectations. The results of this study are fully consistent with the revised formulation, which does *not* predict that equating information not initially defined as task-relevant becomes salient.

In a fourth study, Zelditch, Lauderdale, and Stublarec (1980) extended the investigation of inconsistent status situations from Berger, Fisek, and Crosbie (1970) to deal with situations believed more likely to be conducive to an eliminating explanation. Berger, Fisek, and Crosbie had considered only situations in which both inconsistently allocated characteristics were identified as initially relevant to task performance. Zelditch, Lauderdale, and Stublarec reasoned that, if eliminating was likely to occur in any circumstance, it was most likely in inconsistent situations where only one of the characteristics was the task characteristic (i.e., the ability that is instrumental to success or failure at the task). Under these conditions, the information from the characteristic not directly relevant might very well be ignored. The results showed this not to be the case; actors combined information from the diffuse and the task characteristics in forming expectations. However, the findings from a study by Freese and Cohen (1973) do not seem to accord with the combining argument. This study suggests that two consistent specific status characteristics which were inconsistent with a single diffuse characteristic eliminated the effect of a diffuse characteristic. On the other hand, the results of a partial replication of this study by Webster and Driskell (1979) support the argument that the information in two specific status characteristics is combined with that in an inconsistent diffuse status characteristic.

Finally, an important study by Freese (1974) extended the formulation in a direction that was soon to be picked up in the next, graph-theoretical formulation. Freese considered the impact of *referent actors* (i.e., nonparticipating actors who serve as objects of comparison for interactants). He found that the effect of a referent actor whose statuses are inconsistent with those of the interactants increases with the number of such referents.

The Graph-Theoretical Formulation

In this section we present an informal description of the graph-theoretical version of the status characteristics theory. For a formal treatment of the core theory, see Berger et al. (1977) or Humphreys and Berger (1981).

Scope

A significant expansion in the scope of status characteristics theory occurred with the formulation of a graph-theoretical version of the theory in Berger et al. (1977). This version considered task-oriented situations which could involve any number of actors with any two serving as interactants while others serve as referent actors. Interactants are those directly involved in the interaction at any one time; referents are non-interactants whose status information affects the expectations of interactants. During the course of the interaction, interactants can become referents, and non-interactants can become interactants. Furthermore, interactants and referents may possess any number of status characteristics and characteristics of different types.

New Ideas in the Formulation

The graph-theoretical formulation extensively develops the idea of a path of task relevance introduced earlier. Each path is a connection between the actor and an outcome state, success or failure, of the group's task. Some paths are given in the situation by virtue of culturally established relevance (direct or indirect) of the status and the task, while others are established by virtue of the burden of proof process. New paths may also be introduced through referent actors or by a non-interactant becoming an interactant. Any information added by these methods becomes a part of the status structure of the situation.

Paths may differ in length, and paths of different lengths contribute different amounts to the expectations of an actor. Specifically, the longer the path connecting an actor to a task outcome, the weaker its contribution to the actor's performance expectations. To capture this, we introduce the idea of a decreasing function f from the positive integers to the open interval $(0, 1)$, $f:N \rightarrow (0, 1)$. Note that $f(l)$ is a measure of the strength (or degree) of relevance of a path of length l. We assume that there are characteristic numbers associated with paths of different lengths, and we think of these numbers as representing the *degree (or strength) of relevance* of a path. While it is not necessary to restrict ourselves to a single substantive interpretation of these numbers, we can say that they represent the strength of the actors' expectancy that a certain outcome will be attained, given the information embodied in a particular path.

We assume that the actor combines all information that has become salient and relevant to the immediate task. While, in all likelihood, the process by which this occurs is outside the individual's awareness, we have formulated a theoretical principle, *the principle of organized subsets*, to describe it. In terms of this principle, all status information leading to successful task outcomes is combined to determine a value of positive performance expectations. Similarly, all information leading to unsuccessful task outcomes is combined to determine a value of negative performance expectations. In these combining processes there is an *attenuation* effect. That is, there is a decrease in the increment of expectation values with the addition of each like-signed piece of information. The aggregated expectations for an actor are given by summing these two values. The actor's expectation advantage (or disadvantage) relative to an other is equal to the aggregated expectation for self less that formed for the other.

An actor's position relative to an other in the observable power and prestige order of the group is a direct continuous function of his or her (dis)advantage relative to this other. The more extreme one's expectation (dis)advantage, the greater the differentiation in these positions. This formulation in fact enables us to derive *interval-ordering* predictions regarding such differentiation as well as the more customary ordering predictions.*

Formalization with Graph Theory

Without question, the greatest advance in this third version of status characteristics theory involves its formalization in graph-theoretical

---

*A specific function translating expectation (dis)advantages to behavior has been formulated to predict influence in a standardized experimental situation. (See Berger 1974; Berger et al. 1977.) In addition, Fisek, Berger, and Norman (1991) recently have proposed a second function to translate self-other expectations into behavior for groups of different sizes in open interaction situations (see below). And still more recently, Balkwell (1991b) has proposed a single general function that can be applied to groups of different sizes that may be studied in different types of experimental settings.

terms. Actors, status elements, and task outcomes become points in the graph. Relations among these entities become signed lines linking points in the graph. The status structure of the situation is therefore represented as a series of paths in the signed graph linking actors directly or indirectly with task outcomes.

With this formalization such ideas as the number, length, strength, and task significance of paths are rigorously conceptualized. The principles of attenuation and of subset combining are formulated in a very precise manner, and the impact of a wide variety of status information on the actor's aggregated expectations can be determined. As a result, it becomes possible to represent and make predictions for the behavior of actors in an extremely large number of different types of status situations that all now fit within the scope of the theory.

Another consequence of the formalization is that it makes possible the derivation of abstract and general theorems about status-organizing processes. Humphreys and Berger (1981), for example, show how the relevance of status distinctions, their consistency, and their number are related to the degree of differentiation in the power and prestige order. They also show that there are conditions in which status structures that are markedly different (i.e., involve different configurations of status elements and actors) nevertheless can generate similar behavioral consequences. Although some of the consequences of such theorems are unexpected, their importance does not rest in their novelty alone. It rests also in the fact that they are derived from a basic set of status-organizing principles that are components of a single theory.

Assessing the Theory

The graph-theoretical version of status characteristics theory was originally assessed against data from 55 experimental conditions in 12 studies performed prior to the development of the theory. Since some of the information in those studies was used in developing the theory, the assessment was designed more to determine the consistency of the theory with its resource base than to directly test its predictions. With parameter estimates from a small subset of the studies considered, the empirical fit was very good. A more traditional kind of test, using regression techniques, was conducted on the original data plus additional experimental data by Fox and Moore (1979). They found an even better fit between predictions and observed data than did Berger et al. (1977).

There have been numerous experiments testing different aspects of the graph-theoretical formulation; among these have been experiments on the inconsistency effect. The *inconsistency effect* is the accentuated effect of minority information when it is combined with a predominant amount of opposite-signed information. When the minority information is all positive, the principle of organized subsets predicts a "status positivity effect" and when it is all negative it predicts a "status negativity effect." Experiments by Norman, Smith, and Berger (1988) and Berger et al. (1992) provide evidence for the existence of these effects as predicted and therefore provide support for the argument that they are both consequences of the same theoretical principles.

Most recently Fisek, Norman, and Nelson-Kilger (1992) have analyzed the results of 12 experiments all done subsequent to the publication of the graph-theoretical formulation, in addition to the original 12. Fisek and his colleagues report a good fit between the observed data from these experiments and the predictions from the graph-theoretical formulation.

Collateral Developments: Proliferations and Applications

At the same time that these accounts of status-organizing processes were being developed, expectation states investigators also began pursuing several other issues in a manner that drew heavily on the status characteristics formulations. These included work on distributive justice, on the effects of significant others on self-evaluations, and on major lines of application and intervention research.

Distributive Justice

One major area of concern has been with issues of distributive justice and injustice. How do actors come to determine the justice or injustice of the rewards they receive? How do they respond when they perceive an injustice in the distribution of rewards? The *status value theory* of distributive justice (Berger et al. 1968, 1972) attempted to answer these among other questions.

The status value view of justice was developed originally to challenge an earlier view called *equity theory* (see Adams 1965; Walster, Berscheid, and Walster 1973). Equity theory focuses on the exchange, or consummatory, value of rewards; it assumes that evaluations of justice and injustice are based on comparisons of one actor's ratio of the values of investments to rewards with that of a second actor in the immediate situation. If the ratios are equal, the situation is regarded as equitable and stable; if the ratios are unequal, the situation is inequitable and subject to pressures to reduce the inequity.

However, the ratio comparisons proposed in equity theory have several failings. First, it is difficult to quantify some of the "investments" actors believe they have brought to the situation (e.g., seniority or prestige). Moreover, it is often difficult to determine whether a particular characteristic ought to be treated as a reward or as an investment. For example, is job responsibility an investment or a reward? Even when these problems are not present, the equity equation often fails to adequately distinguish overreward from underreward, self-injustice from other injustice and individual injustice from collective injustice. If actor A's ratio is smaller than B's, does that mean that A is underrewarded or that B is overrewarded? Worse still, many justice situations remain undefined in the absence of a larger social basis of comparison as a reference to indicate what is a customary and appropriate distribution of rewards for actors like those involved in the immediate situation.

Status value theory focuses on the value of objects based on the status they represent (i.e., their symbolic value), rather than on their consummatory value. They are treated as *goal-objects*, not as simply rewards. That is, the theory emphasizes the honorific or status significance of the objects, which can be either positive or negative. Thus, the value of a key to the executive washroom is primarily seen in terms of what it represents regarding the status, honor, esteem, and importance being accorded the executive who possesses it. Justice issues can therefore be seen as involving questions of status consistency and inconsistency. As long as actors receive the status value they expect, the situation is seen as just; however, if actors receive status value different from what they expect, the situation is seen as unjust. This focus parallels Homans's (1953) original exploration of justice issues in his study of cash posters and ledger clerks.

Expectations for reward depend on *referential structures*, that is, on cultural definitions of the association of the status-valued goal-objects with other statuses actors might possess. The activation of referential structures enables actors to relate the general cultural framework within which they operate to their immediate situation of action. When a particular referential structure is activated, actors come to expect to receive rewards commensurate with their relevant status. Basically, "what is," as a matter of culturally defined fact, becomes "what is expected to be" in the immediate situation. Thus, a man (or woman) who believes that men are generally better paid than women in some larger collectivity will expect a higher level of reward for the man when he is interacting with a woman—provided, of course, that gender is a status characteristic to the actors and the relevant referential structure is activated.

The status value theory also argues for the operation of a reverse process, by which allocation of differentially evaluated goal-objects (or rewards) leads to the formation of differentiated expectations for performance that are consistent with the reward levels received. This can occur when the referential structure of concern is activated and the relevant status distinction is principally performance-based.

Several ideas in this theory are linked more or less directly with similar ideas in status characteristics theory. The concept of a diffuse status characteristic is used in specifying the statuses with which rewards are associated in referential structures. Relevance relations define the way in which statuses associated with rewards in referential structures come to be connected to each other in the local situation of action. The theory originally even used graph-theoretic notions to represent properties of the justice situation (Berger et al. 1968; Norman and Roberts 1972), a feature later developed fully in the graph-theoretical version of status characteristics theory.

As a result of its challenge to equity theory, status value theory originally focused on questions of defining different types of situations of justice and injustice and on questions of reactions to these situations (see, for example, Anderson et al. 1969). However, as work on status characteristics theory developed, a concern with other, analytically prior issues has become important. Most notably, this has included a recent focus on how expectations for the allocation of rewards emerge in group task situations, an issue considered in an extension of the graph-theoretical version of status characteristics theory to be discussed in the next section. It has also included a recent concern with how actors choose from among different distribution "rules" on the basis of their reward expectations: Under what circumstances do actors believe that fair allocations involve a principle of proportionality? Under what circumstances do they believe that rewards ought to be distributed equally to all? (See Wagner 1991a, 1991b; and work reported in the next section.)

Sources of Self-Evaluation

Expectation states emerge through a variety of processes. Status characteristics theory describes how societal stereotypes become the basis of expectations. Power and prestige theory explains how expectations may emerge from behavior in the ongoing interaction process. *Source theory* considers how expectations may emerge through the reflected appraisals of significant others. As with status characteristics theory, the original version of source theory (Webster 1969) dealt with the simplest situation first, one with only a single evaluator. Under what circumstances and by what processes, within such situations, do the appraisals of those with the right to evaluate, the evaluators, come to affect the expectations and behavior of others? In answering these questions, source theory makes use of the ideas on unit evaluations and expectations developed in the power and prestige branch as well as ideas from the status characteristics theory.

Basically, the theory argues that the higher an actor's expectations for an evaluator, the greater the likelihood the evaluator will become a *source of evaluations* for the actor (i.e., an evaluator whose assessments matter to the actor). Given that the evaluator is a source, the actor's unit evaluations, expectations, and behavior will be a function of the source's evaluations.

Of course, one's expectations for an evaluator are likely to be strongly influenced by any status characteristics the evaluator possesses. In an extension of the original source theory, Webster (1970) showed that a high status evaluator is more likely to become a source for the actor than is a low status evaluator.

But what if there are multiple evaluators and their evaluations are in conflict? The first version of a multiple evaluator source theory (Sobieszek 1970) considered two conflicting sources and posited that actors would ignore the evaluations of both sources under such circumstances. The data supported this prediction (although several alternative explanations could not be ruled out). However, later work on the topic (see especially Sobieszek and Webster 1973; Webster, Roberts, and Sobieszek 1972; Webster and Sobieszek 1974) suggests that actors in fact combine the unit evaluations of multiple conflicting sources. Thus, actors apparently use source information in much the same way they use status information, processing all the salient cues (in this case, the unit evaluations of significant others) to form expectations.

Recent investigations have extended these arguments still further. Foddy (see Crundall and Foddy 1981; Foddy 1988) distinguishes between the task competence and the evaluative competence of evaluators. For example, an editor may be a competent evaluator of writing without being a good writer. The paths linking evaluatively competent evaluators with self-expectations are less direct than those linking task-competent evaluators. Nevertheless, Foddy's work suggests there are many circumstances under which the evaluations of such an evaluator will have an impact (although the magnitude of the impact is likely to be lower). Finally, Moore (1985) focuses directly on the role of reflected appraisal in determining self-identity through a process of what he calls *role enactment*. He introduces the notion of a *second-order performance expectation* (i.e., actor o's expectations of actor p's expectations for self and o) and demonstrates that the determination of an actor's self-other expectations depends upon his or her role enactment of these second-order expectations.

Application and Intervention Research

Much of the development of status characteristics theory has been directly related to major lines of application and intervention research. Work in the area has been designed to use the theory to understand and alleviate concrete social problems. In addition, the work has had a significant impact on the structure and focus of later versions of the theory.

A major program of applications and intervention research has been that by E. G. Cohen and her associates. An initial focus in this work has been the application of status characteristics theory to biracial interaction among junior high school students (see especially Cohen and Roper 1972). The initial status characteristics theory was used to describe the interracial interaction disability experienced by black students (Cohen 1972). Subsequently, an intervention was developed to help reduce the inequality in power and prestige these students faced. This intervention, "expectation training," involved introducing information about performances that contradicted the racial definitions of the situation. Work on expectation training preceded the publication of the revised theory. In fact, this intervention research served as a stimulus in considering exactly how multiple characteristics situations would operate, and in determining (in conjunction with much other evidence) that some sort of combining mechanism governed the aggregation of expectations in such situations.

Over the years research in the Cohen program has served to identify different concrete social distinctions as status characteristics (e.g., on gender, see Hall 1972 and Lockheed and Hall 1976; on ethnic distinctions, see Cook 1974, Rosenholtz and Cohen 1985, and Cohen and Sharan 1980; on academic reputation and reading ability reputation, see Tammivarra 1982 and Rosenholtz 1985). Also over the years powerful new interventions have been developed within this program (e.g., the use of multiple ability curriculums and the use of referent actors in overcoming the effects of status characteristics; see Cohen 1982). In general, the intervention research in this program has been based on status characteristics theory (as well as source and power and prestige theory) and has also helped to shape the development of status characteristics theory (see E. G. Cohen, this volume).

A second program of intervention research was developed by Webster and Entwisle. As in the previous case, these researchers made use of source, status characteristics, and power and prestige theory in devising interventions. Webster and Entwisle succeeded in developing relatively simple intervention techniques that use unit evaluation and expectation states ideas. These have proven to be extremely effective in changing children's expectations in open interaction school settings. (See Webster and Entwisle 1974.)

Recent Extensions

In recent years, there have been major extensions of the status characteristics theory. Most of these depend heavily on the formulation of the graph-theoretical version of the theory and could not have been adequately developed without the mathematical concepts and principles it introduced. In this section, we describe five of these extensions in some detail, and list additional ones that are being developed.

Formation of Reward Expectations

The first of these extensions linked ideas from status value theory with status characteristics theory in an attempt to account for the formation of reward expectations in status-defined situations (see Berger et al. 1985). The reward expectation theory identifies three different types of referential structures, depending on the kind of characteristic that becomes associated with rewards. *Categorical* structures associate diffuse characteristics with rewards; they invoke criteria of "who you are" in determining rewards. *Ability* structures associate specific task abilities with rewards; they invoke criteria of "what you can do" in determining rewards. *Outcome* structures associate task outcomes with rewards; they invoke criteria of "what you have done" in determining rewards.

Any or all of these structures may be activated in a particular task situation.* When activated, each of these serves as a type of standard in terms of which expectations for reward are formed. If a referential structure is activated, its effect is to induce a path linking the appropriate status elements with reward levels, thereby generating status-based expectations for rewards in the situation. One of the consequences of this process is an increase in the number of paths connecting actors with task outcomes, thus linking reward expectations with expectations for task performance.

This formulation addresses a number of major theoretical questions: Under what conditions will different referential structures become acti-

---

*The current version of the reward expectation theory focuses on situations in which an ability standard is activated in the situation and in which one or more categorical structures can become activated.

vated? If multiple referential structures are activated, how are they organized in the situation? How can we describe the interrelation of task and reward in expectations in the same status situation? Given the actual allocation of rewards in a status situation, how is this allocation related to the task expectations that are formed in the situation? The theory is then used to derive a set of theorems that provide answers to these basic questions: how standards are activated and the information in them is combined to create overall reward expectations; how increases in the number of consistent status characteristics produce increases in the inequality of reward expectations; how increases in the inconsistency of status characteristics produce decreases in the inequality of reward expectations; how changes in task expectations (by adding or eliminating relevant status distinctions) produce correlated changes in reward expectations, and, in turn, how changes in reward expectations (by adding or deleting standards) produce correlated changes in task expectations; and, very important, how the actual allocation of rewards generates task expectations consistent with these rewards (the "reverse process").

Research already exists that is relevant to this formulation and in general supports its arguments. See Webster and Smith (1978) on the role of referential structures in creating reward expectations; see Jasso and Rossi (1977) and Alves and Rossi (1978) on the use of multiple referential structures in American society as well as their combined effect in determining reward expectations. On the relation of task and reward expectations, see Parcel and Cook (1977); and on the generation of task expectations as a consequence of reward allocation (the "reverse process"), see studies by Lerner (1965), Cook (1970, 1975), Harrod (1980), and Bierhoff, Buck, and Klein (1986). In addition, a pair of recent studies (Wagner 1992a, 1992b) provides evidence that male and female allocation preferences for rewards are the outcome of the same status-based processes, a result that is predicted by the reward expectation theory.

The reward expectation theory only partially integrates ideas from the status value theory of distributive justice with status characteristics theory. Many issues remain solely the province of the justice theory. In addition, other theoretical approaches have adopted parts of the status value theory in developing major alternative accounts of justice processes. This has occurred especially in the work of Jasso (1978, 1980, 1983) and Markovsky (1985).

The Evolution of Status Expectations

Up to now our theory has been formulated to describe status-organizing processes in a single task situation, where, although individuals may become or cease to be interactants, most of the status and performance information is available to them at the outset of the interaction. However, individuals often interact with the same or similar others across a sequence of tasks where new status, performance, and evaluational information is acquired at different stages. How do status expectations evolve across such a sequence of tasks? A recent extension of the theory addresses this problem (see Berger, Fisek, and Norman 1989). Specifically, this formulation concerns itself with such basic questions as: Under what conditions will the expectations and behaviors that emerge in one task situation affect those of a subsequent task situation? Under what conditions will there be major changes in the expectations and power and prestige behaviors that evolve across task situations? Under what conditions will the status expectations and behaviors that develop over task situations stabilize? And in this context of stabilization, what happens to status interventions in the later stages of task sequences which have been introduced in the early stages?

Using concepts and an assumption specific to this extension in conjunction with those in the basic theory, we can derive important general results. These describe how expectations on past tasks affect those on current ones; how particular factors such as the external evaluation of group performances can produce major changes in expectations and behavior; how expectations and behavior can stabilize; and how, when interaction is closed to environmental inputs, status interventions can have a diminished, yet lasting effect across task sequences.

A motivation in developing this extension was to determine the ways in which status interventions in one setting affect expectations and behavior in a subsequent setting, and there is research that is specifically relevant to this problem in our formulation. In this connection, see Lockheed and Hall (1976), for research on the effect on female behavior in gender-heterogeneous groups of women's prior experiences in gender-homogeneous groups; see Pugh and Wahrman (1983)* and Markovsky, Smith, and Berger (1984), for research on the transfer of status interventions across status occupants and across tasks. See also Prescott (1986), for research on the transfer of status interventions across tasks and from one actor to a second when the second actor also introduces new status characteristics into the process. The results of this research are in accord with predictions from our theoretical extension and provide support for this extension. Still, much more work will be necessary in order for us to adequately assess this formulation.

---

*The results of this study, while consistent with our extension, are already implied by the Berger et al. (1977) formulation.

Status Cues, Expectations, and Behavior

In many status situations various social cues, many nonverbal, are available to help the actor form expectations: patterns of speech, posture, direct references to background or experience, styles of dress, etc. Status characteristics theory has recently been extended to take into account the role such cues play in generating expectations (Berger et al. 1986).

This extension distinguishes *indicative* from *expressive* cues and *task* cues from *categorical* cues. Indicative cues (e.g., "I'm a doctor") directly label the actor's status state while expressive cues (e.g., a woman's style of dress) provide information from which status states can be inferred. The task/categorical distinction crosscuts the indicative/expressive distinction. Task cues (e.g., fluency of speech) provide information about the actor's capacities on the immediate task while categorical cues (e.g., language syntax) provide information about states of status characteristics actors possess.

A review of the extensive literature on cues generates a set of abstract generalizations that are accounted for by this extension of the status characteristics theory. First, if no prior status differences exist in the group, then differences in task cues will come to determine the distribution of power and prestige in the group. The status theory argument that is used to account for this generalization is that information from task cues is used in the formation of expectations for self and other on the immediate task and such expectations determine power and prestige positions. Second, if status differences based on status characteristics do exist from the outset in the group, then the differentiation in task cues will match the status differences. In this case the status theory argument is that status characteristic differences produce congruent differences in expectations and these in turn determine congruent differences in the rates of task cue behaviors. Consequently, rates of task cue behaviors will be consistent with the initial status differences. (This argument is referred to as the *status governance of task cues.*)

Third, if for some reason, the differentiation in task cues is inconsistent with the differentiation in categorical cues, then both sets will be involved in determining the actors' expectations and behavior. The status theory argument here is that information from both types of cues will be combined in the formation of expectations. However, task cues give information about capacities on the immediate task; categorical cues give information about status characteristics that become relevant to the task. Consequently, the strength of relevance of task cues is greater than that of categorical cues; therefore the effect of task cues will be greater than that of categorical cues when they are inconsistent.

The status cues extension in part responds to challenges from dominance theories (see Mazur 1985; Lee and Ofshe 1981). Generally, these theories argue that dominance behaviors are the primary means by which status differences are established in groups. This extension argues that it is necessary to distinguish high and low task cue behaviors and dominating and propitiating behaviors. The former represent claims about competency at the task; the latter represent attempts to exercise control over others in the group. Unfortunately, these behaviors are often confounded in the literature (especially in the dominance theories). Task cue behaviors are effective to the extent that they have an impact on the actor's performance expectations in the situation. However, dominating and propitiating behaviors are effective to the extent that they reflect a legitimated power and prestige order (see Ridgeway 1984; Ridgeway and Berger 1986). These arguments have led to the development of still another extension of status characteristics theory, that concerned with the process of the legitimation of power and prestige orders. This work will be considered below.

There is an extensive body of background research on status cues which provides support for the extension (see Berger et al. 1986). In addition there is a body of relevant research that has recently emerged (see Tuzlak and Moore 1984; Tuzlak 1988; Mohr 1986; Ridgeway, Berger, and Smith 1985; Rainwater 1987; Riches and Foddy 1989; Sev'er 1989). Of particular interest in this research is the work by Ridgeway (1987), which shows that where we can assume that a legitimated power and prestige order does not exist, high dominance behaviors are no more effective than low dominance behaviors in determining influence in groups. On the other hand, high task cue behaviors are more effective than low task cue behaviors, as well as being more effective than either type of dominance behaviors. (For findings that are related to and extend the research of Ridgeway, see Driskell, Olmstead, and Salas 1992.)

Finally, there is the research of Dovidio et al. (1988) on various types of behavior including task cues such as looking while speaking, looking while listening, and gesturing. They find that status differences generate the usual ordering of these behaviors on tasks identified as masculine or gender-neutral. Thus, for example, males look while speaking more frequently than females when working on a masculine or gender-neutral task. Further, since females are status superiors on tasks identified as feminine, the usual ordering of these behaviors is *reversed*. For example, females exhibit a higher rate of looking while speaking than males. These results provide direct support for the arguments on the status governance of task cues that are developed in this extension. All in all, this has become a very lively area of research.

Legitimation of Power and Prestige Hierarchies

Legitimation is an important factor in status-organizing processes. Research has shown that legitimacy is essential for leaders with traditionally low statuses (e.g., women or minorities) to successfully engage in the directive behaviors ordinarily expected of a leader (see Eskilson and Wiley 1976; Fennell et al. 1978). More generally, legitimacy plays a crucial role in determining the effectiveness of controlling behaviors such as dominating and propitiating behaviors.

A recent extension of the status characteristics theory describes a process and a set of conditions under which a power and prestige order that has emerged in a group becomes legitimated (see Ridgeway and Berger 1986, 1988; Ridgeway 1988). In accord with the reward expectation extension, it is assumed that as part of the social framework, within which actors operate in task situations, there exist consensual beliefs—referential structures—that associate possession of differentially valued status positions with the possession of different states of diffuse status characteristics, or different levels of task capacities, or different levels of task achievements. An example of such a referential structure is the belief that males ordinarily occupy higher-valued status positions than females in American society.

When these beliefs about what is true in the larger society (beliefs which in fact may be true) are activated, they are used to create expectations as to who will occupy high- and low-valued status positions in the immediate situation of action. It is assumed that actors will display differences in respect, esteem, and generalized deference behavior to others in accord with differences in the expectations for possessing valued status positions that they hold for others. When such behaviors are validated by others and when expectations for performances coincide with those for possessing valued status positions, the power and prestige order can become legitimated. An actor's behavior is said to be validated by another if the other engages in similar supportive behavior or if the other's behavior does not contradict the actor's.

With legitimation, assumptions are created about "what ought to be" in the immediate situation. Expectations become normative with the presumption that there will be collective support for these norms. A high status actor has a right to expect a higher degree of esteem, respect, and generalized deference than does a low status actor. At the same time, others have the right to expect more valued contributions from that actor than from the low status actor. In addition, high status actors come to have rights to exercise, if necessary, controlling behaviors—dominating and propitiating behaviors—over the actions of others.

Aside from describing the process of legitimation this theory also describes status conditions that affect the likelihood that a power and prestige order becomes legitimate. These include such conditions as the number of status distinctions that discriminate among the members of the group and the degree of consistency of these status distinctions among the members of the group.

This theory provides an explanation for the resistance that low status members encounter when they engage in power and prestige and task cue behaviors that are above their rank. (For relevant research on race, see Katz 1970, Katz and Cohen 1962, and Cohen et al. 1970; and on gender, see Meeker and Weitzel-O'Neill 1977 and Ridgeway 1982.) It also explains the resistance that women and minorities encounter in mixed-gender and biracial groups when they engage in controlling behaviors even though they are task leaders. Such resistance is due to the fact that these low external status members who have become task leaders are operating from positions in a power and prestige order that is not a legitimated order.

There is much to be done to further develop this extension. We need a more explicit formalization of the theory, we need a further extension of the theory to describe the dynamics of illegitimate power and prestige orders, and we also need research to test its more subtle implications. Such research is now under way.

Integration of Power and Prestige Theory with Status Characteristics Theory

Recently we have considered how the expectation formation process in initially homogeneous status situations and that in initially status-differentiated situations might combine in the development of power and prestige hierarchies (see Fisek, Berger, and Norman 1991). The strategy is to incorporate features of the power and prestige theories (behavior-expectation theories) into the graph-theoretical formulation of status characteristics theory and to generalize the assumptions of the latter to accommodate the more complex situations.

The key idea is that of a *behavioral interchange pattern*, that is, a set of interaction cycles or unit sequences between two or more actors that are consistent in their power and prestige significance. Berger and Conner (1969, 1974) conceptualize interaction sequences or cycles as both decision-making and expectation-forming sequences. For example, if actor A gives B an action opportunity to which B responds with a performance that A accepts, this interchange is a decision-making unit and at the same time a sequence that can result in A and B forming higher performance expectations for B than A. Following Berger and Conner (1974), we can categorize different types of interaction sequences or cycles in terms of their effect in creating expectation differences. A behavioral interchange pattern is a set of unit sequences or cycles in which all the sequences have the same ordering effect in creating expectation differences between the actors involved. These expectation differences are created when they provide new status information (i.e., there are no status distinctions already existing between the actors, or the expectation differences are inconsistent with those that do exist). Once these expectation differences between actors have been created from interchange patterns, they are processed along with other relevant status elements in the formation of aggregated expectations.

An additional feature in this formulation is the extension of the status theory to deal with the simultaneous interaction of multiple actors.* A new measure relating self-other expectations to behavior is introduced, that of *expectation standing*, and an actor's power and prestige behavior is assumed to be a direct function of his or her expectation standing in the multiple actor situation.

This extension also posits an additional process by which the power and prestige hierarchy of the group and in particular the position of the leading actor will come to be legitimated. The argument is that the larger the proportion of actors in a group who have formed low-high behavioral patterns with the actor who is highest in the power and prestige order, the more likely that the position of that actor will come to be accepted as legitimate by the members of the group.

Within this extension a specific model is constructed that predicts participation rates in open interaction Bales-like settings. The fit of the model is assessed against data from groups initially status heterogeneous (Skvoretz 1988; Lohman 1970; Morris 1977; Rosenholtz 1977; Lockheed 1976) and groups initially status homogeneous (Bales 1970). In general, the fit of the model to the data is good.

One of the most interesting features of this extension is that it returns us to some of the issues raised by Bales's research. However, in terms of our present understanding of these matters, the original Bales type of setting can be seen to be very special indeed. In that situation, all or most status information is available at the outset of the process; there is no changeover of interactants; the group's achievements are not externally evaluated; and the group has no past and indeed no future.† In the terms

---

*Previous formulations do cover situations involving multiple actors. However, in these situations only two actors are engaged with each other at any given time and the identity of interactants may change over the course of time.

†It is also the case that studies done in the original Bales type of setting typically involve groups operating over very short time periods so that a structure once formed tends to persist.

of the status evolution extension (see above), groups in such settings are operating under conditions that make them closed to their environment (see Berger, Fisek, and Norman 1989). By making use of the basic status theory and its extensions, we are now in a position to describe the interaction in far more complex status situations as these occur in interpersonal settings, familial settings, and organizational settings. (In this context, see in particular Yuchtmann-Yaar and Semyonov 1979, on status processes in Israeli athletic teams; Gerber 1989, on the status dynamics of mixed-gender police teams; and Cohen and Zhou 1991, on status processes in enduring work teams in organizational settings.)

Other Extensions and Proliferations

In addition to those described above, there have been other recent extensions of the theory, which we briefly describe.

The character of the translation function between expectations and behavior has been the focus òf recent work by Balkwell (1991a). Up to now, distinct translation functions have been required to deal with 2-person and with n-person status situations. In addition, we have assumed that distinct translation functions would be required to deal with each of the variety of experimental situations in which research has been conducted. That is, although the expectation values in the standardized situation, in open interaction settings, in applied situations, and in other settings might remain constant, the translation of the values into behavior would involve a different function in each setting.

Balkwell has now developed a general function that allows the translation of expectation values into behavior in situations involving any number of actors and across different types of experimental situations. The same function can be used for all these circumstances. This represents an important development in the program, one that promises to significantly increase the range of situations to which the graph-theoretical version of the status characteristics theory is applicable.

Foschi (1989) and Foschi and Foddy (1988) have developed a theory describing the operation of multiple standards. An important argument in this theory is that multiple standards, in particular, are invoked in situations involving status inconsistencies and thus are a way of adapting to such situations. Tests of this theory are currently under way.

Johnston (1985) has constructed a theory which is a proliferant of the status characteristics theory to describe the operation of "personality" characteristics. These are evaluated characteristics, constructed from the interaction process, that are assigned by actors to each other. Personality characteristics, under specified conditions, become salient, are used to define situations, are combined, and operate to determine behavior. In structure, this theory is similar to the status characteristics theory, but its explanatory domain is different. Johnston uses the theory to explain rigidities in behavior as these occur in marital and familial systems. (See also Driskell 1982, on the effect of moral characteristics in defining task situations; and Greenstein and Knottnerus 1980, on the effect of differential evaluations in status generalization processes.)

Analytical Review

In this section, we present an overview of the development of the status characteristics program. First, we consider how the program has evolved from the standpoint of the particular relations that obtain between the theories within the program and those in related areas. And second, we present a brief overview of the types of research that exist that constitute the direct and indirect empirical bases for the theoretical research.

Relations Between Theories

Figures 1 and 2 present a schematic summary of the developments that have occurred in status characteristics theory and related areas. The presentation is roughly chronological, although publication dates are notoriously poor as indicators of what work is antecedent to what other work. Instead, the figures more adequately represent analytical dependence; "early" work provides conceptual and empirical foundations upon which "later" work is constructed. The figures are not intended to be comprehensive either; they show only a representative subset of the relevant theory and research.

The structure of development in the program is best characterized using the conceptual apparatus of Wagner and Berger (1985). Status characteristics theory is part of a *branching* program. It is characterized by the *proliferation* of new theories using a common theoretical core to deal with new and different theoretical problems. Power and prestige theory (behavior-expectation theory), status characteristics theory, source theory, and distributive justice theory all represent proliferations. The distributive justice theory is in fact a proliferation from two different theories, status characteristics theory and the rank equilibration theory of Zelditch and Anderson (1966).

In each of these cases further *elaboration* has occurred that extends and refines the analyses of the problems considered in each branch of the program. The elaboration has been most extensive in status characteris-

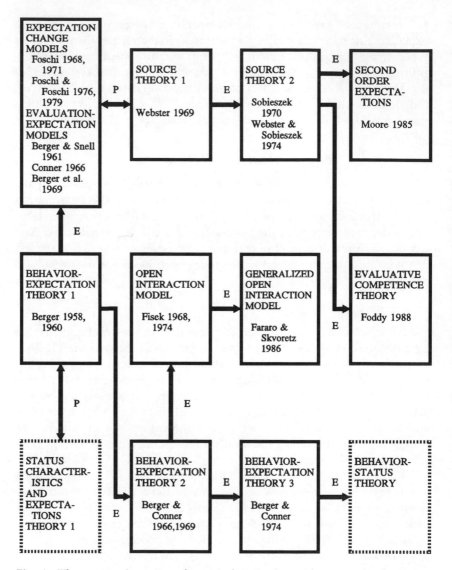

Fig. 1. The expectation states theoretical research program: power & prestige and source branches. E = elaboration; P = proliferation.

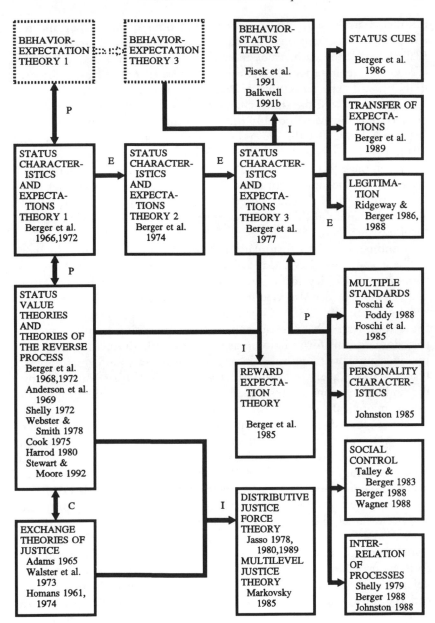

Fig. 2. The expectation states theoretical research program: status, reward, justice, and related branches. E = elaboration; P = proliferation; C = competition; I = integration.

tics theory itself, with three major formulations of the theory and five comprehensive extensions (including two integrations) at this stage. Elaboration of the status value theory of distributive justice has been the least extensive; in fact, only a subset of the issues it raised are considered in the reward expectation theory that elaborates it.

Competition with the status characteristics approach has appeared in a number of cases. Most notably this has occurred in the competition between the dominance theories represented by Mazur (1985) and Lee and Ofshe (1981) and the status cues and legitimation theories (described above) on the effect of dominance behaviors (e.g., deference-demanding behaviors) in the attainment of power and prestige. In the former theories, significantly different theoretical concepts and principles are used to account for some of the same phenomena as in the status characteristics theories.

A number of *variant* formulations have also appeared. After the work of Freese and Cohen (1973), a variant to the revised and graph-theoretical formulations was developed by Hembroff (1982) and Hembroff, Martin, and Sell (1981). (See also Greenstein and Knottnerus 1980 and Knottnerus and Greenstein 1981.) While using concepts and principles similar to those in the status characteristics theory and addressing a similar explanatory domain, this formulation makes use of both eliminating and combining arguments to describe the processing of status information. As a result of recent analytical research, Balkwell (1991b) has concluded that the findings relevant to this variant in fact can be accounted for by the graph-theoretical version of the status characteristics theory.

Although combining seems to be the status-organizing mechanism of choice at the present time, eliminating alternatives remain viable options within the structure of status characteristics theory. In fact, Berger and others have suggested (in Berger 1988 and Berger et al. 1992) that eliminating and combining patterns (as well as oscillating and ambivalent patterns) may be outcomes of the same information-processing principles that occur under different social conditions that are yet to be specified.

A number of significant attempts at *integration* have occurred in the status characteristics program. One is the partial integration of concerns from status value theory with the status characteristics theory that is developed in the reward expectation theory. The other is the recent unification of power and prestige processes with status-organizing processes in a behavior-status theory that also includes some concern with legitimation issues. Both of these efforts have involved integration at the formal level of linking theoretical structures in terms of the concepts and principles of the graph-theoretical formulation. In addition, Jasso (1978, 1980, 1989) and Markovsky (1985) have formulated theories that integrate concepts and principles from the status value and the equity theories of justice.

Relevant Empirical Research

It is not possible here to review in any detail the extensive research testing various formulations in the status characteristics program. This research is of four major types. First, there is background research. Many of the theories in the program build on a body of research that existed prior to their formulation, and some were developed specifically to explain parts of this prior research. See Berger et al. (1966) and Cohen, Berger, and Zelditch (1972), on status characteristics; Berger et al. (1986), on status cues; and Webster and Sobieszek (1974), on self-evaluations.

Second, there has been extensive experimental testing of theories in non-open interaction situations, much of which has occurred in a standardized experimental setting specifically developed for this purpose. On the nature of the standardized experimental situation, see Berger et al. (1977) and Cook, Cronkite, and Wagner (1974); and for reviews of research done in this situation, see Fox and Moore (1979), Berger, Rosenholtz, and Zelditch (1980), and Fisek, Norman, and Nelson-Kilger (1992). In addition, there have been experimental tests of these theories outside of the standardized situation. These include, for example, tests in the Dovidio-Ellyson experimental situation (Dovidio et al. 1988) and tests in the Margolin-Kimberley experimental situation (Balkwell et al. 1992). See also Webster and Driskell (1983) and Yuchtmann-Yaar and Shapira (1981). Third, an important component of the research effort has been pursued in interaction settings. This has been particularly true for application and intervention research. Part of this research has been done in open interaction experimental settings, and part has been done in field settings, most frequently in school situations (see E. G. Cohen, this volume, and Webster and Entwistle 1974; see also Cohen and Zhou 1991, for research on R&D teams, and Gerber 1989, for research on mixed-gender police teams).

Finally, there has also been collateral empirical research, e.g., on conversational interruptions. Such work, in different types of research settings and by researchers working in other theoretical traditions, provides indirect support for status characteristics theories. See, for example, Zimmerman and West (1975), Wood and Karten (1986), Carli (1991), and Lockheed (1985), who presents a meta-analysis of the results of forty-six studies relevant to status characteristics theory as applied to gender.

A proper assessment of these bodies of research is beyond the scope of this paper. But generally speaking we can say that, while there are some ideas that have had to be revised and some ideas that are still matters of controversy, most basic ideas have been supported. Of course, the extent of that support differs from study to study.

Work in Progress

State-Organizing Processes

One of the interesting aspects in the development of status characteristics theory is that in the course of this work we have developed metatheoretical ideas that have shaped our theoretical thinking. Among the better-known of these are the idea of explicitly formulating scope conditions as part of the structure of the theory (see Berger 1974; Walker and Cohen 1985) and the idea of the instantiation of the theory as part of the effort to distinguish between the theoretical elements of an abstract formulation and the factual elements that are involved in applying a theory to a concrete social setting (see Berger et al. 1977). But perhaps the most important of these ideas is our conception of a state-organizing process. This is a metatheoretical scheme that has evolved, in particular, from our experiences in developing status and distributive justice theories. Analyzing the status characteristics theory from this perspective provides us with a more general conception of the structure of this theory and of the type of process it describes. Figure 3 presents a schematic summary of the status characteristics theory as a state-organizing process.

Social framework. In conceptualizing a social process, we distinguish what we call the level of the *social framework* and the level of the *situation of action*. A situation of action occurs within a social framework whose elements are more comprehensive and more enduring relative to those in the action situation. The elements in a social framework may be cultural, including such things as norms, values, beliefs, and social categories; formal, as institutionalized and formalized roles and authority positions; or interpersonal, as enduring networks of sentiments, influence, and communication. As the status characteristics theory is currently formulated, the major elements are cultural: status characteristics with their culturally constructed evaluations and expectations, and referential structures which represent consensual social beliefs that are part of a larger collectivity.

This distinction between social framework and situation of action generates the problem of what elements from the framework become accessed by the actors. The *salience* principles of our theory address this problem in that they describe how and under what conditions different

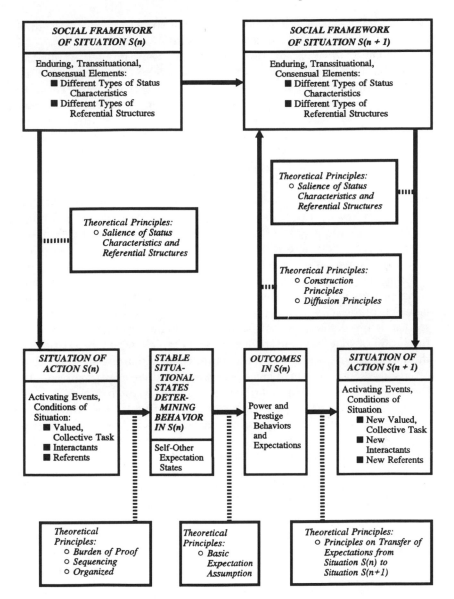

Fig. 3. Status characteristics theory as a state–organizing process.

types of status characteristics and referential structures become significant to the actors in their immediate situation of action.

Situation of action. Social processes occur in situations of immediate
action that have stipulated properties and features. One of the most important components of such situations is the *activating events*. These are
events or conditions that are the focus of the interaction process, they are
the goal-states toward which actors are oriented. In the status characteristics theory they are the collective tasks, the outcome states of which are
capable of being evaluated in terms of team success or failure. In addition, the situation of action is described in terms of properties and components that define the scope conditions of the theory. In the status characteristics theory these conditions are that there are a number of actors in
the situation, that some of them may possess different and others similar
states of status characteristics, that they are task-oriented and collectively
oriented, etc. These activating events and conditions are the theoretical
givens of a situation of action.

Evolution of process. We assume that given the activating conditions the
social process will evolve: behaviors will occur that are addressed to the
demands of the activating conditions, and social information will be used
so that actors define their situation. The outcome of this process is the
formation of states that are stable structures which define the relations of
the actors to each other within their immediate situation. In status characteristics theory, *burden of proof, sequencing*, and *organized subsets* are the
theoretical principles that describe the evolution of the process.

State determined behaviors. Once states are formed, these states determine the behaviors of the actors relative to each other and to the activating events. The theoretical concepts and principles that describe these
relations in status characteristics theory are those of *expectation advantage*,
the *observable power and prestige order*, and the *basic expectation assumption*
that relates positions in the power and prestige order to differences in
expectation advantage. Given that an episode in a situation of action
is completed, that, say, the task has been dealt with by the actors, we
think of the process as deactivating. In the case of status processes, this
could mean that status distinctions which were operating in the situation become latent and that the power and prestige order becomes de-
differentiated.

Transsituational effects. Furthermore, there may be transsituational effects: these are outcomes from one interaction episode that become inputs to a succeeding episode, *succession* effects, or these are outcomes
from one or more interaction episodes that feed back to the level of the
social framework, *construction* effects. Some of the most recent work in
our programs deal with these transsituational effects. We have already

described the work of Berger, Fisek, and Norman (1989) on how expectations formed in one task situation affect expectations formed in succeeding task situations. In addition, Markovsky (1988) has constructed diffusion models which describe how changes in expectations toward members of disadvantaged status classes created in a specific task situation can diffuse through a larger population and thus produce macrolevel changes. And Ridgeway (1991) has formulated a theory which describes how the states of an initially nonvalued characteristic can acquire, from status processes that occur in situations of action, status value and generalized expectations and thus become a status characteristic. These constructed status characteristics then become elements of the social framework.*

This conception of a state-organizing process which has emerged from our work in developing theories has also become a framework for subsequent work on these theories and for constructing theories of different social processes, e.g., theories of interpersonal social control and interpersonal affect processes. As such, this conception now is part of the heuristic structure of the expectation states program.

Other Processes

Within this conception of a state-organizing process we can formulate different theories for the same process. We can also use the same conception to formulate theories for different processes, and this is what has happened. At present there is ongoing research on developing state-organizing theories for interpersonal control processes (see Talley and Berger 1983; Berger 1988; Wagner 1988) and interpersonal affect processes (see Berger 1988).

The Control Process

This process is assumed to occur within a social framework that consists primarily of general norms, rules, and understandings that define what is meaningful, predictable, and accountable interaction in a given type of situation. The process is activated by what, relative to these definitions, is a set of unexpected "should not be" events—major violations of or conflicts in expectations. These events may be ignored or normalized by various kinds of accounting processes. When such maneuvers, if used, have not resolved the problem, actors are seen as engaging in behaviors aimed at managing the problematic events and defining their moral relations to each other. An important outcome of such behavior is

---

*For a more comprehensive and detailed discussion of this conception of a state-organizing process, see Berger, Wagner, and Zelditch 1992.

the construction of situationally stable self-other *control states*, principally "norm carrier" and "norm violator," which determine the actors' subsequent behavior. If the actors come to occupy the complementary states of carrier and violator, they have established for themselves a consensual moral ordering in relation to the "should not be" events. If they fail to establish a consensual moral ordering—say, each seeks the position of norm carrier vis-à-vis the other—intense escalating conflict may result in which such conflict is sustained by what appears to each actor to be the moral nature of his or her claims. If each assumes the position of norm violator in the control structure, conflict, if it occurs, is usually momentary with each actor deferring to the moral claims of the other. Such mutually deferring structures tend to be transitory and often serve as a mechanism to resolve conflicting control episodes.

Whether resolved or not, control processes do become deactivated and have important transsituational outcomes, including the activation of affect states, the creation of rules that are relation-specific, and the assignment of personality characteristics. The last are individual-level stereotypes that, depending upon the course of the process, may be positive or negative and that have strong moral connotations (e.g., "good/bad," "responsible/irresponsible," "mature/immature"). These are attributions, detached from specific acts and specific situations, which define the actors' "deeper reality" to each other.

All of these outcomes—affect states, new rules, and the assignment of personality characteristics—have in common the fact that they can become inputs for the actors in subsequent situations and thus can dramatically change the nature of the process in subsequent control episodes. Finally, it should be noted that audiences can play a critical role in this process, particularly in determining the allocation of control states and in providing validation for the assignment of personality characteristics. For a more detailed description of the control theory, see Berger (1988). For an application of this theory to conflictual divorce situations, see Johnston and Campbell (1988).

The Affect Process

We are also at work in developing a theory of interpersonal affect processes conceptualized in state-organizing terms. Such a process is one in which actors behave in accord with states of diffuse attachment and/or states of diffuse rejection that have been activated in a particular situation.

We assume that general and specific beliefs, norms, and understandings—cultural elements from a more comprehensive collectivity—become inputs to an affect situation and are used to so define the situation and, in particular, to define what are appropriate bonding and rejecting behaviors. We believe that in such a situation the process is activated by interaction events that produce a high level of interpersonal arousal. These interaction events may be positive, such as those involved in sexual gratification and pleasure, or negative, such as those involved in interpersonal conflict and aggression.

With the evolution of the affect process, affect states, which have both emotional and cognitive components, are formed. These states are univalent structures in that actors occupying these states behave toward each other in purely positive or purely negative terms. We believe that when interaction events are producing high levels of interpersonal arousal, actors may form these states by decomposing each other's attributes into positive and negative subsets and use these subsets as a basis for "constructing" the other as a purely positive or purely negative social object. These affect states are generalized and diffuse orientations that actors hold toward each other and typically they cannot be identified with specific emotions such as anger or fear. However, these states may be activated by specific emotional reactions and they may operate to sustain such emotional reactions into new situations, thus creating affect linkages between different types of situations.

We imagine that during the operation of this process actors can oscillate between states that are mutually positive or mutually negative or where one is negative and the other is positive. While they exist, these states determine various types of bonding and rejecting behaviors that are culturally defined as appropriate to the situation. Upon deactivation, the states and the behaviors contingent upon them devolve, and actors may assign to each other positive and negative personality characteristics with strong affective connotations (e.g., "warm/cold," "expressive/inexpressive," "caring/uncaring"). These in turn become inputs to subsequent situations of action (see Berger 1988; Johnston 1988).

The task ahead, in further conceptualizing the control and the affect process, is to specify in explicit form the various theoretical principles—those on the salience of cultural elements, those on the formation of states, and those on the state determination of behaviors—which as a set will constitute a state-organizing theory of these processes.

Interrelation of Processes

While the development of expectation states theories of different social processes is still very much in progress, research has already begun on the problem of interrelating social processes. A number of different approaches have been taken to this problem.

In dealing with the relation of status and socioemotional behaviors, Ridgeway and Johnson (1990) take the view that in the informal task group, these behaviors are closely related. Socioemotional behaviors are elicited by agreements and disagreements with those very task proposals that are involved in forming status hierarchies (see Berger and Conner 1969, 1974). They argue that, in particular, emotional reactions to disagreements are mediated by differentiated performance expectations, so that the individual's expression of such reactions tends to be directly related to his or her status position in the hierarchy, and that status struggles, although they do occur, are relatively uncommon in these task-oriented groups. From this perspective, the expression of negative socioemotional behavior is seen to be a control mechanism which operates to maintain the status order.

On the other hand, positive socioemotional reactions are not constrained by the status hierarchy, and positive socioemotional "chain reactions" occur. As a consequence, the expression of such positive behavior is more common than the expression of negative behavior, which leads to greater levels of group solidarity.

In Ridgeway and Johnson's theory there is a very intimate connection between status and socioemotional processes. Other researchers have conceptualized the different social processes in more distinct terms and have sought to describe their interrelation. One such approach focuses on the interrelation of the states of different processes. This approach assumes that two or more distinct processes have been activated simultaneously, and it deals with the question of how the assignment of different types of states will affect these processes (see Shelly 1979; Wattendorf 1979; and Webster 1980). A basic argument in this approach is what might be called the *congruence principle*. The claim is made that if the states of one process are congruently allocated with those of a second, the first process will accentuate the behavioral effects of the second, whereas if they are incongruently allocated, the first process will constrain the effects of the second. States of two processes are congruent if the relevant states allocated to a given actor have the same sign or evaluation and are incongruent if they have opposite signs or evaluations. By this argument, for example, if status states are allocated incongruently with control states, this will operate to constrain the behaviors determined by the control states, or if sentiment states, say, are assigned congruently with status states, this will operate to accentuate the differentiation produced by status states (see Webster 1980; Shelley 1988).

The congruence approach assumes that states of different processes are already assigned to actors, and it concerns itself with the consequences of different patterns of assignment. This can be seen as but one aspect of the problem of interrelating processes. In situations where more than one process operates at the same time we can also be concerned with how the evolution of one process relates to that of a second. Two processes may evolve simultaneously, with the evolution of one affecting that of the other. This is exactly the case in the reward expectation theory, which describes the simultaneous evolution of reward and performance expectation processes (see Berger et al. 1985). On the other hand, the operation of one process may facilitate the occurrence of a second (e.g., where the conflicting events in a control process may operate to activate an affect process). Or the evolution of an earlier process may directly affect the way a later process evolves (e.g., where an evolving status process determines which actors are assigned to which control states). Or the operation of one process may inhibit the operation of a second (e.g., where the differentiation produced by a status process may inhibit the activation of a mutually positive affect process). (See Johnston's [1988] theory on the interrelation of state-organizing processes.) This "evolution process approach" is particularly attractive. It exploits more fully our conceptualization of social processes as state-organizing processes. However, this approach poses many difficult theoretical problems that remain to be resolved.

Overall, then, we have a good idea about many of the problems that are still to be dealt with. While the ways in which to handle some of these problems may be clear, the ways in which to handle others involve difficult theoretical puzzles. Developing solutions to these theoretical puzzles is the task that now confronts us.

Affect Control Theory: Delineation and Development

Neil J. MacKinnon and David R. Heise

Affect control theory proposes that people cast themselves and others into situational identities and then construct events to validate sentiments evoked by the identities while maintaining the integrity of behaviors and the spirit of settings as well. The normative coherence of social action arises from cultural and institutional shaping of identities, behaviors, and settings. Diversity and innovation in social action arise as different sentiments get evoked in situations and as past events reverberate affectively.

Event construction can occur not only by engaging in behavior but also cognitively by redefining interactants so that their identities fit their actions—the kinds of construction emphasized in sociological labeling theory and psychological trait-inference theory. In affect control theory reidentification processes are comprehended within the same social psychological system that governs action.

Affect control theory regards emotion as the experience of identity validation or invalidation and as a capacity for sensing the social structuring of relationships. Displays of emotion broadcast to others information about what identities one is trying to maintain and how those commitments are faring and thereby provide a nonverbal mechanism for attaining intersubjectivity in definitions of situations.

Having briefly sketched the gist of the theory, we now proceed to our main concerns in this essay. In the next section we describe affect control theory through a systematic statement of the theory's key premises and propositions. Then we turn to describing the development of the theory and a related sociological object—the research program in which the theory developed.*

*This essay, which combines MacKinnon's propositional formulation of affect control theory that he prepared for a book (MacKinnon, forthcoming) and Heise's work on his-

The Theory

This presentation displays the shape of affect control theory at the end of 1990, freely incorporating results of past research. In order to provide an unobstructed overview, we restrict our use of three hallmarks of prior presentations—mathematical equations, citations to the literature, and simulations of social interaction based on a computer implementation of the theory. The interested reader can find equations, citations, and simulation results in abundance by consulting the sources listed in our references. Overviews of affect control theory written by nonparticipants in the research program are available in Stryker and Statham (1985) and Thoits (1989).

We state twenty-four propositions blocked into seven groups. The first group, relating to symbols and affective meaning, sketches the general perspectives and methods involved in affect control theory—the metatheory. The second group, focusing on cognitive operations, outlines an auxiliary theory that is essential in order to apply affect control theory. The third group of propositions presents basic principles of affective response and control. The fourth and fifth groups of propositions relate to event assessment and event production. The sixth group of propositions presents affect control theory's approach to emotion, and the last group of propositions concerns cognitive revision through reidentification of interactants.

Symbols and Affective Meaning

> *Proposition 1.* Social interaction is conducted in terms of social cognitions of the interactants.

The most basic premise of affect control theory is that social interactions is *symbolic interaction*. People manage their interpersonal behavior by cognizing (or recognizing) themselves, others, and objects, including encompassing settings, and by invoking classifications of action to interpret what is happening. Cognitive definitions involved in social interaction are partially determined by the material settings in which people find themselves, but qualitative definitions of situations may differ from one individual to another because different actors have different agendas and

torical analysis of the research program, has benefited from the criticisms and suggestions of numerous colleagues. In particular, we thank Ross Boylan, Larry Griffin, T. David Kemper, Eric Plutzer, Herman Smith, Peggy Thoits, David Zaret, and the editors of this volume. MacKinnon's work on affect control theory has been sponsored by SSHRC Research Grant 410-81-0089. The research also has benefited from NIMH Grant 1-R01-MH29978-01-SSR to Heise and NSF Grant SES 8122089 to Lynn Smith-Lovin.

different histories. Affect control theory makes no claim to predicting individuals' initial definitions of a situation, and indeed those definitions must be available as input data in order to make accurate predictions about social behavior.

Social interaction is influenced by factors other than the social cognitions of actors. Material constraints (physical distance, walls, etc.) limit who assembles with whom, and distributions of material resources (like medical supplies or religious artifacts) limit actions that can be constructed at a given place and time. Thus we keenly appreciate studies in social ecology because they help illuminate constraints on symbolic interaction. Furthermore, opportunities for events change dynamically as action proceeds, resulting in contingencies among events that modify human cognition and motivation, as behaviorists have demonstrated. Thus, we appreciate studies of event contingencies and of their psychological effects in that such studies deepen understanding of processes involved in symbolic interaction.

Proposition 2. Language is the primary symbolic system through which cognitions are represented, accessed, processed, and communicated.

Affect control theory focuses on concepts—cognitions symbolically represented in a language—and uses words to represent social scenes and happenings and to conduct research on interpersonal processes. Moreover, affect control theory's representation of cognitive process is more influenced by linguistic theory than by psychology—for example, events are structured in terms of case grammar, and other grammars are invoked to explain within-event and between-event cognitive constraints. The emphasis on linguistically mediated symbolic interaction reflects the way people talk about their situations and actions, and the approach accords with George Herbert Mead's classic view of the mind as an internal linguistic process of control in which language moderates between sensation and reflective thought. However, we accept that occasionally cognitions can be accessed in a manner unmediated by language, and we suppose (until convinced otherwise) that the principles of affect control theory apply whether constructs are linguistically mediated or not.

Proposition 3. All social cognitions evoke affective associations.

Cognitions have affective connotations that vary in intensity and quality. For example, an attitude—an association along a good-bad continuum—is attached to virtually every cognition. Affective aspects of meaning engage a kind of psychological processing that integrates social cognitions of different types and that is general across individuals.

While situation definitions and other cognitive processes are the framework for social interaction, social dynamics are largely governed by an affective system relating to values, motives, emotions, etc. Classifications of places, people, objects, and behaviors get transformed into a domain of feelings, where things lose their qualitative uniqueness, become comparable to one another, and begin obeying quantitative principles. This is analogous to observing that Sun, Earth, Mars, Saturn, etc., are identifiable by their unique characteristics, but the dynamics of the solar system are governed by the distances, masses, and velocities of these bodies and the operation of physical laws. (Heise 1987: 6)

Proposition 4. Affective associations can be indexed to a large degree on universal dimensions of response.

Affect control theory capitalizes on extensive cross-cultural research with the "semantic differential" which demonstrates that judgments of evaluation (goodness), potency, and activity (*EPA*) are universal dimensions of response to both linguistic and nonlinguistic stimuli. Despite the unfortunate naming of the instrument, measurements made with semantic differentials are affective rather than semantic in nature, as recognized by the inventor of the instrument throughout his later research (Osgood 1962).

Research on affect control theory has employed a single set of scales to measure all kinds of concepts including social identities, interpersonal acts, person modifiers (traits, status characteristics, and labels for emotional states), and social settings. The *evaluation* dimension has been measured on a semantic differential scale employing "good-bad" and "nice-awful" as polar adjectives; the *potency* dimension, "big-little" and "powerful-powerless"; and the *activity* dimension, "fast-slow," "young-old," and "noisy-quiet." For all three dimensions, scale values range from -4.0 (infinitely) through 0 (neutral) to $+4.0$ (infinitely), where a -1 ($+1$) represents "slightly," a -2 ($+2$) "quite," a -3 ($+3$) "extremely." The "assumed" metric has been refined for each dimension using the method of successive intervals to obtain an approximately interval metric. More recent work (e.g., Heise and Thomas 1989; Britt and Heise 1992) implements the scales on computers as graphic rating scales with metric corresponding to visual distances.

An *EPA profile* is an ordered triplet of numbers reporting the evaluation, potency, and activity ratings of some concept within some population. For example, the EPA profile for the social identity "professor" is 1.5, 1.4, -0.6 for Canadian male university students in northern Ontario, and that for "student" is 1.2, 0.2, 1.9. Thus, a "professor" is rated on average in this population as a little above slightly good, slightly powerful, and edging toward slightly slow, old, and quiet. In contrast, a "student" is rated on average as slightly good, neither powerless nor power-ful, and quite active. As an example of a behavioral stimulus, "to assault someone" is rated by the students as extremely bad, slightly powerful, and quite active, corresponding to the EPA profile: −3.0, 1.2, 2.0.

While evaluation, potency, and activity can be considered cross-cultural dimensions of affective meaning, the EPA measurements for par-ticular stimuli are expected, of course, to vary across cultures.

Cognitive Constraints

Proposition 5. Events are constructed in the framework of a definition of the situation that establishes the identities of participants.

Before interaction can meaningfully proceed from one event to an-other in social situations, a plausible interpretation of what is going on has to be settled upon in the mind of each participant. Both cognitive and affective processes operate, but affective processes operate within a cognitive framework.

Central aspects of the cognitive processes develop from defining the situation. Using a linguistic metaphor, we might say that the definition of the situation is a cognitive process that assembles a working "lexicon" of actors who can enter into events: "A definition of the situation iden-tifies the setting and the relevant persons and objects that are present, so it presents the actors and objects that can be combined into recognition of events in that situation" (Heise 1979: 9). Defining a situation involves complex perceptual processing in which various conceptual schemes are raised and entertained, and people's identities are selected so as to be in-stitutionally compatible with each other. The definition of the situation also may utilize knowledge of ritual or scripted behavior, and may in-volve negotiation with other observers present at the scene.

Although early work in affect control theory treated each person at a scene as the carrier of one relevant identity, current work allows that the lexicon of potential social participants at a scene might be complicated by the existence of identity hierarchies for each individual.

Proposition 6. Grammatical structures of various kinds constrain event construction.

Affect control theory considers social events to be organized in terms of case grammar. An *ABO event* consists of an actor (A) performing a behavior (B) on some object-person (O). Smith-Lovin (1979, 1987) ex-tended the case grammar analysis of events to *ABOS events*: an actor performing a behavior on an object-person with the social setting (S) foregrounded, as in the sentence "The priest blessed the soldiers at the battlefront." Averett (Averett and Heise 1987) extended the case grammar idea to incorporate modifiers (adjectives) into identity specifications, as in "The angry mother scolded the naughty child."

Two of the case slots in an event (A and O) get filled from the available social identities at the scene. Selection of a construct to fill the behavior slot is limited by selection of actor and object if we adopt the notion of projection rules (a grammatical principle in semantic theory) and suppose that social identities generally have characteristic acts associated with them. Doctors, for example, are expected to counsel and medicate; patients, listen and obey. Thus, the problem of determining what is happening is constrained by knowledge of who is acting.

The construction of events also is structured by situationally specific grammars of action (which are discussed in the second half of this essay). An action grammar implies that possible event constructions at any moment are limited by logical and causal thinking about what has happened previously and what is supposed to happen in the future.

Affective Response and Control

Proposition 7. The Affective-Reaction Principle. People react affectively to every social event.

This can be considered the first postulate of affect control theory proper. While the idea follows in an elementary way from Propositions 1 and 3, affect control theory expands the idea with the research-based understanding that events generate new affective meanings regarding the actor, the recipient of action, the behavior, and the setting.

According to affect control theory, the affective associations that were attached to cognitions before an event are transformed by the event into new feelings that may differ from prior feelings in direction and/or intensity. Different events produce different effects. For example, "a mother scolding a child" generates feelings that are somewhat negative for both mother and child; but "a mother hugging a child" produces feelings that are positive. The affective responses generated by events are called *transient* in affect control theory, because subsequent events may undo them.

Impression formation equations model the process by which prior feelings about social identities and interpersonal acts combine during event cognition and generate new transient feelings. We will not present impression formation equations here because they are complex with many multiplicative interaction terms, and there is an extensive literature on them that is readily available (see the affect control theory citations in our reference list). However, examining a few predictions from these equations illustrates the processes that the equations represent. Among female Canadian college students "mother" has the EPA profile 2.7, 1.6, 1.0, indicating that in general mothers are considered to be extremely good, quite powerful, and slightly active. The transient feelings for mother after the event "mother scolds child," as generated by the impression formation equations, is −1.4, 0.9, 1.0. Thus, the prediction is that a mother who is seen to be scolding her child (without known justification) becomes somewhat negatively evaluated and viewed as somewhat reduced in potency while the impression of her transient activity level remains unchanged.

Affective meaning for the object-person also undergoes revision as a consequence of the event. The general EPA profile for "child" is 1.7, −1.1, 2.5, indicating that a child is considered quite good, slightly powerless, and extremely active. The impression formation equations predict that the event "mother scolds child" transforms these feelings into the transient impression −0.4, −0.5, −0.6, indicating that the child drops in evaluation or goodness by virtue of being scolded, becomes less powerless, and turns dramatically less active.

Behaviors also get affectively colored by the context of the event. For example, according to impression formation equations, the act of scolding (EPA profile of −0.4, 1.7, 0.7) drops further in evaluation when performed on a good object-person like a child, declines slightly in potency, but remains essentially constant in terms of activity level.

Finally, the affective meaning of a setting is influenced by events when the setting is foregrounded and perceived as a component of the event. "Thus places are viewed as more pleasant when they have been the scene of conciliatory, inquisitive acts like Appease, Consult, Contemplate, Josh and Serve. Conversely, settings which have been defiled by violent, aggressive interactions are viewed retrospectively as unpleasant places or gatherings" (Smith-Lovin, 1987: 91).

Proposition 8. The Affect Control Principle. People try to experience events that confirm fundamental sentiments.

Affect control theory proposes that, apart from transient feelings produced in particular circumstances, every concept carries a fixed affective meaning. This is the affective association of a concept on its own, apart from combinations with other concepts. Called a *fundamental sentiment* in affect control theory, this affective association is operationalized as the average EPA profile for a concept outside of any event context as rated by a culturally homogeneous group of respondents. Fundamental sentiments are highly stable and are cultural in the sense that virtually the same EPA profile for a concept can be obtained by repeated sampling from the same population, although sampling from a different population often yields quite a different result.

One use of fundamental sentiments in affect control theory is to set affective transients in a situation before any events have occurred. However, it is their other function that is theoretically crucial. Fundamental sentiments serve as reference points throughout a social interaction, and transient feelings constantly are assessed in comparison with fundamental sentiments. According to affect control theory, events are constructed in order to control transient feelings and to make transient feelings consistent with fundamental sentiments.

The discrepancy between transients and fundamentals is so important in affect control theory that it is identified by a specific concept. The *deflection* produced by an event is the sum of squared differences between transient feelings and fundamental sentiments, computed across all dimensions of affective response (EPA) and across all components of an event (ABO, or ABOS).

The basic motivational principle in affect control theory is that people construct or reconstruct events so as to maintain consistency between transient feelings and sentiments. The principle is viewed as pervasive in social life. It constrains the interpretation of others' behavior, it guides conduct as one tries to validate identities or to restore meanings after disruptive events, it structures the reinterpretation of others' identities through labeling processes or trait inferences. In all these cases, the theoretical supposition is that individuals are operating in such a way as to generate consistency between transient feelings and sentiments.

The affective-reaction premise pertains to the effect of past events on present affective states. The affect control premise pertains to the return effect that affect has on events via interpretive and constructive work. The two principles conjoined yield a cybernetic model that accounts for affective responses to events and that also predicts cognitive and behavioral constructions.

Just as the affective-reaction premise is operationalized in impression formation equations, the affect control premise is operationalized in *impression management equations*. The impression management equations are derived mathematically from the impression formation equations using the calculus to implement the assumption that a constructed event minimizes discrepancies between transient impressions and fundamental sentiments. We do not present the equations here because they are extremely complex, and ample discussions of the derivations and of the equations are available elsewhere.

Proposition 9. The Reconstruction Principle. Implacable large deflections instigate changes in the sentiments which are being used to appraise the meaning of events such that the new sentiments are confirmed optimally by recent events.

In cybernetic terms, higher-order feedback kicks in to reduce deflections when lower-order feedback fails to maintain consistency between transient impressions and sentiments. In ordinary language, if people cannot confirm fundamental sentiments through action, then they change the sentiments that they are trying to confirm.

An unsolved problem is ascertaining when people will resort to change of sentiments rather than trying to attain confirmation through action. Psychological literature suggests that unexpected events lead to trait inferences about actors, and in affect control theory that would mean that high-deflection events instigate reconstructions. However, some sociological literature and numerous unpublished analyses of personal incidents by college students indicate that people stick to definitions of situations for prolonged periods, even when events fail to confirm sentiments.

At this point, our best guess is that reconstructions get invoked when an event occurs that disconfirms sentiments and later events reveal that the interactants are not engaging in reparative actions. Our formal proposition, however, forgoes such a specification and refers simply to "implacable large deflections."

Later propositions apply the reconstruction principle to cognitive changes—that is, to change in sentiments obtained by reconceptualizing people. We suspect that the reconstruction principle also pertains to how sentiments get attached to cognitions in the first place, though we are not prepared yet to state a proposition on sentiment formation and change.

Event Assessment

Proposition 10. Events are recognized within the framework of a defined situation.

Proposition 11. Grammatical structures constrain event recognition.

These two propositions simply apply earlier propositions to deal with the specific problem of event recognition.

Proposition 12. The likelihoods of event interpretations are inversely related to the affective disturbances they produce.

This proposition is a theoretical derivation. According to the affect control principle, people seek to experience low-deflection events, and therefore given the opportunity to cognize an event in either a low-deflection or a high-deflection way, they will choose the low-deflection interpretation. Thus low-deflection events should be observed more often than high-deflection events.

This proposition provides a basis for understanding how affective dynamics influence event recognition. To illustrate, mean acts would be judged by most people as uncharacteristic of mothers, particularly if directed toward good and vulnerable object-persons like children. If a mother is perceived possibly to be tormenting her child, an alternative act might be selected as a more likely interpretation—perhaps the mother is only teasing, playing with, or bluffing the child. The event, "mother torments child," is avoided, not because it is incompatible with perceptions in this example, but because it is disconfirming of the sentiments for mother and child, and alternative interpretations provide less disturbing experiences for the observer.

Proposition 13. The perceived likelihoods of events are inversely related to the affective disturbances they produce.

This proposition can be viewed as a theoretical derivation obtainable with some auxiliary assumptions. By the affect control principle, people try to experience events that minimize deflection. Therefore, if people have the freedom to exercise their preferences, events that create large affective deflections should be rare. And if people are cognizant of this rarity, they should judge such events as unlikely.

Findings reported by Heise and MacKinnon (1987) reveal that the perceived likelihood of events does indeed vary inversely with the amount of deflection produced by the events, and events that produce massive deflections always are perceived as unlikely. Yet, affective deflections account for only about one third of the variance in ratings of event likelihood because many events that produce little affective deflection are viewed as unlikely anyhow. This result was found in the Heise and MacKinnon analysis of United States data and was replicated in Mac-Kinnon's (1985) Canadian study.

When analyses are restricted to events involving actors with standard institutional identities (e.g., family roles, legal roles, and so on), unlikely low-deflection events are eliminated and high levels of predictability are obtained. When analyses are restricted to events with actors having institutionally vague identities (e.g., child, hero, as well as mildly deviant identities such as smart-aleck, loafer), especially low levels of predictability are obtained. Therefore, Heise and MacKinnon reasoned that institutionally clear identities provide a definite cognitive context and automatically instigate affective processes that govern likelihood assessment. However, identities that are vague call for so much extra cognitive work in order to make sense of an event description that an event may seem far-fetched apart from affective dynamics.

Originally it was believed there would be a tight connection between deflection, perceived likelihood, and the actual probability of an event occurring, but research indicates that the linkage is a loose one. Events that produce little deflection may turn out to be rare because they have no institutional support. Events that produce a great deal of deflection for ego may occur because they are institutionally required, or all that is possible in some circumstances, or because others define the situation differently, or others have different sentiments than ego does. Thus we prefer to interpret the property of events which deflection predicts not as their objective probability but as their singularity. High-deflection events seem singular, unique, extraordinary, and when such events occur, they are experienced as exceptional, out-of-the-ordinary happenings.

Event Production

Proposition 14. A person develops actions by employing situational identities of self and other as actor and object.

Proposition 15. Actions are produced within the constraints of relevant grammars.

Producing an interpersonal event implies filling in the slots of an ABO structure. For the one who is constructing an event, the choice of actor is settled—it is the self (in the guise of a situational identity); in a dyad the choice for object also is obvious—simply the other in his or her situational identity. Of course, the possibility of each individual taking on multiple identities in a situation complicates matters, and in groups larger than a dyad choice of a recipient becomes increasingly problematic. We assume that selections are restricted by the operation of cognitive grammars and minimize affective disturbance.

Selection of a behavior is constrained to the legitimate repertoire of actions assigned to one's identity; this is the projection–rule idea applied to event production rather than to event recognition. Additionally the feasible actions at the moment are limited by what has happened previously—the causal and logical constraints implied by a situational grammar of action. The action grammar also may give salience to some particular behavior that is essential in order to reach a goal event.

Proposition 16. The likelihood that a person will engage in one feasible behavior rather than another is inversely related to the affective disturbances that the behaviors produce.

According to affect control theory, cognitive factors typically limit the choice of behavior to a set of "free variates" (to use another linguistic metaphor), and at that point affective processes narrow the choice to a single option. In particular, a person will enact the behavior that minimizes deflection of outcome impressions from fundamental sentiments. This proposition follows directly from the principle of affect control: people seek to experience events that confirm fundamental sentiments, and therefore, when responsible for the production of a new event, a person will choose a behavior in such a way as to create an event that minimizes deflections.

At one time it seemed plausible that behavioral responses to past events are selected in terms of how much they reduce deflection, but an analysis by Wiggins and Heise (1987: 156) indicated that large current deflections do not increase the likelihood of a restorative event. The construction of events is governed simply by how much deflection they produce, not by how much improvement they offer. Of course, current deflections do influence the character of a subsequent event: if someone has been mortified then events will be built to regain a sense of status and power, whereas an unpretentious response should occur if flattery has made feelings about self too positive. These predictions about the character of responses were supported in a behavioral experiment conducted by Wiggins (Wiggins and Heise 1987).

Affect control theory's proposal that an individual behaves so as to minimize deflections for the self does not mean that events are constructed to confirm the actor optimally but rather to confirm optimally the actor's overall meaning system—the self-identity, the other's identity, and the meaning of the behavior that is chosen. Heise's (1985) studies of differential weighting for these different components of an event led to the general conclusion that confirmation of each component is about equally important.

An act that is confirming for the self may be disconfirming for others if they have different sentiments or a different definition of the situation. Thus social predicaments may arise in which interactants counter each other's efforts to maintain meanings, perhaps even generating unstable increases in deflection that make a sequence of happenings seem more and more singular and incredible to the participants. Such scenes may result in reconstructions of identity, as discussed later.

Proposition 17. In the course of validating social identities people engage in role appropriate acts.

Social identities can be treated as culturally defined social roles subjectively viewed. Thus, in the process of conducting themselves so as to confirm social identities, people theoretically should be enacting social roles.

One of the major research findings arising from affect control theory is that identity-confirming acts do indeed include the functional activities assigned to social roles—for example, "medicating" is an identity-confirming act for a doctor with a patient, "sentencing" is an identity-confirming act for a judge with a thief. Moreover, identity confirmation in the context of disruptive prior events yields sanctioning activities, either positive or negative depending on the circumstances.

The affective system impels people to perform the same role actions that are functional at the institutional level. Moreover, the affective system allows people to improvise creatively in order to perform roles appropriately even when circumstances are so special that no institutionalized response is known.

Social roles typically are defined in terms of social structural position as well as functional conduct. Research in affect control theory adopts a direct translation of an identity's Evaluation and Potency into corresponding role *status* (prestige) and *power*, following Kemper and Collins (1990). For example, male Ontario undergraduates provide the following EPA profiles for father, mother, son, and daughter, respectively: 2.5, 2.6, −0.6; 2.5, 1.0, −0.1; 1.1, 0.4, 1.2; 2.0, −0.2, 1.3. These figures are interpreted to mean that in a typical Ontario middle-class family mother and father have equal and high status, and thereby they garner considerable voluntary compliance in family situations; a daughter also has high status while a son has considerably less than other family members. Meanwhile, the power ranking allows father to have his way regardless of other's wishes, with mother being a powerful subordinate of father and the children being relatively powerless in family situations—daughter even more so than son.

Emotions

> *Proposition 18. The Emotion Principle.* An interactant's emotion following an event reflects the outcome of the event and also the identity that the person is maintaining. Specifically, the emotion is a function of (a) the transient impression of the interactant that was created by the event; and (b) the discrepancy between this transient impression and the fundamental sentiment associated with the interactant's situational identity.

In affect control theory, emotion is modeled as a dynamically varying attribute of self that transforms self-identity into the social impression which has been created by events. The model, developed mathematically from equations defining how modifiers combine with identities, implies that emotion is a function of two factors.

The first factor corresponds to commonsense ideas about emotion. Events that leave us in a positively evaluated state produce positive emotions, events that move us to negatively evaluated states result in negative emotions, events that produce transient feelings of liveliness produce emotional activation, and so on.

The second factor represents a relativistic aspect of emotional response. One's overall emotional state depends not only on how one is doing absolutely but also on how one is doing relative to what is to be expected on the basis of one's identity. For example, events may leave a person in a positively evaluated state, but the person may not be happy if that transient state is less positive on evaluation than expected by virtue of the person's current identity.

The emotion model is a relatively recent addition to affect control theory, and its predictions still have to be tested systematically. However, the model does plausibly specify emotions that might accompany social events. For example, according to predictions from the model (we continue a prior example with Canadian data), a mother who scolds her child should feel irate or mad, and the child being scolded should feel uneasy or remorseful.

Proposition 19. People tend to maintain emotions that are characteristic of their salient identities.

This proposition follows from prior ones with an auxiliary assumption and the understanding that a salient identity is one that gets invoked in many situations. The affect control principle implies that people try to maintain impressions of themselves that match the sentiments attached to their salient identities. Assume that they typically succeed. Then the discrepancy factor in emotion is eliminated, and the emotions they feel as a result of their conduct are a function simply of the impressions produced by that conduct. But because they are successful in confirming their salient identities, these outcome impressions match the sentiments for their identities, so the emotions they feel have profiles matching their identities. Thus, the maintenance of positive identities would lead to the experience of positive emotions, the maintenance of negative identities to negative emotions.

With this proposition affect control theory interprets chronic affective disorders like depression as problems based on the maintenance of negatively evaluated selves.

Proposition 20. Emotion displays facilitate intersubjective sharing of definitions of situations and of the operative social structures that are implied by definitions of the situation.

According to affect control theory, emotion is the experience of one's identity in the context of recent events. Consequently an overt display of emotion by ego shows others how ego is experiencing his or her identity and, given some agreement about events that have occurred, allows others to infer what sentiments ego must be trying to maintain. That is, others can deduce some of ego's definitions—even if they do not initially share them—by observing ego's emotion displays as events occur. "[E]motions arise as events do and do not confirm conventional levels of status, power, and expressivity—the EPA profile—for each person's situational identity. The emotions function as subjective and interpersonal signals concerning how the process of social confirmation is going" (Averett and Heise 1987: 123).

Inferences can be made from emotion displays about how another views the operative social structure in the situation. The point correlates with ideas in the sociology of emotion: emotions reflect social structure, so much so that unauthentic expressions of emotion (emotion work) may be coerced in order to lend powerful interactants an aura of status that they desire.

Cognitive Revisions

Proposition 21. Social labelings render past events more credible by assigning interactants new identities that are confirmed by the past events.

Social labeling processes, a topic studied mainly by sociologists, assign people new social identities in place of old ones. Affect control theory's formulation regarding labeling derives from the reconstruction principle and is as follows.

Suppose that the actor in a recent event is to be reidentified. Then the behavior and the object in the event serve as givens, and the objective is to render the recent event more plausible by redefining the actor in a way that minimizes affective disturbance, in essence asking, "What kind of person would perform such a behavior on that object-person?" Alternatively the actor and the behavior can serve as knowns, and the object-person can be redefined, asking, "What kind of person warrants or seeks that behavior from that actor?" In either case, the given part of the event implies an appropriate sentiment for the person being labeled, and that sentiment can be predicted by employing a variation of the impression management equations. The resulting sentiment guides selection of an explanatory social identity that is situationally appropriate and that fits the event grammatically.

If a stigmatized behavior is involved, then the new identity is likely to be stigmatized as well. For example, given the event "The youth cheats the clerk," affective deflection could be reduced and the event rendered more credible by assigning such labels as "pusher," "mugger," or "evil-doer" to the perpetrator (according to analyses based on the Canadian study). Alternatively a label could be applied to the object-person—e.g., a Canadian youth accused of cheating a clerk might define the clerk as a "grouch," "miser," or "stuffed shirt" according to affect control theory analyses.

Traditional sociological labeling theory focused on acquisition of negative identities, but from the perspective of affect control theory the labeling process is the same regardless of whether the new social identities are stigmatized or respected. For example, a man who uplifts another man might be assigned the label of "pal" (analytic result using the Canadian data). Thus, affect control theory suggests that labeling processes are involved in achieving social regard as well as in receiving social stigma.

Proposition 22. Dispositional inferences render past events more credible by assigning interactants modified identities that are maximally confirmed by the past events.

Dispositional inferences, a topic studied mainly by psychologists, assign an explanatory trait to a person in order to make the person's actions more accountable. Affect control theory's modeling of this kind of re-identification starts off the same as for labeling—a sentiment about the focal person is derived so as to minimize affective disturbance in the key event. However, in the case of a dispositional inference the inferred sentiment does not serve as the template for a new identity but rather defines a result that has to be achieved by modifying the person's current identity.

Affect control theory's empirically derived *amalgamation equations* are employed to model this process. The amalgamation equations define the outcome impression that is produced when a person modifier is combined with a social identity, as in "the wise child." When the equations are applied to dispositional inference, the outcome corresponds to the inferred sentiment that would minimize affective deflection in the key event, the identity is the one which the focal person already has, and the equations are solved to define the EPA profile for an appropriate modifier.

Selection of different kinds of modifiers reflects different social psychological processes. If a personality disposition is selected, then we have the usual kind of trait inference considered by psychologists. If an emo-

tion term is selected for amalgamation with an identity, then we are dealing with attribution of a mood. If a status characteristic is selected (e.g.,
rich, Hispanic, old), then we have attribution of social faculty. If a character descriptor is selected (e.g., evil, noble), then the judgment becomes
a moral attribution.

The amalgamation equations also are used in affect control theory to
specify emotions, but then modifiers are being sought to describe the
relation between an identity and a transient impression rather than seeking a modifier to specify how a person's particular characteristics convert
the sentiment attached to an identity into a different fundamental sentiment that the person confirms through action.

Proposition 23. Dispositional inferences are a more likely form of
reidentification than assignment of new identities through labeling
processes.

Reidentifying people through the attribution of traits, moods, status
characteristics, or moral character, instead of assigning entirely new
identities, has the cognitive advantage of keeping the original definition
of the situation intact. Thus situations promoted by social institutions
can be maintained and individuals' deviant conduct understood simultaneously. For example, it is easier for a family to deal with a "withdrawn
daughter" than with a "schizophrenic" and perhaps easier to deal with a
"brutal father" than with an "alcoholic." As labeling theorists have argued, casting a person into a new identity may require complex confron-
tations, negotiations, and involvements with authorities, and once accomplished the labeling may have unwanted ramifications for one's own
identity. Attributions, unlike role identities, do not have to be validated
institutionally, thus the attributions are more easily applied and even can
be employed tacitly to understand others.

Why, then, are labeling processes ever invoked? One reason is that
reidentification through modifiers can extend only so far. No modifier
can be attached to "friend" to account for a betrayal; only labeling with
an identity like "traitor" yields an event in which the actor is properly
confirmed through betraying others.

Proposition 24. Observers forgo reassessments of an actor's character
after disconfirming events if the person's emotion displays are appropriate to the person's conduct.

Suppose a person in an honorable situational identity engages in an
awful act, thereby generating a very negative impression of himself. By
the emotion principle, his action should generate a negative emotion such

as humiliation, remorse, fear, or rage (whichever is most appropriate). If he does display an appropriate negative emotion, then there is no reason to suppose that he is maintaining an identity different from the one originally supposed. Thus the incident cannot be understood better by assigning him a new identity, and observers have to deal with the affective disruption in some other way—by implementing their own sanctioning events or by reidentifying another interactant in the event.

Similarly, if a person with a menial role performs heroically, then he should feel pride and elation, and if he displays such emotions then there is no reason to suppose that he is other than what he is supposed to be. It would be a display of calm humility that would suggest he had been misidentified and might be cast as a "hero," because only a fundamentally very good and very potent person could be calm and modest after heroism.

Displays of emotion during deviant episodes (or when such episodes are relived in discourse) reveal what identities the interactants are trying to maintain, and thereby observers can deduce whether their identifications of the interactants require revision or not. Moreover, through such displays of emotion each of us can gain some control over how others will view us. "[W]e display negative emotion when revealing our shortcomings to others. Such emotions often are played to and for an audience to authenticate identities and to mitigate the effects of negative information that is revealed through circumstance or self-disclosure" (Smith-Lovin 1990: 250).

Development of the Theory

This is a fitting stopping point for our presentation of affect control theory because the last proposition epitomizes the theory. Social identity, social conduct, and affect intertwine in symbolic representations of social interaction, and together they constitute a control system that impinges on many issues of sociological significance. Now we turn to some factors that were involved in development of this theory. First we try to fathom some of the scientific currents that have fed coherent conceptual growth of affect control theory. Then we describe and analyze the collaborative production system that was the medium for research regarding the theory.

Conceptual Expansion

Affect control theory originated in studies of the affective-reaction principle, which describes how people respond to events. Then the affect control principle was added to explain how people create events. Then the reconstruction principle was brought in to define how people reinterpret past events. Next the conceptualization of events was expanded to incorporate settings and to deal with participants who are characterized by modified identities. Then the emotion principle was added, suggesting how affect control processes are experienced and helping to account for intersubjectivity among interactants. Later the emotion principle and reconstruction principle together led to the idea of emotion displays influencing labeling processes. Each development in this progression of elaborations was integrally related to prior developments, and equations representing the various principles synchronize neatly together.

Elaborations. The coherence of the theory arises partly because empirical research on impression formation applied the same tools repeatedly. Measurements always were made with the semantic differential, prediction equations always were obtained by predicting contextualized meanings from meanings assessed in isolation, and contextual structure always was manipulated in terms of a linguistic case frame. In fact, some theoretical expansions resulted from straightforward case-frame elaborations: this is the way the model was expanded beyond simple actor-behavior-object events to events within specified settings, and it is the way that the theory was expanded so that actors and object-persons can be characterized in terms of identities alone or in terms of modifier-identity combinations. The tools for obtaining empirically grounded impression formation equations continue to be productive. For example, at the time of writing this essay, equations were being obtained to predict impressions produced by self-directed actions using the frame actor-behavior-self (Britt and Heise 1992); and research on cross-cultural comparability of equations was under way in Canada and Japan.

The theory's coherence also arises because some system equations were derived mathematically. For example, the impression management equations were derived from the empirical impression formation equations, in conjunction with the theoretical idea that people try to confirm fundamental sentiments; and attribution and emotion equations were derived from the empirical amalgamation equations for predicting how impressions arise from combinations of a modifier and an identity. Mathematical elaborations of this sort sometimes were an integral step in searching for an affect control theory interpretation of previously reported results regarding some compelling social psychological issue. Thus, the derivation of the construction equations from reaction equations was driven by a desire to account for normative actions associated with institutional roles; and the integration of emotion and impression management equations (Heise 1989a) that underlies Proposition 24 was stimulated by a study showing that people appreciate people who emote negatively over their own deviant behavior.

Expansions through derivations also arose as researchers explored equations mathematically. For example, equations for reconstructing events by selecting a new actor or object identity were obtained as a mathematical variant of the equations for constructing events by selecting a behavior. Equations to predict attributions and emotions became evident when the amalgamation equations were manipulated algebraically so that modifiers were turned into a predicted quantity rather than being one of the predictors.

Mathematical analyses must be tied to substantive concerns in order to constitute theoretical advance. For example, the reconstruction equations became remarkable only when they were interpreted in terms of labeling theory and articulated with research on deviance. Similarly, the amalgamation equations were solved for modifiers soon after being obtained, but a rich interpretation of the results required a decade of work to connect the equations with psychological attribution theory and with the growing body of work on the sociology of emotions. Meanwhile, other derivations led nowhere fruitful. For example, mathematical derivations specified how an event could be reconstructed by redefining the setting, and simulations using the solution yielded results such as: a child punished by his parents might reinterpret his home as a prison. While people do say such things as "This place is like a prison," the prediction of metaphor does not seem connected in any useful way with current sociological concerns. In general, a mathematical derivation assures a high level of conceptual coherence, but it acquires utility only when translated into contemporary theoretical constructs and articulated with prominent issues in the discipline.

Syntheses. Affect control theory addresses a broad range of phenomena, and consequently it competes with a large number of other theories dealing with those same phenomena. For example, in psychology there are alternative formulations of impression formation, of identity maintenance, and of the mind as a control system. In sociology there are alternative formulations regarding identity, role behavior and the social basis of emotions. In some cases the competing theories make virtually the same claims as does affect control theory (e.g., Swann and Hill's [1982] theory of identity maintenance), so the competing theories, and the work they induce, are cited as lending support to affect control theory. In other cases (e.g., Anderson's [1981] approach to impression formation) the competing theory calls for certain refinements that affect control theory does not provide, and in this case we continue working at our chosen level of precision, accepting that ultimately our models might be superseded by more precise ones. In still other cases the competing theory is incorporated as an auxiliary to affect control theory—e.g., Fararo and Skvoretz's (1984) approach to role analysis is adopted more or less intact within our statement of cognitive constraints; and Stryker's (1980) theory of self and identity has been incorporated into some of affect control theory's formulations regarding situational definitions. Wagner and Berger's (1985: 709) contention that "proponents of each theory claim the other is wrong" may be correct sometimes, but researchers sometimes synthesize alternative conceptions with their own.

We can surmise some conditions that contribute to synthesis. First, there must be a discordance within the home theory that cannot be fixed from within. Here are three examples from affect and control theory.

1. Computer simulations revealed that affect control theory is able to predict normative behaviors for particular role relationships, but the predictions sometimes are marred by foolish outcomes like "The doctor baptized the patient." This prediction cannot be fixed from within because it is expressively correct; the problem is that baptizing is not a legitimate expansion of the doctor role. We incorporated projection grammar from semantics into the cognitive component of affect control theory in order to justify a principled elimination of such predictions from results.

2. Affect control theory generates plausible sanctioning sequences in response to deviance, but otherwise simulated sequences of interaction based on affect control theory lack instrumental directionality. That is, while an analyst generally can construct an instrumental sequence from the predicted behaviors that are presented during a simulation, the expressive component of action itself does not organize events so that, say, interactants first greet each other, then work together, then part. It is for this reason that the Fararo-Skvoretz production system approach to roles is incorporated into the cognitive component of affect control theory: a production system model offers a principled basis for selecting among the expressively equivalent actions that are possible at each stage of an interaction in order to produce a functional sequence of action.

3. Affect control theory proposes that people conduct themselves so as to protect sentiments, and this homeostatic approach powerfully explains normative action while also explaining variations in normative behavior by allowing that cultures and subcultures inculcate varying sentiments. However, affect control theory does not address the issue of how sentiments form and get changed and diverge in different groups, and for this task the homeostatic formulation actually is obstructive, since

homeostasis focuses on confluence rather than divergence. Thus it appears that an adequate socialization theory will have to be adopted from outside and synthesized with affect control theory.

In our efforts to expand affect control theory through syntheses with other work on social interaction, we favored external theories that (1) describe phenomena in a succinct and compelling manner and (2) share certain abstract understandings with affect control theory. Theoretical power is the reason we have turned so often to linguistics, a social science that is far advanced over other social sciences in effectively modeling qualitative aspects of human action. Theoretical power also led us to prefer production system models over the script approach to explaining instrumental episodes of social interaction: a production system model is generative and can account for numerous social episodes, whereas a script is static and can account only for sequences that have been stored in a database. Similarly, classic theory on attitude formation and change seems to us less powerful than operant theory's generalizations about how event contingencies influence dispositions, and so our current inclination is to employ operant theory in order to develop a socialization component for affect control theory.

All of the mentioned theories additionally share a key focus with affect control theory in that they emphasize the event as the basic unit of social analysis. Thus it is relatively easy to move back and forth between affect control theory and the alternate theories and see where predictions are the same or different or complementary. Additionally our interest is kindled by theories that interpret structure as a combinatoric ordering of entities in which association modifies properties of the entities while the combination itself operates as a new entity in other combinations. Such parallelism with affect control theory in the meaning of structure inspires efforts to translate dynamic processes in the other theory into the dynamic processes of affect control theory for purposes of comparison and linking.

Syntheses with other theories expanded affect control theory in a different way than mathematical elaborations did. Whereas interpreted mathematical elaborations expanded the scope of the theory, synthesis with other theories set constraints on theoretical principles by acknowledging boundaries between alternative modes of explanation. In general, if a synthesis is successful, the boundaries become seamless in the sense that both theories operate together, one taking over where the other leaves off and each theory permeating the other. We can cite the union of affect control theory with production system theory as an example of this, even though the synthesis is far from complete: production system models pick up where the affect control model falters and show how functionality arises in social interaction; meanwhile, the affect control model picks up where the population system model falters and shows that choices are made among optional actions in order to maintain cultural meanings and social relationships.

The Research Program

We now suspend focusing on the substantive concerns of affect control theory in order to analyze the development of social theory as the outcome of a collaborative production system. In this exercise our focus is on the professional and scientific events that were the medium for developing affect control theory, and the analytic product is an event structure model that accounts for those events.

Event structure analysis (Heise 1989b) adapts production system technology (Newell and Simon 1972; Fararo and Skvoretz, this volume) to the problem of documenting the underlying logic of event sequences through qualitative models that can be viewed as grammars of action. The method's application to ethnographic data is discussed by Corsaro and Heise (1990); its use for content analysis of written texts is illustrated by Heise (1988) and Heise and Lewis (1988); and its use in studying careers is exemplified in Heise (1990).

The data for the analysis were assembled as follows. An initial set of time-ordered events relating to the affect control theory (ACT) research program was obtained from vitae, from reports and publications, and from files. This produced a sequence of career events (degrees, employments, publications, external fundings, editorships) for the key researchers that was supplemented by adding events that seemed to be critical parts of the research process. For example, between funding events and publication events various research events were included—like collecting data, collating data, analyzing data, estimating equations, and so on— and positioned in sequence by searching files when possible, by reminiscing otherwise. Within-university fundings, publication rejections, and grant denials also were added. After the initial list had been compiled by Heise, Lynn Smith-Lovin and Neil MacKinnon examined the listing and provided corrections and expansions related to their own participation in the research program. This procedure resulted in 42 distinct types of events that repeated at different times and with 16 different researchers to yield a time-ordered list of 298 events related to the development of affect control theory from the year 1961 through 1988.

We forgo further discussion of methods and procedures involved in the event structure analysis of the ACT research program since that aspect of the work has been covered in detail elsewhere (Heise 1991).

Table 1 specifies the model verbally. The token in the left column is used as a marker in the logical diagram (Figure 1); bracketed tokens represent publication events and correspond to shaded labels in the diagram. Entries in the second column of Table 1 define the 42 events that occurred in the ACT research program. A terse phrasing in boldface is included for making textual references, and full explanations follow in roman type. The right column of Table 1 identifies direct relations of each event with other events. Events characterized as "required" are the prerequisites of the focal event. The focal event itself is a prerequisite for the events it "may lead to." Appearance of a boldface **and** means that all of a focal event's prerequisites must occur before the focal event can occur; a boldface **or** indicates that occurrence of any one prerequisite is adequate. Event sequences are constrained by the logical dependencies implied in the notion of prerequisite and also by dynamic depletions of the conditions that are generated by prerequisite events. Event consequences do not deplete the focal event unless the word **depletes** in boldface follows the name of the consequence. The focal event has to be depleted by a consequence before the focal event can repeat unless the word **repeats** appears in boldface, in which case an intervening depletion is not required. A focal event does not act as a prerequisite for any of its own prerequisites unless the word **commutes** appears in boldface, in which case the focal event is a prerequisite for one of its prerequisites after an initial priming cycle.

The diagram in Figure 1 presents a graphic representation of the overall logical structure that is implicit in Table 1. The topmost entry, ACT-research, names the model, and below that each event is represented by a token, as assigned in Table 1. Italicized tokens are events that have disjunctive rather than conjunctive prerequisites. Shaded tokens are publication events.

The events in the tier immediately below the topmost entry have no prerequisites specified in the model. The events in lower tiers do have prerequisites that can be identified by tracing lines upward. In general, a prerequisite of an event can be located by following the event's ascending line straight upward to another event, or by following the ascender until it meets a horizontal line and then finding the line that goes straight up from the horizontal line to an event. For example, Fund, Simulat, [Overv], [Meth], [Theory], and Math-method all have Read as a prerequisite; the prerequisite of Expert is Local-funding; and Analyze has two prerequisites, Collate and Utilize.

Indirect implications can be traced using the diagram. For example, [Simulator] (published simulator results) implies Simulat (performed simulation) which implies Read, so publishing simulator results implies

TABLE 1
Specification of the Model for ACT Research Activities

Token	Character of event	Relations to other events
Analyze	**analyzed database**. A researcher extracted new information from a database through transformations of measurements or by focusing on a subset of cases.	Requires *collated data* **or** *utilized existing database*. May lead to *published database study* (**depletes**) or to *wrote research report*. Can **repeat** without depletion.
Certified	**certified in profession**. A researcher obtained a doctorate or other professional credential while not involved in the research program.	No requirements within the model. May lead to *contracted with publisher*, *joined faculty*, or *requested funding*.
Collate	**collated data**. A researcher organized the stimuli used to obtain measurements from respondents, organized and verified the measurements themselves, and then perhaps computed descriptive statistics (e.g., means) that could be the basis for further analyses.	No requirements within the model. May lead to *analyzed database* or *estimated equations*. Can **repeat** without depletion.
Fund	**contributed funding**. A researcher employed personal funds to foster research activities.	Requires *read*. May lead to *gathered database measurements* (**depletes**) or *measured responses* (**depletes**). Can **repeat** without depletion.
Pact	**contracted with publisher**. A researcher obtained a written contract assuring that a publisher would accept a book manuscript for publication.	Requires *certified in profession* **or** *received doctorate*. May lead to *published edited book* (**depletes**) or to *solicited paper*.
Denied	**denied funding**. A researcher received a letter from an external funding agency in which the agency declined the opportunity to support proposed research activities.	Requires *requested funding*. Can **repeat** without depletion.
Refused	**denied monograph publication**. A researcher received a letter from a publisher in which the publisher declined the opportunity to publish a book manuscript reporting research activities.	**Commutes** with *submitted research monograph*—its only requirement. (An initial submission permits a denial of publication; if denial of publication occurs, it **depletes** the submission permitting another submission; another submission **depletes** the last denial of publication, so that denial of publication might happen again.)
Edit	**edited journal issue**. A researcher negotiated with the official editor of a journal and thereby gained editorial control over one issue of the journal for the purpose of promoting a topic or a research program.	Requires *received doctorate*. May lead to *published edited book* (i.e., a special issue of a journal may be published subsequently as an edited book.) Can **repeat** without depletion.

TABLE 1

(*continued*)

Token	Character of event	Relations to other events
Estimate	**estimated equations**. A researcher concretized algebraic portrayals of relations between various measurements by estimating equation parameters as numerical values through statistical analyses of a sample of measurements. Some collation of data is presumed to be part of equation estimation.	Requires *collated data*, measured responses, **or** *utilized existing database*. May lead to *mathematized formulation*, *programmed simulation system*, *published equation estimations*, or *wrote research report*. Can **repeat** without depletion.
Local-funding	**funded locally**. A researcher received funds administered within a university to free a researcher from remunerative activities like teaching or to buy research materials and services.	No requirements within the model (because researchers have an official affiliation with a university). May lead to *gathered database measurements* (**depletes**), *measured responses* (**depletes**), or *ran experiment* (**depletes**).
Funded	**funded externally**. A researcher received funds from a source beyond the researcher's own university to free one or more researchers from remunerative activities like teaching or to buy research materials and services.	Requires *requested funding*. May lead to *gathered database measurements*. Can **repeat** without depletion.
Database	**gathered database measurements**. A researcher measured people's subjective responses to verbal stimuli in order to create a database. (This phrasing applies to survey research as used in ACT research.)	Requires *contributed funding*, *funded externally*, **or** *funded locally*. Can **repeat** without depletion.
Talk	**gave invited talk**. A researcher was invited to speak at a conference or a colloquium outside of the researcher's own university, and the talk led to a publication about the research program by the researcher or by someone in the audience.	Requires *received doctorate*. Can **repeat** without depletion.
Improve	**improved simulation system**. A researcher made the output of a simulation system more realistic by refining the computer program, by incorporating more refined equations and rules, or by refining use of a database.	Requires *performed simulation* **and** *programmed simulation system*. Can **repeat** without depletion.
Issue	**issued simulation system**. A researcher found a way of distributing a simulation program, with databases and instructions, so that people could operate the system on accessible computers.	Requires *performed simulation* **and** *programmed simulation system*. Can **repeat** without depletion.

TABLE 1

(*continued*)

Token	Character of event	Relations to other events
Join	**joined faculty**. A researcher obtained a professorship permitting pursuit of intellectual interests.	Requires *received doctorate* **or** *certified in profession*. (The disjunction here is merely to deal with scholars or researchers whose doctoral work was irrelevant because it occurred before their association with the research program.) May lead to *visited other faculty* during sabbaticals. Can **repeat** without depletion.
Math-theory	**mathematized formulation**. A researcher constructed a mathematical derivation that transformed assumptions about reality along with empirically based equations describing a process into additional equations describing another process.	Requires *estimated equations*. (In the ACT research program, this kind of empirically grounded mathematical work has been conducted only by a researcher whose prior experience in estimating such equations provided incentive for working with the empirical equations.) May lead to *published math derivations* or *wrote research report*. Can **repeat** without depletion.
Math-method	**mathematized methodology**. A researcher constructed a mathematical derivation that resulted in the definition of a complex methodological procedure.	Requires *read* (i.e., some familiarity with both mathematical and substantive literatures). May lead to *published math derivations* (**depletes**).
Measure	**measured responses**. A researcher obtained measurements of people's responses to a number of verbal stimuli presented in a questionnaire or by a computer in order to conduct a specific analysis. (In an experiment the responses of people also are measured in order to conduct a specific analysis, but the stimuli for these responses are real social situations rather than printed presentations. In a database study, the sample of people or the sample of stimuli is sufficiently comprehensive that the data may be broken into different categories for various kinds of analyses.)	Requires *contributed funding* **or** *funded locally*. May lead to *tested theory* (**depletes**), *estimated equations* (**depletes**), or *wrote research report*. The depletions occur because the measurements are tailored to a specific function and are of no further value after the study is done.
Simul	**performed simulation**. A researcher employed a simulation system to enter information about social situations and obtain a computer report about theoretical predictions.	Requires *read*. May lead to *improved simulation system* (depletes—because then old simulations become obsolete), *issued simulation system*, or *published simulator results*. Can **repeat** without depletion.

TABLE 1

(*continued*)

Token	Character of event	Relations to other events
Program	**programmed simulation system**. A researcher programmed a computer in order to implement an empirically grounded mathematical model (plus additional rules) while making use of a database such that a variety of problems can be set up easily and theoretical predictions examined readily.	Requires *estimated equations*. May lead to *improved simulation system* or *issued simulation system*. Can **repeat** without depletion.
[Database]	**published database study**. A researcher published a description of methods and the results of processing a database in order to address some issue.	Requires *analyzed database*. Can **repeat** without depletion.
[Equations]	**published equation estimations**. A researcher published an article describing how some process can be given an algebraic formulation and how numbers were found to make the equations concrete and descriptive of reality.	Requires *estimated equations* **or** *wrote research report*. Can **repeat** without depletion.
[Math]	**published math derivations**. A researcher published a report describing how a mathematical derivation was obtained and how the results are to be interpreted.	Requires *mathematized methodology* **or** *mathematized formulation*. Can **repeat** without depletion.
[Meth]	**published methodology**. A researcher published a report describing a generalized research procedure and discussing its benefits and limitations.	Requires *read* (i.e., familiarity with literature related to the procedure). Can **repeat** without depletion.
[Monograph]	**published research monograph**. A researcher published a lengthy systematic exposition describing activities and outcomes in a research program.	Requires *submitted research monograph*. Can **repeat** without depletion.
[Overv]	**published research overview**. A researcher published an exposition outlining the claims, activities, and products of a research program.	Requires *read* (i.e., familiarity with key publications from a research program). Can **repeat** without depletion.
[Reader]	**Published edited book**. A researcher published a collection of writings by various authors on a particular topic or research program.	Requires *contracted with publisher* (for a book of solicited papers) **or** *edited journal issue* (for reprinting of a special issue of a journal). Can **repeat** without depletion.
[Simulator]	**published simulator results**. A researcher published illustrative simulation results in order to communicate a theory's capacity for portraying reality.	Requires *performed simulation*. Can **repeat** without depletion.

TABLE 1

(*continued*)

Token	Character of event	Relations to other events
[Test]	**published test of theory**. A researcher published a report defining a theoretical assumption or prediction, how the claim was examined empirically, what the results were, and how the results favor or undermine the focal theoretical formulation as well as other theoretical formulations.	Requires *tested theory* **or** *wrote research report*. Can **repeat** without depletion.
[Theory]	**published theory formulation**. A researcher published a statement claiming that some abstracted aspects of reality are interrelated in a principled way.	Requires *read*. Can **repeat** without depletion.
Experi	**ran experiment**. A researcher constructed real social situations representing distinctive circumstances and assessed some aspects of people's responses to the different circumstances.	Requires *funded locally*. May lead to *tested theory* (**depletes**).
Read	**read**. A researcher consumed reports and publications regarding theory, research, or research methods from within the researcher's own research program or from other research programs.	No requirements within the model. May lead to: *published methodology*, *published theory formulation*, *published research overview*, *mathematized methodology*, *performed simulation*, or *contributed funding*. Can **repeat** without depletion.
Reana	**reanalyzed prior study**. A researcher performed new analyses on measurements that were collected previously for a specific study.	No requirements within the model. May lead to *tested theory* (**depletes**—because analyses for a specific test have no utility beyond that test) or *wrote research report*.
PhD	**received doctorate**. A researcher was awarded a doctoral degree certifying the person as a competent researcher.	Requires *wrote research report*. May lead to *contracted with publisher*, *edited journal*, *gave invited talk*, *joined faculty*, or *requested funding*.
Request	**requested funding**. A researcher sought external funding from a government agency or from a foundation or from an outside research institution through submission of a proposal outlining a research plan and a budget for specific research activities.	Requires *certified in profession* **or** *received doctorate*. May lead to *denied funding* (**depletes**) or *funded externally* (**depletes**). Can **repeat** without depletion.

TABLE 1

(*continued*)

Token	Character of event	Relations to other events
Solicit	**solicited paper**. A researcher requested preparation of a report by another scholar or researcher, with assurance that the report would be published in an edited book.	Requires *contracted with publisher* (in order to obtain credibility). Can **repeat** without depletion.
Submit	**submitted research monograph**. A researcher sent a book-length manuscript reporting theory and research to a publisher for possible publication.	Requires *wrote research report.* May lead to *denied monograph publication* (**depletes**) or *published research monograph* (**depletes**).
Test	**tested theory**. A researcher used empirical data to examine the accuracy of a theoretical assumption or prediction. Some collation and analysis of data are presumed to be part of testing a theory.	Requires *measured responses, ran experiment, reanalyzed prior study,* **or** *utilized existing database.* May lead to *published test of theory.* Can **repeat** without depletion.
Utilize	**utilized existing database**. A researcher made use of a collated database in order to conduct some kind of research.	No requirements within the model. May lead to *analyzed database, estimated equations,* or *tested theory.*
Visit	**visited other faculty**. A researcher visited another faculty during a sabbatical leave from his or her own faculty.	Requires *joined faculty.*
Write	**wrote research report**. A researcher prepared a report interpreting literature, describing how an experiment was conducted or how measurements were made, how statistical or other kinds of analyses were done, or how mathematical solutions were derived.	Requires *analyzed database, estimated equations, measured responses, mathematized formulation,* **or** *reanalyzed prior study.* May lead to *received doctorate, published equation estimates, published test of theory,* or *submitted research monograph.*

having read something. Program (programmed simulation system) implies Estimate (estimated equations) which in turn implies either Collate (collated data) or Utilize (utilized existing database), so in ACT research programming a simulation system implies that at an earlier point an existing database was utilized or that raw data were collated.

Professional activities. Figure 1 partitions into a part dealing with research and publication events and another part in the lower left corner mainly consisting of professional activities that depend upon receiving a doctoral degree or equivalent certification. One has to traverse a path

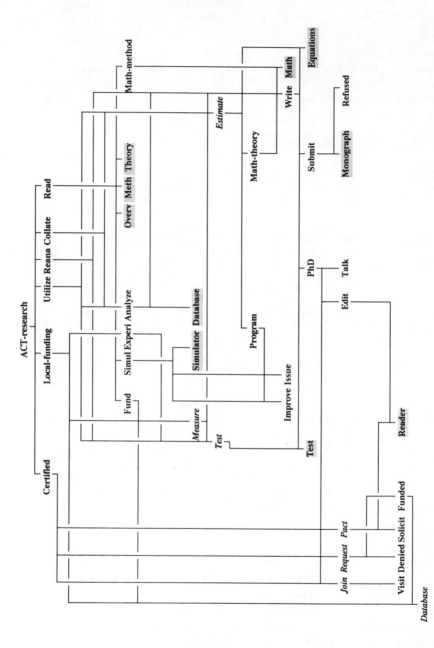

Fig. 1. Diagram of the logical structure of ACT research activities. For the meaning of the tokens, see Table 1. Italicized entries have disjunctive prerequisites; roman type indicates conjunctive prerequisites. Shaded entries are publication events.

through research activities in order to acquire a doctorate, and the doctorate opens opportunities for obtaining resources to sustain a research program. Aside from these institutionalized linkages, though, research activities and professional activities are essentially independent. A doctorate is not a prerequisite for any research activity, and continuous repetition of research activities is not essential to conduct professional activities.

The professional events' relation to resources of one kind or another is especially obvious in the case of *Requested funding*, *Funded externally*, and *Denied funding*. Activities related to control of publications—*Edited journal issue*, *Contracted with publisher*, *Solicited paper*, *Published edited book*—provide publication resources for one's own research program or for exchange with other programs. The academic events, *Joined faculty*, *Visited other faculty*, *Gave invited talk*, distribute researchers' labor and skills to different locales and give researchers access to other colleagues and local resources like university computers.

Data collection activities. Three events relate to data gathering: *Gathered database measurements*, *Measured responses*, and *Ran experiment*. The latter two lead to a series of other research events, as the researcher who gathered the data also analyzes the data and writes a report. In contrast, *Gathered database measurements* is presented as an end product rather than as a step toward other ends. Of course, a database generally is collated and used, but in the ACT research program the collator and the gatherer frequently were not the same researcher, and occasionally the collation occurred long after the data were gathered. This corresponds to Latour's (1987) description of other sciences in which one set of people collect materials at centers of calculation, and there the materials may sit until other people organize them.

The data-gathering activities are elementary in the sense that their only real prerequisite is some sort of funding. This is true even for *Gathered database measurements*, which appears in a lower tier of Figure 1 and therefore appears to be contingent on many other activities; in fact it is dependent only on obtaining a large amount of funding, which requires professional certification of someone, which is the reason the activity appears in a lower tier. (A new technology for obtaining semantic differential ratings with microcomputers reduced the costs of gathering ACT databases so much that Andreas Schneider, a graduate student at the University of Mannheim, assembled a large German database in late 1989 with only local funding.)

Since data-gathering operations do not require mastery of a whole series of ancillary skills, these activities often are handed over to the novices in a research program (or even to complete outsiders in some kinds of social research). A possible disadvantage of letting novices provide the informational inputs is that each data collector may focus on something different. If the flow of information into the program is too diverse and complex to organize, then there may be a lack of progress, as in the case of traditional symbolic interactionism where a plethora of unique field studies defies synthesis. More "scientific" research programs provide standard instruments to data collectors so that the flow of information entering the system is comprehensible and subject to analysis with familiar concepts and methodologies. Thus, data collection in the ACT research program uses the semantic differential (and—as another example—much of the experimentation in the expectation states research program involves application of the program's standard experiment).

The disadvantage of using standardized data collection procedures— the narrowing of vision to what can be perceived through the instruments—seems worrisome in the social sciences, though it rarely is considered a problem in the physical sciences. Perhaps this is because the physical world is simpler than the social world. Or perhaps it is because social scientists have not yet elaborated the reality perceivable through their instruments to the point where that reality seems more compelling than the social realities provided by journalists, politicians, sages, etc.

Descriptive research. Some key activities following data collection— *Collated data, Utilized existing database, Analyzed database*—serve to refine the information provided by the measuring instrument. These activities eliminate noise from data statistically, organize facts so they are accessible, and identify curiosities for special consideration. In the ACT research program some of the facts obtained through these analyses warranted publication on their own. For example, it was found that virtually no emotions are neutral in goodness, according to college students in the United States (Morgan and Heise 1988) and in Canada (MacKinnon and Keating 1989); that gay Christians judge their homosexual identities and activities as good, potent, and lively—contrary to the opinions of other liberal Christians (Smith-Lovin and Douglas 1992); that state policemen have a more positive view of themselves and also of criminals than college students do (Heise 1979).

Performed simulation (which is comparable to hypothesis derivation in other research programs) served a related descriptive function in the ACT research program: simulations allowed the reality defined by instruments and by theoretical principles to be accessed and scanned easily.

A program's descriptive research demonstrates the program's utility to novices and outsiders. Another purpose, especially for advanced researchers, is to identify non–intuitive phenomena, or phenomena that are contrary to competing theoretical realities, whereupon new data can be collected to show that the hypothetical phenomena do exist. Described this way, such work has rhetorical functions, as constructivists like Latour (1987) and Gergen (1985) have argued, in that it justifies commitment of time and other resources to the program by researchers and by outsiders. However, it is to be emphasized that information entering the system through the instruments is not controlled by the researchers (aside from their focusing on a narrow slice of the perceivable world), so research as rhetoric does not present a merely arbitrary world. Moreover, the descriptive work in a research program provides the materials for developing abstractions and rules, and scientists are at least as interested in these intellectual challenges as they are in influencing others.

Theory construction activities. Theory construction is reflected in several different events.

Estimated equations is a form of theory elaboration in that it leads to formulations that are "more comprehensive, more precise, more rigorous, or [with] greater empirical support" (Wagner and Berger 1985: 707). *Tested theory* and *Reanalyzed prior study* function essentially the same way. These forms of theory construction, dealing with middle-level abstractions, are so data-driven that they hardly seem like theory construction at all. However, that is because certain abstraction and organizing processes have been routinized in the form of statistical methodologies. The theoretical nature of the methodologies becomes evident when they themselves are derived, as in the ACT event *Mathematized methodology*.

Mathematized formulation, another form of theory elaboration, better fits the usual notion of theory construction: abstract variables and functional relations are defined so as to maintain (or predict) empirically demonstrable mappings between sets of measurements. (As Abell [1987] observed, this corresponds to the invention of homomorphisms.) In the ACT research program this event always developed from estimation of equations that in turn required contact with some sort of data, and therefore this kind of theorizing implied deep involvement in the research program. It is not the mathematical work that required deep involvement (e.g., *Mathematized methodology* requires nothing more than reading) but rather understanding the substantive phenomena that were to be formally represented.

Programmed simulation system and *Improved simulation system* are additional kinds of theoretical work. Just as statistical methodologies routinize some inductive procedures, simulation systems are intended to simplify and routinize some deductive procedures. For example, program INTERACT (Heise and Lewis 1988) in the ACT research program allows an analyst to specify social interaction input variables in verbal terms, whereupon the program applies equations and then employs databases in order to report results in verbal terms; thus the simulation system is a means of deducing implications of the theory in specific circumstances (Heise 1986). Creating and improving the simulation system required very deep involvement in the ACT research program because it depended on estimating equations and on familiarity with ACT data.

No event in the ACT history specifically accounts for the formation of theoretical statements like those presented in the first part of this essay because such statements evolve rather than emerge suddenly. For example, the affect control principle was first stated as a speculation in a 1969 publication, the idea guided mathematical derivations in the early 1970's, affect control became a key expositional device in the mid-1970's, implications of the idea were tested in various ways in the late 1970's and early 1980's, and in this essay the notion finally is claimed to be a "principle." In general, the evolutionary process depends on finding that an abstract formulation can tie various ideas together, on affirming that empirical reality can be construed as proposed by the formulation, and then—with confidence born of these successes—on advancing the proposition as a fact in discourse with other scientists.

Publication events. ACT research activities generally culminated in publication events of various kinds—e.g., *Published database study, Published equation estimations, Published methodology*, etc. It is notable that most of the publications have no further direct consequences within the model. Publications are final research products, and they have to be utilized by outsiders in order to have impact, as Latour (1987) emphasized. The outsiders may be scientists in other research programs or graduate students who become attracted to participating as a researcher in the program after reading program publications.

Wrote research report is treated as distinct from publication events to allow for the cases where a researcher reported results specifically for internal consumption (as in a thesis, a dissertation, or a technical report). Such documents often had professional consequences for the researcher, and sometimes they were reworked by colleagues for joint publication.

Submitted research monograph can lead to *Published research monograph* or to *Denied monograph publication*, either of which is a possible final outcome of research activities. The potential for being denied publication means that a researcher's work can be invisible to outsiders for lack of access to distribution channels, and being tied to values and gatekeepers in a distribution system may be as important for researchers as it is for the artists that Becker (1982) studied. On the other hand, submission and rejection of a manuscript commute—a rejection primes another submission, and submissions often continue until finally publication is achieved—so the issue may be more a matter of gaining access to a particular audience than of not being able to report at all. (The subsystem relating submission, rejection, and publication of a monograph manuscript applies in principle for publication events involving journals as well as monographs, though the ACT history did not call often for the extra details and so they are not represented in the model for the sake of simplicity.)

Development of a simulation system—a project that received substantial investments of time in the ACT research program—has no standard publication outlet, and therefore such work remains largely invisible to the broader social science community. The quasi-publication event, *Issued simulation system*, arose only in the late 1980's when institutionalized mechanisms for distributing computer simulation systems first began to develop.

Priorities

Figure 1 reveals that research activities are logically structured but also that a researcher usually has options at any point in time. For example, a beginning researcher—say, a graduate student—has the options of reading, collating a database, reanalyzing a dataset, working with an existing database, or obtaining local funding. (Obtaining professional certification also is shown in Table 1, but that is merely a convenience construct used to deal with researchers who entered the ACT project after acquiring professional credentials.) Examining which possible events were implemented promptly and which were deferred provides insights into the values and other facilitators of action that guided activities.

Events from the ACT research program were analyzed, observing which event occurred and which events were possible at each time point and tallying how often an event took precedence over other events that were possible at the same time. The events were ranked in terms of precedence, and Figure 2 shows the results.

Received doctorate appears at the top of the chart, and this means that among ACT researchers virtually no research events intervened from the time a dissertation was completed to the time the Ph.D. was received. This is partly because of short institutional delay times, but it is a matter of personal priorities as well. For example, nearly a year passed from the time that Heise completed his dissertation until he received his doctorate, but he attempted no research while he was completing his language requirement and supporting himself as an instructor.

Published database study is another very high-priority event. In the ACT history, a database analysis was a frequent response to an editorial call for papers, and thus database analyses often were followed by publication of

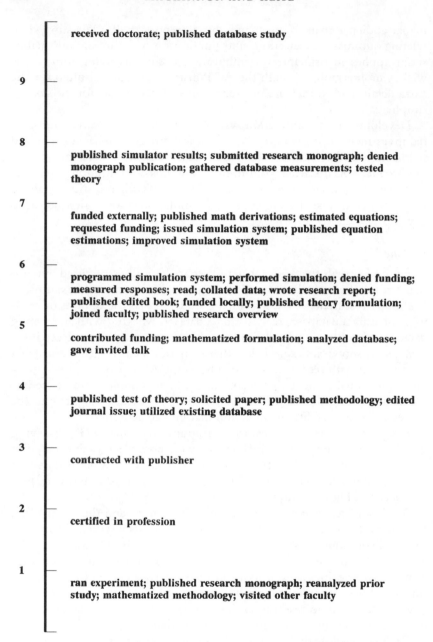

received doctorate; published database study

9

8

published simulator results; submitted research monograph; denied
monograph publication; gathered database measurements; tested
theory

7

funded externally; published math derivations; estimated equations;
requested funding; issued simulation system; published equation
estimations; improved simulation system

6

programmed simulation system; performed simulation; denied funding;
measured responses; read; collated data; wrote research report;
published edited book; funded locally; published theory formulation;
joined faculty; published research overview

5

contributed funding; mathematized formulation; analyzed database;
gave invited talk

4

published test of theory; solicited paper; published methodology; edited
journal issue; utilized existing database

3

contracted with publisher

2

certified in profession

1

ran experiment; published research monograph; reanalyzed prior
study; mathematized methodology; visited other faculty

Fig. 2. ACT research events plotted on a priority range from zero (bottom of
scale) to ten (top of scale).

results with little delay. (*Published simulator results* also has fairly high priority, and the reason is the same.)

Submitted research monograph is a high-priority event. Once the manuscript for a monograph exists (or once it has been rejected by one publisher), little else is done until the manuscript is sent on to a publisher. This is a matter of researcher motivation: a large investment of work offers no benefits until the monograph manuscript is published, so the researcher becomes single-minded about getting the manuscript into the mail. Being denied a monograph publication also is high priority—that is, not much happens between the times of submission and rejection, a fact that mainly reflects rapid response times from editors.

Gathered database measurements is high priority: once appropriate funding is available, researchers move rapidly into the field to implement plans. The precedence of this research activity over other activities reflects the value placed on new data and also the need to spend money while it is administratively available.

Tested theory also is high priority, which is to say that few things interrupt analyses once data for a possible test are ready. This is partly because at that point the test is a fairly easy matter of statistical analyses, and also because scientific culture imbues tests with so much allure that they take precedence over other activities.

(We skip over the large set of events with moderate to moderately high priorities, since these constitute the reference base for judging high and low.)

Published test of theory has somewhat low priority. That probably is an accident of ACT history, since reporting of tests was targeted for a monograph publication that got delayed for years. The relatively low priority of *published methodology* has the same explanation.

Utilized existing database has somewhat low priority because it always was possible though people chose to do other things. The priority would be even lower except that this event was crucial in representing cooperative research projects where one researcher collated a database and another researcher utilized it. The low priority reflects a value among ACT researchers to do many other things rather than mine old data, and also it reflects the fact that funding agencies promote the creation of databases while only rarely supporting the analysis of existing data.

Several editorial activities—*solicited paper, edited journal issue, contracted with publisher*—have somewhat low priorities. In the period studied, ACT researchers focused more on research than on such editorial matters, reflecting their personal values to some degree, but also reflecting the early career development of many ACT researchers. Research programs with more senior researchers (including the ACT program as it ages) can more easily implement such professional opportunities, so the activities might take precedence more often. (Similar interpretations apply also for the very low-priority event *visited other faculty*, which includes honorific visits to research centers: such events might have higher priority among senior researchers who can arrange the visits fairly easily.)

Ran experiment is an event with very low priority in the ACT research program: it was possible nearly all of the time yet happened only once in the time period studied. The low priority reflects the training and early interests of ACT researchers, and the priority undoubtedly would be higher in other research programs. The priority also will rise in the ACT program since Lynn Smith-Lovin began an extensive program of experimentation in 1990 (e.g., Robinson and Smith-Lovin 1992). Similarly, *reanalyzed prior study* had little appeal for ACT researchers, though it is a valued activity among other researchers.

The very low priority of *published research monograph* reflects constraints from the publishing world. Each cycling of a manuscript through submission-rejection caused the precedence of monograph publication to decline. Moreover, the delay after acceptance of a monograph until actual publication always was so long in the ACT research program that many other research events had a chance to intervene.

Mathematized methodology is low priority, being possible virtually all of the time but rarely done. This reflects the research-oriented values of ACT researchers to a degree. However, it also reflects the fact that only Heise undertook such work, so the priority was driven down by others' non-involvement in the activity.

The priority analysis suggests that a variety of factors influence researchers' choice of activities. The culture of science puts high value on new information and on tests of theory, so these activities preempt other activities as soon as they are possible. A particular research program's subculture also sets values concerning what kinds of work are interesting. Researchers' personal motivations lead to high priorities for activities that culminate large investments of work. And vicissitudes in funding and publishing institutions raise and lower priorities of some events.

Conclusion

The event structure model presented above accounts for 298 events occurring over a period of 27 years and involving 16 different people. Thus, it is an empirically grounded and powerful device for explaining how some social psychological research proceeds, though the model describes the activities of only one research program, and changes might be required to account for happenings in other research programs.

The model envisions research as a developmental process in which occurrence of an event may establish necessary conditions for some later events, but no event is sufficient to generate a cascade of later events. Thus, research might start off with a researcher reading and stop there; or it may involve reading and investigating a database and nothing more; analyses might be done and then the research stopped; or perhaps publication is achieved and then the pursuit is abandoned. Past events create opportunities for further events but do not guarantee them.

It therefore is quite remarkable that social theories arise and cumulate over long periods of time. It seems that research programs transform scientific research from an indeterminate developmental process into something more like a causal system. Program funding is a factor, as it increases the rate of research events (an effect that was evident in a conventional time series analysis of the data on ACT), and thereby makes less likely the languishing of a later-stage activity because a required early-stage activity has not been completed. More generally, research programs routinize meetings of research collaborators, assure the availability of facilities which are required for research activities, guarantee that researchers are provisioned with depletable resources (like data), and generate intermediate products that are used by other researchers within the program. Socialization into research roles provides researchers with the skills to perform their duties and with ideologies to sustain their motivation, and imbues scientific standards that keep research products acceptable in the larger scientific community. Thus research programs in the context of academic socialization and institutionalized support operate as productive social organizations that transform empirical observations, scientific literature, and funding into new formulations of reality.

A "Pure Theory" Research Program on Microdynamics

Jonathan H. Turner

It is not always possible, or even desirable, to work within the confines of an explicit "theoretical research tradition." It is critical that a few theorists think globally, putting together concepts from a variety of more delimited theories and metatheories. Using Wagner and Berger's (1985) terminology, I would typify my theory as an "elaboration" of many existing theories in the sense that it is more comprehensive than the theories from which it borrows, and is generally more precise and rigorous. My approach also involves considerable "theory integration" in that it pulls from diverse theories critical concepts and arranges or integrates them in a new way. Perhaps what I do stretches Wagner and Berger's notions of "elaboration" and "integration," but these terms capture a sense of the approach.

I might call this approach a "program," but this implies several things: first, that I have hordes of students carrying forth my ideas, testing them, and training new generations of students; second, that I have always had some vision of where I was going or, at least, what kinds of problems would need to be addressed; and third, that I had designs on systematically testing the theory (by securing research grants, research assistants, and laboratory space). In fact, none of these conditions prevail. The resources for such activities have not been available, but perhaps more important, I would probably not sought them if they were. The reason for this is simple: I am comfortable in a theoretical armchair, and, moreover, I think that it is essential that some of us do this kind of global theoretical activity, lest we not "see the forest for the trees."

It should be emphasized, however, that more than an "orienting strategy" (Wagner and Berger 1985) is offered and that my efforts represent more than a metatheoretical analysis. Rather, I see myself as a theorist who uses metatheory to elaborate and integrate actual theories (somewhat along the lines suggested by Berger, Wagner, and Zelditch 1989). My approach thus seeks to (1) extract useful concepts, propositions, and models from existing theories, (2) extend them to new contexts and problems, (3) integrate them into new models and propositions that address fundamental and invariant (i.e., always present) properties of the social universe, and (4) illustrate the synthetic theory with examples (which can hardly be considered a systematic test of the theory). How, then, have I gone about this "program"?

Inputs into the Initial "Program"

A good deal of my early work involved formalizing discursive theories—from Marx and Spencer to Durkheim, Simmel, Weber, and Pareto through most contemporary theorists (for examples, see Turner 1975a, 1975b, 1979, 1981a, 1981b, 1981c, 1984a, 1984b, 1985a, 1990a, 1990b, 1991; Turner, Beeghley, and Powers 1989; and Turner and Powers 1985). When initially doing this activity (usually involving stating discursive arguments in lists of propositions and in diagrammatic models), I did not have a coherent view of *why* this seemed appropriate. My goal was to get a "handle" on these theories and to present them in a format that communicated their essence without all the distracting detail. For many years, such metatheoretical work seemed to be enough, but increasingly I began to compare, contrast, and reconcile the theories (e.g., Turner 1975a, 1975b, 1984a). Again, I had no grand vision; this just seemed like an interesting thing to do.

And then, perhaps as early as ten years ago, I got more ambitious and decided to develop a synthetic theory of human organization. As soon as this pretension surfaced, however, some questions immediately emerged: What are the fundamental properties and processes of the social universe? And how can these best be represented in sociological theory? To answer these questions required that I pay more attention to strategic issues.

The Theoretical Strategy

In approaching these questions, I found that it was necessary to enter into the debate over the scientific prospects of sociology. Most of the contributors to this volume form a relatively dense network of scholars who rarely have to defend the scientific nature of their work, but as one who lives in broader social theory circles, I sée that the first task is to defend scientific sociology. For there can be no doubt that a clear majority of social theorists do not believe that sociology can or should be a science. As long as I was talking *about* others' theories (even with formal

propositions and models), I was tolerated as a "hard-nosed" metatheo-
rist, but as soon as I began to develop synthetic theories using selected
and modified ideas of the canonized masters and as I began to cut across
the polarized and highly politicized theoretical "camps" of contemporary
sociology, I encountered resistance. When faced with criticism, I found
that it became necessary to defend the emerging research program.
Hence, my strong advocacy for positivism (e.g., Turner 1985b, 1990c)
in the Comtean sense (as opposed to the "logical positivism" of the
Vienna circle or the "raw empiricism" of contemporary critics). I chose
the Comtean vision—perhaps, in retrospect, a mistake—because it was
bold and grand: sociology could denote the basic properties of the social
universe; sociology could develop laws that explained the dynamics of
these properties; and sociology could, thereby, take its place at the table
of science. Whereas Robert Merton (1968: 47) advocated middle-range
theories, arguing that sociology "has not yet found its Kepler—to say
nothing of its Newton, Laplace, Gibbs, Maxwell or Planck," I asserted
that Spencer, Marx, Durkheim, Weber, Pareto, Simmel, and Mead had
been our equivalents of these giants of physics and that it was now time
to "stand on the shoulders" of Spencer, Marx, Weber, Durkheim, Mead,
and others. In my view, these figures had denoted the key properties of
the universe and unlocked many of the secrets in the operative dynamics
of these properties. Such advocacy was considered "naive" by the "sophisticated" social theory crowd, but my early formalizing of these early
masters convinced me that sociology's early burst of creative theory was
over, and yet, we still seemed unaware of how seminal the insights of
these scholars had been. Today, I would go so far as to assert that they
uncovered virtually all of the critical properties of the social universe; and
now, it is time for us to extend and consolidate—or, in Wagner and Berger's terms, "elaborate" and "integrate"—their ideas. But just how is this
to be done?

    For me, the answer to this question has increasingly revolved around
the synergy that results from developing sensitizing schemes, analytical
models, and inventories of abstract propositions (Turner 1985b, 1986b,
1987a). A sensitizing scheme denotes (1) those fundamental properties of
the universe that are to be the subject of theory and (2) those classes of
relations among these properties. An analytical model "fills in" a sensitizing scheme by specifying in visual space (1) those key processes inher-
ing in the properties denoted by a sensitizing scheme and (2) those causal
relations among these processes (including direct, indirect, reverse, and
feedback causal paths). Propositions state in language (1) those critical
relations among processes depicted in an analytical model and (2) those
forces, sometimes exogenous to the model, that influence the values of

variables and the form of relationship among these variables in the model. In essence, a sensitizing scheme alerts us to the fundamental properties of the social universe; an analytical model arrays in visual space the constituent processes of these properties and specifies the configuration of causal connections and paths among them; and a propositional inventory highlights certain causal paths as crucial while at times adding new variables.

Most grand theorizing in sociology operates at the sensitizing scheme level; and, in my view, further specification in detailed models and propositional inventories is the next step in a theoretical research program. A sensitizing scheme, by itself, is too vague and requires more detail, which is provided by an analytical model, but alone an analytical model is untestable because it depicts too many variables and causal paths. And so, by means of selected causal paths converted into propositions, it becomes possible to create a testable theory, or at least portions of a theory. The model provides causal details that are not easily expressed as propositions, even those using the language of mathematics; and the propositions translate selected causal paths into statements that can be tested. By working back and forth between analytical models and propositions—using propositions to sort and translate complex configurations of causal connections into more manageable and testable hypotheses, and, conversely, using models to specify the causal processes operating to produce the relations proposed in a proposition—I find that theoretical growth is encouraged.

Thus, my theoretical research program has, over the years, involved converting existing theories into sensitizing schemes, analytical models, and propositional inventories. Initially, I operated with sensitizing schemes and propositions, but increasingly a major problem emerged: a proposition, even a complex one stated in a formal language, has trouble specifying the *processes* by which the variables in the proposition are connected. A proposition allows the form of the relationship to be specified (e.g., positive, negative, curvilineal, logarithmic, exponential, additive, multiplicative, etc.), but cannot provide a very clear picture of the configuration of processes producing this form. As a result of this problem, I began to draw models, arranging variables in visual space so as to reflect a temporal ordering and, then, inserting lines and arrows to denote the direct, reverse, and feedback causal paths among the variables. Such diagrams provide a sense of process in a more robust manner than is possible with a proposition (or series of propositions). Conversely, the model began to suggest ways that the proposition should be rewritten and reformulated so as to capture some of these more robust configurations. And so, this pattern of moving back and forth between models and

propositions began to typify my research program. At one time, I tended
to start with propositions and then draw a model; but in more recent
years, I usually draw a model first and, at times, simulate it on the computer before translating it into propositions.

This procedure works rather well when analyzing someone else's
theory or, as I often do, when generating a limited middle-range theory
(e.g., Turner 1984b, 1986c; Turner and Bonacich 1980; Turner and Singleton 1978). However, as I approached the task of synthesizing existing
theories in order to produce a general theory of human organization,
another problem immediately surfaced: How does one divide the social
universe into manageable units of analysis? The answer to this question
was, in essence, provided by the long-standing and recently revived issue
of micro vs. macro levels of analysis, and by the corresponding effort to
develop general theories that link these two levels. There are several ways
to address the problem of how to "link" these levels and "fill in" the gap
between them (e.g., see Turner 1983, 1991, for a review), but my conclusion goes somewhat against prevailing opinion: Why try to link the
two and fill in the gap? Too much theorizing in sociology seeks something that may be, in the foreseeable future, unattainable: a unified theory
of human organization. Instead, we should try to develop separate theories of the micro and macro domains, putting off the question of linkage
until we have more adequate theories of the operative dynamics in each
domain. Hence, my theoretical research project deliberately avoids the
issue of reconciling micro and macro. When we wish to explain *face-to-
face interaction among individuals*, we use microdynamic theories; and when
we seek to understand the processes occurring among *populations of actors*, we employ macrodynamic theories. "Meso" theorizing and various
other efforts to connect the two levels are, at the very least, premature;
and we would do better to concentrate our efforts on developing more
precise micro and macro theories.

My research program thus involves (1) analyzing existing theories,
(2) extracting sensitizing schemes, analytical models, and propositions
from these theories, and (3) selectively synthesizing these theories as they
bear on the micro and macro realms of the social universe. Thus far, I
have developed a theory of microdynamics involving a synthetic sensitizing scheme, an analytical model, and an inventory of propositions
(Turner 1988). Currently, I am thinking about the various criticisms of
this theory and considering potential revisions, which can become the
basis for a new round of elaboration and integration. I am also hard at
work on the macrodynamic theory, having constructed a synthetic sensitizing scheme, numerous analytical models, and various propositional

inventories (Turner 1987a, 1990d, 1992). I am not, however, finished with this latter theory, and as a consequence, I will concentrate on the micro theory of this chapter.

The Current Theory of Microdynamics

The Sensitizing Scheme

A sensitizing scheme denotes the basic processes that are to be the subject of a theory. In the development of a theory of microdynamics, three basic processes are considered crucial (e.g., Turner 1986a, 1987b, 1988, 1989a, 1989b; Turner and Collins 1989): (1) *motivating* processes, or those forces that mobilize and energize individuals to initiate and continue interaction with others, (2) *interacting* processes, or those signaling practices by which individuals indicate their lines of conduct and dispositions while interpreting others' internal dispositions and likely courses of behavior, and (3) *structuring* processes, or those procedures by which interaction among motivated individuals is stretched across time and organized in space.

How did I come to divide the micro universe into motivating, interacting, and structuring processes? I initially began to think about microprocesses in much the same ways as other theorists: focus on a specific process and explain its operation. For example, the expectation states research program began by examining a particular process, and over time, the core idea was elaborated in a variety of ways and, then, reintegrated. I began with Mead's (1934) theory of mind, self, and society as my core idea, viewing mind and self as behavioral capacities acquired by virtue of participation in society, or social structures, and as the fundamental behaviors that produce and reproduce social structure. The key process in this reciprocal relation is role taking (with specific others and more generalized others), with the information gathered from such role-taking being used as a basis for self-evaluation and minded deliberations about how to behave in a situation.

Mead's formulation contains the seeds of the division of the micro universe into three constituent processes: people's need to cooperate and sustain a self-concept, and thereby avoid anxiety (or what Mead [1938] termed "disequilibrium with the environment"), represented the motivational dimension; mutual role-taking in terms of significant gestures was the interactional dimension; and society or organized clusters of co-operative activity was the structural dimension. My view of Mead as specifying three constituent processes was not, however, initially clear to me. And as I read other theorists, this core set of ideas in Mead's work could only be seen as a skeletal core; there were, to my way of thinking, many additional processes operating to motivate individuals, to guide the flow of their signaling and interpreting activities, and to structure and organize their interactions. Thus, I was forced to abandon a "strict inter-actionist" view of interaction, but I was confronted with the problem of how to integrate others' concepts, models, and propositions with the Meadian core.

In grappling with how to integrate Mead's ideas with those inside and outside of the interactionist tradition, I finally came to see the underlying dimensions of Mead's work as involving a conceptualization of motivat-ing, interacting, and structuring processes. Once I saw (or, as some say, imposed) this order on Mead, it was much easier to "add on" the ideas of others to this skeleton conceptual core. And as these ideas were added, the main conceptual task became one of integrating them with each other. Propositions and analytical models proved to be useful tools for accomplishing this goal. Thus, the theory of microdynamics "grew" and "proliferated" in my armchair, as I read and thought about the process of interaction. Integration occurred when I tried to reconcile Mead's ideas with other theorists, forcing me to pull out what I saw as the implicit constituent dimensions in Mead's approach.

Schematically, these processes are represented in Figure 1 as a series of interconnected forces, having direct, indirect, and reverse causal effects on each other. That is, motivating processes initiate signaling and inter-preting (or interacting processes), which, in turn, are the vehicles for structuring interaction, but both interacting and structuring processes have causal effects on each other and motivating processes. Figure 1 thus indicates that a *sociological* theory of microdynamics will involve (1) iso-lating those forces that are implicated in motivating, interacting, and structuring and (2) discovering the patterns of causal effects within and among these forces. In seeking to implement the dictates of the sensitiz-ing scheme, I saw the task now become one of (1) constructing analytical models for each of the three basic processes, (2) developing a composite model that links these three processes together, and (3) articulating

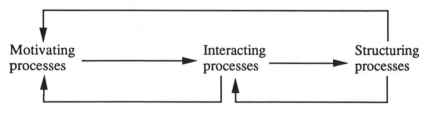

Fig. 1. A sensitizing scheme for a theory of microdynamics.

propositions that highlight certain key processes. I will begin by successively developing analytical models for each basic process—that is, motivating, interacting, and structuring; then I will offer a more general
analytical model that highlights the interconnections among those forces
involved in motivating, interacting, and structuring; and finally, I will
present some propositions that are suggested by the general model.

Motivational Dynamics

In Figure 2, an analytical model of motivation *during the course of interaction** is delineated (Turner 1987b, 1988). As the arrows in the model
flow left to right, time passes; and when arrows move from right to left,
reverse causes or feedback effects are denoted. Variables and arrows
aligned at similar vertical locations are considered to operate simultaneously in time. And the closer two variables and the more direct the causal
paths connecting them, the greater is the hypothesized effect as indicated
by the direction of the arrow.

This model invokes a controversial notion of "need" or "need-state,"
making the theory behavioral (Turner 1989a, 1989b).† That is, when
individuals experience a sense of group inclusion, ontological security,
facticity, self-confirmation, symbolic/material gratification, and thereby
avoid a diffuse sense of anxiety, they feel gratified and are motivated to
engage in those interpersonal behaviors that bring about such gratification; and conversely, when these needs are not met, they experience
deprivation and are motivated to avoid the diffuse sense of anxiety that
comes with such deprivation or to construct lines of interpersonal behavior that enable them to realize some minimal sense of group inclusion,
symbolic/material gratification, self-confirmation, facticity, and ontological security. Thus, from the perspective adopted here, the flow of
interaction and the viability of social structures are always contingent on
the extent to which the fundamental needs are met. What, then, are these
needs?

The notion of *group inclusion* is taken from Durkheim (1954), as his
ideas on egoism were adapted to interpersonal dynamics enumerated by
Goffman (1959, 1967) and Collins (1975, 1986, 1988). Unlike Durkheim,
however, I do not think that individuals need or desire to be fully integrated into all groupings (indeed, I suspect that humans are far more

---

*Obviously, there are other motivating processes, but my purpose is to explain those
guiding human interaction, not behavior in general. Moreover, I am asserting that other motivating processes are channeled through these, *to the extent* that they must be met through
interaction with others.

†I am shying away from the label "behaviorist," since this has very specific connotations. I see my approach as very much on G. H. Mead's (1934) program of "social
behaviorism."

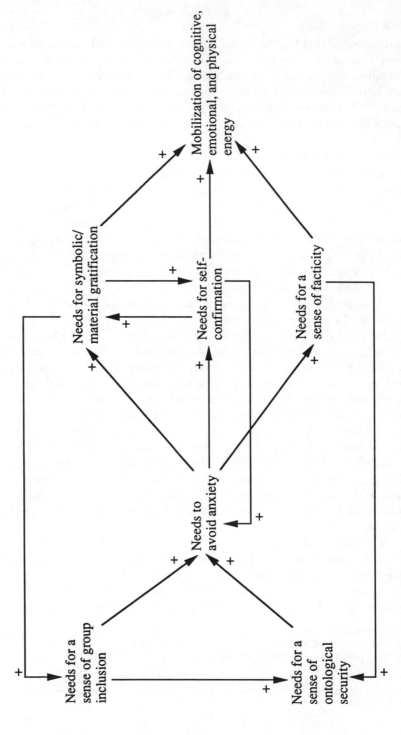

Fig. 2. Motivating dynamics.

individualistic than the sociological tradition would ever admit); instead, they simply need to sense that they are part of the ongoing flow of inter-action. And, as the arrows in the diagram indicate, humans experience considerable anxiety when such is not the case. This anxiety over group inclusion reverberates and increases the sense of deprivation over self-confirmation, facticity, and symbolic/material gratification. More di-rectly, deprivation over group inclusion immediately creates a sense of ontological *in*security which, in turn, escalates the reverberating effects of anxiety.

Ontological security is, of course, an old philosophical idea, but I am borrowing from Giddens's (1984) more recent use of this concept and merging it with Erikson's (1950) well-known notion of "trust." What is denoted by the concept of ontological security is this: people need to sense that the flow of interpersonal events is predictable and that they can trust others to behave in ways that are anticipated. When such is not the case, they experience deprivation, leading to anxiety, which lowers the level of other needs as indicated by the arrows in Figure 2.

Anxiety is one of those all-purpose concepts, but my use of the term is taken from Mead's (1938) analysis of "the act" and is intended to de-note a "sense of disequilibrium" with the environment (the idea was sug-gested by Giddens's [1984] more Freudian formulation). Individuals are motivated to maintain a sense of adjustment and equilibrium to their interpersonal surroundings; and, along with needs to confirm self, satis-fying needs for group inclusion and ontological security are the principal determinants of whether or not people experience anxiety.

Self-confirmation is the implicit motivational force in interactionist theorizing (e.g., Goffman 1959; Rosenberg 1979; Gecas 1985), and the basic argument is that individuals seek to sustain a conception of them-selves as a certain kind of person in interaction.* When this cannot be done, then they experience deprivation, which, in turn, escalates their sense of anxiety. More directly, the failure to confirm self causes people to experience deprivation over symbolic/material needs and needs for facticity; and as a result, they will be particularly likely to seek material objects and symbols confirming self in a situation and to construct ac-counts of the situation that make their self part of what is factual and real.

Facticity is an idea taken from Garfinkel (1963, 1967), although Goff-man (1959, 1967) had also employed the concept to describe similar pro-

---

*Of course, there are many conceptual issues involved in the analysis of self—core vs. peripheral self, stability of self-concepts, the importance of self-esteem, efficacy, or other specific dimensions of self. While all of these considerations are important (see Turner 1988: 43–46, for a review), my general point is that *whatever else* is involved, people seek to confirm self (again, whether core, peripheral, transitory, or some aspect thereof).

cesses. Facticity revolves around a need to construct an implicit account
of a situation which gives individuals a sense—even if illusionary—that
they share similar external and subjective worlds (a point of view clearly
adopted from Schutz 1967). When such is not the case, they immediately
experience deprivation, which escalates needs for ontological security
that can, if sufficiently strong, generate anxiety. Such anxiety can directly, and indirectly through self-confirmation processes, increase the
sense of deprivation over facticity. This potential cycle accounts for the
intensity with which people attempt to avoid, ignore, or gloss over interpersonal "breaches"; such breaches can activate cycles of deprivation
along a number of fronts, as can be seen by following the direct, indirect,
and feedback arrows in Figure 2.

Symbolic/material gratification is a need-state that is implicit in all exchange theories. That is, individuals seek symbols and material objects
that are "valued" in a social context. As the arrows in Figure 2 suggest,
individuals will be particularly attuned to symbols and material objects
that confirm self; and somewhat less directly, they will attempt to acquire
symbols and objects that confirm their sense of group inclusion and ontological security. People's emotions and their mobilization of energy
over exchange ratios (that is, over issues revolving around "justice"* and
"fairness") are intense not just because a sense of justice has been violated, but, more important, because their sense of self, group involvement, and ontological security has been upset.

There are many implications of the model presented in Figure 2,
which I have dealt with at length elsewhere (Turner 1988). Perhaps more
interesting is what I see as areas where the model can be improved.
The most obvious problem is the concept of "anxiety," which glosses
over some important emotional processes. Indeed, I simply incorporated
Mead's idea of "disequilibrium" and modified it with my early reading
of Freud in the 1960's, but increasingly, I see this formulation as flawed.
In the future, I plan to abandon the anxiety variable and to suggest
more specific emotions that are aroused by a sense of deprivation for the
three variables that feed directly into anxiety—group inclusion, self-
confirmation, and ontological security. Some interesting leads along
these lines present themselves—my own armchair version of theoretical
elaboration. Currently, my thinking is most consonant with Kemper's
(1978, 1981, 1987). There is a finite set of biologically based emotions—
fear, anger, satisfaction, sadness/depression, and perhaps a few more—
and these are elaborated through socialization and the establishment of
social relations. Thus, guilt, pride, shame, joy, frustration, anxiety, and

*There is, of course, a huge literature on this topic, but I think that Jasso's formulation
is the most elegant.

other emotional states are socially constructed and built upon a biologically based foundation of emotions. For example, Scheff (1988, 1990) has
argued that "pride and shame" are related to the extent to which social
bonds are sustained; and in terms of the model in Figure 2, shame is
related to the failure to sustain a sense of group inclusion and to confirm
self within an ongoing group context (conversely, the emotion of pride
arises in the opposite situation). Such emotion is, I think, built upon a
biological base of fear, anger and depression (for shame), and satisfaction
(for pride). To phrase the process in Collins's (1975, 1984, 1990) terms,
group inclusion produces enhanced "positive emotional energy" (built
upon satisfaction) and the failure to create a sense of inclusion causes a
reduction in emotional energy (based upon depression). Success in securing valued symbolic/material resources produces socially induced emotions—enhanced emotional energy, contentment, happiness, and grati-
tude—that are built upon the more primary emotion of satisfaction;
failure to secure valued resources, especially if expected, produces anger,
which can be socially channeled into a variety of emotional states—envy,
jealousy, resignation, reduced emotional energy, frustration, etc. Needs
for facticity will produce, as Garfinkel (1963, 1967) discovered, rather
disproportionate anger from those who are subject to breaching tactics
in their social interaction. Thus, I suspect that needs for facticity produce
anger when unmet and that, if deeper needs for ontological security are
also neglected, the emotions of anger and fear are activated. Just what
socially constructed emotions—frustration, contempt, puzzlement, shy-
ness, amazement, anxiety, disgust, etc.—are built upon these emotions
is probably contextually determined.

Obviously, I have not thought these issues out very far. My point here
is not to present a full-blown theory of emotions, but, rather, to suggest
that this microdynamic theory project must incorporate a conceptualization of emotions. As it stands, this fundamental property of interaction
is glossed over, which, in retrospect, seems a rather remarkable oversight
for a model of motivation. This oversight must, in the future, be corrected; and in the attempt to make some corrections, the theory will be
elaborated *and*, then, reintegrated.

Interacting Dynamics

The process of interacting, as I have defined it, involves the mutual
signaling and interpreting of gestures. Such a process depends upon humans' capacities for thought and deliberation—what Mead (1934) termed
"mind"—and use of acquired information about the contextual meaning
of gestures—what Schutz (1967) conceptualized as "stocks of knowledge
at hand." Thus, as individuals are variously motivated and mobilize their

cognitive, physical, and emotional energy, they employ their capacities
for thought and their stores for information about situations and contexts
to emit signals and to read the signals emitted by others. As interaction-
ists (Gecas 1985; Stryker 1980) typically emphasize, this process of signaling and interpreting is influenced by self. The way individuals think
about situations, interpret gestures of others, and emit gestures of their
own is mediated by their conceptions of themselves as particular kinds of
persons. Thus, as individuals mobilize their cognitive, emotional, and
physical energy, their conceptions of themselves circumscribe the gestures they emit and act as a prism through which the gestures of others
are seen and interpreted.

In Figure 3, the process of interacting is modeled. As is indicated
in the model, signaling and interpreting occur against a cognitive and
emotional background of self-references, deliberation, and stocks of
knowledge. The key mediating processes linking these background fea-

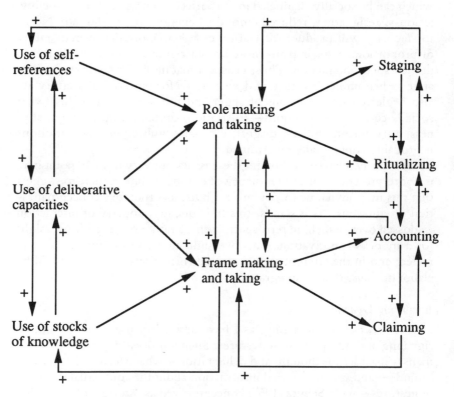

Fig. 3. Interacting dynamics.

tures to signaling and interpreting are role making/role taking and frame making/frame taking. As the model indicates, self-references, or the conceptions of themselves that individuals invoke in a situation, directly circumscribe role making and role taking, whereas stocks of implicit knowledge directly shape frame making and frame taking. Of course, self indirectly influences framing processes, and vice versa, via direct and feedback causal processes that pass through deliberative capacities.

The concept of *role making* is borrowed from R. H. Turner (1962) and involves the process of orchestrating gestures so as to indicate what role one is attempting to play in a situation (a *role* being defined here as a stereotypical syndrome of gestures organizing a person's conduct). *Role taking*, is, of course, Mead's (1934) famous concept and denotes the process of reading others' gestures to determine not only what role these others are attempting to play but also their subjective states. The use of gestures to make a role depends upon actors possessing in their stocks of knowledge information about the kinds of roles appropriate to a situation and how these roles are constructed and communicated. The process of role taking also depends upon possessing a store or inventory of relevant roles, but can also involve more subtle and fine-tuned contextual interpretations of gestures to assess subjective states accompanying a role.

Role taking and role making are also circumscribed by, and at the same time circumscribe, *framing* activities—a concept adapted from Goffman (1959, 1974). A frame is a cognitive-emotional border denoting what experiences are relevant to a situation while indicating what realms of experience are to be excluded by virtue of being outside the frame. Individuals use their stocks of knowledge to *frame-make* or create a cognitive-emotional boundary about what is relevant and irrelevant in a situation; and they simultaneously use these stocks of knowledge to *frame-take* or interpret the contextual meaning of others' efforts at making a frame. As the model also indicates, self-references indirectly impose themselves on these framing activities, and role-taking/making processes directly influence the frames that individuals make and interpret in a situation. Goffman (1974) emphasized the process of "keying" (transforming a frame) and "fabrication" (creating a false belief about what a frame is), and in my view, he overemphasized both. While experience can be "layered" or "laminated" by the successive imposition of different frames and while the fabrication of frames for various purposes does occur, most interaction seeks to create a "primary frame," and when the frame is changed, there are conventionalized ways of doing so (that people carry in their stocks of knowledge). Thus, Goffman's view of individuals is far too cynical, for he sees them as manipulative, mercurial, and mischievous. Extending or elaborating upon Goffman's discussion of "social" and "natural" frames, I discovered five dimensions of framing (Turner 1989b): (1) demographic, or the number, movement, and density of individuals in the interaction; (2) ecological, or the physical props and ecological space to be used in interaction; (3) organizational, or the relevant social unit (dyad, group, organization, societal sphere, etc.) to be used as a reference point for the interaction; (4) cultural, or the type of symbols (values, beliefs, institutional norms, or specific contextual norms) to be used to guide interaction; and (5) personal, or the amount and nature of intimacy, biography, and involvement to be displayed in an interaction. Thus, any interaction is simultaneously framed with respect to demographic, ecological, organizational, cultural, and personal frames; and when rekeying occurs, it involves expanding or narrowing the rim of one, some, or all of these basic dimensions of framing.

As Figure 3 delineates, frame making/taking and role making/taking determine how other gesturing and interpreting processes will occur. Roles are made and interpreted in terms of two major classes of gestures: staging cues and ritual. The notion of *staging* is adapted from Goffman (1959, 1967) and involves the use and interpretation of physical props, ecological space, wardrobe, juxtaposition of bodies, and other physical-ecological features of an interpersonal situation. Individuals use staging tactics to make a role that confirms their self-references, and at the same time they interpret staging tactics of others to determine the role and subjective states of these others. The notion of *ritualizing* is taken from the later Durkheim (1965) as his ideas were adapted by Goffman (1967) and Collins (1975). Ritualizing revolves around the emission of stereotyped sequences of gestures to mark particular points of an interaction and, at times, to charge the interaction emotionally. Such rituals are also used to role-make and role-take. There are, I believe, particular classes of rituals that are crucial to role taking and role making (Turner 1988): (1) opening and closing rituals which indicate the beginning and end of a strip of interaction and which, more significantly, denote the emotional "tone" and "feel" of the interaction that will take place now or in the future; (2) forming rituals which mark the sequence of the interaction and which, also, indicate the pattern, tone, duration, structure, and other features of the interaction as it unfolds; (3) repairing rituals which seek to smooth over the emotions aroused by breached sequences of gesturing and interpreting in the interaction; and (4) totemizing rituals which make an "object" of the interaction and which direct emotionally charged responses toward the interaction as an important reality external to the individuals. Staging and ritual are mutually reinforcing. Rituals accentuate what is being staged by marking the use of props, space, and positioning; conversely, staging often provides the materials by which rituals are organized and performed. Since ritualizing and staging, as mediated by role making/taking, are connected to self-references, it is not surprising that when rituals and staging go awry (when, for example, "personal space" and "turf" are violated or when relevant rituals are not emitted) people become upset and seek to remake and retake roles.

Frames are also imposed and rekeyed in terms of two basic classes of gestures: claims and accounts. Borrowing from Habermas (1970a, 1970b, 1984), but in essence turning his argument on its head, I visualize *claiming* as a process by which individuals implicitly make and interpret assertions over each other's (1) sincerity in the present context, (2) rationality over the means employed to realize goals, and (3) normative appropriateness of the obligations and expectations that are imposed on the situation. Unlike Habermas, however, I argue that people seek to avoid challenging such "validity claims," if they possible can. That is, following Schutz (1967) and Goffman (1967), I find that the last thing that people wish to do is have "discourse" over their validity claims. For if claims are challenged, then cultural, organizational, and biographical frames will have to be rekeyed, thereby stalling the interaction. One way in which claims are sustained is through *accounting* procedures which, following Garfinkel (1967) and Goffman (1967), I conceptualize as the subtle gestures—conversational pauses, turn taking, verbal glosses, questions, quiet assertions, and other "ethnomethods"—used by individuals to create a presumption that they share subjective and intersubjective experiences. Such accounts of "what's real" are constructed within the frame, but they are also a vehicle by which frames are created and imposed on an interaction. Moreover, in so doing, accounts not only reinforce the frame guiding the making and taking of claims, but they also create an additional set of constraints on claims. Conversely, claiming reinforces an account and people's implicit sense of "what's real."

In sum, then, Figure 3 outlines some of the dynamic connections among the processes of signaling and interpreting. And like Figure 2 on motivating dynamics, it represents an effort to integrate very diverse theoretical traditions. Currently, I am trying to provide a more detailed analysis of accounting. Ethnomethodology has become a rather established set of research traditions, but unfortunately, many of these have become somewhat isolated from more general analyses of interaction. Yet, the process of speech and its organization in a setting are crucial to understanding how frames and claims are constructed or changed. And so, one goal of my research project is to interpret conceptually the accumulating empirical literature from "conversational analysis" into the theory outlined in Figure 3. This effort will involve a further armchair elaboration and integration of the general theory of microdynamics.

Structuring Dynamics

Mead's analysis of "society" was the weakest part of his sociology, and so I began with only the general idea that interaction is structured across time. But Mead provided no details, except the notion that role taking was the underlying interactive mechanism for sustaining cooperation. Thus, I had to pull together others' ideas on microstructure and integrate them in a way that allowed me to specify in more detail how interaction produces and reproduces structure. Such an effort began with the recognition, derived from Mead and others discussed above, that structuring depends upon the use of self-references, deliberative capacities, and stocks of knowledge in role making/taking, frame making/taking, staging, ritualizing, accounting, and claiming, but if an interaction is to be structured, these interacting processes must be used in certain ways. That is, what must be done in the course of interaction to structure it in time and space? My answer to this question was this: signaling and interpreting must be used to (1) regionalize, (2) categorize, (3) normatize, (4) stabilize (resource transfers), and (5) routinize the interaction. These structuring processes are modeled in Figure 4.

Regionalization is an idea borrowed from Giddens's (1984) adaptation of Goffman (1959) and is the process of organizing an interaction in space. That is, for an interaction to persist over time, or to be picked up at a subsequent point in time, it is essential that the parties agree on the meaning of space, props, partitions, regions, juxtapositions, and movement in physical space. Typically, regionalization is imposed by macrostructural conditions, but it is still necessary for actors to develop consensus over the features of space and what that means for how they are to relate to one another. Such meanings are stored in people's stocks of knowledge, and they are adjusted to a particular situation as a result of the staging activities of individuals as they use self-references and deliberative capacities to role-make and role-take.

Categorization is, in Schutz's (1967) terms, the process of typifying others and situations as belonging to a certain class, and then responding in accordance with this typification. Following Collins's (1975) adaptation of an earlier set of distinctions by Goffman (1967), one axis of typification is in terms of the ratio of ceremonial, social, and work practical content to be exhibited in a situation. The other axis of typification is the degree of intimacy to be displayed toward others in situations—ranging from efforts at treating others as a mere type of person (e.g., sales clerk, car salesman, etc.) to an intersubjective intimate. These two axes represent a kind of cognitive cross tabulation: How much intimacy should be displayed and what is the ratio of ceremonial, social, and work practical

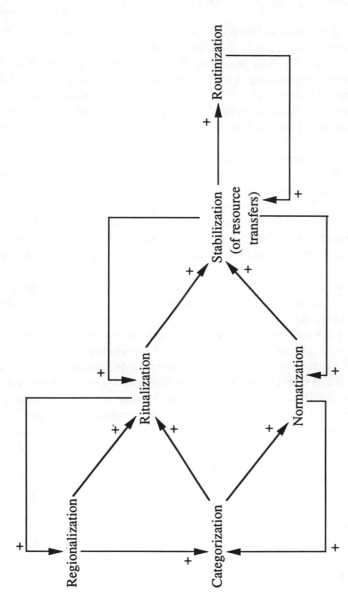

Fig. 4. Structuring dynamics.

content? For a situation to become structured, individuals must agree on this cross tabulation, or, as is illustrated in Table 1, they must find the appropriate "box" for their situation. Such categorization is facilitated by framing and accounting practices, which delimit the range of possible categories, and by regionalization, which imposes physical parameters on how categorization can proceed. But the central point is that without categorization, it is difficult for an interaction to become structured over time.

As Figure 4 delineates, regionalization and categorization dictate the kinds of rituals that will become typical of an interaction over time. For an interaction to be structured, there must be consensus over, and repetition of, certain types of opening, closing, forming, repairing, and, if necessary, totemizing rituals. That is, following Goffman (1967), I argue that a structured interaction must exhibit a high level of *ritualization* in that certain gestural sequences are habitually used to open, close, form, and repair breaches.

Categorization, coupled with claiming activity, is involved in the *normatization* of a situation. The concept of norms has had a controversial history in theorizing, primarily as a result of its association with functionalism (e.g., Parsons 1951), but it is nonetheless a crucial dynamic in structuring an interaction. How, then, can we revitalize the concept of norms in ways that do not overemphasize their dictatorial power over human action and interaction? My answer borrows the imagery or metaphor of structuralist analysis in linguistics: norms are pieces of stored information about (1) rights and duties, (2) interpretative schemata, and (3) organizational principles (for stringing together bits of information). In turn, each of these basic stores of normative information involves additional processes, as is diagrammed in Figure 5. The central point is to avoid viewing norms as static appendages to structural positions; and instead, norms should be seen as constructed assemblages and as potential reassemblages of information along the dimensions outlined in Figure 5. Yet, for a situation to become structured, some degree of consensus over, and stability among, the stores of normative information must exist. I term this effort to achieve consensus and stability *normatization* in order to emphasize that it is a dynamic process of selecting and assembling various types of categorical rights, duties, and interpretative schemata in terms of rules of normative grammar, indexicality, and adjudication. Once such assemblages exist, they can provide a stable set of expectations for how individuals are supposed to behave in a situation.

All interaction involves the exchange of resources—whether material or symbolic. If the interaction is to become structured, the *stabilization of resource transfers* among individuals must occur. This stabilization re-

TABLE 1

The Dynamics of Categorization

Levels of intimacy in dealing with others	Types of situations		
	Work/practical	Ceremonial	Social
Categories	Others as functionaries whose behaviors are relevant to achieving a specific task or goal and who, for the purposes at hand, can be treated as strangers	Others as representatives of a larger collective enterprise toward whom highly stylized responses are owed as a means of expressing their joint activity	Others as strangers toward whom superficially informal, polite, and responsive gestures are owed
Persons	Others as functionaries whose behaviors are relevant to achieving a specific task or goal but who, at the same time, must be treated as unique individuals in their own right	Others as fellow participants of a larger collective enterprise toward whom stylized responses are owed as a means of expressing their joint activity and recognition of each other as individuals in their own right	Others as familiar individuals toward whom informal, polite, and responsive gestures are owed
Intimates	Others as close friends whose behaviors are relevant to achieving a specific task or goal and toward whom emotional responsiveness is owed	Others as close friends who are fellow participants in a collective enterprise and toward whom a combination of stylized and personalized responses is owed as a means of expressing their joint activity and sense of mutual understanding	Others as close friends toward whom informal and emotionally responsive gestures are owed

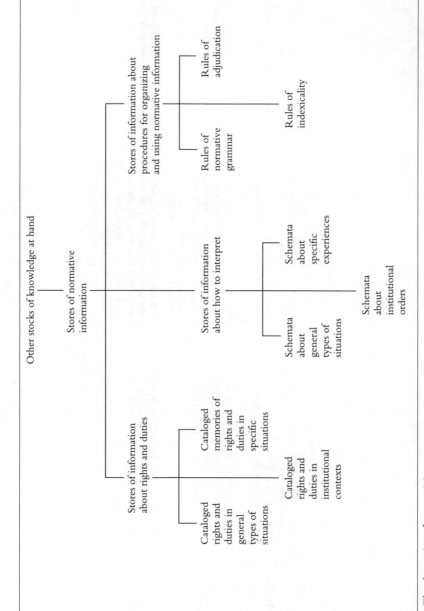

Fig. 5. The dynamics of normatizing.

volves around achieving some degree of consensus over the nature of the resources to be exchanged, the legitimate shares of resources among individuals, and the rates of resource exchange. This stabilization is greatly facilitated, as indicated in Figure 4, by normatization and ritualization. In the large exchange-theoretic tradition, normatization involves creating expectations about what is "fair," "just," and "equitable" in situations; and borrowing from Goffman (1967) and some exchange theorists (e.g., Blau 1964; Collins 1975; Turner and Collins 1989), I view ritualization as smoothing over the inevitable tensions associated with creating and sustaining a given ratio and rate of exchange, especially under conditions of inequality.

Stabilization of resource transfers through normatization and ritualization facilitates the final structuring process, *routinization*, which is an idea I have borrowed in altered form from Giddens (1984). When individuals interact in similar ways, exchanging the same resources, at the same time and place, structuring is greatly facilitated. Moreover, as the feedback arrows in Figure 4 indicate, routinization will reinforce the use of similar rituals and resources for exchange, creating two self-reinforcing cycles that further routinization.

Currently, I am trying to extend the conceptualization of the relationship between normatization, on the one hand, and ritualization, categorization, and stabilization, on the other. The model of normatizing may be too complex, although I am convinced that the emergence of norms is a process of assembling bits of information in terms of implicit generative rules stored in individuals' stocks of knowledge. In particular, in light of the extensive literature on the topic, it should be possible to explore the emergence of justice components of norms and to link them to the process of stabilization of resource transfers and to the processes of categorization and ritualization. That is, by adapting the large literature on justice to a view of norms as an assembled corpus, I should find it possible to see if norms are indeed constructed in this way and to determine how categorization and ritualization influence, and are influenced by, these normatizing processes revolving around assembled notions of "justice" and "fair exchange."

The Overall Composite Model

At various places (Turner 1989a, 1989b), I have sought to combine these analytical models on motivating, interacting, and structuring dynamics into a composite model. Combining the models in this way achieves further theoretical integration of diverse theories. In Figure 6, this overall composite model is presented. The major difference between

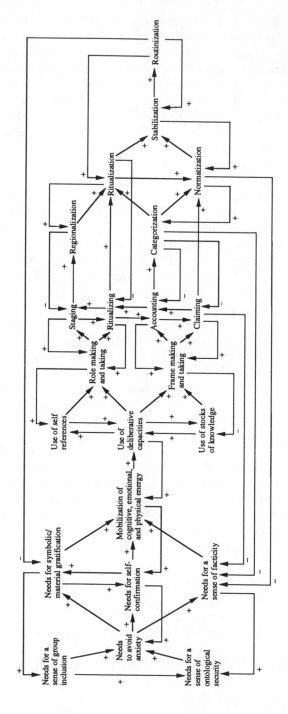

Fig. 6. A composite model of microdynamics.

this model and its predecessors is the longer feedback loops, or reverse causal chains (Stinchcombe 1968), connecting structuring and interacting processes to particular motivating need-states. The reason that these feedback arrows are crucial is that they arrest the potentially ever-escalating cycles of direct and indirect positive connections among the variables in the model. For example, if one were to simulate the model without these long negative causal loops, the values of the variables would continue to escalate. What the model argues is that when structuring occurs, it reduces certain key need-states, which, in turn, will dampen other need-states. And as these motivating need-states and the emotions they arouse decrease in salience, interacting processes will be less animated and visible. Thus, it is structuring that reduces both the mobilization of energy and signaling/interpreting. As the long negative reverse causal arrows indicate, stabilization of resource transfers in particular is crucial for reducing needs for those symbols and objects that signal group inclusion and self-confirmation, whereas normatization and categorization are the crucial structuring processes that dampen needs for facticity and, indirectly, needs for ontological security. Framing is also crucial in decreasing needs for facticity. Let me briefly examine each of these feedback processes separately.

If common frames cannot be imposed on an interaction, then people's sense of a common external and subjective world is disrupted. What I am arguing, then, is that the effects on facticity of using ethnomethods to construct accounts and employing claims to establish means-ends, normative appropriateness, and sincerity are mediated by framing; and to the extent that accounting and claiming do not create an experiential border or "rim" for interaction, facticity is disrupted.

Turning to the long reverse causal loops in Figure 6 from categorizing and normatizing to facticity, I argue that a sense of a common world among interactants depends on the ability to reach an implicit consensus on the appropriate box in Table 1 with respect to the personal intimacy displayed toward others and to the ratio of ceremonial, social, work practical content appropriate to a situation. Thus, as Schutz (1967) implied, a sense of intersubjectivity and, I would add, externality in the world is dependent upon the degree of success in categorization for the course of the interaction. While ethnomethodology has been hostile to the "normative view" of social order (e.g., Wilson 1970) the process of normatizing as I have conceptualized it is perhaps more congenial to ethnomethodological concerns about facticity. Without the ability to construct an assemblage of rights and duties and a common interpretative scheme, individuals will not have a sense of facticity; and this assemblage does not rely solely on ethnomethods, but as the model in Figure 6 indicates, it is the result of successful claiming, categorization, and ritualization as these influence normatization. In emphasizing these long reverse causal loops from structuring processes to needs for facticity, I am also asserting that deep-seated needs for ontological security are mediated by facticity. That is, if the structuring of an interaction, especially with respect to categorization and normatization, cannot create a sense of facticity, then needs for ontological security will not be met, setting into motion an escalation of anxiety (or, as I indicated earlier, a more specific emotion) that, in turn, cycles back to escalate needs for facticity and, potentially, needs for self-confirmation. Such escalated needs will mobilize individuals to signal and interpret in ways that can potentially restructure an interaction (via the various causal paths through interacting and structuring processes). The implication of this argument is that the structuring of an interaction is highly dependent upon the extent to which it directly meets needs for facticity (and indirectly other needs, such as ontological security and self-confirmation). But conversely, when structuring does occur, it is likely to reverse these cyclical processes and decrease needs for facticity and the signaling/interpreting processes that this need-state activates.

Turning to the long causal loop from stabilization of resource transfers to needs for symbolic/material gratification, I find that the critical point is that resource transfers must provide symbolic and material resources that confirm two other need-states, group inclusion and self-confirmation (and in this way, anxiety is reduced). That is, individuals will be particularly attuned to symbolic and material resources that mark group inclusion and that confirm self-references; and to the extent that resource transfers do not enable individuals to acquire symbols and objects marking group inclusion and self-confirmation, escalating cycles of deprivation are created and are likely to mobilize individuals to readjust resource transfers or to withdraw from the interaction. Conversely, when stabilization of resource transfers occurs, it will decrease the salience of these needs for the symbols and material objects confirming self and marking group inclusion. Thus, the variable of symbolic/material gratification is, like facticity, a mediating motive state between interacting and structuring processes as they stabilize resource transfers (or fail to do so), on the one hand, and needs for self-confirmation and group inclusion, on the other. And thus, to the degree that interacting processes—particularly role making/taking, staging, and ritualizing—cannot produce stable resource transfers via their direct effects on regionalization and ritualization, individuals will be motivated to restructure (or abandon) the interaction.

Other, less-extended feedback chains in Figure 6 should also be mentioned. For example, the series of feedback loops that work their way back to stocks of knowledge is also important. The argument here is that the feedback effects among routinization, stabilization, normatization, claiming, and framing all operate to confirm or add to existing stocks of knowledge. And if such confirmation does not occur, or new stocks of knowledge cannot be easily integrated into the old, then interaction will stall and pass through successive waves of mobilizing energy to reframe, reclaim, reaccount, renormatize, restabilize, and reroutinize until new stocks of knowledge are accepted or old stocks are confirmed. But if routinization, stabilization, normatization, and categorization do occur, then these operate to reduce claiming, accounting, framing, and stocking activity (as indicated by the negative sign on the causal loop from categorization to claiming). Another series of shorter feedback loops moves across the top of Figure 6 from routinization through stabilization, ritualization, regionalization, staging, role making/taking, and self-referencing. At any point on these shorter feedback paths, a breakdown will operate to escalate these need–states. Hence, if self-references in a situation cannot be generated, if role making/taking is difficult, if staging is problematic, if regionalization is unsuccessful, and so on for the rest of the variables at the top of Figure 6, there will be escalating feedback effects via self-references. In turn, motivational energies and emotions will be mobilized via the feedback loops emanating from use of deliberative capacities. The central place of self-references in the model is significant, because until individuals create a set of images of themselves in a situation as certain types of individuals, or if these references cannot be confirmed and are, therefore, in disarray, interaction and structuring will cycle around the various direct, indirect, and feedback chains in which self and self-references are implicated.

Developing Propositions from Models

I could continue to trace causal paths in the composite model, but at some point this exercise becomes not only tedious but overly complicated. It is at this point that propositions highlighting certain portions of the model become useful. However, each direct, indirect, and feedback or reverse causal path could be seen as a proposition that could be tested, and as a result, the number of propositions generated by faithfully following every path in the model soon produces an unmanageable number of propositions. Hence, in the development of propositional statements from the model, additional theorizing is necessary and revolves around *selecting* those causal paths for inclusion in a proposition that *seem to be particularly important for understanding microdynamic processes.* Again, I have done this in several places (Turner 1988, 1989a, 1989b), and so the propositional statements here represent a reformulated and truncated version of the basic "laws" of microdynamic processes.

One goal of my microdynamic theory is to reintroduce motivation into sociological theory. Actually, almost all theories of interaction and social structuring have a vision of motivation, but it is often kept implicit. I think that this is a mistake because interaction is voluntarily initiated and sustained only to the extent that it meets basic need-states. And even when macrostructural constraints force people to interact, the nature and form of their interpersonal contacts will be shaped by need-states. Thus, we cannot avoid the topic of motivation, and the question now becomes one of theorizing about its impact on human interaction. As the model in Figure 2 suggests, the basic law of motivation in human interaction is this:

> *Proposition 1.* The level of mobilization of cognitive, emotional, and physical energy during the course of interaction among individuals is a multiplicative function of needs of individuals for group inclusion, symbolic/material gratification, self-confirmation, ontological security, facticity, and anxiety reduction.

We can then use the direct, indirect, and feedback loops in the model to suggest several additional propositions on particular configurations of motivational energy:

> *Proposition 1a.* The level of needs for facticity is an inverse function of the success among interactants in framing, categorizing, and normatizing the interaction, and at the same time it is a positive curvilineal function of needs for ontological security as these escalate diffuse anxiety.

> *Proposition 1b.* The level of needs for symbolic/material gratification is an inverse function of the degree of resource stabilization among interactants and a positive function of needs for self-confirmation and group inclusion as these escalate diffuse anxiety and needs for self-confirmation.

> *Proposition 1c.* The level of needs for self-confirmation is a multiplicative function of needs for symbolic/material gratification as well as needs for group inclusion and ontological security as these escalate anxiety.

> *Proposition 1d.* The level of needs for group inclusion is a positive function of resource stabilization around symbols and material objects denoting group membership.

Proposition 1e. The level of needs for ontological security is an additive function of needs for facticity and group inclusion.

Proposition 1f. The level of diffuse anxiety is an additive function of needs for ontological security, group inclusion, and self-confirmation.

These propositions offer hypotheses about what motivates individuals in various ways and directions. The model in Figure 6 further suggests that the amount of signaling and interpreting will be related to the level of emotional energy, leading to this basic law:

Proposition 2. The degree to which individuals actively use their deliberative capacities, invoke self-references, and search their stocks of knowledge in an interaction is a positive curvilineal function of their mobilization of motivational energy.

This is a curvilineal relationship, because at some point individuals withdraw from interactions that consistently frustrate their need-states (and create depressive emotions or defenses to the more active emotions of fear and anger); or if they cannot withdraw because of macrostructural constraints, they will sluggishly participate and not actively think about, work at, or invest images of themselves in the interaction (Collins 1975). The model also suggests some specific propositions:

Proposition 2a. The level of activation of deliberative capacities around self-references, and the amount of emotion and physical energy devoted to such activation, is a positive function of needs for self-confirmation.

Proposition 2b. The level of activation of deliberative capacities around searches of stocks of knowledge, and the amount of emotional and physical energy devoted to such activation, is a positive function of needs for facticity.

In turn, the specific signaling and interpreting activities are related to whether self-referencing or searching stocks of knowledge is dominant. This line of argument for framing practices can be expressed as follows:

Proposition 3. The level of frame making and frame taking in an interaction is an additive function of the multiplicative relation between deliberative capacities and searches of stocks of knowledge, the multiplicative relation between deliberative capacities and role-taking/making activity, and the multiplicative relation between claiming and accounting activities.

In turn, we can construct a series of subpropositions from the model in Figure 6 that summarizes those forces influencing the values of variables in Proposition 3 above. Hence, in addition to Propositions 2a and 2b on deliberative practices, the following propositions can be stated.

Proposition 3a. The level of accounting activity in an interaction is a positive function of the multiplicative relation between claiming and framing and the level of ritualizing activity, and is an inverse function of the degree of categorization.

Proposition 3b. The level of claiming activity in an interaction is a positive function of the multiplicative relation between accounting and framing, and is an inverse function of normatization.

Turning now to role-taking/making processes, where self-referencing is the dominant process, I state the following propositions as suggested by Figure 6:

Proposition 4. The level of role making and role taking in an interaction is an additive function of the multiplicative relation between deliberative capacities and self-references, the multiplicative relation between deliberative capacities and framing activity, and the multiplicative relation between staging and ritualizing activity.

Proposition 4a. The level of staging activity in an interaction is an additive function of the multiplicative relation between ritualizing and role taking/making, and is an inverse function of the degree of regionalization.

Proposition 4b. The level of ritualizing activity in an interaction is an additive function of the multiplicative relation between staging and role taking/making and the level of accounting activity.

We can now turn to structuring processes and begin with a general law of microstructuring:

Proposition 5. The degree of continuity of an interaction over time and its level of organization in space are a multiplicative function of the degree of regionalization, ritualization, stabilization, categorization, normatization, and routinization.

In turn, various subpropositions on those forces influencing each of the variables in Proposition 5 can be offered, and in this way the proposition will be less tautological.

Proposition 5a. The degree of regionalization of an interaction is an additive function of the degree of success in staging and the degree of ritualization.

Proposition 5b. The degree of ritualization of an interaction is an additive function of the multiplicative relation between regionalization and categorization, and the multiplicative relation between stabilization of resource transfers and routinization.

Proposition 5c. The degree of stabilization of resource transfers in an interaction is an additive function of the multiplicative relation between normatization and ritualization and the multiplicative relation between ritualization and routinization.

Proposition 5d. The degree of normatization in an interaction is an additive function of the degree of success in establishing validity claims, the degree of stabilization of resource transfers, and the degree of categorization.

These five propositions, and their constituent subpropositions, summarize what I feel are the basic laws of microdynamics. They denote the crucial causal paths in the composite model and, in so doing, explain microdynamic processes. Of course, the values for the variables in these processes are not entirely endogenous to the composite model presented in Figure 6. Macrostructural conditions often determine these values, independent of the causal effects among the endogenous variables in the model. Yet, with the model and the predictions implied by these five propositions, it would be possible to understand the direction of interaction, once macrostructural forces have loaded the variables in various ways. At least this is the presumption and rationale behind the theoretical research strategy advocated here.

Conclusion

The theoretical research program outlined here is decidedly an armchair theorist's orgy. Those who prefer precise and narrow theories about a specific process will be suspicious of this kind of grand theorizing. Such suspicions can stem from several sources: (1) the lack of any suggestions about how to test the theory, (2) the failure to introduce data sets assessing the plausibility of the propositions, and (3) the failure, in fact, to offer the reader anything more than my views about how the microdynamic universe operates. I confess to all of these "sins," but I make no apologies. This is a "pure theory" project, and it assumes a division of labor between theorists and researchers—a division that is not always necessary but is at times useful. Far too much emphasis in sociology has been placed upon making theorists researchers and pretending to make researchers theorists. If what I have said seems misguided, then it will become yet another dead theory in sociology's graveyard. If, on the other hand, at least portions of the project are interesting, I invite others to assess the plausibility of these portions.

My theoretical strategy begins with the assumption that it is reasonable to develop, at least initially, separate micro and macro theories. Too much agonizing over the micro-macro gap has consumed sociological theorizing during the past decade. I have reported on my micro theory project in this chapter, primarily because it is further along than the macro project (Turner 1992). For both the micro and macro project, the theoretical strategy is the same: (1) begin with a sensitizing conceptual scheme that roughly denotes the domain of inquiry, (2) develop more precise analytical models for the properties denoted in the sensitizing scheme or, alternatively, articulate some abstract propositions specifying relations among the forces that explain these properties, and (3) move back and forth between the model and the propositions. In a very real sense, this chapter has performed strategy 3, because I have reworked both the model and the propositions in these pages. A "pure theory" project can continue along these lines, and several future avenues of further conceptual work have been suggested. Of course, empirical assessment is needed, and, perhaps, this missing ingredient can be added by others.

The theory presented here is, in a sense, an effort to consolidate what I see as the essential ingredients of numerous theoretical programs. These programs are not always well developed, like most of those reported in this volume, but they represent theoretical traditions with varying lines of research flowing from them. These programs—ethnomethodology, exchange theory, interaction ritual theory, psychoanalytic theory, structuration theory, symbolic interactionisms, dramaturgical theory, role theory, and phenomenology—do not constitute clear linear conceptual traditions which have become elaborated by careful research (with the exceptions, perhaps, of exchange theory and ethnomethodology), nor do they represent unambiguous patterns of internal competition and reconciliation. Rather, they are somewhat general, sensitizing perspectives which reveal many diverse practitioners and positions, most of which cannot be seen as either competing strands or as clear pieces of coherent whole. For me, they each represent key insights into an important process; and the goal of my approach is to select these key insights and integrate them into a reasonably coherent whole. However, it is very likely that those from whom I borrow will reject the selective requisition of ideas from *their* tradition, with the result that few would want to test the ideas presented in the models and propositions outlined above. For while practitioners working within one of these traditions may not constitute a coherent program, they are often highly resentful of those, such as I, who invade their conceptual turf.

Yet, having said this, I think that it is still critical that the proliferation of micro theoretical perspectives be pulled together periodically. This is what the "pure theory" research program outlined in this chapter has sought to do, even if the effort is resented by some. For we must do more than work within established theoretical programs; we must also try to pull what are very different programs together, "kicking and screaming" if need be. Only in this way can sociology as a whole cumulate knowledge.

PART III

Theoretical Research Programs:
Conflict and Bargaining

The Game of Conflict Interactions: A Research Program

Bruce Bueno de Mesquita

At least since Thucydides contemplated the causes of the Peloponnesian War, students of international relations have been interested in constructing models of conflict. Often these models are motivated by a desire to distill and understand a particular event, such as World War I or the Cuban missile crisis. Sometimes the informal modeling process concentrates on providing insights into a few important but rare events, such as hegemonic or power transition wars. Sometimes, as in Jervis's (1976) research on the relationship between misperception and conflict behavior, or North's event-interaction studies of crises, the goal is the identification of lawlike generalizations. Such models often are ambiguous and implicit in the researcher's analysis, and only occasionally are they explicit and formalized.*

Since the end of World War II, there has been a proliferation of theorizing about international relations. Morgenthau (1973) suggested a model of the balance of power at roughly the same time that Brodie (1946) introduced a general model of deterrence. As a counterpoint to their perspectives, Organski (1958) developed the theory of the power transition as a way of explaining cataclysmic great power wars while Modelski (1987) suggested a model of long cycles. While these *Realpolitik* theories dominated discourse, Deutsch (1953, 1963) and Haas (1957, 1976), and later Keohane and Nye (1977), promulgated models of cooperation and integration as an alternative viewpoint. And, of course, many other prominent theorists proposed equally interesting and provocative models of conflict processes. These efforts varied greatly in their attentiveness to logical rigor and internal consistency, just as they varied

*I would like to thank Joseph Berger, James Morrow, and Brian Pollins for helpful comments on an earlier version of this essay.

greatly in the motivation to provide explanations of rather specific events or of broad ranges of international interactions.

The competing perspectives among international relations scholars generally have been stimulated by a desire to resolve the fundamental issues in international affairs. These include concerns with whether foreign policies are motivated by the quest for power and security or by the search for harmonious and cooperative interactions, as well as whether national motivations matter at all. A central debate is focused on the extent to which international interactions are best understood from a structuralist perspective that allows only minimal latitude for variation in choices at the national level or from a more decentralized perspective that envisions structural constraints as the aggregated product of numerous individual, national actions.

My principal purpose here is to explain the research program in which I am engaged. I trace its evolution and its implications, beginning with a focus on system-wide characteristics that might account for war, and then turn to an evaluation of individual choices under uncertainty and risk. In that discussion, I suggest ways in which this research program has addressed questions of ordinary domestic policy choices and individual competition well beyond the domain of international disputes and war. I also discuss the current locus of the research on a limited information, game-theoretic model of interactive decision-making, and its earlier manifestations in decision theory. I note that the latest efforts incorporate the results from the earlier, decision theoretic analyses while adding substantially to the range of phenomena accounted for by the research program.

Impetus to the Research Program

Throughout most of the postwar period, international relations scholars have focused on structural parameters of the international system as determinants of war and lesser conflicts. The distribution of power, for instance, is widely regarded as central to understanding whether the international community faces a high or a low risk of war. Balance of power theorists generally contend that a rough equality in the distribution of military and industrial resources across nations enhances the prospects of peace. Yet those who subscribe to the hegemonic stability or power transition perspective maintain that cataclysmic wars are most likely exactly when such resources are about equally divided among the "great powers." The differences in the arguments supporting these apparently contradictory claims reside in alternative assumptions about how decision makers respond to uncertainty and to risks.

Differences in assumptions about how leaders react to risky or uncertain situations are at the core of almost all disagreements among theorists who focus on system-level attributes in accounting for war. The view, for instance, that the chances of victory are too small to warrant waging war when power is roughly equally divided among rivals is predicated on the unstated assumption that national leaders tend to be risk averse. Hegemonic stability theorists, on the other hand, claim that the joint probability that force will be used by two rivals is maximized when their power is roughly equal. They base their argument on the notion that only when the risk is about the same for both sides can the expected benefits for each side be large enough to outweigh the anticipated costs. This argument depends on the unstated belief that decision makers are risk neutral or risk acceptant in the face of uncertainty.*

The importance of assumptions about risk and uncertainty in international affairs is not limited to debates over the distribution of power. All researchers who focus on the polarization of interests in the international system maintain that multipolar structures contain greater uncertainty than do bipolar structures. But such scholars disagree markedly on how the uncertainty of multipolar structures influences behavior. Those, like Waltz (1964, 1979), who claim that bipolar systems tend to induce stability rely on the argument that decision makers are risk acceptant in the face of uncertainty. Those, like Deutsch and Singer (1964), who claim that multipolar systems tend to be more peaceful than bipolar systems, rely on the assumption that decision makers are cautious or risk averse in the face of uncertainty.

The views of these competing schools of thought about systemic characteristics and the likelihood of war informed my earliest research on conflict. The realization that these perspectives relied upon assumptions of *uniform* behavioral reactions to risks and to uncertainty provided the foundation for the development of a research program that deviates markedly from the perspective of classical, systemic theories.

While theories focused on system-wide, structural characteristics contain the concepts generally considered to be at the core of international relations, these theories are, at root, not really about the structure of the international system at all. Instead, these are theories in which the risks and uncertainties faced by national leaders are shaped by the structure of the international environment. For those who believe that structure *determines* relations between states, variations in national characteristics, in leadership, in institutional arrangements, and in domestic politics in general are all irrelevant. None of these features are believed to be capable of influencing the "high" politics involved in the promotion of national se-

---

*These competing claims also depend upon the unstated assumption that the *objective* probability of success is known, so that estimates of such a probability are not subjective.

curity and the quest for power. Indeed, from this *realist* perspective, only power and security are considered viable national objectives. According to this point of view, all international interactions are governed by the overarching proposition that national leaders respond uniformly to foreign policy challenges.

An alternative viewpoint suggests that the structure of the international system acts as a constraint on choices, rather than as a determinant of behavior. In a world in which decision makers vary markedly in their reaction to risks and uncertainty, system-wide characteristics would not be significantly correlated with such outcomes as the occurrence of peace or war.

The assumption of uniformity or near uniformity in risk-orientations seems to me to be too restrictive analytically, inefficient in generating propositions, and empirically unrealistic. Indeed, the empirical literature that evaluates these competing systemic theories finds little support for any of them (Singer, Bremer, and Stuckey 1972; Bueno de Mesquita 1978; Organski and Kugler 1980; Moul 1988; Bueno de Mesquita and Lalman 1988b; Ostrom and Job 1986; James and Oneal 1991). The restrictiveness of their assumptions and their lack of empirical support seem to provide a firm impetus for examining international affairs through a somewhat different lens.

The research program described here takes as its point of departure the belief that individual decision-makers vary in their subjective estimations of costs and benefits even when faced with the same objective information. Thus, the way in which system-wide characteristics act as potential constraints on decision-makers may vary from person to person in theoretically identifiable ways. Consequently, the core concepts in my research program relate to individual decision-maker calculations of costs and benefits in a constrained environment, and not to system-wide structural features of international relations. By drawing attention to variations in individual responses to constrained choices, my colleagues and I try to clarify some of the confusing results of systemic theories. I have reviewed several of the difficulties with such systemic approaches elsewhere and so shall not focus on them here (Bueno de Mesquita 1980, 1985a, 1985b). Instead, here I draw attention to the evolution of the research program in which I am engaged, with the hope of delineating a theoretically sound and empirically useful account of decisions to engage in violent or nonviolent behavior.

A Brief Overview of the Research Program

The research program in which my colleagues and I are engaged focuses on foreign policy choices as the product of rational, strategic calculations by national leaders. The research program's evolution can be divided roughly into four phases. These phases represent developments over an eleven-year span ranging from a decision-theoretic model applied to a single foreign policy choice—to join an ongoing war or not—to the present game-theoretic specification of the necessary and sufficient conditions for a wide variety of policy choices involving the prospects for cooperation or conflict. The research in its current guise is as concerned with analyzing domestic political considerations as it is with accounting for war.

The first phase—hereafter referred to as T_1—reflects the initial efforts to develop a decision-theoretic model of conflict choices. T_1 was dominated by two publications: "Choosing Sides in Wars," which I co-authored with Michael Altfeld (1979), and *The War Trap*, published in 1981. In T_1 emphasis was placed on the derivation and empirical assessment of broad propositions about the selection of adversaries; the role of allies in militating or mitigating disputes; the effectiveness of threats as deterrents to war; and the evaluation of conventional variables having to do with cultural or historical differences across states as potential means of encouraging or discouraging violent conflict.

The second phase— T_2—was dominated by the publication of "*The War Trap* Revisited" (1985b) and *Forecasting Political Events* (with David Newman and Alvin Rabushka, 1985). In T_2 I attempted to improve the way in which the value of the status quo was specified; to introduce an endogenously derived, theoretically motivated measure of risk-taking propensities; to develop new propositions regarding the role of misperception in encouraging or discouraging conflict escalation; and to expand the model's domain to include the analysis of policy choices in non-international settings and in real time. Most of the developments in T_2 depended upon the introduction of a theoretically grounded method for estimating the willingness of decision makers to take risks and the incorporation of that measure into the estimation of the shape of individual utility functions. This measure, validated empirically (1985) and theoretically validated for most cases in a subsequent study by Morrow (1987), enriched the decision-theoretic model by permitting the derivation of propositions related to the risk of escalation and the perceptions of decision makers.

One year after the inception of the second phase, a further development advanced the research program sufficiently to warrant being called Phase 3. With the publication of "Reason and War," which I co-authored with David Lalman (1986), the model was advanced in several new directions. First, the estimation of the value attached to not challenging a rival's policies was enriched to include estimations of possible improvements or declines in the relations between states in the absence of direct pressure for such changes. Thus, the specification of the status quo branch of the decision problem now included a rational expectations component. Second, the model developed in "Choosing Sides in Wars" (at the inception of T_1) was combined with the risk-taking component from T_2 to permit the estimation of each actor's subjective probability of success, taking into account the expected behavior of each third party. Most important, in T_3 David Lalman and I expanded the model's international relations applications to include outcomes other than war or peace and to include theoretically derived, continuous probability estimates of the likelihood of each type of event. By T_3 the model had evolved from the specification of only the necessary conditions for war to a probabilistic estimation of the conditions governing the likelihood of war, capitulation, or the negotiated resolution of disputes. With the introduction of a continuous, rather than ordinal, framework for estimating the likelihood of various types of events it became possible to subsume within the model additional arguments and predictions concerning the balance of power, power preponderance, deterrence, misperception and uncertainty, arms races, and the like and to reconcile seemingly contradictory predictions from several of these competing theories.

Phase 4, which is most clearly represented in *War and Reason* (with David Lalman, 1992) and in a series of articles that preceded its publication, is a substantial departure from T_1–T_3. The first three phases represented enrichments of a decision-theoretic model that took strategic interaction into account indirectly through the introduction of a rational expectations component as looked at by one decision-maker at a time. In T_4, however, the modeling specifies strategic interaction in a game-theoretic framework. Whereas prior efforts focused on necessary conditions or on probabilistic predictions, Phase 4 specifies the necessary and sufficient conditions for two types of war, capitulation, and acquiescence, as well as for negotiations and the maintenance of the status quo under full information conditions and under a variety of limited information circumstances. The model—now called the international interaction game—also introduces domestic political considerations for the first time, and makes predictions about the evolution of norms of behavior that might induce cooperation. T_4 permits the integration and translation of a very broad array of seemingly competing theories into its framework. Thus, even the apparently fundamental distinction between so-called *realists* and so-called *idealists* or *liberals* in international relations—between those who believe international politics is governed by the search for power and security or by the promotion of values and shared, integrative goals—can be accommodated within the international interaction game. As with each previous phase, T_4 includes extensive empirical analysis and comparisons with previous stages of the model.

In developing the research program that is discussed more fully in the following pages, I have attempted to build in a cumulative way on previous efforts. Thus, virtually all deductions from T_1 can be deduced from T_2, as well as new propositions; virtually all results from T_2 can be derived in the formulation represented by T_3, as well as a new set of propositions; and virtually everything that is logically true in T_3 can be deduced from T_4, which also adds new propositions to the research enterprise. Each phase represents an effort to improve upon deficiencies of earlier phases, some of which were well known to my colleagues and me as we began our research and some of which were highlighted by our constructive critics (Zagare 1982; Wagner 1984; Moul 1987; Nicholson 1987; Hussein 1987).

Current Formulation: The International Interaction Game

No two interactions in international politics are likely to be exactly the same. Yet there are essential features in the development of any relationship between states. These features concern sequences of decisions that lead to friendly or hostile relations. To describe these essential features, the scaffolding from which foreign policies are built, I begin with the common assumption that each nation can be treated as a unitary actor. I distinguish between a strong unitary actor assumption and a weaker variant. In the strong version, a single decision-maker is assumed to be responsible for selecting foreign policy goals for his or her nation, as well as being responsible for selecting the tactics and strategies by which the goals are implemented. In the weaker version, the unitary actor is only responsible for selecting tactics and strategies while the domestic political process is assumed to foster the selection of goals. In the application of these unitary actor assumptions, then, I recognize that the metaphoric unitary actor is responsive to domestic political considerations as well as to calculations of support from its allies and support for its enemies from their allies (Altfeld and Bueno de Mesquita 1979; Siverson and King 1980; Iusi-Scarborough and Bueno de Mesquita 1988). I also recognize that this is a controversial assumption, both from the perspective of systemic theorists who discount the importance of individual states and from the perspective of those who investigate bureaucratic processes. I have defended the unitary actor assumption *when studying phenomena that threaten a state's sovereignty* elsewhere (Bueno de Mesquita 1981b; Bueno de Mesquita, Siverson, and Woller 1992). Here I merely note that heads of government bear direct costs for failed foreign policies that eventuate in unsuccessful wars and reap direct benefits from successful military campaigns (Bueno de Mesquita, Siverson, and Woller 1992). There can be little doubt that national leaders have strong incentives to act *as if* their welfare and the welfare of the state are the same when sovereignty is at risk.

Any international interaction is assumed to arise in a context that provides one or another state with an opportunity to take the initiative in shaping relations, an initiative which may govern the future development of events. Each state shapes its relationship with each other state through the selection of strategies. States may, for example, make demands or not make demands. Leaders may elect to acquiesce to a rival's demands or they may choose to try to negotiate over their differences. And, of course, leaders may choose to use force rather than capitulate to a rival's wishes.

Different combinations of strategies result in different political outcomes. If, for instance, two states exchange demands and each state uses force to try to accomplish its demanded goal, then a war ensues. If the interaction between two states involves no demands, then each has elected to live with the status quo. The selection of strategies is a function of the value states attach to alternative outcomes and the beliefs they hold regarding how their adversary will respond to their strategic decisions.

I assume that decision makers respond to circumstance by making the choice they believe maximizes their expected utility from that stage of the game onward. They cannot pre-commit themselves to a future course of action—in the largely anarchic system of international relations no binding authority exists to enforce agreements against the participants' own will—but they can act in anticipation of their opponent's choices. That is, I assume subgame perfection in which forward-looking decision-makers contemplate the consequences of their current strategic choices for an entire sequence of interactions (Selten 1975).

The state, which I call state A, that has the opportunity to initiate an interaction can choose to make a demand (D^A) or not make a demand ($-D^A$) of another state. The demand may be about anything. I am not concerned here with the specific content of prospective disputes so much as with the *process* by which interactions evolve.

Once A makes its move, state B has the opportunity to select a course of action by making a demand or not. Using superscripts to name the actor selecting a strategy, we can say that if the initial sequence is $-D^A$, $-D^B$, then the outcome is the maintenance of the status quo. If the sequence is D^A, $-D^B$, then B is said to acquiesce to A's demand. Should A forgo the opportunity to initiate a demand and allow B to initiate ($-D^A$, D^B), then A has the opportunity to acquiesce to B's demand

$(-D^A, D^B, -d^A \rightarrow$ Acquiescence to B's demand) or to make a counter-demand $(-D^A, D^B, d^A \rightarrow$ Crisis). Similarly, if the initial sequence of strategic choices were D^A, D^B, then by A's second move there is also a crisis. Failure by both parties to abide by the status quo and failure by either party to acquiesce to the other's demand results in a crisis (Lalman 1988; Powell 1987).

In a crisis, a state may choose to escalate the dispute further by using force or it can attempt to defuse the situation by offering to negotiate: abiding by the status quo ante is no longer an option (Lalman 1988). If there is an offer to negotiate, the rival can reciprocate by not using force or it can exploit the offer to bargain by attacking the rival itself. Anytime a state escalates a dispute by using force it can expect one of two responses by its adversary. The adversary can capitulate to the attacker's demands, thereby cutting its battlefield losses, or the adversary can retaliate, escalating the dispute further so that it becomes a war.

The extensive form of the international interaction game is depicted in Figure 1, with the crisis subgame labeled in the lower right. In the crisis subgame, A offers to negotiate by not initiating the use of force $(-F^A)$ or A escalates the dispute by using force to back up its demand (F^A). If A elects to escalate the dispute, then B must choose between capitulating to A's first strike $(F^A, -F^B)$ or striking back by using force itself (F^A, F^B). In the latter case, the strategy sequence D^A, D^B, F^A, F^B results in a war initiated by state A.

Should A elect to offer to negotiate $(-F^A)$ at the outset of the crisis, then B's choices can lead to negotiations $(-F^A, -F^B)$ or to escalation $(-F^A, F^B)$. If B selects the escalatory path, then A must make a final strategic determination: to capitulate to B's enforcement of its demand $(-F^A, F^B, -f^A)$ or to retaliate $(-F^A, F^B, f^A)$, resulting in a war initiated by B.

As is evident from Figure 1, international interactions can culminate in the following eight different generic outcomes:

Status Quo	Acquiescence by B to A's Demand (Acq$_B$)
Acquiescence by A to B's Demand (Acq$_A$)	Negotiate
Capitulation by A (Cap$_A$)	Capitulation by B (Cap$_B$)
War Initiated by A (War$_A$)	War Initiated by B (War$_B$)

The structure of the international interaction game establishes a simplified view of the foundations of all international relations, but it does not provide sufficient information to make positive statements about behavior. The game requires further elaboration in the form of assumptions

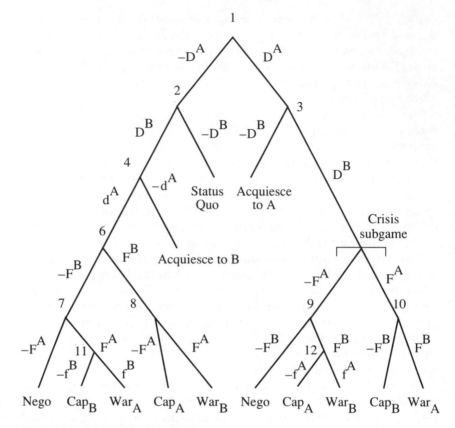

Fig. 1. International interaction game.

that establish the feasible range of preferences over the game's outcome events. The value national leaders associate with each of the game's outcomes, and therefore the set of admissible preferences over the outcomes, is determined in accordance with the following assumptions:

Assumption 1. The players choose the strategy with the greatest expected utility given that they are playing subgame perfect strategies.

Assumption 2. The ultimate change in welfare resulting from a war or from negotiations is not known with certainty. Hence, arriving at a war node or at negotiations yields an expected value, assessed according to the subjective probabilities of gaining welfare and the subjective probabilities of losing welfare. We restrict the probabilities in such lotteries: $0 < P < 1.0$.

Assumption 3. In contrast to Assumption 2, acquiescence and capitulation result in changes in welfare that are certain rather than probabilistic. The probability that the state that gives in loses is 1.0, as is the probability that the challenging state wins its demand.

Assumption 4. All nations prefer to resolve their differences through negotiations rather than through war.

Assumption 5. Measured from the status quo (SQ) are $U^i(\Delta_i)$, the expected *gain* in utility by successfully obtaining one's demands, and $U^i(\Delta_j)$, the expected *loss* in utility by acceding to the adversary's demands. All terms are positive: $0 < U^i(\Delta_j) < U^i(SQ) < U^i(\Delta_i)$.

Assumption 6. Each outcome has a set of potential benefits and/or costs appropriately associated with it. We make restrictions on the various costs such that α, τ, γ, $\varphi > 0$; and $\tau > \alpha$. Here α is the cost in lost life and property associated with fighting *away* from one's home territory; τ is the cost of lost life and property of fighting at home as the *target* of an attack; γ is the cost in life and property from a first strike to which the attacked party *gives in*; and φ is the domestic political cost (separate from life and property) associated with *using force*. Assume further that the costs involving lost life and/or property decrease for nation i as P^i increases and that domestic political costs for i increase as P^i increases.

Assumption 7a. What is demanded (D^A, D^B) is determined as an endogenous function of the international interaction game; or

Assumption 7b. What is demanded (D^A, D^B) is determined as an endogenous function of domestic political processes.

Assumption 1 stipulates that nations are led by rational, forward-looking, expected–utility–maximizing leaders.* Assumptions 2 and 3 are concerned with the probability of success given alternative mixes of strategies for A and B. If either decision-maker initiates a strategy of force, the adversary has the option to defend itself. A decision not to defend oneself in the face of a forceful challenge is assumed to be a decision to accept defeat (Assumption 3). This means that if the opponent does not respond with force, the challenger using force obtains with certainty whatever benefits were sought. For all events other than capitula-

---

*This need not imply that a single decision-maker forms foreign policy. Rather, Assumption 1 implies that whatever the internal political process by which policy preferences are revealed, national policy follows directly from the ordering emerging from that internal process.

tions (or acquiescence before force is used), the gains and losses are not determinate but are probabilistic. For real world decision-makers, the outcome of war is not known with certainty at the time they choose to use force. The risky prospects of conflict are represented by assuming that the likelihood of alternative outcomes is weighted in accordance with the relative capabilities of the adversaries, reflecting their gambling odds (Bueno de Mesquita 1981b, 1985a, 1985b; Morrow 1985, 1989; Bueno de Mesquita and Lalman 1986; C. Kim 1991; W. Kim 1989; Wu 1990).* Nations A and B select their strategies on the basis of estimated values for these events.

In the case of negotiation, the outcome is expected to be partially dependent on the relative capabilities of the antagonists (and their respective coalitions of supporters). Negotiations are considered as if they result in compromises that are somewhat akin to a weighted view of the common notion of "split the difference" (Rubenstein 1982). Assumption 4, in conjunction with Assumption 6, stipulates that the expected outcome from negotiations (Ω) is greater than the expected value of the outcome of war. Thus, $\Omega^i > P^i U^i(\Delta_i) + (1 - P^i) U^i(\Delta_j) - \varphi^i - \alpha^i$ for all $i, j \varepsilon$ set of nations.[†]

The game imputes a first-strike advantage by Assumption 6 ($\tau > \alpha$). A main advantage to the initiator is the enhanced ability to select the venue of the fighting. The costs to a nation of being engaged in combat on its own territory are greater than the costs incurred when combat takes place on someone else's territory. The rationale is that combat on someone else's territory involves greater control over losses; the number of combatants and the amount of military matériel committed to the fight are at the discretion of the nation's political leadership. In contrast, fighting on one's own territory usually involves lost civilian lives and non-military property in addition to military losses. These costs are not so easily controlled unless one capitulates.

---

*That is, I assume that the probability of a side emerging victorious from a war increases as the side's capabilities increase relative to the capabilities of the rival side. This stands in contrast to the more restrictive assumption, common in many game-theoretic models of conflict, that the side with greater resources wins with certainty (see, for instance, Niou, Ordeshook, and Rose 1989). I prefer to assume a probabilistic view of war outcomes for several reasons. Of course, ex post, one can always say that the winner must have had greater resources or power (Blainey 1973), but ex ante it is common for rivals to view their prospects in war as risky. Empirical assessments of war choices that are based on probabilistic models of war outcomes seem to provide a stronger fit with the historical record than do models that assume outcomes are not risky (Organski and Kugler 1980; Bueno de Mesquita 1981b; Bueno de Mesquita and Lalman 1986; Midlarsky 1988).

†That is, the value of negotiations exceeds war even under the lowest war-cost conditions.

TABLE 1

Expected Utilities Associated with Each Possible Outcome

Outcome	A's expected utility	B's expected utility
Status Quo	$U^A (SQ)$	$U^B (SQ)$
Acq_B	$U^A (\Delta_A)$	$U^B (\Delta_A)$
Acq_A	$U^A (\Delta_B)$	$U^B (\Delta_B)$
Negotiate	$P^A U^A (\Delta_A) + (1 - P^A) U^A (\Delta_B)$	$P^B U^B (\Delta_B) + (1 - P^B) U^B (\Delta_A)$
Cap_B	$U^A (\Delta_A) - \varphi^A P^A$	$U^B (\Delta_B) - \gamma^B P^B$
War_B	$P^A U^A (\Delta_A) + (1 - P^A) U^A (\Delta_B) - \varphi^A P^A - \tau^A (1 - \varphi^B P^B)$	$P^B U^B (\Delta_B) + (1 - P^B) U^B (\Delta_A) - \varphi^B P^B - \alpha^B (1 - P^B)$
Cap_A	$U^A(\Delta_B) - \gamma^A (1 - P^A)$	$U^B(\Delta_A) - \varphi^B P^B$
War_A	$P^A U^A (\Delta_A) + (1 - P^A) U^A (\Delta_B) - \varphi^A P^A - \alpha^A (1 - P^A)$	$P^B U^B (\Delta_B) + (1 - P^B) U^B (\Delta_A) - \varphi^B P^B - \tau^B (1 - P^B)$

Assumption 6 also recognizes that losses arise in relation to decisions to use force. These costs (φ) are primarily political in nature. They entail domestic political opposition to using force in order to achieve policy goals. Immanuel Kant specifically addressed this cost when he wrote:

If . . . the consent of the citizens is required in order to decide whether there should be war or not, nothing is more natural than that those who would have to decide to undergo all the deprivations of war will very much hesitate to start such an evil game. For the deprivations are many, such as fighting oneself, paying for the cost of war out of one's own possessions, and repairing the devastation which it costs, and to top all the evils there remains a burden of debts which embitters the peace and can never be paid off on account of approaching new wars. (Friedrich 1977: 438)

Assumption 7a represents the *Realpolitik* view that foreign policy choices are independent of domestic affairs (with the exception of the imposition of ex post costs for employing a failed policy that ultimately required the use of force). Assumption 7b adopts a different perspective by attributing the origin of foreign policy demands to the domestic political process of the country in question.

The strategies available to nations A and B are the means by which they can realize gains or losses. Except for strategic combinations that eventuate in some form of submission, gains and losses are probabilistic, so that decision makers must choose across lotteries. Table 1 gives the values associated with each event described at the terminal nodes of the international interaction game depicted in Figure 1.

The international interaction game associates a skeletal structure of sequential decisions with outcomes in the international environment. As will be evident later, the game is readily adapted to applications outside the international arena, including policy forecasting, domestic political conflict, and, perhaps, even interpersonal conflict. Here, however, I examine some of the theoretical implications that can be deduced from the international interaction game in the context of relations between nations.

International Interaction Game: Some Implications

Although the international interaction game is relatively simple, it provides for a rich variety of possible circumstances. The few fundamental assumptions accompanying the theory restrict the number of ways decision makers might order the game's outcomes from 8! (40,320) to 52. While a great many orderings are assumed away, still there are 52 × 52 (2,704) possible pairings of preferences for actors A and B. These orderings and the game's structure allow the deduction of numerous propositions and theorems, several of which seem counterintuitive. It also casts serious doubts on many previous categorizations of international interactions. Before I turn to specific theorems, let me pause briefly to discuss this latter point.

Categorization of Disputes

Most research on international conflict conceptualizes war and peace as mutually exclusive and exhaustive events (Singer, Bremer, and Stuckey 1972; Blainey 1973; Bueno de Mesquita 1978; Gilpin 1981). That the pairings of strategies in the international interaction game lead to mutually exclusive events is clear. It is also evident from the strategy paths that war and peace do not exhaust the set of possible outcomes. If peace is taken to mean the absence of violence, then four of the game's outcomes represent distinct conditions of peace:

1. Maintenance of the status quo;
2. Acquiescence by A to B's demands, in which case the status quo shifts in B's favor;
3. Acquiescence by B to A's demands, in which case the status quo shifts in A's favor; and
4. Negotiated settlement of a dispute, in which case the outcome could remain at the status quo or shift in either player's favor.

Peace, then, is a complex concept, involving quite discrete outcomes and alternative strategic paths. The same is true for the use of force. War is but one of three circumstances in which violence is utilized as a foreign policy tool. War occurs when both parties to a dispute elect to use force, whereas a capitulation arises when either A or B strikes the other, forcing a surrender without retaliation. These latter sorts of events are more common than wars, have long been known to exist, and yet were over-looked or inexplicable by previous research on international conflict. The structure proposed here (T_4) and earlier variants of it (T_1–T_3) not only identify distinct conditions underlying each of these events but have also proven relatively successful empirically in accounting for them (Bueno de Mesquita and Lalman 1986; Banks 1990).

In Bueno de Mesquita and Lalman (1986), for instance, we assume that the probability with which a decision maker would resort to force is a monotonically increasing function of that decision maker's net expected utility from challenging an adversary (T_3). Banks (1990) subsequently proved that this monotonicity condition *must* hold for any Bayesian asymmetric information game in which any rational actor faces a choice between using force and offering to negotiate a settlement of differences. With the monotonicity assumption, Lalman and I deduced specific probability functions in the expected utility polar coordinate space im-plied by the theory. A unique probability function is associated with each outcome of the crisis subgame. These functions were tested on European dyadic conflict data for the years 1816 to 1970 (Bueno de Mesquita and Lalman 1986, 1987). Each probability function proved to be quite signifi-cantly related to the outcome it was expected to predict and insignifi-cantly related to all other outcome events. What is more, each probability function was shown to improve significantly upon the ability to discrimi-nate across outcomes from earlier formulations of the model (1981b, 1985a, 1985b). The theory has provided a foundation for specifying the conditions related to a wider variety of outcome events than had previ-ously been possible, and has been shown to be consistent with the record of historical disputes. Indeed, the addition of the monotonicity condition allows us to explain why balance of power and power preponderance theorists can both marshal substantial evidence in support of their own claims and in apparent refutation of the hypotheses of the opposed theory (Bueno de Mesquita and Lalman 1989a).

Figure 2 shows that two points exist in which expectations about the consequences of challenging an adversary (and its coalition of supporters) are balanced. Since the probability of war, given monotonicity, is high when rivals A and B each *expect* large gains from a challenge (i.e., angle $\theta = 45°$), the probability of war is high at the point marked X in Figure 2. At the point marked Y, where expectations are low (angle $\theta = 225°$), the probability of war is low. Balance of power theorists fail to distinguish these two radically different conditions of balanced expecta-tions. Likewise, areas C and D represent situations of imbalanced expec-tations. In one such instance (area C), the probability of war is high. In the other (area D), the probability of war is low.

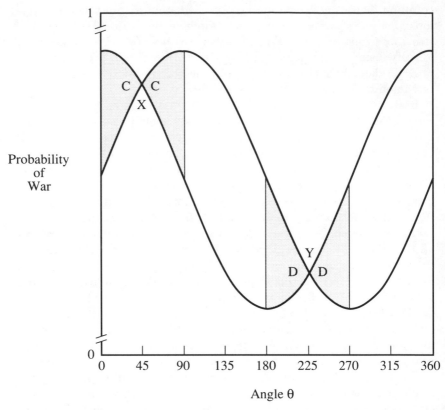

Fig. 2. Probability of war.

Points X and Y depict the crucial moment of the "power transition" in which one hegemon is surpassed by another (Organski 1958; Organski and Kugler 1980; Gilpin 1981; Organski and Kugler 1986; Kennedy 1987). At point X, B overtakes A, at least in terms of expectations. At point Y, A overtakes B. These two transitions are accompanied also by a high and a low probability of war. The empirical attention of those supporting a balance of power perspective seems focused on situations typified by point Y or area C. Power preponderance theorists seem to have their attention drawn to situations characterized by point X or area D. Preponderance theories do not isolate such circumstances as point Y or area C in which balanced expectations lead to peace. Balance of power theories overlook conditions under which balance implies war (point X) or imbalance implies peace (area D).

A critical aspect of Figure 2 is that it differentiates situations with high or low risks of war as a function of the rational expectations of gains by adversaries. The historical record should be, and is, consistent with this perspective. In fact, the vast majority of the crises in Europe since the Napoleonic Wars for which estimations of expected utilities place the dispute in the neighborhood of point X ended in war. None of the crises in the neighborhood of point Y resulted in war (Bueno de Mesquita 1985a, 1985b; Bueno de Mesquita and Lalman 1989a). The critical distinctions in Figure 2 are derived from our focus on rational-choice, expected-utility-maximizing behavior. That focus on individual choices rather than systemic structure provides a reconciliation of the seemingly contradictory balance of power and power preponderance perspectives with regard to the risk of war. Thus, by translating the war-related predictions of those theories into expectational terms, we are able to integrate these theories within our framework (T_3 and T_4).

Theorems Derived from the Game

The international interaction game (T_4) specifically provides a foundation for searching for the necessary and/or sufficient conditions that account for the types of relations nations can have with each other. The game also permits an evaluation of the dependence of the deduced relationships on specific information conditions, so that we can identify how uncertainty influences behavior. Several of my colleagues and I have utilized the structure summarized here, or variants of it, to deduce theorems about each of the game's outcome events and about associated phenomena. A sampling of the analytic results is presented below:

Basic War Theorem. With perfect information, war can arise in the crisis game if and only if demands arise in response to domestic politics (Assumption 7b) and the preferences over the outcomes are

$$\text{For } A\text{: } \text{Cap}_A > \text{War}_B, \text{ War}_A > \text{Acq}_A$$

$$\text{For } B\text{: } \text{Cap}_A > \text{Negotiate}, \text{ War}_A > \text{Acq}_B.$$

This first, basic theorem (Bueno de Mesquita and Lalman 1989b) implies several corollaries, a few of which I mention here:

Negotiation Corollary 1. Let Doves be those who prefer negotiations to exploitation of rivals (defined as compelling a capitulation) and let Hawks be those who prefer to exploit an adversary rather than negotiate. With common knowledge of a rival's type, pairs of Doves with a conflict of interest will always reach a negotiated settlement of their disputes (Bueno de Mesquita and Lalman 1989b) or they will maintain the status quo.

Negotiation Corollary 2. Neither dovishness nor hawkishness is necessary or sufficient for disputes to be settled through negotiations (Bueno de Mesquita and Lalman 1989b).

Pareto-Inferior Corollary. War can occur even when rational leaders know that they can gain more by negotiating with each other than by fighting (Bueno de Mesquita and Lalman 1989b).

Dove Corollary. Doves are not immune from initiating war, provided they face (or *believe* sufficiently that they are facing) a Hawk (Bueno de Mesquita and Lalman 1989b).

Dove Uncertainty Corollary. *Weak* dovish *A*'s are more likely to initiate violence than are strong dovish *A*'s, with the likelihood diminishing asymptomatically as *A*'s subjective estimate of its probability of success increases. If *A* and *B* are Doves uncertain of each other's types and if *B* is not the type who retaliates if attacked, then the likelihood that *B* acquiesces to *A*'s initial demand increases exponentially as *B*'s subjective estimate of *A*'s probability of success in a confrontation with *B* increases (Bueno de Mesquita and Lalman 1992).

Democracy Corollary. Democratic institutions signal higher than average domestic costs associated with using force, implying that adversaries confronting a democracy hold an unusually high prior belief that the democracy is Dove-like. Consequently, democracies confronting one another are unlikely to use force, whereas democracies confronting non-democracies are likely to use force (Bueno de Mesquita and Lalman 1992).

Hawk Corollary. Hawks are not excluded from reaching peaceful, negotiated settlements of their disputes, even if they know that their rivals are also exploitative Hawks (Bueno de Mesquita and Lalman 1989b).

Deterrence Corollary. With incomplete information, deterrence policies appear efficient when they are wasteful. This inefficiency arises in such a way that tests of deterrence theory contain unintentional data selection biases that inflate the apparent empirical support for deterrence (Bueno de Mesquita and Lalman 1988a).

Self-Defense Corollary. If each adversary is sufficiently confident that were it to initiate the use of force, its rival would retaliate with force, then the crisis between the rivals is certain to be resolved through negotiations (Bueno de Mesquita and Lalman 1989b, 1992).

Arms Race Corollary. Arms races are neither a necessary nor a sufficient condition for war or for peace (Bueno de Mesquita and Lalman 1988a).

Status Quo Corollary. A highly valued status quo does not ensure peace, and a hated status quo does not make war more likely (Bueno de Mesquita 1990b), regardless of information considerations.

Costs of War Corollary. The expected stakes in war bear a positively sloped, heteroschedastic relationship to the expected costs of war, with an intercept value of zero (Bueno de Mesquita and Lalman 1992).

Cost War-Risk Corollary. For wars that have the prospect of being very costly, the risk of war is maximized when side A believes its probability of success is greater than 0.5. For lower-cost wars, the would-be initiator can believe that the probability of success is high or low (Bueno de Mesquita and Lalman 1992).

Also demonstrated within the context of this research program are theorems about domestic politics and war, successful and unsuccessful deterrence, war among allies, and so forth. A sampling of these theorems is summarized below:

Allies Theorem. War is at least as likely between close allies as it is between enemies, but such wars must necessarily be low in costs (Bueno de Mesquita 1981b, 1992).

Domestic Politics Theorem. If either A is uncertain about B's domestic political costs or B is uncertain about A's domestic political costs, so that those costs are either φ or $\delta\varphi$, $0 < \delta < 1$, and if there is a positive probability that one type of nation A or one type of nation B does not hold the preferences delineated in the Basic War Theorem, then there is no value of δ such that either A or B can engage in strategic deception that successfully revises the rival's belief about the magnitude of its opponent's domestic political costs sufficiently to induce negotiations when war would otherwise have occurred (Bueno de Mesquita and Lalman 1990, 1991; Ahn 1990).

The domestic politics theorem, in its fully specified form, implies several significant, counterintuitive conclusions. Beliefs about domestic political opposition to conflicts prove not to be easily manipulated. Building a reputation as a nation with a relatively hawkish (or dovish) domestic opposition also proves more difficult than one might have thought. Under the conditions stipulated, the theorem reveals that nations (and perhaps individuals too) cannot readily step out of character so as to deceive a rival into a course of action that otherwise would not have been taken. But the theorem also indicates that domestic politics is far from irrelevant in shaping international disputes. In this regard it directly contradicts a fundamental tenet of the dominant, *realist* paradigm in which system-wide structural variables wash out the relevance of variations in domestic circumstances. Yet an increasing body of empirical analysis reinforces the implications of the domestic politics theorem (Ostrom and Job 1986; James and Oneal 1991; Morrow 1991; Morgan and Campbell 1991; Bueno de Mesquita and Lalman 1992).

Initial beliefs about the magnitude of a state's domestic opposition profoundly influence the course of events in crises. This certainly is a lesson demonstrated not only by the game but also by the American experience in Vietnam and, perhaps, by the Soviet experience in Afghanistan. The theorem points to the conviction that honesty about domestic attitudes toward foreign policy is not only ethical but also strategic. It is apparently counterproductive for foreign policy leaders to pretend that their domestic political circumstances are different from what they really are. By doing so, such leaders fail to alter the behavior of their foreign adversaries, but they raise the domestic political costs that they must endure.

Several theorems and corollaries not summarized here have been derived regarding negotiations, acquiescence, and pursuit of the status quo. Also of interest is a three-player variant of the international interaction game that has been developed by Wu (1990). He proves and tests empirically several important theorems regarding the necessary and sufficient conditions for extended deterrence to be successful. Two are summarized here:

> *Extended Deterrence Information Theorem.* A successful extended deterrence policy requires the presence of incomplete information (i.e., uncertainty) (Wu 1990).

> *Extended Deterrence Counterproductivity Theorem.* A counterthreat from a defender can be counterproductive in that it can *increase* the probability that the defender's protégé will give in to the would-be attacker's demands (Wu 1990).

Wu's primary theorem directly contradicts the widely held view that clarity of commitment is necessary for successful deterrence (George and Smoke 1974; Lebow 1981) and thereby establishes a critical, testable issue. His empirical tests of the theory account for as much or more variation than do the best rival formulation of the extended deterrence problem (Huth 1988; Huth and Russett 1984, 1988), thereby providing support for the view of his results as a progressive addition to our knowledge about the elements governing deterrence crises.

The above sampling of analytic results suggests some of the phenomena addressed by the international interaction game. Most of these and other deductions have been subjected to empirical investigation and have found strong support in the historical record. At the same time, the models and the measurement procedures that compose this research program have undergone substantial modification over the past ten years.

Evolution of the Research Program

In *The War Trap* (T_1) I set out a decision-theoretic model of necessary, but not sufficient, conditions for conflict choices that was rooted in the assumptions of expected-utility-maximizing behavior. That formulation was accompanied by extensive empirical tests of nine principal propositions. All nine, as well as several ancillary hypotheses, were strongly supported by the evidence. However, the model's specification contained several limiting features, some of which I recognized at the outset (Bueno de Mesquita 1981b), others I became aware of through my own research, the research of colleagues, and helpful critiques (Zagare 1982; Wagner 1984; Nicholson 1987; Moul 1987; Hussein 1987).

In particular, the original model did not adequately treat rational expectations in the absence of a dispute. Consequently, the model tended to overstate the risk of conflict. The initial version also suffered from an inadequate treatment of the risk-taking characteristics of individual decision-makers. This limitation seriously restricted the empirical referents of the research and encouraged interpersonal comparisons of utility. Finally, the operationalization of key concepts in *The War Trap* gave a false impression that the theory was zero-sum in orientation. Thus, while the *theory* was decidedly not zero-sum, the *measurement procedures* tended to make empirical estimations appear zero-sum. Each of these deficiencies has been eliminated or diminished in subsequent developments of the research program.

In *The War Trap* decision makers were assumed to calculate how the policies of their rivals might change in the absence of any direct pressure from the state in question. However, those calculations were treated as if they could be estimated by decision makers only under conditions of *extreme* hostility or *extreme* friendship toward the "other" state. In "*The War Trap* Revisited" (T_2) a technique was introduced for estimating the value each actor attached to the continuation of the status quo. In this way, the earlier estimate of future expectations in extremis were extended to encompass any circumstance. With the removal of this important limitation, it became possible to test a variety of new propositions, especially about expectations and the avoidance of crises (Bueno de Mesquita and Lalman 1987), and to extend tests of earlier propositions to a broader array of circumstances. The support for the theory in the tests based on the revised model proved to be significantly stronger than the already statistically significant results reported in *The War Trap*.

Still, the improved estimation of the value attached to the status quo did not adequately resolve the rational expectations component of the model. To do so required the introduction of a fuller estimation of possible future states of the world in the event that there was no dispute between nations A and B. In "Reason and War" (T_3) such a fuller specification was introduced. There, Lalman and I exploited important properties of the median voter theorem (Black 1958) by noting that the most secure position a nation or interest group could adopt was the position supported by the "median voter" or "median nation."* This extension of the median voter theorem into the realm of international politics rests on the supposition that power is to interstate relations as voting is to elections and that the side that can marshal a majority of *available* power behind its objectives is the side whose objectives will prevail.

We define this median by taking the sum of the capabilities of each state, discounted by each state's intensity of preference for any given policy outcome relative to its most preferred policy outcome. We then locate the Condorcet winner among all pairwise comparisons of possible policy outcomes.† Thus, power discounted by preferences is treated as the analogue in international politics to voting in domestic politics.

Newman (1982), as part of the broader research program, had already shown that the selection of alliance partners gravitated toward the pairing of states that enhanced each other's security, defined as the minimization of putative opponents' expected utilities for challenging the state in question. The issue-specific median nation's policy position is, by definition, the *most* secure policy stance a participant in the international interaction game can take (Bueno de Mesquita, Newman, and Rabushka 1985). With the assumption that nations would gravitate toward this median nation position, it became possible to estimate the direction of change, if not the exact state of the world, that was most likely between A and B on any given issue provided these nations did not engage in a forceful dispute with each other.

The improved specification of the rational expectations component of the model again significantly increased the goodness of fit between the

---

*Briefly, the median voter states that if preferences are single-peaked, so that they diminish as the Euclidean distance between an outcome and one's ideal point increases, and if issues are unidimensional, and if a majority of votes (or power, in our context) is required for victory, then the outcome preferred by the median voter is the winning outcome.

†The Condorcet winner is that alternative which always wins in head-to-head competition with each other alternative. There must be a Condorcet winner (and it must be the median voter) if issues are unidimensional and preferences are single-peaked. Otherwise, of course, there may not be a Condorcet winner.

theory and the data over previous formulations. At the same time, the rational expectations component added a feature that is now more fully exploited in the international interaction game. In particular, several researchers have shown that decision-theoretic results tend to converge on game-theoretic equilibria when the decision theory model contains a rational expectations component. Thus, the enhanced specification of expected future states of the world provided a bridge from the earlier, decision-theoretic models to the limited information, sequential game version that represents the current state of my research.

Risk Modifications

The original motivation behind the research program discussed here was, as mentioned earlier, a realization that many crucial hypotheses about conflict were rooted in the assumption that all decision-makers respond in the same way to risks and to uncertainty. Even in the earliest formulations, I was motivated by an interest in evaluating the impact of risk and uncertainty on conflict choices. Lacking an adequate means to evaluate risk-taking propensities, in *The War Trap* I developed four *ad hoc* rules that captured the "flavor" of classical economic views of risk taking, but did not permit me to estimate the curvature of utility functions. In "*The War Trap* Revisited" (T_2) I was able to abandon those *ad hoc* procedures, replacing them with a theoretically informed operationalization of risk-taking propensities. That procedure greatly expanded the potential explanatory power of the models and, incidentally, eliminated the troublesome tendency toward zero-sumness and toward interpersonal comparisons of utility that were prevalent in the original phase of the research (T_1). The empirical fit between the indicator of risk-taking propensities and actually risky behavior (Bueno de Mesquita 1985b), as well as subsequent research by others (Morrow 1987), supported the usefulness of the risk refinement.

By incorporating a theoretically meaningful approach to risk taking, I was able to expand significantly the model's explanatory power beyond its earliest construction. In "*The War Trap* Revisited" I demonstrated that all previous deductions followed from the revised model; that the goodness of fit was improved; and that it was possible to deduce propositions regarding the impact of misperception on rational actors. The highlighting of misperception represented the first rational-choice focus in international relations research that contained both an axiomatic theory about misperception and systemic empirical tests of the theory's implications. In contrast to many arguments prevalent in the literature (Stoessinger 1974; Jervis 1976), I showed conditions under which misperceptions could *decrease* as well as increase the risk of war (T_2). Those conditions occur frequently in the empirical world and yield behaviors consistent with the deduced expectations from the model.

The introduction of the risk-taking component of the model permitted several other developments. In 1981a I showed that the likelihood of war was not dependent on the distribution of power among nations, but rather covaried with the distribution of *both* risk-taking predilections and the power with which to implement those predilections. Subsequently (1985b), I reported that the risk indicator turned out to be approximately normally distributed and centered on risk neutrality. That distribution helped explain the failure of researchers to find strong empirical support for the competing systemic hypotheses about the likelihood of war that had motivated my original concerns. In particular, it made clear why no consistent pattern of evidence emerged in the debate between those who believe that bipolarity encourages peace and those who subscribe to the notion that multipolarity diminishes the risk of war. Empirical assessments bore out the expectations from the research program I was developing (Iusi-Scarborough and Bueno de Mesquita 1988; Bueno de Mesquita and Lalman 1988b).

Additionally, the new risk indicator facilitated the development of refined, ordinal estimations of *subjective* beliefs, including not only what state A expected to impose on state B but also state A's perception of state B's beliefs about what B could impose on A. The model also included estimations of A's perception of B's beliefs about nation C and so forth. This latter refinement freed the model from its limited empirical focus on international conflict, allowing me to develop tests of the model in entirely new settings.

Application of the Model to New Settings

In a brief paper (1984) and then more fully in *Forecasting Political Events* (Bueno de Mesquita, Newman, and Rabushka 1985) and other publications (Beck and Bueno de Mesquita 1985; Bueno de Mesquita 1990a) (T_2), my co-authors and I refined the model from "*The War Trap* Revisited" into a tool for forecasting policy decisions and sources of domestic political instability in any political setting. The theory's scope was expanded in such a way that any political issue involving competing interests could be assessed *provided* the issues in dispute were separable rather than linked.* The expanded domain of the theory required no modifica-

---

*More recently, the restriction that issues must be separable has been dropped, through the incorporation of a model developed originally by Shepsle and Weingast (1981, 1987) for assessing congressional committee decision-making. Also, see Bueno de Mesquita and Stokman (forthcoming) for a dynamic version of the model and for a comparison to logrolling models.

tion in the formal, mathematical structure of the model, although it did require additional definitions to make it usable outside the international context. In particular, to apply the model to policy decisions required the specification of relevant actors, defined as any individual or group of individuals who have the following three characteristics in common:

1. Access to a common pool of resources or capabilities with which to influence policy choices;

2. A shared view of what constitutes the most preferred outcome on the issue in question; and

3. A common willingness to spend a particular share of the available resources in pursuit of the group's objectives on the issue in question.

If any one of these three conditions is not satisfied among members of a tacit or explicit group, then the group is viewed as fractionalized and is treated as multiple groups, so that each faction satisfies the three restrictions just enumerated. Adapting the model to a real-time policy setting also required a fundamental adjustment in terms of prospective sources of data. Whereas the research on historical conflicts depends on readily available data, the application to policy issues requires tapping into the expertise of area or issue specialists who possess the relevant information on group preferences, resources, and issue salience, but who do not necessarily believe that such a modeling enterprise is a reasonable way to investigate questions of interest to them. Fortunately, despite the reasonable skepticism of area specialists, it proved possible to obtain data on an extremely wide variety of issues with which to test the applicability of the model to this new setting. Furthermore, the basic operationalizations of utilities, probabilities, risks, and so forth on which my earlier empirical research depended proved readily adaptable to this new, broader empirical setting.

The adaptation to an issue-specific policy setting also led to an increase in the range of uses that the model could have. By capitalizing on the perceptual components developed during the second phase of my research program, I was able to analyze issues not only in terms of expected outcomes but also in terms of possible strategic interventions that could alter anticipated outcomes. Indeed, the model has found broad use and proven highly reliable as a vehicle for testing—before the fact—alternative scenarios designed to manipulate the ex ante predictions of the basic model. Such strategic scenario tests have proven sufficiently accurate that the model has found extensive use in several departments of the United States government and in several large, multinational corporations. A description of some applications to scenario testing as well as to policy forecasting can be found in *Forecasting Political Events* (1985). The book contains forecasts about the future of Hong Kong and China that result from the decision-theoretic model as formulated in "*The War Trap Revisited.*" The important departure in the book is that it demonstrates the robustness of the theory when applied to entirely new forms of data and to entirely new subject areas. The model has now been utilized to forecast policy decisions and political interactions in over sixty countries, encompassing more than two thousand distinct political issues. A sampling of such applications is provided below.

1. The ascent of Yuri Andropov as successor to Leonid Brezhnev was forecast while Andropov was still with the KGB, before his rise to the Politburo and well before he was viewed as a serious contender by most other analysts (Bueno de Mesquita 1982).

2. Italian deficit policy, and the attendant fall of the Spadolini government in Italy in 1982, was predicted months in advance. The forecast was that Fanfani would succeed Spadolini and that his government would ultimately be threatened by a policy shift of the Communist party of Italy toward greater support for austerity programs, leading to the rise of Craxi. Spadolini fell several months after the forecast analysis was completed. He was succeeded by Fanfani, who fell to Craxi on the heels of shifting economic policy by the Communists. The model's forecast of the Italian Parliament's deficit policy for 1983 was within 99.2 percent of the actual policy, despite wide-ranging speculation at the time that the government would adopt a deficit program anywhere between 60 trillion and 100 trillion lira (Beck and Bueno de Mesquita 1985).

3. Successful elections were predicted for El Salvador in 1981 and again later. The model predicted that the Duarte government would fall to a coalition led by d'Aubisson in 1981, as it did, despite widespread speculation in the American press that the Left would prevent the elections from occurring in the first place.

4. The shift in Iran of Rafsanjani from a hard-line stand promoting a military solution to the Iran-Iraq war to his stance in favor of economic sanctions and a less bellicose resolution of the dispute was predicted in early 1984 (Bueno de Mesquita 1984). The same article also forecast increasing movement in Iran toward more open, free market policies in response to pressures from the Bazaaris. Rafsanjani was described in the *Wall Street Journal* in the summer of 1984 as having surprised everyone by his shift to a pacifist position on the war. In August 1984, the *Washington Post* reported: "Revolutionary leader Ayatollah Ruhollah Khomeini has come down firmly on the side of Iran's bazaar merchants in a simmering political and ideological dispute over whether they or the state should control the country's foreign trade. Western diplomats here described his intervention, which steers Iran away from further state monopolies and encourages free enterprise, as a development likely to de-

termine the future course of its Islamic revolution" (*Washington Post*, August 30, 1984, A38).

5. In the same article (Bueno de Mesquita 1984), I predicted that in post-Khomeini Iran "the ability to dominate Iran's politics resides with Khameini and Rafsanjani" (p. 233). At the time this prediction was made, both Khameini and Rafsanjani were viewed as minor figures on the Iranian political scene. Indeed, Khomeini had designated Ayatollah Montezari as his successor, a designation widely believed to be definitive by Iran specialists in the mid-1980s. Of course, following Khomeini's death, Khameini was designated as the interim president. Subsequently, Rafsanjani and Khameini forged an alliance that paved the way for Rafsanjani to assume Iran's presidency and for Khameini to assume a key leadership position in the government.

6. A dispute between Chen Yun of the ideological faction of the Communist party of the People's Republic of China and Deng Xiao Ping on the issue of free market reforms was forecast well in advance of its occurrence. In *Forecasting Political Events*, my co-authors and I noted that *"the modernizers have seriously misperceived their ability to implement Deng's policies. . . . [T]he modernizers believe they can resist the demands of the ideologues. . . . However [the ideologues] . . . believe they can successfully counter the modernizers. . . . Such perceptions will produce costly mistakes for Deng's successors among the modernizers. . . . Thus, domestic pressures will ultimately force Deng's successors to compromise with those seeking a more regulated economic system"* (Bueno de Mesquita, Newman, and Rabushka 1985: 149–50; italics in the original). In short, the analysis anticipated a serious dispute over market reforms between the ideologues and the Deng faction within the People's Republic of China. The analysis also anticipated a compromise settlement that would slow economic reforms in China. That these forecasts were surprising at the time is highlighted by the coverage given the actual dispute. On the first page of the *International Herald Tribune* it was reported on September 24, 1985, that:

The Communist Party of China closed its national conference Monday with an unusual public airing of the policy differences that have created tensions between Deng Xiao Ping, the reform-minded veteran who is the country's paramount leader, and more doctrinaire figures in the party hierarchy. The conference was summoned by Mr. Deng to entrench his open-door economic policies in the five-year plan for 1986–1990. . . . It ended on a discordant note as Chen Yun, a Marxist conservative, made a brusque speech that challenged Mr. Deng's position on . . . the play given to market forces in the economy. . . . With Mr. Deng seated on the podium nearby, Mr. Chen quoted Mao to warn of possible social disorder. . . . Still more sharply he reminded delegates that "we are a Communist country," and said that central planning had to remain the pillar of the economy, not market regulation that meant "blindly allowing supply and demand to determine production."

7. In February 1989, in a talk delivered at Gettysburg College, I used a refined version of the model in *Forecasting Political Events* to bring up to date earlier analyses on reforms in China. In that talk, I predicted that China was facing a period of severe political instability in which relative hard-liners were likely to slow or stop economic and political reforms and in which students and other reform-minded interests would face severe repression. Tragically, just such a consequence arose following the student uprising in the spring of 1989.

8. In a conference on the future of Nicaragua, held in October 1988, the model was used to predict accurately the cohesion of the Chamorro coalition during the campaign, and the defeat of Daniel Ortega and the Sandinista government by the Chamorro coalition in an election held in early 1990. Even on the eve of the election, virtually all polling agencies reported that Ortega would win by a substantial margin (Bueno de Mesquita and Iusi-Scarborough 1988).

9. The model was used by the State Department in October 1989 to help develop a strategy that would lead to the signing of a peace agreement among the relevant parties to the dispute in Cambodia. The report to the State Department anticipates an agreement almost identical to the one signed in November 1991 (Decision Insights, Inc. 1989).

10. The admission of both Koreas into the United Nations was predicted in an article written in advance of the decision, although published after the United Nations decision was made. The publisher notes that the article was received well before the United Nations decided the issue favorably, an outcome which many observers thought was all but impossible only a few months before the United Nations voted (Bueno de Mesquita and Kim 1991).

This sampling of forecasts highlights the ability of the model to predict policy formation and political conflict accurately within democratic and authoritarian regimes, in purely domestic, international, or mixed situations; to deal with socialist and capitalist settings for decision making; and to cope with policy decisions in virtually every type of cultural, political, economic, and social setting.

Modeling Continuous Processes

Although the model revisions through 1985 improved upon earlier efforts, still there were several significant limitations of which I was aware. The role of third parties as potential supporters, adversaries, or bystanders in international interactions was not well developed in the early formulations. This was true despite the fact that Michael Altfeld and I (1979) (T_1) had already developed and tested an expected–utility–maximization model of third-party decisions to join one or another side in ongoing wars. The tests showed that the model correctly categorized third-party decisions to join the stronger initial belligerent or the weaker initial belligerent or to remain neutral in well over 90 percent of the cases. In fact, our approach to the problem led to a two-thirds proportionate reduction in error. This is twice as large a reduction in error as occurs in the closest rival model of third-party decisions (Siverson and King 1980). More recently, C. Kim (1991) has extended the theory of third-party decisions and has refined the testing procedures, yielding still stronger support for the Altfeld–Bueno de Mesquita model. In "Reason and War" (T_3), Lalman and I incorporated the Altfeld–Bueno de Mesquita model into our estimation of each actor's subjective calculation of the actor's probability of success or failure in a confrontation with a specified rival. By doing so, we simplified the calculation of subjective probabilities over earlier formulations while providing a stronger linkage between our axiomatic structure and our operationalizations.

The Altfeld–Bueno de Mesquita model also proved useful in accounting for seemingly contradictory hypotheses about the role of alliances in war. Balance of power theorists contend that alliances are short-lived, non-ideological marriages of convenience that are highly effectual in shaping the course of war. Power transition theorists argue that alliances are long-term, ideologically or policy oriented marriages of like-minded states that cannot be effectual in war. The Altfeld–Bueno de Mesquita model allowed the specification within a single framework of when the balance of power expectation or the power transition expectation about alliances would prove to be true (Bueno de Mesquita 1989).

The key difference in assumptions about alliances set out by power preponderance and balance of power theorists is readily formalized. Let C_A be the power of the most powerful nation or alliance of nations. Let C_B be the power of A's rival B. Let C_K be the power of a third nation or coalition of nations K. Organski and Kugler's (1980) power transition argument that alliances are ineffectual in wars among the most powerful states is driven by the assumption that

$$C_B + C_K < C_A.$$

Morgenthau and other balance of power theorists, however, maintain that

$$C_B + C_K \geq C_A.$$

A rational actor's expected-utility-maximizing view of third-party choices to join side A or side B encompasses the generalizations of both balance of power and power preponderance theorists. Assume that the choice to join A, join B, or remain nonaligned is determined by expected-utility-maximizing criteria. Further assume that the amount of effort third party K makes on behalf of A or B increases continuously and monotonically with K's expected utility for its choice. That is, the more K expects to gain from helping a nation at war, the larger the commitment K is willing to make in pursuit of those gains.

According to the Altfeld–Bueno de Mesquita model, K's choice between joining A and joining B depends on the probability of A winning given help from K (P_{AK}), the probability of A losing even though K helps A ($1 - P_{AK}$), the probability of B winning (A losing) given that K helps B (P_{BK}), the probability of B losing (A winning) even though K helps B ($1 - P_{BK}$) and the utility—or degree of motivation—K attaches to the two possible outcomes. Let the utility to K of A winning = $U(W_A)$, and let the utility to K of A losing and B winning = $U(L_A)$. Expressed algebraically, K's expected utility for joining A or B equals

$$E(U)_K = [P_{AK}U^K(W_A) + (1 - P_{AK})U^K(L_A)]$$
$$- [(1 - P_{BK})U^K(W_A) + P_{BK}U^K(L_A)].$$

The terms may be rearranged by factoring to yield

$$E(U)_K = [P_{AK} + P_{BK} - 1][U^K(W_A) - U^K(L_A)].$$

This reorganization of the terms helps make clear that since the value of $[P_{AK} + P_{BK} - 1]$ can only be greater than or equal to zero, the sign of the expression—and, therefore, the predicted behavior—is determined by the relative magnitude of the utilities or preferences of K for victory by A or B. How much effort K makes depends both on the intensity of K's preference for one or the other side and on K's power. To see this, assume no nation enters a conflict with the expectation of harming the side it chooses to join, so that the *a priori* probability of A winning if K abstains is not larger than the probability of A winning if K joins A, and likewise the *a priori* probability of B winning is not diminished by K joining B. That is, I stipulate that

$$P_{AK} \geq P_{Ab}; \ P_{BK} \geq P_{Bb} = (1 - P_{Ab})$$

where P_{Ab} and P_{Bb} are the respective probabilities of A and B winning a *strictly bilateral* dispute (as estimated by K).

Once P_{Ab} and P_{Bb} (which sum to 1.0, and represent the probabilities when A and B act alone) are subtracted (as dictated by $P_{AK} + P_{BK} - 1$), all that remains is K's marginal contribution to the probability of the outcome. This can be seen most easily by adding an operational assumption. Let $P_{AK} = (C_A + C_K) / (C_A + C_K + C_B)$, where, as before, C refers to the capabilities or power of the subscripted actor. Similarly, let $P_{BK} = (C_B + C_K) / (C_A + C_B + C_K)$. Then

$$
(P_{AK} + P_{BK} - 1) = \frac{C_A + C_K}{C_A + C_B + C_K} + \frac{C_B + C_K}{C_A + C_B + C_K}
$$
$$
- \frac{C_A + C_B + C_K}{C_A + C_B + C_K} = \frac{C_K}{C_A + C_B + C_K}.
$$

Now, under the power transition condition stipulated above and with the assumption that effort increases monotonically with expected utility, we see that C_K is small compared to C_A and C_B. Therefore, with utilities held constant, K's expected utility must approach zero for a finite value of $(U[W_A] - U[L_A])$ compared to the conditions stipulated for the balance of power (where C_K is *relatively* large). Given monotonicity of effort with expected utility, these expressions reveal that alliances are less important when third parties are weak compared to initial belligerents and are more important when third parties are relatively strong compared to initial belligerents. Thus, the balance of power and power transition hypotheses are not incompatible at all. Rather, they are each special cases of behavior under the axioms of expected utility maximization as modified by the assumption of monotonicity (T_3).

The monotonicity restriction allows the derivation of continuous estimates of the likelihood of each type of conflict outcome. In this way, that assumption enhanced the ordinal predictions that were possible from the perceptual model in "*The War Trap* Revisited" and in *Forecasting Political Events*. The continuous form of the probability estimates, as noted earlier, also greatly increases the model's explanatory power, reducing significantly the mistaken predictions from the earlier formulation. The movement toward a continuous probability function was accompanied also by movement toward a specification of the expected utility associated with a continuous stream of outcomes (Morrow 1985), rather than the discrete outcomes specified in the earlier research. The continuous form as developed by Morrow led to the derivation of several significant theorems related to bargaining in crises.

The International Interaction Game and Future Developments

Each of the refinements developed over the past several years has now been incorporated into the international interaction game (T_4). These refinements, however, represent only a portion of the important analytic growth of this research program. The most consequential development for the future of this research is the shift from a decision-theoretic focus to a focus on sequential games with limited information. With the move from a decision-theoretic to a game-theoretic approach, it has become possible to expand and enhance further the explanatory potential of the research program. Decision-theoretic models of the sort that characterized earlier analyses in this research program identified only partial equilibrium conditions. *The War Trap*, for instance, focuses only on necessary conditions for war. The game structure, as noted earlier, allows the specification of necessary and sufficient conditions. Consequently, the model has now moved to a position where it fully specifies equilibrium conditions for a wide range of observable events. In dozens of empirical tests of the game's equilibrium conditions, Lalman and I (1992) have found the game to be a significant tool in accounting for the origin, escalation, and resolution of disputes.

The utilization of techniques developed in economics for analyzing decisions under incomplete information further enhances the prospective explanatory power of the international interaction game. Analyses under complete and perfect information facilitate the identification of boundary conditions governing behavior. But such a perspective greatly limits our ability to comprehend how leaders learn from the behaviors they observe. The incorporation of Bayesian learning into the limited information, sequential equilibrium analyses of the international interaction game provides a foundation for evaluating signaling and learning in situations that are potentially conflictual.

Complete information models do not adequately inform us about how decision makers *manipulate* beliefs to shift their rival's strategies in ways that enhance their own welfare. The incomplete information analyses of the game, however, focus our attention on the manipulability of beliefs. In the domestic politics theorem, reviewed above, we have an example of a circumstance in which the limited information analysis reveals, surprisingly, that beliefs about domestic opposition cannot be effectively manipulated under a wide array of precisely specified circumstances (Bueno de Mesquita and Lalman 1990; Ahn 1990). The game structure, however, also reveals important circumstances in which uncertainties about other features of decision making—the cost of a first strike or the probability of gaining a demand or the likely value of a negotiated settlement—might be manipulable. These are the issues to which my colleagues and I have now turned our attention.

Analyses of the international interaction game suggest important limitations in previous data collection efforts, both in terms of sampling biases and in terms of misplaced reliance on ex post observations where ex ante expectations were critical. For instance, disputes settled through negotiations have historically lasted for a shorter time than have disputes settled through warfare. Yet, rational-choice models generally lead us to expect that disputes settled through negotiations were feared to have the potential to be costlier than were those disputes that became wars. That is, a partial equilibrium condition for war is that the expected benefits exceed the expected costs, a condition that is difficult to satisfy if the anticipated costs are very high.

By regressing such costs as battle deaths or duration on estimates of expected benefits for wars and then extrapolating the function to negotiated disputes, we can estimate the *expected* costs for disputes that were settled through negotiations. The observed battle deaths for such events are, of course, zero, and the observed duration is short. However, the *ex ante expected* costs, as predicted, were greater for disputes that ended in negotiations than for disputes that ended in war (Bueno de Mesquita 1989; Bueno de Mesquita and Lalman 1992).

Results such as those just reported suggest how important it is to develop data sets about beliefs and perceptions, both for cases of violent conflict and for cases of peaceful interaction. This is a fundamental empirical direction for the future. Theoretically, we continue to be sensitive to the great demands that rational actor models make on the care with which decision makers select among alternatives. In this regard, the research program continues to be informed and motivated by the realization that science progresses by discovering which of our beliefs are wrong, and so we must not hold rashly to any conviction when logic and evidence contradict.

Metatheory and Friendly Competition in Theory Growth: The Case of Power Processes in Bargaining

Edward J. Lawler and Rebecca Ford

This paper analyzes the theoretical development taking place in a program of research on power processes in bargaining (see Bacharach and Lawler 1976, 1980, 1981a, 1981b; Lawler and Bacharach 1976, 1979, 1987; Lawler, Ford, and Blegen 1988; Lawler and Yoon 1990; Lawler 1986, 1992).* The theoretical program takes as its starting point a situation where individuals, groups, organizations, or even societies with conflicting interests voluntarily enter into explicit bargaining. Explicit (as opposed to tacit) bargaining assumes the mutual acknowledgment of negotiations, conflicting issues along which compromise is possible, and open lines of communication through which parties can exchange offers and counteroffers in an attempt to resolve the issues that divide them (Schelling 1960; Bacharach and Lawler 1980; Boyle and Lawler 1991). The scope of this theoretical research program assumes further that the parties have a power capability, that they use this power tactically in an effort to achieve desired outcomes, and that they strive for a favorable position during the bargaining process.

Despite mutual acknowledgment of conflict and despite open lines of communication, explicit bargaining is usually fraught with ambiguity. Given uncertainty about the other's action, each party will likely make inferences about the other party's intent, the importance of the issue(s) to them, the extent to which they are likely to yield during negotiations, and what tactics might produce the most yielding. Questions considered by parties themselves probably include whether or not the opponent will

*The authors thank the editors of this volume and Jeongkoo Yoon for helpful comments on an earlier draft. The first author also expresses appreciation to Samuel B. Bacharach, with whom some major parts of the program were developed. Two research grants from the Sociology Program of the National Science Foundation were critical to the development of this theoretical research program.

exploit every advantage, follow through on threats, adopt a hostile stance, reciprocate concession making, or be trustworthy in general. The parties are likely to use some combination of conciliatory and hostile tactics to influence each other, and these patterns of influence should have important effects on the prospects of conflict resolution. Under the conditions of primary concern to our theoretical research program, coming to a workable agreement is far from a foregone conclusion.

The fundamental theoretical question addressed by our program is: How do the power capabilities of two parties with a relationship affect their use of that power in bargaining? Power is defined broadly as a structurally based capability to modify valued outcomes or resources of another (Emerson 1972). A power process consists of the following distinct but complementary components: (1) the structural potential or capability to influence (e.g., Cook and Emerson 1978; Molm 1987, 1990); (2) the tactical use of the capability by the parties (e.g., Bacharach and Lawler 1981a; Lawler 1992); and (3) the actual or realized power, i.e., the influence produced by tactical action or the structural capability (e.g., Willer, Markovsky, and Patton 1989). While these distinctions are somewhat standard among contemporary social exchange theories of power (Emerson 1972; Cook and Emerson 1978; Cook 1987; Molm 1987, 1988; Markovsky, Willer, and Patton 1988; Yitzhak and Zelditch 1989), our program incorporates a sharper distinction, both conceptually and empirically, between power capability and power use and also between power use and actual power. Thus, a power capability may or may not be used (e.g., a union may have a sizable strike fund, but never use it); and if power is used, it may or may not result in actual influence over the opponent (e.g., union workers may walk off their jobs, but management may have sufficient inventories and access to alternative sources of labor, so that the walkout is ineffective). Of particular importance, actual power is analytically distinct from both the underlying power capability and power use in the theoretical program.

Two Themes

In analyzing this theoretical research program, we develop two themes. The first is the import of metatheory in theory growth. A metatheory is defined as a set of assumptions, epistemological and ontological, that orient and direct the form or content of theorizing about some phenomenon. We distinguish for heuristic purposes the *orienting* and *directing* facets of a metatheory. The orienting part of a metatheory constitutes a set of very broad assumptions about the social process under study, suggesting a problem focus. The directing elements of a metatheory specify how the key constructs within the problem focus should be conceptualized. We term the former the "orienting assumptions" and the latter the "metatheoretical core." A theory, on the other hand, is a set of abstract claims or propositions that are testable, directly or indirectly (Wagner and Berger 1985).

Our argument is that the orienting and directing facets of a metatheory are indispensable parts of the theorizing process, because any theoretical statement must be based upon some prior assumptions and a set of conceptualizations that are taken for granted (see also Berger, Wagner, and Zelditch 1989). Even though metatheoretical assumptions may not be explicitly articulated in a theoretical research program, they affect theories and stimulate theoretical growth in a variety of important ways. For example, metatheories define the substantive problems of theoretical interest, dictate how those problems should be investigated, and establish boundaries for the sort of theoretical solutions that are deemed satisfactory (Wagner 1984).

Metatheories not only initiate theorizing but often guide extensions of extant theories in implicit, unacknowledged ways. While metatheories should be assessed in terms of their instrumental or heuristic value—indicating where they lead, what theories they spawn, etc.—we suggest that theories with explicit, acknowledged metatheories will have richer patterns of growth resulting from periodic reexamination or fleshing out of metatheoretical premises. A metatheory may be the source of a new concept that alters or conditionalizes previous theoretical predictions; it may suggest a new problem focus or branch; or it may contain an assumption that, upon reflection, leads to a new theoretical claim. Explicating the metatheories underlying theories seemingly can yield important benefits to theories, which are often formulated with a determined avoidance of metatheoretical issues. In this context, our analysis will make explicit the metatheoretical foundation of the program on power processes in bargaining formulated by Bacharach and Lawler (1981a, 1981b) and will show how the original premises have shaped recent theorizing on bilateral deterrence and conflict spiral (Lawler 1986; Lawler, Ford, and Blegen 1988; Lawler 1992).

The second theme to be developed here is the role of "friendly competition" in theoretical growth. In Wagner and Berger's (1985) terms, friendly competition refers to a particular relationship between two "variants" of a theory. Two theories are variants of each other if they address the same theoretical questions, issues, or phenomena, and contain both common and contradictory predictions. Friendly competition should engender "theory elaboration" and, as such, should lead to increases in scope, rigor, precision, or the empirical adequacy of each theory (Wagner and Berger 1985). In this context, contradictory predictions of two theoretical formulations identify critical issues that need to be resolved in a theoretical research program and also key points around which conditionalization is necessary. When using a strategy of "friendly competition," the theorist pits one theory against another, not to choose between them as in a critical test, but to pinpoint their differences and to understand the conditions under which their respective predictions are likely to occur. In sum, friendly competition is a form of "theory variation" that stimulates "theory elaboration" (see Wagner and Berger 1985).

To create friendly competition, each theory is developed as an alternative to another. This implies more explicit construction of opposite characterizations of a social process and the use of contradictory predictions to clarify the main propositions of concern. Rather than seeking to dispense with or blend theoretical differences quickly, contradictory predictions from alternative formulations are used to fuel theoretical growth by uncovering new theoretical issues that need to be dealt with, by clarifying more precisely the set of conditions to which a theory applies, or by developing an integrative theory that is better than either of the original theories. Thus, various forms of theoretical growth conceivably could be stimulated by "friendly competition."

The subsequent analysis is divided into five sections. The first synthesizes the main features of the program as a whole. This summary introduces the basic elements of the theoretical research program and identifies the metatheoretical starting points (i.e., orienting assumptions). The section also explicates a set of core metatheoretical ideas that capture the conceptual foundation for the program, encompassing in particular some important assumptions about power. The second section describes the developmental steps in two branches of the theoretical research program, one on power dependence and the other on punitive power. Greater emphasis is placed on the punitive power branch because it has explicitly used the strategy of "friendly competition." The third section discusses a recent theoretical convergence of these two branches (Lawler 1992). The fourth section describes incipient developments from the theoretical convergence. The fifth and concluding section discusses the general implications for theory growth.

Elements of the Program

This section describes the main elements of the theoretical research program. Figure 1 contains a general diagram of the program and provides the basis for several descriptive points. First, the background of the

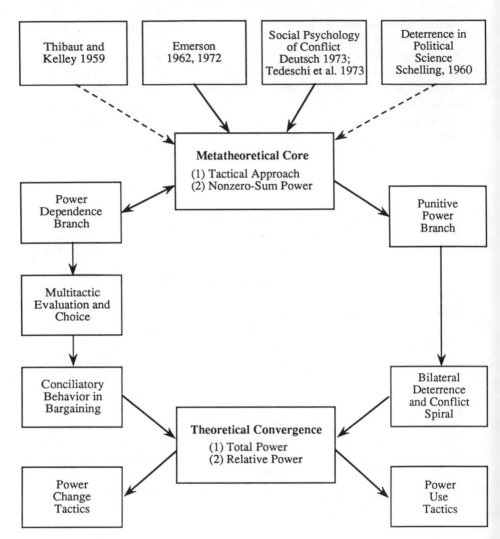

Fig. 1. Diagram of program.

program combines features of both sociological and psychological literatures. Thibaut and Kelley (1959) serve as an important backdrop for the
program because of their cognitive or interpretative conceptualization of
rewards, and their treatment of social relationships as an interdependent
matrix of choices. Emerson's (1962, 1972) theory of power dependence
and social psychological research on conflict (primarily by psychologists)
combine to form a dual emphasis on *power* and *tactics*. Finally, Schelling's

(1960) classic analysis of threats, which emphasized the perceptual and impression management aspects of coercive tactics, and also his persuasive critique of game theory strengthened the problem focus drawn primarily from these other sources.

Second, the diagram identifies two ideas, which formed the metatheoretical core of the program: a tactical approach to power use and a nonzero conception of power. This metatheoretical core developed primarily from several features of the background: Emerson's (1962, 1972) power dependence theory, social psychological research on conflict and bargaining (Rubin and Brown 1975; Pruitt 1981), as well as some classic social psychological and political science theory on power processes (Thibaut and Kelley 1959; Schelling 1960). However, the solid arrows indicate the two most important sources of the metatheoretical core. Emerson's theory is the source of a structural, nonzero-sum approach to power, and selected social psychological work is the primary basis for a conception of power use as tactical action.

Third, the diagram indicates that the program has two theoretical branches addressing complementary problem areas (see Wagner and Berger 1985, for a discussion of branching programs). The power dependence branch has analyzed the impact of dependence on conciliatory tactics while the punitive power branch has examined the impact of coercive capability on the use of hostile tactics, i.e., those that inflict punitive damage (see Lawler and Bacharach 1987, for some research; and Lawler 1992, for some further discussion of this contrast). As will become more evident later, these two branches actually developed in sequence, with the power dependence branch coming first. The reciprocal relationship of the metatheoretical core and the power dependence branch reflects the fact that early research within the power dependence branch provided part of the basis for the development of the metatheoretical core. This is important for understanding the metatheoretical foundation of the punitive power branch, and also serves to illustrate how empirical results might facilitate theoretical growth through feedback on metatheoretical underpinnings.

In the sequence of development, the power dependence branch began by exploring two related issues: (1) how the dimensions of power dependence (i.e., the value of the outcomes at stake and the availability of alternative sources for those outcomes) are used by parties to form judgments about each other's power capability, and (2) how parties use their own and another's power position to choose among a range of tactic options (Bacharach and Lawler 1976; Lawler and Bacharach 1976, 1979; Bacharach and Lawler 1981b). Once the metatheoretical core crystallized, this branch took up the issue of how power dependence relations

affect concessions tactics in two-party bargaining, which became the focus of Bacharach and Lawler (1981a).

The punitive power branch developed as we became more concerned
with the impact of punitive power in conflict settings—in particular,
with the relationship between Emerson's power dependence theory and
notions of deterrence in political science and social psychology. Emerson
had begun with the fairly standard notion that power is the ability to levy
costs, yet power dependence theory really only incorporated one form of
cost—opportunity costs (i.e., the value forgone when a choice is made).
Thus, power dependence theory did not really account for the imposition
of retaliation costs, i.e., costs which can be levied above and beyond
opportunity costs (see Bacharach and Lawler 1981a; Molm 1987). This
omission is particularly problematic for conflict settings, where actors
attempt to resist each other's demands (Bacharach and Lawler 1981a;
Blalock 1989).

The idea that punitive or damage tactics play an important role in
conflict processes can be traced to earlier social psychological work by
Deutsch (1973) and Tedeschi, Schlenker, and Bonoma (1973). Their research stressed the importance of tactics which levy costs (or threaten to)
above and beyond those forgone when a choice is made. For instance, in
choosing to withdraw from negotiations, a country forgoes the benefits
associated with reaching an agreement. The same country may experience retaliation costs (for withdrawing) imposed by the opponent in the
form of tariffs, trade embargoes, and the like. With the use of "friendly
competition," this branch of our program made it apparent that there
actually were two contradictory positions in the literature on how a coercive power capability affected the frequency of threatening or damaging action in a conflict. These contradictions were explicated by Lawler
(1986) in the form of "bilateral deterrence theory" and "conflict spiral
theory."

The final part of the diagram shows a theoretical convergence around
the concepts of relative and total power in a relationship. This convergence pulls together the common implications for power capability and
power use from both power dependence and punitive power branches
(Lawler 1992). The recent convergence, in turn, forms the basis for incipient work on tactics of "power change" and tactics of "power use"
(e.g., Lawler and Bacharach 1986; Blegen 1987; Lawler, Ford, and Blegen 1988; Blegen and Lawler 1989; Lawler and Yoon 1990). The incipient
power-change branch attempts to utilize power dependence to develop
notions about power struggle in ongoing relations and dyadic commitment in exchange networks, and the punitive power branch attempts to

understand better the conditions under which unequal power relations produce resistance rather than intimidation by lower-power actors.

Orienting Assumptions

The diverse background, portrayed in Figure 1, is the basis for three orienting assumptions. These assumptions stipulate that the conflict has a structural foundation, that actors' subjective interpretations of the structure are crucial to their power use, and that a conflict activates the power capabilities which are present in the relationship. Together, these assumptions imply that bargaining is a fundamental social process within which to examine how action reflects or departs from the tendencies and constraints embedded in a social structure. This is not a trivial point, given the relative paucity of work on bargaining by sociologists (for exceptions, see Strauss 1978; Bacharach and Lawler 1981a; Schellenberg 1982; Heckathorn 1985; and Patchen 1987).

Structuralist assumption. The theoretical research program adopts the sociological premise that social conflict—whether between individuals, groups, organizations, or societies—has a social structural foundation (Simmel 1950; Dahrendorf 1959; Cook and Emerson 1978; Wright 1985; Willer, Markovsky, and Patton 1989). The principal units of social structure are sets of interrelated "positions," abstractly representing the places or social locations that people or groups can come to occupy in a differentiated, hierarchical system. "Interests" are attached to each position; occupants represent these interests; and the interests are passed on to successive occupants of the positions. From a purely structural standpoint, the primary cleavages in a social structure are grounded in the differential interests of the positions interconnected within the social structure.

A structural approach stipulates that bargaining most likely occurs in response to structurally based conflicts—i.e., when the positions in a social structure create conflicting interests among a set of actors while simultaneously making it necessary for them to interact. Negotiation is understood in such contexts as a form of conflict management, rather than conflict resolution per se. Thus, while bargaining may resolve particular time-bound issues, new conflicts will likely emerge time and time again, given that the structural conditions remain unchanged. The recurrence of conflict reflects the persistence of the divergent interests of the positions occupied by actors (e.g., labor vs. management, husbands vs. wives, blacks vs. whites, and so on). In fact, because social structures tend to persist as occupants leave and are replaced, conflict with a structural foundation is likely to recur frequently and be difficult, if not impossible, to resolve in the absence of structural change. In this respect, the theoretical research program borrows a bit from conflict theory (e.g., Dahrendorf 1959).

A structuralist perspective emphasizes the competitive side of the mixed-motive dilemma and views conflict resolution as highly problematic. One critical, concrete implication is that the likelihood of agreement on a set of conflicting issues is an important phenomenon to be explained, even independent of the nature of the agreement. While this may seem obvious at first glance, it should be noted that economic and game-theoretical approaches to bargaining typically assume an agreement, given the incentives of the game, and attempt to predict the nature of that agreement (Rapoport 1966; Harsanyi 1977). The scope conditions of our program of work assume a much lower probability of conflict resolution than that found implicitly in most game-theoretical work. This is due, in part, to the focus on conflict with a social structural foundation.

A structuralist approach to conflict differs in important, but subtle, ways from the interpersonal approach that is implicit in most bargaining literature (see Rubin and Brown 1975; Pruitt 1981). Pruitt (1981) exemplifies the interpersonal approach. He conceptualizes negotiation as ". . . a process by which a joint decision is made by two or more parties [with opposing interests]" (Pruitt 1981: 1). To say that parties have opposing interests is to say that they have different *individual* (emphasis is ours) needs that lead them to incompatible preferences (Pruitt 1981: 1); moreover, "interests should never be regarded as inherently opposed" (Pruitt 1981: 4). An interpersonal approach, such as that offered by Pruitt, implies that negotiation in mixed-motive contexts is primarily a form of cooperative decision-making by individuals. With emphasis on the cooperative side of the mixed-motive dilemma, the task of parties is to reconcile individual needs and opinions. While both structuralist and interpersonal approaches have their place in the bargaining literature, the structuralist approach is underrepresented.

Interpretation assumption. The second assumption is that parties interpret and make concrete the interests attached to their structural positions (see Bacharach and Lawler 1981a; Lawler 1992). In other words, the social structure does not fully dictate or determine the tactical action of the parties in conflict. This follows from a concept of power use as tactics which may or may not be adopted or can be used in different ways. Parties have the latitude to bridge their differences and otherwise mitigate the conflict embedded in the social structure, i.e., adopt conciliatory tactics. They also have the discretion to exert pressure and risk exacerbation of the conflict, i.e., adopt hostile tactics.

The most general point is that the social structure "frames" or limits the action of parties by establishing some sort of implicit agenda. Yet this agenda is interpreted, refined, and essentially completed by the parties themselves in the course of bargaining (Strauss 1978; Zelditch et al. 1983; Lawler 1992). This means that parties might adopt tactics that are not congruent with the power relationship between them and that the joint effects of their tactics may not follow from the structural power conditions. For example, parties with lower power may exert more influence than predicted by their power position and power struggles over time may have an integrative or cohesive effect on the relation (Lawler 1992; Lawler and Yoon 1990). An approach to bargaining which fails to give sufficient attention to "bargaining actors as agents" and to "bargaining processes as emergent" will find it difficult to explain the effects of power on the use of tactics and on conflict resolution.

Activation assumption. Conflict is the social condition that activates a power process. Activation means that power capabilities become salient to actors, and tactical options are devised, assessed, and chosen. While the structuralist and interpretive assumptions, in combination, lead to an emphasis on power as a structural condition and tactics as an interpretive condition, the activation assumption makes clear that it is conflict which renders power capabilities salient and tactical options operative. Without a conflict, the effects of structural power are much more subtle and the assumed cognitive/interpretive task faced by parties is likely to be minimal.

The main rationale for the activation assumption is that conflict makes the interaction "problematic" to parties. Most of the problems connect in some way to uncertainty about the intentions of the other, and the fact that the "problems" do not fit available routines, habits, or recipes. The result is that actors search for and "read" available cues in the situation. One obvious cue is the nature and form of power in the relationship, e.g., the degree of power equality or inequality. In sum, uncertainty serves to make power a salient feature of the relationship and to transform power use into a tactical issue for each actor. With the activation assumption, our theoretical program tends to stress how actors *perceive* and *define* the power in their social relationships (Bacharach and Lawler 1976; Lawler and Bacharach 1976; Hegtvedt 1988) more than most social-exchange approaches (e.g., Cook and Emerson 1978; Molm 1987; Markovsky, Willer, and Patton 1988). It should also be noted that the activation and interpretation assumptions are closely related and complementary.

The three orienting assumptions represent fairly pervasive themes in theorizing and research within the program of work. Each orienting assumption represents a strategic ontological claim, designed to shine a "searchlight" on selected features of a social relationship. First, the structuralist assumption maintains a focus on power capabilities as a causal force. Second, the activation assumption suggests that a conflict situation is an important scope condition for the study of power processes. Finally, the interpretation assumption supports the emphasis on uncertainty as a scope condition and impression management as integral to tactical action. The relationship of these assumptions to specific theorizing is primarily intuitive, rather than logical. For example, the program's problem focus—the impact of power capability on tactics in two-party bargaining—has not been derived logically from the orienting assumptions, but one can easily discern a linkage.

Metatheoretical Core

A "metatheoretical core" is defined as a small set of fundamental *conceptual* directives for theorizing about the problem focus. We characterize the metatheoretical core of this particular program as consisting of two primary conceptual twists: (1) a tactical approach to power use, and (2) a nonzero-sum approach to power capabilities. Orienting assumptions underlie the basic problem focus while the metatheoretical core conceptualizes broadly the key phenomena of theoretical concern. In the case of our program, a focus on power capability is suggested by the structuralist orienting assumption, and the metatheoretical core offers a conceptual directive about how to treat power capabilities; and a tactical conception of power use is implied by a combination of the interpretation and activation assumptions. The importance of each conceptual component of the metatheoretical core is discussed, in turn, below.

Tactical conception of power use. The first conceptual twist concerns the meaning of a tactic. Tactical behavior refers to a move or set of moves directed at influencing another's cognitions or behavior in the here and now, or in the future. By definition, these moves are a response to resistance (anticipated or real) from the other and involve some intervening cognitive or subjective process. A tactical approach to power stresses the importance of impression management in the bargaining process, and suggests that tactics flow from conscious or nonconscious judgments in which power is estimated, alternatives assessed, and consequences predicted (Bacharach and Lawler 1981a). While this implies a rational choice process, it is highly bounded and subjective, especially given the level of uncertainty and ambiguity inherent in the conflict settings of primary concern. A tactical approach to power focuses attention on one part of the bargaining process.

Our conceptualization distinguishes two broad classes of tactics likely to be used during negotiations: hostile and conciliatory. Hostile tactics are punitive behaviors that communicate an intent to compete, intimidate, and resist. Such tactics may inflict damage on the other's outcomes or involve a threat to harm. When actors use punitive tactics, they do so either to punish the opponent for engaging in noncompliant behavior, or to influence the opponent to engage in some preferred behavior (Schelling 1960). Conciliatory tactics are positive acts that communicate an intent or willingness to compromise. Within explicit bargaining, conciliatory tactics often take the form of concessions (i.e., movement toward the other party's position) designed to stimulate concessions by the opponent or avoid reprisals for not making concessions.

A distinction has emerged in the theoretical research program between "power use" and "power change" tactics (e.g., Blegen and Lawler 1989). Power use tactics are those that actors use to deal with the immediate conflict or bargaining situation; they are directed at influencing an opponent in the here and now. Examples include tough concession behavior, testing the resolve of the other, threatening to leave a relationship, and punitive tactics such as strikes or other actions that inflict damage. Power change tactics, on the other hand, are efforts to alter the power of either or both actors in the relationship. Such tactics presume an ongoing relationship, anticipate future conflict, and implicitly acknowledge the pervasiveness of the conflict underlying the immediate matters at hand. If successful, power change tactics obviously have important effects on future conflicts.

To illustrate the difference between power use and power change tactics, we contrast a threat to leave the relationship with Emerson's (1962, 1972) "extending the power network" tactic. A threat to leave uses the existing power capability (that is, the available alternative relationships); extending the power network is an effort to change the power base itself (that is, the availability of alternative relations underlying such threats to leave). Overall, power change tactics have the potential to significantly affect immediate bargaining episodes as well as the relationship itself over time. If a party is able to significantly improve the availability of alternative relations, then that party acquires a power advantage in bargaining.

Nonzero-sum conception of power. The second conceptual twist in the metatheoretical core stipulates that power is a nonzero-sum phenomenon. This approach to power is based on implications of power dependence theory and it contrasts with nearly all other approaches. Other approaches to power tend to adopt a zero-sum conceptualization in practice, if not always in principle (see Gamson 1968; and Kanter 1977, for exceptions). A zero-sum approach assumes a fixed sum of power in a relationship or set of relationships, such that a change in one actor's power capability will produce an equal and opposite change in the other's power capability. From a zero-sum perspective, there is, by definition, a perfect negative correlation between the power capability of one party and the power capability of the opponent (see also Lawler 1992).

In contrast, a nonzero-sum conception assumes that the absolute or total amount of power in a relationship can vary, so that a gain of power capability for one party does not necessarily imply a loss of power capability for the other. From a nonzero-sum perspective, it is conceivable that in a dyad, both actors can increase their own power capability, both can lose power capability, or one can gain power while the other's remains constant. To illustrate, if power is a fixed sum, a union which increases its power capability by building a strike fund automatically decreases management's power; however, if power is a nonzero-sum phenomenon, then both the union and management could increase their power capability within the same period of time—i.e., management could increase inventories in order to support a possible lockout, and the union could build its strike fund. The basic point is that with a nonzero-sum conceptualization the power capability of each can move in the same direction, in opposite directions, or one can become stronger while the other remains the same. Thus, a nonzero-sum metatheory raises several questions and issues about power that are neglected or defined away by a zero-sum metatheory.

The nonzero-sum conception can be traced to an implicit and undeveloped notion of "absolute power" in Emerson's (1962, 1972) power dependence theory. In Emerson's formulation, the power capability of A is based on B's dependence on A for valued resources, and vice versa. It is particularly noteworthy that A's power resides in B's dependence on A—not A's dependence on B; likewise, B's power resides in A's dependence on B—not B's dependence on A. This means that theoretically the absolute power of each actor is not related a priori in a particular way and that the amount of power in the relationship can vary as can the power distribution across actors.

The major conceptual directive of a nonzero-sum conceptualization is a contrast between the "total power" in the relationship and the "relative power" in the relationship. Such a distinction subsumes elements of the zero-sum approach within a nonzero-sum metatheory. Total power refers to the sum of each actor's absolute power (Pab + Pba), and relative power refers to the power difference or ratio of each actor's absolute power to the total in the relationship: Pab/(Pab + Pba). Given equal power, increases or decreases in total power involve proportional changes in the degree of mutual dependence, or what Emerson (1972) essentially termed "relational cohesion," and what Molm (1987) has recently labeled "average power." Shifts in relative power occur when existing power is distributed unequally or when total power changes and these changes are distributed unevenly within the relationship.

The major implication is that the relative and total power in a relationship can change in a variety of interesting and somewhat independent ways. If two nations over time become the exclusive providers of valued commodities, then the total power in the relationship has grown without a change in the relative power as long as the net growth of each party's absolute power is equal. Similarly, if actors in a close relationship each develop their own set of friends, then mutual dependence (and, hence, the total power in the relationship) declines without necessarily changing the relative power of the actors; but if only one actor develops such a set of friends, a change in both total and relative power occurs, though in this case all of the change in total power would be an artifact of the change in relative power. These examples suggest that total and relative power may affect tactical action somewhat independently.

An abstract example will further clarify the implications of the distinction between relative and total power. Assume that each actor's absolute power can vary from 1 to 10 units, and therefore that the total power in the relationship can vary between 2 and 20 units. A nonzero-sum conception leads us to ask a question that a zero-sum conception would not pose—specifically, whether a relationship in which each actor has 2 units (total power = 4) will produce different rates of conflict behavior than a relationship in which each actor has 9 units of power capability (total power = 18).

Now, compare a context in which party A has 2 units of power while party B has 8 units of power with another in which A has 4 units of power while B has 6 units of power. Both relationships have a total power of 10, but differ in relative power. A more complex situation might involve a change from 2 units of power capability for A and 8 units for B to 4 units for A and 7 units for B. In this case, total power has increased (from 10 to 11) while relative power has decreased (from 6 to 3). A nonzero-sum approach would take account of these various patterns of change for relative and total power, and a zero-sum approach would attend only to the changes in power difference. As Lawler (1986) has shown, empirical research on power which confounds relative and total power yields results that are difficult to interpret.

This simple contrast, derived from a nonzero-sum metatheoretical directive, raises a number of issues that warrant theoretical analysis. For example, given that each actor's absolute power is independent theoretically, is power use or certain tactical forms of it related in different ways to one's own power capability than to the other's power capability? Perhaps the most important factor in determining the choice of tactic is the other's power capability—regardless of one's own power. These would be "absolute power" effects. Or, in view of the total power in the relationship, do higher degrees of total power increase or decrease the level of conciliation or hostility in the relationship? These questions, and others like them, stem from the orienting assumptions and the metatheoretical core of the program. Our theoretical research program illustrates how fairly simple metatheoretical shifts can raise new questions about power.

Two Branches

The metatheoretical core has spawned two branches of theoretical and empirical analyses, one dealing with power dependence processes and the other with punitive power processes. Both lines of endeavor examine the impact of power capabilities (either dependence or coercive) on the tactical use of that power in a conflict; both treat power capabilities as in part cognitive; and both define power use in tactical terms. Each branch addresses the same general questions about power in social relationships and about patterns of conflict and bargaining, and each adopts a very sharp distinction among power capability, power use, and actual power. Nevertheless, several differences between the branches are important to note at the outset.

First, the power dependence and punitive power branches deal with somewhat different forms of power capability and different types of tactical power use. The power dependence branch stresses concession tactics in bargaining or, more specifically, the impact of dimensions of dependence (i.e., the value of the resources at stake and the availability of alternative actors from whom the resources might be acquired) on the toughness of concession behavior and the probability of reaching agreement (Bacharach and Lawler 1981a). The punitive power branch stresses the effect of coercive capabilities on punitive action, i.e., tactics that damage the outcomes of the opponent (Lawler 1986; Lawler, Ford, and Blegen 1988). The forms of power underlying these two branches essentially represent a difference of focus on opportunity costs vs. retaliation costs.

Opportunity costs are of primary concern to the power dependence branch (see also Emerson 1972; Cook and Emerson 1978; Cook et al. 1983), and retaliation costs are of primary concern to the punitive power branch (Tedeschi, Schlenker, and Bonoma 1973; Lawler and Bacharach 1987; Molm 1987; Lawler 1992). Opportunity costs refer to the outcomes forgone when a choice is made among mutually exclusive options. Applied to bargaining, opportunity costs are the benefits forgone by remaining in a given bargaining relationship, e.g., the anticipated payoff from bargaining with an alternative other. Opportunity costs essentially involve a comparison of the benefits from a choice made with those that might have accrued from an option forgone. Retaliation costs, on the other hand, are negative actions by an opponent that directly damage or punish the actor independent of those costs that would be incurred if the opponent simply withdrew from the relationship. The costs and the different forms of power might be incorporated into a power dependence framework (see Bacharach and Lawler 1980: Chapter 5; Molm 1987); however, empirical evidence indicates the these forms of power have distinct behavioral effects in both bargaining and nonbargaining settings (Gray and Tallman 1987; Molm 1988; Lawler and Bacharach 1987). Lawler (1992) has recently identified the elements for a new theory organized around theoretical principles applicable to both power dependence and punitive forms of power (see Lawler and Bacharach 1987, for relevant empirical evidence).

A second contrast is that the two branches have a different connection to the nonzero-sum part of the metatheoretical core. The reciprocal relationship between the metatheoretical core and power dependence branch in Figure 1 reflects the fact that the nonzero-sum assumption actually emerged in our research on power dependence. Specifically, some early findings (see Bacharach and Lawler 1976; Lawler and Bacharach 1976, 1979) indicated that people in conflict acted as if power was nonzero-sum in nature, and subsequently Bacharach and Lawler (1981a) used the nonzero-sum assumption heuristically in their work on concession tactics in bargaining. Then Lawler (1986) made the nonzero-sum conception central to his bilateral-deterrence and conflict-spiral formulations and to an integration of the power dependence and punitive power branches (Lawler 1992). The overall point is that the power dependence branch is actually part of the foundation for the punitive power branch.

The third difference between the branches is the role of empirical research in the theoretical development. The power dependence branch began as a problem-driven enterprise designed to apply Emerson's ideas on tactics of influence (Emerson 1962) to social conflict. We weren't testing Emerson's theory explicitly but were using it, along with a variety of social psychological work (Thibaut and Kelley 1959; Michener and Suchner 1972), to develop and test theories about perceptions of power and the choice among influence tactics in a conflict. In contrast, the punitive power branch began as a theory-driven enterprise (see Chapter 4 of Bacharach and Lawler 1981a) and was able to take advantage of the earlier theoretical and empirical work in the power dependence branch. The problem-driven vs. theory-driven character of each branch will be evident in the following discussion.

Power Dependence Branch

The power dependence branch was stimulated by a critical reaction to a growing body of social psychological literature on tactics of influence (for relevant reviews, see Tedeschi, Schlenker, and Bonoma 1973; Deutsch 1973; and Michener and Suchner 1972). Bacharach and Lawler began with three interrelated criticisms of this literature. First, while the literature contained many interesting ideas and research findings, it was highly fragmented and in need of an integrative theory. Second, it seemed incongruous that so much work on conflict could be done with relatively little reference to or systematic use of the concept of power (see Michener and Suchner 1972, for a noteworthy exception). Third, given that in most conflicts actors face an array of tactical options, we were interested in developing a theory that would facilitate understanding of multi-tactic evaluations and choice. Emerson's 1962 formulation of power dependence theory, because of its emphasis on power-based tactics, served as the starting point. All of this early work focused on two-party conflicts primarily between an employer and employee.

The first step in the branch consisted of a series of papers addressing two questions: (1) To what extent do actors in conflict use the dimensions of power dependence, specified by Emerson (e.g., actor A's alternative outcomes source and outcome value, actor B's alternative outcome sources and outcome value), to estimate each other's power? (2) How will such actors use the dimensions of dependence as a basis for evaluating and choosing among a range of tactic options? We assumed that an overt conflict would make power salient, motivate actors to assess each other's power capability, and lead them to develop "plans of action" on this basis (see in particular Bacharach and Lawler 1976; Lawler and Bacharach 1976).

To address the above questions, Bacharach and Lawler used a series of vignette studies, pitting an employee of a small store who wants a pay raise against an employer known to be leaning against it. The findings generally supported hypotheses developed from power dependence theory. For example, each of the four dimensions of dependence affected perceptions of self and other's power in a manner consistent with power dependence hypotheses (Bacharach and Lawler 1976; Lawler and Bacharach 1979); and, furthermore, different dimensions of dependence were used by actors to evaluate and decide on different tactic options (Lawler and Bacharach 1976; Bacharach and Lawler 1981b). This work culminated in a classification of tactics and a set of predictions based on the assumptions that (1) dimensions of dependence identify points of strength and weakness in an actor's power position, (2) different tactics deal with different points of strength or weakness, and (3) actors will choose tactics that produce the most significant improvement in their power position by capitalizing on points of particular strength or removing points of particular weakness (Bacharach and Lawler 1980: 160–65).

There was, however, an anomalous finding in this work. Our framework included four tactics, one each for the four dimensions of power dependence, and our theorizing stipulated that an actor will use the corresponding dependence dimension to decide on given tactics. However, the results revealed that actors attributed more importance to their own dependence on the opponent, rather than the opponent's dependence on them, when assessing a series of tactic options. In other words, they were more likely to use or use more heavily their own alternative outcome sources than the opponent's alternative outcome sources to make tactical decisions. The implication was that absolute power or dependence was more important to them than their relative power or dependence position. This led us to question the prevailing zero-sum conceptions of power and ultimately to develop the nonzero-sum facet of Emerson's (1962, 1972) formulation of power dependence theory.

In their book on bargaining, Bacharach and Lawler (1981a) developed the nonzero-sum conception of power and elaborated their theoretical analysis of the cognitive facets of power. They distinguished the absolute power of each bargainer from his or her relative power and also from the total power in the relationship, and they argued that the effect of these is contingent on actors' cognitive imagery of power. If actors adopt a nonzero-sum imagery of power, then they presumably will respond to variations of total power in the relationship and stress their own absolute dependence in tactical decisions; if they adopt a zero-sum imagery, they will attend only to the comparison of their power and that of the other. In brief, Bacharach and Lawler (1981a) developed a theoretical argument leading to two fundamental predictions assuming a nonzero-sum imagery. First, the concession behavior of an actor would be a function of his or her own dependence not the other's dependence; and second, the greater the total power (i.e., mutual dependence) in the relationship, the greater the likelihood of conflict resolution, presumably because each actor responds in accord with the first prediction.

The results of the Bacharach and Lawler (1981a) experiments generally support these predictions. The concession behavior of an actor was primarily a function of whether the actor could expect a good or poor agreement from an alternative party with whom he or she might negotiate, and greater total power in the relationship produced higher average rates of concession across actors. Moreover, across a number of experiments, rates of agreement were significantly higher (e.g., 75 percent, 63 percent) when each actor had an alternative bargaining opponent from whom a poor agreement was likely than when a good agreement was anticipated from the alternative (e.g., 13 percent, 19 percent). These results might be interpreted as the "relational cohesion effects" alluded to by Emerson (1972) in a brief reference to the importance of mutual dependence. Such effects probably reflect the opportunity costs of leaving the current relationship to negotiate with another from whom a poor agreement is likely.

At this juncture, there are several unresolved issues in the power dependence branch, each of which might provide the basis for future theoretical work. The first is the impact of equal vs. unequal power dependence in a conflict. Bacharach and Lawler (1981a) offered some preliminary evidence indicating higher rates of agreement when actors had equal vs. unequal dependence on each other, but a recent study integrating dependence and punitive forms of power found that such effects occur only when actors are equal with regard to both dependence and coercive capabilities and also when mutual dependence is high (Lawler and Bacharach 1987). The interactive effects of dependence and punitive power on conflict resolution warrant further attention (see also Molm 1989).

The second unresolved issue concerns the value of the outcomes at stake. Our vignette and laboratory work empirically disentangles the alternatives and value dimensions of power dependence, and the results for alternative outcome sources are consistent with power dependence, while those for outcome value tend to diverge from power dependence predictions. More specifically, if a party highly values the outcomes controlled by an opponent, it enhances the opponent's power capability, but also motivates the party to exert substantial effort to overcome his or her power disadvantage. The result is that in a conflict the value of the outcomes at stake produces effects on tactics that are the opposite of those predicted by power dependence theory (e.g., see Lawler and Bacharach 1979; Bacharach and Lawler 1981b).

The third unresolved issue concerns both the sort of tactics examined in this tradition and the integrative effects of power suggested by a non-zero-sum approach. With a basis in the distinction between power use and power change tactics discussed earlier (see Blegen and Lawler 1989), virtually all of the work in the Bacharach/Lawler power dependence branch has dealt with "power use" tactics, i.e., those tactics that use available power to exercise influence in the immediate situation. Other tactics can actually change the power position of actors and have an impact on future encounters. For example, if both actors successfully increase the other's dependence on them in the course of dealing with a particular conflict, the total power in the relationship (i.e., mutual dependence) will grow, producing an integrative effect on the social relationship (Bacharach and Lawler 1980; Lawler and Bacharach 1986; Lawler 1992). In this sense, tactics designed to gain advantage in the short run may, in combination and as a by-product, change the power in the relationship over time and enhance the prospects for conflict resolution in future bargaining encounters.

In conclusion, the development of the power dependence branch illustrates the potential importance of metatheory to theory development. In this case, the *metatheoretical* implications of research on how actors treat power dependencies transformed a problem-driven enterprise (see Bacharach and Lawler 1976; Lawler and Bacharach 1976) into a theory-driven enterprise (Bacharach and Lawler 1981a). It is not that the results failed to support our derivations from Emerson's power dependence theory, but that in reflecting about the broader implications of the work, we found gaps in Emerson's and in our own analysis. The theoretical problem was resolved by adopting explicitly a nonzero-sum conception of power, which then provided a metatheoretical backdrop for analyses of punitive power.

Punitive Power Branch

This branch responds to an incomplete analysis of punitive power in Bacharach and Lawler (1981a), and addresses a contradiction in the social psychological literature on threat and punishment tactics in conflict. Two theoretical formulations, termed "bilateral deterrence" and "conflict spiral," suggest divergent relationships between coercive capabilities and punitive tactics, based on assumptions about the meaning or interpretation actors will place on their own and the other's coercive capability. Before discussing each theory, we note that both theories have the same problem focus; both are based on the same metatheoretical premises; both contain common theoretical concepts such as "coercive capability" and "punitive tactics"; and both specify the same type of predictions about power in the relationship (e.g., the impact of equal vs. unequal power). The theories also have the same scope conditions, i.e., both are designed to apply to conditions where actors are seeking to resolve a conflict through explicit bargaining, where each actor has a coercive capability, and where they know both their own and the other's power capability. In the context of such similarities, the theories of bilateral deterrence and conflict spiral differ in important ways, and this program of work emphasizes the differences rather than the similarities in order to promote theoretical development. Thus, it is this branch that has used "friendly competition" as a method of theory growth.

Our analysis identifies five phases in the growth of the punitive power branch. The *first phase* was essentially problem definition. It involved the identification of two classic social psychological arguments linking the magnitude of a punitive capability to the use of that capability through threats or punishments. The argument from Deutsch and Krauss's (1962) research on the famous trucking game indicated that if actors in conflict have the capability to inflict damage upon each other, they will indeed use that capability. The reason is that an actor with a power capability, who faces resistance from another, will succumb to a temptation to use whatever means are available to overcome the other's resistance. Larger power capabilities, by implication, will create more temptation. Once the use of the power capability occurs, a use-counteruse spiral ostensibly will develop in which actors continue to express hostility over time, in part because to do otherwise entails a loss of face (Deutsch and Krauss 1962; Deutsch 1973).

An alternative point of view was suggested by social psychological research implicitly or explicitly using deterrence principles (Tedeschi, Schlenker, and Bonoma 1973; Michener and Cohen 1973; Hornstein 1965). Most notably, research by Tedeschi and associates (1973) showed that a large punitive capability for A reduced B's competitive behavior in a prisoner's dilemma setting. Tedeschi and associates found that the magnitude and credibility of threats determined threat effectiveness in a social situation with rather large power differences between the threatener and the target. We noticed that the ideas underlying such social psychological work dovetailed with some political science research on deterrence processes. The basic idea drawn from the political science literature (Schelling 1960; Morgan 1977) was that actors' use of punitive tactics would be an inverse function of the other's absolute power capability, primarily because the other's capability produces a "fear of retaliation." Bacharach and Lawler (1981: Chapter 4) developed an initial formulation of bilateral deterrence and conflict spiral based on the contrasting arguments implicit in social psychological work by Deutsch and Krauss and by Tedeschi.

The *first phase* of development made it clear that there was a contradiction between the two classic arguments. The *second phase* of theoretical development accentuated and sharpened the differences between the classic arguments in order to reveal the primary source of the contradiction (see Lawler 1986). Figure 2 portrays the contradictions for a dyad with equal power (coercive capability). Note that consistent with the

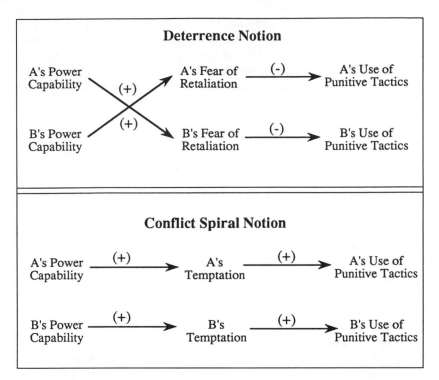

Fig. 2. Classic views.

nonzero-sum concept of power, the absolute power of each actor is treated separately.

Two differences are indicated by the theoretical construction in Figure 2. First of all, the intervening cognitive or interpretive variables (i.e., fear of retaliation vs. temptation) are distinct and essentially reflect disparate inferences from absolute power in the situation (see Lawler 1986; Lawler, Ford, and Blegen 1988). Second, the relationship of power use to absolute power capabilities is different. Deterrence theory traces power use primarily to the *opponent's* (absolute) power capability, and conflict spiral theory traces power use primarily to the *actor's own* absolute power.

By pitting the classic arguments against one another in the spirit of "friendly competition," we revealed a puzzle or anomaly—*each incipient theory traces power use to either, but not both, an actor's own or the other's power capability.* The conflict spiral tradition suggests that actors use power because *they* have it, and the deterrence tradition suggests that actors do *not* use power because *their opponent* has the power to retaliate (Lawler 1986). Neither theoretical position connected the punitive tactics of an actor to his or her own power capability *and* that of the other. This puzzle served as the impetus for the *third phase* of development in both theories. Intuitively, it seemed critical to have a theory that traced the punitive tactics of an actor to both the actor's own and the other's power capability, without resorting to a zero-sum conception of power. So the nonzero-sum conception of power framed our explication of the implicit contradiction of deterrence and conflict spiral arguments and revealed a theoretical anomaly.

The "solution" to the puzzle was to add a common intervening variable to each theoretical formulation: each other's expectation of attack by the opponent. The notion that an actor might be influenced by expectations that the other would use his or her power capability was not new; in fact, this idea came from Schelling (1960). He had proposed that the successful deterrence of an actor by an opponent was contingent on two factors—a reciprocally high fear of retaliation on the part of each actor and a perception by each that the other is not likely to attack because of this fear (Schelling 1960). Moreover, social psychological research has suggested that actors form an "expectation of attack" when confronted with a powerful opponent and, in turn, tend to increase hostility in advance of anticipated attacks (Rubin and Brown 1975; Pruitt 1981; Nemeth 1972). Thus, the intervening variable "expectation of attack" seemed to be an important omission from the classic arguments. Adding such a concept incorporated each actor's perception of "what the other thinks," because the formation of an expectation of attack would involve such inferences.

To build expectation of attack into each theory, Lawler (1986) made the simplifying assumption that actors would expect each other to use the same criteria for deciding on punitive tactics. From the perspective of bilateral deterrence, actors would be influenced by their own fear of retaliation, and they would assume that their opponent would be influenced similarly. This means that the actor's own fear of retaliation would be based on the opponent's power capability—the more powerful the opponent, the more fearful the actor. Similarly, the actor's own power capability became the basis for his or her expectation of attack by the opponent; the greater the absolute power of the actor, the more fearful the opponent ostensibly would be to initiate an attack (Lawler 1986). Thus, in the revised formulation of bilateral deterrence theory (see top panel of Figure 3), each actor's use of punitive tactics was now a function of both the actor's own and the other's power capability, but the intervening mediating processes were different.

In conflict spiral theory, the assumption of similar criteria for choosing punitive tactics meant that actors would anticipate that their opponents

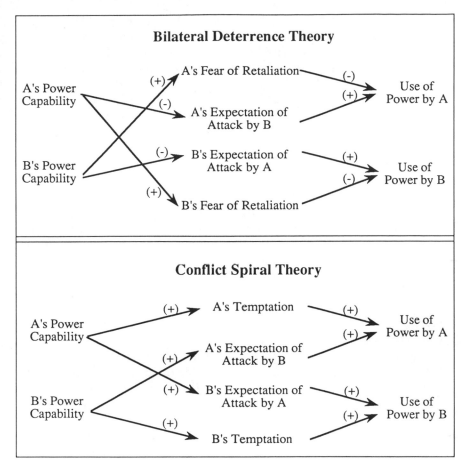

Fig. 3. Reformulation of classic views.

would be tempted to use power, contingent on the magnitude of the opponent's absolute power. From the point of view of the actor, the more powerful an opponent, the more tempted that other would be to use his or her power capability—just as the actor's own power capability would underlie his or her own temptation. Conflict spiral theory essentially translated an actor's perception of the opponent's temptation into an expectation of attack (Lawler 1986). The relationships, posited by the revised theoretical formulation, are depicted in the bottom panel of Figure 3. Once again, each actor's power use is now a function of both the actor's own and the other's absolute power.

By means of the strategy of "friendly competition," the addition of "expectation of attack" as an interpretive intervening variable had the effect of further sharpening the source of contradiction between classic views. From the revised formulation (Lawler 1986), bilateral deterrence theory predicts that higher power for both actors results in each having a higher fear of retaliation (due to the other's high power) and also lower expectations of attack (due to his or her own high power); these conditions, in turn, produce lower rates of inflicting damage (i.e., power use). In contrast, spiral theory predicts that higher total power in the relation will increase the temptation of each actor to use his or her power (due to the actor's own power) while also increasing their expectation of attack (due to the other's power).

In conclusion, the competition of the theories is made "friendlier" by the addition of the common mediating cognitive phenomenon (i.e., expectation of attack). At the same time, the differences are further explicated by the fact that expectations of attack are based on a party's own power in bilateral deterrence theory, and the other's power in conflict spiral theory. The puzzle or anomaly found in the classic arguments now was solved, because in each theory the power use of actors was a function of both their own and the other's power capability. Moreover, this conceptual improvement was accomplished without resorting to a zero-sum conception of power.

The *third phase* of development was stimulated by the importance of extending the theories to account for possible differences between equal and unequal power relationships. To this point, the focus of the theoretical development had been on each other's absolute power and on the total power in the relationship. But if the predictions of each theory for equal power relationships (see Figure 3) are simply transposed to an unequal power relationship, we would conclude that both theories predict *no difference* in the rate of punitive tactics (*at the level of the dyad*) between equal and unequal power relationships. In the case of unequal power, the rate of power use by the lower-power actor would diminish while the higher-power actor's rate of use would increase proportionately. This implication is not consistent with Emerson's (1962, 1972) analysis of power-balancing tactics or Bacharach and Lawler's (1981a) discussion of the instability of unequal power relationships.

An abstract example, once again, may serve to illustrate the problem. Assume a situation where both A and B have the capability to reduce each other's outcomes by 50 percent and one where A can reduce B's outcomes by 60 percent and B can reduce A's outcomes by 40 percent (note that total power is constant at 100). Bilateral deterrence theory would suggest that as A's power increases to 60 and B's decreases to 40, A's fear of retaliation and expectation of attack would go down, whereas

B's fear of retaliation and expectation of attack would increase. If we assume that changes in the fear of retaliation and expectation of attack are proportional, any increase in *A*'s use of punitive tactics would be offset by a corresponding decrease in *B*'s use of punitive tactics. The same result is produced by applying conflict spiral theory to this example. Overall, such reasoning indicates that without additional assumptions, both theories would predict no difference between equal and unequal power at the dyad level as long as the total power in the relationship remains constant.

This problem was resolved by thinking more about how actors might interpret absolute power levels in the context of unequal power. Lawler (1986) stipulated that in an equal power relationship, the actors would give equal subjective weight to the fear of retaliation and expectation of attack in the case of bilateral deterrence theory, or equal subjective weight to temptation and expectation of attack in the case of conflict spiral theory. A shift from power equality to power inequality ostensibly produces an unequal weighting of the intervening cognitions, reflecting a significant change in how actors interpret power in the relationship. The extension of the theories to the contrast of equal with unequal power situations, therefore, hinges on an assumption that higher- and lower-power actors stress different mediating cognitions.

Let us consider the higher- and lower-power actors from the standpoint of bilateral deterrence theory. The argument is that higher-power actors would exploit their power advantage, simply because there is little to prevent them from doing so, i.e., the lower-power actor cannot inflict retaliation costs comparable to those of the higher-power actor. The higher-power actor presumably places more emphasis on the fear of retaliation (which is now lower than under equal power) than on the expectation of attack (also lower but less relevant). Similarly, the lower-power actor is more likely to use power now than under equal power, but for different reasons—namely, higher expectations of attack. The lower-power actor ostensibly accords greater weight to the expectation of attack (now higher) than the retaliation costs. Consequently, the lower-power actor will use power more than would be implied by the power difference itself.

Bilateral deterrence theory makes sensible this rather counterintuitive claim about power use by lower-power actors in unequal power relations. In the face of a power disadvantage, a lower-power actor has essentially two choices: resist or submit to the demands of the higher-power actor. Given its scope conditions, bilateral deterrence theory suggests that resisting intimidation is generally the more likely choice for two reasons. The first is that the use of punitive tactics by the lower-power actor demonstrates to the higher-power actor that attempts to exploit his or her power will not go unpunished. The second reason is that submission by the lower-power actor does not preclude the possibility (or likelihood) that the higher-power actor will continue to inflict costs in the form of minimal concessions or even punitive tactics. Thus, given that the lower-power actor has a "significant" amount of absolute power (a key scope condition), that actor is likely to adopt hostile tactics in the hope of minimizing losses in the long run. Implicitly, lower-power actors will be more concerned about averting a pattern of attack by the opponent than they are about immediate retaliation.

In conflict spiral theory, the assumption is that higher- and lower-power actors respond differently to temptation and expectation of attack. From the perspective of the lower-power actor, there is little to be gained by using power (and possibly much to lose); thus, temptation is likely to have more effect on the lower-power actor's choice of tactics. In contrast, higher-power actors are likely to be aware that lower-power actors have little to gain by using their power, and thus do not expect them to initiate attacks. This suggests that higher-power actors expect the structural power difference itself to produce desired outcomes (given their low expectation of attack). In sum, from the conflict spiral perspective, each actor in unequal power relationships will use fewer punitive tactics than actors in equal power relationships, a prediction opposite to that of bilateral deterrence theory (see Lawler 1986).

With the completion of the third phase, we had resolved the primary issues involved in linking total and relative coercive power to the use of damaging tactics in bargaining. The *fourth phase* of theoretical development was designed to address two unanswered questions that raise some ancillary issues. The first was whether the predictions for punitive tactics could be generalized to concession tactics. The second was how to conditionalize each theory, taking account of their similarities. Each of these questions resulted in a modest extension of bilateral deterrence and conflict spiral theories.

Generalization to Concession Tactics

Once the theories were developed, it became clear that they have implications for concession behavior in bargaining, if one simply assumes a negative correlation between the rate of hostile and conciliatory tactics in a conflict (see Michener and Cohen 1973; Rubin and Brown 1975; Bacharach and Lawler 1981a). Specifically, bilateral deterrence theory indicates that conciliatory tactics are most likely to occur when actors maintain high levels of punitive capability; also, compared to equal power relationships, unequal power relationships are likely to produce lower rates of conciliation (Lawler 1986). Conflict spiral theory, in contrast, suggests that a decrease in punitive capabilities will increase actors' use of conciliatory tactics and, compared to equal power relationships, unequal power relationships will produce more use of such tactics, probably reflecting the submission of the lower-power actor (Lawler 1986). Given this simple extension of each theory, the comparative rates of conciliatory and hostile tactics should vary with the relative and total power in the relationship. The main problem with this extension is that while conciliatory and hostile tactics are correlated, the correlation is far from perfect. Whether conciliatory and hostile tactics should be considered flip sides of the same coin remains an open question.

Conditionalization Principle

The contradictory predictions of the two theories raises the question of what conditions will elicit deterrence effects and which ones will produce conflict spiral effects. Since the most fundamental difference between the theories boils down to how power is interpreted by the actors, the starting point is to identify how structural conditions would have to change actors' interpretive processes in order to produce bilateral deterrence vs. conflict spiral results. The initial conditionalization, offered by Lawler (1986), stresses the salience of the intervening cognitions (see Figure 3) and addresses only the equal power case where total power can vary.

In brief, the basic conditionalization principle is: Any condition that makes the relative salience of retaliation costs greater than the temptation will produce bilateral deterrence effects; whereas any condition that makes the relative salience of the temptation greater than the retaliation costs will produce conflict spiral effects. Stated somewhat differently, the more salient the retaliation potential embedded in the opponent's coercive capability, the stronger the bilateral deterrence effects; while the more salient the temptation associated with the actor's own power, the stronger the conflict spiral effects. Conditions that should produce shifts in relative salience include (a) the degree to which actors are more concerned with minimizing losses than maximizing gains (Tversky and Kahneman 1986; Bacharach and Lawler 1981a), and (b) the incentive attached to initiating an attack (Schelling 1960; Lawler, Ford, and Blegen 1988). While the conditionalization principle is a reasonable starting point (see Lawler 1986, for more discussion), the task of translating this general condition into more specific theoretical predictions is unfinished at this point.

The *fifth phase* of the punitive power branch was empirical research.

We pitted bilateral deterrence and conflict spiral theories against one another, focusing on the predicted impact of punitive capabilities on the frequency of action that damages the opponent's resources (Lawler, Ford, and Blegen 1988). This research utilized a fairly standard two-party bargaining (laboratory) setting in which subjects exchanged offers on an issue across a series of bargaining rounds (e.g., Siegel and Fouraker 1960; Komorita and Barnes 1969; Chertkoff and Esser 1976). In addition, subjects could levy punitive damage against their opponent during each round (e.g., Michener and Cohen 1973).

In the experiments, subjects represented the interests of a group in conflict with another group, giving the bargaining a minimal intergroup character. Instructions encouraged an individualist orientation, i.e., maximization of the payoffs for their own group without regard to the payoffs of the opposing group. Punitive capability was manipulated by varying the maximum amount of an opponent's resources that the subject could destroy, say, 10 percent vs. 90 percent (e.g., Lawler, Ford, and Blegen 1988). Punitive behavior was measured by the frequency (with a fixed magnitude) of punitive tactics summed across both actors, and conciliatory behavior was measured by the total amount of yielding in the dyad (summed across both actors) and also the likelihood of agreement.

The empirical evidence, thus far, supports the predictions of bilateral deterrence theory over those of conflict spiral theory. In two studies, the total punitive capability had a negative impact on the use of punitive tactics, with one study indicating that this effect occurred mainly in the later phases of the bargaining after subjects had experienced the negative consequences of power use (Lawler and Bacharach 1987; Lawler, Ford, and Blegen 1988). Furthermore, punitive tactics were used more frequently in unequal power relationships than in equal power relationships, and there were no differences between high- and low-power actors' rate of using punitive tactics (Lawler and Bacharach 1987; Lawler, Ford, and Blegen 1988). Similar (though weaker) support for bilateral deterrence occurs for conciliatory tactics. Actors in relationships with high total power made larger concessions overall than those in relationships with low total power, and they made larger concessions when in relationships with equal, compared to unequal, power. Significant effects were not observed for the likelihood of agreement across two experiments (Lawler, Ford, and Blegen 1988).

Given the empirical evidence in support of bilateral deterrence theory, there are at least two unresolved issues in this branch of our theoretical research program. The first stems from a plausible interpretation of the failure of conflict spiral theory—namely, that the salience of temptation associated with the actor's own absolute power is generally lower than the salience of retaliation potential attached to the other's absolute power capability. Given many real-world examples of conflict spiral, there must be some particular conditions which evoke conflict spiral processes, and these conditions need to be identified. The second unresolved issue stems from support for the bilateral deterrence prediction that lower-power parties will resist efforts at intimidation and essentially use power as much as the higher-power actor. An effort is needed to understand further the conditions under which unequal power relationships will produce resistance rather than compliance by the lower-power party. This requires that at least one more conditionalization principle be added to the theory.

In conclusion, two forms of theory growth actually come together in the punitive power branch. Each theory—bilateral deterrence and conflict spiral—is developed in part as a "theoretical elaboration" of earlier ideas about threats and damage in conflict; at the same time, each theory constitutes a variant of the other, addressing the same research problems with the same concepts but with different predictions (see Wagner and Berger 1985, for a similar conclusion about this program). We have specified more precisely the type of "theoretical variation" found in the program (i.e., friendly competition) and also shown the importance of certain metatheoretical elements (i.e., the metatheoretical core) to theory growth.

A Theoretical Convergence

Each branch of our theoretical research program—power dependence and punitive power—developed somewhat independently. However, a similar set of orienting assumptions and an identical metatheoretical core provided a series of unifying themes tying the branches together. Recently, a convergence of the branches has been formulated (see Lawler 1992). The theoretical convergence is organized around the metatheoretical core; in fact, it is probably the case that an explicit metatheoretical core was necessary to foster a convergence at this point in the program.

The theoretical convergence is captured by two core propositions that have emerged from the theoretical and empirical work. Based on the metatheoretical core, one proposition deals with total power and the other with relative power or power differences, as follows:

Total Power Proposition. Given equal power between two parties in bargaining, higher levels of total power in the relationship will decrease hostility and increase conciliation.

Relative Power Proposition. Given that each party has a "significant" amount of absolute power, a relationship with unequal power will produce more hostility and less conciliation than a relationship with equal power.

The propositions apply to both dependence and punitive forms of power and incorporate both types of power use tactics (hostile and conciliatory). These are core propositions in the sense that they express the most central and basic ideas of the theoretical research program. The core propositions also can integrate ideas from the larger power dependence and deterrence literatures. Next, we discuss how the convergence pulls together implications of diverse literatures and, thereby, poses new issues.

The Total Power Proposition is consistent with Richard Emerson's power dependence theory and also selected theorizing on deterrence in international contexts (Emerson 1972; Morgan 1977; Blalock 1989; Lawler 1992). In Emerson's terms, total power constitutes the level of mutual dependence or "relational cohesion" in the relationship. Higher total power in a relation essentially produces an increase in the opportunity costs associated with leaving the relation (Lawler and Bacharach 1987; Lawler 1992). With higher total power, parties have a larger stake in the bargaining and, more specifically, in bringing it to a reasonable conclusion. One obvious implication from the power dependence branch of our program is that bargaining in relationships with higher, rather than lower, total power generally should be more cooperative and produce more mutually satisfactory agreements. While counterexamples to this general pattern might be identified, this is the basic idea implied by power dependence theory (Emerson 1972).

The punitive power branch extends the Total Power Proposition to coercive or punitive capabilities. Indirect support for this extension can be found in one part of the deterrence literature on international relations, in particular, research dealing with war or warlike action in bilateral and multilateral power systems. From this literature, if two or more parties develop and maintain high levels of coercive power (i.e., capability to damage each other), then each will not use that capability or use it less frequently, because they fear the costs of retaliation by another. This is termed a "general deterrence" process by Morgan (1977), and it receives some (though certainly not universal) support in research on international relations (e.g., Thompson 1986; Houweling and Siccama 1988). Interestingly, from both the power dependence and bilateral deterrence formulations, the primary reason higher total power in a relation produces less use of that power is the cost associated with power use, i.e., opportunity costs for power dependence and retaliation costs for bilateral deterrence.

In the case of the comparison of equal and unequal power, the core proposition subscribes to the view that relationships with unequal power tend to be less stable than ones with equal power. A major reason, particularly important in explicit bargaining, is dissensus over the legitimacy of the power differences or, specifically, whether and how such differences should affect the negotiated solution. With an unequal power relationship, the disadvantaged party may resist agreements that reflect his or her power differences, and the advantaged party may firmly advocate exactly those agreements that provide a payoff advantage proportional to his or her power advantage (Bacharach and Lawler 1981a: Chapter 6; Lawler 1992).

Certain aspects of explicit bargaining should accentuate the tension generated by unequal power. The mutual consent typical of explicit bargaining should give the lower-power actor a rationale for pushing for agreements that are more equal than the power in the relationship; the structural, intergroup nature of the bargaining context should increase the constituent pressure toward unequal agreements in the case of the higher-power actor. As Lawler (1992) recently argued, if power capabilities are unequal and parties agree to engage in explicit bargaining, then the legitimacy of the power difference is likely to be contested. This should complicate the issues or agenda faced by the actors and, thus, reduce the prospects for conflict resolution.

Emerson's analysis of power balance (i.e., power equality) complements the analysis of unequal power in Lawler's (1986) theory of bilateral deterrence. Emerson's (1962, 1972) formulation suggests that balance occurs over time through one or both of the following processes: (1) continual power use by the higher-power actor reduces the dependence of the lower-power actor, and/or (2) power change tactics by the lower-power actor increase the dependence of the higher-power party or decrease his or her own dependence. Implicitly, it is *power use* tactics by the higher-power actor and *power change* tactics by the lower-power actor that underlie the movement toward power equality over time.

While Emerson's principles of power balance provide an explanation for the instability or change of unequal power relations across a series of negotiations, Lawler's (1986) bilateral deterrence theory accounts for instability in the short term or within a particular bargaining episode. This instability is reflected in the tendency of both actors in an unequal power relationship to use power, but for somewhat different reasons. As indicated earlier, the higher-power actor will respond more to his or her lower fear of retaliation, and the lower-power actor will respond more to his or her greater expectation of attack by the other. Overall, and in combination, power dependence and bilateral deterrence theories might account for power use tactics (i.e., ones that assume a given power relation) and also power change tactics (i.e., ones that attempt to change the power relationship). Bilateral deterrence theory seems to capture a basic process embedded in power dependence relations, and power dependence captures the importance of the larger power struggle within which bilateral deterrence processes affect particular negotiations.

The theoretical convergence brings to the forefront some new theoretical issues. First, since the distinct effects of relative and total power have been pulled apart and isolated, more work is now needed on the joint effects. Clearly, these facets of power capability have some sort of joint or interactive effect on power use. Second, given the empirical support for bilateral deterrence and the parallels between bilateral deterrence and power dependence processes, how might each theory contribute to the other? Bilateral deterrence could capture the logic underlying the relational cohesion effects suggested by Emerson, and the power dependence relation may determine whether bilateral deterrence effects occur (e.g., Bacharach and Lawler 1981a; Molm 1989; Lawler, Ford, and Blegen 1988). As will be evident in the next section, work on the first issue is further along than work on the second issue.

Incipient Theoretical Directions

The theoretical convergence and related nonzero-sum conception of power are the basis for several emerging theoretical efforts. In accord with Figure 1, we treat these as incipient extensions or elaborations of prior branches, one on power change tactics and one on power use tactics. The power change variant is an elaboration of the power dependence branch, and the power use variant is an elaboration of the punitive power branch. In each case, there is at least one new theoretical question underlying the extension and each (if successful) would produce simultaneously two forms of theoretical growth in Wagner and Berger's (1985) terms, i.e., elaboration within each branch and proliferations from the theoretical convergence. An elaboration adds scope precision or rigor while proliferants involve distinct explanatory domains.

Power Change

The power change proliferant is an effort to develop notions about power struggle implicit in Emerson's (1962, 1972) formulation. The primary purpose is to take the concept of total power and address the following question: When will tactics of power change, designed to gain individual advantage, produce structural changes in the power relationship? Contingent on the nature of these changes, the prospects of conflict resolution should become better or worse in future episodes of bargaining.

The initial proposition is as follows:

Power-Struggle Proposition. If parties have an ongoing relationship, in which conflict and bargaining occur regularly, they will strive to improve their power position by either increasing their own absolute power or decreasing the other's absolute power (Lawler 1992).

Such efforts by actors to improve their power positions are termed a "power struggle." Given this proposition, any continuing relationship in which conflict and bargaining occur is likely to be somewhat unstable over time, regardless of whether it is balanced or imbalanced in Emerson's (1962, 1972) terms. Structural balance will not eliminate each actor's incentive to seek an advantageous power position, and, therefore, Emerson's condition of power balance is vulnerable to the same sort of problem found with mutual cooperation in an iterative prisoner's dilemma game (Blalock 1989; Lawler 1992).

The key to understanding the effects of power struggle on the prospects of conflict resolution is the concept of "total power." This is the nonzero-sum aspect of power dependence, and either actor can improve his or her power position in the long run by (1) decreasing his or her own dependence or (2) increasing the opponent's dependence (Bacharach and Lawler 1980; Lawler and Bacharach 1986; Lawler 1992). These are two major classes of power change tactics, and each constitutes a tactic for gaining individual advantage. However, if we assume that both actors in a two-party conflict want to improve their power position and both have these same options, the joint effects of their tactics are of particular importance. If both actors successfully decrease their own dependence by developing alternative outcome sources, then the total power in the relation (i.e., mutual dependence) will decline and the conflicting issues should be more difficult to resolve as they emerge over time. In contrast, if each party successfully increases the other's dependence on him or her, then total power in the relation will increase and, correspondingly, so will the structural pressures toward conflict resolution when bargaining occurs. Thus, a key concept of our theoretical approach, derived from the metatheoretical core, has important implications for the new question about power struggle. If actors in an ongoing relationship repeatedly and effectively use the same class of power change tactics, then their individual efforts to gain advantage will change the structure of the power relationship. Depending on the nature of these changes, the result will be an integrative or disintegrative impact on the relationship (see Bacharach and Lawler 1980; Lawler and Bacharach 1986; Lawler 1992).

The impact of power struggle on changes in structural power raises a larger question about the integrative or cohesive effects of power dependence relations (Lawler and Yoon 1990). Recall that Emerson (1972) put forth, without much development, the notion that greater mutual dependence (or total power, in our terms) increases the relational cohesion within a dyad. In a recent theoretical analysis, Lawler and Yoon (1990) offered a modification of Emerson's notion, treating it as a joint function of both a larger total and lower difference of power within the relation. One key idea is that *if total power in a relation increases and also the power difference decreases, then greater commitment will develop in that relation.* Greater commitment implies easier negotiations and more satisfactory agreements (Lawler and Yoon 1990). This revised concept of relational cohesion could expand the analysis of power struggle to take account of how power change tactics simultaneously affect both the total power and power difference in the relation.

Power Use

The power use proliferant is an effort to work further on the conditionalization of conflict spiral theory and also the bilateral deterrence analysis of unequal power. Despite the fact that research has supported the predictions of bilateral deterrence theory over conflict spiral, it would be premature to reject conflict spiral theory at this time. In fact, to reject it would be inconsistent with the idea of friendly competition. Friendly competition capitalizes on a common metatheory by pitting against each other contradictory predictions from theories with virtually identical assumptions. "Competition" in this sense leads not to "critical tests" with a primary object of rejecting one of the theories, but rather to comparative tests designed to ferret out a set of conditions under which the theories hold. Conditionalization is one important way for friendly competition to stimulate theoretical growth (e.g., Cohen 1980).

Our efforts to conditionalize the theories, at this point, focus on the incentives associated with the initiation of an attack. Based on the salience assumption discussed earlier, the main proposition is as follows:

Incentive-Mediation Proposition. If power use (i.e., initiating damage) provides a direct, unmediated benefit to the user, then greater total power in the relationship will increase power use (i.e., a conflict spiral effect); whereas if the benefit to be derived from power use is mediated by the response of the other, then greater total power in the relationship will decrease power use (i.e., a bilateral deterrence effect).

Tactics that redistribute outcomes, such as taxes, tariffs, and fees, exemplify actions that not only damage the outcomes of another, but provide a direct benefit to the party using the tactic. Outcome reduction tactics, such as strikes, work slowdowns, and war, exemplify tactics that may provide indirect benefits, mediated by the response of the opponent. The rationale is that an incentive involving a direct, unmediated benefit will enhance temptation to use power.

Turning to the other conditionalization issue (i.e., the impact of unequal power in bilateral deterrence theory), we raise the question: Under what conditions will a lower-power actor in a conflict use power to resist the higher-power party? The prediction of bilateral deterrence indicating that lower-power actors will use power as much as higher-power actors is quite provocative, because it contradicts the conventional wisdom expressed by substantial social psychological and political science work (see Rubin and Brown 1975; Morgan 1977; and Blalock 1989). Our hunch is that the magnitude of the lower-power actor's absolute power is critical to the effect of bilateral deterrence. The conventional notion that the lower-power actor complies or submits often has been investigated with rather low levels of power available to the lower-power actor.

In conclusion, the agenda embedded in the incipient theoretical directions identifies two elaborations of the power dependence branch—power struggle and relational cohesion—and two elaborations of the punitive power branch. The agenda also suggests that our work is far from complete. It should be clear that the metatheoretical core and strategy of "friendly competition" will continue to have an important role as we more explicitly analyze power change tactics and explore further the relationships between bilateral deterrence, conflict spiral, and power dependence theories.

Conclusion

The theoretical research program described here is an effort to understand and explain the impact of a structurally based power capability on the use of that power in two-party bargaining. The program brings together diverse strands of thought on this relationship. At the outset, we identified two themes to be developed. The first was the importance of metatheory to theoretical growth. We argue that a metatheory shapes theoretical content in subtle ways and contributes to theoretical growth by orienting theoretical efforts and resolving key conceptual issues. The second was to show how "friendly competition" among theories with a common metatheoretical foundation can stimulate more precise theorizing and raise important issues of conditionalization.

Role of Metatheory

In developing our general argument about the role of metatheory, we distinguished "orienting assumptions" from the "metatheoretical core" and showed how the explication of the metatheoretical core of a program can bring it unity, focus, and clear direction. Orienting assumptions cut a wide pathway across a theoretical landscape, whereas conceptual twists of the metatheoretical core settle on a particular route within the pathway. The distinction between orienting assumptions and a metatheoretical core is a heuristic one. The general message for theoretical research programs is that by identifying and making explicit those ideas that link theories to their metatheoretical parentage, we can clarify concepts, raise new questions, and bridge the disparate branches in a program. In our particular program, the metatheoretical core accomplished these purposes and also laid the groundwork for a theoretical convergence, now serving as a reference point for new theoretical efforts.

This example of a theoretical research program leaves two kinds of questions about the role of metatheory incompletely resolved. The first stems from the fact that the nonzero-sum conception in the metatheoretical core developed partially from rather subtle implications of research findings in the power dependence branch. These implications easily could have been missed. The question is: Under what conditions will feedback from empirical work to the underlying metatheory stimulate theoretical growth, as it did in this particular case? Is it helpful to examine findings produced by a theory-driven research program periodically from the broader metatheoretical standpoint? Aside from making tacit assumptions clear, this sort of theoretical activity could produce new insights or problems for systematic theoretical analysis.

A second question concerns the role of a "metatheoretical core" in theoretical research programs. In the program we studied, it was obviously critical, but is this necessarily applicable to all programs? Are there properties of our program that made this part of a metatheory particularly important? While we would argue that every theoretical research program has a metatheoretical core and would benefit from its explication, we wouldn't necessarily suggest it will produce the same level of benefit as it did for this program. For instance, it is possible that explication of the metatheoretical core is most helpful to programs attempting to integrate ideas from a wide variety of sources. For such programs, the metatheoretical core may introduce the focus necessary to permit more precise theorizing. Our program certainly had an explicit integrative purpose at the outset, and one can argue that it was insufficiently focused until we developed the metatheoretical core more explicitly.

Friendly Competition

Our other major theme was to illustrate how "friendly competition," as a strategy of theoretical development, stimulated the punitive power branch of the theoretical research program. In brief, friendly competition is a form of "theoretical variation" (Wagner and Berger 1985) in which the difference between two theories is substantial, because they make directly opposite predictions about some central part of a social process. Each theory has a common metatheory (i.e., the same orienting assumptions and metatheoretical core); each has the same concepts with identical definitions; and the theoretical structures are virtually identical. The difference lies in the predicted relationship between a key independent variable and the primary dependent variable; and this difference is traceable to some part of the explanation for that relationship. That is, differences in explanation lead to a divergent prediction about the relationship of key independent and dependent variables.

In terms of our program, several points are worth emphasizing. First, without a common metatheoretical core, it is unlikely that the precise contrast of bilateral deterrence and conflict spiral theories could have been accomplished. The contrasting implications of different lines of social psychological work (Deutsch and Krauss vs. Tedeschi) had gone unnoticed, and it was the metatheoretical core that suggested the relevant questions and the most important independent and dependent variables. Thus, we infer that friendly competition can occur primarily when there is a common metatheoretical core. Second, each theory—bilateral deterrence and conflict spiral—seems most useful in juxtaposition to the other. The contradiction, alone, sharpens and makes the theories more precise, thereby facilitating the "elaboration" of each theory. The implication is that if theoretical research programs self-consciously develop contrasting accounts or explanations for those specified in the program, each theoretical account may benefit from the contrast. In friendly competition, neither theory is treated as a "straw man," because elaboration efforts are meant to produce parallel development. Parallel development should engender further theoretical growth in the form of conditionalization or convergence.

In comparison to Wagner and Berger's (1985) notion of theoretical variation, the strategy of "friendly competition" emphasizes a bit more the importance of a common metatheoretical foundation, in particular an identical metatheoretical core, and explicit efforts at parallel development. In addition, the difference between the theories in question becomes more significant, given that an opposite prediction is made on a central theoretical question. Yet our analysis is intended not to suggest a new category of theory growth, but only to specify an important subcategory within Wagner and Berger's (1985) concept of theoretical variation. Friendly competition should be distinguished from other forms of "variation" on the basis of (1) how central the contradictory prediction is to both theories, (2) the existence of an identical metatheoretical core, and (3) parallel development of two theories.

To conclude, we have analyzed one program in which we have a substantial investment. Our investment could, of course, color our analysis; and the fact that we have only a single case could limit the applicability of what we have learned to other programs. However, we offer both examples of growth that can be compared with examples from other programs, and we suggest some conceptual ideas for interpreting our program that should help to interpret the growth found in some other programs as well. Using the Wagner and Berger (1985) approach, we demonstrate the role of metatheory in theory growth and the importance of friendly competition as a form of theoretical variation.

PART IV

Theoretical Research Programs:
Justice, Structural Power, and Legitimacy

Nisi Dominus aedificaverit domum,
in vanum laboraverunt qui aedificant eam.
—Psalmus 126

Sonnet 29

When, in disgrace with Fortune and men's eyes,
I all alone beweep my outcast state,
And trouble deaf heaven with my bootless cries,
And look upon myself and curse my fate,
Wishing me like to one more rich in hope,
Featured like him, like him with friends possessed,
Desiring this man's art, and that man's scope,
With what I most enjoy contented least;
Yet in these thoughts myself almost despising,
Haply I think on thee, and then my state,
Like to the lark at break of day arising
From sullen earth, sings hymns at heaven's gate;
   For thy sweet love rememb'red such wealth brings
   That then I scorn to change my state with kings.
—William Shakespeare

Building the Theory of Comparison Processes: Construction of Postulates and Derivation of Predictions

Guillermina Jasso

1. Introduction

We begin with first principles. The goal of sociology is to accumulate reliable knowledge about behavioral and social phenomena. To achieve that goal, we use the scientific method. Accordingly, we operate on two fronts—a theoretical front and an empirical front. Both theoretical knowledge and empirical knowledge are required for command over a field of phenomena.

With respect to theory growth—the subject of the conference for which this paper was written—we may distinguish between the growth of *theoretical knowledge* and the growth of *a theory*, the latter being a special case of the former. The purpose of a scientific theory is to yield testable propositions concerning the relationships among observable phenomena. Given that a theory is a structure consisting of two parts— the first part containing the assumptions or postulates and the second part containing the predictions deduced from the postulates—assessing the growth of a theory means assessing the growth of each of the two parts. The more general problem of assessing the growth of theoretical knowledge encompasses not only assessment of the growth of *a theory* but also investigation of the connections among the postulate sets and prediction sets of *two or more* theories. For example, while assessment of the growth of *a theory* may focus on growth in the number of predictions derived from a set of postulates, assessment of the growth of *theoretical knowledge* may focus on the connections between theories, such as, for example (1) the case where the postulate part of one theory becomes the prediction part of another theory, or (2) the case where the postulate parts of two theories, when combined, yield an entirely new set of predictions to add to the prediction sets of the two separate theories. The task of investigating processes of the growth of theoretical knowledge has received ground-breaking attention in a recent paper by Wagner and Berger (1985).*

This paper examines the growth of one theory, the theory of comparison processes. The theory describes the operation of the fundamental human impulse to compare oneself to others—more precisely, to compare the amounts or levels of the goods and bads received in social allocations and in the natural lottery to the amounts or levels deemed just or desirable for oneself—an impulse generating a class of comparison-based sentiments and judgments, including happiness, satisfaction, well-being, self-esteem, relative deprivation, and distributive justice. Formal description of the elementary comparison process enables derivation of a large number and variety of predictions for a wide range of social and behavioral phenomena.

We begin, in Section 2, with a few general remarks concerning the question of how a theory grows. To systematize the results of theoretical work, we develop two record-keeping devices; we call these Merton Charts, in honor of Robert K. Merton, who has long advocated codification of theoretical work in social science. Section 3 reviews briefly the growth to date of comparison theory. To illustrate the theory's growth, Section 4 reports two new sets of derivations. Section 5 discusses some practical matters concerned with testing the theory. A short note concludes the paper.

2. How Does a Theory Grow?

Growth of a theory refers to growth of the theory's assumption set and prediction set. Because a key goal of theoretical work is to minimize the size of the assumption set and to maximize the number and variety of the predictions, the term "growth" must be interpreted differently for each of the two parts.

With respect to the postulate part, in the early phase of a theory's development, the number of postulates may grow until it reaches a size sufficient to facilitate abundant prediction. But, as understanding grows, it may become clear that some of the postulates are unnecessary (for example, being themselves implied by other postulates). And, thus, we may say that *the growth curve of the postulate part of a theory is nonmonotonic, at first increasing, subsequently decreasing.*

---

*Of course, assessment of the growth of *scientific knowledge* requires assessment of the growth of both *theoretical knowledge* and *empirical knowledge*. Assessing the growth of scientific knowledge thus must attend very particularly to the empirical testing of predictions derived from theories. For analysis of the testing process, see Popper (1935, 1963), Kuhn (1962), and Lakatos (1970), and for brief discussion, Jasso (1989a).

In contrast, the prediction part of the theory must increase without limit. Moreover, not only is quantitative growth required but so also is qualitative growth, in particular, the continual derivation of novel predictions—predictions for phenomena and relationships not yet observed.* Thus, we may say that *the growth curve of the prediction part of a theory is increasing, and so also is the growth curve of the subset containing novel predictions.*

It is obvious that growth of the prediction part of a theory presupposes a postulate part. It is less obvious that growth of the postulate part presupposes a wealth of insights and pre-postulate propositions. The initial postulate(s) must come from somewhere; often they come from a distinguished history of thought about a field of phenomena. Because thinking about the human condition, as thinking about physical nature, antedates development of tools for reasoning—of logic and mathematics—there exists an abundance of insights and propositions that are not formally expressed and that, indeed, may be quite hidden. The theorist searching through such insights often encounters or unearths some likely candidates for postulates. Other times, a postulate arrives in full dress; but note that even in such cases, the postulate's relationship to earlier insights can often be precisely mapped.

The collection of insights and early propositions may be called the *foundation* of a theory. This foundation often begins with a list of questions, which can be condensed to a few central questions. Each question may be accompanied by attempts to answer it in words. Formalization begins when the answers to the questions are represented in a formal language—notably as a set of equations. At this early stage the equations may be written in a general manner that assumes nothing. Once an assumption is made, the equation has become a postulate. The temporal sequence of these activities may be quite jagged. It is possible, for example, that one question may, in short order, receive first a verbal answer, second a general-function answer, third a specific-function answer—where the specific function makes assumptions not made by the general function. Concomitantly, other important questions may become lodged at the general-function stage, with no new insights on the horizon to enable passage to a specific function.

Accordingly, at any given time, a particular field will have a variety of ongoing theoretical investigations. Some scientists will be working on a question whose development is at the general-function stage; others will be deducing predictions from postulates; still others will be attempting to craft postulates more fundamental than those in the current inventory.

*For lucid discussion of the requirement that a theory predict novel facts, see Lakatos (1970).

With such varied activities at hand, it would seem most useful to follow the advice proffered by Merton almost a half century ago and *codify* the results of theoretical work.* To that end, Jasso (1988b) proposed the use of "Merton Charts" as outlines of current theoretical knowledge. As part of the work undertaken for the present paper, two such Charts have been developed. These are in a preliminary stage and will no doubt undergo many changes before a sizable group of theorists find them useful enough to adopt as part of routine record-keeping. Both Charts are titled "Merton Chart of Theoretical Codification." The first, reproduced here as Table 1, is subtitled "Chart One: Foundations, Formalizations, and Unsolved Problems"; it contains space to write the central questions of the field, together with space to write the current formal answers to the questions as well as the current research agenda, including the major unsolved problems. The second, shown as Table 2, is subtitled "Chart Two: The State of the Theory"; it is organized as a "spreadsheet" with "Postulates" as the column designator and "Predictions" as the row designator, so that for each prediction one may mark which postulates were used in its derivation. Chart Two, if fully filled out (as of a given date), would tell at a glance which postulates are "productive" and which not, and which predictions are "expensive" and which not. Both Charts have a final section, "Notes."

Note that each Chart may require extensive supplementary pages, containing definitions, proofs, references, etc. Notwithstanding the importance of full documentation, we believe that the most useful Chart will be the simplest one. Note also that this manner of codifying the state of a field generates many new questions, both substantive and formal. For example, the simple fact, in a theory's Chart One, that the current answer to a central question remains a general function proposed twenty years earlier may stimulate a fresh search for a specific function. Similarly, the visual information, in a theory's Chart Two, that a given postulate is seldom used may lead to recognition of its limited tractability or of the need for new tools and thereby generate mathematical advances. Finally, note that using these Charts may suggest many important modifications in the Chart forms.

For a workable Chart, it is necessary to have a form that can be easily generated or printed and that the working theorist can fill out, at the beginning and at the end of a project—thereby answering the question,

---

*A reading of the work of Merton and Lazarsfeld (and a remembrance of the things each emphasized in seminars and informal conversations during the early 1970's at Columbia University) suggests that, while both advocated codification, Merton championed the cause of theoretical codification and Lazarsfeld that of empirical codification. A notable early example of empirical codification is Berelson and Steiner's (1964) *Human Behavior: An Inventory of Scientific Findings*.

Theory:_____   Date:_____

Page:_____

I.   FOUNDATIONS

II.   FORMALIZATIONS

III.   UNSOLVED PROBLEMS

NOTES:

TABLE 2
Merton Chart of Theoretical Codification

CHART TWO: THE STATE OF THE THEORY

*Theory:*_____				*Date:*_____	
				*Page:*_____	

PREDICTIONS	POSTULATES				

NOTES:

What have I learned? What do I now know that I did not know when I started this work?—or may consult when curious or when inspiration strikes. Note that it would be straightforward to write a computer program that automatically repeated the Chart shell at the top of each page (dating and paginating each), so that the length of each section could be variable.

3. Tracing the Growth of Comparison Theory

3.1 Preliminaries

This paper focuses on the theory of comparison processes. As discussed in Jasso (1988b, 1989a) and following classical thought, we believe it may be useful to regard all observed human behavioral and social phenomena as the product of the joint operation of several basic forces. From this perspective, we may think of comparison processes as possibly constituting one of these ultimate engines of behavior. Of course, it is possible that comparison processes are not fundamental but rather arise from the interplay of yet more basic forces.*

Even if comparison turns out to be a basic force, it is only one basic force. Thus, it is useful for the theorist (and the reader) to keep in mind the limitations inherent in comparison theory—as in any theory of a single force or process. In particular, note that all predictions of comparison theory are *ceteris paribus* predictions; observed phenomena will reflect the operation not only of comparison processes but also of other basic forces.

The multiforce perspective tempers the claims that might be made for comparison theory. It also underscores both the larger theoretical challenge—to identify the basic forces and describe their operation—and the empirical challenge—to discern in observed phenomena the interplay of the basic forces.†

3.2. Growth of the Postulate Part of Comparison Theory

3.2.1. The Classical Idea of Comparison. The Mertonian starting idea for comparison theory is the classical insight, discussed as early as Genesis and the classical Greeks and formalized in the work of Marx (1849), William James (1891), and Durkheim (1893, 1897), that humans compare

---

*See Jasso (1989a, 1989b), for brief discussion of this matter. Jasso (1989b: 383) also lists four candidates for basic forces governing human behavioral and social phenomena.

†It could be said, paradoxically, that the more absorbed one is in working with a particular theory, the more pressing appears the need for new theories of new forces; similarly, the more engaged one is in theoretical work, the greater the importance one attaches to empirical work.

their attributes and possessions to those of others and/or to some desired
or expected level and thereby experience particular magnitudes of well-
being, self-esteem, happiness, relative deprivation, and the sense of being
justly or unjustly treated in the distributions of the natural and social
goods.* As would be expected, pertinent literatures include both the literature on comparison per se and the literatures on the sentiments and
judgments generated by comparison activities. Though all these literatures are densely intertwined, we shall attempt to isolate some strands in
this brief sketch.

The modern development of comparison theory begins with a trio of
nineteenth-century accounts describing how satisfaction, self-esteem,
and happiness are generated by comparison processes. The first account
we owe to Marx (1849) who, in the celebrated thought-experiment on
the hut and the palace, argued that satisfaction arises as the outcome of a
comparison, specifically comparison of one's material possessions to the
material possessions of others. Next, William James (1891) proposed a
formulation in which self-esteem is produced by the comparison of a
person's actual holding of a good to the desired amount or level of that
good. Finally, Durkheim (1893) argued that happiness arises from comparison with others.

These three classic analyses have had a profound effect on twentieth-
century social science, as noted by Merton and A. Rossi (1950) and Merton (1957, 1967). A rich variety of applications, formalizations, and extensions will be found in Stouffer et al. (1949), Festinger (1954), Thibaut
and Kelley (1959), Homans (1961), Runciman (1961), Wright (1963),
Blau (1964), Berger et al. (1972), Emerson (1972), Cook (1975), Sprague
(1977), and Goode (1978). Further evidence of the importance of the
founding formulations comes from the several review articles in the *International Encyclopedia of the Social Sciences* that invoke them. For example, Lipset's (1968: 312) article on social stratification quotes Marx's
account of the hut and the palace; Hyman's (1968: 354) article on reference groups and Sherif's (1968: 157) article on the self concept utilize
James's reasoning; and Zelditch's (1968: 253–54) article on social status
treats as a vital foundational account Durkheim's comparison-based formulation of happiness.

As shown in Jasso (1988b), the central elements in the starting idea can
be formalized as the Received Axiom of Comparison, which specifies the
class Z of human individual phenomena which are produced by the comparison of an Actual Holding (A) of a good to a Comparison Holding

---

*For discussion of the part played by a "starting idea" (to use Merton's apt phrase) in
the construction of a theory, see Merton (1967) and the commentary in Jasso (1988b).

(C) of that good, such that Z is an increasing function of A and a decreasing function of C:

$$Z = Z(A,C), \quad \partial Z/\partial A > 0, \quad \partial Z/\partial C < 0. \tag{1}$$

Thus, the insights of Marx, James, and Durkheim can be straightforwardly expressed as a general mathematical function, a function that makes claims only about the direction of the effects of the two arguments.

3.2.2. Developments in the Theory of Distributive Justice. Meanwhile, work on the positive theory of distributive justice, spearheaded by the theoretical formulations of Homans (1961) and of Berger et al. (1972) and by the inductive empirical explorations of P. Rossi and his associates (Jasso and Rossi 1977; Jasso 1978; Alves and Rossi 1978; Alves 1982), led to two new developments.* The first was the growing recognition that the scientific problems of distributive justice and equity could be reduced to three sets of questions, questions whose answers could be represented by equations, each feature of each equation (variables, parameters, functional form, subscripts) addressing a specific question; Jasso (1978: 1400, 1417–18) provides a brief statement of the three central questions and Jasso (1989b) a comprehensive elaboration of the three-equation framework. The second development was an axiomatization of distributive justice processes, an axiomatization whose key postulate, the Postulate of the Logarithmic Specification of the Justice Evaluation Function, specifies the function that combines the Actual Reward and the Just Reward to produce the Justice Evaluation; the logarithmic specification was proposed in Jasso (1978) and initial statement of the developing axiomatization appeared in Jasso (1980).

3.2.2.1. The three central questions of distributive justice. In the scientific study of the operation of distributive justice processes, three sets of questions are central:

1. What do individuals and collectivities think is just?

2. What is the magnitude of the perceived injustice associated with given departures from perfect justice?

3. What are the behavioral and social consequences of perceived injustice?

The three central questions are listed in the top panel of Table 3, which reports a recent attempt to describe in a Merton Chart One the foundations, formalizations, and unsolved problems of the theory of distributive justice.

Of course, each question is really a set of questions, encompassing

*For brief discussion of the distinctive questions posed, respectively, by normative and positive analyses of distributive justice, see Jasso (1978: 1399–1400).

TABLE 3

Merton Chart of Theoretical Codification

CHART ONE: FOUNDATIONS, FORMALIZATIONS, AND
UNSOLVED PROBLEMS

Theory: Distributive Justice   *Date*: 11 July 1989
                                   Page: 1

I. **FOUNDATIONS** -- <u>The Three Central Sets of Questions</u>

    1. What do individuals and collectivities think is just?

    2. What is the magnitude of the perceived injustice associated
        with given departures from perfect justice?

    3. What are the behavioral and social consequences of perceived
        injustice?

II. **FORMALIZATIONS**

    1. <u>**Just Holding Function**</u>

        $$JH_{brots} = h_{brots}(X_{brots}; B_{brots}),$$

where X denotes the vector of holding-relevant characteristics, B denotes a
parameter vector, h denotes the functional form, the subscripts *brots*
denote, respectively, the benefit/burden, the recipient, the observer, the
time period, and the society, and where the JH and the X may appear in
either cardinal or ordinal form.

    2. <u>**Justice Evaluation Function**</u>

        $$J_{brots} = \theta_{brots} \ln \frac{A}{C_{brots}},$$

where J denotes the justice evaluation, A denotes the Actual Holding, C
denotes the Just Holding (viz., Comparison Holding), θ denotes a constant
that transforms the experience of a justice evaluation to the expression
thereof, and the subscripts are as in the JHF.

    3. <u>**Justice Consequences Function**</u>

        $$\Xi_{brots} = \xi_{brots}[T_{brots}(J), \Gamma_{brots}, \tau_{brots}, G_{brots}; \epsilon_{brots}],$$

where Ξ denotes the behavioral or social consequence, ξ denotes the functional form, T denotes the transformation of J (e.g., absolute value of J or
an aggregation of J over persons, resources, time, etc.), Γ denotes a vector
of other factors relevant to Ξ, τ and G denote a parameter and parameter
vector, respectively, and ϵ denotes the stochastic disturbance.

TABLE 3 (*continued*)

| *Theory*: Distributive Justice | *Date*: 11 July 1989 |
| | *Page*: 2 |

III. CURRENT RESEARCH and UNSOLVED PROBLEMS

  1. Construct a postulate describing determination of the Just Holding. Reduce the number of unknowns in the Just Holding Function.

  2. Find theoretical reasoning to provide independent warrant for the logarithmic specification in the case of ordinal goods.

  3. Continue deriving predictions so as to build a library of testable propositions for the JCF class.

NOTES:

many subquestions and unsolved problems. Moreover, some of the questions in each set are related to questions in the other sets and related as well to the questions of other theories, that is, to the operation of other forces. For example, one of the important elements in distributive justice theory—the individual's Actual Reward, which aggregates to form the collectivity's actual distribution of resources—arises by the operation of other forces (forces which are studied in social stratification, biology, labor economics) and arrives to play a part in the second set of questions; at the same time, phenomena analyzed by the third set of questions include the alteration of actual rewards.

A comprehensive analysis of the three central questions in the scientific theory of distributive justice appears in Jasso (1989b). There it is shown that each of the three questions leads to a distinctive equation, so that the general theory of distributive justice may be formalized by a basic framework of three generalized equations. The three equations are shown in the second panel of Table 3.

The first equation—the Just Holding Function (JHF)—represents a formalized answer to the first set of questions, What do individuals and societies think is just? What is the just reward for an individual of specified characteristics? What is the just distribution of resources?

The Just Holding Function, which reduces to a Just Reward Function (JRF) in the case of a good, expresses the Just Holding of any good or bad as a function of relevant recipient characteristics:

$$\text{JHF:} \quad JH_{brots} = h_{brots}(X_{brots}; B_{brots}), \tag{2}$$

where X denotes the vector of holding-relevant characteristics, B denotes a parameter vector, h denotes the functional form, and the subscripts $brots$ denote, respectively, the benefit/burden, the recipient, the observer, the time period, and the society. Just Reward Functions were estimated empirically by Jasso and Rossi (1977), Jasso (1978), Alves and Rossi (1978), and Alves (1982).

Jasso (1983a) showed that the Just Reward Function is fully derivable from the verbal formulation of Berger et al. (1972). Given that Berger et al. (1972: 128) intended their formulation to encompass bads as well as goods, we may think of the more general Just Holding Function as similarly a formalization of Berger et al.'s (1972) work.

Jasso (1983a) also showed that there are strict connections between the Just Reward, the Just Reward Function, and the Just Reward Distribution—thereby establishing the links between the micro and macro principles of justice. For example, given the Just Reward Function and the distributions of the reward-relevant variables, the shape of the Just Reward Distribution is fully entailed.

The JHF may be expressed in cardinal, ordinal, or mixed cardinal-ordinal forms. Moreover, as described in Jasso (1981a, 1989b), the JHF may appear in a theoretical version or an observable version, and may be represented by a second-order version, as in the case where the arguments are not recipient characteristics but rather a magnitude of the Just Holding corresponding to another individual or to a parameter of a distribution.

The second equation in the second panel of Table 3—the Justice Evaluation Function—represents a formalized answer to the second central question, What is the magnitude of the injustice associated with specified departures from perfect justice?

Empirical analyses of justice judgments obtained by P. Rossi's method suggested a specification (Jasso 1978) in which the Justice Evaluation J varies as the logarithm of the ratio of the Actual Reward to the Just Reward:

$$J = \theta \ln \left(\frac{Actual\ Reward}{Just\ Reward} \right), \tag{3}$$

where θ is a positive real constant. The logarithmic specification has several good properties: First, it enables representation of J by the full real-number line, with zero representing the point of perfect justice, positive numbers representing degrees of unjust overreward, and negative numbers representing degrees of unjust underreward. Second, it quantifies the common human opinion that deficiency is felt more keenly than comparable excess. Moreover, the logarithmic specification makes it possible to link the heretofore disparate conceptions of the two major "schools" of distributive justice, Homans's (1961) notion that the Justice Evaluation involves a ratio (of the Actual Reward to the Just Reward) and Berger et al.'s (1972) notion that it involves a difference (between the Actual Reward and the Just Reward).

The logarithmic specification, though found empirically while analyzing factorial-survey data collected by P. Rossi's method, may be regarded as a natural development occurring in a line of notable developments: (1) Homans's (1961, 1976: 232–33) and Berger et al.'s (1972: 123–24) insight that there are three qualitative conditions—perfect justice, under-reward, and overreward—and that these correspond exactly to a relationship between what today we call the Actual Reward and the Just Reward; (2) Blau's (1964: 148) recognition that, holding expectations constant, as the Actual Reward increases, satisfaction increases at a decreasing rate (expressed in distributive justice terminology, that, holding constant the Just Reward, the second partial derivative of the Justice Evaluation with respect to the Actual Reward must be negative); (3) Berger et al.'s (1972:

143) explicit characterization of a three-category "reward state" variable whose three categories may be represented by the mathematical signs of zero, minus, and plus; and (4) Jasso and Rossi's (1977: 643–44) explicit representation of the Justice Evaluation variable by the full real-number line, with zero representing the point of perfect justice and the negative and positive segments representing, respectively, degrees of underreward and overreward.

Like the Just Holding Function, the Justice Evaluation Function (JEF) may be generalized to reflect the operation of the benefit/burden, recipient, observer, time period, and society:

$$\text{JEF:} \quad J_{brots} = \theta_{brots} \ln \left(\frac{A}{C_{brots}} \right), \tag{4}$$

where A denotes the actual amount or level of the benefit/burden, C denotes the just amount or level of the benefit/burden, and θ is a real constant whose sign indicates whether the subject of the Justice Evaluation is a good or a bad (positive in the case of a good, negative in the case of a bad) and whose magnitude transforms the experience of a Justice Evaluation into the expression thereof.

As will be seen in Section 3.2.3, recent theoretical work, reported in Jasso (1990a), has strengthened the foundation of the logarithmic specification of the Justice Evaluation Function for the case of cardinal goods/bads.

The third equation in the three-equation framework formalizes the operation of the Justice Evaluation and its transformations and aggregations in the determination of observable behavioral and social phenomena. This equation, called the Justice Consequences Function (JCF), is written

$$\text{JCF:} \quad \Xi_{brots} = \xi_{brots}[T_{brots}(J), \Gamma_{brots}; \tau_{brots}, G_{brots}; \epsilon_{brots}], \tag{5}$$

where Ξ denotes the behavioral or social consequence, ξ denotes the functional form, T denotes the transformation of J (for example, absolute value of J or an aggregation of J over persons, goods/bads, resources, time, etc.), Γ denotes a vector of other factors relevant to Ξ, τ and G denote a parameter and parameter vector, respectively, and ϵ denotes the stochastic disturbance. The equation is written with full subscripts for the benefit/burden, recipient, observer, time period, and society. Of course, appropriate parametrization may differ across the behavioral and social consequences of interest; for example, the specification of a social consequence would not be indexed over individuals.

A wide range of behavioral and social phenomena can be expressed as consequences of the sense of justice. For example, as discussed in Jasso

(1986b, 1987, 1989a, 1989b), the JCF formalization permits specification of both responsive and purposive behaviors.* Moreover, as also discussed in several papers, most fully in Jasso (1980, 1989b), the relevant transformation of J can be any transformation, including (1) parameters of the Distributive Justice Profile, which maps an individual's time series of Justice Evaluations, and (2) parameters of the instantaneous distribution of Justice Evaluations in a collectivity.

The final panel of Table 3 outlines the current research agenda. The tasks associated with the second and third questions/equations appear to be straightforward; for example, as we shall see below, the current postulate set is already capable of generating literally hundreds of predictions. In contrast, the task associated with the first question—to construct a postulate describing determination of the Just Reward—would appear to constitute a major unsolved problem.

3.2.2.2. Axiomatization of distributive justice. The goal of theoretical work is a theory. Given the bipartite structure of theory, the goal of foundational reasoning of the sort just summarized in Section 3.2.2.1 is to produce postulates. The foundational reasoning about the sense of distributive justice did just that, for it was quickly seen that the logarithmic specification of the Justice Evaluation Function provided an ideal postulate—an ideal starting point for a positive theory of distributive justice. Thus, the new Justice Evaluation Function proposed in Jasso (1978) became the cornerstone of the new theory proposed in Jasso (1980) and developed in subsequent papers.

The axiomatization which ensued provides a mathematical description of the process whereby individuals compare their holdings of the goods they value (such as beauty, intelligence, or wealth) to the holdings they deem just for themselves, experiencing a fundamental instantaneous magnitude of the *Justice Evaluation* (*J*), which captures their sense of being fairly or unfairly treated in the distributions of the natural and social goods. This process generalizes in (at least) two ways: (1) to include judgments about the justice or injustice of another person's situation, and (2) to include burdens as well as benefits. As in the classic

---

*See Coleman (1973) for what to my knowledge is the earliest discussion of the distinction between responsive and purposive behaviors. As discussed in Jasso (1989b: 384), Coleman (1973) distinguishes between "causal" models and "purposive" models, noting that what he terms "causal" model appears in psychology under the rubric of "stimulus-response" model—and hence Jasso's (1986b) use of the term "responsive" instead of "causal"—and that what he terms "purposive" model appears in psychology as "purposive action" model and in economics as an "optimizing" model. Closely related to the distinction between responsive and purposive phenomena is the distinction arising in econometrics between the "behavioral equations" and the "technical equations" of a simultaneous-equation model; Judge et al. (1985) provide useful exposition. Note, however, that we use the term "behavioral" to encompass both responsive and purposive phenomena.

literature, this instantaneous experience of being fairly or unfairly treated (or of another's being fairly or unfairly treated) in the distributions of the natural and social goods (and bads) is regarded as having the most wide-ranging and diverse consequences for virtually every area of human individual and social behavior.

Early efforts to deduce predictions from the Postulate of Logarithmic Specification alone indicated that, although predictions could be derived, their number would be few. Immediately attention focused on what appeared to be two main obstacles to the abundant generation of predictions; the first concerned the measurement properties of the good and the second the theorist's information, especially about the Just Reward. As will be reviewed below, the first of these problems—the problem of measuring ordinal goods—was described in Jasso (1980), which also proposed a procedure to deal with it. The second problem—the theorist's ignorance of an individual's Just Reward—was raised in several papers, beginning with Jasso (1980) and continuing with Soltan (1981), Cook and Messick (1983), Harris (1983), and Gartrell (1985); an initial, relatively restrictive procedure to deal with it was proposed in Jasso (1980) and elaborated in Jasso (1981a), and a new nonrestrictive and more satisfying procedure, of which the initial procedure is a special case, was proposed in Jasso (1986b).

It is obviously easy to measure the Actual Reward and the Just Reward when the good under consideration is a cardinal good, say, when the good is land, cattle, or wealth. But cardinal goods are not the only goods about which individuals experience the sense of distributive justice. Goods not susceptible of cardinal measurement—e.g., beauty, intelligence, athletic skill—also play important parts in the individual's justice life. Hence, a measurement rule was proposed (Jasso 1980), which states that additive, transferable goods are measured in their own units (the amount denoted by x), and non-additive, non-transferable goods are measured by the individual's relative rank $[i/(N + 1)]$ within a specially selected comparison group, where i denotes the rank-order statistic in ascending order of magnitude and N denotes the size of the group or population. Following Campbell (1921), we term the goods, respectively, quantity-goods and quality-goods. The population counterpart of $[i/(N + 1)]$ is α, which appears in the ordinal-outcome form of the Just Reward Function discussed above.*

Note that the measurement rule introduces the population size N as a factor in distributive justice processes. Thus, the theory will be able to

*Further analysis of the properties of goods and of goods sets is found in Jasso (1987, 1991a).

produce predictions concerning the effects of population size for a wide range of observable phenomena.

From the theorist's perspective, the original Justice Evaluation Function contains a second rather large problem: while the Actual Reward is easily observed, the Just Reward is not. Accordingly, the Just Reward must be recast in a more accessible form, if *a priori* work is to proceed. This recasting has followed two directions. The first is to make additional assumptions concerning the Just Reward. The second is to represent the Just Reward in a more tractable yet equivalent way.

Following the first direction, the Just Reward may be assumed to be either a constant or a variable quantity. If the Just Reward is assumed to be a constant, then the theorist may further assume its magnitude. For example, Jasso (1980) proposed a special case of the Justice Evaluation Function in which the Just Reward is fixed at equality. This procedure has the virtue of fidelity to many classic accounts—e.g., Plato, Cervantes, Simmel—but the obvious problem is that counterexamples abound, or, put differently, that its scope is restricted and not yet well defined.* Jasso (1981a) noted, in response to Sołtan (1981), that the Just Reward need not be fixed at equality but may be any constant, thus reducing somewhat the restrictiveness of the earlier special case.

If the Just Reward is assumed to be a variable, then the theorist has even further interesting alternatives, including that of assigning it a probability distribution and that of assigning it a correlation with the Actual Reward. For example, if the Actual Reward and the Just Reward are dependent, then the Just Reward is potentially expressible as a function of the Actual Reward—hence rendering the Just Reward knowable.

Of course, it is preferable to address the Just Reward problem without incorporating additional assumptions. A useful device by which the theorist can partially overcome the problems arising from ignorance of the Just Reward is that of representing it by an equivalent quantity. To this end, Jasso (1986b) proposed an identity representation of the Just Reward. This new representation, based on the fact that any value in the domain of a good—and hence any Just Reward—can be expressed as a transformation of the good's arithmetic mean, expresses JR as the product of the mean and an individual-specific parameter ϕ, where ϕ captures everything that is unknown about an individual's JR.

---

*The proposition that "justice is equality" can be traced back at least as far as Plato's *Gorgias* (where it appears as words of Socrates); lucid analyses include William James ([1891] 1952: 887) and Goode (1978: 349–56). For further discussion of this proposition and of Simmel's (1950) closely related sociability hypothesis, see Jasso (1980, 1988a). See also Blau (1960) and Blalock (1967), who conjecture that individual behavior might be responsive to the difference between the individual's rank on some attribute and the mean rank in the society.

The identity representation of the Just Reward possesses the additional virtue that it enables theoretical prediction of the effects of the mean's constituent factors, which in the case of a quantity-good are the sum S of the good and the population size N.*

Combining the logarithmic functional form, attentiveness to the type of good (quantity-good vs. quality-good), and the phi-including representation of the Just Reward yields the following goods-attentive formula for J:

$$J = \begin{cases} \theta \ln (xN/\phi S), & \phi > 0, \quad \text{quantity-good} \\ \theta \ln \{2i/[\phi (N + 1)]\}, & 0 < \phi < 2, \quad \text{quality-good} \end{cases} \quad (6)$$

Thus, the basic part of the postulate set contains three postulates—the logarithmic specification of the Justice Evaluation Function, the measurement rule for ordinal goods, and the identity representation of the Just Reward. This simple set is sufficient to generate literally hundreds of predictions.

Other postulates have been formulated and used, adding to the postulate part of the theory. These include the Postulate of Multi-Good Justice Evaluation, the Social Welfare Postulate, and the Social Cohesiveness Postulate (Jasso 1980, 1988a, 1989b, 1990a).

The Postulate of Multi-Good Justice Evaluation, proposed in Jasso (1980) and further discussed in Jasso (1981a, 1989b), states that the instantaneous J experienced about k goods is equal to the arithmetic mean of the corresponding single-good J scores:

$$J^* = (1/k) \Sigma J. \quad (7)$$

The Multi-Good Justice Evaluation J^* can be expressed in several equivalent ways, including statement as a weighted sum and, given the logarithmic form of J, a variety of statements highlighting geometric means of the Actual Reward, the Just Reward, and of the ratio of the Actual Reward to the Just Reward.

The Postulate of Social Welfare, proposed in Jasso (1980) and further discussed in Jasso (1982, 1991a, 1991b), states that the instantaneous Social Welfare SW experienced by a collectivity is equal to the expected value of the distribution of Justice Evaluations:

$$\text{Social Welfare} = E(J). \quad (8)$$

The Social Welfare, too, can be expressed in several equivalent ways, including a variety of statements highlighting the geometric means of the Actual Reward and of the Just Reward.

---

*As discussed in Jasso (1986b), assessment of the constraints imposed on theoretical prediction by ignorance of phi, under alternative characterizations of phi, becomes an integral component of distributive justice analysis.

The Postulate of Social Cohesiveness, proposed in Jasso (1980) and further discussed in Jasso (1983b, 1988a), states that the instantaneous Social Cohesiveness *COH* experienced by a collectivity is equal to the negative of the Gini's Mean Difference of the distribution of Justice Evaluations:

$$\text{Social Cohesiveness} = -GMD\ (\,J\,). \tag{9}$$

3.2.3 Convergence and Generalization. By early 1988 it had become clear that the axiomatization of distributive justice enabled derivation of a large number and variety of predictions for a wide range of behavioral and social phenomena. A sampler of predictions was published in Jasso (1988b). Momentum was on the side of continued theoretical derivation; it seemed that no matter what topic one thought of—monastic and mendicant institutions, eating disorders, gift and bequest behavior—distributive justice theory could produce some not uninteresting predictions.

But what if the foundation were defective? In particular, what if the Postulate of Logarithmic Specification turned out to possess no stronger warrant than ten other functional forms? This question had first been raised by Sołtan (1981); other colleagues raised it in seminars and in correspondence. Of course, many of the predictions did not require the logarithmic form, being derivable solely from the direction of the effects of the Actual Reward and the Just Reward, together with the identity representation of the Just Reward, which brings in the population size and wealth factors. Yet concern persisted.

Eventually, work on theoretical derivation was brought to a halt; and attention turned to the Justice Evaluation Function and its specification. As discussed in Jasso (1990a), it quickly became obvious that justification for the form of the Justice Evaluation Function must be obtained by theoretical methods; almost a decade earlier, Alwin et al. (1980) had suggested that it might be possible to theoretically derive the logarithmic specification.

Renewed investigation of the foundations of the Justice Evaluation Function quickly showed that the essential element of the Justice Evaluation Function was the *comparison* between the Actual Reward and the Just Reward. A rereading of the old texts—Berger et al. (1972: 122–24); Jasso and Rossi (1977: 647); Jasso (1978: 1400–1401, 1416–17); Jasso (1980: 5–6)—underscored the centrality of comparison. Accordingly, we were led to the view that the operation of distributive justice is a comparison process, and understanding it requires and entails understanding the more general comparison process. Thus, as described in Jasso (1990a), what began as a search for a functional form for the Justice Evaluation Function became a search for a functional form for comparison processes. And the Received Axiom of Comparison provided the new foundation for all comparison processes, including distributive justice.

Recognition that the operation of distributive justice shares fundamental elements with other comparison processes—with the production of happiness, well-being, and self-esteem—led quickly to the view that the axiomatization of distributive justice could serve as an axiomatization of the wider class of comparison processes. It became clear that (1) J is a special case of Z and the Just Holding a special case of the Comparison Holding; (2) Z, like J, can be aggregated over goods/bads, persons, and time; (3) the Comparison Holding, like the Just Holding, can benefit from the identity representation; and (4) Z's, too, arise from ordinal as well as cardinal goods and bads. Accordingly, the basic axiomatization was restated in terms of comparison, as shown in Table 4. For simplicity, Table 4 omits the Multi-Good and Social Cohesiveness Postulates, although, of course, they too belong in the new theory of comparison processes.

It also quickly became evident that the Axiom of Comparison could be generalized to include bads as well as goods. Panel A of Table 5 reports the statement of the Generalized Axiom of Comparison.

The search for a functional form for the general comparison function began with a rereading of the literature on comparison processes, with the goal of finding conditions that the admissible functional form must satisfy. This search produced five conditions, three of which—a zero point for the Z variable, additivity, scale-invariance—had stronger warrant than the other two. Of these, scale-invariance pertained only to cardinal holdings. These conditions were expressed mathematically, in the form of partial differential equations and a calibration restriction, shown in panel B of Table 5. Solution of the resultant systems of partial differential equations, subject to the inequality restrictions in the Received Axiom of Comparison, indicates that the three most basic of the further conditions constrain the functional form to the logarithmic family, for comparison processes involving cardinal goods and bads; the two conditions applicable to comparisons of relative ranks constrain the admissible functional form to the more general family, $[\,f(A) - f(C)\,]$, of which the logarithmic form is a special case. The Z function includes a multiplicative constant—the Signature Constant θ, which by its sign indicates whether the subject of the comparison is a good or a bad and by its magnitude transforms the experience of Z into the expression thereof. These results are expressed as a theorem and proof, shown in panels C and D of Table 5.

As so often happens in science, solving one problem has generated new problems. An interesting new question that arises concerns the

TABLE 4

Basic Elements of the Theory of Comparison Processes

A. RECEIVED AXIOM OF COMPARISON

$$Z = Z(Actual Holding, Comparison Holding)$$

where

$$\frac{\partial Z}{\partial A} > 0, \qquad \frac{\partial Z}{\partial C} < 0$$

B. THREE-SENTENCE BEGINNING OF THE POSTULATE SET

1. Postulate of Logarithmic Specification

$$Z = \ln \frac{A}{C}$$

2. Measurement Rule for Goods

$$A,C: \begin{cases} x, & \text{quantity-good} \\ \dfrac{i}{N+1}, & \text{quality-good.} \end{cases}$$

3. Identity Representation of Comparison Holding

$$C = \phi E(A) = \phi S/N.$$

C. BASIC COMPARISON FUNCTION

$$Z = \begin{cases} \ln \dfrac{xN}{\phi S}, & \phi > 0, & \text{quantity-good} \\ \ln \dfrac{2i}{\phi(N+1)}, & 0 < \phi < 2, & \text{quality-good} \end{cases}$$

D. POSTULATE OF SOCIAL WELFARE

$$SW = E(Z)$$

$$SW = \begin{cases} \ln \delta - \ln[G(\phi)], & \text{quantity-good} \\ \ln(2/e) - \ln[G(\phi)], & \text{quality-good} \end{cases}$$

NOTES: The symbol i denotes the rank-order statistics arranged in ascending order of magnitude, in a population of size N. The symbol S denotes the total amount of the quantity-good and ϕ the individual-specific parameter. $E(\cdot)$ and $G(\cdot)$ denote, respectively, the expected value and the geometric mean. The symbol δ denotes the measure of inequality proposed by Atkinson and defined as the ratio of the geometric mean to the arithmetic mean.

TABLE 5

Form of the Comparison Function: Overview of Theorem and Proof

---

A. GENERALIZED AXIOM OF COMPARISON

There exists a class Z of human individual phenomena which are produced by the comparison of an Actual Holding (A) of a good(bad) to a Comparison Holding (C) of that good(bad), such that Z is an increasing(decreasing) function of A and a decreasing(increasing) function of C:

$$Z^* = \theta[Z(A,C)], \quad Z_A > 0, \quad Z_C < 0, \quad \theta > 0 \text{ for a good, } \theta < 0 \text{ for a bad.}$$

B. ADDITIONAL CONDITIONS ON THE COMPARISON FUNCTION

    1. ZERO-POINT PROPERTY. If A equals C, Z must equal zero:

$$Z(a_0 = c_0) = 0.$$

    2. ADDITIVITY PROPERTY. The effect of A on Z must be independent of C, and the effect of C on Z must be independent of A:

$$Z_{AC} = 0.$$

    3. SCALE-INVARIANCE PROPERTY. In comparison processes that involve cardinal holdings, the Z function must be homogeneous of degree zero:

$$AZ_A + CZ_C = 0.$$

C. THEOREM. FORM OF THE COMPARISON FUNCTION

Consider the comparison function Z^*, defined above. The zero-point, additivity, and scale-invariance conditions constrain Z^* to the form:

$$Z^* = \begin{cases} \theta[\ln(A) - \ln(C)], & \text{cardinal holding} \\ \theta[f(A) - f(C)], & \text{relative-rank holding,} \end{cases}$$

where f is an increasing function.

D. NOTES ON THE PROOF

    1. The zero-point and additivity conditions jointly constrain Z to the form $[f(A) - f(C)]$. By the Axiom's sign conditions, f must be increasing.

    2. Additivity and scale-invariance jointly constrain Z to the logarithmic form $[k \ln(A) - k \ln(C) + b]$. The zero-point condition further constrains b to zero.

mechanism by which members of the Z class become differentiated. We raise the questions intuitively: Why do some comparisons lead to sentiments of happiness while others lead to self-esteem and still others to justice sentiments? What accounts for intra-personal as well as inter-personal variation in the configuration of these outcomes? Why do some individuals become "captured" by self-esteem interpretations of their comparisons while other individuals assign a justice interpretation to all of their comparisons? As a starting approach, it may be useful to conceptualize the process as one controlled by a "switch-box" which feeds comparisons onto alternative Z "tracks." Future work will no doubt make vigorous attacks on this question. Note that an understanding of this switching mechanism would shed light on one of the more intriguing questions faced by students of distributive justice, namely, why the condition of being overrewarded sometimes leads to bliss and other times to guilt and/or to redressing behaviors.

Similarly, consideration of the general Z class leads to a new distinction between reflexive and nonreflexive Z's. Reflexive Z's arise from comparison of the individual's *own* Actual and Comparison Holdings of a good or a bad. Nonreflexive Z's arise from comparison of *another's* Actual and Comparison Holdings; these include assessments of another's happiness or well-being as well as judgments concerning whether another is justly rewarded and, if unjustly rewarded, the magnitude of his/her unjust over- or underreward. Note that the class of nonreflexive Z's may be further divided according to whether the Comparison Holding is that which the individual perceives the other to have or is instead that which the individual considers correct for the other, that is, whether the Comparison Holding is formed descriptively or prescriptively. The case of distributive justice judgments about another's situation, in which the individual experiencing Z compares the other's Actual Reward to what the first individual regards as the Just Reward for the other, exemplifies prescriptive formation of the Comparison Holding; this is the case intensively investigated in Jasso and Rossi (1977), Alves and Rossi (1978), Alves (1982), and Jasso (1978, 1989b, 1990a).

3.2.4. Reflections on the Growth of the Postulate Part of Comparison Theory. The foregoing account indicates how the postulate part of comparison theory grew from a single postulate, restricted to the sense of distributive justice about cardinal goods, to a set of three fundamental postulates, augmented by three aggregative postulates (one aggregating over subjects of comparison, two aggregating over individuals)—the new axiomatization applicable (1) to all comparison processes (not only distributive justice), (2) to ordinal as well as cardinal holdings, and (3) to bads as well as goods. It may be useful to cast these developments in the framework proposed by Wagner and Berger (1985). Any assumption (or set of assumptions) which describes the operation of a process and from which predictions may be deduced may be said to constitute the postulate part of a theory, even if prediction has not been attempted. We shall refer to such postulate sets by the lowercase letter t, with subscripts to identify distinct sets.

In this light, the theory of comparison processes begins with a set of insights and a set of terms, dating from classical antiquity and achieving scientific precision in the work of Marx (1849), James (1891), Durkheim (1893, 1897), Simmel (1896–1917), Merton and A. Rossi (1950), Merton (1957), P. Blau (1960, 1964), Homans (1961), Blalock (1967), Berger et al. (1972), Jasso and Rossi (1977); and Goode (1978). The principal terms are the Actual Reward and the Just Reward (the Just Reward being a special case of what may be termed a Comparison Reward). The principal insights are: (1) that happiness and self-esteem arise from comparison of the Actual Reward and the Comparison Reward; (2) that the Justice Evaluation arises from comparison of the Actual Reward and the Just Reward, leading to the conditions of unjust underreward, perfect justice, and unjust overreward, according to whether the Actual Reward is, respectively, less than, equal to, or greater than the Just Reward; (3) that the Justice Evaluation arises both about oneself and about others; (4) that the Just Reward arises by the combination of several inputs and their associated weights; (5) that the Just Reward may be represented by the mean reward in a group or collectivity; and (6) that as the Actual Reward increases, happiness increases at a decreasing rate. These terms and ideas together constitute the postulate part of a theory, which we could present in axiomatic form and from which predictions could be deduced. That this set of ideas was never axiomatized in no way detracts from its status as the postulate part of a theory. We thus call it t_1.

The first attempt at axiomatization occurred when Jasso (1978) proposed the Postulate of the Logarithmic Specification of the Justice Evaluation Function, which states that the Justice Evaluation varies as the logarithm of the ratio of the Actual Reward to the Just Reward. The resultant postulate set—call it t_2—used all the insights in t_1 except the idea that the Just Reward may be represented by the mean reward in a group or collectivity, adding to t_1 the following: (1) formalization of the key terms Actual Reward, Just Reward, Justice Evaluation, Just Reward Function, and Justice Evaluation Function; (2) the logarithmic specification of the Justice Evaluation Function; and (3) the explicit statement that the Justice Evaluation Function is applicable to judgments and sentiments both about oneself and about others. Like t_1, t_2 confined itself to goods (although classical insights since the Book of Job took account of the distribution of bads); however, t_2 was narrower than its predecessor t_1 in that it applied only to cardinal goods, whereas t_1 encompassed both cardinal and ordinal subjects of comparison (albeit without express concern for their measurement). Although few predictions were attempted in the interval between Jasso (1978) and Jasso (1980), t_2 could have produced predictions in abundance. Indeed, all predictions describing the effects of a cardinal good on the sense of justice or on justice-dependent behaviors are derivable from t_2 alone. This set includes, for example, all the predictions describing the effect of own wealth on the propensity to steal and on a victim's well-being after a theft (reported in Jasso 1988b).

The next development occurred when Jasso (1980) proposed a theory which included not only the logarithmic specification of the Justice Evaluation Function but also the measurement rule for cardinal and ordinal goods, the Postulate of Multi-Good Justice Evaluation, the Social Welfare Postulate, and the Social Cohesiveness Postulate; moreover, the multiplicative scaling constant in the Justice Evaluation Function, first described in Jasso (1978: 1415–16), was given fresh meaning as an individual-specific Signature Constant (Jasso 1980: 11). The new postulate set t_3 also incorporated the idea from t_1 that under certain conditions the Just Reward may be represented as the mean reward in a group or collectivity. Manipulation of t_3 produced, and continues to produce, many predictions. These include predictions for marital cohesiveness (Jasso 1983b, 1988a), for eating disorders, and for the rise of inequality-reduction schemes and of the division of labor (Jasso 1991b).

A year later, in response to criticism that the Just Reward was too narrowly conceived (discussed in Section 3.2.2.2 above), Jasso (1981b) expanded the representation of the Just Reward from the mean reward to a reward constant but not necessarily fixed at the mean. This development—t_4—also noted that even if the Just Reward were fixed at the mean reward, the formalization was far less restrictive than it appeared, since, as in Blau (1977: 46–47), any collectivity could be regarded as a collection of subgroups, for each of which the subgroup mean could with some justification be thought of as the Just Reward. Mixtures of distributions provided the relevant mathematical tool for studying such collections of subgroups.

Two years later, Jasso (1983a) formalized the Just Reward Function and the Just Reward Distribution, implicitly adding the Just Reward Function to the postulate part of the theory and thereby producing the new postulate set, t_5. In Section 4.2 we derive predictions for the behavior of rewardees vis-à-vis reward distributors, based on t_5.

The next major development occurred in 1986, when Jasso (1986b) proposed the identity representation of the Just Reward. Because the identity representation introduces into the postulate part of the theory two new terms, the population size N and the collectivity's affluence S, the new postulate set—t_6—has produced an explosion of new predictions. These predictions include the disaster predictions to be reported in Section 4.1 below. Note that, as described in Section 3.2.2.2 above, t_6 was developed in response to criticism that representing the Just Reward by a constant, such as the mean reward, was unduly restrictive.

The most recent development was reported in Jasso (1990a), which showed that distributive justice is a special case of comparison processes and that the theory formulated to date was applicable to the general set of comparison processes and to all subjects of comparison, bads as well as goods. This new postulate set—t_7—considerably enlarges the domains covered by the theory. It also enlarges the operation of the Signature Constant θ, which now indicates by its sign whether the subject of the comparison is regarded as a good or a bad. As with t_4 and t_6, t_7 developed in response to criticism, as discussed in Section 3.2.3 above, in this case the view that there was inadequate justification for the logarithmic specification of the Justice Evaluation Function. The search for the specification of the Justice Evaluation Function, using theoretical methods alone, not only produced the result that for cardinal goods/bads the logarithmic specification uniquely satisfies three relatively mild requirements but also led to the enlarged comparison theory.

Except for t_2, each successive postulate set has retained all the assumptions of the preceding postulate set and added to them; the two features of t_1 not included in t_2— applicability to ordinal goods and the idea that the Just Reward may be represented as the mean reward of a group or collectivity—were included in t_3. Thus, t_3 incorporates all of both t_1 and t_2; and, beginning with t_3, each postulate set is nested in its successor. Note that the Merton Chart Two, by making it possible to see which postulates were used in the derivation of each prediction, makes it possible to learn which predictions could have been derived at an earlier date, that is, from a postulate set earlier than the current one.

3.3. Growth of the Prediction Part of Comparison Theory

Table 6 reports a Merton Chart Two for the theory of comparison processes. Space is provided for five postulates; the postulates included are the logarithmic specification, the measurement rule, the identity representation of C, the Social Welfare Postulate, and the Social Cohesiveness Postulate. The first step in generating predictions is to make explicit all the basic relations embodied in the postulates. The second step is to deduce, from subsets of the postulate set, new propositions for particular behavioral and social phenomena or particular classes of phenomena. To that end, Table 6 separates the predictions into two groups, the first labeled "Basic Relations Embodied in the Postulates," the second simply labeled "Some Predictions." It is too early to tell what further subdivisions may prove useful in a Merton Chart Two.

The most basic relations embodied in the postulates are the effects on Z and on its transformations (e.g., the Social Welfare and the Social Cohesiveness) of the constituent factors. As an illustration, the three rows of panel A of Table 6 report the basic relations embodied in the Social Welfare Postulate. These were obtained by straightforward algebraic manipulation, as described in Jasso (1980, 1988b, 1991b). For example, the effect of inequality on the Social Welfare is obtained by showing that in the quantity-good case $E(Z)$ is equivalent to the natural logarithm of δ (the measure of inequality defined as the ratio of the geometric mean to the arithmetic mean) minus the natural logarithm of the geometric mean of the individual-specific parameter phi (as reported in panel D of Table 4). The measure δ, arising in Atkinson's (1970, 1975) family of inequality measures and described in some detail in Jasso (1982), has bounds of zero and one and decreases as inequality increases. Thus, as inequality in the distribution of the valued quantity-good increases, the collectivity's Social Welfare declines.

Similarly, consider the effect of the population size in a quality-good regime. The term containing N is the natural logarithm of the ratio of the Nth root of N-factorial to the quantity $N + 1$. This ratio has an exciting history in higher mathematics. It can be shown to decrease as N increases, approaching the quantity $1/e$ as its limit. Thus, as population size increases, the collectivity's Social Welfare decreases; however, at "large" population sizes the effect is negligible.

Once the basic relations embodied in the postulates have been established, it is natural to move immediately to deriving predictions for interesting behavioral and social phenomena. Panel B of Table 6 provides as illustration some of the many predictions that have been obtained as of November 1990.

There are many possible ways of deducing predictions. One of the simplest is to investigate the effect of an event or action on an individual. Letting Z_1 describe the individual's well-being prior to the event and Z_2 his/her well-being after the event, the effect of the event may be represented by the change in Z—denoted CZ—and written

$$CZ = Z_2 - Z_1. \tag{10}$$

If CZ is zero, then the event has had no effect on the individual; if, however, CZ is negative, the event has left the individual worse off; and,

TABLE 6

Merton Chart of Theoretical Codification

CHART TWO: THE STATE OF THE THEORY

Theory: Comparison Processes				*Date*: 1 November 1990 *Page*: 1	

PREDICTIONS	POSTULATES				
	Individual-Level			Social-Level	
	$Z = \ln \dfrac{A}{C}$	$A.C = \left\{ \begin{matrix} x, \ \text{quan} \\ \frac{1}{N+1}, \text{qual} \end{matrix} \right\}$	$C = \phi E(A)$	$SW = E(Z)$	$COH = -GMD(Z)$
	1978	1980	1986	1980	1980
A. **Basic Relations Embodied in the Postulates**					
In all societies, the Social Welfare increases with variability in what individuals regard as just for themselves.	x			x	
In quantity-good societies, the Social Welfare decreases with the inequality in the good's distribution.	x	x		x	
In quality-good societies, the Social Welfare decreases with population size.	x	x		x	
. . . . .					
B. **Some Predictions**					
A person will prefer to steal from a fellow group member rather than from an outsider. This preference is stronger in poor groups than in rich groups.	x	x	x		
Informants arise only in cross-group theft, in which case they are members of the thief's group.	x	x	x		
A society becomes more vulnerable to deficit spending as its wealth increases.	x	x	x		

TABLE 6 (*continued*)

Theory: Comparison Processes	*Date*: 1 November 1990
	Page: 2

PREDICTIONS	POSTULATES				
	Individual-Level			Social-Level	
	$Z = \ln \dfrac{A}{C}$	$A,C = \left\{ \begin{smallmatrix} x, \ quan \\ \frac{i}{N+1}, qual \end{smallmatrix} \right\}$	$C = \phi E(A)$	$SW = E(Z)$	$COH = -GMD(Z)$
	1978	1980	1986	1980	1980
Given a society that values wealth and a cloistered sub-group characterized by both individual and corporate poverty, the greater the societal wealth inequality the greater the benefit conferred by the cloister to the society.	x	x		x	
In wartime, the favorite leisure-time activity of soldiers is playing games of chance.	x	x			
The phenomenon of "finding the motive" in the murderer-detection enterprise and the associated literary genre arises only in societies which value wealth.	x	x	x		
Societies in which population growth is welcomed must be societies in which the set of valued goods includes at least one quantity-good, such as wealth.	x	x	x	x	
In societies which value wealth, when wealth inequality approaches or crosses $2/e$ on Atkinson's δ (viz, $\frac{G(A)}{E(A)}$), a guardian will exhort the people to value things other than wealth.	x	x	x	x	
. . . .					

if positive, better off. Because there are many events that affect the constituent factors of Z, this simple procedure can be used for a wide variety of cases. For example, theft affects x and may affect S (depending on whether the thief and victim are from the same group); murder affects N, may affect x and S depending on bequests and relationship to the victim, and may affect i in a quality-good regime; gifts affect x and S but not N; etc.

At this early date, there are already hundreds of predictions derived by means of this simple procedure. For example, the initial predictions for theft-related behaviors (stealing, informing, being victimized, etc.)—derived by considering the simplest possible case (i.e., where there is a single good of value) and counting both first and second partial derivatives—already number 18 in the case where theft is from a fellow group member, 40 in the case where theft is from an outsider, and 5 for the choice between insider and outsider theft (Jasso 1986b, 1988b). These predictions include those reported in the first two rows of panel B of Table 6: (1) that a person will prefer to steal from a fellow group member rather than from an outsider, and that this preference is stronger in poor groups than in rich groups; and (2) that informants arise only in cross-group theft, in which case they are members of the thief's group. Of course, the number of predictions grows greatly when complexity is introduced. For example, research currently under way introduces other goods into the theft problem, including the prospective thief's reputation.* For each new combination of number of goods and types of goods, another 63 primary predictions are obtained—plus new predictions expressing the difference between the one-good environment and the two-good environment, etc.

Other predictions have been obtained in other ways. For example, the cloister-effect prediction (row 4, panel B, Table 6)—that, given a society that values wealth and a cloistered subgroup characterized by both individual and corporate poverty, the greater the societal wealth inequality the greater the benefit conferred by the cloister to the society—is one of a set of predictions we derived by letting the cloistered group assume the lowest places in the distribution of a valued good and then using probability-distribution theory to learn how the good's type, distributional form, and inequality affect the Social Welfare of the non-cloistered; the full investigation of cloister effects is reported in Jasso (1991a). For still another example, the prediction, reported in Jasso (1983b, 1988a), that, if both spouses work full-time, marital cohesiveness increases with the ratio of the smaller to the larger earnings, was derived by instantiation of the Social Cohesiveness Postulate.

---

*This two-good case was suggested by Thomas J. Fararo.

As a final example of procedures to generate predictions, consider the problem of representing the instantaneous distribution of Z in a collectivity. Jasso's (1980) early approach was to hold the Comparison Holding constant and, using change-of-variable techniques, show how the distributional pattern of Actual Holdings determined the distributional pattern of Z. For example, if A is Pareto, then Z will be exponential; if A is lognormal, then Z will be normal; etc. Subsequent removal of the restriction that C be constant transformed the problem into one of deriving the distribution of a function of two variables. Jasso (1989b: 373–74) reports that if A and C are independent lognormals, then the distribution of Z will be normal; if A and C are independently and identically distributed (iid) Paretos, then Z will be a double exponential (often called Laplace). More recent, unpublished work shows that, for A and C iid, if A and C are power-function (including the rectangular, which describes the distributions of ordinal goods), then Z will be Laplace (just as in the case where A and C are Paretos); if A and C are exponential, then Z will be logistic. Distributions of Z have also been derived for several cases where A and C are correlated. An important direction for further research is to seek distribution-free results. Along this line, Jasso (1989b: 373–74) shows that if A and C are iid, then Z will be symmetric about zero; Jasso (1990a: 397) notes that, for C constant, the mean of Z, $E(Z)$, must be less than $\ln[E(A)/E(C)]$, and, hence, if $E(A) = E(C)$, then $E(Z)$ must be negative.

Even a cursory look at Table 6 shows that there are two "workhorses" in the task of theoretical derivation: the logarithmic specification of the Z function and the identity representation of the Comparison Holding. Given that the identity representation requires no behavioral assumptions and is thus virtually cost-free, it would appear to be an exceptional "value."

We note that it might be useful to group the predictions in several alternative ways. For example, the predictions could be grouped by the main substantive topic: family predictions, crime predictions, etc. Lists could also be generated of all predictions in which particular variables play a part, for example, all predictions that describe effects of education, whether for crime behavior, family behavior, etc., or all predictions that describe determinants or consequences of laws. Moreover, separate lists could be generated of predictions that link two or more principal topics, for example, predictions that link disasters and migration or that link bequests and migration. We note also that we expect elaborate deductive schemes to appear in the future, including multi-period models, in which the predictions cover the trajectory of Z as a result of configurations of events in each period.

4. Observing Growth in Comparison Theory:
Two New Derivations

We now illustrate the process by which the prediction part of the
theory grows. We do so by deriving two new sets of predictions.

4.1. Disaster: Death and Destruction

The first step in formulating the disaster model is common to many
applications of comparison theory. Given that we are to investigate an
event and its effects, we utilize the CZ formulation introduced above.

In general, disaster events have three immediate effects: death, destruction of material possessions, and personal injuries. Thus, disasters
affect three elements that play a prominent part in comparison theory.
Through the effect on death, disasters alter the population size N in both
quality-good and quantity-good regimes; by destruction of material
possessions, disasters alter both the wealth x of survivors and the total
wealth S of a collectivity; and through personal injury, disasters may
affect an individual's rank on a valued quality-good. For example, an
airplane crash may leave an athlete physically impaired, destroy homes
and businesses in the area of the crash, and kill persons both in the air
and on the ground. As well, disasters have non-immediate effects, such
as payment of compensation for the death of kin.

In this paper we restrict attention to quantity-good regimes, focusing
on the immediate effects of death and destruction of property. Future
work might develop a disaster model for the case of quality-good regimes, as well as formulate a more general model that includes simultaneous valuation of quality-goods and quantity-goods and that spans several periods, so that both immediate and non-immediate effects may be
analyzed. In the present case, we substitute the formula for quantity-
good Z into Formula 10 for CZ, obtaining:

$$CZ = \ln\left(\frac{x_2 N_2 S_1 \phi_1}{x_1 N_1 S_2 \phi_2}\right). \tag{11}$$

Formula 11 is the basic formula used in all comparison-theory-based
analyses of the effects of events which alter individuals' holdings of material possessions. For example, it was used to derive predictions for
theft-related phenomena (Jasso 1988b) and for gift/bequest behavior
(Jasso 1990b).

We now introduce ingredients specific to the disaster application. We
analyze CZ for a survivor. Let t denote the material loss incurred by a
survivor and L the material losses incurred by others in the group, where
t and S are measured in units of x; let D denote the number of deaths.

For simplicity, in this paper we analyze the eight simplest cases. In these cases, a surviving individual's wealth can be altered only by a property loss; that is, the survivor whose CZ is analyzed does not inherit anything as a result of the disaster, nor does he or she receive compensation for the death of kin. Thus, the survivor's x_2 equals $x_1 - t$. Moreover, the property of decedents is either all destroyed or else is inherited by other members of the group. Thus, S_2 equals $S_1 - t - L$. Finally, the population size is altered only by the deaths resulting from the disaster; that is, the disaster does not engender either immigration or emigration. Thus, N_2 equals $N - D$. Letting the three factors t, L, and D each assume either zero or positive values, the number of possible cases equals eight ($2 \times 2 \times 2$), of which one is the null case of zero on all three factors—a convenient benchmark.

Of course, in the general case own property loss t, others' losses L, and deaths D are not the only effects of a disaster. Decedents may bequeath undestroyed property to survivors in the group, thereby altering x in a new way (besides t) or may bequeath undestroyed property to outsiders, thereby altering S (in a way other than through t and L). Moreover, compensation to survivors for the death of kin may alter x and S. As mentioned above, the disaster may lead to either or both in- and out-migration. Future work might analyze these more elaborate cases.

The next step is to write Formula 11 in versions specific to the survivor in each of the special cases examined in this paper. Table 7 reports the formula CZ for each of the eight cases defined by the three-factor event configuration. The CZ formulas express the change in the survivor's well-being due to the disaster events. There are two main sets of questions to be asked, each illuminating different aspects of disaster-related phenomena and singly or in combination yielding a variety of predictions. These two main questions are: (1) What is the sign of CZ? (2) What are the effects on CZ of the three disaster factors—own loss t, others' losses L, and deaths D—and the three pre-disaster characteristics—own wealth x, group wealth S, and the population size N?

The sign of CZ indicates whether the individual is better off, worse off, or unaffected by the disaster. We turn to examine the sign of CZ for the special cases in Table 7. The formulas for CZ include the phi component; and thus it is not possible to know the sign of CZ without making an *a priori* assumption about phi. It is not unreasonable that phi, for a given individual, remains constant across the two time periods. The most parsimonious assumption is that $\phi_1 = \phi_2$. It can also be argued that even if the Comparison Holding does change, it does not do so immediately; and hence there may be an important period (of unknown dura-

TABLE 7

Effect of a Disaster on a Survivor, by Configuration of Own Loss t,
Others' Losses L, and Deaths D

Case	Event Configuration			Effect CZ	
	t	L	D	$\ln \dfrac{(x-t)(N-D)S\phi_1}{xN(S-t-L)\phi_2}$	Sign
1	0	0	0	$\ln \dfrac{\phi_1}{\phi_2}$	0
2	0	0	+	$\ln \dfrac{(N-D)\phi_1}{N\phi_2}$	–
3	0	+	0	$\ln \dfrac{S\phi_1}{(S-L)\phi_2}$	+
4	0	+	+	$\ln \dfrac{(N-D)S\phi_1}{N(S-L)\phi_2}$	– 0 +
5	+	0	0	$\ln \dfrac{(x-t)S\phi_1}{x(S-t)\phi_2}$	–
6	+	0	+	$\ln \dfrac{(x-t)(N-D)S\phi_1}{xN(S-t)\phi_2}$	–
7	+	+	0	$\ln \dfrac{(x-t)S\phi_1}{x(S-t-L)\phi_2}$	– 0 +
8	+	+	+	$\ln \dfrac{(x-t)(N-D)S\phi_1}{xN(S-t-L)\phi_2}$	– 0 +

NOTES: Negative (positive) signs indicate negative (positive) quantities.
Survivor's pre-disaster wealth is denoted by x, and population's pre-disaster
size and wealth by N and S, respectively. The sign of CZ is calculated for
the case where ϕ_1 equals ϕ_2. For simplicity, cases investigated refer to
situations in which the survivor does not inherit property as a result of the
disaster and a decedent's property is either inherited by others in the group
or is destroyed.

tion) when $\phi_1 = \phi_2$ and this assumption yields an accurate assessment of CZ. The rightmost column of Table 7 reports the sign of CZ, assuming $\phi_1 = \phi_2$. As shown, CZ is of course zero in the null case. It is negative in cases 2, 5, and 6, positive in case 3, and may assume any sign in cases 4, 7, and 8. Thus, if a disaster produces only deaths or if the survivor is the only person experiencing a property loss, then CZ is negative; of course, if these two occur together as the only events, CZ is *a fortiori* negative. Negative CZ means that the survivor's well-being Z is reduced by the disaster; we may say that the survivor is made worse off by the disaster or that he/she experiences pain, distress, or the negative sentiments associated with post-traumatic stress syndrome. In case 3, however, in which there are neither deaths nor a personal property loss, but only the property losses of others, the non-victim survivor is made better off by the disaster; we may say that the survivor experiences positive sentiments such as relief and even euphoria. The three cases in which others' property losses occur together with either deaths or own property loss lead to a magnitude of CZ which may be of any sign, depending on the magnitudes of the disaster factors.

To express in words the results of Table 7, consider the situations described in cases 2, 3, and 4. The case 2 formula for CZ leads to the following prediction: If in a disaster there is no property damage but at least one death occurs, then all survivors will experience psychological distress. We may call this the John Donne effect, after the famous lines, "And therefore never send to know for whom the *bell* tolls; It tolls for *thee*."

The case 3 formula leads to the prediction: If in a disaster there is property loss but no deaths, then non-victims will experience a rush of energy and euphoria. This prediction sheds new light on the casual impression that hurricanes, tornadoes, and little earthquakes—in which there are no deaths—rouse in non-victims an extraordinary energy that enables them to help their neighbors, sort through rubble, and rebuild their homes, all the while with something of a carnival spirit that prompts them to say to those who have lost their homes, "Be joyous, be thankful; you have your lives."

The formula for CZ in case 4, in which there are deaths and property damage but the survivor does not suffer a property loss, can be algebraically manipulated to lead to the prediction: If in a disaster there are both deaths and property damage, then a surviving non-victim will need psychological relief if and only if the ratio D/N exceeds the ratio L/S. This prediction can be helpful to disaster relief organizations, for it enables them to know whether a given site will need many or few emotional counselors. Moreover, note that disasters characterized by much larger ratios of D/N than of L/S—such as many airplane crashes—can be psychologically devastating to survivors. In contrast, disasters characterized by few deaths and much property damage can be psychologically energizing.

The results reported in Table 7 can be further manipulated to yield new insights. For example, one may ask whether a person who suffers a property loss is ever made euphoric by a disaster. Table 7 shows that in cases 7 and 8 the survivor can have a positive magnitude of CZ. Case 7 is relatively easy to analyze. Algebraic manipulation indicates that

$$CZ > 0 \text{ iff } (t + L)/S > t/x, \tag{12}$$

which can be restated as

$$CZ > 0 \text{ iff } x/S > t/(t + L). \tag{13}$$

In words, a survivor who suffers a property loss is better off if and only if the ratio of the total property loss $(t + L)$ to the group's pre-disaster wealth exceeds the ratio of own loss t to own pre-disaster wealth x, or, equivalently, if and only if the ratio of own pre-disaster wealth to group pre-disaster wealth exceeds the ratio of own loss to total loss. Indeed, we can revert to the more general notation of Formula 11, bypassing t and L, to write

$$CZ > 0 \text{ iff } x_2/S_2 > x_1 S_1 \tag{14}$$

and

$$CZ > 0 \text{ iff } x_2/x_1 > S_2 S_1. \tag{15}$$

The first expression is particularly useful. In words, a survivor who suffers a property loss is better off if and only if his/her share of the wealth after the disaster exceeds his/her share of the wealth before the disaster. There is, however, a certain crassness about this formulation, and a disaster relief worker would probably be prudent to focus on losses, calculating only privately changes in the wealth shares of survivors.

We turn now to the second main set of questions, questions addressing the effects on CZ of the several variables in the formulas. Table 8 reports, in panel B, a decomposition of CZ into its four components—two individual-specific components, reflecting a survivor's own property loss and the survivor's idiosyncratic phi parameters, and two common components, reflecting loss of life and total property damage. The decomposition indicates that the effect of a personal property loss is always negative, as is the effect of loss of life; however, the effect of total property damage is always positive.

Panel C of Table 8 reports the first and second partial derivatives of CZ with respect to each of the six arguments; the signs of the deriva-

TABLE 8

Effects of Survivor's Pre-Disaster Wealth x, *Population's*
Pre-Disaster Size N *and Wealth* S, *Survivor's Loss* t,
Others' Losses L *and Deaths* D

A.   Effect of Disaster

$$CZ = \ln\frac{(x-t)(N-D)S\phi_1}{xN(S-t-L)\phi_2}$$

B.   Decomposition of Effect of Disaster

$$CZ = \ln\frac{x-t}{x} - \ln\frac{S-t-L}{S} + \ln\frac{N-D}{N} + \ln\frac{\phi_1}{\phi_2}$$

C.   First and Second Partial Derivatives of *CZ*

Factor	First Derivative		Second Derivative	
1. Pre-Disaster Factors				
x	$\dfrac{t}{x(x-t)}$	> 0	$-\dfrac{t(2x-t)}{[x(x-t)]^2}$	< 0
S	$-\dfrac{t+L}{S(S-t-L)}$	< 0	$\dfrac{(t+L)(2S-t-L)}{[S(S-t-L)]^2}$	> 0
N	$\dfrac{D}{N(N-D)}$	> 0	$-\dfrac{D(2N-D)}{[N(N-D)]^2}$	< 0
2. Disaster Events				
t	$-\dfrac{S-L-x}{(x-t)(S-t-L)}$	< 0	$-\dfrac{(S-t-L)^2-(x-t)^2}{[(x-t)(S-t-L)]^2}$	< 0
L	$\dfrac{L}{S-t-L}$	> 0	$\dfrac{L}{(S-t-L)^2}$	> 0
D	$-\dfrac{1}{N-D}$	< 0	$-\dfrac{1}{(N-D)^2}$	< 0

TABLE 8 (*continued*)

D. <u>**Non-Zero Second-Order Mixed Partial Derivatives**</u>

	Derivative				Derivative	

$$CZ_{xt} = \frac{1}{(x-t)^2} \qquad > 0 \qquad\qquad CZ_{ND} = \frac{1}{(N-D)^2} \qquad > 0$$

$$CZ_{St} = -\frac{1}{(S-t-L)^2} \qquad < 0 \qquad\qquad CZ_{tL} = \frac{1}{(S-t-L)^2} \qquad > 0$$

$$CZ_{SL} = -\frac{1}{(S-t-L)^2} \qquad < 0$$

tives are also reported. Here no assumption need be made concerning phi; all effects are independent of phi and its possible changes. The first-derivative results indicate that, other things the same, the effects of pre-disaster own wealth x and of pre-disaster population size N are positive while that of pre-disaster group wealth S is negative; the effects of own loss t and of deaths D are negative while that of others' losses L is positive. Thus, in advance of a disaster, and holding constant the disaster events, wealthier individuals are expected to suffer less trauma as are persons in large collectivities; however, the more affluent the population, the greater the expected trauma. The effects of the disaster events are negative for own property loss and for deaths and positive for others' property losses.

The six factors give rise to fifteen second-order mixed partial derivatives. Five of the mixed partials are non-zero; these are shown in panel D of Table 8, along with their sign. The results can be interpreted in several ways that illuminate diverse aspects of the disaster situation. For example, the results indicate that the bad effect of own loss is mitigated by own pre-disaster wealth and by others' property losses but is exacerbated by the group's pre-disaster wealth. The good effect of others' losses is intensified by own loss and tempered by the group's pre-disaster wealth. The negative effect of the group's pre-disaster wealth is intensified both by own loss and by others' losses. The salutary effect of population size is intensified by deaths; the bad effect of deaths is tempered by population size.

At this stage of the work, we pause to ask the question, What do I now know that I did not know before? We begin our answer by examining the results of the work to date. From this initial investigation of predictions of the theory of comparison processes for disaster phenomena, we have produced the following: (1) the formula expressing the general effect of a disaster on a survivor; (2) a typology of eight distinct types of survivor experience, together with predictions concerning which survivors are positively affected by the disaster, which negatively affected, and which are unaffected; (3) a decomposition of the disaster effect into its four components; (4) six each first partial and second partial derivatives, expressing the effects of the three disaster events and of three initial conditions on the experience of a survivor; and (5) fifteen mixed partial derivatives, of which five are non-zero, expressing the interactions of the disaster events and the initial conditions. As well, we are preparing a checklist such as relief organizations might use to decide in advance how much psychological relief is required. And for all this, the total price was only the logarithmic specification of Z and the identity representation of C. To illustrate how a Merton Chart Two would sum-

Theory: Comparison Processes *Date*: 5 November 1990
Prediction Subset: Disaster *Page*: 1

PREDICTIONS	POSTULATES				
	Individual-Level			Social-Level	
	$Z = \ln \dfrac{A}{C}$	$A,C = \left\{ \begin{array}{c} x, \text{ quan} \\ \frac{i}{N+1}, \text{qual} \end{array} \right\}$	$C = \phi E(A)$	$SW = E(Z)$	$COH = -GMD(Z)$
	1978	1980	1986	1980	1980
A. Summary					
Effects of six factors: (i) three initial conditions -- own wealth x, societal wealth S, and population size N; and (ii) three disaster events -- own property loss t, others' property loss L, and deaths D.	x	x	x		
. . .					
B. Some Predictions					
If in a disaster there is no property damage but at least one death occurs, all survivors will experience psychological distress.	x	x	x		
If in a disaster there is property loss but no deaths, then non-victims will experience a rush of energy and euphoria.	x	x	x		
If in a disaster there are both deaths and property damage, then a surviving non-victim will need psychological relief if and only if the ratio D/N exceeds the ratio L/S.	x	x	x		
. . .					

marize this work, Table 9 reports a partially filled-out Merton Chart Two, tailored for a prediction subset.

Of course, many new predictions can be derived from the initial set. To illustrate, consider the decomposition of the disaster effect, shown in panel B of Table 8. As noted above, the decomposition indicates that the effects of a personal property loss and of loss of life are always negative, but that the effect of total property damage is always positive. Thus, the general principle is that property damage mitigates the ill effects of deaths, the relevant comparison being between the ratio of fatalities to the population and the ratio of property damage to total wealth. Applying this general principle, we may deduce many new predictions, among them: (1) Post-traumatic stress is more severe for the survivors of conveyance disasters than for the survivors of natural disasters; and (2) To reduce pain, survivors will substitute subpopulations with fewer dead, e.g., "my section" instead of "my plane," or "my railroad car" instead of "the train," blocking out the memory, say, of the first-class section in the Sioux City airplane crash, or of persons they saw boarding the railroad cars that are now destroyed.

As well, some of the predictions in the initial set alert the theorist to more general predictions applicable to phenomena in several topical domains. For example, applying to war the general principle stated and applied in the preceding paragraph leads to the following prediction: Post-traumatic stress is more severe among armies not fighting on their home soil; post-traumatic stress would thus be greater for Union army survivors than for Confederate army survivors, and greater for Americans than for most other combatants in all the wars fought by the United States in this century.

4.2. Differences in Ideology and Information Between Rewardee and Distributor

In the study of distributive justice it is sometimes suggested that ideological differences between a rewardee (e.g., a worker or a student) and a distributor (e.g., a wage setter or a teacher) are sufficient for the rewardee to challenge the legitimacy of the distributor. We now use properties of the Berger et al. (1972) Just Reward Function to show that such ideological differences are not sufficient to produce a legitimacy challenge.

To begin, recall the Just Reward Function (JRF) to which the Just Holding Function reduces in the special case of goods:

$$\text{Just Reward} = h(X; B), \tag{16}$$

where X denotes the vector of reward-relevant characteristics, B denotes the parameter vector, and h denotes the functional form. An individual's

Just Reward Function captures the individual's *ideology* concerning the question of what constitutes a Just Reward for persons of specified characteristics.

Consider now that the Just Reward Function appears twice in a distributive justice problem involving a rewardee and a distributor. First, the rewardee has his/her own Just Reward Function, by means of which the rewardee's Just Reward for him/herself is generated. The rewardee's Just Reward Function is denoted JRF^R, with the superscript ^{R} to indicate that this is the rewardee's JRF. Second, the distributor also has a Just Reward Function, denoted JRF^D (the superscript ^{D} indicating that this is the distributor's JRF), which guides him/her in the task of setting the reward for the rewardee; the distributor calculates a Just Reward for the rewardee and this Just Reward becomes the rewardee's Actual Reward.

The rewardee's reflexive Just Reward, produced by JRF^R, reflects (1) the rewardee's JRF, that is, the *rewardee's ideology*, and (2) the *rewardee's knowledge* of his/her magnitudes on the reward-relevant variables. The rewardee's Actual Reward, which is the distributor's Just Reward for the rewardee and produced by JRF^D, reflects (1) the distributor's JRF, that is, the *distributor's ideology*, and (2) the *distributor's information* concerning the rewardee's magnitudes of the reward-relevant variables. Panel A of Table 10 summarizes these basic elements of the rewardee/distributor problem.

This approach highlights the fact that a discrepancy between the rewardee's Actual Reward and his/her reflexive Just Reward can arise from two sources. First, it can arise if rewardee and distributor have different JRF's, that is, different ideologies—$JRF^D \neq JRF^R$. Second, a discrepancy can arise if rewardee and distributor place different magnitudes of the X reward-relevant variables into the JRF's, that is, if their information differs—$X^D \neq X^R$.

To investigate the operation of ideology and information in generating a discrepancy between the Actual Reward and the Just Reward, we set up a fourfold table, shown in panel B of Table 10. It is obvious that if rewardee and distributor have identical JRF's and identical information on the magnitudes of the X variables, then there can be no discrepancy between the Actual Reward and the Just Reward. It is also obvious that if rewardee and distributor have identical JRF's but different information on the reward-relevant variables, then the Actual Reward and the Just Reward must differ. When rewardee and distributor have different JRF's, however, regardless of whether they have identical or different information on the reward-relevant variables, the Actual Reward may or may not equal the Just Reward. For example, two different JRF's, evaluated for the same inputs, may intersect at one or more points. Similarly, two

TABLE 10
*Ideology, Information, the Discrepancy Between the Actual Reward
and the Just Reward, and Behavioral Outcomes: Model Based on Berger, Zelditch,
Anderson, and Cohen (1972)*

A. <u>Elements of the Problem</u>

   Given: An individual's Actual Reward and reflexive Just Reward.

The Just Reward (*JR*) is produced by the individual's own Just Reward Function, denoted JRF with the superscript R for rewardee. The Actual Reward (*AR*) is produced by the distributor's Just Reward Function, denoted JRF^D. Thus, both JRF's have the same formal ingredients, a set of arguments X, the associated parameter vector B, and a functional form *h*.

$$\text{JRF}^R: \quad \textit{Just Reward} \; = \; h(X;\; B)$$

$$\text{JRF}^D: \quad \textit{Just Reward} \; = \; h(X;\; B)$$

The Actual Reward reflects both (i) the distributor's JRF, and (ii) the distributor's information concerning the magnitudes of the rewardee's X.

B. <u>Generating a Discrepancy between the Actual Reward and the Just Reward</u>

A discrepancy between AR and JR can arise from two sources: (i) JRF^D $\neq$ JRF^R; and (ii) $X^D \neq X^R$. These two sources generate a fourfold classification:

Information	Ideology	
	JRF^D = JRF^R	JRF^D $\neq$ JRF^R
$X^D = X^R$	*AR = JR*	*AR* may or may not equal *JR*
$X^D \neq X^R$	*AR $\neq$ JR*	*AR* may or may not equal *JR*

continued

TABLE 10 (*continued*)

C. **Behavioral Outcomes**

1. If $AR = JR$, none.

2. If $AR > JR$, then curiosity about JRF^D and X^D. Further behaviors are not well understood; these may include behaviors listed in section 3 below.

3. If $AR < JR$, then

    a. Learn JRF^D and X^D.

    b. If $X^D \neq X^R$, then inform distributor, thereby obtaining new Actual Reward.

    c. If $JRF^D \neq JRF^R$, then one or more of the following alternatives:

        i.   Change magnitudes of reward-relevant characteristics.

        ii. Revise own Just Reward Function.

        iii. Persuade distributor to change his/her Just Reward Function.

        iv. Challenge legitimacy of distributor.

D. **Conclusions**

The results and relationships in sections B and C indicate:

1. Ideological differences between distributor and rewardee are neither necessary nor sufficient to generate a discrepancy between the Actual Reward and the Just Reward, and therefore neither necessary nor sufficient to generate the behaviors in sections C.2 and C.3.

2. Informational differences between distributor and rewardee are neither necessary nor sufficient to generate a discrepancy between the Actual Reward and the Just Reward, and therefore neither necessary nor sufficient to generate the behaviors in sections C.2 and C.3.

3. Ideological and informational agreement are jointly sufficient but not necessary to generate equality of the Actual Reward and the Just Reward.

different JRF's, evaluated for different inputs, may coincide at one or more points. Thus, due to the operation of information on the reward-relevant variables, a discrepancy between the Actual Reward and the Just Reward is neither prevented by ideological agreement nor guaranteed by ideological disagreement; and equality of the Actual Reward and the Just Reward is neither guaranteed by ideological agreement nor prevented by ideological disagreement.

Panel C of Table 10 systematizes the alternative behavioral outcomes. First, if the Actual Reward equals the Just Reward, then distributive jus-tice theory predicts that the system is in equilibrium and the rewardee will not engage in any justice-dependent action. Second, in the case where the Actual Reward exceeds the Just Reward, distributive justice theory is somewhat murky, but suggests that if justice sentiments are activated, as opposed to, say, happiness or well-being sentiments, then the rewardee may challenge the distributor or may keep the money but feel guilty; at the very least, it is likely that the rewardee will become curious about the distributor's JRF and information on the rewardee's attributes. Third, in the case where the Actual Reward is less than the Just Reward—and here distributive justice theory comes into its own—the rewardee will be roused to activity. The first objective will be to discover the distributor's JRF and X^D. If the source of the inequality be-tween the Actual Reward and the Just Reward is an informational dis-crepancy, then the rewardee will merely inform the distributor, thereby obtaining a new (and "correct") Just Reward. If, however, the source of the reward discrepancy is an ideological difference, then the rewardee has a new set of alternatives; these include revising his/her own JRF, altering his/her magnitudes of the reward-relevant variables, persuading the dis-tributor to revise his/her JRF, and, finally, challenging the legitimacy of the distributor.

Panel D of Table 10 lists the major conclusions of the analysis, ex-pressed as statements concerning the necessity and sufficiency of ideo-logical and informational differences for generating a discrepancy be-tween the Actual Reward and the Just Reward.

Again, we ask, What do I now know that I did not know before I did this work? This is a little model, and the answer is modest. For the special case of a worker and a wage setter, we now know that ideological differ-ences between a worker and a wage setter are neither necessary nor suf-ficient to generate a discrepancy between the worker's Actual Wage and Just Wage; and, similarly, that information asymmetries are neither nec-essary nor sufficient to generate a discrepancy between the worker's Ac-tual Wage and Just Wage. Modest as this answer is, it has some implica-tions for related phenomena; for example, ideological differences by themselves are not sufficient to generate conflict or to lead to a worker's challenge of the legitimacy of the wage setter. If a wage setter "makes mistakes"—from the worker's perspective—in assessing the worker's worth, such mistakes may compensate for the ideological differences.*

These predictions were inexpensively obtained. Logic alone—logical manipulation of the Berger et al. Just Reward Function—produced them. The results of this little exercise are summarized in Table 11, which reports a Merton Chart Two for the project.

5. Toward Empirical Test of the Predictions of Comparison Theory

• To date, the theory of comparison processes has generated literally hundreds of predictions. Indeed, such is the ease with which it enables theoretical derivation that by the time this paper goes to press the number of predictions could be in the thousands. How does one test so fecund a theory?

• Few among us would claim that comparison processes constitute the sole ruler of human behavior, or even that there might exist behavioral domains subject only to comparison processes. Thus, all predictions of comparison theory are *ceteris paribus* predictions. How does one test *ceteris paribus* predictions?

• The theorist who has contributed a postulate cannot be assumed to be indifferent concerning the fate of the postulate. However obsessed with the hunt for truth the theorist may be, however profuse with postulates, even handing out contradictory postulates, the theorist may retain a certain residual affection for the postulates and hence for their progeny, the predictions. How does a theorist preserve the proper skepticism?

• A theorist is, almost by definition, a generalist. As such, the theorist often has wide knowledge of many behavioral domains. Yet the theorist seldom knows as much as the empirical specialist about any particular behavioral domain. The predictions of comparison theory are for highly specialized contexts and they are *ceteris paribus* predictions, requiring for their rigorous test the most minute knowledge of all the factors thought to operate in the given situation, their measurement properties, the available data sets, and the results of previous empirical work. Under what conditions is it prudent for theorists to test the predictions of their theories?

• Contemporary sociology has inherited a strongly inductivist bent, an emphasis on "letting the data speak for themselves." Con-

---

*Readers will be familiar with the special case of student and teacher where the grade is the reward set by the teacher.

Theory: Distributive Justice
Prediction Subset: Ideology and Information

Date: 10 July 1989
Page: 1

PREDICTIONS	POSTULATES				
	Individual-Level			Social-Level	
	$J = \ln\dfrac{A}{C}$	$A,C = \left\{ \begin{array}{l} x, \ quan \\ \frac{1}{N+1}, qual \end{array} \right\}$	$C = \phi E(A)$	$SW = E(J)$	$COH = -GMD(J)$
	1978	1980	1986	1980	1980
A. Summary					
Logical statements express-ing the effects of the four combinations of two binary conditions -- (i) reci-pient/distributor (dis)-agreement on the Just Holding Function, and (ii) recipient/distributor assessments of recipient's holding-relevant character-istics -- on the discrep-ancy between recipient's Actual Holding and Just Holding.					
B. Some Predictions					
Ideological differences between worker and wage-setter are neither neces-sary nor sufficient to produce a discrepancy between A and C.					
Ideological agreement between worker and wage-setter is neither necessary nor sufficient to produce an Actual Wage equal to the reflexive Just Wage.					

TABLE 11 (*continued*)

Theory: Distributive Justice					
Prediction Subset: Ideology and Information				*Date*: 10 July 1989 *Page*: 2	
Differences between worker's and wage-setter's assessments of worker's reward-relevant characteristics are neither necessary nor sufficient to produce a discrepancy between *A* and *C*.					
Congruence between worker's and wage-setter's assessments of worker's reward-relevant characteristics is neither necessary nor sufficient to produce an Actual Wage equal to the reflexive Just Wage.					

NOTES:

comitantly, it is difficult for empirical specialists to learn of theoretical results pertinent to their specialty. Predictions are often published in papers whose principal "topic" is the basic process, not the predictions for disparate domains. How can topical sets of predictions be made accessible to empirical specialists?

The foregoing are some of the practical issues that arise when one begins to think seriously about testing a theory. That is, after the philosophical questions are aired and the canons for assessing the empirical validity of a theory are established—matters treated in Jasso (1989a: 140–41)—the practical issues reduce to questions of which and how many predictions can be tested and who is best suited to test them.

In principle, one would like as many of the predictions as possible to be tested. How long would it take to test a theory? Designing and implementing an empirical test, as is well known, is not easy. In the most blessed of circumstances—data already available, a seasoned researcher already knowledgeable about the pertinent matters of model specification and choice of estimation procedure—a test of one prediction might take three months. At the other extreme, it could take years for execution of an empirical test, if the right data have to be collected and/or the test has to become technologically feasible. To calculate a crude index of the time required to test a theory, let us assume that each testing project can test ten related predictions and that it takes a year to complete. Then it would take one hundred project-years to test each thousand predictions. If the researchers were extremely capable and could design and implement a test in six months, the number of project-years required to test a thousand predictions would be reduced only to fifty. Put another way, it would take fifty researchers to test a thousand predictions in one year.

Of course, the time required to test a prediction is highly variable. In particular, empirical specialists already working on a particular topical domain would be able to test a prediction in the minimum time. Efficiency is one important reason for bringing theoretical results to the attention of empirical specialists.

The quality of an empirical test also varies. In particular, it varies with the researcher's experience of the questions and data at hand. *A priori* it would seem highly desirable to interest empirical specialists in testing, alongside other hypotheses, the predictions of comparison theory for phenomena studied by their particular specialty.

Of course, at this stage in the development of the social sciences many theorists also do empirical work. It may happen that some theoretical predictions fall within the theorist's empirical interests. Such has been the case with comparison theory. To date, only two predictions of comparison theory have received rigorous empirical assessment.

The first—that, among couples where both spouses are employed full-time, martial cohesiveness increases with the ratio of the smaller to the larger earnings while, among other couples, marital cohesiveness is equal to that of couples whose earnings ratio is one-half—was first reported in Jasso (1983b). The empirical test, with marital coital frequency as an indicator of marital cohesiveness, was reported in Jasso (1988a); the results were consistent with the prediction. In this case, the test required familiarity with the sexuality literature and with the literature on age-period-cohort effects, matters studied by Jasso (1985, 1986a).

The second prediction that has received empirical assessment dates to Jasso's (1980: 11) suggestion that each person has a Signature Constant that appears in the Justice Evaluation Function, reflecting the individual's style of expression. Jasso (1990a) established that such a Signature Constant—currently denoted θ, as shown in Equations 3 and 4 and Table 5—performs two functions: (1) by its sign, it indicates whether the subject of the comparison is perceived as a good or a bad (positive for goods, negative for bads); and (2) by its magnitude, as proposed earlier, it transforms the experience of Z into the expression thereof. Estimates of θ were obtained in Jasso's (1990a) reanalyses of the Jasso-Rossi data on the justice of earnings. Statistical tests indicate that the two hundred respondents in that sample have unique values of θ. Moreover, two of the two hundred respondents consider earnings a bad rather than a good.

In order to have tests of many theoretical predictions and to have rigorous tests, it would appear necessary for such tests to be conducted by researchers with experience of the particular topics. Accordingly, the task is for theorists to widely disseminate prediction subsets among empirical specialists. This can be accomplished in two principal ways: first, by publishing in specialty journals; and second, by participating in specialty conferences. For example, the predictions concerning disasters reported in Section 4.1 above could be presented in a manner more accessible to disaster researchers and published in a disaster research journal. Note that some of the predictions concern natural disasters and others concern conveyance disasters, and thus it might be necessary to refine even further the presentation. Similarly, the predictions derived in a recent project on gifts and bequests (Jasso 1990b), which include predictions for grief behavior, burial goods, intergenerational transfers and co-residence, and seasonal gift expenditures, could be reported to audiences of specialists on these topics. Again, several specialties are involved and, indeed, several disciplines, as, for example, psychologists might be interested in the grief predictions and anthropologists in the burial-goods predictions. As a final example, the predictions for behavior associated with monastic and mendicant institutions (Jasso 1991a) should be brought to the attention of sociologists of religion; while they were not published in a sociology of religion journal, reprints can be widely circulated.

Sometimes everyday facts seem consistent with a theory's predictions. For example, comparison theory yields the following prediction subset (Jasso 1990b):

In families with more than one child (excepting the case where all the children have the same birthday), parents will tend to give fewer and less-costly birthday presents and more and more-costly presents at an annual gift-giving occasion—such as Christmas. The larger the average family size in a society, the greater the likelihood that annual gift-giving occasions will arise. Schools will reinforce this tendency—regardless of family size—because the re-definition of hierarchies that follows gifts not only deflects attention from intellectual pursuits but also can be socially disruptive.

As it turns out, the toy industry in the United States reports that 70 percent of all sales occur in the fourth quarter. This implies, assuming that births are distributed uniformly across the year and that all children receive both birthday and Christmas gifts, that 40 percent of toy sales are for birthday gifts (10 percent per quarter) and 60 percent are for Christmas gifts. Thus, the typical child's Christmas gift is worth 1.5 times as much as his/her birthday gift. And the typical parents spend 40 percent of their toy budget on birthday gifts and 60 percent on Christmas gifts. The facts seem to be exactly in line with the first prediction in the subset. Yet there is no substitute for a rigorous test, one that takes account of fluctuations in the economy and of the age distribution; as well, it would be useful to test the other predictions in the subset, for example, those concerning family size and school influences. It would seem that only a specialist on parental expenditures for toys or on intergenerational transfers can properly test these predictions.

6. Concluding Note

We end with first principles. The goal of sociology is to accumulate reliable knowledge about behavioral and social phenomena.

On the theoretical front, we have reviewed the growth of the theory of comparison processes, describing growth of the postulate part and growth of the prediction part of the theory. We believe that the prediction part will continue to grow and that new theorists, schooled in new methods of mathematical analysis, will deduce from the simple postulates of comparison theory predictions of unprecedented subtlety and complexity. Indeed, new theorists will restate the postulates in forms simpler and more elegant than we can imagine.

On the empirical front, we believe that the predictions old and new will receive precise and rigorous test at the hands of sagacious empirical analysts. Some of these tests will be astonishingly inventive, making use of future technologies both for observing and measuring physiological processes and also for the conduct of everyday life in an inter-galactic environment.

Whatever the fate of comparison theory, the knowledge and experience gained by both theorists and empiricalists who work with it will directly assist in the larger task of identifying and describing the operation of the basic forces governing human behavioral and social phenomena.

The Mathematical Elaboration of Small Group Power Structure: From Naive Empiricism to Theoretical Enhancement

Louis N. Gray

Introduction

Since its development in the late 1960's our approach to small group power structure and process has gone through five developmental periods: (1) initial empirical and definitional development (approximately 1966–72), (2) basic theoretical development and elaboration (1972–76), (3) experimental investigation of the theory using a revised experimental structure (1976–82), (4) revision of the experimental procedures, development of the theory along traditional design approaches, incorporation of an individual choice model (1982–88), (5) revision of the nature of the theory, recognition of parallel processes within interaction structures, elaboration of the mathematics of behavioral power structures (1988–   ). Each of these relatively distinct periods involved a number of persons contributing to the development of a research program, each contributing his or her own ideas and experiences to the general development of the current theory. I shall proceed through the stages listed above, identifying the most important of the developments and the persons responsible for them in our growth. I shall conclude with a fairly detailed explication of the state of the theory at the present time. Each section will be accompanied by a fairly complete bibliography of the material published during that period.

The First Period (1966–72)

Our approach to social power was generated through a series of discussions between Bruce H. Mayhew, Jr., and me which began shortly after we arrived as beginning faculty at Washington State University, in the fall semester of 1966. Both of us had a behavioral orientation toward sociology, that is, we felt that the study of behavior was the best ap-

proach to detailing social structural phenomena. In addition we shared
the belief that the advance of sociology lay not in the study of individuals
and their similarities or differences, but in the study of groups as groups;
this, we felt, was the central subject matter of sociology and would serve
to differentiate sociology from psychology in a way that much of the
current research did not.

Another shared concern was the advantage of observation (experimental or otherwise) as a tool for measurement. We did not feel that
questionnaire responses meant very much or were reliable enough for
the systematic study of human social systems. Mayhew was less concerned with small group behavior than I, but he recognized the value of
the small group as a simulated organization under certain conditions and
the relative ease of measurement in small social systems. As might be
anticipated, we both held an interest in influence processes.

As was normal for beginning sociologists in the 1960's we had been
fairly thoroughly trained in methods and statistics (this trend probably
continues). Due to this background we took the generally positivistic
view of the day and assumed that appropriate methods and applications
of statistical techniques would give us the answers to questions we
wanted to ask. In these early days we did not concern ourselves with
theory, but with the methods we might use to uncover principles of human behavior. Both of us had experience with theory, but we saw no
existing theory of the behavioral sort which applied directly to power or
influence, and made detailed predictions. Thus we began by developing
an experimental situation which would allow us to measure behavioral
aspects of power in somewhat restricted situations.

Mayhew had developed a basic category system for power related behavior which we adopted (eventually published as Mayhew, Gray, and
Richardson 1969). This category system divided behavior into directive
acts (acts which specify their own reinforcements and may order, direct,
implore, etc., another to engage in some specified activity), compliant
acts (acts which supply the reinforcer requested in a directive act, i.e.,
follow the order, etc.), and non-compliant acts (acts which do not reinforce the directive) (see Adams and Romney 1959). Later we tended
to label such non-compliant acts as "rejective," though this application
only holds for the kinds of experiments we have engaged in, and need
not apply in general. What was needed was a situation in which we
could observe and record the instances of directive, compliant, and non-
compliant acts. While we understood that some sort of game situation
would be appropriate, we had not envisioned the exact details.

Shortly after the beginning of 1967 we pooled our experience with
parlor games and settled on a restricted version of Scribbage as the heart

of our experimental design. This game, similar to Scrabble, uses dice with English letters printed on the sides to form words. Although the game was designed as a competition among individuals we decided to modify it such that groups would work collectively for solutions. The points gained in playing the game would count toward the winning of prize money (or some other payment method). In this situation directive actions would be indicated by the suggestion of a group member that a particular word should be formed by the group. Compliant and rejective actions would be indicated by the occurrence of a "yes" vote or a "no" vote. The voting would be indicated by two colored chips held in the subjects' hands under the table, so that those voting on a suggestion (excluding the person who made the suggestion) would not directly interact about their choice. A unanimous vote was required in order to form the word. If the subjects had adequate vocabularies it should be the case that the better suggestions would be accepted (complied with) while those of inferior value (based on point count) would be rejected. As we had designed the game, coding of behaviors was simple and reliable.

The reader should note that at this point we have no theory. We have not specified any relations between the variables or their frequencies. What we have is a situation in which we can view rudimentary behavioral power relations. The methods we adopted at this time were purely descriptive: we had found an experimental situation in which we could observe the behaviors we were interested in through a controlled setting and with high reliability. We as yet did not know exactly how these behaviors would be used in some kind of analysis that would be theoretically informative.

The initial set of data was collected in the spring of 1967 at Washington State University. A total of twenty sex-homogeneous triads were run, half male and half female. Two communication structures were utilized: (1) spontaneous activity structures in which anyone could initiate a word suggestion, so long as no other suggestion was pending, and (2) cyclical, in which directives proceeded around the group in order, as in most parlor games. There were five triads in each of the four treatments. The data collected included the identification and nature of each suggestion (directive), and the response of each other group member to the suggestion. The number of directives a person initiated had to be equal to the sum of the compliances and rejections of each other actor (the initiator could not vote on the suggestion). Totally, then, there were twice as many reactions (compliances and rejections) as there were proactions (directives).

Since our focus was on the influence or power of individual positions within the group, our initial approach to the data was to calculate $Pr(C)$, the probability of a compliance (acceptance) occurring either in a specific dyad or for the group as a whole. Examination of these quantities allowed, for each triad, the construction of a quantified digraph indicating the nature of the relations between the positions. Our initial attention was concentrated on the specific groups, rather than on differences between them or on the relations of $Pr(C)$ to other variables that could be defined.

James T. Richardson, however, in developing a summary of our experimental results, noted that in spontaneous groups there was a strong association between the frequency of directive activity initiated by an individual and the frequency of compliance received. This finding began the developments that started us thinking along theoretical rather than methodological lines in regard to power and influence structures. The initial idea lies in elementary reinforcement theory.

We assumed that compliance received operated as a reward or reinforcer for directive action. This seemed to suggest a curvilinear relationship between directive activity and compliance received. Persons initiating relatively more directive activity would be those receiving proportionally more compliance and directing proportionally more of the group's work. This approach led to the development of an equation which suggested that

$$Pr(C) = r \, Pr(A)/(S_i \, r \, Pr(A)), \tag{1}$$

where $Pr(C)$ is the probability of receiving compliance for a member of a dyad or triad out of all compliance received in the dyad or triad; r is the conditional probability of receiving compliance, given that a directive activity has been initiated; $Pr(A)$ is the probability of initiating a directive activity out of all those initiated; and S_i indicates the summation over all members of the dyad or triad considered.

While this equation fills all the requirements of probabilities, it adds little to our understanding, since it is tautological for appropriately chosen values of r. The equation did, however, provide the basis for the examination of processes involved in the acquisition of power by a particular occupant of a position in a group. In order to understand the utility and importance of the equation it is necessary to look at some of the simple models of learning which were influential in the theoretical development. Some learning models (see Bush and Mosteller 1951; Estes 1959) suggest that responses often tend to occur in proportion to the amounts of reinforcement they receive. In relationship to Equation 1, such an idea suggests that $Pr(A)$ would tend to vary with r. In a relatively natural interaction situation, however, there are no externally controlled reinforcement probabilities such as those found in simple learning situations. Instead, control of such probabilities lies with the other members of the group who reward or punish an initiator with respect to the types and amounts of directive activities that person generates. From this, it may be expected that there exists a relationship between $Pr(A)$ and r and that it is a two-way relationship of mutual adjustment of both values rather than a causal chain from reinforcement to response as in individual learning experiments.

The process may be explained more clearly by dealing with the dynamics of talent or skill. Presumably, in stranger groups of relatively homogeneous composition, a prime mover to initiating directive activity would be skill. If some relevance attaches to the successful completion of a group task, we would then expect a person's directivity to be complied with to the extent that the person actually was directing the group activity more effectively than others. Thus talent or skill should be a determining factor in both $Pr(A)$ and r.

If we are willing to assume that the problems of mutual adjustment of activity and reinforcement are not too different from those of a simple learning model (though one of group learning), then we might expect that the values of $Pr(A)$ would converge to some limit proportional to the values of r (which are also converging). These coincident convergence processes could be thought of as the results of a relatively simple multiperson learning process which requires the balance of initiation and reward as persons become aware of each other and the types of responses they receive from each other. The final limiting values would represent some sort of optimum level of participation and reward to maximize some salient aspect of group operation (e.g., group reward). At such points of balance we would be assured that even talented individuals did not overparticipate and that the amount of directive activity provided by each member would be proportional to that member's ability on whatever criterion was important for reinforcement in the group.

The model suggested here we called the "contingent" model of group influence, since the probability of receiving reinforcement was dependent on the initiation of directive action. Some simple simulations indicated that the final relationship should yield a curve resembling an S bend. For hypothetical data we observed that the relationship was approximately linear over most of its range, but curvilinear aspects were evident at the extremes. Thus for an application of linear regression between $Pr(C)$ and $Pr(A)$ we should find a negative intercept and a slope greater than one. This was observed for male triads in the spontaneous situation (intercept = $-.12$, slope = 1.35, $r^2 = .97$).

A second form of the model might be called "non–contingent," indicating that the receipt of reinforcement was independent of directive activity. At the limit in such a case, we would find approximate equality among the values of r calculated for the different members of the group. Such a condition would result in a simple linear relationship between $Pr(C)$ and $Pr(A)$, with an intercept of zero and a slope of one. This was observed for female triads in the spontaneous situation (intercept $= -.01$, slope $= 1.02$, $r^2 = .98$).

We realized at the time that the employment of linear models with these data was inappropriate. The application of mathematical learning theory to our results indicated that the relationship for the contingent model was non-linear, though its central area could be linearly approximated. At the time of our first paper (Gray, Richardson, and Mayhew 1968) we did not have the analytical tools to examine non-linearity (due to small sample sizes) and, further, did not have a useful functional form for the non-linearity we presumed to be present. Equation 1 did not provide a useful functional relation between $Pr(C)$ and $Pr(A)$, due to the presence of r. While it allowed simulations to be made, it did not give us an abstract form which could be used in analysis.

The difference between male and female spontaneous groups was striking and significant. While both linear applications fit well, it was clear that there were differences. More specifically, male triads exhibited a positive linear trend between r and $Pr(A)$ ($r^2 = .35$), but female triads exhibited no association between these variables ($r^2 = .02$). This meant that males probably varied more in skill level and functioned on that basis while females did not vary much along this dimension, leaving socialized activity levels to determine the relationship. Although this was initially considered a gender effect, it needed to be considered in terms of the more general theoretical approach we were developing.

In this first stage of our theory development we began with a simple descriptive measurement scheme. When results began to come in we adapted the structure of psychological learning theory to attempt to make sense of the exchange of interactions occurring among participants. While the theoretical development at this stage was largely borrowed from individual psychology, we were beginning to do something new. We were applying the concepts and principles across interacting individuals: all the relationships we studied involved at least two persons, neither of whom was an experimenter. Unlike psychological studies in which the experimenter may control the behavior of the subject organism, we were overtly dealing with subjects who responded naturally to each other in the course of the gamelike experiment. Since the principles of psychological learning theory still seemed to hold, this initial step in our investigations set the stage for a later development of learning in groups as analogous to that of individual organisms. Our first task, however, was to attempt to systematize a model which would apply more generally than simple substitutions on Equation 1. Before we began that task in earnest, however, we engaged in several replications or partial replications of the original experiment, in an attempt to investigate the generality of our original findings, their stability, and additional features of the organization of social power structures (von Broembsen, Mayhew, and Gray 1969; Gray and Mayhew 1970). While the strength of the relationship varied over different experiments, it remained high ($r^2 > .90$), so that it seemed our initial work was no accident.*

The Second Period (1972–76)

We were well aware that the linear model examined during the first period was inadequate to systematize the general nature of the relationship between the relative frequency of compliance and the relative frequency of directive activity. The relationship should be fundamentally non-linear, though monotonic, with a linear relationship as a special case. The studies of the first period used a number of statistical learning theories as their base. In general, these learning theories may be thought to be related to the "Law of Effect." The Law of Effect may be stated as follows: the probability of a specified response occurring is a positive function of the probability of that response being reinforced (rewarded). This definition is a simple equivalent of those presented by Thorndike (1913), Skinner (1938), and Herrnstein (1970). While this basic principle may be widely accepted for individual behavior, it is difficult to apply to relatively unstructured social situations.

The question we addressed was whether or not the underlying principles present in the individual level Law of Effect could be generalized to social settings, thereby, perhaps, providing the functional form needed for generalizing the relationship between directive activity and compliance. Our starting point lay in the suggestion that what happens in groups is similar to what happens in individuals, except for the comparisons available to the organisms involved.

We were primarily concerned with subsets of interaction in which the following variables could be identified: (1) a, the activity or response rate of an organism, and (2) c, the reinforcement rate of an organism. The use of the variables a and c corresponds to the directive activity and com-

*First period references are as follows: Gray, Richardson, and Mayhew 1968; Richardson, Mayhew, and Gray 1969; Mayhew and Gray 1969; von Broembsen, Mayhew, and Gray 1969; Mayhew, Gray, and Richardson 1969; Gray and Mayhew 1970; Bolton, Gray, and Mayhew 1970; Mayhew and Gray 1971, 1972; Gray and Mayhew 1972; Richardson et al. 1973; Gray, Mayhew, and Campbell 1974; Williams, Gray, and von Broembsen 1976.

pliance rates initiated and received by a position in a group setting. To limit further the range of discussion we assumed that these variables are measured as proportions of their maximum and lie between zero and unity; and that, in social situations, they represent proportions of the total initiated activity or the total reinforcement received. Thus the individual values of a and c sum to unity over all positions in the group. This restriction indicates that we assumed the social system to be closed; the occurrences of activity or receipt of positive reinforcers were bounded and finite within the social system under consideration.

In individual learning an organism is subjected to reinforcement contingencies by the experimenter. In no way does the organism know the contingencies before the experiment, nor does it know what might be happening to other organisms in similar experimental situations. When we move to social situations, however, organisms usually can see what happens to other organisms in the same context—thus a comparison process evolves (Thibaut and Kelley, 1959).

While participating in social situations the individual organism will compare its level of reinforcement or response with that of other organisms in the same social situation. The question we addressed at the time, however, was how this comparison should be symbolically represented. There were essentially two choices here: (1) the difference between two inputs or outputs (subtraction), or (2) the ratio of two inputs or outputs (division). The first of these choices was dismissed, since the range of outcomes was constrained to the interval $(-1, +1)$, and because the negative signs which were likely to occur in some groups were mathematically troublesome. The second choice yielded values with infinite range (thought not symmetrical) and gave no problems with signs: thus the odds ratio approach was accepted as the appropriate operational and symbolic analogue of the comparison process we envisioned.

We suggest, then, that the appropriate unit for analysis in a group situation is not simply the probability of an event but the odds ratio of the event. In addition to specifying appropriately the comparison process we believed to occur, it also had the mathematical advantages of allowing transformations which we needed to provide estimates of parameters in the model under development, parameters which would allow the generalization of the original model.

With group situations, the functional relation is made not between the raw probabilities in the equation for single organisms but between the odds ratios of activity and reinforcement. Even though reinforcement in social situations is often highly difficult to measure with any degree of precision, we still expect that the activity of one person relative to others should be related to the perceived levels of such ratios in reinforcement.

The basis for the comparison, then, is the functional relationship between the odds ratio for activity and the odds ratio for relative reinforcement. It is not how much one does or gets per se, it is how much, relatively, one does or gets. The general expectation for the social situation lies in Equation 2 below:

$$c/(1 - c) = f(a/(1 - a)). \tag{2}$$

We now attempted to examine the nature of f and to develop a mathematical equivalent to the individual Law of Effect which applies to group processes. To do this we must first start with the notion of the odds ratio itself. Terms of this type vary from zero to infinity and thus do not encompass the whole range of real numbers. It would be preferable to have a situation in which the value varied (theoretically) from minus infinity to plus infinity. This could be easily accomplished by taking the logarithm of each side of the equation. Once this is done a first approximation to the functional form can be generated by a linear function, i.e.,

$$\ln (c/(1 - c)) = D (\ln (a/(1 - a))), \tag{3}$$

where ln indicates the natural logarithm and D indicates the single parameter of the system. It has often been suggested that an intercept term be added to the equation, but our assumption was that the means of both sides of the equation should be equal (to zero) under general conditions in which each position in a dyad (or dyad within a larger group) was equally likely to be selected as the first (numerator) member of any dyad studied. A somewhat more complex model was suggested for groups of larger size, but the model is more clearly viewed in the dyadic format. For larger groups predictions can be made by examining all the dyads contained therein, assuming homogeneity of the function across dyads (see Gray et al. 1976; Gray and von Broembsen 1976).

In this form (Equation 3) the model contains a single parameter, D. For expository purposes we choose to call D the differentiation parameter of the system, since it tells the extent to which group members are differentially rewarded or punished and also indicates the extent to which a non-linear structure emerges in a group. The value of D allowed the definition of four exhaustive types of group structures: (1) simple structures ($D = 1.00$); (2) differentiated structures in which some persons are overrewarded for high input while others are underrewarded for lower input ($D > 1.00$); (3) undifferentiated structures in which persons receive relatively the same reinforcement regardless of input ($0.00 < D < 1.00$); and (4) redifferentiated structures in which reinforcement is inversely related to input ($D < 0.00$). While we expect that all these types of structures could arise under the appropriate circumstances, it seems most likely that the values of D will be relatively close to 1.00 in groups without formal structure and with relatively homogeneous reinforcement schedules operating.

The development of this model (Equation 3) yielded the formulation we sought. When the value of D was unity, the model yielded a perfect linear relationship between the probability of compliance and the probability of activity (equivalent to the non-contingent version of Equation 1). When the value of D was greater than unity, the equation yielded an S-shaped bend with a slope (linear approximation) that was greater than one. Thus, at least two forms of the model could be used to reproduce the results found for males and females in our first study. Moreover, the revised form of the model did not suffer from the ordinary linear approximations problem of predicting values outside the zero to one range. Additionally, as a power function (in its general form) it was similar to formulations developed by S. S. Stevens (1957) and others for dealing with the stimulus value of psychological phenomena. It was also almost identical to William Baum's (1974) generalization of the matching law for operant psychology. The model worked effectively for a variety of data we had access to, much of which was from other researchers, and was tested by Doreian (1978) on data he had collected. In all instances the general form of the model seemed adequate to the task.

Nevertheless, it seemed clear that the value of D varied substantially from situation to situation and was often greater than 1.00 (it was sometimes slightly lower, very rarely negative). This led us to concentrate on the value of D as a regressionlike parameter and attempt to explain the reasons for its varying value. While some of the variation was certainly stochastic in nature, there were enough large differences that could not be so simply explained. It was logical, then, that in the next period of theoretical development we would attempt to deal with explanations of the value of the differentiation parameter. The elaboration of a theory of group power structure based on a theory of group learning had led us immediately to a new problem to be solved.*

The Third Period (1976–82)

The third period began with a series of wide-ranging discussions involving M. H. von Broembsen, M. J. Sullivan, W. I. Griffith, and myself. Our basic question was: How could differentiated structures be explained? We had been aware for some time that the frequency of noncompliant (rejective) activity was important in partially determining the conditions for differentiation. It will be recalled that our first work indi-

*Second period references are as follows: Gray and von Broembsen 1974; Gray et al. 1976; Gray and von Broembsen 1976.

cated that a positive association between the conditional probability of compliance and the marginal probability of directive activity would be sufficient to create an *S*-shaped curve, and a lack of such association would result in a linear relation (see Equation 1). Such an association can only exist if some persons receive rejections: in the event that no rejections occurred in a group, the linear model ($D = 1$) would be the only possible outcome.

We had been aware of such a limiting result for some time, and modifications to the initial experiments had been made to encourage rejection in the interactive word game. While our attempts to increase rejection had met with some success, we were still having difficulty achieving mean conditional acceptance rates below 80 percent. Our discussions directed us back into the structure of psychological learning experiments and the features that led to their impressive results. The idea occurred to us that groups tend to mimic, in some manner, their environments. That is, groups which receive little reward from their environment find rewards scarce and thus, in their dealings with other group members, distribute internal rewards sparingly. Groups which receive a high rate of reward from their environment, however, tend to give rewards relatively frequently in their internal interaction. In our experiments to this point we had accepted almost everything groups had accomplished in counting toward their point total and subsequent environmental rewards (the exceptions being misspelled words, nonexistent words, etc., which occurred relatively rarely). Essentially, then, we were rewarding the groups at a high rate (over 90 percent of the time), which contributed to their tendency to reward each other at high rates. How could we break this trend?

The most obvious solution was to introduce an additional factor into the interactive situation—explicit environmental rewards. In such situations groups received immediate feedback from the experimenter on the acceptability of a word they had formed. This was explained as a computer-generated reward schedule, with the suggestion that the computer program was selecting certain features of words chosen as the basis for granting or withholding rewards. Such an environmental schedule could be set at any desired rate of richness, depending upon the experimenter's purpose; the group attempted to learn the patterns the computer would accept, even though in actuality there were no such explicit patterns involved in the computer program.

We hypothesized that a primary factor affecting a group's reaction to its environment was the rate of positive reinforcement which it received from its environment. If the rate of reinforcement from the environment was high, then the group need do little to meet the requirements successfully and should rapidly tend to develop an equitable structure and a differentiation parameter of 1.00.

If, on the other hand, positive reinforcement from the environment was at a relatively low level, then the group must attempt to develop strategies for increasing, if possible, the rate of external reinforcement. Low levels of reinforcement should cause groups to engage in exploratory and even superstitious behavior to attempt to find the behaviors which will result in increased levels of external reward. Such exploratory behavior should manifest itself in the discrimination process by which individuals are differentially reinforced with compliance in the group setting, thus producing differentiated structures with differentiation parameters greater than 1.00 (see Michaels and Wiggins 1976).

Once a group had maximized its level of environmental reinforcement, or found that it could not improve the rate of environmental reinforcement, the process of the movement toward equity should begin. For groups with low levels of reinforcement we should find differentiated structures in initial stages, but this differentiation should diminish over time as satisfactory or optimal solutions to the environmental demands were reached.

An additional characteristic of environmental reinforcement which should affect the structure which evolves in groups was the contingency of the reinforcement (i.e., the extent to which the environmental reinforcer depends on some characteristic or quality of the reinforced response). It is possible to distinguish between at least two basic situations: (1) non-contingent (or random) reinforcement, in which the probability of reinforcement is independent of any characteristic of the response, and (2) contingent reinforcement where the probability of reinforcement depends on some characteristic of the response.

These two types of reinforcement should have direct effects upon the differentiation of structures in groups. Most notably, the presence of a non-contingent reinforcement schedule indicates that the group can do nothing to increase their rate of reinforcement. The group, however, attempts to find ways of increasing the rate and correspondingly spends more time on exploratory behavior. This should result in more rejection and consequently more differentiated, yet less stable, structures than would be the case for corresponding groups with contingent reinforcement schedules.

Groups with contingent reinforcement schedules can influence the rate of reinforcement from their environment simply by following the contingencies. They should learn from the situation with relative rapidity and develop structures which are stable and which approach equity relatively soon. While exploratory behavior should still occur with contingent situations, we suspected that such exploration should soon be re-warded through location of an appropriate solution so that exploratory behavior would no longer be necessary. It was expected that the general model would fit better for groups operating under conditions of contin-gent than non-contingent reinforcement situations.

The results of an experiment testing these ideas is reported in Griffith and Gray (1978). The results supported the general theory, with richly rewarded groups achieving relative equity over time and differing little from equity at any time. Sparsely rewarded groups, on a non-contingent schedule, were highly differentiated and unstable, though they did move toward equity over time. Contingently rewarded groups tended toward stable differentiation and did progress toward equity. This experiment tended to show that our thinking was essentially correct and that we could in part account for the appearance of differentiation over the short term in groups. It did not explain how differentiation (or some other non-equitable structure) might persist over time. While previous studies had revealed that most groups tended toward a matching relationship over time, empirical observations of general group structures often yielded differentiated structures (see Michaels and Wiggins 1976).

The solution to this kind of problem was most easily approached by consideration of the general learning theory which underlay our concep-tualization of power. In order to do this, we could list the various types of reinforcers which may impinge on the group situation. We suspected that three basic reinforcers affected one's tendency to initiate directive activity in a group situation: (1) self-reinforcement, which is the ten-dency of individuals to reward themselves for the simple event of acting in group situations; (2) internal or group reinforcement, which is the reinforcement an individual receives from being rewarded by members of the group (e.g., receiving compliance); and (3) external reinforcement, which refers to the rewards, if any, that are received by members of the group from some source outside itself.

Following Killeen (1972) we assumed that odds ratios across pairs of positions in a group could be combined multiplicatively among sources of reinforcement to predict the directive activity odds ratio for a dyad (by itself or within a larger group). This is a form of the matching law applied to groups in which activity matches with the product of the probabilities of the three types of reinforcers. Utilizing Baum's (1974) generalization of the matching law and assumptions from our original study, we could show that the value of D would be greater than one when positions in the dyad had different proportional levels of environ-mental reinforcement. That is, an individual level of contingency (success depends on the position of the actor) is a sufficient condition for the generation of differentiation parameters greater than one. While this outcome does depend on the number of reinforcers operating in a situation (an infinite number of reinforcers yields simple structure), a relatively small number, such as that assumed, will tend to yield differentiation under these circumstances. Such differentiation should persist over time and not be reduced to an equitable relationship, since no amount of alteration of behavior can effect the relative frequency of environmental reinforcement contingent on the position receiving compliance. In this sense, it is possible for the group to learn to overreward one position with compliance, since such overreward will always result in greater success for the whole group. It is impossible to learn the repertoire of a successful player to improve one's own performance when a position contingent schedule is applied.

Results of the initial experiment testing these ideas (reported in Gray and Sullivan 1978) confirmed our general ideas, though some deviations occurred. The groups tended to be differentiated and remained so for a period of six sessions, generally confirming our contentions. Thus by considering the reinforcement nature of the group situation we were able to isolate at least some of the conditions which produced inequitable (differentiated) structures in groups. But it should be pointed out that the conditions specified here are not the only conditions which might result in differentiation. Any condition which produces a conditional probability of compliance which is not constant over all positions should operate to effect differentiation. Among those conditions are such things as status or performance cues which may operate to affect the responses of group members. It may be suggested, however, that such cues are actually operating as external reinforcers to group interaction situations.

These theoretical developments are important because they examined the conditions under which certain structures could be developed or maintained. These developments represented a step beyond earlier work, since they sought to do more than just examine the effects of various types of external reward and proposed to apply theoretical principles as they were understood at this stage in the development of the theory. The most complete statement of the theory at this time is contained in Gray et al. (1982a).

The theory developed had many implications for the elaboration and utilization of social power theory. In addition to specifying the conditions under which differentiated or simple power structures would emerge in social situations, it also specified the conditions which could be utilized to produce groups with such characteristics. The theory told us what to do in order to produce groups with differentiated structures or to produce groups with simple structures.

Michaels and Wiggins (1976) suggested that most groups use differential distributions of reinforcement. If this contention is true, then we should expect to find that most groups are differentiated in structure to some extent. Our suggestion would be that the reason for observed stratification would then follow if it were the case that contingent reinforcement distributions were generalized in some sort of halo phenomenon to formal levels of stratification within the group. While we take differentiation or contingency of external reinforcers as given by experimental conditions, they may well arise for the reasons Wiggins suggests.

Inequitable local exchanges seem to be continued in the event that more profitable alternatives are unavailable. This would occur precisely because there are additional reinforcers which apply to the situation and bring it into balance. The point is that distributive justice and equity may be served by these additional reinforcers when the total system is examined, but a researcher, focusing upon a local segment of the entire transaction, may be misled to read inequity into the operation when the appropriate inclusion of additional reinforcing variables may allow the overall transaction to be viewed as balanced and equitable. The matching law predicts that the entire situation will be characterized by a balanced loss, not that each local segment of the situation will have equitable results.*

The Fourth Period (1982–88)

To this point, we had not directly considered the exchange relations between the environment and the internal group behavior. We had taken the environmental reinforcers as given for a situation and had not dealt with changes in the behavior of reinforcers stemming from such sources. This seemed to represent an important elaboration of the theory.

A modification of the basic relationship (Equation 3) had been proposed by Hamblin (1977, 1979). His modification adds a power of an additional variable—the magnitude of reinforcement. Since the probabilities of external reinforcement had been employed in earlier explications of our theory, this seemed a natural extention. While we had been successful in earlier applications, the relationship between the external reinforcement occurring in the course of an experiment and the internal behavior of a group had not been well developed.

The inclusion of a variable representing rewards to a group generated by an external environment but contingent upon a single position is par-

*Third period references are as follows: Griffith and Gray 1978; Gray and Sullivan 1978; Gray, Griffith, von Broembsen, and Sullivan 1982; Gray, Griffith, Sullivan, and von Broembsen 1982; Elworth and Gray 1982.

ticularly salient. Hamblin (1979) notes that many matching theorists have not taken into consideration the fact that organisms have the problem of adapting to changing environmental demands. Presumably, organisms do not generally operate in isolation from some kind of external evaluation of their task resolution, when such is forthcoming. In a group situation individuals are likely to take into account the internal reactions of other group members as well as reactions from some environment external to the group itself.

At this point in our theoretical development we assumed that group behavior should come into agreement with external contingencies and these external contingencies should serve to structure the behavior of individuals occupying positions in groups. On this basis we proposed the following model of behavior,

$$c/(1 - c) = (a/(1 - a))^D (e/(1 - e))^{1/d}, \qquad (4)$$

where e represents the proportion of environmental reinforcement accruing to the group on the basis of agreement with the first position, and $1/d$ indicates the inverse of the discrimination parameter (the extent to which positions are influenced by environmental requirements). The inverse of the function derives from developments in Gray et al. (1982a). Fits of this model were generally good (see Griffith and Gray 1985; Gray and Griffith 1984). Nevertheless, the fits were not as strong as those obtained in the early experiments and seemed to be influenced by factors we were not considering or aware of.

The fourth period also involved extensive changes in the experimental design and attempts to elaborate the model beyond the initial paradigm of the word game, as well as the elaboration of the model to more general circumstances. While the developments were along traditional lines, and achieved some success, they were less adequate for the development of the theory than those that have occurred more recently.

The redesign of the experiment followed criticisms that our word game was too limited and not generalizable to ordinary situations. With the development of more restricted techniques (see Molm 1981a, 1981b, for example) we developed more controlled experimental conditions than had been pursued earlier. Specifically, games were played by dyads (the simplest of groups) against a computer. Persons could initiate a directive action which attempted to predict the decision a computer program would make in a two-alternative situation. Once a directive was initiated the other person could either agree or disagree. A disagreement not only signaled a rejection but also initiated a new directive act (since there were only two alternatives). This somewhat more abstract situation was developed because we felt that ordinary vocabulary skill differences were influencing the behavior we would like to control.

In the latest experiments there can be no skill differences among occupants of positions which are not, at least probabilistically, controlled by the experimenter. There may still be status differences or other cues persons can use to influence the behavior of others. Such an abstract game often tends to be relatively boring, but we felt this was a necessary expense for the improvement of the design. Throughout this period we found relatively good fits to Equation 4, though the coefficients of determination were not as high as we had hoped, or as high as those of earlier experiments. Since these experiments generally tended to reward differentiation, that was observed in the behavior of the groups. Particularly of interest were differences in the parameters of the model which seemed to be effected by the gender composition of the group: females seemingly were more attentive to variations in the external reinforcement structure than were males. This stands in contrast to some of Molm's (1985) work that indicates little in the way of a gender effect.

During this period Gray and Tallman (1984) developed a "satisfaction balance" model of individual choice and decision-making. Since this model includes magnitudes of reinforcements and punishments rather than simply probabilities, it could be used to develop more detailed statements of group behavior by appropriately replacing individual characteristics with those of an interactive setting. Generally these applications yielded models of group choice which were generally in accord with the models previously suggested, though some additional effects were noted. Application of a satisfaction balance model of group choice to some of Molm's (1985) data was quite effective in increasing explained variation. For our own data these applications yielded no increase in predictive power, leading us to believe that the initial (and somewhat simpler) formulations were, in fact, group generalizations of the satisfaction balance approach which were simplified somewhat by the restrictions in our experimental designs and the limited nature of communication in our groups. Either approach leads to the development of models which relate odds ratios and powers of odds ratios: in either case linear applications can be done appropriately by taking the logarithms of both sides of the power functional models.

The final application of this period involved changing environmental reward structures over time. Discussions with Dean Judson led to an experimental design which used the computer matching interactive design but incorporated the initial establishment of status differences among players of opposite sex. Initial manipulations, similar to those of the expectation states tradition (see Berger, Rosenholtz, and Zelditch 1980) were used along with traditional criteria to yield groups in which the male player had (or was supposed to have) an initial power advantage.

The actual experiment consisted of systematically varying the environmental reinforcement (our analogue of "skill" or "talent") in favor of the female. We reasoned that the systematic alteration of environmental reinforcement in favor of the low-power position would result in the "shaping" of group behavior in such a manner that initiation of directive activity, receipt of compliance, and receipt of rejection would move to create greater equality in the group and, perhaps, alter the power structure in favor of the initially less powerful position. Indeed, this happened over a relatively short (100 trial) experiment. In fact we were able to reverse the direction of the initial inequality in position. By altering the receipt of environmental reinforcement in the group we were able to alter, relatively rapidly, the interactive relations of the participants and overcome the initial advantage offered to the male position (see Judson and Gray 1990). The implication of this experiment is that manipulation of environmental rewards and punishments can be successfully used to modify the internal behavior of groups, creating whatever type of inequality (or equality) is desired for a particular group structure.

Theory development during this period was basically elaborative, and except for the impact of satisfaction balance, little in the way of new development occurred. Nevertheless, the work in this period set us thinking about the generality and applicability of the theory and focused our attention on additional aspects (much of this due to the influence of Molm and her work in groups). We began to see that much of the work in traditional exchange theory could be modeled by the kinds of equations we had developed, and applications to others' data were encouraging. Thus this period set the stage for the current development of the theory and the mathematical enhancement that it has undergone over the last few years.*

The Current Status of the Theory (1988–)

Thinking in the last few years has centered on some of the omissions of the theoretical framework and the nature of the relation between those variables which characterize the internal (interactive) structure of groups and those which characterize the environment in which the group operates. These two systems, which must be related, are at the core of any attempt to apply generalized learning principles to group behavior. In the course of such developments we have attempted to broaden the theory and determine precisely those relationships which exist. While our past work had been productive, it still did not portray the fundamen-

---

*Fourth period references are as follows: Gray and Tallman 1984; Gray and Griffith 1984; Griffith and Gray 1985; Gray and Tallman 1986, 1987; Gray and Stafford 1988.

tal relationships we believed existed in group power structures. Additional dimensions can be developed through classifications such as proactions and reactions (Murray 1951), and reactions may themselves be classified as positive or negative (Bales 1950). Of the possible dimensions which might be defined we have, in our work on internal social power, concentrated on three: (1) proactions, or, more specifically, directive actions; (2) reactions which are compliant in nature; and (3) reactions which are rejective (or at least non-compliant) in nature. The great majority of research and theory on internal relations has concentrated on the relation, or extensions of the relations, between the receipt of compliance and the initiation of directive activity; that is, we have examined the relations between two of the three internal dimensions of power-related interaction.

More recently we have begun to examine the addition of rejective behavior to this original bivariate relationship, with substantial success. If we conceive of power-related interaction as consisting of three variables (directive activity, compliance, and rejection), then we not only reach higher levels of explanatory power but also show the interdependence of *all* the relevant dimensions in producing the general interaction structure we observe in groups. It is the interrelation of these dimensions which constitutes the interaction structure of groups. It is this interactive *structure* which should be produced by variables constituting the consequences of the interaction structure (either scheduled or obtained). Thus, instead of studying the relation between a single dependent variable and one or more independent variables, we need to study a set of dependent variables and their relation to a set of independent variables, as well, of course, as the interrelations of the variables in each of the two sets.

For each group we can define a vector $S = (f(a), f(c), f(r))$ expressing that group's position on directive activity ($f(a)$), compliance ($f(c)$), and rejection ($f(r)$), the three dimensions describing power relations defined by Mayhew, Gray, and Richardson (1969). The functional notation ($f(.)$) implies that the proportional measures defined by Mayhew, Gray, and Richardson must be operated upon to achieve easily manipulable mathematical expressions. The work of Gray and von Broembsen (1976), Griffith and Gray (1978), and Gray and Sullivan (1978) provides us with a suggestion of this form, i.e., $f(x) = \ln(x/(1 - x)) = L(x)$, or in other words a logit transformation, where x is a proportion of a total accruing to a specific position in a dyad, i.e., $x = X_1/(X_1 + X_2)$, and X_i represents the frequency of a specified class of behavior for a position in the dyad. While this approach has worked well in a variety of applications (Gray et al. 1982a; Griffith and Gray 1978), it seems to suffer a logical failing. For example, suppose $x = .67$. This proportion can be based on as few as three discrete acts or a number approaching countable infinity. That is, while x or $L(x)$ gives us an indication of departure from equality within a particular interactive setting, it gives no indication of the amount of activity which has departed from equality. As suggested by Thianisia Gaskins, $L(x)$ provides a kind of "velocity" away from equality, but gives no indication of the "mass" which has been moved. For this reason we suggest an alternative functional form: $p(x) = (X_1 + X_2)L(x)$, which is the total frequency on which the proportion is based times the appropriate logit. Thus $S = (p(a), p(c), p(r))$ and reflects the location of any group on the three power relevant dimensions of interaction structure. It is easy to see that S may be represented by a point in a three-dimensional space.

Several aspects of a group's power structure are evident in such a geometrical representation. The length of the line connecting S with the point $(0,0,0)$ describes the extent to which the group differs from perfect equality along all three dimensions, and can be measured through use of the Pythagorean theorem. This global amount of inequality can be calculated as $H(p) = (p(a)^2 + p(c)^2 + p(r)^2)^{.5}$. The direction of the line indicates the extent to which the power structure is influenced by the dimensions, and its projected angles with the three axes describe this relative impact of the variables. The cosines of these angles can be calculated by dividing $p(x)$ by $H(p)$ for any particular group. In these senses the structure of interaction can be described by a new derived composite in the three-space which characterizes the relative contribution of each of the dimensions to the overall "structure" of group interaction. Such a structure, which may be represented as a canonical variate, can then be related to the set of variables which arise as consequences of the interaction structure developed by a group. Before examining this interrelation, however, let us turn our attention to the internal structure of S.

Internal Structure of Power Dimensions

The three dimensions of internal structure related to power can be depicted (for a dyad) in a simple 2×2 tabulation, as shown below. The two reactive dimensions (compliance and rejection) must be structured so as to sum to the proactive dimension of directive activity, at least within the kinds of experiments we have utilized.

	Compliance	Rejection	Directive Activity
Position 1	$A_1 - R_1$	R_1	A_1
Position 2	$A_2 - R_2$	R_2	A_2
Sum	$A. - R.$	$R.$	$A.$

This tabulation, designed for groups in general, suggests that the amount of directive activity initiated by an individual in a position can be seen as the sum of two components: (1) the compliance received for a directive act, and (2) the rejection received for a directive act. This view of groups suggests that each directive act received exactly one reaction (either a compliance or a rejection) from the other member of the dyad. Under such restraints it is clear that groups larger than two would develop SA. reactions, where S is the size of the group. This kind of balance between proactions and reactions is suggested by Bales (1955), though data from some experiments indicate that it need not occur (Tallman, Marotz-Baden, and Pindas 1983), but definitions of types of actions may obscure this feature of interaction in those data.

Most of our prior research suggests a relationship between the column headed "Compliance" and that headed "Directive Activity." Clearly this ignores one of the columns in the tabulation, and thus ignores the full range of interaction which can occur in groups. As Mayhew, Gray, and Richardson (1969) suggest, power can be developed not only on the basis of the receipt of compliance, but on the basis of the delivery of rejections. Thus attempts to view the structure of interaction as bivariate (directive activity and compliance) is misleading, since it ignores the information provided by the examination of rejections in the interaction structure.

A consistent question which has followed this line of research concerns the character of the dependent variable in an equation. For the most part we have utilized compliance as the dependent variable, though many persons have suggested that activity should be so designated. Since the system we are attempting to describe is defined as a feedback system in which directive activity effects compliance and rejection, compliance and rejection effect directive activity, and compliance and rejection may be correlated due to the requirement that they sum to directive activity, it must be the case that any of the variables could be considered dependent under appropriate viewpoints. There is no direct causal ordering of these variables over a series of trials long enough to give us a realistic picture of the interaction structure. Like any learning system dealing with obtained behavioral events that are the results of a feedback process, there is no clear rationale for identifying any specific variable as dependent. In the present analysis we shall designate directive activity (proactions) as the dependent variable. While this is not necessary, is seems reasonable in light of the symmetry between proactive and reactive behaviors which appears in the tabulation, and because the larger frequencies render this variable somewhat more stable than the two reactive measures (compliance and rejection). Nevertheless, any of the variables might appear in this role for specific theoretical or practical purposes.

Our general theory is that changes in the proportion of directive activity initiated in the first position of a dyad will be proportional to the changes in the proportions of compliance and rejection. The major question lies in how these changes will be represented; that is, changes relative to what? Since the terms we choose to deal with are proportions, their changes must be relative to some baseline from which change can be measured. We suggest that they be measured relative to their variance. A change in the proportion P, dP (using a differential as an estimate of a difference), would be measured relative to the variance of the proportion, $P(1 - P)$. Thus for a given change, dP, the effect is greater if the change occurs near the extremes of 0 or 1, rather than the mid-point of .5. This makes intuitive sense in that a given amount of change at the extremes is more significant than the same amount of change around the center. The variance of outcomes (in a binomial-like sense) is greater near the center of the distribution ($P = .5$) than near the extremes. The dynamic equation connecting the dimensions of power-related interaction may be given by

$$F(A)da/[a(1 - a)] = F(C)dc/[c(1 - c)] + F(R)dr/[r(1 - r)], \quad (5)$$

where da is the differential (difference) in the proportion of directive activity initiated by position 1, dc is the differential (difference) in the proportion of compliance received by position 1, dr is the differential (difference) in the proportion of rejection received by position 1, a, c, and r are the raw proportions of directive activity, compliance and rejection prior to a change for position 1, and $F(A)$, $F(C)$, and $F(R)$ are constants representing the total frequencies of directive activity, compliance, and rejection. We may divide both sides by $F(A)$, yielding constants of proportionality on the right-hand side, $Pr(C)$ and $Pr(R)$, which indicate the relative frequency of compliant activity out of all behavior in the group and the relative frequency of rejective activity out of all behavior in the group. Clearly, $Pr(R) = 1 - Pr(C)$.

Integrating this equation over both sides yields the following model for the internal interaction structure of groups,

$$L(a) = Pr(C)L(c) + (1 - Pr(C))L(r), \quad (6)$$

where $L(x)$ is the familiar logit. The two constants of proportionality indicate the relative impact of the two independent logits (for compliance and rejection). It should be noted that this form also yields the somewhat simpler expression

$$p(a) = p(c) + p(r), \quad (7)$$

in which constants of proportionality are unity.

In Equation 7 we see that a balance is formed consistent with the tabulation above. That is, the weighted term for directive activity is equal to the sum of the weighted terms for compliance and rejection, the reactive dimensions. Thus this form of analysis is consistent with our observations of the structure of the data matrix and with the notion of balancing mechanisms between proactions (directive activity) and reactions (compliance and rejection) (see Bales 1955). An additional aspect of this approach is that each group must be considered individually. The constants of proportionality (see Equation 6) and the "masses" (see Equation 5) are functions of the marginal frequencies of the interactive events that occur. Since these are generally unique to individual groups and their interactive habits, it should be seen that each group needs to be considered individually in analysis. The success of aggregate parameters in many of our early studies simply indicates that there was not much difference from group to group. Later studies show much more variation in the proportions of compliance and rejection, resulting in a less adequate fit.

At this point it is important to investigate the fit of Equation 7 to data. As a preliminary step this is most easily accomplished with OLS regression over available research sets. Estimates of parameters for $p(c)$ and $p(r)$ can be made and compared with results from a restriction setting these parameter estimates at 1.00. The major basis for comparison is the R^2 associated with the two approaches: while restricted estimates should be lower, they should also be close if our theoretical estimate of the relationship is correct.

The mean R^2 for the OLS estimators is .993, indicating an excellent fit for the general form of Equation 7. The mean R^2 for the model restricted to parameters of 1.00 is .976, also indicating a good fit. The fit is certain to be better for the general model but the restricted model appears to provide a decent approximation. The regression parameters for the OLS model are approximately equal at .92, somewhat below the hypothesized value of 1.00. Nevertheless, it is to be expected that these values are attenuated estimates of the true values. The independent variables (reactions) in this model are certainly measured with error; they are random variables, not fixed known values. Thus the appropriate regression would take into account the fact that the residual terms for these variables are correlated with the observed values of the variables themselves. If we assume that the general model is functional in nature (Graybill's Model 2 in Graybill 1961), then our estimates of the parameters by OLS will be biased downward from their true value. In other words, the estimates should be closer to 1.00 than appears from OLS. While it is not possible, without further information or assumptions, to estimate the extent of attenuation in these data sets, it seems reasonable to conclude that the specific model presented in Equation 7 represents a good approximation of the relationship, especially when frequencies are fairly large.

Interface Between Internal and External Structures

One of the variables we have discussed is common to both the internal interaction structure and the external reinforcement structure: compliance. It is through compliance that the group confronts its environment. This particular form of reaction constitutes the work accomplished (or avoided) by the group and thus forms the linkage between the internal interaction structure of the group and the external environment. While the compliance structure is a reaction (output) of the internal system, it serves as an input to the external system. Only when a group has decided to take some action or make some decision (or refused to take some action or make some decision) can the external environment operate on that behavior. When contingent reinforcement schedules (known or unknown) are in effect they can only operate on the behaviors engaged in by the group.

Two types of events can occur once a group has made some sort of decision, i.e., when compliance with a directive act has occurred: (1) the external system may reinforce (reward) that group's choice of behavior, or (2) the external system may fail to reinforce (punish) that group's choice of behavior. If we assume that one of these types of events has to occur following each instance of group behavior (compliance), then it can be seen that a tabulation similar to the one above can be used to represent the frequencies of events at the interface between the two systems. Here the receipt of environmental events is depicted for each of the positions that may have received compliance.

	Reward	Punishment	Compliant Activity
Position 1	E_{r1}	E_{p1}	C_1
Position 2	E_{r2}	E_{p2}	C_2
Sum	$E_{r.}$	$E_{p.}$	$C.$

Such a matrix suggests that we can form measures based on the proportions of column totals. While this has already been done for compliant activity, it is also possible to develop proportional measures for environmental reward and punishment. Similarly, it is possible to take the logits of these proportions, multiply them by the appropriate frequencies, and develop a model for the interface of the internal and external systems. Thus in addition to $p(c)$, already defined, we propose $p(e_r)$ and

$p(e_p)$ to reflect the inequalities along these external dimensions. A dynamic equation for this kind of relation can be developed which is parallel to Equation 5. If we follow the analogue developed in the internal system and note that the structure of the data is identical, we should propose that

$$p(c) = p(e_r) + p(e_p). \tag{8}$$

This equation, similar in form to Equation 7, also yields an expression in the logit's equivalent to Equation 6, i.e.,

$$L(c) = Pr(E_r)L(e_r) + (1 - Pr(E_r))L(e_p), \tag{9}$$

which shows that the logit of compliance is a weighted average of the two environmental logits it gives rise to. The weights are simply the probabilities of external reinforcement and external punishment, which sum, for our designs, to unity. This approach seems consistent with the additive nature of the frequencies in the second tabulation, which is a parallel to the additive nature of the frequencies in the first.

It is now of interest to examine the fit of Equation 8 to available data sets, both with parameters free to vary and with parameters restricted to 1.00 for both independent variables.

The mean R^2 for the OLS estimators is .994, indicating an excellent fit for the general form of Equation 8. The mean R^2 for the model restricted to parameters of 1.00 is .980, also indicative of a good fit. Tests of the significance of the restriction can be made, but are of limited usefulness. The problem lies in the high values of the R^2s; they are so close to their maximum that differences which have little substantive importance are likely to be statistically significant. To our way of thinking an *a priori* model that makes no use of information from the data, yet explains 98 percent of the variation, is of more use than a model that makes use of information from the data (therefore having to be estimated) and explains only an additional 1 percent of the variation. Effectively this is the same situation that arose with Equation 7.

The estimates of the two parameters (if we assume them to be equal) are about .92, approximately the same figure obtained for Equation 7. As before, these values are attenuated due to error in measurement in the independent variables. Since the environmental frequencies of reinforcement and punishment are produced through application of a probability generator to compliance frequencies, it can be seen that these environmental elements can hardly be measured without error. Thus the estimates of the parameters in the OLS model are too low. It might be suggested that we attempt to search for some theoretical values, other than 1.00, which would be identical for both independent variables and give a slightly better fit than the restrictions we have employed. While this would be an interesting search, it appears that the values of 1.00, indicating an equal balance between input and output (for both Equations 7 and 8), provide the most theoretically appealing solution to the problem.

It should be evident at this point that we have constructed a vector in a three-space describing the external structure of the group. Thus we define the vector $E = (p(c), p(e_r), p(e_p))$, which represents the external structure. Clearly the point $p(c)$ is common to both the internal and external systems. This is appropriate, since this feature of behavior provides the interface between the two systems, which are clearly *not* independent. Again we can define the appropriate point in our three-space and measure its distance from (0,0,0) by $H(p_e) = (p(c)^2 + p(e_r)^2 + p(e_p)^2)^{.5}$, which is a measure of global inequality in the external system. The cosines of the projective angles in the three-space can be calculated by dividing each $p(.)$ by $H(p_e)$.

Relations Between the Internal and External Structural Systems

Two summary, global measures have been developed to describe the inequality that exists in the internal structure of an interactive system, and the inequality that exists in the external structure of an interactive system. These two measures, $H(p)$ and $H(p_e)$, contain a common member, the interface $p(c)$. Thus it is to be expected that these two measures are correlated. Due to the square root function applied to these measures, it is simpler to develop the relationship between $H^2(p)$ and $H^2(p_e)$. Some algebraic manipulation shows that we expect inequality in the internal and external systems to be related by the function

$$H^2(p) = H^2(p_e) + 2p(a)p(r) + 2p(e_r)p(e_p). \tag{10}$$

That is, the global internal structural inequality of the dyadic system is directly related to the global external structural inequality of the system as modified by two terms: one representing the interaction of dimensions within the internal system, and one representing the interaction of dimensions within the external system.

As one might expect, there is a good deal of collinearity between the terms in this equation. Clearly, $p(a)$ and $p(r)$ are components of $H^2(p)$, and $p(e_r)$ and $p(e_p)$ are components of $H^2(p_e)$. Attempts to fit such an equation involve a high degree of dependence, and thus potential parameter estimates are suspect. Similarly, the problem of correlated error we have encountered before is still present and attenuates the parameters entering Equation 10 in its abstract form.

The general application of the model fits the data well, with a mean R^2 of .995. Similarly, it is clear that estimates of the general parameters are highly variable and inconsistent. While the standard errors associated with the parameters are not large, as might be expected in the presence of multicollinearity, it appears that something unusual is going on in these data. To examine the structure more completely, we first estimated the value of the right side of Equation 10 and then examined the relationship of this composite variable with the left side of the equation. It was not possible to arrive at solutions from a model restricted to the theoretical parameters of Equation 10 for most of the data sets, since the specific structure of data entry in these files renders the matrix singular.

The fit to the composite variable is quite good (mean $R^2 = .990$), but the weighting parameters appear to be less than the theoretical value of 1.00. In fact the mean parameter value (.87) is approximately the square of the mean parameter value estimated for Equation 8, which might be expected due to the square form of Equation 10. While we know that the values of the parameter are attenuated, it seems unlikely that the attenuation would be this great, though multicollinearity may add to this result. Thus it seems that attention needs to be paid to the parameters in Equation 7 and Equation 8, to investigate the possibility that the parameters in these equations are not 1.00, as hypothesized. Nevertheless, we should be aware that the errors in measurement and attenuation posited for Equation 7 and Equation 8 are compounded in Equation 10, and this compounding may have resulted in the kinds of results we observed.

Clearly, however, we have derived a relationship between the structure of the internal interaction system and that of the external system, though this relationship is modified by the presence of interaction terms representing each of these systems. *Ceteris paribus*, the degree of inequality in the internal interaction system is a function of the degree of inequality in the external system, building a total system structure composed of these two parts. These are not independent systems, but function with each other to create the structures we observe in interaction both within groups and between groups and their environment.

An additional canonical relationship between the internal and external systems can be derived by use of Equations 7 and 8. Solving both of these equations for $p(c)$ and equating them, we arrive at the canonical relation

$$p(a) - p(r) = p(e_r) + p(e_p), \tag{11}$$

which again suggests a direct relationship between the interactive internal system of groups (the left-hand side) and environmental processes (the right-hand side). This kind of canonical relation shows more clearly than Equation 10 the relationship between the two systems. Since this association is essentially functional in nature, we see the inherent relationship between the elements of the closed system we have developed in our experiments. The mean canonical coefficient of determination for available data sets is .992 (allowing the coefficients in the canonical equation to vary). When the coefficients are constrained, as in Equation 11, the mean canonical coefficient of determination is .987. There is evidence that the sum on the right-hand side of the equation is somewhat larger than that on the left-hand side, but further investigation is necessary to determine whether this apparent effect is real. Again, there is some reason to suggest that the coefficients operative in Equations 7 and 8 might be somewhat different from these hypothesized; however, the evidence is not conclusive given the equation errors which are inevitable and the correlated error involved. Additional theory about the nature of error and the interdependence of elements is necessary before final conclusions can be made. For now I prefer to think that we can at least get good approximations of the relationships using Equations 6, 7, 8, 9, 10, and 11.

Independence of Terms in the Equations

From the definition of terms in the equations representing the internal and external structures, it can be seen that the terms are not independent in their formation. For example, the association between the internal dimensions can be alternatively represented as

$$(A_1/A_2) = (C_1/C_2)^{Pr(C)} + ((A_1 - C_1)/(A_2 - C_2))^{(1 - Pr(C))} \quad (12)$$

where $Pr(C) = (C_1 + C_2)/(A_1 + A_2)$, $1 - Pr(C) = (A_1 - C_1 + A_2 - C_2)/(A_1 + A_2)$, and $R_1 = A_i - C_i$. This form can be derived from Equation 6 and clearly shows that the A_i frequencies appear on both sides of the equation; in this form the equation involves only two variables. A parallel form can be derived for the relationship depicted in Equation 9 with the same presence of a variable (C_i) on both sides of the equation. Clearly this equation is not linear and not simply reducible to a linear form.

Given the obvious possibility of mathematical dependence between the two sides, it should be clear that our regression applications may be a result of this feature. While not perfect mathematical tautologies, these relations are somewhat stronger than might be anticipated if we were able to remove the dependent variable from the right-hand side of the structural equations. This is not possible if a closed form solution is desired. However, it is possible to develop iteration techniques which allow us to estimate the dependent variable from the kind of equation cited above.

Since we really have two equations that connect at the interface (compliance), it is possible to develop a sequential iteration procedure that can be used to predict all the frequencies in either the internal or external tabulation. If we begin with an iterative procedure, based on E_{ri}, that is used to develop predictions for the C_i, and then if these predicted values are used, in a second iterative procedure, to generate predictions for the A_i, we can construct tabulations for both the internal and external structures. The predictions made for the A_i and the C_i can be tested against the observed values by chi-square type methods.

It might appear that we have generated the entire structure of group interaction from knowledge of external features, but this is not really the case. Equations 7 and 8 represent a theory regarding the interrelations that will occur in both internal and external structures. This theory in conjunction with knowledge of the total amount of directive activity and the total amount of compliance can yield predictions, given knowledge of the reinforcement received from the environment. In this sense we have shown that a balancing mechanism of the sort posited will enable specific predictions to be made regarding the nature of group interaction and the interface between a group and its environment. Of considerable importance in our work here is that such structural relationships are, most generally, specific to a group and not amenable to the averaging of behaviors over several groups unless experimental conditions are so rigid as to constrain the proportional receipts of compliance, rejection, environmental reward, and environmental punishment. That is, groups are most properly treated as individual cases with unique properties and unique parameters (see Equation 6, for example), rather than replications in a particular experimental design. Aggregate features of such structures can only be dealt with after the unique (group specific) features have been addressed. The search for generalities across groups must begin with the understanding that all groups are not identical.

Another implication of this approach, given that the constants of proportionality for the specified relationships are known, is that attention needs to be paid to the particular values of the variables for any specific group. Most sociological work concentrates on the general form of relationships. Here, assuming these relationships are known, we must focus on the specific values of the variables in a group and the manner in which they change over time. Thus, instead of concentrating on the general form, we must concentrate on the specific development of power structures (internal and external) in groups. This kind of orientation is much more compatible with the development of therapies which could, conceivably, correct power imbalances or produce groups designed to achieve certain results through their interaction. Such practical applications of sociological theory are clearly needed to improve the status of the discipline and the abilities of persons entering it.

Conclusions

The history of these developments related to behavioral social power extends over a period of about twenty-four years. During this period we have attempted to develop mathematical expressions for the interactive relations between positions in small groups. While the development has moved in fits and starts, it seems close to accomplishing our initial goal of understanding the mathematical structure of power relations. With such an understanding it is possible to explain and predict the kinds of structures developed in interactive systems and the dynamics which lead to changes in such systems. Most important, it is possible to understand the geometry of the structures and use this for the development of new applications and extensions of the current formulation. Clearer understanding of dynamic processes is sorely needed, but current work in this area seems promising.

Most of the alternative theories in this area do not deal with all the variables we have used. Most particularly, other applications have not allowed the initiation of directives to vary as widely as we have or have not dealt with the probability of outcomes imposed by the environment. My suggestion would be that many other research endeavors could substantially benefit from application of the types of mathematical expressions we have developed and their sources in mathematical learning theory. Through such a mathematical medium we can communicate more precisely with other theorists and develop potentially informative research concerning the areas of difference between theories.

While we see little in the way of directly competitive theory, our developments have been informed by several alternative approaches. These approaches include expectation states theory (Berger, Rosenholtz, and Zelditch 1980), behavioral power dependence developments (Molm 1981a, 1981b, 1985), and exchange theory applications (Cook and Emerson 1978; Cook et al. 1983). I tend to see these alternative approaches as complementary to ours and not competitive. Each of them emphasizes aspects of behavior which are ignored or controlled in our own research, but focuses on the successful completion of some type of interaction between participants. Expansion of these alternative approaches in terms of the mathematics we have developed would be informative and potentially expand the explanatory power of such alternatives. Most other applications do not specify functional forms for relationships (except for the traditional linear model or ordinal analogues) and therefore are of limited use in generating predictions beyond the specific experimental application. The reason for this lies in concentration on the significance of terms in the models rather than on theoretically meaningful constants of proportionality that enlarge the scope of experimental findings. We realized early on that emphasis must be placed on the value of such constants rather than on the significance or nonsignificance of general effects. Concentration on the appropriate mathematical forms ensures this outcome.

While our approach can be developed further, especially through application to communication networks which are not completely connected, the basis for a sound mathematical application to group power and communication structures has been laid. Further developments require applications outside of our basic experimental paradigms and to situations with either greater or fewer restrictions on the nature of interaction. We have been able to show that applications of external reinforcement and punishment may be used to systematically alter the power structures of groups. While much remains to be done before a thorough understanding of such phenomena is achieved, here is a foundation on which further growth can be achieved. Such additional growth is of interest not only for its scientific value but also for applications in group-based therapy and in other social instantiations.

Exchange Relations and Exchange Networks: Recent Developments in Social Exchange Theory

Karen S. Cook, Linda D. Molm, and Toshio Yamagishi

Cumulative theorizing is a major aim of sociologists interested in theory growth. Various strategies for analyzing theory growth have been proposed in the social sciences. For our purposes, however, the general strategy outlined by Wagner and Berger (1985) and Berger, Wagner, and Zelditch (1989) will serve to provide a set of concepts for describing recent developments in exchange network theory (Emerson 1972a, 1972b; Cook and Emerson 1978, etc.). Given space limitations this chapter can only cover the major developments in this particular theoretical research program over the past two decades. The review of relevant work is thus more illustrative than exhaustive.*

Our goal is to trace the development of exchange theory since the explicit introduction of network concepts and propositions into social exchange theory (S.E.T.) by Emerson in his seminal formulation written in 1967 and published subsequently in 1972 (a, b). This theoretical framework was based on power dependence notions first proposed by Emerson in work published in 1962 and 1964. While there were other theoretical influences on his work which can be traced to related exchange theories developed at about the same time by Homans (1961), Blau (1964), and Thibaut and Kelley (1959), we will treat a detailed analysis of the relations among these variants of exchange theory as outside the scope of this review chapter. This restriction also applies to key anthropological formulations and related work within economics. These linkages have been addressed to some extent elsewhere (e.g., Cook 1982, 1987; Emerson 1976, 1981; see also Turner 1986).

*The authors' names have been listed alphabetically; we share joint responsibility for the development of this chapter. We would also like to acknowledge the support of various National Science Foundation grants for the research reported here. Without this support programmatic research efforts such as this one would not be possible.

Plan of the Chapter

Given this somewhat limited scope, the chapter is organized into Sections I and II, two major divisions, followed by a set of concluding remarks about future developments in the theoretical research program (Section III). The two major sections represent what we refer to as different *branches* of the theoretical research program on exchange networks originating in the most extensive treatment of the basic theoretical premises presented in Emerson (1972, 1972b). There are important links to other theoretical research programs (e.g., Willer and his collaborators; see Willer and Markovsky, this volume) and related unit theories (e.g., equity theory) that will not be developed in this chapter given space constraints. First, we describe briefly the character and scope of the original formulation; then we present an overview of the development of the two branches of this research program.

Figure 1 is a simple diagram representing the two major branches of the theoretical research program on exchange relations and exchange networks that have developed based on Emerson's (1972a, 1972b) power-dependence formulation. The work of Cook and Emerson (1978), representing one branch, initiated the empirical development of exchange network theory through an extended series of experimental studies of exchange networks and a wide range of related topics (e.g., coalitions, commitment formation, equity, network centrality, and various forms of exchange). Another branch, representing the work of Molm, was initiated by a series of experiments (e.g., Molm 1981a, 1981b) on exchange relations and the dynamics of power use and includes subsequent theoretical extensions on the use of punishment power and models linking strategic action and structural sources of power. These theoretical and empirical developments are detailed after a brief description of the original power-dependence formulation.

Emerson's Original Formulation

In "Exchange Theory, Part I: A Psychological Basis for Social Exchange" and in "Exchange Theory, Part II: Exchange Relations and Networks," Emerson (1972a, 1972b) developed a comprehensive, though incomplete, theory of exchange building, in part, on the groundwork laid by Thibaut and Kelley (1959), Homans (1961), Blau (1964), and Kuhn (1964). Emerson was drawn to this work primarily because of his interest in power. As he put it: "My initial reason for beginning the work set forth in these two chapters was to formulate a more encompassing (and hopefully enriching) framework around previous work on power-

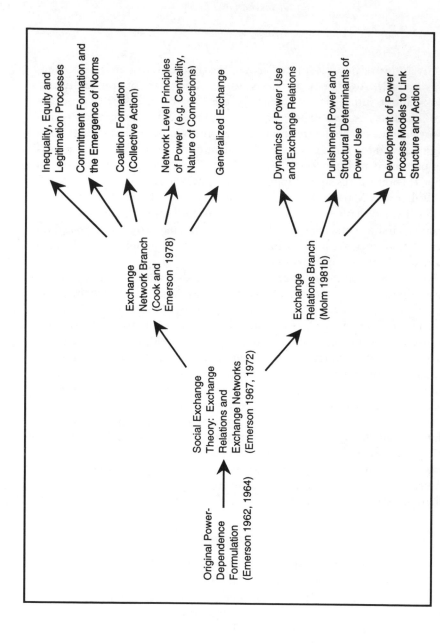

Fig. 1. Theoretical and empirical extensions of the power-dependence formulation of social exchange theory (selected topics).

dependence relations" (Emerson 1972a: 39). He continued: "Exchange is more general and fundamental than power. As a result, I now am concerned with exchange theory in general." In these two companion chapters he presented an explicit formulation of the psychological basis for social exchange theory (Part I), which he extended in Part II to apply to the analysis of social structure and structural change. In Part II he examined both networks (connected exchange relations among sets of actors) and groups (or corporate groups) as different forms of social structure. Our emphasis in this chapter is a review of the work that has grown out of the theoretical focus on exchange networks; we comment less on the topic of corporate groups, except in the concluding section in which we describe the preliminary research on coalition formation.

Part I includes basic concepts and propositions derived primarily from operant concepts and principles relating to the definition of the basic unit in the theory—the exchange relation. These terms and general propositions are reviewed briefly in Section I of our chapter. It should be noted that this initial formulation used operant psychology as the explicit psychological underpinning for the "more sociological" version of the theory presented in Part II for several reasons. First, the operant concepts and principles were "exceptionally operational," allowing Emerson to use them in developing his own theory without committing himself to a particular theory of motivation (see Emerson 1972a: 42). He viewed the "atheoretic" character of operant psychology at the time as a benefit, since he could use the concepts without adopting any particular motivational or cognitive baggage. In fact, he criticized operant psychology because it contained few "cognitive" concepts, and he indicated that in his own theory development he would find "reason to weave some cognitive dimensions into the otherwise operant framework" (1972a: 43). Further developments of exchange theory since that time have continued this rather eclectic approach of weaving into the theory operant (e.g., reinforcement, stimulus, etc.) as well as more "cognitive" concepts (e.g., uncertainty, risk, comparison level, etc.). What remains is the more difficult task of theory reformulation which clarifies the boundaries of these concepts and propositions and indicates where each applies in the broader exchange formulation under development. (See Emerson 1987, in which he states that the goal is to indicate how these formulations can be integrated into a more complete theory of the factors that govern exchange relations.)

Part II of Emerson's formulation takes the psychological underpinnings developed in Part I for granted and constructs on this basis a "theory of social exchange in which *social structure* is taken as the dependent variable" (Emerson 1972b: 58). In the introduction to Part II he clarifies the primary focus of social exchange theory: "The concept of an exchange relation, and the principles which surround it, provide a basis for studying the formation and change of social structures as enduring relations among specified actors, with the exchange relation as the structural unit." Both branches of the research program that have developed subsequently have continued to adopt this primary focus. Molm's work (see Section I) investigates the nature of the power dynamics and power use which occur within exchange relations, and Emerson, Cook, Gillmore, and Yamagishi's work (see Section II) examines the structural determinants of the distribution of power in exchange networks and mechanisms of structural change.

Emerson (1972b) and subsequently Cook and Emerson (1978) indicate the limitations of adopting a strictly microeconomic approach to exchange relations, since "market economics (traditionally) focuses upon the $x : y$ transaction (or resource exchange) as a unit, with actors interchangeable." In contrast, Emerson argues, "the exchange relation $Ax : By$ focuses attention upon relatively enduring interaction between specified actors A and B." This important distinction delimits the focus of social exchange theory, but does not preclude the use of microeconomic concepts and propositions as they inform the analysis of social exchange processes. In fact, as Cook and Emerson (1978) indicate, social exchange theory is developing in such a way as to define the neoclassical economic market as one specialized type of exchange network (see also Turner 1986, for this discussion). Of greater interest to social exchange theorists are the social structures that emerge as a result of exchange relations and the connections among the actors involved in various types of exchange networks. In Part II Emerson (1972b) developed concepts and propositions to describe the nature of the connections among actors involved in exchange relations that create networks, social circles, or corporate groups and the mechanisms that transform these structures (e.g., exploitation, division of labor, stratification, and norm formation). Only parts of Emerson's original formulation have been extended and empirically investigated in subsequent research over the past fifteen years; much theoretical and empirical work remains to be done. The next two sections summarize some of the work that was inspired by Emerson's original formulation.

Section I. The Behavioral Formulation of the Theory (Part I)

In this section we describe the concepts and principles of the initial behavioral formulation of the theory (Emerson 1972a), and the branch of the program of research that developed from those roots.

Basic Concepts

Earlier efforts to develop a behavioral approach to social exchange (Homans 1961) were criticized for being tautological and reductionistic. Emerson believed these problems stemmed not from the psychological base of the theory per se, but from the failure to recognize that the concepts of operant behavior, reinforcer, and discriminative stimulus form a single conceptual unit, with each concept defined in terms of the others. Together, they compose the psychological equivalent of an exchange relation between an organism and its environment. By maintaining the integrity of this conceptual unit, Emerson established the social relation, rather than the individual actor, as the unit of analysis of the basic theory.

To make the transition from operant psychology to social exchange, Emerson defined social equivalents of these operant terms. An "exchange opportunity" is a situation in which there are discriminative stimuli; these stimuli evoke "initiations" of exchange, which are the operant responses; and a "transaction" is a positively reinforced initiation. A series of temporally interspersed opportunities, initiations, and transactions is an "exchange relation" (1972a: 45). When theoretical development moves beyond the exchange relation of an organism and its environment to social exchange relations in which the "environment" is another social actor (either individual or corporate), transactions become reciprocally reinforcing events that can be initiated from either end of the relation. The exchange relation is the smallest unit on which the theory is based, and the building block for larger structures.

At the time that Emerson was writing his theory of exchange, psychologists were beginning to analyze behavioral choices rather than simply the strengthening or weakening of a single behavior (e.g., Herrnstein 1970). For applying operant principles to social exchange, this was an important development. The analysis of behavioral choice led directly to two key variables of the theory, value and alternatives, and their convergence in the central concept of dependence. Actors typically confront choices among two or more reinforcers, and among two or more exchange relations. The first choice leads to the concept of value, the second to the concept of alternatives. Both affect dependence: an actor in an exchange relation is dependent on the other for reinforcement, and the magnitude of dependence is a joint function of the strength of the reinforcer (its value) and the degree of its contingency on the other person (Emerson 1972a: 49–51). Reinforcer strengths can be compared both within and across exchange domains, which Emerson defined as a class of functionally equivalent reinforcers. Exchange relations within a single domain for an actor are alternative relations for that actor. The contingency of a given reinforcer on a specific exchange relation varies inversely with the availability of alternative relations that are sources of reinforcers in the same domain.*

Emerson proposed that the strength of reinforcement, whether measured within or across exchange domains, is a direct function of the uncertainty of receiving reinforcement. This was an intriguing and creative use of the variations in operant schedules of reinforcement (reinforcement is more uncertain when schedules are variable); but it has remained little more than that. The concept of value remains one of the least developed concepts of the theory. Emerson (1987) was continuing to work on a theory of value at the time of his death. Recognizing the problem of interpersonal utility comparisons which the concept of value poses (Heckathorn 1983; Emerson et al. 1983), Emerson originally suggested that value could be measured, behaviorally, by initiations (1972a: 63). But this solution makes it impossible to test the effect of value-based dependency on initiations. In practice, research programs on power dependence relations have not defined value in terms of uncertainty, but simply as the unit value of the resources exchanged (e.g., Cook and Emerson 1978; Yamagishi, Gillmore, and Cook 1988; Molm 1988).

The concept of dependence is the foundation on which the theory is built. From this single concept, Emerson derived definitions of power, power imbalance, and cohesion, and predictions of the initiation of exchange behavior and the resulting distribution of resources. These concepts and predictions were developed at the relational level; later extensions to exchange networks consisted of analyzing the power dependencies in the component relations of a network. As we discuss later on, efforts are now under way to develop definitions of power at the network level.

Emerson defined each actor's power as synonymous with the other actor's dependence; i.e., the dependence of actor A on actor B (Dab) equals the power of actor B over actor A (Pba). Because the power/dependence of each of the two actors in an exchange relation can vary, Emerson further defined two dimensions of the power/dependence in the relation: balance/imbalance, and cohesion. An exchange relation is balanced when $Dab = Dba$, and imbalanced to the extent that the two

---

*In Part I of his 1972 treatise, Emerson defined dependence as a function of four variables rather than two. In addition to value and alternatives, he proposed that dependence varied directly with comparison level (CL), a concept borrowed from Thibaut and Kelley (1959), and with primacy, the number of domains in which transactions within the relation occur. CL and primacy disappeared when he moved to his analysis of power and dependence in Part II, however. CL resurfaced to some degree in his analysis of the tendency for relations to move toward balance, but primacy remains a largely unexplored, yet important, subject for research.

actors' power dependencies are different. An imbalanced relation gives a power advantage to the less dependent actor.

The cohesion of the relation, which Emerson treated much more briefly, is defined as the average of the two actors' power dependencies, $(Dab + Dba)/2$. Some concept of the mutual power in a relation, as well as its imbalance, is theoretically important because of Emerson's assertion that power is fully operative even in balanced relations. "In a highly cohesive relation, both members are significantly controlled 'by the relation'" (Emerson 1972b: 76). At the same time, it is questionable whether this dimension of the power relation is an appropriate measure of cohesion. Cohesion may be affected by relational dimensions other than average power, including power imbalance. Only a few researchers have examined the effects of what Emerson called cohesion, and they have referred to it by more neutral terms: mutual dependence (Michaels and Wiggins 1976), total power (Bacharach and Lawler 1981; Lawler and Bacharach 1987), or average power (Molm 1989b). As Bacharach and Lawler (1981) have emphasized, it is important to distinguish this dimension of power from power imbalance because of the potential interaction of the two.

Power balance and cohesion (or average power) are structural attributes of exchange relations and the networks in which they are embedded; the theory predicts that they will affect the structure of behavioral interaction of the actors in those relations. Both initiations and transactions are expected to vary with power dependence. Initiations are predicted to vary directly with dependence; thus, they are more likely from the more dependent actor in an imbalanced relation, and both actors are more likely to initiate exchange, the greater the cohesion of the relation (see Michaels and Wiggins 1976). Second, the reward levels of transactions change in favor of the less dependent party in imbalanced relations, and they increase for both actors with the cohesion of the relation. In an imbalanced relation between *A* and *B* in which *A* has a power advantage, *A*'s power use increases over time, as evidenced either by increased rewards for *A* from *B*, or by decreased rewards for *B* from *A* without decreased rewards for *A* from *B*. In short, the exchange ratio of the relation changes in favor of the more powerful, less dependent actor (Cook and Emerson 1978; Molm 1981b) until an equilibrium is reached when *B* gets no more from *A* than *B* can receive from alternative partners.

Actors in power-imbalanced exchange relations or power-imbalanced exchange networks (including more than two actors) can engage in what Emerson (1972b) referred to as power-balancing mechanisms. The specific mechanisms included in his theory were the following: (1) withdrawal from the exchange relation, (2) network extension or the addition of alternative sources, (3) "status-giving" (i.e., altering the value of the resource obtained from the other party), and (4) coalition formation or a reduction in alternative relations (i.e., network consolidation). Actors could engage in these activities in order to alter the balance of power in the exchange relation or network. Withdrawal from the relationship and "status-giving" represent ways of altering the value of the resources at stake in the exchange (one of the key determinants of dependence and thus power in the relationship). To "devalue" what another offers in exchange removes that actor's source of power in the relationship. "Status-giving" represents the opposite; it is an example of value enhancement. When the power-imbalanced relationship is embedded in a network in which other actors are potential exchange partners, then either through coalition formation with other power-disadvantaged actors or through seeking out new sources of valued resources the power relations in the network can be altered. Either mechanism changes the structure of the network and thus reduces the positional advantage of more powerful actors. Emerson (1972b) formulated some preliminary notions about the conditions under which the various power-balancing mechanisms were likely to be used. Subsequent research, however, has begun to specify more precisely the conditions under which these different processes occur (for example, see the discussion on coalition formation in Section III).

Research in the Behavioral Tradition

The publication of Emerson's theory coincided with the emergence of "behavioral sociology," an approach that applied the principles and experimental methods of operant psychology to various forms of social phenomena. Emerson's theory of social exchange was part of that more general perspective, as evidenced by the publication of another essay by him in Burgess and Bushell's 1969 book, *Behavioral Sociology*. The central concept of behavioral sociology is the "social contingency," which differs from the individual contingencies of operant psychology in that it describes the conditional relation between one actor's behavior and another actor's rewards. When the relation between two actors is described by reciprocal social contingencies, we have Emerson's original definition of a social exchange relation.

Emerson's work provided a much-needed theoretical framework for researchers interested in a behavioral approach to questions of social interaction, exchange, and cooperation, and research by behavioral sociologists provided some of the earliest tests of the theory. The initial research in this tradition focused not on power per se, but on more general questions about the structural conditions under which exchange relations will be established, maintained, and disrupted (Burgess and Nielsen 1974; Michaels and Wiggins 1976; Molm and Wiggins 1979; Molm 1981a). Later research, particularly by Molm, concentrated specifically on the central variables and issues of power dependence relations.

This line of research is clearly part of the same theoretical program pursued by Cook, Emerson, and their associates, but it is distinctive enough in some of its assumptions, its methodology, and its propositions to constitute a separate branch of the program. As the Cook and Emerson program has developed, it has focused on how different structural configurations of networks affect the distribution of power in the network as a whole and has paid less attention to the interaction processes in the component exchange relations. They have also attempted to integrate into the basic framework cognitive concepts and principles from the rational choice perspective (see Heath 1976; Cook and Emerson 1978; Cook, O'Brien, and Kollock 1990; and Cook et al., forthcoming). The approach taken by Molm and other behavioral researchers, however, has developed in ways that reflect its closer ties to Emerson's original formulation and its theoretical predecessors (Homans 1961; Thibaut and Kelley 1959).

The behavioral branch of the program makes several assumptions about social exchange that are consistent with Emerson's original behavioral formulation, but depart from the theory's subsequent development in the network branch of the program.

1. An actor's resources in an exchange relation are behaviors in that actor's repertoire that produce rewarding consequences for the other actor; these rewards are not assumed to be transferable or divisible.

2. Exchange behavior is choice behavior. The structure of exchange relations provides actors with a set of opportunities to choose among alternative exchange relations and, within those relations, alternative behaviors.

3. Actors make choices individually, typically without formal negotiations and without explicit agreements of whether or when others will reciprocate.

As a consequence of points 2 and 3, exchange relations develop as longitudinal sequences of interactions in which the "returns" for one's investment are uncertain, discrete transactions are difficult to identify, and the degree and timing of reciprocity are revealed only over time. The power use in an imbalanced relation is determined by the distribution of behavioral resources in the relation over extended interaction.

The methodology used by researchers in this branch of the program reflects these assumptions as well as other characteristics of a behavioral approach. Consistent with the behavioral emphasis on learning, exchange relations are typically studied over hundreds of exchange opportunities. Actors participate in social exchanges without formal bargaining, without agreements on the amount or timing of reciprocity, and often without knowledge of the other's intent to reciprocate. The behaviors that actors exchange usually have consequences of fixed value for each actor, reflecting the assumption that social reinforcers are often nondivisible. Finally, the unit of analysis in this research is the exchange relation, even when relations are embedded in larger social networks. In some studies, the alternatives are individual task alternatives rather than alternative social partners; that is, actors choose between a social exchange relation and an "individual-environment" exchange relation comparable to those that Emerson described in the first part of his theory (e.g., Burgess and Nielsen 1974; Molm 1981a). In other studies, the alternatives are social (e.g., Molm 1989a, 1989b), but the focus is on understanding how the structure of opportunity in the network affects the power dependencies and the process of power use in particular relations. The structural power in an exchange relation is a function of the actors' control over each other's outcomes relative to that of actors in other potential exchange relations in the network. Molm (1987), for example, defines A's power over B as the proportion of the total units of value potentially available to B in an exchange network that are controlled by A. The power imbalance in the A-B relation is the difference between the individual power-dependencies of A and B, defined in this manner, and its effects on exchange in the A-B relation are studied.

In general, the behavioral branch of the program shares the theoretical predictions of the general theory. But it differs in two important respects. First, researchers working in this tradition distinguish between power dependence as a structural attribute of exchange relations, and power use and its outcomes as behavioral attributes (see, for example, Burgess and Nielsen 1974; Michaels and Wiggins 1976). This position is at odds with Emerson's statements that actors who use power will lose power, and that imbalanced relations tend toward balance (1972b: 66–67). Emerson argued that as the more powerful actor obtains increasing benefits from the relation, the accumulation of those benefits increases the actor's dependence. In other words, dependence is a function not only of the structural potential to affect another's outcomes, as determined by value and alternatives, but of the actual rewards obtained over time. Those working in the behavioral tradition prefer to keep these two levels distinct, with the definition of structural power-dependence unaffected by the actual rewards received in the course of exchange. This is consistent with the behavioral distinction between schedules of reinforcement and actual reinforcement received. The exchange outcomes of structural power might lead to behavioral efforts to change the power structure (e.g., through coalition formation or network extension), but the outcomes do not in and of themselves affect the structural dependencies in the relation.

Second, the assumption that actors initiate exchange without knowledge of the terms or timing of the other's reciprocity means that actors are making choices under conditions of greater risk and uncertainty. Both economists and psychologists distinguish between risky choices, in which the probabilities that alternatives will yield particular outcomes are less than 1.0, and riskless decisions, typified by transactions in which the terms of exchange are specified before agreements are reached (see, for example, Kahneman and Tversky 1984). In the latter, actors choose between alternatives with known advantages and disadvantages; in the former, they act on the basis of subjective expectations of what those advantages and disadvantages are likely to be. When outcomes are known, structural power is more likely to determine the distribution of resources as long as actors try to maximize their outcomes. When the probabilities of outcomes are uncertain, structural power only sets the boundaries within which interaction processes operate. Exchange outcomes are then a joint function of structural power and the process of social interaction.

Recent Developments

Molm's recent work within this tradition extends the theory in two ways. First, it broadens the scope of the theory to include power dependence relations based on control over negative as well as positive outcomes for another, thus incorporating "coercive" power and "reward" power within a single theoretical framework (Molm 1987, 1988, 1989a, 1989b).* Second, by analyzing not only the structure but the process of power use, it lays the groundwork for developing models that specify the linkages among structural power, strategies of actors, and power outcomes (Molm 1989c).

Coercion and punishment have traditionally been excluded from the scope of social exchange, partly because of erroneous beliefs about the effects of punishment at the time that the classic exchange theories were written (see Anderson and Willer 1981). Emerson, like Blau, excluded aversive acts from the province of social exchange and conceptualized power only in terms of dependence on another for rewarding outcomes. His analysis of cost is restricted to opportunity costs, or "rewards forgone" from exchange relations not chosen. As some have argued (e.g.,

---

*Other efforts to integrate analyses of reward-based and punishment-based power, in different theoretical traditions, include Lawler and Bacharach (1987), Anderson and Willer (1981), and Gray and Tallman (1987).

Heath 1976), however, there is no theoretical imperative for this restriction. From a behavioral perspective, reinforcement and punishment are parallel concepts. Dependence results from control over the quality of another's outcomes, whether those outcomes are positive or negative. And power derived from either source of dependence provides equivalent structural capacity to change another's outcomes (in opposite directions). In most exchange relations, actors control a range of outcomes for one another that vary from positive to negative: employers have the capacity to hire or fire employees, to promote or demote them, and to praise or criticize them; family members control a wide range of positive and negative outcomes for one another; and of course nations engage in both trade agreements and war.

Empirical findings show that the two bases of dependence affect attraction to the relation in similar ways: social exchange is more frequent in relations in which actors jointly control either greater rewards or greater punishments for one another, and exchange is less frequent in relations in which power imbalance on either base is greater (Molm 1989c). But their effects on the distribution of resources in power-imbalanced relations are quite different. The effects of punishment power are consistently weaker than the effects of reward power, and punishment power imbalance primarily affects the distribution of exchange when it opposes reward power imbalance (Molm 1989b). Under those conditions, actors who are disadvantaged on reward power can use a punishment power advantage to improve their benefits from the relation; i.e., the structural power to punish acts as a power-balancing mechanism, thus extending Emerson's original formulation of these mechanisms. Under other conditions, it has little effect.

These empirical differences are related to important theoretical distinctions. The two bases of power provide different structural incentives to use a power advantage, by withholding rewards or administering punishment. Structural power imbalance can directly induce the use of reward power, but not the use of punishment power. The reason lies in the different effects of alternatives. Regardless of awareness of power or the intent to influence, imbalanced reward power will lead to reduced exchange by the more powerful actor simply because that actor has more valuable alternatives. The alternatives provide the structural incentive to withhold rewards from the more dependent actor. Reward exchange can be withheld intentionally and strategically, to influence the other's behavior, but it need not be.

In contrast, the use of punishment power must be an intentional response to another's behavior. Alternative sources of punishment affect actors' relative abilities to inflict harm on one another, compared to other actors in the network, but these alternative sources do not make actors use punishment. As a result of this difference, it is likely that additional variables, of a more cognitive nature, must be introduced into the theory to explain the use and effects of punishment power. These should include variables that affect the incentive to use punishment, such as risk assessment, and variables that are relevant when the use of power is intentional, such as justice evaluations. Recent work in cognitive science and decision theory offers fertile ground for expanding the theoretical analysis of actors' choices in exchange relations.

The second focus of theory expansion, now in progress, is an effort to develop models of dynamic power use that will increase the theory's predictive power. As Turner (1988) has noted, theories of social exchange say little about the actual process of interaction. If structural power determines power outcomes, then the strategies and interaction processes of actors are unimportant theoretically. But if structural power only sets the boundaries within which power use must occur, then developing models of the process of using power is an important theoretical task. A number of empirical studies have found that power use falls below the maximum predicted by the structural power advantage. Analyses by Bacharach and Lawler (1981), Markovsky (1987), and Michaels and Wiggins (1976) suggest that actual power use is determined jointly by the strategies of individual actors and the structure of the power relations among them.

Within the context of exchange theory, the crucial aspect of power processes is how actors use the resources of structural power in "contingencies of action," i.e., the contingent use of reward and punishment. By selectively giving or withholding rewards or punishments for exchange partners, contingent on the other's prior behavior, actors can use their power resources to alter the frequency and distribution of exchange outcomes in the relation. The classical theories of social exchange viewed contingencies of action as mediating the relation between structure and outcomes. For example, Thibaut and Kelley (1959) explicitly proposed that "fate control" (structural power) can be converted to "behavior control" if actors make their valued resources contingent on others' behavior. This is a straightforward behavioral prediction; i.e., to the extent that one's control over another's rewards and punishments is used contingently, to reward desirable behaviors and punish undesirable behaviors, structural power should be more effective. Emerson considered contingencies as part of exchange relations by definition. But because he viewed structural power as determining power use, he did not consider how variations in the strength and asymmetry of the contingent use of power might influence the outcomes of exchange.

Molm (1989c) has recently found that incorporating contingencies of action in the theory significantly increases its predictive power, but contingencies do not in general mediate the relation between structural power and exchange outcomes. Instead, the structural potential for power and the contingent use of that power are best conceptualized as distinct determinants of exchange outcomes. Obviously, structural power is a prerequisite for the contingent use of that power, but variations in the magnitude and asymmetry of structural power do not, in general, affect exchange outcomes by producing comparable variations in the magnitude and asymmetry of contingencies of action.

This line of theoretical development remains in the early stages, but it suggests that more attention needs to be paid to strategies and processes of power use by actors. As we discuss later, one of the strengths of exchange theory is its potential for linking macro and micro, structural and individual levels of analysis. This effort requires further elaboration of both levels. In addition, the analysis of power processes provides an opportunity for the integration of behavioral and rational choice perspectives on social exchange. Analysis of the interactive processes through which actors influence one another involves both the traditional behavioral questions of how the contingent use of rewards and punishments affects behavior, and the more cognitive issues of how actors make choices that influence the structure of these contingencies. Sometimes actors engage in the deliberate calculation of strategies of influence; these cases can be subsumed under the model of rational choice.

While this branch of the research program on exchange theory growing out of Emerson's original formulation has more fully developed the underlying behavioral processes that operate within the structure of exchange relations, the other branch of the research program, which has proceeded in a parallel fashion, has addressed the effects of different structural properties at the network level of analysis. We turn now to a brief description of this branch of the larger programmatic research effort.

Section II. The Network Formulation of the Theory (Part II)

In this section we trace how Emerson's original insights and ideas have developed into what is now called exchange network theory. Emerson's original ideas that set the direction for the development of theory and research in this area include the following key precepts.

1. The power of each partner in a dyadic exchange relation is determined by the availability of desired resources from alternative exchange relations (as well as the value of the desired resources). From this it fol-

lows that the network structure of exchange relations determines the distribution of power among actors within an exchange network. The subsequent work on exchange networks has all been inspired by this insight (Cook and Emerson 1978; Cook et al. 1983; Markovsky, Willer, and Patton 1988; Yamagishi 1987; Yamagishi, Gillmore, and Cook 1988).

2. One of the most important contributions made in Emerson's (1972b) earlier work was the explicit introduction of the concept of "network connection" and the definition of exchange networks as consisting of mutually "connected" exchange relations. The concept "network connection" made it possible to distinguish two major types of exchange networks and to predict the differential effects of network structure on the distribution of power in these two types of networks.

3. Another significant contribution made in Emerson's earlier work (1972b) is the distinction between exchange opportunities and exchange relations. Possible exchange opportunities may or may not be used as exchange relations are formed between pairs of actors; the opportunities between connected exchange partners may develop over time into exchange relations. This distinction opened the door to the study of network transformation (e.g., how relatively stable exchange network structures emerge from unstable and less structured networks of exchange opportunities). Although this particular issue (network transformation) has not been explored for some time, renewed interest is emerging in this topic.

Before discussing the development of exchange network theory, we will first outline the basic exchange network concepts to be used in our discussion.

Basic Network Concepts

Exchange network. An exchange network can be defined as consisting of (1) a set of actors (either natural persons or corporate groups), (2) a distribution of valued resources among those actors, (3) for each actor a set of exchange opportunities with other actors in the network, (4) a set of historically developed and utilized exchange opportunities called exchange relations, and (5) a set of network connections linking exchange relations into a single network structure (Cook et al. 1983).

Actors and positions. Some of the actors in an exchange network may occupy "structurally equivalent positions." Two actors are defined as occupying the same position when the two have identical relations with all positions in the network. According to the definition of structural equivalence used by most social network theorists, two points are structurally equivalent when their relations to other points are similar or identical (Breiger, Boorman, and Arabie 1975; Burt 1976; White and Breiger

1975; White, Boorman, and Breiger 1976). However, we adopt another, graph-theoretic definition of structural equivalence that is more congruent with the exchange-theoretic conception of networks. Graph theoretically, two actors are structurally equivalent when the residual graphs for the two actors are isomorphic, i.e., the graphs representing the network structures that remain when all the exchange opportunities related to the actor involved are removed have the same shape (see Yamagishi 1987, for more details of this definition and related issues). In the following discussion, we treat actors occupying the same position as interchangeable; we focus only on the structural characteristics of the positions occupied by the actors, not their individual characteristics.

Connections. An important contribution made in Emerson's (1972b) formulation was the introduction of the new concept of "network connection" and the definition of exchange networks as consisting of "connected" exchange relations. Thus, in his terminology, two exchange relations, *A-B* and *B-C*, are defined as forming the exchange network *A-B-C* only when exchange activities in one relation affect exchange activities in the other relation. Cook and Emerson (1978: 725) provide formal definitions of network connections and exchange networks based on Emerson's (1972b) earlier discussion.

An "exchange network" is a set of two or more connected exchange relations. Two exchange relations are connected to the degree that exchange in one relation is contingent upon exchange (or nonexchange) in the other relation. Network connections can be either positive or negative, depending on whether exchange in one relation affects exchange in the other positively or negatively (Emerson 1972b). That is, (a) the connection is "positive" if exchange in one relation is contingent upon exchange in the other relation, and (b) the connection is "negative" if exchange in one relation is contingent upon nonexchange in the other relation (Cook and Emerson 1978: 725).

Recent studies of exchange networks have shown that the nature of the connections in a network fundamentally alters the distribution of power among network positions, as discussed below (see Cook et al. 1983; Yamagishi, Gillmore, and Cook 1988). Recent work on "power domains" and "flow networks" by Willer and Markovsky also indicates the importance of network connections. Markovsky, Willer, and Patton (1988), for example, use the term "power domain" to refer to what Emerson calls an exchange network. Within each power domain (or network, to use Emerson's terminology) exchange in one relation affects exchange in another, whereas exchange in one relation has no effect upon exchange in another relation across power domains (or across networks). Each power domain can and should be analyzed as an independent ex-

change network, as Emerson suggested. Willer also uses a different terminology for negative and positive connections (exclusive and inclusive
networks). Their unique contribution on this topic is the introduction of
various degrees of negativity of connections rather than treating negative
and positive connections as dichotomous concepts.

Resource flow. The above distinction between positive and negative
connections involves different forms of resource flows within networks.
Suppose two actors A and B exchange resources x and y; A trades the
resource she or he controls, x, for another resource y, controlled by actor
B. This exchange relation can be expressed as $(Ax : By)$. Suppose further that in another exchange relation with actor C, B trades resource x
which she or he obtained from A in the $(Ax : By)$ exchange relation. In
return, B obtains resource y from C. The second exchange relation can
be expressed as $(Bx : Cy)$. These two exchange relations are positively
connected at B, since B has to obtain y in the $(Bx : Cy)$ exchange to use
it in the $(Ax : By)$ exchange, and B has to obtain x from the $(Ax : By)$
exchange relation to use it in exchanges with C. Thus the $(Ax : By)$ and
$(Bx : Cy)$ exchanges are mutually positively contingent. In this positively
connected three-actor network, $(Ax : By) + (Bx : Cy)$, resource x originating at position A flows to C beyond the immediate exchange partner
B. (The symbol $+$ can be used to represent the fact that the two relations
are positively connected.) Similarly, resource y originating at C flows to
A beyond the immediate exchange partner B. Resource flow beyond immediate exchange partners is an important aspect of positively connected
exchange networks.

Note that in the above three-actor positively connected exchange network, B receives different kinds of resources, x and y, from his or her
two exchange partners, A and C, respectively. The nature of the exchange network dramatically changes when both A and C, the two exchange partners to B, offer the same resource x in exchange for y. Now,
the two exchange relations are expressed as $(Ax : By)$ and $(By : Cx)$. Emerson (1972b) referred to these two exchange relations as belonging to
the same exchange domain. This three-actor exchange network, $(Ax : By)$
$- (By : Cx)$, involves a negative connection (represented by the $-$ symbol) at B. In exchange networks consisting solely of negative connections, resources do not flow beyond immediate exchange partners.

Thus far we have discussed two basic types of exchange networks:
(1) positively connected exchange networks and (2) negatively connected
exchange networks. Another important type of exchange network is
(3) a "mixed" network, involving both positive and negative connections. In mixed networks resources flow beyond immediate exchange
partners and some of the actors have more than one alternative source for

at least one of the resources he or she desires. Mixed networks represent one class of more complicated network structures. Having clarified the distinctions between different types of network connections, let us discuss the principles that determine the distribution of power in different network structures.

The Distribution of Power in Negatively Connected Networks

The early stage of development of exchange network theory was characterized by its focus on negatively connected networks (e.g., Stolte and Emerson 1977; Cook and Emerson 1978; Cook et al. 1983). These studies showed that (1) the distribution of power in negatively connected exchange networks is a function of structurally equivalent network positions, and (2) the distribution of power does not necessarily correspond to the centrality of positions in the network (Cook et al. 1983). These early studies stimulated further interest in power processes in exchange networks and the development of various measures to predict positional power (Cook et al. 1983; Bonacich 1987; Markovsky, Willer, and Patton 1988). Each measure has its own limitations, thus the development of a general measure of the distribution of power in exchange networks remains an unfinished task. (See Yamagishi and Cook 1990, for a discussion of the Markovsky, Willer, and Patton [1988] measure.)

The Distribution of Power in Positively Connected and Mixed Networks

As discussed earlier, power is a function of dependence which, in turn, is a joint function of the value of the desired resources and the availability of those resources from alternative sources. These two factors—value and availability of the desired resource—determine dependence and thus power in exchange relations and are both affected by the nature of the exchange connections in the network.

Availability of the desired resource from alternative sources. When two or more exchange relations are negatively connected at an actor (or position) *A*, that actor has alternative sources for the desired resource. This makes *A*'s dependence less on each of his or her exchange partners for the desired resource, and thus *A* has a structural power advantage. That is, a negative connection makes the pivotal actor less dependent on each of his or her exchange partners and thus makes him or her more powerful in each exchange relation (see Cook et al. 1983).

Value of the desired resource. In a positively connected exchange network, the first factor—availability of the desired resource from alternative sources—should not affect the power processes in the network, since such a network does not involve negative connections or alternative

sources. Thus, value of the desired resource is the only factor affecting power processes in positively connected networks. Of course, the unit value of a particular resource may vary among actors; however, we are less interested in such "individual" differences in the value of particular resources than in variations in value as a function of the network structure.

Assuming that the resources exchanged in an exchange network are governed by the principle of satiation (or declining marginal utility), Yamagishi, Gillmore, and Cook (1988) argue that the unit value of the resources to be exchanged in a positively connected exchange network varies directly with the local scarcity of resources, which, in turn, is a function of the aggregate supplies of the resources and the distance of a particular actor from the supply source of each resource of value. That is, to the extent that total or aggregate supply of a particular resource is limited, the resource is hard to obtain for the actors and thus is more valuable. In addition, the resource becomes more scarce and thus more valuable as an actor is located farther from the supply source. Suppose, in the five-actor positively connected network ($Ax : B : C : D : Ey$), in which resource x is supplied at position A (i.e., A is the supply source of x) and flows to E through B, C, and D and resource y is supplied at position E and flows to A through D, C, and B, the aggregate supplies of x and y are identical. The scarcities and thus value of the two resources in a particular exchange relation, for example ($Ax : By$), are determined by the "distance" of each actor from the supply source of the resource he or she controls. That is, A is the supply source of x (i.e., the distance to the source of x is zero), whereas B is three relations away from the supply source of y. This implies that the resource controlled by B, y, is more scarce than the resource controlled by A, x, in the ($Ax : By$) relation. Thus y is more scarce and more valuable to A than x is to B. It was predicted that B would be more powerful than A; similarly, it was predicted that D would be more powerful than E, and C would be more powerful than B or D. These predictions were clearly supported in an experiment (Yamagishi, Gillmore, and Cook 1988). Yamagishi, Gillmore, and Cook (1988) also predicted and found that the locus of power shifts toward the supply source of the resource with the lowest aggregate level of supply.

How these two factors—availability and value—are combined to determine the distribution of power in mixed networks remains to be investigated in future research. One possible avenue for analyzing power processes in mixed networks is to break them into negative connections and positively connected chains. For example, the eight-actor mixed network shown in Figure 2 (from Yamagishi, Gillmore, and Cook 1988) can

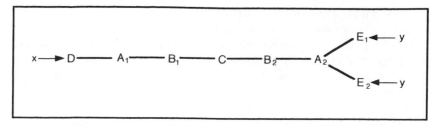

Fig. 2. An example of a mixed network (adapted from Yamagishi et al. 1988).

be decomposed into a positively connected chain ($Dx : A_1 : B_1 : C : B_2 : A_2y$) and a negative connection of two relations at position A ($A_2x : E_1y$) $-$ ($A_2x : E_2y$). The negative connection affects the total or aggregate supplies of x and y in the positively connected chain ($Dx : A_1 : B_1 : C : B_2 : A_2y$), such that the aggregate supply of x at A_1 is less than the aggregate supply of y at A_2. This is because A_1's relative power over D in the ($Dx : A_1y$) relation is less than A_2's relative power over E_1 or E_2 in the negatively connected subnetwork ($A_2x : E_1y$) $-$ ($A_2x : E_2y$); A_2 can obtain more y from E_1 or E_2 than A_1 can obtain x from D. The distribution of power in the positively connected chain ($Dx : A_1 : B_1 : C : B_2 : A_2y$) may then be analyzed in terms of the differential aggregate supplies of the desired resources as discussed above for simple positively connected chains. Further research on the principles governing the distribution of power in "mixed" network structures is currently under way.

Research in this branch of the program has used a set of experimental operationalizations in the laboratory distinctly different from those used by researchers working within the behavioral tradition described in Section I. The differences are driven in part by differences in the nature of the research questions under investigation, and they also reflect the different relative influences of operant psychology and rational choice theory (see Heath 1976) on the two branches. Whereas Molm (as well as other behavioral researchers) has studied exchange as a sequence of mutual behavioral choices in which the terms and timing of reciprocity are unspecified, Cook et al. (forthcoming) have studied exchange as a bargaining process, in which actors explicitly negotiate exchanges through a series of offers and counteroffers until an agreement is reached or a stalemate occurs (see also Cook and Emerson 1978; Cook et al. 1983; Yamagishi, Gillmore, and Cook 1988). Early research in this tradition investigated the nature of the network structural constraints on the exercise of power as indicated by the differential rates of exchange in vari-

ous structures. Exchanges were explicitly negotiated between actors in different types of exchange networks. Under experimental control were the nature of the exchange opportunity structures and the types of exchange connections as indicated above, as well as the differential values of the resources to be exchanged. That is, some actors had access to resources of greater value than others, as determined by the exchange profit overlaps (see Cook and Emerson 1978, for example). In these fairly simple initial network studies, principles were developed to allow us to predict the relative power of actors within these structures (as measured by the distribution of exchange outcomes or the differential rates of exchange which emerged). Subsequent research (including Cook and Emerson 1978; Cook and Hegtvedt 1986; and Cook, Hegtvedt, and Yamagishi 1988, etc.) investigated factors which restrict the use of power (e.g., equity concerns and reactions to inequality).

The experimental paradigms described above differ in other respects (in Molm's experiments actors exchange resources that have a fixed value for each; in the Cook et al. experiments actors negotiate mutually profitable exchanges based on varying profit overlaps, or ranges of mutually beneficial trades, without exact knowledge of the constant sum to be divided), but these differences tend to be related to the first, more fundamental, difference in the two paradigms. These different operationalizations of exchange are theoretically driven, and each is appropriate to the central research questions of that branch. The exchange conditions represented in each laboratory paradigm are typical of some forms of social exchange relations, but not others. The development of two very different experimental paradigms within a single theoretical research program illustrates that there is no single "right" way to operationalize the concepts of exchange theory. The same theoretical concepts can be operationalized in different ways in different research contexts. The primary advantage of standardized experimental settings for any branch of the research program is that of comparability across studies and cumulative theory development. The advantage of having more than one standardized experimental setting (e.g., Molm's laboratory paradigm versus the Cook et al. laboratory paradigm) is that similar results found in different experimental settings show that the findings are not unique to a particular laboratory setup; that is, the theory is robust. And, indeed, despite the differences between the experimental settings and the research questions of the two branches, they have reported similar findings in support of the most basic principles of the theory; for example, the effects of structural power imbalance on the distribution of exchange resources.

Section III. Related Unit Theories in the Research Program and Future Developments

In the previous two sections we have outlined the key developments in exchange network theory that trace directly to Emerson's original formulation. Within each branch of the theoretical research program theory growth to this point can be described primarily as linear development consisting mainly of theory elaboration (Wagner and Berger 1985). However, at this stage theory proliferation is beginning to occur, in part through the development of what some theorists (e.g., Willer and Patton 1987; Markovsky, Willer, and Patton 1988) define as "competing" theories. Since elementary theory as developed by Willer is described elsewhere in this volume, we have not attempted to specify the nature of the links between that theory and our own theoretical and empirical work except as it relates directly to specific experiments that have been conducted in the exchange network research program (Markovsky, Willer, and Patton 1988; Markovsky 1987; Willer and Patton 1987). It is not clear to what extent this theory represents a competing theory (i.e., an alternative theoretical framework) or should be treated as theory proliferation (i.e., the application of some of the core ideas of exchange network theory to new areas). Some features of the underlying frameworks differ in terms of key concepts and core ideas, but there is also a great deal of overlap and similarity among the basic concepts between these two research programs.

Theory elaboration within the domain of the behavioral formulation of social exchange theory has occurred by extending the basic concepts and propositions and by providing empirical tests of propositions that had previously been unexamined empirically. In this process, represented primarily by the work of Molm (1981a, 1981b, 1987, 1988, 1989a, 1989b, 1989c, etc.), several aspects of the original formulation in Part I of Emerson (1972a) have been extended. First, the scope of the theory has been extended to include punishment-based power (i.e., the control over negative outcomes or the capacity to reduce positive outcomes for another actor) in addition to reward-based power. This is a major extension because, as suggested in Section I, different theoretical principles are required to explain the effects of imbalanced reward- and punishment-based power. Second, the theory is being elaborated to incorporate models of dynamic power use to increase the theory's predictive accuracy. This work derives from the empirical insight that structural power relations are not sufficient under certain conditions to predict actual patterns of power use; attention to strategies and processes of power use by actors is also required.

Section II details the core set of experiments conducted to test key propositions concerning the distribution of power in different types of exchange networks. Based upon subsequent developments in exchange network theory (Emerson 1981; Cook and Emerson 1978; Cook 1977; Cook et al. 1983; Yamagishi, Gillmore, and Cook 1988, etc.), this work specifies the conditions under which network structural properties (like centrality) facilitate the prediction of the network power distributions. Theory growth in this branch of the program can be classified as linear (Wagner and Berger 1985: 710–14), with each step building directly upon the prior empirical results and theoretical reformulations. Several theoretical problems identified in this research program remain unresolved, a primary example being the formulation of an adequate network-level measure for the distribution of power. (As suggested in Section II, there have been various attempts to solve this measurement problem, but the existing measures each have limitations that restrict the scope of their applicability.) Current research efforts are being devoted to extending the theory to apply to larger, more complex network structures and to incorporate different fundamental types of exchange processes—for example, generalized exchange and indirect exchange relations (see Cook and Yamagishi, unpublished). While Emerson's original formulation (1972b, 1976) described different forms of exchange (elementary and productive exchange relations), there have been few empirical studies of exchange relations that are not "elementary" exchange relations, in his terminology. An exception is a recent article by Stolte (1987) examining the implications of different types of exchange (elementary vs. productive) for the emergence of norms concerning the distribution of exchange benefits (i.e., equality vs. equity-contribution rules for "fair" distribution).

Related Theoretical Work Within the Program of Research

We have been purposely selective in the substantive topics we have chosen as the focus of our review of the development of the basic research program consisting of two key branches on exchange relations and exchange networks. Now we would like to describe briefly the other major topics of research that have been investigated. In some cases these topics represent distinct unit theories, in other cases they would be best described as theory proliferation (i.e., the application of core ideas to new areas of inquiry). The two topics we will discuss are commitment formation and coalition formation; research on equity concerns in exchange relations will not be discussed, since its theoretical lineage is more complicated.

Commitment formation. Cook and Emerson (1978, etc.) present an extension of the theory to deal with the phenomenon of commitment formation among exchange partners, though the process has not been fully explored empirically. This work is an attempt to identify the structural conditions under which certain types of exchange opportunity structures result in different patterns of committed exchange relations (e.g., one such pattern is a set of mutually, exclusively committed dyads). Commitment is hypothesized (in Cook and Emerson 1978) as resulting from various structural conditions that foster uncertainty. For example, in power-imbalanced exchange networks less powerful actors, dependent upon more powerful actors, are likely to experience greater uncertainty about obtaining valued resources (as a consequence of the competitive relations fostered among powerless actors in negatively connected networks). One mechanism for reducing uncertainty (and often the corresponding risk of not being involved in an exchange at all) is for power-disadvantaged actors to seek to form an exclusive relationship (or some form of exclusive contract) with the more powerful actor. Various examples of these processes exist in the form of contracting, norms which foster exclusive relations, and other similar mechanisms of reducing competition. Of course, different mechanisms exist among powerful actors to restrict commitment formation in order to keep open alternatives and foster competition (in negatively connected, power-imbalanced network structures). While many of these issues have not been experimentally investigated yet, preliminary studies suggest that they are important processes within exchange networks that function to alter the underlying structure of the network. In this way commitment formation can be defined under certain circumstances as a power-balancing mechanism (see Cook et al., forthcoming). In this respect it also represents theory elaboration, providing an extension of Emerson's original formulation of the various power-balancing mechanisms. This topic also raises the issue of the formation of a different class of norms which potentially regulate exchange processes. (The other class of norms often investigated in the context of exchange relations are equity norms. See Cook and Emerson 1978; Stolte 1987, for examples.) Fundamental theoretical and empirical questions remain concerning the conditions under which commitments form and the behavioral and structural consequences of such commitments in exchange networks. It is evident in the results presented in Cook and Emerson (1978), for example, that commitment serves to temper the exercise of power in power-imbalanced networks when it emerges, since it fundamentally alters the opportunity structure, reducing the access of powerful actors to valued resources (in this case through a reduction in perceived alternatives).

Coalition formation. In a similar manner coalition formation has been investigated within the framework of the exchange network research program (see Gillmore 1983; Cook and Gillmore 1984; Gillmore 1987). This research represents a theoretical elaboration of Emerson's original formulation, extending the framework to predict specific conditions under which this form of power-balancing will occur in power-imbalanced networks. As Gillmore (1983, 1987) and Cook and Gillmore (1984) indicate, coalitions are likely to form in power-imbalanced networks, but the larger the coalition, the more difficult it is for actors to coordinate activities in such a way as to form effective coalitions (i.e., the costs of coordinating activities increase with an increase in the size of the potential coalition). Gillmore (1983, 1987) examines in greater detail the structural conditions which facilitate coalition formation among less powerful actors in power-imbalanced networks. This research remains limited to small networks and relatively small potential coalitions. Further research is necessary to extend the empirical basis of this theoretical work. Current efforts include theoretical integration and attempts to link this work not only with the extensive body of research and theory on coalitions but also with the more recent experimental and theoretical literature on the logic of collective action.

Future Developments

In addition to the developments indicated in the previous sections, other issues for further investigation involve fundamental unresolved theoretical questions concerning various aspects of the original power-dependence formulation of exchange network theory. A major theoretical effort is being undertaken by Molm and by Cook and Yamagishi to reformulate the basic theoretical framework to take into account major strides that have been made in the empirical testing of the original propositions. In the early 1970's when these research efforts were initiated the primary problem was that there was so little empirical research on even the most basic propositions. Over the past decade the situation has changed and now, not only is there a large body of experimental work on these topics (see Cook 1987), but there are also more empirical attempts to investigate exchange networks using other methodologies (e.g., field studies and historical studies). These efforts are made possible in part by the theoretical refinements which have resulted from the two major sustained research programs described in this chapter.

A second overarching concern which has emerged within the larger research program is what might be labeled the "link" between structure and action. The two major branches of the program have in different ways addressed how structure determines exchange processes and the dynamics of power use. What remains to be investigated in full is the specific nature of these exchange processes and how they, in turn, determine, modify, or transform the structures involved (and how structures emerge from these processes). These research questions will involve the development of more refined dynamic models of the processes involved (e.g., coalition formation, strategic power use, coercive mechanisms, norm formation, division of labor, commitment formation, etc.) and the investigation of the effects of different characteristics of actors on such processes (e.g., individual vs. corporate actors, individual difference factors like level of trust, etc.). This implies development of a more complete model of the actor (individual or corporate) as well as the formulation of more detailed models of the processes involved (e.g., see Molm's [1987] process analysis) and the resultant structural consequences. This work also has the potential to further bridge what has been labeled the "micro-macro gap."

Our review of this particular research program in sociology has been selective, focusing on the major theoretical developments. The application of power dependence principles and exchange network theory to the analysis of interorganizational processes (see Cook 1977; Cook and Emerson 1984, etc.) and to other network-level phenomena (e.g., social support networks, professional referral networks, etc.) has not been discussed. Related applications of Emerson's formulation and subsequent theoretical developments, including the use of these concepts and principles in the analysis of relationship dissolution, elder abuse, urban policy networks, networks of access to medical care, and models of physician-patient relations, among others, are also not discussed in this chapter due to space limitations. In subsequent work Molm and Cook intend to discuss more fully the many arenas in which exchange network principles have been applied outside the laboratory. This work will provide the ultimate test of the significance of this programmatic research effort.

Elementary Theory:
Its Development and Research Program

David Willer and Barry Markovsky

Introduction

Elementary theory (ET) is a network-relations theory that takes its name from its mode of construction—a construction that begins, as Einstein advised, with "irreducible elements as simple and few in number as possible" (Einstein 1954 [1933]: 272). Unlike theories that are named for their substantive foci (e.g., "equity theory"), ET covers a variety of theoretical issues and empirical phenomena. These include social and economic exchange relations, relations of conflict and coercion, and communal property systems, each in a variety of structural configurations.

The most central question for the theory is, How are actions in relations conditioned by structures? Most work, however, has focused on the somewhat narrower question, How is power in the form of exploitation and domination structurally produced? The theory was originally developed for historical/comparative research. It was not originally anticipated that, as described below, most of its tests would be conducted in laboratory settings.

ET has a research program, the various branches of which are related by common principles and modeling procedures. Work has proceeded incrementally, from simple theoretical models and experimental investigations, to the more complex structures and conditions presently under investigation. This paper will trace the growth of the theory temporally.*

Theory growth began after certain theoretic methods were adopted. The first section traces the origin and workings of these theoretic methods. The middle sections describe the theory's growth along several dimensions, including centralized exchange and coercive networks, hierarchy and mobility phenomena, and the structural conditions of "inclusion" and "exclusion." The subsequent discussion of recent formula-

*Both authors thank the National Science Foundation for grants supporting parts of the reported research.

tions covers a model that predicts power in a general class of exchange networks and in flow networks—structures in which resources can move through multiple network positions. We conclude with two final sections: current issues in simulation, experimental and nonexperimental research, and an examination of ET as a program of theory-driven research.

Theoretic Method and Basic Concepts

Method

ET uses a theoretic structure, including modeling procedures, principles, and laws, like that of physical theory (Willer 1967; Willer and Willer 1973; Willer 1987). One hopes to gain breadth and precision by adopting a proven theoretic structure. Adopting a particular type of theoretic structure cannot by itself ensure breadth or precision, however. To the contrary, achieving these qualities depends on the successful prediction and explanation of empirical phenomena.

Our theoretic method begins with the recognition that to understand the world, we identify relations among objects and events. Although objects and events are observable, all theories face the problem that relations among objects are generally unobservable. The solution is to construct an abstract, theoretical world of objects and events, and relate these elements to one another in known ways. These are theoretic models. In explanation and prediction, theoretic models are applied to objects and events in the observable world. Perhaps the first known example of this was Archimedes' formulation of the equilibrium of planes that, in application, were his laws of levers (Archimedes 1897 [230 B.C.]). According to Windelband (1958 [1901]: 388ff), it was Galileo's (1954 [1665]) development of theoretic models that launched modern science.

Modeling procedures are methods for constructing theoretic models. Different models will lead to different conclusions. For example, for Galileo and Newton, space is a nothingness upon which a grid is conceptually imposed. For Einstein, space itself gives shape to the grid. In sociology Simmel (1964 [1917]) was the first to propose the formal development of a social space with "spacial forms" subject to "isolation and recomposition."

Theoretic models and the real world phenomena to which they apply are often conflated. Motion in the real world consists of very complex events, e.g., boulders with uneven surfaces bounding down bumpy slopes, retarded by friction and drag. Motion in a theoretic model is relatively simple. Objects move in geometrically perfect straight lines unless acted on by external forces, all of which are assumed to be fully known. Sociologists who confuse the realms of theory and reality assert that the subject matter of the social sciences is far more complex than that of the physical sciences, and that social scientific theories must reflect this (e.g., Blalock 1969). Willer (1987: ch. 7) argues the opposite. In fact, the theoretic models of sociology should no more account for all of the fine-grained contingencies of reality than theoretic models of physical motion should take into account the unique projections and depressions of the rolling boulder's surface, or the shrubs and gopher holes to be found on a particular slope.

Clearly distinguishing abstract from phenomenal worlds leads to two important conclusions. First, principles and laws are not applied to the world. Instead, principles and laws connect the abstract objects and events of models, thus standing for the connections of the world that cannot be observed. Second, theory is applied through explicitly linking objects and events in the theoretical realm to objects and events of the world. These linkages are known as "operationalizations" or "instantiations." Thus, the operationalization of a theoretical concept such as "power" consists of a set of empirical properties or events that conform to the set of abstract properties or events specified in the conceptual definition of power. Explanations of and predictions for events in the real world are based on results obtained from applying principles and laws to models and relating the whole to the observable world.

Toulmin (1953) has illustrated these applications for the case of optics. In optics, a light ray diagram is a model drawn in accordance with the principle that "light travels in straight lines." The model is solved using the law of reflection—that the angle of incidence of a light ray equals the angle of reflection—or using Snell's law for refraction (1953: 42–62). Toulmin suggests that physical theories are stratified with principles at a higher level and laws at a middle level, but these are not levels of abstraction or logic. According to Toulmin, principles are not more abstract than laws and laws cannot be deduced from principles. While this asserts that the two are different, it does not entirely clarify the nature of that difference.

Though principles and laws are in continual use in physical theory, we know of no physical scientist or philosopher of science, other than Toulmin, who has formally differentiated the two. The following distinction will suffice for our purposes. In theory, problems are formulated by applying principles to models. Problems are solved by applying laws. For example, in geometric optics thinking about a ray diagram in accordance with the principle that light travels in straight lines leads to a class of problems. How is the direction of the light ray at this point related to its direction at a second point? If between the two points the light ray was reflected, the law of reflection is used to derive the relation between the two directions. If the light ray is refracted, then Snell's law is used. Examples from the history of ET given below illustrate the formulation of problems with models and principles and their solution using laws.

Theory is used to design experiments. When a social structure is to be experimentally investigated, a theoretically modeled structure of social relationships becomes the design for the structure to be observed in the laboratory. The model's initial conditions are the initial conditions of the experiment. Applications of the theory's principles and laws produce theoretic processes and outcomes that are the predicted results of the experiment. If successful, the experiment's dynamics and outcomes will correspond to those which occur in the model. These issues are discussed in greater detail in Willer (1987), where theory is used to design experiments.

Over the past two decades in sociology, experimentation has become the preferred method for many theorists. Simulations can also aid theory development by providing constructed worlds for deriving complex theoretical implications. At the beginning of a theoretic research program, the theoretic models subject to experimental study are usually quite simple, in contrast to the complex phenomenal world. They are simple by necessity because theory moves from simple to complex formulations. This simplicity, however, raises issues of substantive significance.

We suggest that theory development can take one of two paths. One path leads from initial formulations directly to complex formulations and applications to contemporary and historical examples. This was the path taken in the classic theories of Marx and Weber. One reason for this choice was their assumption that experimental investigation of social structures is impossible (1967 [1867] and 1968 [1918], respectively). Yet both recognized the very great difficulty in using theory without experimentation to reach naturally occurring cases.

The second path leads less directly to contemporary and historical applications. When experimentation is the predominant mode of testing a theory, the theory's growth is incremental, going forward step by step in ongoing contact with research results. The design of experiments challenges the precision of theory. The outcomes of experiments evaluate derivations and form the groundwork for new constructions. In this process experimentation is the test, theory the driving force. The advantage of the second path over the first lies in the greater precision demanded and in the ability to extend theory one step at a time.

Methodological choices in the development of ET have led to a particular pattern of theory growth. The point of departure is fundamental concepts that are given a network interpretation and then combined to form increasingly complex derived concepts. Early in this process principles and then laws are deployed (Willer 1984). The development of increasingly complex entities results in branching as, for example, the investigation of coercive structures which are distinct from exchange structures and, as detailed later, the investigation of exclusion and inclusion in social exchanges which are distinct structural conditions. The program of expectation states theory has also branched while it has grown (Wagner 1984; Wagner and Berger 1985).

Insofar as the history of ET is concerned, issues of theoretic method and structure were settled *before* substantive formulations were developed. That is, it was decided that the theory would have a modeling procedure, principles and laws. The first step was the development of the modeling procedure. During that development it was realized that the conception of the social world implicit in the modeling procedure might ultimately prove fruitless. This was seen as a reason for caution. No attempt was made to formulate a fundamentally new conception of the social world. Instead, the modeling procedure was constructed to formalize concepts of actor and agency, social relationships, and social structure that were seen as common to Marx, Weber, and Simmel.

The conception of theoretic methods given in this section was the conception held prior to the development of the theory. Though it was realized that, in the exact sciences, theory was used to design experiments, this was not generally the case in sociology. The comments above on theory and experimentation benefit from hindsight. Thus, the vital ongoing role that experimental research would take in theory growth was initially a surprise. It should not have been. The expectation states program was already under way and was already demonstrating the power of experimentation in sociology.

Basic Concepts

Figure 1 shows the set of *points* and *signed arcs* that are used to develop the fundamental concepts of ET. Points represent *social actors* endowed with preferences, beliefs, and decision-making capabilities. Each arc represents an act called a *sanction*. In Figure 1a there is a positive sanction transmitted by A and received by B. In 1b no act occurs, and in 1c a negative sanction is transmitted by A and received by B. Sanctions are treated as flows of quantity x with unit valuation v such that P_A, the payoff of any actor A, from r, a resource flow received by A, is given by the equation

$$P_A = v_r x_r.$$

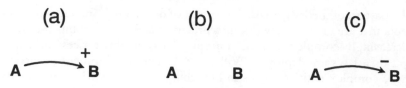

Fig. 1. Sanctions.

This is the First Law of the theory. (Note that, unlike operant theory, v is not a function of x.) These sanctions can be used to build a simple preference structure for B that orders the three payoff states in a manner that is consistent with the sanctions' signs. For any $A - B$ flow, B prefers any positive sanction flow to no sanction flow, and no sanction flow to any negative sanction flow.

Principle 1. All social actors act to maximize their expected payoff state.

Payoff states are defined in terms of the sanction flows of Figure 1 and in terms of the First Law. For B, a change of state from 1b to 1a—from no sanction flow to a positive sanction flow—is a positive payoff, and a change from 1b to 1c is a negative payoff.

The First Law is used to quantify the payoff states of sanction flows. The sign of v is negative for a negative sanction flow and positive for a positive sanction flow while v's absolute value and the size of x determine the amount of positive or negative payoff to the actor. In later figures, sanctions may have both these signs of reception and signs of transmission. In that case, v_t and x_t will indicate transmission signs.

Only actors transmitting sanctions act, and only they can decide to transmit or not transmit a sanction. Therefore, the application of Principle 1 to Figure 1 produces no activity. In that figure, only A is endowed with the capability to act—to transmit sanctions to B. Since in that figure only reception produces a payoff, only B's payoff state can be altered. Since sanctions separate action from payoff, neither A nor B can act to maximize its payoff state.

This conceptualization points to the limitations of "action theory." For rational choice theory in its most extreme form, the world is a cafeteria in which action is a mechanical selection of valued things. In this form, action theory offers only one explanation of all human behavior. "People do what they want to do." By contrast, application of Principle 1 to sanctions poses new problems by placing action in an interpersonal context. As developed below, the solutions to those problems drive theory beyond individual action to a consideration of relationships. This step corresponds to the one taken by Weber (1968 [1918]). Contrary to Parsons, for Weber social actions were not themselves the subject of theory. Instead, social actions were elements combined to form social relationships.

Modeling Interactions

Figure 2 displays the three logically possible social relationships that can be constructed using two actors and two sanction types. The three are theoretically pure types of social relationships called exchange, conflict, and coercion. Simple representations such as these can have a number of uses. As shown in later figures, the relations can be the parts of more complex wholes. Alternatively, as illustrated in Figures 4 and 5, the relations can be analyzed into component sanctions and ordered to represent preferences. As shown in Figure 4, beliefs can be represented using the same component parts. Focusing on dyads this subsection illustrates how the modeling procedure, Principle 1, and the First Law can be used to pose and solve problems. The discussion will begin with exchange relations, and then move through conflict to coercion.

The modeled structures of ET are frequently drawn as bisigned directed graphs as in the two types of exchange illustrated in Figure 3. As indicated by these graphs, the actors' payoff states are altered by either transmitting or receiving sanctions. The addition of a transmission sign (in parentheses) permits the definition of two types of exchange. In *social*

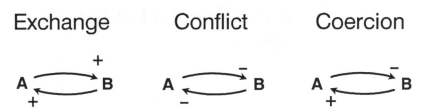

Fig. 2. Relations.

Fig. 3. Exchange as Bisigned Digraphs.

a) A's Preferences

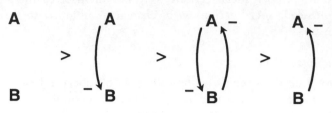

b) B's Preferences

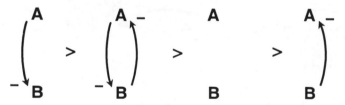

c) B's Beliefs Concerning A's Preferences

Fig. 4. Conflict.

exchange, both signs are positive, so both transmission and reception are gains. Examples include the exchange of friends' favors discussed by Hansen (1981) and Loukinen (1981) and the relations of primitive exchange discussed by Sahlins (1972).

In *economic exchange*, the loss and gain of each flow produce interest

a) A's Preferences | b) B's Preferences

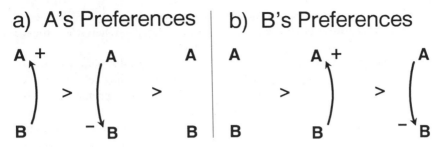

Fig. 5. Coercion.

opposition between A and B. A's maximally preferred payoff state occurs when the quantity of B's transmissions is maximized and its own minimized; exactly the opposite is preferred by B. Let $v_t(a)$ be A's valuation of a unit transmission and $v_r(a)$ be the valuation of a unit reception, and similarly for B. Then an $A - B$ exchange is possible when

$$v_r(a)v_r(b) - v_t(a)v_t(b) > 0.$$

Note that this inequality follows from the First Law and Principle 1 and, when satisfied, exchange can produce positive payoffs for both A and B. The size of this difference is the *exchange potential* of the relationship.*

Other possible relations aside, the greater the exchange potential, the greater the range of possible exchange rates, and the greater the interest of one, the other, or both actors in exchanging—depending upon the exchange rate being negotiated. (*Exchange rate* is defined as the ratio of the two sanction flows.) If 3b is the whole social world of A and B, and the above inequality is satisfied, then Principle 1 asserts that exchange will occur. Not explained, however, is the rate of the exchange.

The problem of exchange rate in isolated dyads or "bilateral monopolies" is more than 100 years old, having been first formulated by Edgeworth (1881). As an economist, Edgeworth chose to leave the problem of exchange rate in the dyad indeterminate, a practice still frequently followed in economic theory and consistent with its focus on markets. Sociology, being as interested in dyads as markets, cannot avoid attempting a determinate solution to the problem. In ET, the solution is provided by the *resistance* model, covered below.

In *conflict*, as depicted in Figure 2, neither actor benefits. Applying Principle 1 to the conflict relation implies that no informed actor will exchange in this relation. This follows because only negative payoffs are

---

*The term "exchange potential" was suggested by Norman Hummon (in personal communication).

possible in a relation containing only negative sanctions. Therefore conflict can occur only when the relation is not isolated—when it is a means to an end—or when actors have false beliefs.

One scenario in which conflict can occur due to false beliefs is drawn in Figure 4. Figures 4a and b order the acts of the conflict relation by A's and B's preferences for the different payoff states. The preferences arbitrarily assigned to A and B are mirror images of each other, and one of a set of possible preference orders consistent with Principle 1. Applying Principle 1 means that if both have accurate information of the other's preferences, each will choose to transmit no sanction and conflict is not actualized.

Now assume that B's beliefs concerning A's preference are incorrect, as shown in 4c. For this preference order, Principle 1 implies that A will transmit its negative sanction regardless of B's choice of action. This would narrow B's choices to its third- and fourth-ranked payoff states. As theorists with full information we know that A will not act. Thus B acts first in the mistaken belief that only its third and fourth payoff states are possible. Acting on Principle 1 and preferring the third-ranked state, B chooses to transmit its negative sanction. In terms of A's actual preference ordering, B's transmission moves A to its least preferred payoff state. Preferring the third over the fourth, A transmits its negative sanction and conflict occurs.

There are empirical examples that correspond to this scenario. These range from the overly defensive individual who strikes out at others wrongly believed to be aggressors, to the nation-state whose leaders decide to attack another nation because they mistakenly believe that the other intends to attack. It is obvious, however, that conflict need not be based on false information because it may occur as a means to an end. In Carneiro's (1970) theory, for example, conflict occurs in state formation as a precondition to coercion.

Coercion poses other problems for the theorist. Bierstedt (1976: 140) defined coercive power as "the ability to use force, not its actual employment." If analysis is limited to ordinary language, however, Bierstedt's definition could easily be taken as a senseless paradox. Of what use is a threat if it is not used? If the threat is not used, what makes power happen? An example solves this problem while posing a second.

The preference orders given in Figure 5 and Principle 1 form a point of departure for a coercive scenario. Assume that the beliefs of each actor accurately reflect the payoff ordering of the other and contain an array of possible offers and threats. In the language of the theory, offers and threats are formed by relating pairs of payoff states. For example, one possible threat that A could send to B is, "Transmit your positive sanction or else you will receive my negative sanction." The problem is to use Principle 1 to select the best offer or threat.

Initially in the scenario, no sanction is transmitted and A is in its least preferred state. A's most preferred state, receiving the positive sanction from B, can occur only if B decides to transmit it. At first, however, B is not acting, preferring no act to transmission of the negative. As we have seen, one possible threat from A is, "Transmit your positive or receive my negative." This maps onto B's preferences, blocking B's preferred state limiting B's choices. Either B chooses to transmit its positive or A transmits its negative sanction. Applying Principle 1, B chooses to transmit the positive sanction to A, and interaction ends with A in its most preferred state.

The coercive scenario solves the apparent paradox of threat and power in coercion. If A's threat is effective, B transmits the positive sanction. Only if A's threat is not effective—that is, if B does not believe A— would the negative sanction be transmitted. Thus the existence of the threat—more accurately, B's *belief* that there is a threat—is a necessary condition for B's transmission. This solution, however, leads to a second question, How much can A extract from B for a given threat? This issue concerns the rate of coercion and, like rate of exchange, is addressed by the resistance model.

Though sometimes far removed from the objects and events of the world, even simple constructions can lead to useful inferences that are by no means self-evident. For example, according to Weber, the state is that organization which monopolizes the means of violence over a given geographical area. In terms of the three pure relational types, there is one and only one structure that satisfies Weber's definition: a structure like Figure 6 below, in which one coercer is central and a number or coercees are peripheral. This construction relates Weber and Carneiro. The coercive state, as defined by Weber, is the end point of Carneiro's conflict process of state formation.

Further inferences may be drawn. Historians have long viewed state centralization and commercialization in Europe as independent processes. However, models of coercion and exchange imply that the two are necessarily related. The centralization of coercion was the result of a long process in the development of the modern state (Gilham 1981). A necessary result of this process is that actors subject to the state are left with only positive sanctions. Exchange is the only relation in which only positives occur, and commercialization is no more than the spread of exchange relations. Therefore, it is not accidental that commercialization accompanied the centralization of coercion by the state.

Since state centralization and commercialization are necessarily related, it follows that the frequency with which we encounter exchange is not itself a demonstration of its inherent superiority over other kinds of relations, as once asserted by Homans (1967) and Blau (1964); exactly the opposite could be the case. Assume, contrary to Homans and Blau, that coercion is "more effective" than exchange. If so, coercive relations will rapidly centralize, forming the organizations that we call states. As we have already seen, however, state centralization implies commercialization and the ubiquity of exchange. Thus if coercion is "more effective" than exchange, then most relations daily encountered would be exchange.

Resistance and Power in Simple Structures

Resistance and Relational Power

According to Weber, "power is the chance of a man or number of men to realize their own will in a communal action even against the resistance of others" (1964 [1918]: 180). In ET, power is a potential associated with a relation or structure. When that potential is actualized, it is observable as a rate of exchange or coercion. Departing from Weber, we have a model for *resistance* to predict and explain the use of power. That is, resistance predicts rates of exchange and coercion from conditions of relations and structures.

In comparison to resistance, negotiation schemes like Nash's (1950, 1953) are restricted to the prediction of compromise outcomes in isolated exchange relations. The scope of resistance is broader, for, beyond exchange dyads, it is used to predict power outcomes in exchange structures, isolated coercive relations, and coercive structures. The broader scope of resistance is due to its use of two terms: $P_{\max}$, the actor's maximum payoff, and P_{con}, the payoff at confrontation. As we saw in the coercion scenario above, at confrontation—that is, when the two actors cannot agree—the coercer transmits the negative sanction. In contrast, in the exchange relation at confrontation, there is no exchange and no sanctions flow.

The resistance equation is formally expressed as

$$R_A = \frac{P_{A\max} - P_A}{P_A - P_{A\text{con}}},$$

which is the Second Law of the theory. Intuitively, it expresses a prediction for the actor's resistance to a given profit level by comparing its difference from the best possible value to its difference from the value received at confrontation.

Principle 2. Compromise occurs at the point of equiresistance for un-differentiated actors in a full information system.

Thus, when an exchange relation is settled by compromise, the predicted rate of exchange is derivable by the assertion that $R_A = R_B$. Principle 2, however, does not rule out the possibility that settlement may occur by means other than compromise.

Logically, the first use for resistance equations is to define equipower and differential power conditions. For a number of years, however, the terms "exploitation" and "domination" were used instead of power. As Weber wrote somewhere, power is an amorphous concept. Better to de-lay introducing the term and get it precise from the outset.

The particular problem with power is that equal power obtains at equiresistance, but not all equiresistance points are equipower—a point illustrated in the following example. Assume that A and B are actors in an exchange relationship who bargain to a compromise rate of exchange at equiresistance. Call this rate equipower. Suppose, then, that A is not satisfied with the compromise rate and introduces a threat of negative sanction. This transforms the relationship into one of mixed exchange-coercion. Prior to the threat $P_{Acon} = P_{Bcon} = 0$, and, after bargaining, preliminary agreement occurred at the exchange rate for which $R_A = R_B$. Now, due to A's threat $P_{Bcon} < 0$, and this increases the size of the denominator of B's resistance equation. For the previously agreed–upon rate, $R_A > R_B$, and equiresistance is now at a rate of exchange that is more favorable to A. Certainly, the first exchange rate should be called equipower and the second differential power. This conclusion leads to the following stipulation:

Equipower occurs at equiresistance when $P_{con} = 0$ for both actors.

This stipulation allows consistent use of the term "power" across ex-change, coercive, and mixed relations. By definition all coercive relations are power relations, as are all exchange relations into which coercion is mixed. Further, the stipulation points to an array of conditions of ex-change relations that are not coercive, but which, nevertheless, produce power. These are conditions under which $P_{con} < 0$ when non-completion of exchange has negative outcomes.

For example, in explaining power in modern societies, Weber (1968 [1918]) noted that the capitalist holds workers' families for ransom. That is, the worker who is a concerned spouse and parent fears the effects of unemployment on the family. Then P_{con} will be much smaller than zero, which, compared to the $P_{con} = 0$ condition, greatly reduces the worker's resistance to offered wages. Conversely, $P_{con} > 0$ when opportunities are forfeited by completion of an exchange. This increases resistance to previous offers and shifts the rate of exchange at equiresistance relative to the case where $P_{con} = 0$.

Because research has leaped past relations to focus on structural conditions, there is no evidence directly supporting these expected shifts in rate of exchange when P_{con} is varied. It would be good if there was. Nevertheless, resistance has predicted rates of exchange when $P_{con} = 0$ for both actors, and rates of coercion when $P_{con} < 0$ for one actor but not the other. Thus, there is indirect evidence that leads us to believe that resistance can predict rates in mixed exchange-coercive relations and other relations in which P_{con} values are varied.

Experimental research has used three prototype relations: an exchange relation, a coercive relation, and a resource pool relation that simulates exchange. Here the equiresistance points for each will be derived beginning with the resource pool relation, as its derivation is the simplest. All derivations assume that the relation is isolated and that actors have sufficient information, so that P_{max} and P_{con} rates are known. Also assumed is the opportunity to make and receive offers.

In resource pool relations, a pool of exchange units or "points" is placed between positions that can be divided if the A and B actors in the two positions agree upon a division. A pool of 24 resource points has been used in most experiments. Principle 1 asserts that 1 point is the least that either actor will accept. Thus $P_{max} = 23$ for each. Also, if no exchange occurs, there is no loss or gain—no positive or negative payoff. Thus $P_{con} = 0$ for both, and

$$R_A = \frac{23 - P_A}{P_A} = R_B = \frac{23 - P_B}{P_B}.$$

Furthermore, $P_A + P_B = 24$ by design. Substituting, we find that both P_A and P_B equal 12 when $R_A = R_B$. Therefore, a 12-12 split of the pool occurs at equipower.

Now consider an exchange relation for which A initially holds 1 unit resource that is valueless to A but worth 10 points to B. B holds 10 resource units each worth 1 point to A and 1 to B. The differential valuation of A's resource produces an exchange potential of 10. At one extreme, A could transmit its resource and receive 9 of B's in return, i.e., $P_{Amax} = 9$. At the other extreme, A's resource is exchanged for one of B's and $P_{Bmax} = 9$. At no exchange $P_{con} = 0$ for both. The exchange potential of 10 means that $P_A + P_B = 10$. Then

$$R_A = \frac{9 - P_A}{P_A} = R_B = \frac{9 - P_B}{P_B},$$

and compromise occurs when $P_A = P_B = 5$. At compromise, B transmits 5 sanctions and receives A's sanction in exchange. Since A's sanction is valued at 10 by B, this may be called a 5/10 rate. Since the rate occurs when both P_{con} values are zero, this is the equipower rate.

Finally, consider a coercive relation in which the coercer C holds a negative sanction that is worth 1 point to C if retained, and reduces D's preference state by 10 if transmitted. D holds positive sanctions worth 1 point each to D and 1 each to C. Confrontation occurs when the negative sanction is transmitted, for which $P_{Ccon} = -1$ and $P_{Dcon} = -10$. According to Principle 1, the most that D will transmit to avoid the negative is 9. Thus, $P_{Cmax} = 9$. The least that D will transmit if C does not transmit the negative is zero sanctions—thus $P_{Dmax} = 0$. This is because the transmission of the sanction is costly to C, being a loss of 1. If it were costless, D would transmit 1 sanction to avoid the negative and the compromise point would shift favoring C. In resistance terms,

$$R_C = \frac{9 - P_C}{P_C - (-1)} = R_D = \frac{0 - P_D}{P_D - (-10)}.$$

Since $P_D = -P_C$, when we solve for equiresistance, $P_C = 4.5$ and $P_D = -4.5$. That is, C and D will bargain and compromise at the point where B transmits 4.5 sanctions to A. Relative to the resources initially held by D, this is a 4.5/10 rate of coercion. Note that this rate, though at equiresistance, is not an equipower rate. At equiresistance C is exercising coercive power over D.

These examples illustrate the use of resistance to obtain bargaining solutions for isolated dyads. In exchange and resource pool division examples, $P_{con} = 0$ for both actors and equiresistance is equipower. In coercion, relational power occurs in the perfectly isolated dyad because $P_{Dcon} < 0$. More precisely, power occurs because P_{con} is much smaller than zero for the coercee. In the next section these relations will be composed into simple structures in order to investigate structural power.

Recently, Fararo and Skvoretz (1989) have shown that equiresistance points shift when certain kinds of nonlinear payoff functions are differentially attributed to actors. This raises the possibility that compromise points may be unique to each pair of persons. Whereas Fararo and Skvoretz's point is logically possible, at issue is whether it has practical consequences. Up till now $P = vx$. That is, the payoff function of all actors is a linear function of x, and it has been suggested that this formulation is more general than might seem to be the case at the outset (Willer 1981: 113).

If the payoff functions of actors varied widely, it would not be possible to predict the amount of power use from relational or structural conditions without also knowing each actor's unique payoff function. In fact,

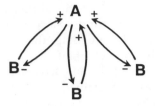

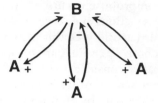

Fig. 6. Centralized coercion.   Fig. 7. Coercee central.

predictions that assume $P = vx$ for all actors have been routinely supported in a variety of relations and structures. Nevertheless, Fararo and Skvoretz have raised an important new issue for research, for it is logically possible that predictions have been thus far supported, and effects of differential payoff functions masked, due to a combination of the robustness of predicted effects and measurement imprecision which misses more subtle effects.

Building Structures

Each of the prototype relationships discussed above has been used to build larger structures. Structures are built by connecting the relations. For example, a centralized structure can be composed by connecting a number of resource pool relations at A. Exchange relations (A with one unit valued at ten by B, B with ten units valued at one each by A) have been combined to form two types of centralized structures, those with A central to three, four, or five B's, and those with B central to three, four, or five A's. Centralized structures with either coercers or coercees at the center have been tested. Figures 6 and 7 display coercive structures with, respectively, the coercer central to three coercees, and a coercee central to three coercers.

In building structures, we follow certain conventions that result in "baseline" conditions from which variations may depart. Unless otherwise specified, the constructions maintain the conditions of each of the relational types. Foremost of these conditions are exchange resources and exchange opportunities. For example, when A is connected by resource pool relations with two B's: (1) the number of profit points in each relation is the same as in the prototype resource pool dyad used to build the structure and (2) A can divide pools with both B's. Similarly, when A is connected by exchange relations with two or more B's: (1) A's resource units are multiplied by the number of those relations and (2) A is allocated as many opportunities to exchange as there are relations. The same is true when B is connected to two or more A's.

Precisely the same conventions are followed when coercive structures are assembled. Unless otherwise specified, when the coercer is central, it is allocated resources for negative sanctioning in each of its relations. Finally, for both coercive and exchange structures, all actors act independently. Unless otherwise specified, coalition formation and collective action are disallowed. In Willer (1987) rates of coercion were predicted before and after coalition formation, and experiments supported the predictions.

Structural Power and Exclusion

Exclusion produces centralized power by changing actors' resistances. Contrary to conventional wisdom, centralization alone does not produce power of the central actor over peripheral actors. That is, merely connecting relations together at one position in the manner described above does not alter the rate of exchange from rates of baseline dyads. The resistance model shows why that is the case.

To see that centralization alone does not produce power, let two exchange relationships be connected at A. Then, for A, the value of P_{max} doubles while P_{con} remains zero. Also, the expected value of P doubles, since payoff from two relationships is now at issue. In general, when n relationships are connected at A, P_{max} and P both increase n times:

$$R_A(n) = \frac{n(P_{Amax} - P_A)}{nP_A} = R_A = \frac{P_{Amax} - P_A}{P_A}.$$

Since $R_A(n) = R_A = R_B$, the compromise rates reached in any branch built in this way are identical to the isolated dyad. Thus centralization alone does not produce power differences. This conclusion is supported by extensive experimental findings, some of which are described below.

Structures that maintain the conditions of each relationship have no structural effect and are thus termed *null connected*. In theory, a null connected 3-branch, like that of Figure 8a, is not one structure but three dyads incidentally connected at A. Both A-central and B-central null connected 3-branches have been investigated experimentally. With A central, B's transmitted an average of 4.5 sanctions in exchange for A's resource, a 4.5/10 rate. With B central 6.9 sanctions were exchanged for A's resource, a 6.9/10 rate. The predicted rate was 5/10 in both experiments. In each case, the direction of deviation of the rate of exchange indicated a small degree of power used by peripherals over the central subject.

These experiments used the "interaction setting" detailed in Willer (1987). This setting allows face-to-face interactions among subjects who are connected by exchange relations. Non-connected subjects are separated by dividers that block eye contact but allow subjects to hear all other negotiations. The experimental design controlled all material pay-offs, but subjects could and did introduce symbolic sanctions, including equity demands. This may explain the small amount of power use by peripherals: central subjects may have been influenced by the asymme-try—the convergence of three on one that would shift the equiresistance point. If so, a design that did not allow subjects to introduce symbolic sanctions would produce equipower. Recent experiments using ExNet, an electronic experimental PC network described below, allowed isola-tion of subjects in separate rooms and controlled the content of bargain-ing. Preliminary research on a null connected 3-branch using the 24-point resource pool relation shows practically no deviation from 12-12 equipower rates.

Exclusion, not centralization, produces centralized power in branches. More generally, if a structure permits one set of actors to exclude a subset of the actors to which they are connected which cannot exclude in return, then the first set develops power over the second. The simplest case, when one actor excludes members of a set of connected actors, occurs in branches like those in Figure 8b and c. In Figure 8, exchanges are indi-cated by solid lines and exclusions by dashed lines.

Early experimental research used the following distinctions. Let N_p be the size of a position's *potential network*—the set of positions with whom an actor can negotiate—and N_m be the size of its *maximum possible net-work*—the number with whom the actor may exchange during a given time period. Let $N_p = N_m$ for all peripherals. Then for the central posi-tion in a branch, the number of its structural exclusions is $S_x = N_p - N_m$. Only if $S_x > 0$ is the central position high in power. For all Figure 8 networks, $N_m = 3$. If $N_p = N_m$ as in 8a, the central position is null connected and there are no exclusions. If $N_p > N_m$ as in 8b and 8c, the central position is exclusively connected (Willer and Anderson 1981).

As indicated by the solid lines and dashed lines of Figure 8, there is no exclusion in 8a, and one and two exclusions in 8b and 8c, respectively. In 8b, B_2 is pictured as being excluded by A. At some future time, how-ever, the exclusion could occur between A and any other B, and similarly for the two exclusions of 8c. A "centrality index," $C_p = N_p / N_m$, was introduced by Willer (1981) to predict power in such branches. When $C_p = 1$, there is no exclusion and no power at A. In contrast, when $C_p > 1$ as in 8b and 8c, A is a high power position and the B's are low. In 1981 Brennan showed that there is a change of power over time for the 8b and c networks the rate of which was predicted by C_p. In 1987 Willer and Patton proposed an array of procedures for the location of power in branch structures, all of which (including C_p) have now been subsumed by GPI, a more comprehensive model described below.

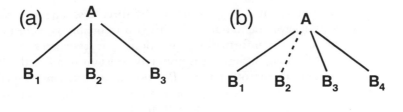

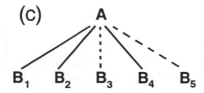

Fig. 8. Three exchange networks.

C_p predicts which branches have centralized power, and the rate of development of power use. However, it does not address a variety of actor-level questions. For example, does the use of power require deliberate adoption of a strategy by actors in high power positions? Alternatively, is the development of power driven by low power actors? To answer these questions requires an actor-level analysis that relates actors' decisions and actions to structural exclusion.

The resistance model explains why exclusion produces power differences. Assume that all actors know their own and others' initial P_{max} and P_{con} values, and have ongoing information concerning other offers in the structure. Apply the resistance model to 8b and assume that there is tentative agreement between A and three of the B's for any rate of exchange less than $P_A = P_{Amax}$. If A exchanges with the fourth B, the payoff (P_A) from one of these exchanges will be lost. As a result, for the fourth exchange, $P_{Acon} = P_A$. That is, A's payoff when agreement cannot be reached with the fourth B is the payoff of exchanging with any of the other B's. This considerably increases A's resistance in negotiating with the fourth B.

A's resistance is maximal if the fourth B offers A an exchange equal to rates previously offered. Then $P_A = P_{Acon}$, the denominator of the resistance equation is zero and resistance is infinite. Offers at infinite resistance are rejected. Thus the fourth B must better the offers of the other three or face exclusion. With that offer, A's resistance relative to another B goes to infinity, and the same is true for the set of B's. By extension, the process continues until $P_{A\max}$ is offered by three B's. The process is similar for 8c, but more rapid due to the larger proportion of exclusions.

Under the assumed information conditions, the resistance of low power actors also changes. Since A is infinitely resistant to a fourth offer equal to the offers of the other three B's, no rate of exchange equally favorable or more favorable to the fourth B is now possible. Therefore, $P_{\max}$ for the fourth B declines to equal P_B for the best offer that A will accept. For that offer, $P_{B\max} = P_B$. Since $P_{B\max} - P_B = 0$, for the fourth B, $R_B = 0$ and the offer is made. With that offer, $R_B = 0$ in sequence for the remaining B's. These changes in resistance that initiate the power process continue for rates successively more favorable to A.

The power process is driven by the very high resistance of high power actors and very low resistance of low power actors. There are structurally induced changes in resistance of high and low power actors because $P_{\max}$ and P_{con}, initially set by the conditions of the exchange relationship, vary over time. Under the assumed information conditions, the power process entails bidding: low power actors make offers with incrementally higher payoffs to the high power actor. At the extreme favoring the high power actor, the resistance values of high and low power actors are both zero and exchange occurs. This contrasts with bargaining where two actors equal in power move from extreme, conflicting offers toward a medial compromise rate.

The resistance model demonstrates that power use does not require actors in high power positions to adopt a particular bargaining strategy. To the contrary, under the given information conditions, power is not produced by the activities of the high power actor alone. Typically, low power actors actively offer a sequence of bids at rates increasingly favorable to the high power actor.

Once the extreme offers are reached, exploitation, as measured by the rate of exchange, is at its maximum. Also present at the extreme (and as the extreme is approached) is the condition that Weber called domination. Domination is simply the obverse of obedience, a condition assured in these structures by the zero resistance of low power actors. According to Weber (1968 [1918]), dominated actors have only a minimal interest in obedience. This condition corresponds to the point at which power is maximized, the end of the power process explicated above. The apparent paradox, that the dominated have only a minimal yet determinant interest in obedience, is resolved when we note that, even at the extreme, the resistance of the dominated is zero.

The processes and outcomes of experiments on exchange branches strongly support the resistance analysis. The rate of exchange moves through a bidding process, and that rate is a positive function of numbers of exclusions. The end point of the process is the rate maximally favorable to the high power position. Under the relatively complete information conditions of the interaction setting, the maximally favorable rate of the central, high power actor has been routinely attained (Brennan 1981; Willer 1987). These conclusions are also supported by recent results using ExNet, where 3-branch networks with one and two exclusions were investigated (Willer and Skvoretz 1989).

Power and Hierarchy/Mobility

As Weber (1968 [1918]) noted, modern organizations have hierarchical structures in which officials in higher positions are privileged in money and status relative to those in lower positions. Because officials do not appropriate offices, there is mobility from lower to higher positions. Mobility in a hierarchy is a power condition structurally similar to exclusion—a similarity that can be uncovered by looking at qualities of exclusion from the perspective of mobility in a hierarchy.

When exclusion is possible, positions may be described as either exchanging or excluded in a given period. Structural power occurs when low power actors prefer exchanging to exclusion, and when it is effectively costless for the high power actor to move low power actors from one to the other status. Similarly a two-level hierarchy has two statuses, one more and the other less preferred by low power actors, and in which it is effectively costless to move actors from one level to the other. Hierarchy/mobility works like exclusion, except that actors move between levels of the hierarchy instead of being excluded. Hierarchy without mobility, like a branch without exclusion, is not a power structure.

Willer (1987) conducted experiments on power in branches that were hierarchies. High and low status positions were produced by dividing peripherals into two sets. There was a high status set with two members who were each allowed to exchange for any mutually agreeable rate with *A*. The four members of the low status set were allowed to exchange for at least two fewer points than the first exchange. This produced two levels, with the rates of exchange of the two related but free to move relative to agreements of the more privileged. Movement of the rates in a direction favorable to the central actor indicated an increase in centralized power.

Two conditions were investigated: "fixed," in which designated *B*'s have the first two opportunities to exchange; and "mobile," in which any of the *B*'s could make either of the first two exchanges. There were no exclusions under either condition. As predicted, the mobile structure moved rapidly by a bidding process toward the rate maximally favorable to the central A. Bargaining in the fixed structure produced rates that remained at or near equipower.

Life in contemporary society is increasingly dominated by large formal organizations, and contrary to Weber's focus on legitimation, hierarchy/mobility may be the condition that centralizes power in these organizations. If so, that power condition occurs between all pairs of levels in the hierarchy, and between each pair of levels of job ladders built into each position. More work in theory development supported by experimentation and field research is needed to infer to multilevel organizations. Preliminary work, however, suggests that the conditions for power centralization in modern organizations are particularly strong. This suggestion is by no means a new one, but its basis in hierarchy/mobility is new. Given the empirical significance of organizational phenomena, this direction of research deserves more work.

Power in Coercive Structures

As we saw above, coercers exercise power over coercees in isolated coercive relations. Connecting a number of coercive relations at the coercer, therefore, results in a branch like that shown in Figure 6, where the central coercer has power over peripheral coercers. *This is not structural power.* Instead, it is an example of combined power relations. Like the null connected exchange branch, the rates of coercion observed at equiresistance occur through bargaining to compromise, not through power processes like those found in exclusionary exchange structures (Willer 1987). Nonetheless, coercive networks with power processes that are similar to exclusionary exchange networks have been constructed.

In theory, there are coercive networks that are *structurally similar* to exclusionary exchange networks. The similarity lies in the way that the costs of confrontation are structurally redistributed in the power process. A coercive network contains a structural condition similar to exclusion when the central coercer has an interest in transmitting negative sanctions to any subset of coercees—unless that subset offers the rate of positive sanction flow maximally preferred by the coercer. Threat of transmission successively increases power over subsets until power is maximized across all peripheral coercees. When information is relatively complete, the power process is a bidding process. The process is sustained, just as in exchange, because the resistance of the central actor is very high and the resistance of peripherals is very low.

Willer (1987) investigated coercive structural power in a number of experiments. First, a coercive network without structural power was constructed. The prototype coercive relation was used to build a 5-branch, an expanded version of the 3-branch of Figure 6. In the 5-branch, the central coercer was allocated resources for only two negative sanctions. The coercer needed only two negative sanctions to coerce five actors because, when threats succeed, negative sanctions are not transmitted. The observed mean rate of coercion was .538, somewhat higher than the predicted rate of .45. As predicted, these rates were reached through a bargaining process.

To produce structural power, the two negative sanctions were changed such that their transmission confiscated the resources of the peripheral receiving the negative. Previously the negative sanction simply eliminated the value of the coercee's resources. Although the effect on the peripheral coercee is no different from before, now the central coercer has an interest in transmitting the two negatives unless the maximum rate of coercive exploitation is offered. In the experiment a power process was generated and the rate of coercion moved toward .9, theoretic maximum. The overall observed mean was .841, and the modal rate was .9, the predicted maximal rate. Resources confiscated through transmitting negative sanctions were not included in the calculation of rates. These rates included only sanctions transmitted under threat. The process and outcome of this structure are similar to the 5-branch exchange network with two exclusions.

The similarity of exchange and coercive structures is more transparent when the coercive relations in the branch are reversed, so that B, the coercee, is central to three peripheral coercers, as in Figure 7. Let it be a condition of this structure that B can negotiate with the three A's but must enter into relations with only one. For example, B might be a corporation seeking to locate a plant in one of the three states represented by the three A's. Since only one A can enter into relations with B, only one can benefit while the other two A's will be excluded. In experimental tests (Willer 1987), prospective coercers bid against each other and rates of coercion approached .1, the minimum possible rate. Like interactions observed in the experiment, plant locations are also accompanied by bidding among states that offer increasingly favorable tax incentives, i.e., diminishing rates of coercion.

Inclusion

Inclusion conditions exist when, in order to receive benefit from exchanging, an actor must complete exchanges with (or "include") two or more others. In the history of the development of ET, the discovery and investigation of these conditions occurred after the investigations of complex networks, reported below, were well developed. Inclusion is discussed here because its theoretical and experimental investigations have been restricted to simple branch structures. Furthermore, inclusion logically completes the first part of the research program. Taken together with exclusion and null relations, inclusion exhausts the logically possible conditions of structural power.

Consider the conditions of connection possible for a central position in a 2-branch exchange network.

1. The central position seeks to exchange in either or both of the relationships. This is the null connection which, as was seen above, has no structural effect on the process and outcome of relationships.

2. The central position may exchange in either relationship but not in both. This is exclusion, and it produces power in the center of the branch.

3. The central position *must* exchange in both relationships, or else realize value in neither. This is inclusion, and it produces power at the peripheral positions of a branch.

Inclusion appears quite frequently in exchange networks. Households seek food, shelter, and clothing, none of which can be substituted for the other. Organizations use a wide variety of resources, the absence of any one of which can bring activity to a halt. As noted in Patton and Willer (1991), the condition of inclusion is not found in the classic works of Marx and Weber, though exclusion is.

Inclusion and exclusion are mutually exclusive only in the 2-branch. Let N_q be the size of a position's minimum necessary network—the network in which the position must complete all exchanges to realize value. Then for a 3-branch like Figure 5a, if $N_p = 3$, $N_m = 2$, and $N_q = 2$, A excludes one B and must include both remaining B's to realize value for either exchange. More generally, if $N_p > N_m = N_q \geq 2$, both exclusion and inclusion are present. A resistance analysis predicts the direction of the effects of inclusion and the combined effects when both inclusion and exclusion are present.

A position's connection is purely inclusive when $N_p = N_q$. Assume that A is inclusively connected in a branch with $N_p B$'s. Let A's negotiations with B_1 result in exchange at equiresistance with a payoff of $P_A/B_1 > 0$. Because the results of the first exchange are lost if the second is not completed, $P_{Acon} < 0$ for A's second exchange with B_2. More precisely, $P_{Acon} = -P_A/B_1$ and A's resistance for the second exchange is

$$R_A = \frac{P_{Amax} - P_A/B_2}{P_A/B_2 - (-P_A/B_1)} = \frac{P_{Amax} - P_A/B_2}{P_A/B_2 + P_A/B_1}.$$

Since A's resistance is now reduced and B_2's is unchanged, the point of equiresistance is shifted in favor of B_2. In general, for a sequence of exchanges in a branch, later exchanges are increasingly favorable to the peripherals. But if all exchanges are simultaneous, then all should be affected equally. Under that condition for the inclusive branch

$$R_A = \frac{P_{A\max} - P_A}{N_q P_A}.$$

Patton and Willer (1991) experimentally demonstrated that inclusion conditions create power differentials. This research used the interaction setting in which subjects have relatively complete information. Though a sequential ordering of rates was found, simultaneous exchange was more frequently observed. Given knowledge of rates gained by others, subjects could easily recognize that the last to exchange gained the best rate. Frequently, all waited to the last moment, and all exchanged at the same time and for the same favorable rates.

Work is now under way to theoretically and experimentally investigate branches in which inclusion and exclusion are both present. When peripherals act independently, the combined effect of the two should be identical to exclusion alone. This follows from the resistance model because (1) the effect of inclusion on the central actor is much less than the effect of exclusion and should thus be completely wiped out, and (2) inclusion does not affect peripherals' resistance while exclusion reduces their resistance to zero. Extensive research has recently been completed on mixed exclusion-inclusion branches. Though data analysis has not been completed, from looking through data we believe that there is support for resistance predictions. Certainly, exchange rates favor the central over peripheral positions. Whether mixed exclusion-inclusion structures have outcomes identical to pure exclusionary structures as predicted by resistance or whether the two are merely similar must await detailed analysis.

A second mixed type is also logically possible, a type which mixes null and inclusion conditions. For branches with three or more peripherals, the connection is null-inclusion when $N_p = N_m > N_q \geq 2$. Resistance suggests that null-inclusion connections are like null connections; that is to say, the process and outcome of each relation are predicted to be exactly as they are when the relation is observed in isolation. Though a number of mixed null-inclusion branches have been run, we have not looked closely at results. It is evident, however, that when mixed with null, the effect of inclusion is weakened, for rates do not strongly favor peripherals. Determining whether rates do not significantly favor peripherals as we expect must await completion of the analysis.

Power in Complex Exchange Networks

Theory Competition: The Power Dependence Approach

In 1983, Cook, Emerson, Gillmore, and Yamagishi published theoretical, experimental, and simulation analyses of several social exchange networks. The Cook et al. article was instrumental in motivating the initial collaboration between the authors of this paper, and will therefore be reviewed in some detail.

Cook et al.'s research demonstrated a variety of interesting and sometimes counterintuitive network exchange phenomena, along with informal analyses based on the power dependence (PD) perspective (Emerson 1972a, 1972b). Their experiments and simulations involved sets of actors related in networks who negotiated in resource pool relations. In cases where an actor's position had multiple relations, s/he could negotiate with all partners, but ultimately could exchange with only one per experimental round. After the completion of a round, resource pools were replenished and negotiations began anew. Over a series of negotiation periods, highly significant differences in resource divisions occurred across positions. Some of the results have been reproduced schematically in Figure 9.* All four networks were run through computer simulations, and 9a was also tested experimentally. As displayed, solid nodes represent points at which advantageous outcomes accumulated, i.e., high power positions. Open circles represent low profit, low power positions.

It is especially interesting that in all four networks, the positions that are central are disadvantaged, being low in power use. The reasons for this involve the joint effects of the network structures and the "1-exchange rule" (our term) enforced as part of the experimental procedures. In 9a, for example, consider which positions are potentially excluded in a given round of exchanges. Number the positions from 1 to 5, starting at the lower left and moving clockwise. If we assume that no actor purposely abstains from an agreement, a round of negotiations may have one of three possible outcomes in terms of who reaches agreement with whom: 1-2, 3-4; 1-2, 4-5; or 2-3, 4-5. It is important to note that only positions 2 and 4 appear in all three combinations, indicating that positions 1, 3, and 5 all face possible exclusion in any given round of negotiations. If actors are excluded in a given round, then to avoid exclusion on a subsequent round they must bid their way back in by offering position 2 and/or 4 increasingly favorable outcomes. Under the 1-

---

*"Low profit" relations with reduced resource pools connected some positions in the networks studied by Cook et al. For clarity, we have dropped these relations. They do not affect the central issues of this analysis or the outcomes of experiments.

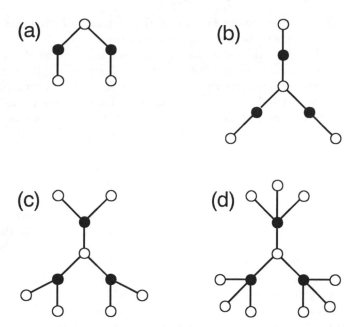

Fig. 9. Power dependence networks.

exchange rule in these networks, the central position is not exempt from exclusion. Therefore, its disadvantage is comparable to that of positions 1 and 5.

Our computer simulations of 9a corroborated these results. Simulated actors were programmed to accept their best offer in each round, to lower their offer in the subsequent round after completing a deal, and to raise their offer after being excluded. Networks 9b, c, and d were simulated under the same conditions, with the pattern of results reflecting those in 9a. Cook et al. recognized the structural similarity of the four networks by identifying just three distinct positions in each: center, off-center, and peripheral. More formally, all of the networks have a diameter of 4—the maximum length of the path connecting any two positions without passing through any position more than once. Inspection reveals that b, c, and d are actually variants of the simpler a, hence the similar results across the four.

One reason why central positions were disadvantaged in these networks was the restricted distance that resources could flow. Power use entails a flow of resources, and *a necessary condition for power relations between actors is that they be linked either directly or indirectly by a flow of resources.* If resource units flow only from a pool between positions to adjacent positions, then power in structures composed of resource pool relations can occur *only* between adjacent positions.

Cook et al. (1983) did not explain power by exclusion, as above. Instead, they proposed an analytic procedure, "vulnerability," for predicting which network positions would or would not have structural power advantages and favorable exchange outcomes. Lacking this procedure, their hypotheses were, strictly speaking, not theoretically derived but based on interpretations and intuitions (Markovsky, Willer, and Patton 1990).

Let the 5-actor line "1-2-3-4-5" represent 9a for the calculation of vulnerability. Assume that each relation contains a pool of 24 profit points and that the 1-exchange rule is in effect. First, the maximum resource flow (MRF) for the network is given by the maximum number of exchanges that can take place in a round, multiplied by the size of the resource pools. As we have already shown, MRF = 2 × 24 = 48. Next, the reduction in maximum flow (RMF) is obtained for each position by observing the effect on MRF if it is removed. In the case of the 5-actor line, removing either position 2 or 4 results in RMF = 24, whereas RMF = 0 for positions 1, 3, and 5. Vulnerability is asserted to be directly related to RMF, and power is determined by vulnerability. (More fully, a position's power is determined by the network's vulnerability to resource flow disruptions caused by the removal of that position.) In this case, positions 2 and 4 are correctly identified as having high power, as are all of the off-center positions in all four networks of Figure 9.

Despite its success in the Figure 9 networks, vulnerability has important limitations. First, it does not square with the PD perspective used to explain the same results. True, it was described as a "first step toward a formal procedure," but its links to existing theory were not explicated. Second, and much more important, Willer (1986) demonstrated that vulnerability predicts impossible outcomes for even some very simple networks—impossible, that is, under the experimental conditions used by Cook et al. (1983) and in previous PD research (Stolte and Emerson 1977; Cook and Emerson 1978). Figure 10a shows the vulnerability predictions for a 5-position T-shaped network. As indicated by the large shaded circles, three consecutive high-power positions along the vertical line are predicted. Given the zero-sum nature of profit point divisions in the PD research, this vulnerability prediction is an impossible event.

In replying to Willer's comments, Cook, Gillmore, and Yamagishi (1986) concurred and proposed a modification to the vulnerability measure. Although we could not reproduce the predictions which they claimed to obtain from their model (see Markovsky, Willer, and Patton 1988: n. 3), they are shown in Figure 10b. Now the bottom-most posi-

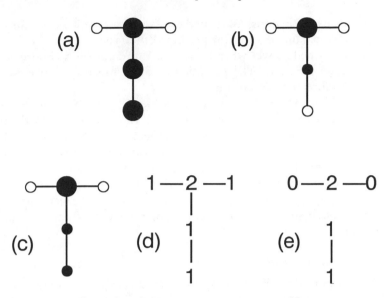

Fig. 10. Conflicting predictions.

tion is low power, the next position up intermediate, and only the position with three branches is predicted to have high power.

The revised vulnerability measure produced tenable predictions for the Figure 10 network. The exchange process that would have to transpire for its realization, however, would contradict the PD perspective. The reason is that for the bottom position to have low power relative to its partner, the partner would have to have some basis for its power advantage—presumably, in this case, its second branch. That second branch connects to the position with the highest power of all. This is decidedly disadvantageous and does not provide a basis of power for the second position from the bottom. At best, that position would simply avoid the high power position and deal exclusively with the end position on an equal footing, as shown in Figure 10e.

Willer's (1986) critique identified a logical flaw in the vulnerability predictions, but did not present an alternative metric for power in exchange networks. Our collaboration began with a long series of communications and idea exchanges, with the goal of devising such an alternative. Ideally, we wanted a measure that (1) was consistent with the logic of ET, (2) was consistent with the Cook et al. (1983) experiments and simulations, as well as ET experiments, (3) included explicit scope conditions that subsumed the conditions employed in the PD experiments, (4) relied on a rigorous procedure and not interpretations or intuitions for its predictions, (5) treated the 1-exchange rule as but one level of a variable parameter, and (6) predicted the type of network decomposition described above, whereby one or more positions choose not to utilize certain relations. The C_p index, though too restricted in scope, suggested a direction for our thinking.

The problem was to develop an index like C_p, but one that also took into account distal network effects. In the spirit of Karl Popper, the process of development was truly one of "conjecture and refutation." Many times over the course of approximately a year, one of us was certain he "found it," only to have the other identify some flaw or critical limitation. There is no doubt that the procedures we ultimately published, including the "graph-theoretic power index" (GPI), were greatly strengthened for having survived this process. The theory is summarized in the next section.

A Graph-Theoretic Alternative

Our procedure for predicting power in exchange networks is predicated on a set of provisional scope conditions. These require that (1) actors use identical strategies in negotiating exchanges, (2) actors consistently excluded from exchanges raise their offers, (3) actors consistently included in exchanges lower their offers, (4) actors accept the best offers they receive and choose randomly among tied best offers, (5) each position is related to one or more other positions, (6) at the start of an exchange round, equal pools of positively valued resource units are available in every relation, and (7) two positions receive resources from their common pool if and only if they exchange. All of the simulations and experiments discussed above that used resource pools satisfied these conditions.

The underlying logic of the graph-theoretic power index (GPI) is simple: it is advantageous to be connected to positions that have few alternatives relative to the number of exchanges they seek, and disadvantageous to be connected to positions that have many alternatives relative to the number they seek. Although the PD perspective also treats "number of alternatives" as crucial, it does not clearly condition this factor by the number of exchanges sought. Nor does the vulnerability measure address the problem. Thus, for example, as was shown earlier, if B in the A-B-C network seeks two exchanges and can exchange with both A and C in the same period, then B has no more power than A or C, despite having the greater number of exchange alternatives.*

*One could defend the PD approach by arguing that A and C are not actually "alternatives" under such conditions. Certainly A and C are not exclusive alternatives. It is not

Under the 1-exchange condition, each position's index of power is calculated by first counting the number of nonintersecting paths of each length up to g, the network's diameter. Two paths from the point i are nonintersecting if they share only i and no other point. For example, in Figure 8a, none of A's paths are intersecting while B_1's paths to B_2 and B_3 intersect at A. In lines no paths intersect. In the 5-actor line 1-2-3-4-5, for example, position 1 has one nonintersecting path of length 1 and also one each of length 2, 3, and 4. Position 2 has two 1-paths (paths of length 1), one 2-path, and one 3-path. Position 3 has two 1-paths and two 2-paths. Position 4 is identical to 2, and position 5 is identical to 1. Then $p_i(1)$, the graph-theoretic power index for position i under the 1-exchange rule, is given by the equations

$$p_i(1) = \sum_{k=1}^{g} (-1)^{(k-1)} m_{ik},$$

and

$$p_{ij}(1) = p_i(1) - p_j(1),$$

where m_{ik} is the number of nonintersecting paths of length k stemming from position i. The function $(-1)^{(k-1)}$ makes the value of m negative for paths of even length, and positive for paths of odd length. Thus, for the 5-actor line, the $p(1)$ values are 0-2-0-2-0. The $p(1)$ prediction that the even-numbered positions are high power fits Cook et al.'s experimental findings. The $p(1)$ values for all of the other Figure 9 networks conform to Cook et al.'s simulations.

Intuitively, the procedure works by treating nonintersecting paths of odd length as advantageous and those of even length as disadvantageous. For instance, a 1-path from position i(i-j) provides an exchange partner for i, and this is advantageous; a 2-path i-j-k means that j now has an alternative to i, a situation that is disadvantageous for i. The 3-path i-j-k-q provides an alternative for k, that weakens j, that is good for i, and so on. The reason for counting only nonintersecting paths is a bit more subtle. Given i-j-k, if j is given an additional partner z, this makes no qualitative difference from the standpoint of i. That is, from i's perspective, j is a potential exchange partner who has alternatives to exchanging with i. Whether there is one z or many does not change the direction of i's power relative to j's. The magnitude of the difference between adjacent actors' p indices does reflect relative power, however. In this case, j's index will be 3 compared to i's 0, and so $p_{ji} = 3$. In the i-j-k line, p_{ji}

---

clear, however, whether the term "alternatives" in the PD approach should be restricted to the "exclusive alternative" meaning.

= 2. Thus, the effects of intersecting paths are taken into account via the relative power index, p_{ji}, without having to count all paths for every position.

The equation for $p_i(1)$ is Axiom 1 of the theory. The remaining axioms allow predictions regarding network decompositions.* In the axioms, "power" refers to the value of p_{ij}.

> *Axiom 2.* i seeks exchange with j if and only if i's power is greater than j's, or if i's power relative to j equals or exceeds that in any of i's other relations.

> *Axiom 3.* i and j can exchange if and only if each seeks exchange with the other.

> *Axiom 4.* if i and j exchange, then i receives more resources than j if and only if i has more power than j.

To "seek exchange" means to attempt to make competitive offers. Also, note that the mutual seeking of exchange, as in Axiom 3, entails negotiation but not necessarily the completion of a deal. Finally, Axiom 4 provides the explicit link between the potential power induced by the network and the observable use of power manifested in resource distributions.

Figure 10d shows the $p(1)$ values for every position in the 5-actor T-network discussed earlier. By Axiom 2, the actor in the central position, for which $p(1) = 2$, will seek exchange with the actor in the position below it in the figure. The reverse, however, will not be true because that lower-power position can form an equipower dyad with the bottom position. This prediction is shown in 10e, with p values recalculated to reflect the break in the network. Both the predictions for relative power and this predicted break in the network were borne out in experimental tests (Markovsky, Willer, and Patton 1988; Willer, Markovsky, and Patton 1989).

The GPI was also generalized to the case of "multi-exchange networks," i.e., those in which positions seek exchange in up to e different relations in a given period. To calculate GPI under e-exchange conditions, the concept of e^+ and e^- positions was needed. An e^+ position is one having more than e relations, and an e^- position has e or fewer relations. The calculation of $p(e)$ is simplified in e-exchange networks because it is calculated for separate network domains rather than for the entire network. Whether or not two positions are in the same domain is determined as follows:

---

*In their appendix, Markovsky, Willer, and Patton (1988) express the axiomatic theory in predicate logic, along with four key derivations and proofs.

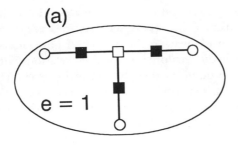

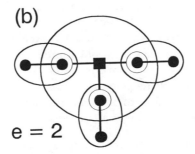

Fig. 11. Shifting domains.

Given the set V of all positions on a path between i and j, i and j are in the same domain if and only if there exists a path such that either (1) $V = \{\ \}$, or (2) all members of V are e^+ positions.

The GPI is now called $p_{id}(e_d)$, or the p index for position i in domain d under the condition that i may exchange up to e times in that domain. Its formula is

$$p_{id}(e_d) = [1/e_d] \sum_{k=1}^{h} (-1)^{(k-1)} m_{idk}.$$

Note that paths are only counted within a given domain.

Figure 11a is equivalent to 9b, but redrawn to differentiate e^+ and e^- positions (boxes and circles, respectively) and to illustrate domains. When $e = 1$, all positions are in a single domain and $p_i(e) = p_i(1)$. The filled boxes indicate the high power positions, and unfilled elements indicate low power positions.

Figure 11b shows the same network when $e = 2$. Now, any position with two or more relations may exchange once each with up to two different partners in the same round. Only one position is e^+, and four domains emerge. Calculating p for every position, we find that the center position has high power and the off-center positions low power within their shared domain. (The off-center positions are open circles within this central domain.) However, the off-center positions are also drawn as filled circles within dyadic domains for their relations with the peripheral positions. In these domains they have equal power. These predictions were all supported in experiments (also in Markovsky, Willer, and Patton 1988): the off-center positions averaged one-third the profit of the center position when they exchanged, but equal profit when dealing with the peripherals.

In sum, $p(e)$ accurately predicted radical differences in the distributions of power and resources stemming from small changes in the conditions of exchange. The extension to e-exchange networks points to important ways that prior research under 1-exchange conditions masked a variety of interesting exchange phenomena waiting to be addressed theoretically. Current work (Markovsky et al. 1991) is further refining and generalizing the GPI to provide "iterative analyses" of even more complex networks, taking into account interaction effects involving actors' strategic choices and their structural locations.

New Computer Simulations

Computer simulations strike an attractive balance between theoretical rigor and empirical complexity. As the types of networks, exchange conditions, and negotiation strategies that we wish to study become increasingly varied and complex, the use of simulations is becoming essential. Recent work by Markovsky (summarized in Markovsky 1989) has taken up where the earlier simulations of Cook et al. (1983) left off. The newer simulation program, X-Net, (1) provides nonprogrammers and inexperienced computer users the opportunity to "experiment" with network exchange simulations, (2) includes numerous adjustable parameters for exploring variations in networks, exchange conditions, and actors' strategies, (3) is written in a popular high-level language (Microsoft Quick-BASIC), thus facilitating its manipulation by interested programmers at all skill levels, and (4) is highly modularized to facilitate comprehension and continued growth. In fact, the gross structure of the program conforms fairly closely to the experimental paradigms used to test ET.

X-Net Program Structure

X-Net has a four-level structure. Each level, except for the lowest, contains a loop that invokes the next lower level. The program begins at Level One, the *Experiment* level. Here, the user sees X-Net's main program menu, with options to (1) receive information about the program, (2) create or delete a network, (3) run a simulation, or (4) leave X-Net.

If the user chooses to run a simulation, he or she is first prompted to select a network, and then given the option to run the simulation with default parameter settings, inspect or change parameter settings, or turn data recording on or off.

If the user decides to change program parameters, s/he is shown a menu containing options to change the sizes of resource pools, the maximum number of deals per round, the number of experiments or rounds per experiment, or the decision strategies to be employed by actors. The user may also choose to return to the previous screen or immediately run the simulation. With the options to change resource pool sizes or maximum number of deals, the user receives further options as to whether these changes will apply to all actors or to selected actors. To actually make these changes, the user merely responds to a series of simple queries from the program.

When the network is chosen, the parameters set, and the simulation begun, the program runs a series of experiments. Within each experiment, there is a series of *rounds*. These rounds compose Level Two. With each round, actors make an adjustment to each of their offers based on the results (exchange or non–exchange) of the prior round, and check the offers received from others.

Within each round, actors check their potential exchange partners one at a time in systematic fashion to determine if they are still negotiating and, if so, whether their offers are acceptable. A *cycle* consists of a completed series of such checks, wherein every actor has checked every potential exchange partner once. Thus, the cycle composes Level Three of the simulation. A single round may contain one, two, or many more cycles.

Several critical operations occur within each cycle, and these constitute Level Four. First, the program determines whether and with whom each actor has reached compromise agreements on the division of resource pools. If the simplest decision strategy was chosen, and an actor reached multiple compromises, then one of the potential partners is selected at random and flagged. (If the actor is permitted to complete *e* exchanges in a round, then at this point there could be up to *e* flagged partners.) The program then checks for reciprocated flags and in such cases assigns "deal" status to the pair. Finally, actors that have already made deals, or no longer have potential exchange partners, are pulled from the list of active negotiators. As long as there remains the possibility of a deal for any pair of related actors, another cycle is run. When no such possibility exists, the program returns to Level Three.

Reentry to Level Three signals the completion of a round. The program tallies the profit received by every actor and notes from which relation it was received. It then determines how actors will change their offers for the next round of negotiation. If an actor completed the num-

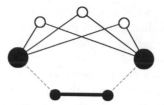

Fig. 12. X-net simulation result.

ber of deals it sought, then it will try to make out a little better in the next round. Otherwise, it makes concessions to those with whom exchanges were sought but not completed.

After these new offers are established, the program pops up to Level Two, where it combines the latest data with those gathered across multiple rounds. Finally, after all experiments are run, the program returns to the top level and provides the user an opportunity to run a new simulation.

A graphical display of resource accumulations is updated at the end of each experiment. The program shows the network positions spaced around the screen in an elliptical pattern, with lines connecting pairs of related positions. After each experiment, the size of the node for a given network position is increased in proportion to the resources it accumulated during the last few rounds of the experiment. At the conclusion of a simulation, the weight of the lines connecting actors is reduced according to the relative frequency of exchanges between actors; the more frequently used a relation, the more solid its line.

Figure 12 illustrates the results of a simulation for a 7-position network. There were 10 experiments, 25 rounds each. (This executes in under 15 seconds on a fast personal computer.) In accord with the GPI predictions, there are two high power positions, three with low power, and two with intermediate power. The weight of the lines representing the relations also shows that, in accord with the axioms of the theory, the positions with moderate power exchanged only with each other, essentially breaking away from the more powerful positions. Note also that the exchange frequencies between the high and low power positions are evenly distributed across relations.

Future Simulation Research

Work with X-Net is in its early stages at this writing, but its potential is quickly becoming evident. Even in its first incarnation, the program is consistent with all previous experimental work. In its most recent form (Version 3.1) it is being used to explore the effects of variations in resource pool sizes, numbers of exchanges permitted each actor per round, opportunities to open new relations, and more realistic decision strategies on the part of actors.

A new program, F-Net, is also currently under development. To the user, this simulation operates much the same way as X-Net. Instead of actors negotiating over resource pools, however, they negotiate over the actual exchange of different kinds of valued resources. Thus, each actor begins with a certain quantity of one or more different types of goods, and each actor may desire certain goods or goods-combinations to different degrees. Such "flow networks" are clearly more complex than those addressed by the GPI. They are also much richer in their empirical implications. Yamagishi, Gillmore, and Cook (1988) have conducted some experimental and/or simulation research using this type of network, but do not provide a model for generating predictions. Marsden (1983) provided a model, but did not state scope conditions for the behavior of actors in the network. (Actors have control over goods and evaluations of goods, but there is no model for individual action.) It is impossible to identify empirical applications that might constitute appropriate tests of his theory. However, its mathematical rigor recognizes, controls for, and even accommodates the variability of individual decision strategies.

All of the foregoing issues entail violations of the scope conditions initially drawn for the GPI procedures. Not surprisingly, when GPI is applied to these cases outside its scope limits, results generally vary from predictions. Thus, the simulations are already suggesting new directions for theoretical scope expansion. They also intimate that analytic solutions such as GPI may be unavailable under more complex combinations of exchange conditions and decision strategies.

Some Concluding Thoughts on the Research Program

The concept of a scientific research program presented by Lakatos (1970) was introduced to sociology by Berger, Conner, and Fisek (1974). According to Lakatos, "Mature science consists of research programmes in which not only novel facts but, in an important sense, also auxiliary theories, are anticipated; mature science—unlike pedestrian trial-and-error—has heuristic power" (1970: 175, emphasis removed). Within a program, Lakatos emphasized, discovery occurs as part of a process of "continuous growth" (ibid). Figure 13 reproduces a figure from Willer (1987) that indicated the main branches of theoretical and experimental work up to that time. As can be seen, only some of these branches have been reviewed here.

Within a research program, even small advances seem to take inter-

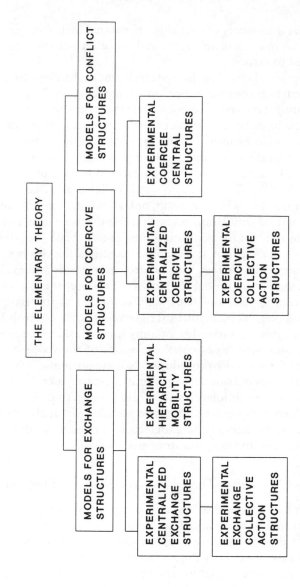

Fig. 13. Structure of the program.

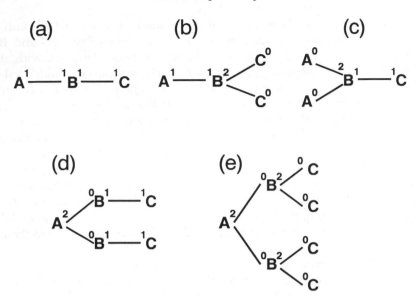

Fig. 14. Flow networks

minable periods. It is with considerable astonishment that one realizes how much has occurred since Figure 13 was drawn. As detailed above, the investigation of complex networks has added a further lateral branch under "Models for Exchange Structures." The complexity encountered and managed in those investigations has moved much farther in a vertical direction than any of the investigations noted in the figure. The discovery of inclusion adds a further branch under "Exchange Structures."

Growth continues. Some present and future work was noted in the section above. For purposes of illustration, two recent developments deserve mention: the investigation of transitive power in flow networks and the development and anticipated uses of ExNet, an electronic computer network for experimental research.

Traditionally, definitions of power have been concerned with one-step phenomena—the power of A over B (cf. Dahl 1957; Lukes 1974). Power relations in all of the networks discussed above were limited to adjacencies. Not addressed have been issues of power transitivity. For example, if A has power over B and B over C, are there conditions in which A can exercise power over C through B? Given in Figure 14 are networks designed to address that and related questions. These networks use extensions of the prototype exchange relation introduced and discussed earlier. In this case, A initially holds a resource valueless to A, worth five points to B and ten to C. B and C initially hold resources that, like a medium

of exchange, are similarly valued at all positions. Each branching indicates exclusion. For example, in 14e A excludes one of two B's and B
excludes one of two C's. Since B exchanges on two sides, once with A
and once with C, applying $p(e)$ means each B is assigned two index values, one relative to A and one relative to C. The $p_{BA}(e)$ applies to the
$A - B$ side of the network and the $p_{BC}(e)$ applies to the $B - C$ side.

Results from only two of these networks will be mentioned. Figure 14a is the flow network equivalent of a dyad: according to $p(e)$, there
is no basis for power. At equiresistance under full information, all should
benefit equally with B paying A 3.33 for A's resource and selling it to C
for 6.66. Figure 14e is an instance of transitive power. Since A has power
over B and B over C, A should gain all the benefit in the system save for
the minimum going to B and C. In terms of rates of exchange, B should
pay A 8 and sell to C for 9. Experimental results correspond well to these
predictions.

All of the experimental investigations discussed in this and in previous
sections have occurred under relatively open information conditions.
This format was chosen because it fitted well certain implications of ET.
For example, the resistance analysis suggests that the use of power develops more rapidly under conditions of more rather than less complete
information. This follows because certain kinds of information restrictions can halt the decline of resistance of low power actors. For example,
if low power actors do not know the offers of rivals, their resistance does
not go to zero, as it does under more complete information conditions.
In that case the power process is sustained only by the very high resistance of the high power actor while the unchanged resistance of low
power actors is like friction drag, slowing the process. Something other
than the usual interaction setting is needed to investigate these inferences.

ExNet (as distinguished from X-Net) is an electronic experimental
network which was developed by John Skvoretz with the assistance of
Willer. ExNet is a set of linked PCs through which experimental subjects
can interact making offers and counteroffers, accepting or rejecting the
offers of others. Whereas subjects are currently limited to relations in
which profit point resources are divided, other relations are now under
development. Since our first concern was to compare ExNet results with
previous experimental results, a relatively complete information design
is now being used. Later investigation will focus on the effect of information on the power process. In addition to exclusion, we are interested
in the effect of information restrictions on inclusion, where high power
positions are decentralized in the branch. Later studies will investigate
flow networks that are longer than the ones considered thus far.

As the growth of ET continues, scope restrictions are pushed back and increasingly complex structures are investigated. Increasingly precise theoretic and simulation procedures are developed. With the recent establishment of experimental laboratories in Krakow, Poland, cross-national investigations by Jacek Szmatka have replicated experiments on the Figure 10 network *and* on all of the structures noted in Figure 13 but exchange with collective action (Willer and Szmatka 1993). In spite of important social structural differences which existed between Poland and the United States at the time of the studies, in all cases results were very similar for the two settings. That they were similar indicates that application of elementary theory is not restricted to the special conditions of time and place of the U.S. studies. That is to say, similar results support the universality of the theory.

The long-term goal is the development of increasingly realistic models, experimental replicas, and simulations that will, of necessity, be increasingly complex. With that development we hope to move precisely and seamlessly, using theory, from experimental laboratory and simulation to contemporary and historical cases.

Power, Legitimacy, and the Stability of Authority: A Theoretical Research Program

Henry A. Walker and Morris Zelditch, Jr.

Introduction

In this paper we analyze a program of theoretical research concerned with the process by which legitimacy makes a system of authority more or less stable.*

However, most of the peculiar characteristics of this program grow from the fact that the stability of authority was not its starting point. Its starting point was the stability of unequal distributions of rewards rather than authority. Even this is somewhat misleading, because our original concern was less with the stability of reward inequalities than with a particular effect, that individual-level pressure to redistribute rewards often has no effect on their aggregate distribution.

Thus, the problem driving the program shifted substantially during its course. Nor was this just a matter, common to any such program, of a progressive shift in the unsolved problems to which at any given moment its research was oriented. It was the fundamental phenomenon with which the program was concerned that shifted.

This progressive problem-shift, and the fact that we began with an effect rather than a theory, gives the present program a somewhat differ-

*We would like to acknowledge the support of NSF Grants No. SOC 7817434, SES 8420238, and SES 8712097. In addition, we are grateful for the help of a rather large number of students and colleagues who have participated in this research. Especially influential in the development of the project were Joan Ford, Bill Harris, and George Thomas. Responsible for one or more of the experiments of the program and co-authors of various papers in the attached references were Dorine Barr-Bryan, Ed Gilliland, John Hooper, David Lineweber, Tormod Lunde, Kathy Lyman, Larry Rogers, and Louise Smith-Donals. In addition, we would like to thank Terry Amburgey, Kelley Massey, Val Valdez, and Kelli Wong for their assistance in carrying out these experiments. Finally, we are grateful to Yitzhak Samuel for his contributions to our understanding of power; to two postdoctoral fellows who contributed to the development of the experimental setting, Wendy Harrod and John Stolte; and to two undergraduates whose honors thesis made an important contribution to our understanding of relations among multiple objects of legitimation, Chris Erlin and Bonnie McLean.

ent character than any program analyzed by Wagner and Berger (1985). Effect programs develop by simplifying the phenomenon with which they are initially concerned, as one can see by studying any Lewinian research program, and they typically compare and contrast alternative explanations of the effect. Both were true of the early stages of development of the present program. It began with attempts to understand a quite complex phenomenon, involving a number of theoretically distinct processes, and we first formulated the phenomenon from the point of view of two rival theories. Only later did our research begin to take the shape of a theoretical research program. (See Figure 1.)

Two Theories of Nondecision Making

The effect with which we started was called a "nondecision." The alternative theories we considered to explain the effect were Bachrach and Baratz's theory of nondecisions (1962, 1963, 1970) and Dornbusch and Scott's theory of authority (1975).

The Effect

Although it can be generalized to other contexts, the concept of a "nondecision" first arose from the study of redistributive politics. In this context, a nondecision is the failure of individual-level pressures to redistribute rewards to affect the aggregate distribution of rewards. If one can show that the individual members of a social system felt its injustice, it is reasonable to infer from a nondecision that some process has suppressed the individual-level pressure for change. Thus, the concern with nondecisions is essentially a concern with the politics of the suppression of redistributive issues in a group. The effect is virtually unknown in the experimental study of injustice (for a review, see Cook and Hegtvedt 1983), but is common in its nonexperimental study (an important example is Moore 1978).

That nondecisions are a complex phenomenon, involving several more fundamental processes, is evident from some of the factors that the existing literature has felt are relevant to it. Four such factors are listed below.

First, pressures to change a distribution of rewards are individual-level responses to injustice. The accomplishment of actual change is collective action. Collective action is widely understood to be problematic, and the whole logic of collective action (from Olson 1965 on) is one fundamental process underlying nondecision making.

Second, the effect of collective action on the redistribution of rewards depends on action by some organized polity. That is, while the distri-

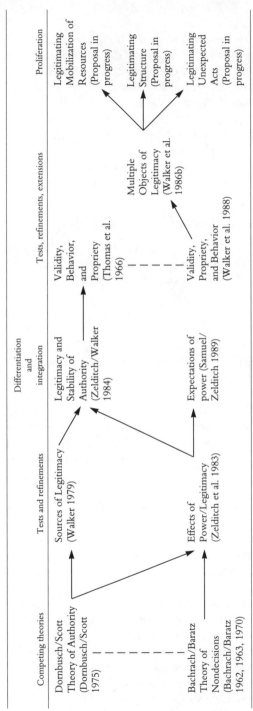

Fig. 1. Evolution of the Walker–Zelditch program of theoretical research on power, legitimacy, and the stability of authority. A broken line indicates competition. A solid arrow from X to Y indicates any form of elaboration of X by Y or proliferation from X to Y, including tests of X, refinements or extensions of X, and applications of the concepts of X to new phenomena. Two arrows to Y, from two different sources, X and X', indicate integration of X and X'.

bution of rewards may be determined in whole or in part by a market process, and long-term changes in it also may be, wholly or partly, determined by markets, short-term pressures to redistribute rewards are collective choices made by politically organized communities of actors. That the logic of collective choice, the logic relating the preferences of members to the actions of a group, is as problematic as the logic of collective action has been emphasized by Bachrach and Baratz's theory of nondecisions. The logic of collective choice is thus a second process underlying nondecision making.

Third, a long tradition of Western social thought relates the logic of collective action to the logic of collective choice by means of power (in the narrow sense of positive and negative sanction capabilities). This tradition assumes that inequalities in resources and rewards are highly intercorrelated, an assumption that is particularly plausible when a reward, like income, is also a resource. When the two are intercorrelated, the "haves" are also the powerful and have not only the motive but also the capacity to prevent change. Even if one gives more emphasis to plural, uncorrelated resources, it remains plausible that power, however distributed, plays a role in the redistribution of rewards.

Fourth, a tradition almost as old relates the two logics by means of processes of legitimation. Reward inequalities are stable if they are justified, either by an ideology of worthiness defining the haves as more deserving than the have-nots or by an ideology of causality attributing inequalities to dispositions of the actor rather than to external system forces, or both. The concept of a nondecision presupposes injustice, implying that legitimacy is therefore not a factor in causing the effort. But legitimacy of reward inequalities may not be the only kind of legitimacy that is relevant. If redistributive pressures are suppressed by power, the legitimacy of power may be an independent factor in the stability of a reward distribution. Another long tradition in Western social thought is that naked power is unstable. (Power, in this tradition, is "naked" if use of rewards or punishments is not legitimate.) It is costly, inefficient, and undependable, because arbitrary use of it increases public but decreases private compliance and because instruments of force not bound by legitimacy are as dangerous to the authority that uses them as to the populations they control. Without any very good reason, legitimacy has often been thought of as an alternative that competes with "pure" power as an explanation of order. But they are not necessarily mutually exclusive, and legitimacy may be a fourth process underlying nondecisions.

All this suggested two ideas to us: that inequality of rewards was embedded in other inequalities that therefore became relevant to their stability; and that redistributing them was a collective-, not individual-, level process. Our task was therefore to explain the gap between injustice and its redress in terms of the effects of power and legitimacy on collective action oriented to collective choice. We thought we understood justice (in terms of Berger et al.'s theory, 1972) and that resource mobilization theory (McCarthy and Zald 1977; Oberschall 1973; Tilly 1978) understood collective action. The task, therefore, was to understand the effects of power and legitimacy on the effect collective action has on collective choice. This understanding of our initial task led us to two competing theories.

Theories

One of the two theories was Bachrach and Baratz's theory of nondecisions (1962, 1963, 1970). In Bachrach and Baratz's theory, legitimacy and power combine to suppress emergence of a redistributive issue at the level of collective choice, preventing the issue from being decided. Our chief interest in this theory, which at the time dominated the literature on community power structure, was its understanding of collective choice in institutionalized polities as a multistage decision process in which outcomes are sometimes determined before an issue ever comes to the point of a decision. Thus, we followed it in focusing on "agenda," i.e., predecision, politics. In Bachrach and Baratz's conception of predecision politics minorities control them. The minority that controls them is, because of the high intercorrelation between rewards and resources in a society (presupposed by their theory), the haves of the society. While normal politics, which they identify with distributive politics (Lowi 1964), is the politics of competing interests that divide the haves, redistributive issues tend to unite them. Because have-nots are in the majority, this unity would not be enough to determine the outcome if redistributive issues came to the point of a vote, but it is sufficient to give them control over the polity's agenda. United, the minority has power that is often sufficient even to prevent the have-not majority from voicing its grievances, owing to the "law of anticipated reactions," i.e., pure power. If this is not enough to prevent the have-not majority from voicing grievances, however, the minority of haves still controls the political agenda and, by "mobilization of bias," i.e., by manipulating the rules that legitimate political behavior, can determine what actors have access to the polity, what issues are seen to be within its jurisdiction, and what tactics will be recognized as legitimate ways of raising them.

The other theory was Dornbusch and Scott's theory of authority (1975). Dornbusch and Scott were concerned with organizations rather than communities, but the domains of the two theories overlapped in a concern for what happens to pressures to change the structure of a system. As with Bachrach and Baratz, the two chief factors at work in Dornbusch and Scott's theory are power and legitimacy. But where Bachrach and Baratz's approach is neo-Marxist in origin, Dornbusch and Scott's is Weberian. This gives it a quite different concept of the relation between power and legitimacy: in Bachrach and Baratz, power creates legitimacy; in Dornbusch and Scott, legitimacy creates and regulates power.

Bachrach and Baratz's is a conflict theory. In it, legitimacy is reduced to material causes. Within the family of conflict theories, it is an instrumentalist theory in which power manipulates legitimacy in order to mask its real interests. Over and above power to coerce quiescence, it controls the media, church, education, and other cultural mechanisms that justify manipulation of the polity's agenda.

The most sharply contrasting view would be a consensus approach to power and legitimacy in which behavior is rule-governed, the rules are shared, acts are legitimate if they accord with the rules, and compliance derives from voluntary consent, without being either coerced or manipulated.

Weber is sometimes thought to be the father of such a theory, but in fact his theory is a mixture of conflict and consensus. In this he is followed by Dornbusch and Scott, for whom conduct is neither all coercion nor all consent, but a mixture of both, the task of theory being to work out the details of the mix.

Our chief interest in Dornbusch and Scott's theory was its emphasis on authority as a system rather than a relation. The exercise of authority by *A* over *B* requires the cooperation of other agents of a larger system who both participate in executing a directive and back it when it is challenged. While a professor may exercise power over a student by control over grades, s/he cannot grade the student if the registrar does not record his/her action, and control cannot be enforced if Chairs and Deans do not back the grade when a student protests that it was unfair.

In Dornbusch and Scott, authority's behavior is rule-governed but the rules are not necessarily shared, at least not in the sense that each individual must personally believe in them. A system of authority, and the rules that govern it, can be said to be "valid" if the system behaves in accord with the rules whether a particular individual, say *p*, believes in them or not. (In this they follow Weber.) If *p* believes in a rule, that is, believes that it is "right," is how it ought to be, then the rule, and the system, is "proper." But propriety and validity are two distinct concepts. "Propriety" is legitimacy at the individual level, "validity" is legitimacy at the collective level. From *p*'s point of view, validity means that others can be expected to behave in accord with the rule. It will be "normative" for *p*, "shared" or not, because sanctions enforce it.

Dornbusch and Scott's theory was formulated to explain the cause, not the prevention, of change. It formulated pressures to change in terms of the "compatibility" of bundles of authority rights that, because authority is a system rather than a relation, come to be divided among actors. We had no interest in compatibility, since we already had a cause of pressure to change in the inequity of rewards. What was important for our purposes was how the theory explained the frequent failure of incompatibility to cause change.

If incompatible, a system becomes improper, but it may nevertheless remain valid. Validity prevents change in four ways. First, it directly dampens challenges, defining them as inappropriate behavior in a particular system of authority. Second, it has an indirect effect through propriety. Through social influence, validity can form individual-level beliefs that a system is "right." In addition, it acts on other actors' support for, backing of, the system of authority. But with respect to support, Dornbusch and Scott take into account the fact that some people matter more than others, distinguishing support by A's superiors and equals from support by B's peers. The former is "authorization," the latter "endorsement." Thus, if the registrar records and the Dean backs a grade by a professor, his/her authority is "authorized." This is a third mechanism by which validity prevents change. If other students treat B's grade as perfectly within the rules, the professor's authority is "endorsed," a fourth mechanism by which stability of authority is maintained.

Like Weber, therefore, Dornbusch and Scott think of a variety of motives for compliance with authority, only one of which is personal belief that it is legitimate. Prudence also maintains authority. Once empowered, authority can enforce itself on those who dissent. But without legitimacy it is not empowered.

For this reason, it makes sense to say in Dornbusch and Scott's theory that power is normatively regulated, unlike power in Bachrach and Baratz, or conflict theory generally. It is not, as in a consensus theory, regulated by A's voluntary constraint, but by the fact that an authority system requires cooperation if it is to act. Rules regulate power because authorization and endorsement depend on validity.

It was the process of refining and testing these two theories that gradually led to a shift in problem from explaining nondecisions to understanding power and legitimacy processes. This in turn led to differentiation of our program into two distinct lines of theoretical development, one elaborating Bachrach and Baratz's theory of power and the other integrating the two rival theories of legitimacy into one theory of the stability of authority.

Differentiation and Integration of Theories of the Program

The key development in the program with which the present paper is concerned was the integration of the authority and nondecision theories into one theory of legitimacy and the stability of authority. But integration of the two theories was not exactly immediate. It came only after a progressive simplification of effects, of analyzing a complex effect of the interrelations of two processes, power and legitimacy, into two more unitary processes, one concerned with power compliance and the other with legitimation. This, in its turn, led to differentiation of the program into two distinct programs of theoretical research.

Differentiation

One of these two programs was concerned with public, as distinct from private, compliance. In Bachrach and Baratz and in Dornbusch and Scott, legitimation has the effect of empowering authority. That is, it mobilizes resources of members or the environment and places them in the hands of agents of collective purpose. Once empowered, authority is enabled to compel public compliance with its decisions and directives, whether or not compliance would occur if authority was unable to monitor it.

Although the two theories had similar conceptions of power, Bachrach and Baratz's had somewhat more emphasis on power's less visible aspects, and it was to these aspects that we devoted particular attention. Our theoretical research on power compliance was devoted especially to power expectations, especially to the effects of potential power and anticipated reactions, on which Bachrach and Baratz depended for their explanation of the invisibility of power compliance. This body of research resulted in a theory refining and extending Bachrach and Baratz by capitalizing more than they did on the possibilities of forming and maintaining expectations about the amount and use of power (Samuel and Zelditch 1989). This theory involves the expectations not only of the less but also of the more powerful actor, and not only first-order but also second-order expectations (e.g., what a more powerful actor expects a less powerful actor to expect, etc.). This reformulated theory was used to predict how the amount of power is amplified by expectations, how it is made stable by them, how it emerges more rapidly because of them, and how it is made virtually invisible by them.

The differentiation of a second path of development, concerned with legitimation, is really to be understood as differentiation into two programs, not proliferation of the branches of the program. "Proliferation" is the extension of the concepts and propositions of one theory to a second phenomenon (Berger and Wagner 1985). Had the Samuel-Zelditch theory been used to explain power compliance as one phenomenon and then applied to legitimation as another, one could describe our "program" as one program with two branches, one the proliferant of the other. But the two "branches" not only differ in their domains of explanation, they also differ in the concepts and propositions employed to explain them. About all they share is a body of metatheoretical assumptions and methods of observation and inference.

Our second program grew out of tests of Bachrach and Baratz's "mobilization of bias" and refinements and extensions of Dornbusch and Scott's validity, propriety, authorization, and endorsement. These refinements and tests led to integration of the two theories into one theory of the effects of legitimation.

Integration

Tests of the two theories confirmed the hypotheses they had in common, all of which had to do with effects of power and legitimacy on the suppression of dissent by less powerful, underrewarded actors. These tests were carried out in experiments that created centralized communication networks in which rewards for performance of a collective task were inequitably allocated, in which the subjects (S's) were in the less powerful, underrewarded positions, and in which the dependent variable was any attempt to change the structure of the network, called a *change-*, or *C-*, *response*. The manipulated independent variables, which varied from experiment to experiment, were various features of power and/or legitimacy.

While tests of these predictions, because of their similarities, could not have discriminated between the two theories, one anomaly in our findings tended to question the instrumentalism of Bachrach and Baratz's theory. Bachrach and Baratz formulate both the "mobilization of bias" and "law of anticipated reactions" in terms of specific acts by specific actors. Our findings, on the contrary, suggested a more structural interpretation, in which—given legitimacy, or the sheer existence of a structure of power, or both—suppression of dissent did not depend on whether any particular actor specifically acted to prevent redistribution.

Tests of differential predictions of the two theories also favored Dornbusch and Scott over Bachrach and Baratz. Differential predictions were largely confined to behavior of powerful, overrewarded actors. They were tested in the same settings as less powerful, underrewarded actors, but with S's at the center of the communication structure instead of at the periphery. Centrality is effectively control of collective choice because any proposal to change the structure of the communication network must pass through the center. For S's at the center, a C-response is forwarding such proposals. Bachrach and Baratz's nondecision is in our experiments operationalized by a not-C-response $(-C)$ by the center. Tests of Bachrach and Baratz's "mobilization of bias" hypothesis found that $-C$-responses, the suppression of dissent, did not depend on gain, nor did threat of loss prevent C-responses, redressing inequity, unless, independent of the motives of the central actor, the existing communication structure was valid. Finally, power was normatively regulated in much the way it is described by Dornbusch and Scott. Not that their theory escaped untouched; but it was theoretical rather than empirical considerations that led us to considerably refine the mechanisms through which validity accomplishes the stability of authority.

Despite the fact that our tests tended to favor Dornbusch and Scott over Bachrach and Baratz, there were certain features of Bachrach and Baratz that we found compelling and certain features of Dornbusch and Scott that we found unnecessary for our purposes (such as the compatibility hypothesis). Thus, we were led to integrate the two into one formulation that had some but not other features of both.

From Bachrach and Baratz we took four ideas: (1) that redistributive politics are collective choices; (2) that collective choices are multistage processes, in which agenda politics play an especially important role; (3) that members' pressures for change are effective only if mobilized as collective action; and (4) that the effect of collective action depends on the legitimacy of actors, issues, and tactics. From Dornbusch and Scott, we also took four ideas: (1) that authority systems are cooperative systems; their distinctions between (2) validity and propriety and (3) authorization and endorsement; and, because of the results of our first wave of experiments, (4) also their view of legitimacy as empowering (rather than Bachrach and Baratz's view that power legitimates).

This process of integrating the legitimacy ideas of two theories led us to what must properly be called the initial theoretical formulation of our program of theoretical research on legitimacy and the stability of authority.

Initial Formulation of a Theory of the Effects of Legitimacy on the Stability of Authority

Delegitimated, reward inequalities threaten to destabilize not only rewards but also a system's structure of power. But power has other sources of legitimacy besides its relation to rewards. The independence of these sources from reward inequalities gives to authority the capacity to resist pressures to change.

The theory we have formulated is addressed to the mechanisms of this resistance. *Change-responses* are the specific domain of the theory, i.e., challenges to an existing structure (of any kind). The theory also concerns itself with how others react to change-responses, in terms of their *support* of them. This admittedly imprecise term covers various kinds of exchanges of resources among actors that either increase or decrease the probability of change-responses, especially (1) positive or negative sanctions, either formal or informal; and (2) mobilization of resources, such as labor or capital, either to facilitate or prevent challenges.

The scope of the theory is limited to corporate groups oriented to collective goals, the polity and practices of which are institutionalized. To be a corporate group there must be some means by which collective choices are made that, once made, are unitary acts of the group by which members are bound. The polity of a corporate group is the structure that makes such choices, being institutionalized to the extent that there is a recognized procedure by which recognized authorities make decisions with respect to a recognized jurisdiction and membership, and members' access to procedures is defined. The means by which goals are pursued are also assumed to be institutionalized: that is, the goal to which members are oriented is for them a task the practices of which are governed by recognized rules.

It is with reference to the institutions of a corporate group that we define the terms of the theory. For any particular member, *p* (for "person"), we can say that an object of orientation such as an act, rule, person, position, or structure of positions is "proper" or "improper":

Definition 1. (Propriety.) The conduct of an object of orientation is *proper* if and only if *p* personally believes that it is morally right.

If *p* personally believes in a social order as morally right, we assume *p* will voluntarily comply with it, whether it is backed by power or not. Further, we assume that *p* will not try to change it and will resist attempts by others to change it.

Assumption 1. The probability of a *C*-response by *p* is inversely proportional to the propriety of the authority system to *p*.

The probability of a *C*-response denotes both attempts by one actor to change a system and reactions by any other actor that facilitate such change. Thus, given a simple order relation such that $A > B$, *B* is less likely to attempt to change the relation and *A* is more likely to resist such a change if the relation is proper. The same assumption could be written for other features of an authority system besides change-responses, such as compliance, or competing directives.

If, however, the system is improper to *p*, it does not follow that change automatically occurs. Change is problematic because, independently of propriety, the validity of an authority system may delay or prevent change.

Definition 2. (Validity.) An act is valid if it is in accord with a rule that is valid. A rule is valid if it is in accord with the institutionalized practices of a group or if the procedure that made it is valid. A procedure is valid if it is in accord with the institutions of the polity of the group.

The concept of validity is sometimes ambiguous because it is easily confused with authorization and endorsement, terms which refer to how it is backed. This arises from the fact that any particular member *p* may be unsure of the rules, inferring them from the behavior of other members. Thus, one knows a rule is valid if authorities or peers behave in accord with it. However, to define validity in terms of authorization and endorsement is to introduce an undesirable circularity into the theory, and we have tried to provide a definition that does not depend on them. But this definition becomes difficult to apply in uninstitutionalized systems to which, eventually, we would like to be able to apply the theory. This will be a key to extension of the theory because validity is its key concept. It is the key concept of the theory because of the direct and indirect ways in which it acts to delay or prevent change.

First, independent of propriety, validity has a direct effect on the probability of a *C*-response:

Assumption 2. The probability of a *C*-response by *p* is inversely proportional to the validity of the group's authority system.

But in addition to this direct effect, validity also has indirect effects on the rate of *C*-responses by means of three intervening mechanisms: the first is that, through social influence, validity can increase individual-level propriety and, through it, reduce the rate of *C*-responses.

Assumption 3. Propriety is directly proportional to validity.

In addition to its effect on any individual's sense of legitimacy, validity also affects whether and how a structure is supported by others. Because the reactions of actors differently located in the system can be assumed to have differently weighted effects, we distinguish among different sources of support.

Definition 3. (Authorization.) Assume an order relation $A > B$, with any number of actors at each level and any number of levels above A and below B. Then an act of an authority system is *authorized* if and only if actors at A's level or higher provide resources to authority and withhold them from challengers.

The theory then assumes that:

Assumption 4. The probability of the authorization of an act is directly proportional to its validity.

Assumption 5. The probability of a C-response by p is inversely proportional to the probability of its authorization.

While less powerful, the peers of a challenger nevertheless are important because without support a challenge is unlikely to occur. Thus, endorsement is also a factor in change or resistance to change.

Definition 4. (Endorsement.) An act of the authority system is *endorsed* if and only if actors at the same level as the challenger or lower provide authority with resources and/or withhold them from the challenger.

While there are other sources of endorsement, the theory assumes that:

Assumption 6. The probability of endorsement of an act is directly proportional to its validity.

Assumption 7. The probability of a C-response by p is inversely proportional to the probability of its endorsement.

Endorsement, and even authorization, will of course also depend on propriety. But insofar as resources are employed as sanctions we assume that propriety is not sufficient—i.e., it is not sufficient ground for an actor p to sanction another. Hence,

Assumption 8. Sanctions, especially negative sanctions, are directly proportional to the product of the validity and propriety of an act by another.

The theory, of course, could be expressed more economically by taking into account the fact that the various elements of it, because they are independent, are additive. Thus, probability of a C-response is determined by the joint effects of propriety, validity, expected authorization, and expected endorsement, condensing Assumptions 1, 2, 5, and 7, and so on.

The theory as written describes the acts of individuals. Whether the outcome at the system level is stability or not depends on a complex interaction among A and B, A and other A's, B and other B's. Nor is stability necessarily any individual's intention. At the individual level many motives are at work—belief in the system, belief that others believe in the system, the desire to do one's job or to complete the group's task, concern for the welfare of the group, desire for advancement, personal loyalties to others, fear, apathy, the belief that change is impossible and challenge futile, as well as calculation of gains from the status quo, losses from change, and other prudential calculations of advantage or disadvantage. It is not necessary that any individual think in terms of preserving the stability of the system of authority for the outcome of his/her interaction to be system maintaining.

Elaboration of the Initial Theoretical Formulation

Once the legitimacy process had been differentiated from the power compliance process and Bachrach and Baratz's and Dornbusch and Scott's theories of legitimacy had been integrated into a single theoretical formulation, the subsequent development of the legitimacy program followed the pattern of elaboration described by Wagner and Berger (1985). The chief elaborations of the theory had to do, first, with the relation between validity and propriety and, second, with the fact that there are not only a number of sources, there are also a number of objects of legitimacy.

How Is Validity Related to Propriety?

The theory described in the previous section assumes that validity directly affects propriety, which then affects the rate of C-responses. But *post hoc* analysis of post-session questionnaire responses by S's in an early test of the theory called this assumption into question. A more consistent interpretation of the post-session questionnaire data was that actors formed their judgments of propriety after their behavior, which had been determined by validity. Self-justification seemed to bring their legitimation of the communication network into line with how they had behaved toward it (Thomas, Walker, and Zelditch 1986).

But the self-justification hypothesis did not survive in a better-designed replication of the experiment—better designed, that is, to clarify the time order of the relations among validity, behavior, and propriety.

Formulating two competing theories of their causal relations, we designed an experiment that would choose between them. In this more precise experiment, validity both directly increased propriety, before action was required by S, and also acted to buffer initially given levels of propriety against the subsequent impact of inequity. S's often begin our experiments feeling that a centralized network, because efficient, is the appropriate way to structure the task. It is inequity that undermines the propriety of this structure. If a centralized structure is also valid, inequity reduces propriety much less than if such a structure is not valid. This effect occurred before rather than after C-responses (Walker, Rogers, and Zelditch 1988).

Multiple Objects of Legitimation

Our first test of Dornbusch and Scott manipulated the endorsement of a centralized communication network by peers of an S on the periphery of the network and found that endorsement markedly reduced the probability of a C-response. Endorsement is the one hypothesis in our theory which has a substantial earlier literature (see Walker, Thomas, and Zelditch 1986, for a review of these results). The results in this literature give the hypothesis very mixed support. But replicating our experiment, we again confirmed the hypothesis. Seeking to clarify the mixed nature of previous results, we found it necessary to distinguish not only multiple sources of legitimacy and support (validity, propriety, authorization, and endorsement) but also multiple objects of legitimacy—acts, persons, and structures. Confounding the three had often obscured the endorsement effect (Walker, Thomas, and Zelditch 1986).

But once the objects had been distinguished, the obvious question arose of how they were related to each other. It is equally possible to suppose that legitimacy is an all-or-none phenomenon or that each object has an independent effect on total legitimacy. Non-compliance is a 0,1 phenomenon. If an act is not legitimate, surely that is sufficient to assure non-compliance. If the person performing an illegitimate act also has no legitimate title to authority, or the structure of authority is also illegitimate, can the illegitimacy of the person or structure add anything more to the effect of the illegitimacy of the act on the probability of non-compliance? On the other hand, in cases such as Reagan's mining of Nicaraguan harbors, perhaps it makes sense to say that even if an act is illegitimate, there is some effect of the legitimacy of person and structure on compliance. But if that is true, then each object of legitimation must be supposed to have an independent effect on total legitimacy and, hence, compliance.

A rather elaborate experiment, in a new setting invented for the purpose, found that compliance is indeed a 0, 1 variable at the individual level, perhaps even legitimacy is, but the aggregate rate of compliance is the additive outcome of three independent effects, legitimacy of act, person, and structure (Walker, Rogers, and Zelditch 1989).

Current Theoretical Formulation

The results of these further tests and refinements of the theory led to one important modification of the initial theoretical formulation, an assumption attributing independent effects on the rate of C-responses to legitimacy of acts, persons, and structures. The experimental support for this reformulation did not study C-responses, it studied compliance. But it seems to us implausible to suppose that legitimacy behaves additively for compliance but not for C-responses.

One way to incorporate this modification is to rewrite each assumption. For example, one could rewrite our first assumption so that it had three lines, one for acts, one for persons, and one for structures, each of which expressed the effect of the object of legitimacy as independent of any other. An alternative is to add an additional assumption, which we will do here to save time and pages. To do this, however, requires some generalization of terms: we assume i objects (i = acts, persons, and positions or structures of positions) and use *legitimacy* to refer to either propriety or validity or both. Then,

Assumption 9. The effect of the legitimacy of the ith object on the probability of a C-response is independent of the effect of the legitimacy of any other object.

New Directions

While previous growth of the theory has been a matter first of differentiation and integration and then of elaboration, we believe future growth of the theory will mostly involve proliferation. This follows from what we believe to be an important feature of the nature of legitimacy as a social process. For some time we have been trying to decide for ourselves whether legitimacy is one social process or many. There appear to be a very large number of different things that can be legitimated—power, rewards, rules, status, mobilization of resources, unexpected acts, and sanctions, among others. Equity theory, for example, is a theory of legitimacy of rewards. Is the process it describes the same as the process that legitimates power?

It does not, at the moment, seem to us plausible to believe that there is one unitary process of legitimation. Rather, it seems more plausible to imagine it as one aspect of many, possibly all, social processes—that aspect that causes the stability or instability of whatever the process is. It is possible that there are some common features of legitimacy in all processes, but, just as an example, it does not seem likely that there is a common dependent variable in all such processes. Thus, we are likely to require a number of distinct theories, each with a different domain, in order to understand legitimation.

Three domains are of immediate concern to us. The first has to do with how legitimacy affects resource mobilization. Resource mobilization turns out to be crucial to any Dornbusch-Scott kind of theory because it is by pooling resources to be committed to collective purposes that one creates the power that is deployed by valid authority. But in resource mobilization theories there turns out to be no theory of how resources are mobilized, and often they view legitimacy as simply one among a number of resources (McCarthy and Zald 1977; Oberschall 1973; Tilly 1978). This makes no sense, since with a lot of legitimacy and no resources it does not seem to us that you can do much collective action, and with lots of resources and no legitimacy it does not seem likely that one can mobilize them. Hence, we require some kind of interactive legitimation hypothesis and some way to test it.

A second domain that immediately concerns us has to do with legitimating rules, institutions, or structures. This derives in part from the fact that up to this point our theory has been concerned with the effects, not the causes, of legitimacy and in part from the need to distinguish between acts and rules. Because our focus has been on a particular act, change-responses, we have been able to think of legitimacy as a cause, without a theory of how it is itself caused. This is not really bothersome if one considers only particular acts, because the "cause" of the legitimacy of an act is often a straightforward application of the common definition of legitimacy as "in accord with a rule." Thus, if one asks whether Reagan was legitimately president of the United States, the answer depends on whether he won a majority of votes in an election, not whether one likes him or not. But that leaves unanswered the question of how to legitimate elections. The causes of the legitimacy of rules, institutions, or social structures such as elections, capital punishment, and capitalism are a quite separate question (Rawls 1955). A second proliferant of the program, therefore, would be a theory of the causes of the legitimacy of rules, institutions, or structures.

A third direction of theoretical development has to do with the legitimacy of acts. While what we have said in the previous paragraph appears to make this question trivial, the existing literature on "accounts," which are legitimations of unexpected actions, raises serious questions about the basic nature of legitimacy. Our conception of legitimacy departs from a conflict theory above all in the view that power cannot make an act legitimate. It of course can make people publicly comply, but that is not the same as making something legitimate. In the accounts literature, however, there are very mixed results about the effects of power, some of which imply that power legitimates and some which do not (Blumstein et al. 1974; Scott and Lyman 1968; Shields 1979). We believe this is due to confusing status with power, hence public with private compliance. What we require is a theory of the relation of status and power to legitimacy, and a method by which to study accounts that separates status from power and public from private honoring of them. If it turns out that power can legitimate an act, we will have to fundamentally rethink the basic assumptions of our theory.

PART V

Application and Integration

From Theory to Practice: The Development of an Applied Research Program

Elizabeth G. Cohen

Picture interracial groups of schoolboys arguing over which way to go on a gameboard entitled Kill the Bull. The two black and two white subjects in each group have come to Stanford University as paid participants in a study of interracial interaction. One white subject is doing most of the talking about which path the group should take. One black subject, although attentive to the proceedings and agreeable to the suggestions made, says very little. When he does suggest a move by tracing out a path on the board, the other group members act as if he were invisible. The engaging game of Kill the Bull was constructed to meet the scope conditions of status characteristics theory (Berger, Cohen, and Zelditch 1966), and the purpose of the study was to see if whites were more active and influential than blacks in a free interaction situation as predicted in the theoretical description of the process of status generalization. That study (Cohen 1972) took place in 1968 and marked the beginning of the research program.

At the present time, teachers in various parts of California and in Israel make regular use of treatments designed to modify undesirable dominance of high-status students and to raise the expectations for competence for low-status students. The total number of classrooms where children are experiencing such treatments is now in the hundreds. Teachers-in-training learn about status characteristics theory and the strategies derived from this theory as part of their regular coursework in the California state university system. These techniques, along with the curriculum strategies and a system of classroom management that have been developed under the aegis of the Program for Complex Instruction at Stanford, are gaining attention in countries where previously homogeneous school populations have become increasingly diverse and include low-status language minority students.

The status treatments are typically incorporated in a method of instruction that employs small groups of students talking and working together to solve problems in mathematics and science. A system of organizational support for classroom teachers using these methods has been developed and is implemented with variable success in the context of the loosely coupled organization that is the public elementary school in the U.S.

What can we learn about the growth of an applied research program from reviewing this development? There are two major themes of this chapter; the particulars from the program of applied research are intended as illustrative of these themes. The first theme is the role of theory in the program's initial stages and continuing development. The second theme pertains to the stages in growth of the research from applied science to engineering. B. Cohen (1989: 52) makes the following useful distinctions: *basic science* is oriented to the production and evaluation of knowledge claims; *applied science* is oriented to the discovery of new uses for knowledge claims that have been previously evaluated and tentatively accepted; *engineering* is oriented to the solution of technical problems where the problem to be solved is regarded as given.

The chapter is organized around the two phases of the applied research program: the applied science phase and the engineering phase. The program started in a search for practical problems that status characteristics theory (in its earliest form) could solve. Thus, in Cohen's terminology, the program began as applied science. The section of the chapter on this initial phase summarizes the studies of instantiation. These studies used the already developed theoretical propositions concerning status generalization. Essentially, they located problems of status generalization in the interaction of school-age children who were working in mixed-status groups. The phase of applied science also includes the experimental studies of various interventions designed to create equal-status interaction. In designing interventions, the researcher finds new uses for the knowledge claims of status characteristics theory; from the theoretical model of the process of status generalization, inferences are made about how outcomes could be altered. These propositions are tested in controlled experimental settings.

In his distinction between engineering and applied science, B. Cohen emphasizes that solving practical problems involves more than scientific knowledge: "A scientific principle in and of itself almost never provides the optimal solution to a problem. . . . The solution nearly always involves extrapolating from what is known" (1989: 56). The organization of the chapter reflects this challenging transition from applied science to engineering. The section entitled "A Shift in Goals and Values" deals with the complex of issues confronted in the move toward the production of equal-status interaction in normal classrooms. With this shift, there arose a concern with practical issues such as curriculum and with larger educational goals such as equity in racially, ethnically, and academically heterogeneous classrooms. In addition, as the laboratory treatment entered the arena of classrooms where learning outcomes are the major basis for legitimacy of any innovation, there was a shift in goals. Although an applied sociologist may be content with having achieved equal-status behavior, most schools are unwilling to make time-consuming and costly changes unless they are convinced that the innovation will have an impact on achievement scores. Thus the program staff became concerned with the broader problem of how the achievement of low-status students might be improved.

The engineering phase began as program staff sought to make selected interventions a standard part of classroom practice. Making the intervention attractive and practical for classrooms engendered a whole new set of problems requiring the application of various propositions from organizational sociology. The section on educational engineering highlights the ways in which multiple theories became relevant as staff tackled problems of classroom management, problems of teacher training, and problems of organizational support.

After this account of the two phases of applied research, the role of theory in applied research is reviewed. The chapter then closes with a discussion of how and when the researcher lets go of the program of applied research. The issue of when to let go is tied to the problem of the poor chances of survival of both effective and ineffective educational innovations.

Applied Science: An Initial Grounding in Theory

The purpose of the initial study was not to develop interventions, but to demonstrate that formal equality in cooperative groups in a desegregated setting produces not equal-status behavior but its opposite. Allport's (1954) theory of equal-status contact as a means to produce true integration was, at that time, widely cited as the basis for the design of desegregated situations. If status characteristics theory were correct (Berger, Cohen, and Zelditch 1966), bringing blacks and whites together in formal equality, as in a cooperative, collective task, would actually activate expectations for lesser competence from blacks than from whites. Instead of integration, the theory predicted that a self-fulfilling prophecy would take place in which racist notions about blacks being less competent intellectually would be enacted in terms of the less active and influential role played by blacks as compared to whites.

A second purpose of the first study was to see if status characteristics theory could be applied to a free interaction situation in which the subjects were seventh- and eighth-grade students. All the laboratory studies based on the theory had used highly controlled interaction settings and college-age subjects. The question this study asked was: Was black-white interaction on a task designed to meet scope conditions of the theory an instance of status generalization? We designed a criterion task based on scope conditions specified in Berger, Cohen, and Zelditch (1966). This collective task, the game initially called Kill the Bull, became the standardized criterion task for many of the laboratory studies. Subjects were asked to make collective decisions as to which way they were to proceed on the game board. A Host Experimenter rolled a die and determined how many steps the group could advance along the path chosen. The square on which the playing piece landed determined the number of points the group earned for that move. The group had to reach the goal in fourteen turns and was instructed to earn as many points as possible.

The earliest version of status characteristics theory only dealt with one status characteristic at a time. Thus the sample differed on race with two white and two black boys in each group. They were of the same age and social class background. They did not know each other prior to the study.

In order to measure the prestige and power order in the group, we utilized the work of a second branch of expectation states theory, the early work on performance expectations (Berger 1958; Berger and Conner 1969, 1974). This work provided observable indicators of the prestige and power order: concepts such as action-opportunities, performance outputs, and communicated unit evaluations. Observers scored videotapes of group interaction for the number of these kinds of speech acts that could be attributed to each actor.

In fourteen of the nineteen interracial groups of boys, a white actor was the most active on the task; and in thirteen groups a black member was the least active (Cohen 1972). Although earlier studies by Katz and associates (Katz and Benjamin 1960; Katz, Goldston, and Benjamin 1958) had demonstrated the problem of white dominance in interracial groups, this study was the first to formulate the problem as an instance of generalization of expectation states and to show, within scope conditions, that the phenomenon fit the predictions of that theory. The problem illustrated by the study was named "interracial interaction disability."

Subsequent Instantiation Studies

My graduate students and I conducted a series of studies examining other instances of status characteristics. These studies were always of situations restricted to variation on a single characteristic. We used the same criterion task and the same scoring system, so that studies could be compared. Prior to studies of intervention, it was important to demonstrate that we were dealing with a genuine instance of a status characteristic. Because the theory states that whether or not a particular distinction is a diffuse status characteristic varies with time and place, one must gather empirical evidence that a status distinction in a given setting functions as a status characteristic. For example, in testing whether or not being a Mexican-American was the low state and being Anglo was the high state of ethnicity as a status characteristic, Rosenholtz and I (Rosenholtz and Cohen 1985) found that this was true in the San Jose area only when the Mexican-American had a distinctive ethnic appearance. If we had assumed that a Hispanic surname was adequate to activate expectations based on the status characteristic of ethnicity, we would have tried to treat mixed ethnic groups in which the status characteristic would never have become activated even without intervention.

Other instantiation studies showed that Indian vs. Anglo (Cook 1974) and Middle Eastern vs. Western Jewish Israeli (Cohen and Sharan 1980) were also examples of diffuse status characteristics. As we moved to different cultural settings, we began to understand what generalizability across cultures might mean in the work with status characteristics theory. Although the theory was generalizable, not all the indicators worked in the same way in different cultural settings. Interaction varied more with culture than did the direct measures of influence. For example, in Israel, where both Middle Eastern and Western Jews enjoyed discussing issues, there was comparatively little difference in interaction rates between the two status groups, but the difference between the groups when it was a matter of whose suggestions were adopted as a final decision (a direct measure of influence) was much more marked.

Because the research program was located in a school of education, doctoral students were interested in exploring the utility of Expectation States Theory (EST) in explaining specifically educational problems. They were greatly aided in this work by the extension of the original formulation of status characteristics theory from diffuse to specific status characteristics (Berger and Fisek 1974). Specific status characteristics are social characteristics which have performance implications for a specified task (Berger et al. 1977: 91). Hoffman (Hoffman and Cohen 1972) demonstrated the effects of perceived academic ability on interaction and influence among junior high school students, and Tammivarra (1982) and Rosenholtz (1985) showed the capacity of perceived reading ability to produce status generalization among elementary school students.

Applied Science: Using Theory to Design Interventions

The early formulation of status characteristics theory explicated the stages of a process and the sufficient conditions for that process. Therefore, it was possible to infer a number of different ways to modify its outcome. For example, if expectations for competence attached to states of a diffuse status characteristic were activated by the situation, then one might find a way to avoid activating those expectations. Alternatively, if those expectations for competence had already been activated, they might be modified by combining them with contrasting expectations for competence before they had a chance to become attached to a new collective task. Finally, if the process of status generalization had already taken place, one might still interfere with the way expectations are translated into behavior by inserting specific norms for how people are to behave in groups.

The Use of Inconsistency to Produce Equality

The earliest attempt at intervention, Expectation Training I, utilized a simple inference from the first formulation of the theory (Berger, Cohen, and Zelditch 1966). "If both blacks and whites experienced the reverse of their general expectations on a new performance characteristic, they might then transfer these altered expectations to the game task where we could see evidence of interaction of an equal status variety" (Cohen et al. 1970: 5). In this early experiment, blacks were simply given better instructions than whites on how to build a radio; four-person interracial groups then worked together to build a radio prior to playing the game task. The theory of that time did not specify how the effects of the intervening experience would generalize from task to task. The intervention clearly failed to change the tendency of whites to be more active and influential than blacks on the game. Even when outside observers saw that blacks were more competent than whites on the radio task, the blacks did not perceive themselves as such. We concluded, as a result of this experiment, that the method of assigning competence to blacks had to be unmistakable to both whites and blacks.

Expectation Training II (Cohen and Roper 1972) was the first successful intervention. In this treatment, black students became teachers of white students in building a radio. Theoretically, the low-status person was assigned a high state on two new specific status characteristics: the ability to build the radio and the ability to teach this skill to someone else. The idea of two training tasks came from Freese (1976), who proposed that assignment of competence on task characteristics which were consistent with each other was likely to become relevant to a new task, whereas this would not occur if the characteristics were inconsistent.

In order to avoid threatening the high-status subject, the white was told that the black had been through a teacher-training program; presumably, the white could have been equally skillful if he had been through the training. Special procedures assured that the assignment of competence to the low-status student was believable. The black student was not permitted to act as teacher until he met a criterion level of competence following meticulous coaching by a black trainer. A videotape of competent performance of building the radio by the black members was shown to each four-person interracial group before the teaching session. The black trainer pointed out how competent each black member was as a radio builder (the first specific status characteristic). Moreover, a second videotape was made of the teaching sessions and was played back with the black trainer pointing out black competence in teaching (the second status characteristic).

This treatment greatly reduced the expectation advantage (the average difference in rates of interaction and score on influence between the races) of whites on the game in comparison to a condition where blacks experienced successful building and teaching the radio task only with their black trainer and where white expectations were untreated prior to the playing of the game task. This latter condition was seen as an analogue to many compensatory education programs in which black students are given success and reinforcement in an attempt to raise their self-esteem, but in which whites are untreated. The failure of this strategy to change the tendency of whites to dominate blacks was widely cited as a result of this study. The most effective condition in producing equal-status behavior contained an extra step of spelling out the relevance for the blacks of their competent behavior in the radio–building episode to their coming performance on the game task. The strategy of building a relevance bond came from the early work of Berger and Fisek (1970) on performance expectations. They had hypothesized that specifying relevance would raise the probability of transfer by the principle of perceived similarity.

In designing Expectation Training, we were forced to leapfrog the theory available at the time. There was no clear theoretical basis for knowing whether insertion of assignment of competence on two performance characteristics that were inconsistent with expectations based on the diffuse status characteristic of race would eliminate or only modify the effect of these general expectations. There was also no specific assurance from the theory that expectations modified by a training task would transfer to an unrelated task.

Expectation Training was replicated by Riordan and Ruggerio (1980) on blacks and whites. Subsequently, the treatment was applied to whites and Indians in Canada (Cook 1974); to Western and Middle Eastern Jews in Israel (Cohen and Sharan 1980); and to Anglos and Mexican-Americans in San Jose, California (Cohen 1982). The treatment was consistently successful in producing equal-status behavior with the one exception of the study of Mexican-Americans and Anglos (Cohen 1982). For a comparison of observed percentages among treated groups in these various studies, see Cohen's review (1982).

The Multiple Ability Treatment: Another Use of Inconsistent Expectations

In a multi-characteristic situation such as a classroom, actors combine all units of status information which are salient to form aggregated expectation states for self and other. If the information is inconsistent, such that there are both positive and negative expectations for the competence of actors in a given status state and they are of equal relevance, then these can average with each other (Berger et al. 1977; Humphreys and Berger 1981). Once this combining principle was formulated, it became possible to conceive of introducing specific status characteristics on which high- and low-status individuals received inconsistent assignments. Because people combine these high and low expectations, the net effect is to reduce the expectation advantage of the high-status person. In contrast to Expectation Training, where the inconsistency lay between the expectations based on the diffuse status characteristic and the expectations based on specific status characteristics, in this case the inconsistency lies between the expectations for different specific status characteristics. In a multiple ability treatment, students are told that many different abilities are relevant to the collective task they are about to undertake. Furthermore, they are told that no one student can be good on all these abilities and that each student will be good on at least one. Theoretically, these are new specific status characteristics with a direct relevance to the collective task. If students are convinced that this is the case, they will assign to themselves and others both high and low states on these new characteristics. These expectations, when combined with expectations based on a status characteristic such as academic or reading ability, will result in less of an expectation advantage for the student with higher academic or reading status than would be the case without this treatment.

Tammivaara (1982) carried out the first laboratory experiment using the multiple ability treatment. She used reading ability as a status characteristic with students who assigned to themselves and were publicly assigned high and average states. Experimental groups experienced a discussion task which was described as requiring many different abilities. Subjects were told that reading was irrelevant, that everyone was expected to be good on at least one ability, and that no one was expected to be good on all the abilities. As a result of this simple change in the definition of the situation, Low Readers were significantly more active and influential on the game in comparison to Low Readers who had experienced the same intervening task without the multiple ability introduction.

Use of Norms for Equal Participation

Morris (1979) demonstrated that it was possible to intervene in order to produce rational and harmonious discussion groups that were not marred by the dominance of high-status students. This intervention was of great interest to educators who are very concerned with the way students treat each other. Morris achieved this effect by introducing special norms for equal participation in a practice session prior to a problem-solving task requiring discussion. The guidelines included listening to others and giving everyone a chance to talk. The results of his experiment showed that those with high reading status had significantly lower initiation rates on the game in treated groups as compared to untreated groups. However, the high-status students continued to be much more influential than the low-status students. This experiment illustrated an important principle: although the internalization of a set of norms concerning more equal participation will alleviate undesirable dominance behavior, it will not, in and of itself, change expectations for competence.

The results had major significance both practically and theoretically. Theoretically, this experiment demonstrated that it was possible to intervene in such a way as to produce equal-status interaction after the process of status generalization had taken place but before the interaction on the new collective task. Moreover, the altered patterns of interaction would transfer to a dissimilar task. The fact that the status-organizing processes remained untouched was shown by the continuing imbalance in influence.

In practical terms, educators frequently advocate cooperative learning as a method of working with interracial and interethnic classrooms. Although it is true that these methods produce increased friendliness and trust, Morris's experiment showed that norms for cooperative discussion do not alter differential expectations based on competence emanating from status characteristics. Nonetheless, the use of norms for cooperation, *in addition to* direct treatments for status effects, is highly desirable from an educational point of view. Treating the status problem will not, in and of itself, produce socially and educationally desirable discussion and group interaction.

Experimenting with Interventions in Classrooms

The Center for Interracial Cooperation was an ambitious field experiment designed to determine whether Expectation Training would work in a field setting and would be sufficiently robust to maintain equal-status behavior over time, when interracial groups continue to work with each other on collective tasks (Cohen, Katz, and Lohman 1976). The experiment was run as a six-week summer school program in a junior high school in Oakland, California, that was to be integrated in the fall. Among the volunteer students recruited for the program, the blacks were markedly lower in social class than the whites. Expectation Training in this setting used four separate tasks, two of which were academic and two of which were non-academic. After a week of training just for the black students and one week of Expectation Training in which the black boys and girls trained white same-sex partners, there was a first round of measurement on the game task. Whites experienced four different black trainers, one for each of four different Expectation Training tasks.

Results of the first round showed approximately equal-status behavior for males and a reduced expectation advantage for white girls over black girls in comparison to previous studies of untreated groups. Four weeks of classroom experience followed this first round of measurement. The composition of each classroom was single-sex but interracial; the teaching staff was always an interracial team. The curriculum stressed small cooperative groups in which each person had a different role to play. The content of the curriculum was highly intellectual and creative, but did not require any reading or writing. Groups made movies with a Super 8 camera. They studied the difference between facts and inference in a curriculum that included archaeological digs.

In the last week of the summer school, students played the game once more, in newly composed groups whose members had not functioned as teachers and students of each other during Expectation Training. In the second round, there was a tendency toward black dominance in the male groups and equal-status behavior in the female groups. It was clear that under these conditions, Expectation Training could produce robust results that could grow stronger over time. The presence of powerful black adults in the roles of teachers and an experimenter may have acted as referent actors (Humphreys and Berger 1981), boosting the expectations for competence of the black males during the weeks of the summer school. Expectation Training was successful in producing equal-status behavior (and, in some cases, black dominance) even when students were not matched on SES and academic skills. Finally, the effects of treatment could evidently generalize beyond the individuals who had undergone the initial treatment together.

The multiple ability treatment, described above, grew out of the unexpected success of an alternative condition in the experiment at the Center for Interracial Cooperation (Cohen, Katz, and Lohman 1976). Students experienced a variety of new skills and abilities in interracial groups during the first week of the experiment. Close supervision by an adult in each group and much use of turn taking provided success experiences for each child. Results on the game showed equal-status behavior for boys that persisted to the end of the summer school experiment. Tammivarra (1982) interpreted this result in terms of combining the mixed expectations for competence developed by students in the small groups where they experienced success with many different skills and abilities.

Classroom Experiments with Multiple Abilities

Because the graduate student–researchers in this program were dedicated educators, they pushed for moving not only out of the laboratory, but toward normal classroom settings where academic issues would be confronted. Rosenholtz (1985) was not content with Tammivaara's strategy of telling students that reading was irrelevant to the collective tasks. This was unrealistic in classrooms where reading was always relevant to curriculum activities. Therefore her experiment took place in normal classrooms where a wide socioeconomic range among white students produced large differences in reading skills. Her control groups in untreated classrooms were composed of students perceived to have "High" and "Average" reading ability or "Average" and "Low" reading ability. The students were selected on the basis of their rank ordering of classmates on reading ability. With the standard game task, the results revealed the strongest status characteristic yet studied in the history of the program. These results also revealed that Average Readers would act as low status when combined with High Readers and high status when combined with Low Readers.

In the treated classrooms, Rosenholtz's multi-ability curriculum reflected her own successful and innovative practice in her career as an elementary teacher. Students were not told that reading was irrelevant to the experiences they were about to undergo. The curriculum focused on abilities that were said to be relevant to successful adult experience— visual, reasoning, intuitive, and spatial abilities. Each student had a high probability of experiencing success in one of the abilities because of creative and varied group tasks, several representing each ability; none of them required conventional academic skills. The probability of an individual's success was also enhanced by systematic turn-taking in guessing the solution to problems and by an adult supervising the experience of each small group. Although the results did not produce equal-status behavior because of the strong and continuing influence of expectations based on reading ability, the expectation advantage of the High Readers in the treated groups was significantly reduced in comparison to the High Readers in untreated groups.

Emboldened by the success of Rosenholtz's multi-ability curriculum in all-white classrooms, we planned a major field experiment (The Status Equalization Project) in a set of desegregated schools. This was a multi-characteristic situation where the black and the brown students were typically of a much lower social class than the white students and where classrooms exhibited an even wider range in reading skills than in the Rosenholtz classrooms (Cohen 1984b). There were three conditions in the field experiment: control, multi-ability curriculum, and multi-ability curriculum plus Expectation Training. To measure the effects of these interventions, 97 pairs of students played the game. Same-sex pairs were selected from the same classroom; they had not selected each other as close friends on a sociometric measure; they were matched on perceived social influence as measured by the questionnaire item, "Who in the classroom is most able to get you to do things?" Some pairs were differentiated on both race and reading while others were all-black and differentiated only on reading.

The results did not clearly show the effects of intervention. Despite our efforts to control perceived social influence within the pairs, it turned out to be the case that in 57 of the pairs, the black Low Reader was perceived as more influential *by classmates* than the white High Reader. In these 57 pairs, the interaction was clearly equal-status, even in the control condition. In the remaining pairs, there was a strong expectation advantage for High Readers in the control condition. When the social influence of the High Reader was higher than that of the Low Reader, either intervention condition reduced the expectation advantage of the High Reader. In all-black pairs, the addition of Expectation Training produced marked dominance of the Low Readers, although with the small number of pairs left in this analysis and with complex interactions between school and treatment, the differences were not statistically significant.

With this experiment, we had taken the plunge into a multi-characteristic setting with very wide differences in relevant status characteristics. Furthermore, we had important differences between schools and between informal peer relations within the sample. Before doing this experiment, we had no clear idea just how important these factors could be in influencing the effects of treatment and our ability to measure the effects of treatment in a field setting.

There were several important lessons learned from this experience. First, peer status was a status characteristic that had to be taken into account in the multi-characteristic situation of the classroom. Second, the strong effects of school on these data illustrated the power of the organizational context in which the treatment is taking place. The relationship of popularity to academic status appeared to be an effect of organizational context. If, as was the case in two of the three schools in this study, peer status is uncorrelated or negatively correlated with academic status, it has a powerful, independent effect on expectations for competence. The occurrence of socially dominant black boys in one of the schools made it very difficult to disentangle the effects of treatment from the contradictory effects of an academic status characteristic and a peer status characteristic. Academic status acted to raise expectations for High Readers who were white while peer status simultaneously acted to raise expectations for many Low Readers who were black. Even without the intervention, the net result of these inconsistent status characteristics was equal-status behavior.

In the one school where peer status, ethnicity, and academic status were highly intercorrelated, status imbalance was quite resistant to treatment. This occurred despite the finding that in this school the interracial climate was far more harmonious (even utopian) than in the other two schools. This was also a school with very few black or brown faculty in contrast to the other schools. In theoretical terms, the lack of competent referent actors (Humphreys and Berger 1981) may have exacerbated the status problems at this school.

Our one unsuccessful experiment with Expectation Training and the succeeding experiment by Robbins (1977), in which he was able to correct the difficulty, had taught us the importance of competent adults in authority who are of the same race-ethnic group as the low-status student. If there are no such adults, the status treatments are very likely to fail. The failed attempt at Expectation Training (Cohen 1982) used an Anglo middle-aged male as a Host Experimenter. Younger community college students with a Mexican-American background assisted him in preparing the Mexican-American students for their role as teachers of Anglos. In the Robbins (1977) study, this situation was repeated with an Anglo in charge of a subordinate Mexican-American assistant. In a contrasting condition, the Anglo and the Mexican-American modeled an equal-status relationship in which they solved several "staged problems" by working collaboratively in the presence of the students. Expectation Training was effective in the latter condition but not in the former.

The third lesson had to do with the creation of multiple ability curricula that would incorporate academic tasks. In the experiment proper, we had utilized the Rosenholtz multi-ability curriculum. However, if the intervention were ever to gain wide acceptance in school, we would have to deal with academic tasks and a classroom that did not require six adults. Our attempts at getting the teachers to create new multi-ability curriculum tasks following the completion of this experiment revealed to us that moving beyond Rosenholtz's delightful experimental curriculum was going to prove very difficult. Busy teachers do not have the time or the background for curriculum construction. We were unprepared to show them how to integrate more conventional academic skills into multi-ability curriculum tasks. Teachers needed to understand more of the theory behind curriculum construction than we could give them in impromptu conferences or in after-school sessions. Furthermore, teaching in small groups meant a major change in the teacher's role, which necessitated serious retraining. In order to make these changes, schools and teachers would need to be reassured that improved achievement would result. In other words, the time had come to embark on the engineering phase of the research program.

A Shift in Goals and Values

As we began to work with normal rather than experimental classrooms, a major question arose: Just which status characteristics should we be treating? Although major work had been done on treatment of expectations based on race and ethnicity, the most relevant characteristics in the classroom are academic status and peer status based on personal attractiveness and popularity. Ethnicity (when it is closely associated with social class) tends to be correlated with academic status in mixed-status classrooms and cannot easily be separated in the field situation. Furthermore, given what we knew about combining in a multi-characteristic situation, it was necessary to take the most relevant characteristics and to assume that their effects would be combined in the observed interaction within classroom groups. We made the decision to focus on a combination of peer and academic status.

Safety of the Intervention

Effectiveness in producing equal-status interaction was not the only value to be maximized in selecting interventions for use by busy teachers.

Issues of safety were of prime importance. Expectation Training, although probably the most powerful treatment of competence expectations yet devised, is not the safest classroom treatment. Unless the low-status student is carefully coached to attain a criterion level of competence on the new status characteristic and is also coached on how to teach the new skill, he or she may very well turn in a poor performance with a potential backlash. Under ordinary classroom conditions, teachers cannot give that much attention on an individual basis. We therefore chose the multiple ability treatment, perhaps not the strongest intervention, but certainly one of the safest and one that did not require visible selection of low-status students for treatment.

Broad Goals of Equity

As we entered the engineering phase, goals broadened in an almost imperceptible manner. We now hoped to undermine the way social class and the external societal status system are reproduced in classrooms. We argued that the phenomenon of status generalization in the classroom helps to perpetuate educational failure from one generation to the next. As students enter the classroom without the standard middle-class repertoire that makes for school success, they are relegated to low-ability groups and to a curriculum that is below grade level. Students with low expectations for competence make little effort and fail to initiate toward the teacher or toward peers in a task setting. The combination of depressed expectations for success and exposure to curricula that are below grade level perpetuates school failure from one generation to the next.

Clearly, we were extrapolating from other studies of classroom interaction and from studies of ability grouping and social class in coming to this conclusion. We were also assuming that the process of status generalization operates under typical classroom conditions. However, ordinary interaction in the classroom is teacher-dominated and does not clearly fit the scope conditions of a collective task. Nonetheless, there is considerable empirical evidence that students with high academic status initiate toward the teacher at a much greater rate than students with low academic status; they also spend much more time engaged in their schoolwork. These results suggest that status generalization operates under these relaxed scope conditions.

A major influence on the evolution of this ambitious goal for the program was the changing demographics of the California school population. With approximately half the school population belonging to some racial, ethnic, or language minority group, teachers face incredible academic and linguistic diversity within their classrooms. No longer can teachers who only want to teach white middle-class students take refuge in the suburbs. These schools also reflect the more general demographic changes. Many of the minorities are experiencing grave academic difficulties in the schools, so that linguistically and racially diverse classrooms also tend to have a very broad range of academic skills. The broader the range of academic skills, the more severe is the status problem (Cohen 1988). Teachers and teacher educators are quite aware of these status differences, but they lack effective instructional strategies for such diversity as well as direct ways to ameliorate the status problems.

Social engineering necessitates clarity about the values one is choosing to maximize in putting interventions in place. An honest and clear enunciation of these values brings the researcher together with the practitioner who is working for the same ends and enables a firm partnership between the two. In our case, these values were phrased as "the importance of giving minority students alternative futures that permit them to be more successful than their parents." Some teachers and administrators, particularly those from minority communities, are interested in the goal of improving the status of the child who has very low expectations for competence. These are the strongest allies of the researcher trying to treat status problems.

These values and goals concerning equity, however, are not enough to convince many school administrators and school boards. The goals of the applied researcher who has undertaken educational engineering must take into account the major objectives of teachers and administrators who work with students performing well below grade level, e.g., improvement in scores on standardized achievement tests. The only way to persuade most school authorities to commit themselves to change is to show them that these changes represent ways to reach their own goals, or, more concretely, the link between innovative strategies and improved test scores.

Although there is no tradition of sociologists working in the area of curriculum, we were forced to include changing the curriculum as a program goal. If teachers and students are supposed to see multiple abilities as relevant to the classroom, the biggest obstacle is the conventional curriculum. Typical classroom work represents a very narrow range of abilities exemplified in paper and pencil tasks and recitation. In order to enable students to assign themselves and others to the high state on new status characteristics, it is necessary to introduce new kinds of intellectual activities to the classroom. For example, introducing spatial and visual means of problem solving not only fulfills the technical prerequisite for successful use of the multiple ability status treatment, but it actually provides new opportunities for learning for children who are generally un-successful with purely verbal and symbolic media. Broadening the cur-riculum to include multiple abilities actually has two consequences: (1) it makes a multiple ability treatment workable and believable, and (2) it produces desirable learning outcomes in a much wider variety of students than does the more conventional curriculum (Bower 1990).

Changing the curriculum to embody multiple abilities while at the same time producing achievement gains on standardized tests represented a challenging goal. We probably would never have achieved this goal had it not been for our collaboration with E. DeAvila, a development psy-chologist, who had developed a new instructional approach for working with the children of migrant laborers.

DeAvila's curriculum materials had already shown surprising achieve-ment gains in basic skills in a pilot project; he came to us for sociological help in designing implementation of a complex and sophisticated method of instruction so that the program would survive under normal school conditions. Finding Out/Descubrimiento (FO/D), DeAvila's bilingual approach to the development of thinking skills in math and science, played a critical role in this program of applied research. Here was an already developed curriculum that used many different intellectual abili-ties. Children learned concepts by experimenting, hypothesizing, and solving problems using manipulative materials; several activities illus-trated each basic concept so that if a child did not understand the concept underlying one activity, he or she would have the opportunity to under-stand through another activity that used very different materials and re-quired different intellectual skills. Here was a curriculum that had already demonstrated that it could develop basic skills at the same time that it was developing higher-order thinking skills. Because all materials are in Spanish and in English, FO/D solved the problem of linguistic access for the large number of Spanish-speaking students in the schools of Califor-nia. Last, this curriculum was so attractive to teachers, with its hands-on learning and its high-prestige subject matter of physics and chemistry, that they would be willing to invest the considerable effort required to learn to manage a classroom with multiple activities and groups, to say nothing of the science underlying the activities.

In many classrooms with language minority children, instructors are so busy trying to teach English that children have little opportunity to study higher-level concepts in math and no opportunity to study science. These were the conditions that impelled DeAvila to develop his ap-proach. DeAvila saw these materials, not as a conventional curriculum, but as a model of a different instructional approach. Once teachers had grasped the basic principles of this type of instruction with this set of curricular materials, they would be able to adapt and to use other curricula that are available.

Engineering Phase

Once applied researchers have settled on a practical problem or an issue of practice to address, they must undertake a whole new set of empirical studies and development tasks. Multiple theories are necessary to deal with different practical problems. If the goal is a model for practice that can be disseminated while retaining its effectiveness, working with a theoretical framework that permits generalizability is more important than ever. In this program, the goal of the engineering phase was the incorporation of the interventions into regular classroom practice.

Status Problems in FO/D Classrooms

The first question the researcher should ask when putting an intervention into practice is: What form does the phenomenon I am trying to change take in the field setting where I will be working? Before we could incorporate status treatments as part of the new instructional approach, it was necessary to document the phenomenon of status generalization in classrooms implementing FO/D. Our experience in schools had led us to be very cautious about assuming that the process of status generalization took place in an uncomplicated way in mixed-status groups of students specifically assigned a collective task, let alone in interaction between students in a classroom.

In the first study of interaction in FO/D classrooms (Cohen 1984a), it was not clear that the children were engaged in a collective task meeting scope conditions. There were approximately six learning centers per classroom with about five students per center. Each learning center had a different set of activity cards in English and in Spanish. Each student had a worksheet to fill out as a result of completing the task at a given learning center. Students were supposed to complete work at each learning center before the end of the unit. However, they were not assigned to any particular group and could move on to the next problem, if there were space available at the learning center. In this first version of implementation, students were permitted and encouraged to ask each other for help and to give assistance. The two rules were: You have the right to ask for help from anyone at your learning center, and You have the duty to assist anyone who asks you for help at your learning center. Thus lateral relations were permitted but not mandated.

It was necessary to develop simple measures of status and interaction that could be used without benefit of laboratory conditions and video-tapes. To measure status, we used a sociometric measure that asked the children to circle the names of their classmates who were their best friends and those who were best at math and science. The distribution of choices for each child for each of these criterion questions was then divided into quintiles within each classroom. Each child received a score of 1 to 5 on the dimension of attractiveness/popularity and on the dimension of academic status. Using the principle of combining, we reasoned that states on these two characteristics should be combined to produce the status score of any given individual. The total of the two numbers was called the costatus score.

There were nine classrooms in this first study of implementation of the program. The classrooms ranged from grades two through four; many were formally designated as bilingual or ESL (English as a Second Language). The children came from working-class families and were largely of Mexican-American backgrounds. Many had only limited proficiency in English. The sample of target children chosen for observation represented a range of English proficiency and included children for whom the teacher judged this type of instruction to be particularly "problematic."

Children were observed for three minutes as they worked at the learning centers. Observers counted the number of task-related speeches and the frequency of working together. Multiple observations were taken on different occasions. An average rate of task-related interaction was then calculated for each target child.

Results showed what was indeed a problem of status generalization. Even the momentary interdependencies between children were sufficient to activate expectations for competence. High-status children were interacting more than low-status children at the learning centers. Interaction was, in turn, related to learning gains. If their pretest scores on a test related to the content of the curriculum are held constant, those who interacted more frequently did better on the post-test than those who interacted less frequently. This meant that some low-status children were failing to gain access to the interaction. Many of these children needed help from others in order to read the activity cards and the worksheets. Some were even failing to gain access to shared curriculum materials. In the meantime, the more popular children and the children with higher academic status were benefiting from the process of talking and working together. In other words, the "rich" were getting richer.

After finding out that there was a severe status problem, we began training the teachers to use the multiple ability treatment in the subsequent rounds of implementation. Evaluation of the effectiveness of this treatment in 1982–83 revealed that the effects of status on interaction were somewhat weakened in comparison to the first implementation, but by no means eliminated (Cohen, Lotan, and Catanzarite 1988). The most surprising result was that the effect of status on learning outcomes was eliminated. It was actually easier to treat the problem of differential learning gains than it was to treat the problem of status generalization.

Some of the reduced effect of status on achievement gains was due to major changes in the methods of classroom management put into operation in 1982. In the new management system, children were assigned to particular learning centers and to heterogeneously composed groups. All children went through a set of training exercises prior to the first unit of FO/D. They learned new norms for cooperation such as asking questions, explaining how, and helping others without doing their work for them. In addition, each child had a role to play and the roles rotated. An important role for guaranteeing access of all children to the learning experience was that of facilitator. The job of a facilitator was to see to it that everyone got the help he or she needed to complete the task. Another important role was that of the checker who made sure that everyone had finished his or her worksheet.

These changes in classroom management had the effect of boosting everyone's rate of interaction as well as the effect of ensuring access to materials and interaction for all students. Low-status children who had difficulty with reading and writing were less likely to be shut out of the tasks by not understanding what they were supposed to do or by being unable to put their thoughts into writing on the worksheet. Even if they didn't know how to read or write, they were expected to use their peers as resources and to obtain the necessary help to complete the task and the worksheet. Thus, even without total success in treating competence expectations, we were able to prevent the negative effects of status on learning gains.

Combining Status Treatments

Rather than work with one intervention at a time, as in the phase of applied science, it often becomes desirable, in the engineering phase, to *combine* several treatments. In addition to the multiple ability treatment, a new treatment, called Assigning Competence to Low-Status Students, was developed, building on the work of Webster and Sobieszek (1974). The teacher, as a high-status source of evaluations, can manipulate student evaluations of competence of self and other. Webster and Entwisle (1974), using source theory to test this proposition, found that students who had received positive evaluations from the teacher were more likely to raise their hands to volunteer a response than students who had not received positive evaluations from the teacher. In our classroom settings, teachers who use this treatment watch for instances of low-status students performing well on the intellectual abilities of reasoning, being precise, or being able to use visual thinking—abilities that are relevant to success on FO/D tasks. The teacher then provides the student with a specific favorable and public evaluation so that high-status members of the group will also hear and accept the teacher's evaluation. Furthermore, the teacher spells out the relevance of this intellectual ability to adult problem-solving experiences, or the teacher explains to the group how this student's ability constitutes a valuable resource for the group's task.

In the application of theoretically based research to practice, it becomes necessary to see if interventions work in the field setting for the reasons theory says they should. The most recent evaluation of the effectiveness of the use of these status treatments in classrooms where the FO/D curriculum was implemented in 1984–85 showed that the more frequently teachers were observed using these two treatments, the lower were the correlations observed between status and interaction rates in that classroom (Cohen 1988).

Interaction and Achievement

As educational engineers, we believe it is essential to understand how interaction relates to learning outcomes. From the first study of implementation in 1979, we consistently found that the higher the average proportion of students talking and working together in a classroom, the higher were the average gains in math concepts and application and in computation (Cohen, Lotan, and Leechor 1989).

For a theoretical explanation of this association, we turned to organizational theory concerning the problem of uncertainty among workers. Perrow (1967), Galbraith (1973), and March and Simon (1958) argue that lateral communication helps in dealing with uncertain tasks because it increases the amount of information being processed and is associated with higher-level search procedures. Finding Out tasks are highly uncertain from the students' point of view. For example, students are asked to "measure the waist of a dinosaur." The students must grapple with the following problems: Where is the waist on a dinosaur? And if we decide on the answer to that question, how are we supposed to measure it when the only equipment we have is a string, a large inflated plastic dinosaur, and a metric ruler?

By conceptualizing the students as workers grappling with a task that requires creative problem-solving, we had found a way to understand the importance of interdependence and interaction in helping the students benefit from the curriculum materials. Maintaining a high proportion of students interacting became a central goal of the training of teachers. They understood the research results and realized that no matter what changes they might want to make to deal with the particular problems of their classrooms, they should avoid cutting down on student interaction in any event.

Uncertainty at the individual level is increased if reading skills are inadequate to understand the activity cards and worksheets. Leechor (1988) found some support for the proposition that those students who were well below grade level in reading benefited even more from interaction than those who were reading at grade level. Thus, another reason that interaction leads to improved test scores is that students are using one another as resources to gain access to beneficial learning tasks.

Organizational Context of the Intervention

Interventions take place in an organizational context; the developer inevitably faces problems of how to produce consistent implementation in the field setting. In the first round of implementation, some of the teachers had great difficulty with managing multiple groups, each of which was working at a different task. As a result, some teachers reduced the complexity by lowering the number of groups to two or three, thereby cutting down on student interaction and the size of the gains in achievement (Cohen and Intili 1981).

In order to help teachers maintain the desired complexity of the technology, we decided that teachers needed more help in delegating authority to lateral relations. This decision was based largely on the work of Perrow (1967): once the technology has become more complex and uncertain, two necessary changes should be made in order to maintain or increase organizational productivity. The first is based on the need for more delegation of authority to the workers. The second is based on the need for more lateral communication among the workers.

From a practical point of view, we could see that teachers were fearful of losing control of the classroom without the assistance of direct supervision, that is, telling all the students exactly what to do. This was one of the reasons that we developed the new system of classroom management in which teachers delegate authority to groups of children at assigned learning centers. The use of cooperative norms does much to reassure the teacher that children will behave themselves constructively without direct oversight. The use of roles delegates to the children many of the functions that the teacher usually carries out as direct supervisor.

Teachers are trained to develop these roles and to rely on their enactment rather than on direct intervention in the groups when things are not going well. Teachers hold students accountable for managing many of their own interpersonal and procedural problems in the group. Teachers also hold students accountable for the completion of their worksheets while allowing the groups considerable latitude in the means they use to solve their problems.

In addition to helping teachers delegate authority, the new management system was designed to increase the level of student interaction. If interaction led to desired learning outcomes, then we wanted to develop a system that would help the teacher maximize the proportion of children interacting.

We train teachers to avoid hovering over the children and to intervene only when necessary to get the group going, to carry out status treatments, or to ask questions that will stimulate thinking. Evaluation of this management system showed that it produced excellent consistency of implementation between classrooms (Cohen and DeAvila 1983). Teachers maintained multiple small groups, and on the average, less than one child per classroom was observed to be disengaged from his or her task. The obverse of delegation of authority is direct instruction of the students. When teachers failed to delegate authority and used direct instruction while the students were at the learning center, the result was lowered rates of interaction between the students (Cohen, Lotan, and Leechor 1989).

Organizational Support for the Teacher

As technology grows more complex and non-routine, interdependent work arrangements become critical at the level of the classroom and the school. From the first round of implementation in 1979 (Cohen and Intili 1982), we therefore mandated two persons per classroom to manage the complexity of the technology. Previous research on individualized instruction (Cohen et al. 1979) had shown that such a technology would require two persons.

Just as it was necessary to train students how to work together, it was necessary to develop practical ways to train this classroom team to work together. Beyond the classroom, all the teachers implementing FO/D at a school also compose a team. Increasingly, with experience, we have realized the importance of building up a team of teachers within the school who can support each other and who can, if necessary, work for the survival of the program.

Intervention in the classroom does not take place without critical support from the principal. The principal plays a key role in coordinating personnel and logistics necessary for the collection, organization, and storage of curriculum materials (Ellis 1987). Two investigators have found significant associations between the principal's coordination and the character of implementation observed in the classrooms in the first year of training (Parchment 1989) and in a follow-up study up to five years after initial training (Dahl 1989). Teachers' perceptions that the principal expects them to follow through on implementation of the program is also a strong predictor of quality of implementation during the first year (Cohen and Lotan 1990). Thus, it was important to develop strategies for involving the principal from the beginning of the training cycle and to provide training for the role he or she was to play.

Issues of Persuasion and Education

No matter how valuable the researcher might think an intervention is for education, it is never possible to direct teachers to learn how to use it. Even among administrators of American schools who supposedly have authority over teachers, it is widely understood that one does not tell teachers how to carry out instruction. One must persuade teachers of the value of the intervention and provide the type of education and follow-up that will enable them to implement under a wide range of conditions.

The initial persuading of a teacher to use a status treatment requires recognizing the problem as one encountered in the classroom and one he or she wants to do something about. Beyond this step, the multiple ability treatment presents a special challenge in the preparation of teachers. It requires that teachers view human intelligence as multidimensional, so that they really believe that their best students will not be able to excel at all aspects of Finding Out tasks. Even more difficult for teachers to believe is that students who are very poor in reading and computation can make intellectually valuable contributions such as reasoning, visual thinking, or manipulative problem-solving. Since educators have generally regarded intelligence as unidimensional, this represents a major change in worldview.

We had to develop a number of strategies to help teachers to see intelligence differently and to provide practice and reinforcement for giving multiple ability orientations at the start of each day's session when the children were going to work at the learning centers. Even those teachers who were excited about the potential of a multidimensional view of intelligence found it strange and difficult to say, "No one will be good at all these abilities. Everyone will be good on at least one."

Learning how to assign competence to low-status students (the second status treatment) required that teachers learn how to observe the intellectual contributions of low-status students. It was then that they saw that such children could make important contributions to these rich tasks. What they found shocking is how blind they had been to competent behavior from these children (Benton 1992).

The most common method of training practitioners is to give them recipes, to tell them exactly how to do things. The major difficulty with this approach is that without a more fundamental understanding, the practitioner has no way to adapt the intervention to the myriad exceptions that any concrete setting will involve. Many a developer has been horrified to find that his or her intervention is hardly recognizable in the hands of a practitioner who has the best of intentions.

In order for teachers to implement properly, they must grasp the underlying theory (Lotan 1985). Lotan found that the teachers' grasp of the theory predicted the quality of their classroom implementation. In Lotan's formulation, the mastery of a body of theoretical knowledge permits teachers to use analyzable search procedures when faced with non-routine situations in the classroom. For example, having mastered a body of theoretical knowledge, teachers will be able to analyze observed low-status behavior and select competent behavior for assigning competence. The methods for preparing teachers we have developed start with a firm basis in the sociology underlying status treatments as well as the sociology underlying the system of classroom management. We provide practice for teachers in analyzing concrete cases, using these principles and making decisions; they work on these problems in small groups during the full two weeks of a summer workshop. In addition, they have a week of practice during the summer with a special heterogeneous group of students. They observe each other and discuss the translation of theory into practice.

There is no magic workshop that will guarantee that practitioners will apply what they have learned with skill and understanding. Practitioners require systematic feedback on their performance along with an opportunity to reach a deeper understanding through talking with a trainer. In order to provide soundly based evaluations and to ensure thorough understanding by the teachers, we drew upon the work of Dornbusch and Scott on evaluation and authority (1975) and upon the application of that work to evaluation of teachers (Roper and Hoffman 1986). Theoretically, clarity of criteria used in evaluation is a requirement in an evaluation system if workers are to perceive that evaluation as soundly based. Clarity is achieved by using criteria for effective implementation supplied by the research that correlated theoretically important dimensions such as interaction with desired outcomes such as achievement. For example, one important criterion is that, on average, more than 30 percent of the students should be talking and working together. Teachers learn to use research instruments to observe each other. First-year teachers are systematically observed by means of these instruments and given three feedback sessions using criteria such as the percentage of students observed interacting and the frequency with which the teacher was observed talking about multiple abilities.

Adequacy of sampling by the evaluator is another criterion for soundly based evaluation. To meet this criterion, we base each feedback session on three classroom observations. There are separate observations of the teacher and of the engagement and interaction of the students.

In addition to clarity of criteria and adequacy of sampling, the feedback given to teachers is highly specific (Gonzales 1982). Data from observations are compiled into bar charts in which the teachers can see information such as the proportions of students engaged in various activities and the number of times they have administered status treatments. These data provide an ideal opportunity for confronting problems, for coming to understand underlying theory more thoroughly, and for discussing various problem solutions. By keeping past records, teachers can see their progress in solving the problems that have been identified.

There is research evidence for the effectiveness of these methods of providing evaluation for the teacher. In the first year of training, Ellis (1987) found that the frequency of feedback to the teacher was correlated with implementation of some of the most challenging non-routine behaviors of the teacher. Feedback to the teachers that is perceived to be based on clear criteria, is derived from an adequate sampling of classroom observations, and is seen as highly specific predicts high-quality implementation in the first year of the teacher's experience with complex instruction. When feedback from trainers shifts to feedback from colleagues in the years following initial training, Lotan (1989) finds that this evaluation is associated with the maintenance of high-quality implementation.

Role of Theory in Applied Research

The conventional view of applied research is that theory, if it plays any role at all, has its primary impact in the formulation and initial testing of interventions in a controlled setting. Theory supposedly fades as the intervention is moved into field settings. Our experience has been that theory has played and continues to play a major role throughout the phases I have called applied science and engineering.

Expectation States Theory

Within expectation states theory, we have made broad use of three different branches: status characteristics theory, performance expectations, and source theory. The original formulation of status characteristics theory lent itself to the formulation of interventions. The description of the process of activation of expectations based on status characteristics and the spread of those general expectations to new tasks permitted us to infer a variety of interventions. The powerful analytic tool of scope conditions allowed us to move across a range of situations in experiments and in actual classrooms.

In later work, we made extensive use of the reformulation of the theory for multi-characteristic situations (T_2 and T_3). The principles of combining and relevance helped us to conceptualize the multi-characteristic nature of the classroom and to understand the impact of status on behavior in this setting. The theory provided a basis for selecting the most relevant status characteristics, academic and peer status, and for aggregating them to represent a single status variable. Relevance bonds were also used to strengthen assignment of competence both in Expectation Training and in Assigning Competence to Low-Status Students.

The concept of referent actor (Humphreys and Berger 1981) proved useful for analyzing key features of the organizational environment that can affect the success of treatments for status problems. For example, we have found that the lack of an authority figure, a competent referent actor of the same race/ethnic background as the low-status student, can negate the effects of a status treatment.

A second branch of the theory, the performance expectations branch (Berger 1958; Berger and Conner 1969, 1974), was fundamental to understanding specific status characteristics such as academic ability in the classroom. This branch of the theory also provided us with a way to operationalize the power and prestige order when categorizing free interaction. In the course of the early studies, we found that there was such a strong intercorrelation between the various interaction behaviors and between the initiation rates and rates at which actors received outputs from others, that eventually we shifted to a simpler index of task-related interaction and to an independent measure of exercised influence. In field settings, we found that the basic indicator of task-related action was a sufficiently simple yet valid and reliable measure of the prestige and power order that could be used by on-site observers who counted interaction among children working in groups at the learning centers in a noisy classroom.

The source theory branch (Webster and Sobieszek 1974) was used to create an adaptation of Webster and Entwisle's intervention of using the teacher as a high-status source to make positive evaluations of the competence of low-status students. Although simple in principle and attractive to teachers, this intervention has proved extremely challenging to implement. Teachers tend to view low-status students as problematic. They check them out for confusion, wandering, trouble making, or disengagement. If they are showing none of these problems, the teacher then shifts his or her attention to other students, thus overlooking positive examples of the contributions these children make to the group. Some of this problem is undoubtedly due to the warping effects of teachers' low expectations on their perception of the behavior of low-status students. This interesting new twist to the process of status generalization emerged from the work of J. Benton (1992), who has been conducting experiments on the question of how best to train teachers to use this intervention.

The work of applied science can have an impact on the work of basic theorists. The success of Expectation Training raised important theoretical questions concerning the multi-characteristic situation. What was the nature of the process by which inconsistent expectations became the basis for assignment of competence on a new task? A series of experiments by the basic researchers followed this applied study. The results of this research were incorporated into a reformulated version of the theory (Berger et al. 1977; Humphreys and Berger 1981). The nature of this process turned out to be one of combining in which subjects combine the expectations based on the diffuse status characteristic with the expectations based on the specific status characteristics. Even though the effects of the diffuse status characteristic are not eliminated, the net effect is one of lessening of inequality.

Another issue of interest to the basic researchers was whether or not the effect of a status treatment would generalize beyond the people directly involved in the intervention. The study of the Center for Interracial Cooperation demonstrated in 1972 that Expectation Training effects would last for six weeks, and that equal-status behavior was observed in interracial groups whose members had not directly been involved with each other as teachers and students in Expectation Training. This issue was specifically raised and tested by the basic researchers many years later (Pugh and Wahrman 1983; Markovsky, Smith, and Berger 1984).

Use of Other Theories

It has been necessary to use multiple theories to deal with very different kinds of problems. Within social psychology, the work of Bandura

(1969) has been very useful in laying down the prerequisites for the rapid internalization of new socially desirable behaviors. Propositions from organizational sociology have also proved useful in designing classroom management systems, in developing a model of organizational support for the teacher, and in providing a type of evaluation system that will ensure good implementation.

In the applied science phase, we began to make use of Bandura's work on modeling (1969) in order to create competent behavior in low-status students as quickly as possible. Role modeling was used during Expectation Training to convince black students learning how to build the radio that they could be very competent at this task.

Bandura's basic ideas concerning social learning have provided a way to internalize cooperative norms in the classroom (Cohen 1986). Today, teachers, trained in complex instruction, routinely use these techniques in preparing children so that they can manage lateral relations in a classroom where authority has been delegated.

The basic insight of Perrow (1967) has been very practical for teachers trying to manage classrooms with multiple groups and activities, i.e., delegation of authority to lateral relations as a way to manage complexity. Interdependence for both students and teachers has become a standard method of managing uncertainty (Thompson 1967). In a related application of organizational theory, the role of the principal has been conceptualized as one of coordination essential to a program of complex classroom technology that mandates interdependent work arrangements in the school (Perrow 1967; Thompson 1967). We have made major use of the theory of evaluation and authority (Dornbusch and Scott 1975) to design an evaluation system that will be perceived as soundly based.

The Role of Theory in Preparing Teachers

The Program for Complex Instruction has designed a full year of staff development for teachers and principals, including two weeks of instruction prior to implementation in the classroom. The teachers are taught the elements of status characteristics theory and the organizational theory that are basic to the program. They are also instructed in the relationship between this theory and observable features of the program such as the number of students talking and working together. Armed with this knowledge, they are able to make various changes in the program in response to the particular challenge of the schools and classrooms they face. Because they understand the critical features of the program that must be maintained, they do not unwittingly destroy the program's effectiveness in an attempt to solve particular practical problems. For example, in a classroom where the students speak several dialects of the mountain peoples of Vietnam, the teacher instructed the aides who spoke these dialects to translate the materials for the children but to avoid staying with the groups in such a way as to cut down on their level of interaction.

The Importance of Practical Knowledge

The engineering phase calls for a blend of the application of multiple theories with a thorough understanding of the particularities of the field setting. For example, without theory I would never have recognized the value of FO/D, the fact that it was a multiple abilities curriculum. However, without the practical experience of working with FO/D, I would not have known that teachers will put forth great effort and make costly changes in order to work with an attractive and practicable curriculum.

The program would never have achieved its present acceptance in schools without the contribution of graduate students with extensive practical experience in inner city classrooms, in bilingual education, and in administration. They contribute a deep understanding of the problems and pressures of classroom teaching. They have the legitimacy in working with teachers that a sociologist will never achieve. Each of their dissertations focused on some aspect of the classroom or school organization, giving us a systematic knowledge base for the program that is most unusual in education research and development.

When Does the Researcher Let Go?

An appropriate question to ask is: If the major engineering and scientific questions at the classroom level have been answered, why not let the status interventions loose from the researchers' guidance and consider the work of the program essentially complete? Unfortunately, the organization of schools is such that most innovations, effective and ineffective, tend to disappear over time. Meyer and Rowan (1977, 1978) describe schools as preoccupied with their legitimacy in the surrounding community and society. This leads to a situation, called "loose-coupling," where little attention is paid by district officials to the quality of implementation of last year's innovation; little attention is paid to what actually goes on in classrooms in individual schools. Because administrators receive rewards for being up-to-date and innovative, they take on some new innovations each year while allowing the old ones to languish without support and without resources for continuing to train new teachers.

Innovative instruction is also threatened by instability of personnel.

Principals are routinely shifted between schools in a district. Teachers shift between grades, schools, and districts and in and out of the labor force. In her follow-up study of teachers in the program, Dahl (1989) found that instability of personnel was the greatest threat to the continuation of implementation. Therefore, we are now engaged in a study of conditions for institutionalization of complex instruction.

Unlike the field of engineering, this one has no trained personnel who might be described as educational engineers. There are people who do in-service staff development, training in various practical techniques, and curriculum development. However, they are divorced from theory and research and almost never do systematic studies of how well their techniques are implemented in classrooms. Thus, unless we want to see our work gradually undone, we must continue to search out ways to assist the survival of these effective classroom strategies.

Looking back over the process of research and development in this program reveals a long road beginning in applied research when we found instances of status generalization and ran experiments to test the effectiveness of interventions in modifying that phenomenon. That first phase of the program, categorized as applied science, was guided by a single family of theories. The sharpest turn in that long road was where we began to incorporate our interventions into local classroom practice. With this shift into the engineering phase, we were forced to develop a whole new set of goals and concerns as well as to make eclectic use of sociological theories for the solution of a variety of practical problems. Success in solving problems at the classroom level only led to more questions concerning success at an organizational level and finally to questions of institutionalization of changes in practice.

If there is one central message that has been learned from this long-term program of applied research, it is that theoretically oriented sociology is enormously practical. And that has probably been the best-kept secret in the history of the field.

Methods and Problems of Theoretical Integration and the Principle of Adaptively Rational Action

Thomas J. Fararo and John Skvoretz

In this paper we have two main objectives. First, we want to address problems and methods of integration in sociological theory and to draw upon our previous work to illustrate our general ideas about theoretical integration. Second, we want to produce the beginnings of a new episode of theoretical integration that is specially addressed to the group process research programs represented in this volume. We proceed in three parts. The first sets out a general perspective on the overall problem of unification in general theoretical sociology. It makes the important claim that the structure of scientific theory has four distinct levels, each of which comes into play in the search for unifying themes and principles. Obstacles to and opportunities for unification can occur at any of these levels. The second part illustrates these points by drawing heavily on our previous attempts at theoretical unification: social network representations with expectation states theory and Blau's social differentiation theory with Granovetter's strength of weak ties principle. The third part treats unification of group process research traditions.*

Our discussion is motivated by a spirit of unification which attempts to advance general theoretical sociology. A more extensive explanation of what is meant by "the spirit of unification" occurs elsewhere (Fararo 1989b). For present purposes, three key ideas need to be emphasized. First, we do not envision some single all-embracing feat of theoretical unification at one fell swoop. Rather, unification is a process which occurs in episodes and involves recursion. That is, the outcome of any one integrative episode may enter into further such episodes. Also, any one episode may be only a partial unification of the entities brought into integrative connection, so that there is almost always a sense of "more to be done."

*The comments of Douglas Heckathorn and David Willer on earlier drafts were very much appreciated.

Second, proliferation and unification are both essential processes in science. If *only* proliferation were to occur, a field would spawn endlessly branching discrete ideas and give rise to a sense of intellectual chaos. If *only* unification were to occur, a field would eventually arrive at a non-growth condition in which integration would have gone as far as it could with the given intellectual materials. In real theoretical sciences, *both* processes occur together. But fields differ in their relative weight. In some sciences, despite proliferation, a sense of movement toward more and more comprehensive theory exists even as new problems and theories continue to be generated. In other sciences, despite occasional episodes of integration, the predominant tendency is to ever-increasing proliferation with insufficient integration. In sociology, the latter is the case.

This leads us to the third key idea. The spirit of unification in its most general sense is a value commitment to activities that, while not theory-integrating episodes as such, are important to the creation of an intellectual situation that produces such episodes. This means that not only direct theory integration is valued, but so are other sorts of unifying intellectual activities. Thus, we think that the spirit of unification can be embodied in at least four distinct modes of inquiry. The first mode is the *intra-program mode*, in which the concern is the integration of theories *within* a given general framework, paradigm, or research program. Wagner and Berger (1985) have identified this mode in their discussion of theory growth in sociology.

The second mode is the *comprehensive tradition mode*, in which attempts are made to unify general theoretical frameworks or research programs in sociology treated as a comprehensive theoretical tradition. As an example here, consider the network analytic tradition (see the papers in Leinhardt 1977) on the one hand, and Blau's (1977) macrostructural research program on the other. Despite common elements, differences in concept and method have led some observers (see Marsden and Laumann 1984) to explicitly set aside Blau's research program as external to the network research program. Similarly, in a recent article, Blau (1988) treats his approach as distinct and different from that of network analysis. Both programs, however, acknowledge Nadel (1951, 1957) as a common ancestor (Lorrain and White 1971; Blau 1977: 3). The very distinctiveness of these two bodies of ideas, the perception that they stand in external relation to one another, and the recognition of their common ancestry make their unification a significant task within the comprehensive theoretical tradition of sociology.

The third mode is the *methodological mode*, in which the search is for integrative theoretical methods that can be deployed in diverse unification attempts. These methods are "neutral" with respect to substantive content, providing the would-be unifier a tool kit with which to construct unified accounts. Generative structuralism and biased network methods are two such integrative devices highlighted in later sections. More generally, what is needed is not another trotting out of more general methodological ideas about the hypothetico-deductive method. Rather, the methods needed must be adapted to the conceptual structures and theoretical problems of sociology: they must stand to the enterprise of theoretical sociology as our data analysis methods stand to the enterprise of empirical research. (See Jasso 1988, for further discussions of the distinction between theoretical and empirical analysis and of the need for methods of theoretical analysis.)

The fourth mode is the *philosophical mode*, which involves the formulation of a philosophy of theoretical sociology that displays two important integrative attributes. First, there is an explicit, comprehensive "worldview" that has an integrative function with respect to the different worldviews associated with the distinct research traditions that collectively compose the comprehensive research program of general theoretical sociology. Second, there is an integration of valuable features of the three contending and contentious philosophies of science, instrumentalism, positivism, and realism, which have legitimated various methodological claims in diverse subtraditions of sociological theory. This mode forms the general conceptual backdrop for the actual work of unification.

Integrative Philosophical Models

The tasks for the philosophical unifier are many. The ones most relevant to the purposes of this paper are (1) the development of a view of theory structure and the nature of explanation which unifies disparate philosophies of science; and (2) the development of a comprehensive understanding of what the fundamental analytical focus of general theoretical sociology ought to be. The first task is quite general, and the resulting integrative synthesis of philosophies of science is applicable to all fields of scientific inquiry. The second task is particular to sociology and arises out of approaching the basic problem of holism versus methodological individualism in the spirit of unification. Standing behind these tasks is a "process worldview," rooted in the philosophical writings of Whitehead (1978) and adumbrated elsewhere (Fararo 1987a). The overall logic of this discussion of integrative philosophical models is shown in Figure 1.

The Structure of Theory and the Nature of Explanation

There are a variety of philosophies of science today. Some theorists find great merit in the logical positivist formulations of, for instance,

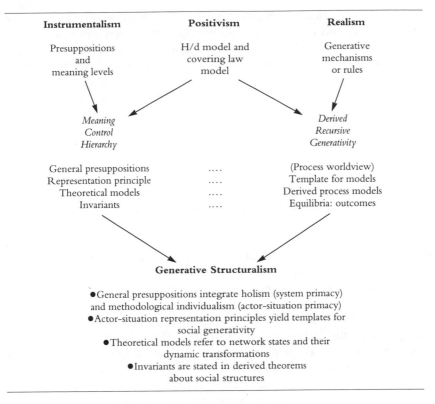

Instrumentalism

Presuppositions
and
meaning levels

Positivism

H/d model and
covering law
model

Realism

Generative
mechanisms
or rules

*Meaning
Control
Hierarchy*

*Derived
Recursive
Generativity*

General presuppositions	....	(Process worldview)
Representation principle	....	Template for models
Theoretical models	....	Derived process models
Invariants	....	Equilibria: outcomes

Generative Structuralism

● General presuppositions integrate holism (system primacy)
and methodological individualism (actor-situation primacy)
● Actor-situation representation principles yield templates for
social generativity
● Theoretical models refer to network states and their
dynamic transformations
● Invariants are stated in derived theorems
about social structures

Fig. 1. Integrative philosophical models.

Braithwaite (1953) and Hempel (1965). Others favor the post-positivistic critics of logical positivism—such as the "instrumentalist" views of Toulmin (1953), who was influenced by the later Wittgenstein, and Kaplan (1964), who was influenced by Dewey's (1938) pragmatist views—or the "scientific realist" approach (Harré and Secord 1973; Hacking 1983; Leplin 1984). In this section we first consider the problem of characterizing the structure of theory. Here the concept of a meaning hierarchy will be advanced, incorporating ideas from the positivist and the instrumentalist traditions. We next consider the nature of explanation, integrating the positivist and realist conceptions around the idea of the role of generativity in theoretical explanation.

The structure of theory has four levels which form a *hierarchical meaning control system*: (1) general presuppositions; (2) representation principle; (3) theoretical models; and (4) invariants. Invariants are uniformities of some kind, derived within theoretical models and corroborated by observations. Or, alternatively, they are discovered empirically through the study of data and then rationalized by derivation from some postulated theoretical model. The theoretical meaning of the invariant depends upon the theoretical model. Included in this category are constants in laws and the laws themselves in the natural sciences. Theoretical models are constructed within some mode of representation defined by a principle. Finally, principles are formulated within some set of nonempirical assumptions guiding the theory enterprise. These general presuppositions are ultimate for the given structure. Thus the interpretation of invariants presupposes models which presuppose modes of representation which presuppose general presuppositions about the world, the subject matter and the knowledge process.

Calling this a meaning control hierarchy is intended to emphasize that higher levels constitute commitments that "inform"—enable and constrain—the lower level activities or discoveries. Bearing in mind that the lower levels depend on connection with the world through observation, we have reciprocal control in that the reconstruction of particular representations (models) or of the entire framework for such representations (specified through the representation principle) depends on the fit of inferences from models with relevant observations. Ultimately, the presuppositions themselves are not absolutes: through reciprocal feedback we may articulate them more carefully, revise or abandon them, and these decisions have an impact on lower levels of the hierarchy.

The key level is *the representation principle,* a generalized way of mapping an entire class of phenomena into some class of models. For instance, the idea of mapping balance phenomena in social and psychological structures into signed graphs is a representation principle. Historically, the work of Heider (1946) was the background for the formulation of such a principle by Cartwright and Harary (1956). Their famous structure theorem holds for a rigorously defined class of such graphs, signed graphs, of particular interest in Heider's formulation of psychological balance problems. These authors presupposed that discrete representations of subjective phenomena were important and, in application, would provide a route to empirical knowledge of uniformities. They also presupposed the importance of the axiomatic method, in the sense of modern mathematics. Any family of graphs, in their sense, defined and studied through some assumptions about processes and structures of interest to us counts as a theoretical model. At this level one can envision Newcomb's (1953) famous ABX argument, which concerns consensus and dissensus in social interaction and the conditions of their respective production in communicative processes. Once balance theory is formalized in terms of signed graphs, the ABX idea can be cast in terms of them. Thus, we could embed Newcomb's ideas at the third level in an appropriate balance-theoretical model—ideally by actually constructing a dynamic process in which the state of the graph changes over time in ways corresponding to the implications of balance phenomena. The well-known observations that liking and consensus and disliking and dissensus tend to go together is an invariant that one would hope to rationalize by derivation from the model.

The four-level structure of theory blends instrumentalist and positivist philosophies. The instrumentalist insists on the importance of representation principles and the fact that particular models presuppose them (Toulmin 1953). Indeed, science is the search for novel, interesting, and revealing types of representation. In form a representation principle is a general *nonhomogeneous* statement in which the grammatical subject is the substantive subject matter and the predicate designates a general mode of representation of that subject matter for the purpose of theoretical and empirical analysis. The essential function of the representation principle is to structure scientific problem-solving—to define, in the terms of Newell and Simon (1972), a "problem space." Different representation principles may produce very different problem spaces for what is ostensibly the "same problem." Adoption of a particular principle provides a flexible *generalized* basis for constructing scientific problem spaces. The principle is a generalized symbolic medium for scientific cognition. It is public, not private. We orient to the mode of representation as we find it in use (object of cognition), and it also structures our problem-solving activity (mode of cognition). We can change the *particular* representation (some specific model) in favor of an alternative, using the same generalized mode of representation. We discard the entire principle when it leads to problem spaces that cannot effectively structure our relevant problem-solving activities. (In this respect we are much like Newell and Simon's cryptarithmetic problem solvers: representations in which letters stand for numbers have much greater chances for success than ones in which surface features of letters are mapped onto numbers.) This focus on problem solving, on symbolic representations and communication, is pragmatic and instrumentalist in spirit.

Where does the positivist conception fit? The positivist model is the familiar hypothetico-deductive system, which, in its most austere version, is understood to involve a purely formal system together with an interpretation linking the formal terms to observables. The deductions are secure because they involve only the form, not the content provided by the interpretation. Such a formal system, a deductive hierarchy with a generic interpretation, however, is a special case of the idea of a representation principle, no more and no less. For instance, corresponding to the mathematical theory of games, a mathematical axiomatic system, is the representation principle we can put in the form "A rule-governed interactive choice situation is a game." Particular game-theoretical models, working within the framework defined by this principle, attempt to construct and strategically analyze particular families of games (see Fararo 1973: pt. 4).

Our view differs from the well-intended but mostly unproductive attempts to use a kind of verbal axiomatics in sociological theory. Such positivistic work embodied a conception which overlooked the crucial role of theoretical models. The element of models appears in the positivist image as some unnecessary appendage to the main element, the *sentential* structure of the theory. But all the imagination involved in theorizing is focused on the model objects, the idealized representations guiding our scientific problem-solving. The sentences written down are only the vehicles for observing such models and talking about them. Without the models, the sentences have the feeling of vacuity that the nonmathematical reader senses without being able to pinpoint. Sentences in a deductive system are not the sort of entities our scientific problem-solving activities operate on or with respect to. They may be adequate as summaries of what we learn by studying models, but they are no substitute for the creative process of constructing models and studying their properties.

Before closing this brief treatment of the structure of theories, we offer a few further remarks about the idea of a representation principle that may help to clarify the intended meaning. Such principles may vary in the precision of the formal predicate and in the scope of the empirical subject matter. By precision, in this context, we mean that predicate P is more precise than predicate Q if P implies Q but Q does not imply P. In his paradigmatic example of how models function in science, Toulmin (1953) formulates the fundamental principle of geometric optics as "Light travels in straight lines." A less precise principle would be "Light traces out a continuous curve in space." Yet both of these formulations qualify as representation principles. Clearly, the fundamental principle of geometric optics is more precise than the weaker, perhaps working, principle that merely proposes thinking of light as tracing out some sort of curve in space. The first clarifying point, then, is that it makes sense to think of a process whereby a relatively imprecise representation principle initiates a line of inquiry and is subsequently modified, depending on the experience with it. Such a process is likely to move the principle from a less precise to a more precise state.

There is a second general clarifying point to be made. A representation principle defines a framework, it enables and constrains a family of models. A weak, or imprecise, representation principle does not constrain particular models very much. This suggests another image of change in the structure of theory. Namely, model builders seek more precise principles that constrain particular theoretical models more definitely than the overarching framework principle. This leads to a set of variants, as it were, in which various families of models are organized under subordinate representation principles that exemplify the general principle but with greater precision. Also, it may be an ultimate goal of research to attain a more precise version of the general principle. It is this latter situation which characterizes our later work in this paper. Action is adaptively rational is our general form of principle, with two more precise forms specified. The agenda for our work includes the important quest for some integration of these two forms that will later become the more precise general form.

We turn now to the nature of explanation. Realism and positivism are integrated in our view of the nature of explanation. Realism stresses generative mechanisms, positivism stresses derivation from more general premises. Integrating the two, we say that a satisfying sense of explanation is associated with the construction of models of generative mechanisms and with the derivation of those models within a general framework that both enables and constrains such model construction. Ideally we want both elements. Without a common conceptual scheme and some basis for the derivation of such generative models, a field would simply be a series of independently devised accounts without unifying principles. This is where the positivist view of explanation is relevant. However, the covering law version of this view, which is emphasized in the best logical positivist account (Hempel 1965), needs to be construed more processually and more in terms of models than in terms of relationships among sentences. So the point is that we construct or derive the generative process model within the framework defined by some representation principle. For the sake of generality, however, we want that principle to enable and constrain process representations.

For example, consider the ABX model, in which the invariant—consensus with liking, dissensus with disliking—begins as an empirical generalization. Researchers find a positive correlation between consensus and mutual liking. Why should this relation hold? The ABX answer, framed exactly and studied deductively in a balance-theoretic structure, shows this correlation is expected in the equilibrium condition of the interpersonal communication process. One can "read off" a property of the balanced graphs that corresponds to the empirical generalization and, in that sense, explains it. This interplay between graph and generalization is not really the sort of explanatory logic that the sentential "covering law" paradigm describes, at least as discussed in a sociological context. This context tends to regard definite models as part of the "operationalization" of theories that are framed and discussed in intuitive language. Our image of the structure of theory, by contrast, places models as intrinsic to the theoretical analysis and not as after-the-analysis operationalizations of informally developed ideas. The corresponding logic of explanation then is modified in the direction of how inferential techniques with models function in the explanatory process. The idea that one "reads off" the empirical generalization is an example of what is intended. In other cases of explanations involving formal theoretical models, the connection between what is derived and what is observed may be less direct than the expression "read off" suggests.

As it stands, the ABX example is not a satisfying explanation from a generative or realist standpoint. What must be shown is how communication—through the change it produces in people's perceptions and feelings—*recursively generates* a changing state of the ABX system. Then, under some conditions, this process will yield one or more states of equilibrium. Such a state is balanced, and it is the system state from which we "read off" the empirical generalization. The model objects— the signed graphs and the mathematical representation of the processual transformation of such graphs—are thereby the crucial entities in the theoretical model that would account for the generalization. (At the present time, while it is not hard to show how the generalization corresponds to the balanced state, we do not have a process model that generates such balanced states as derived equilibria.)

In general, then, scientific *realism* demands that observable properties or regularities be generated from some sort of formal model that represents how a system of interacting entities is constituted. What the *positivist* wants is that the particular theoretical model that formulates the generative mechanism be an instance of a more general pattern to be expected under the given circumstances. And this demand is quite as important in formulating a philosophical model of explanation as the scientific realist's call for generativity. In short, in an integrated philosophy of explanation, we formulate a *dual ideal*: to specify generative mechanisms in terms of recursive process models and to derive such generative mechanisms within a more general framework. (Much more can be said about generativity, but see Fararo [1987b], for such extended discussion.)

Our integrative philosophy of theory structure and our integrative philosophy of explanation meet here (as shown in Figure 1). *The representation principle level of theory structure defines a kind of template for an unlimited number of explanatory models of the generative type.* The birth-and-death template of demography does this; so does the supply-and-demand template of economics; so does the force-acceleration template of classical mechanics. In all these and analogous instances, theorists frame comprehensive representation principles leading to templates. Such a template enables the construction of an unlimited number of explanatory theoretical models satisfying the template and depending upon the circumstances to which the theory is applied. Each particular theoretical model is really a family of models, since it will be expressed in terms of parametric variables corresponding to sets of possible conditions in which the referent system may exist. So each theoretical model will have some general properties, and their deduction is an essential feature of theoretical activity.

The Proper Analytic Focus for General Theoretical Sociology

The proper analytic focus for general theoretical sociology emerges from a consideration of the problem of holism and methodological individualism in the philosophy of theoretical sociology. It is a focus on social structures: their emergence and form, their maintenance, their comparison, and their change. This focus on social structures means that all questions and all answers are in relation to the entity that features the emergent or sustained structure—an entity best thought of as a network of interacting units. Or, as Mayhew (1980: 338) put it, "[A communication] network, the interaction which proceeds through it, and the social structures which emerge in it are the subject matter of sociology."

The holistic element of this focus on social structures is the concern with the dynamic transformations of a social network. It is properties of the whole (the network) whose stability or change is scientifically problematic: how a certain structural pattern characterizing the interaction system—not the units interacting—is maintained or altered. Yet, if we ask in detail about the generator of the process, we find that we are ultimately asking how the nodes in the communication network act and react relative to each other, either because the structure of interest is defined in terms of a pattern in their action and reaction or because the maintenance/stability of a structure depends on nodal activity. Hence every intelligible theoretical system in sociology requires grounding in some principle of action that governs the activity of the nodes in the network. This constitutes the element of methodological individualism in the analytic focus on social structures.

Some name is needed for the strategy of formulating theory structures that contain *both* methodological individualism and holism in one framework. In a recent book, Fararo (1989a) used the name *generative structur-*

alism to describe the general position of which this strategy is a component. The term "generative" refers to the behavior of actors, the term "structuralism" refers to the analytic focus on the system, the network of interacting units and the structures that their interactions produce or reproduce. The guiding principle for theory construction is that the basic nature of any group process resides in how networks of relations differentially affect information and other input to nodes and in how these similarly endowed nodes respond to the input in ways that sustain or alter the outcomes of the group process.

If actors obey the rational choice principle, we are close to the viewpoint expressed by Coleman and by Wippler and Lindenberg in their contributions to a recent collection of papers on the macro-micro linkage (Alexander et al. 1987). Other action principles are possible. For instance, actors can be endowed with the capability of executing production systems whose processes involve explicitly represented symbolic structures (actor know-how in latent form). Then, institutionalized social action turns out to be much like a language: an infinite set of distinct behavior sequences each of which is well formed in a socially normative sense (Skvoretz 1984). Thus, multiple frameworks based on distinct modes of representation can achieve the objective of generative structuralism. We return to the problems and methods of theoretical integration starting from a rational action foundation in the third part of this paper.

Theoretical Integration in the Comprehensive Mode

For more than a decade, our joint work has involved at least three efforts at theoretical integration in the comprehensive mode. The first and most long-standing of these efforts concerns what we may call the theory of institutionalized social action. This is the most complex and, although potentially the most theoretically significant, the most difficult to describe in a compact way. Thus, we confine ourselves to a few brief remarks. The fundamental idea is to treat conceptual totalities of "normal forms" of social interaction as generated by systems of "production rules" which are distributed in modules to distinct types of actors. In spirit and in technique, the work draws upon the tradition of modern cognitive science (Axten and Fararo 1977). But in sociological content, its integrative thrust has been reflected in the connections made to Parsonian action theory (Fararo and Skvoretz 1984; Skvoretz and Fararo 1989), to the social networks tradition (Fararo and Skvoretz 1986a), to affect control theory (Skvoretz and Fararo 1989), and to a variety of "interpretive sociologies," including reality construction theory, ethnomethodology, symbolic interactionism, and structuration theory (Fararo

1989a: ch. 3). This work exhibits what may be a distinguishable mode of integration, which we might call the conceptual mode. The very concept of institution, as the core of social reality and with its centrality to social structure, is what is mapped onto a formal mode of representation. Yet, the work is very much in its infancy, and uncertainty exists as to the likely achievement of its programmatic aims. Hence, having mentioned it as one of our key efforts, we move on to our two other examples.

Both are efforts that illustrate the bridging or linking of subtraditions within the general comprehensive tradition of theoretical sociology. These are not examples of unification of theories within a single research program, and so more difficult issues are raised—for instance, how is it possible to unify two frameworks that differ or even contradict each other at the presuppositional level? The general character of these two episodes of unification is shown in Figure 2.

The first case is an example of the development of *integrative theoretical methods*: Fararo and Skvoretz's (1986b) E-state structuralism, which unites network analysis and expectation states theory. The method is integrative in that it links a construct and a theoretic procedure of one subtradition to the presuppositional basis and methods of a second subtradition. It shows how a system model can be derived from an actor-situation model so as to define a social generating process whose derived equilibrium states correspond to certain social structures. In short, it implements the generative structuralism approach.

The first step in the integration is to take the abstract form of expectation states theory and express it generatively. In a simplified notation, let E be the actor's expectation state; let I be some information input to the actor and B the actor's observed behavior. The recursive generativity of the actor's state (E) and the behavior (B) may be expressed by

$$B = f(E, I)$$
$$E' = g(E, I).$$

The first expression states that the current behavior is a function of the actor's expectation state and information input, in a given situation. The second expression says that the information input, given the situation and the current state E, transforms the expectation state. The recursive character of the process is shown when we subscript with respect to time with zero as the initial time:

$$B_0 = f(E_0, I_0)$$
$$B_1 = f(E_1, I_1) = f(g(E_0, I_0), I_1)$$
$$B_2 = f(E_2, I_2) = f(g(E_1, I_1), I_2) = f(g(g(E_0, I_0), I_1), I_2).$$

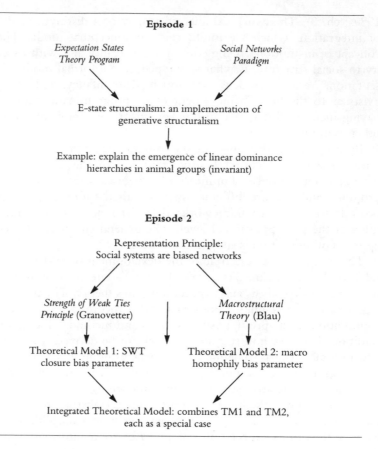

Fig. 2. Integration in the comprehensive mode: Two episodes.

Thus the recursion implies a specific form of dependence of B_2 on the initial expectation state and on the information input up to time 2:

$$B_2 = F_2(E_0, I_0, I_1, I_2).$$

Similarly, for any time t, the behavior function is given by

$$B_t = F_t(E_0, I_0, I_1 \ldots, I_t),$$

which says that the current behavior is a function of the initial expectation and the complete history of information inputs since the initial time. What the initial expectation state does is sum up the prior history of situational information processing: all actors whose past experience led them to the same state are equivalent as far as the theoretical model is concerned. In this way, the theory takes the form of a state space approach (Fararo 1973: ch. 8)—recursive state transformations take place "in the small" in the sense of a transition between t and $t + 1$. For any t, the final equation shows the "long-range" consequence and the dependence of the outcome on the whole history of inputs.

E-state structuralism takes this generic picture of the individual unit in a situation and embeds it in a network of interacting units that are generating or regenerating social structure. The information inputs become related to the behaviors of other units. The E-state aspect is the individualist element with the analytical object of interest being the social system of interaction. The *system state*, as contrasted with the actor's E-state, is a pattern of E-state relations (represented in a matrix or graph).

For instance, in Fararo and Skvoretz (1986b) the system is a triad of interacting units where the interactions involve attacks or functionally equivalent threat symbolism. The initial system state is "no structure," in the sense that E-states—and so relations between them—are not yet defined. The objective is to show how E-states emerge and the patterns among them are transformed in interaction such that a stable hierarchy occurs with a definite probability. For any given dyadic interaction, the third party is a bystander. An implied consequence of the action-situation model is that the bystander's E-state can change as a result of observing the others interact. The problem for the structuralist part of the theory is to show how such a bystander element enters into the generative process which yields one or another type of emergent social structure.

In particular, starting from the "invariant" that animal encounters give rise to dominance hierarchies, the theoretical model—not the generic E-state theoretical procedure—has as its aim the generation of the equilibrium forms of dominance. Indeed, the structural model, which is derived from axioms about the actor-situation E-states and encounters with a bystander effect, shows that, for the triad, the probability is extremely high that a linear hierarchy will be observed while a cycle of dominance relations has only a very small probability of occurrence. Here a dominance relation is defined in terms of a conjunction of E-states, "ready-to-dominate" and "ready-to-be-dominated." In short, the model generatively explains a known empirical generalization of cross-species type. The same method can underlie the richer theories of expectation states that treat human interactions. The complexity of E-states depends on the capabilities of the species whose social structures are of interest. Human capacities for speech and for implied self-indications mean that E-states become complexes of self-other expectations in the sense stressed by a variety of theorists. In this way, the E-state method can be employed in cross-species models and allow a more generalized sociology to emerge from a conjunction of theory and research.

In relation to the four levels of theory structure, this example is an instance of work at the theoretical model level. The representation principle involves E-states and networks, and the invariants include the emergence of linear hierarchies of dominance in animal groups. The critical importance of developing a theoretical model is also illustrated in the next effort we discuss.

Research traditions can be bridged when theories in distinct frameworks can be integrated. Fararo and Skvoretz (1987) offer an example in which a theoretical method (biased networks) is used (a) to formalize a theory in the social network tradition, Granovetter's (1973) weak ties theory; (b) to formalize a theory in the macrostructural tradition, Blau's (1977) differentiation theory; and then (c) to construct a third theoretical model that formally links the first two and captures them as special cases. It is interesting to note that this episode of theoretical integration represents a fourth type of integration not discussed by Wagner and Berger (1985). In this fourth type, theories with different explanatory domains and different principles of explanation are consolidated under one conceptual "umbrella." Wagner and Berger's integration of variants and integration of competitors refer to the unification of theories which have the same explanatory focus; the third type, integration of proliferants, refers to unification of theories created by extending the explanatory ideas of one of them to a new problem or data base. Following Fararo (1989a: 149f) and Merton (1968), we call this type "integration by consolidation."

The essential interest of this case is the common representation principle without which the integration could not proceed. The principle is that social systems are biased networks. A network is described in probabilistic terms but is only a "random net" when the social structural "biases" are not present. The bias parameters are of various types, but two are important to the integration. One, the homophily bias, relates to the common empirical finding that actors' associations tend to be (at a greater than chance level) with those like themselves on relevant social dimensions. It makes more probable than chance that a relationship will be between persons in the same group or stratum. The other bias parameter applies to triads and is called the closure bias. It makes more probable than chance that two actors who are each known by a third will themselves be acquainted.

The homophily bias relates to what Blau (1977) calls the salience of a dimension of social differentiation. The closure bias relates to what Granovetter (1973) treats as a probability-one idealization: two persons strongly tied to a third will become linked. When we relax the idealization, we obtain Granovetter's basic theory in quantitative form, and, similarly, the biased network concept permits a formal representation of Blau's theory. The common image emphasizes differentiation of ties into strong and weak and differentiation of nodes by group or status membership as both features impact simultaneously and concrescently on the formation and location of ties between nodes. The key step in the unification of the two subtraditions is the construction of theoretical models that specify in detail the means or mechanisms through which the effects postulated by the two theories come about. As we have said elsewhere:

The task is to find the fundamental, nonrandom aspects of social structure to which the theories refer and represent them by appropriate bias parameters. . . . A natural consequence is consistency in the formalizations, and this, in turn, creates the possibility for their articulation as one unified theory. Given two theories, or principles, T and T', their unification proceeds by their formalization in terms of corresponding bias models B and B' and then the creation of a third model B", which subsumes both B and B' and has the property that both B and B' are special cases. (Fararo and Skvoretz 1987: 1188f)

Thus we arrive at a position to guide our unification efforts in the next section. At the level of *general presuppositions*, our commitment is to the strategy of generative structuralism. But this idea can be implemented at the *representation level* in various ways. We need a good template for building to the next level, that of theoretical models, within the group process research traditions. The models will be instantiated forms of the template. Various simple properties that can be derived from them suggest possible invariants. But, just as important for purposes of unification, these models serve as the piers for the integrative bridge. In the next section we pursue the idea that the representation principle that action is adaptively rational can provide the common framework.

Rational Action Theoretical Models
in Group Process Research Programs

To say that "action is adaptively rational" when the process emphasis of generative structuralism is presupposed is, in the general case, to envision a recursive process in which an actor adapts to a changing situation of action, each change of action depending on the actor's values (or preferences) and the structure of alternatives given in the situation. In the case of social generativity, two or more actors are each behaving in accordance with some specific form of the adaptive action principle, and one problem is to formulate the general form of interaction of such actors—the basic template for further specification. Two basic variants of the adaptively rational action principle exist in the literature. In the first type the principle is that action changes in accordance with the sanction signification of outcomes, as found in the Homans-Emerson tradition and its behavioral basis. In the second type, the fundamental representation principle involves the conception of dynamic utility.

The first principle has recently been given formal exposition by Fararo (1989a: ch. 3), using the operator model proposed by Bush and Mosteller (1955). The actor's state is a vector of probabilistic dispositions over alternatives, and outcomes depend jointly on the actor's choice and on a situational response. When a reward occurs—an outcome favorable from the actor's standpoint—the probabilistic disposition of the action that led to it is increased and the disposition probabilities of the alternatives are correspondingly decreased. Similarly, outcomes that count as punishments reduce the disposition probability of the action that led to them and increase the probabilities of the alternatives. At the level of the general action principle, the abstract form is

$$\mathbf{p}' = T(\mathbf{p}, x),$$

where T is an "operator" that transforms the disposition vector $\mathbf{p}$ given the outcome x, defined by the conjunction of the actor's choice and the situational response into the new disposition vector $\mathbf{p}'$. (In the particular form used in Fararo [1989a], the operators are linear.) The template for social generativity follows directly by generalization in which the state of each actor is a probability vector, each outcome is defined by the conjunction of their actions and residual situational response, and each vector is transformed depending on the outcome.

Formally, let $\mathbf{S}$ be the matrix of the $\mathbf{p}$ vectors and let x represent the list of outcomes defined by joint actions and situation response. Then social generativity is given by

$$\mathbf{S}' = T(\mathbf{S}, x).$$

Here T transforms a matrix into a new matrix. As in the general actor-situation model, a recursive generativity is implied at the social level. When the T relation between $\mathbf{S}$ and $\mathbf{S}'$ is linear, the social template becomes more definite, and particular models can be specified and consequences derived. For instance, in Fararo (1989a), the iterated two-person prisoner's dilemma is modeled with eight linear operators to represent the dynamics of adaptation of each actor's dispositions to the other's actions, and of special interest, of course, is possible convergence on the cooperative solution.

The second type of rational action principle also holds that an actor's choice of an action influences outcomes over which preferences are held. It introduces the idea that in a small interval of time, the action is chosen so as to increase the utility of the anticipated outcome relative to the most recent outcome. The actor climbs a gradient. Utility refers to a numerical representation of an actor's preferences over the domain of outcomes, each of which depends on the actor's action and on other factors. For a continuous time and continuous space case, the abstract form of this principle is

$$dx/dt = \partial u(x, y, \ldots)/\partial x.$$

Here u is the utility of the outcome $(x, y, \ldots)$ for the actor, and variable x ranges over a domain from which the actor makes a choice. In words, in a small interval of time dt, the change dx is chosen so as to move upward in utility, subject to constraints. In most cases, the overall utility of any outcome for an actor may be analyzed as the difference between the benefits and the costs, each expressed in utility terms. Hence, the term dx may be positive or negative, depending upon the difference between the marginal benefit and the marginal cost. Thus, although "more is better" often describes the domain of x, in some cases the costs attaching to "more" may make it rational to choose "less." In other words, dx becomes negative when the marginal cost exceeds the marginal benefit: this is implied by the dynamic utility representation. Also, an equilibrium point for the dx/dt process is one at which the marginal benefit equals the marginal cost.

In the social template, each actor controls a domain, and the form becomes a coupled system as in, for two persons,

$$dx/dt = \partial u(x, y, \ldots)/\partial x$$
$$dy/dt = \partial v(x, y, \ldots)/\partial y.$$

The second actor controls y, and the utility to him/her of the outcome corresponding to the joint action (x, y) plus additional factors is $v(x, y, \ldots)$.

The movement process continues until a local maximum is reached where each actor is "satisfied," that is, can do no better, given the situation. At that point, the gradient is zero. But in the social template, such a point of relative satisfaction must be the same for all parties. In the two-person case,

$$\partial u(x, y, \ldots)/\partial x = \partial v(x, y, \ldots)/\partial y = 0$$

at the joint action (x, y) and under specific additional conditions. An outstanding example of this form of adaptively rational action has been proposed by Rapoport (1960: ch. 4) to study production and exchange. His model yields three types of outcome. Depending on the parametric con-

ditions, there is (a) no production and no exchange, (b) cooperative production and mutual exchange, or (c) exploitative production with one
producer who gives up part of his or her product to the other. The third
outcome arises when the point of joint exchange is unstable, so the dynamic utility process takes the system state to a boundary on one of the
two axes (where the initial state determines which axis and so who is
exploited).

To sum up this type of theory structure for implementing the idea of
adaptively rational action, we note that the general action principle takes
the form of gradient dynamics. In a small time interval, the actor changes
action in the direction of increasing utility under given conditions. The
actor adjusts to these conditions, which include the choices made by
other actors, by choosing to improve the situation within those constraints. When a number of actors are considered in the same situation of
action, then each provides conditions for the others and the outcome
reflects their mutual rational adjustment processes.

Let us now consider some of the research programs treating group
processes from the standpoint that actors are adaptively rational. Moreover, let us see if we can formulate those processes in a way that illumi-
nates their relationship to the above discussions of the social templates
for adaptively rational action. It may not be possible to set up an exact
correspondence, but the work to follow is informed by the ideal of setting out theoretical models in which (a) each actor is adaptively rational
in a sense that is specific enough to define a model at the individual level
and (b) through the coupling of such models of actors, the social interactions and their outcomes are recursively generated. In addition to this
ideal of theoretical adequacy, we also aim for empirical adequacy—
theoretical models that account tolerably well for the major findings in a
research program. Because of space limits, remarks here are necessarily
brief but, it is hoped, sufficient to give the reader a sense of the empirical
adequacy of the various models.

Programs we consider include the power dependence and negotiation
research programs (Lawler and Ford; Cook, Molm, and Yamagishi; and
Willer and Markovsky) and the legitimation, justice equity, and status
expectations research programs (Walker and Zelditch; Jasso; and Berger
and colleagues). The first set contains programs for which "resistance
theory" (Heckathorn 1980) provides a suitable framework for integration. The second set contains programs that focus more on collective
problems of action, problems where outcomes are sought from which
all benefit.

The suitability of the rational action principle for both types of programs should come as no surprise. In each program, there are actual or

implied payoffs that "drive" the action or the actors' choices. Further, analysis based on adaptively rational action is common in the bargaining and negotiation literature. Also, rational action frameworks have been creatively applied to collective-good problems (Oliver and Marwell 1988; Marwell, Oliver, and Prahl 1988) and to the generation of solidarity (Hechter 1987, 1989). We cannot treat in detail all group process research programs. But even those we overlook should be amenable to a process of integration founded on the adaptively rational action template.

We begin our integrative episode with the programs in which the concept of an actor's "resistance" to particular outcomes is a key determinative factor in driving negotiations. While resistance theory is not completely satisfactory in ways we will point out, it does approximate our aim of recursive generativity in how it can be deployed to describe the bargaining/negotiation processes that are at the heart of these research programs.

Resistance Theory

Our presentation of resistance follows Heckathorn (1980). The key concept is an actor's resistance to an outcome. It is expressed as a function of three variables: the payoffs from that outcome, the actor's best hope outcome, and what is termed the "conflict" outcome. In the bargaining context, both the best hope and the conflict outcomes have a precise technical meaning. The conflict outcome is the outcome reached in the absence of cooperation from others. In the two-person bargaining case, the conflict outcome results from failure to reach an agreement. Any outcome that yields payoffs just as good as or better than the conflict outcome is said to be in the "contract zone." Then an actor's best hope is the outcome in the contract zone that yields his or her maximum payoff.

As an illustration, consider the classic experimental paradigms of Cook and colleagues and Willer and colleagues. In these experiments, dyads negotiate over the division of a fixed pool of payoff points, receiving nothing if they cannot agree, but if they agree, they receive the shares agreed upon. Each point translates into a small amount of money, and subjects may or may not know one another's "payoff schedule." There is a tendency in these programs to use directly the raw payoff points or the equivalent monetary amounts as measures of the "utility" a subject receives from an outcome. For basic theoretical work, this tendency *must be avoided* because it leads to enormous confusion about whether invalid interpersonal comparisons of utility are being made (Emerson et al. 1983; Heckathorn 1983b). Consequently, we present the resistance concept in terms of the utilities of outcomes $(x, M - x)$, where x refers to the points A receives and $M - x$ the points that B receives. Failure to agree results in the outcome $(0,0)$.

Formally, let $u(x, M - x)$ be the utility to person A from $(x, M - x)$. Player A's best hope is $(M, 0)$, which has utility u_{max}. The conflict outcome is $(0,0)$, which has utility u_{min}. The resistance of person A to outcome $(x, M - x)$ is defined as

$$R_A(x, M - x) = [u_{max} - u(x, M - x)]/[u_{max} - u_{min}].$$

This is an application of Heckathorn's (1980) definition. Clearly, as $u(x, M - x)$ approaches u_{max} the resistance of person A to outcome $(x, M - x)$ declines to zero, and as it approaches u_{min} resistance increases to unity. A similar definition, in which, in our terms, u_{max} in the denominator is replaced by $u(x, M - x)$, is offered by Willer (1981, 1987). Under the assumption that A's preference order over the pure outcomes and over gambles of pure outcomes satisfies the von Neumann and Morgenstern (1947) axioms, u is unique up to linear transformations, $u'(x, M - x) = \alpha u(x, M - x) + \beta$. If all u values are so transformed and a new resistance value calculated, it is easy to see that $R'_A(x, M - x) = R_A(x, M - x)$, that is, an actor's resistance to a particular outcome is invariant under linear transformations of utility. A similar expression for person B's resistance uses v to indicate B's utility function:

$$R_B(x, M - x) = [v_{max} - v(x, M - x)]/[v_{max} - v_{min}]$$

In the payoff point division experiments, the $(M,0)$ outcome maximizes u while on the v-scale it ranks equal to $(0,0)$ outcome, which minimizes v. The $(0,M)$ outcome maximizes v but on the u-scale ranks equal to $(0,0)$ outcome, which minimizes u.

According to Heckathorn (1980), resistance operates as follows. An outcome is identified with a particular division of the pool, and a particular outcome occurs if both parties agree to it. Agreements which do not exhaust the pool can be eliminated from consideration if we assume that subjects always behave with Pareto optimality. The likelihood of agreement is governed by the resistance of each actor—outcomes with high resistances are more unlikely to be agreed to than outcomes with low resistances. But generally outcomes to which one party has little resistance are outcomes to which the other has much resistance. More to the point of recursive generativity, however, resistance is held to govern the process of concession by which agreement is (contingently) achieved. In idealized terms, a negotiation is a sequence of proposed divisions which can either terminate in an agreement or in $(0,0)$ if time runs out. Heckathorn (1980) proposes that the player with the lower resistance to the current proposal makes the next concession (when a next one occurs), and when resistances are equal and minimal, agreement occurs. Minimality is guaranteed if divisions that do not exhaust the pool are ignored. The occurrence of agreement (in full information conditions) when resistances are equal is called the *Principle of Equiresistance*. Agreement occurs on an outcome $(x^*, M - x^*)$ such that

$$R_A(x^*, M - x^*) = [u_{max} - u(x^*, M - x^*)]/[u_{max} - u_{min}]$$

$$= [v_{max} - v(x^*, M - x^*)]/[v_{max} - v_{min}]$$

$$= R_B(x^*, M - x^*).$$

How does this formulation relate to the social templates of adaptive rational action? Clearly, actors are coupled through their reactions to the current proposals. Since it is the actor of lower resistance who is hypothesized to be more likely to offer a concession and since a concession is an offer to which this actor is more resistant, the offer of a division has *lower* utility to him or her than the current offer. It may seem that this does not fit the dynamic utility framework in which the actor acts in a small unit of time to move upward in utility. But considering that offers and not just outcomes are involved, we would argue that the concession represents an increase in expected payoff, given the negotiator's assessment of how much the likelihood of agreement is increased. If it is increased sufficiently, the apparent loss of outcome utility can be offset and the concession becomes adaptively rational. The point here is the treatment of dynamic utility as a template which is, in itself, not empirically falsifiable. That is, apparent inconsistency only means that deeper and further consideration must be given to find the proper correspondence between situation and template. While a template can yield an interpretation of any situation, it may prove ultimately to be generally unsatisfactory and will be abandoned by a scientific community.

Note that the concession may make agreement more likely and that agreement is a reward potentially reinforcing the other's concession-making behavior. This suggests an application of the dynamic learning template. In fact, the general nature of concession making in a similar kind of experimental task (but without attention to resistance) has been modeled as a Bush-Mosteller learning process by England (1973), whose research could serve as a point of departure for a more rigorous treatment of the concession process implied by the intuitive formulation of resistance (see Skvoretz, Willer, and Fararo, 1993).

Let us sum up before we proceed. Rational choice models usually focus on specific choices in static situations. The actor has a utility function and, under the given constraints, makes a choice that maximizes utility. Our emphasis on generativity, when combined with rationality, implies the need for process representations. The situation is not static, and so the rational actor must adapt to its changes. Ideally, the notion that action is adaptively rational would be ready for application to group processes as a general and precise representation principle. It is not. Instead, we must find one or more ways to formulate it such that it is a genuine representation principle, i.e., the predicate is formal. On the one hand, the behavioral or sanction response model enables the representation of change via experience, with the change mechanism embodying the classic reinforcement idea used in learning theory. This is one meaning of adaptive rationality (March 1986: 149). On the other hand, the dynamic utility model starts with a classic utility function formulation but adds the recursion element. We have tried to embed the resistance concept in this latter context, first framing it in relation to the utility concept in this section. In what follows, we add the recursion element to obtain some first-approximation theoretical models of group processes that occur when adaptively rational actors engage in various forms of interaction.

Power, Dependence, Exclusion, and Branching

As suggested in the presentation of resistance, application to the research programs of Cook and colleagues and Willer and colleagues is straightforward, except in one very important respect. In these programs, payoff point divisions when agreement is reached are used to indicate whether a position in a network of such exchange/division relations is a position of power. A classic demonstration is that the center position in a branching structure when the peripheral alternatives are "negatively connected" (Cook and colleagues) or subject to "exclusion" (Willer and colleagues) is a position of power. The degree to which divisions favor the center differs between the experimental setup of Cook and colleagues and that of Willer and colleagues, but this is arguably a function of differences in the information environment subjects confront. The Willer format is one of open face-to-face interaction with physical barriers preventing communication where no resource division is possible. The Cook format filters offers and counteroffers through computer terminals and thus limits the knowledge subjects have of anything but their own offers to and from those to whom they are immediately connected.

The troublesome point is the formal warrant by which exchange rates are held to indicate the presence or absence of power differences. Consider two simple cases, the dyad and the branch structure. The latter consists of one central and two peripherals where the center can make one exchange. The intuitive idea is that the center is powerful in the

branch because the actor in that position is always included in any agreement, whereas peripherals are not powerful because one of them is always excluded from a bargaining round. Hence the peripherals bid to be
included by offering divisions that are increasingly favorable to the center. These intuitive dynamics do not characterize the dyad: both are either included (if agreement is reached) or excluded (if agreement is not
reached). Intuitively, for a dyad, one expects a near-equal division of the
pool to be the point of agreement. Yet it is easy to show that a reasonably
extreme division in favor of one member of the dyad is entirely possible
and consistent with the Equiresistance Principle.

Suppose the total pool to be 3 points. With the canonical von Neumann–Morgenstern utility representation, where the best hope outcome has utility 1 and the conflict outcome utility 0, let $u(2,1) = .75$,
$v(2,1) = .50$, $u(1,2) = .50$, $v(1,2) = .50$, $u(0,0) = v(0,0) = 0$, and
$u(3,0) = v(0,3) = 1$. These assignments have predictive consequences.
In particular, the two actors differ in the utility they assign to intermediate outcomes: for instance, A is indifferent to getting 1 point for sure
and a gamble of a 75 percent chance of 2 points and a 25 percent chance
of 0 points, whereas B is indifferent to getting 1 point for sure and a
gamble of a 50 percent chance of getting 2 points and a 50 percent chance
of getting 0 points. Applying equiresistance, we find that the actors are
equally resistant at the $(1,2)$ outcome. Hence, equiresistance predicts an
average division of 1 point to A and 2 points to B, apparently indicating
that B is in a more powerful position. (Note that the player who "values"
less his or her second- and third-best outcomes is more powerful as measured by advantage in raw payoff points. This observation is reminiscent
of the second "value" component in Emerson's [1972, 1987] formulation
of power dependence theory.)

This example shows that without an additional assumption about how
utilities are related to the payoff point schedule, differences in exchange
rates could merely indicate (idiosyncratic) differences in utility evaluations of outcomes rather than systematic effects of positional power differences. That additional assumption is often made when the utilities of
the outcomes are treated as linearly related to the payoff points they provide. That is, if we assume that each actor's utility function is a linear
transformation of the payoff points, then even though the specific transformation may differ from actor to actor, the Equiresistance Principle
implies agreement at a 50/50 split in the dyad and so any departure from
this equidivision would indicate power differences. But it must be
pointed out that this assumption implies there is a linear relationship between the two actors' utilities and thus that, however indirectly, interpersonal comparisons of utility are being made possible. (The same result

holds if utilities are assumed to be linear functions of the log of payoff points.) This may be a reasonable assumption for the types of experiments investigated in the dependence, bargaining, and negotiation research programs. Adopting it for the purpose of further applications and discussion gives a version we term "linear resistance theory." Further, because of the assumed linearity, utilities of both actors can be expressed directly in terms of the point payoffs without loss of generality.

Returning to the simple cases, we can easily show that linear resistance theory predicts each actor gets $M/2$ points in the dyad, where M is the pool size. To analyze the simple branch, consider the relationship between adjacent rounds as follows (Willer 1984). Let x_1 denote the points received by the central node in the first round in the exchange concluded with one of the peripherals, who receives $M - x_1$ points. The other peripheral is excluded and receives 0 points. In the second round, neither peripheral can expect to do better than the payoff earned by one of them in the first round. That is, each peripheral's best hope is no longer M for self and 0 for the center, but $M - x_1$ for self and x_1 for the center. For the peripherals, v_{max} in the second round changes from M to $M - x_1$. For the center node, it is the payoff from disagreement with any one peripheral that changes. The center made a deal in the first round for x_1, and that amount now becomes the payoff from conflict with the other peripheral, that is, for the center u_{min} is now x_1. Thus the resistance equation for the second round with actor A the center node and B a peripheral node becomes

$$R_A = [M - x_2]/[M - x_1]$$
$$= [(M - x_1) - (M - x_2)] / [(M - x_1) - 0] = R_B,$$

and solving we get $x_2 = (M + x_1)/2$. The same logic applies to the next round and then the next round. If x_n is the equiresistance offer on the nth round, the equiresistance analysis provides the following recursive relation between agreements on adjacent rounds:

$$x_n = (M + x_{n-1})/2,$$

which reaches a limit of $x = M$ rather quickly, regardless of the initial points the center has. Therefore the linear resistance theory predicts that the center eventually obtains its best hope outcome as the peripherals bid each other up.

In practical terms, of course, this prediction is incorrect because it implies that peripherals will agree to give the entire pool to the center node and accept a payoff equal to that earned from no agreement at all. However, the general tendency for rates to become more favorable to the center over time is evident in the experimental traditions of both Willer and colleagues and Cook and colleagues. Furthermore, the center's advantage tends to appear more quickly and be more extreme in the Willer experimental setup of full information than in the Cook setup of restricted information.

Power and Nonexchange Alternatives

A set of experiments related to network exchange is that by Molm (1985, 1987). Here one alternative for subjects is to exchange with their partner (who may or may not reciprocate). This exchange alternative provides a payoff to other but not to self. The second option is to choose an "individual" response, which simply results in a payoff to self. This may then be added to the payoff one gets if other has chosen the exchange response. The key dependent variable is the proportion of times a subject chooses the exchange response, and a typical experimental run manipulates the payoff of the individual response for the two subjects, creating situations of varying dependence of each on exchange for quality payoffs.

Specifically, let I_α denote α's payoff from the individual response and E_α denote α's payoff from the exchange response by other, where $\alpha = A$ or B. The payoff matrix in Molm's experiments has the form below:

		B	
		Ind	Exch
A	Ind	(I_A, I_B)	$(I_A + E_A, 0)$
	Exch	$(0, I_B + E_B)$	(E_A, E_B)

For example, in experiments reported in Molm (1985) nine experimental setups were generated by allowing I_A to be 3, 4, or 5 points; I_B was 0, 1, or 2 points; and $E_A = E_B = 4$ points. The idea was to create a grid of conditions in which both A's and B's dependence on exchange for quality outcomes varied from high to low with A always less dependent than B. In some of these conditions, the payoff structure is that of an (asymmetric) prisoner's dilemma. In these conditions, the experiment constitutes an iterative PD game, thereby suggesting the relevance of Axelrod's (1984) work on the evolution of cooperation. Space does not permit further exploration of this linkage, which is, in any event, not recognized or exploited in Molm (1985, 1987).

To analyze this setup, we assume that the subjects' choices are independent on any one round, although the level at which A chooses exchange may depend on the level at which B chooses it. Let p_α denote the probability α chooses the exchange response, where $\alpha = A$ or B. Then $p_A p_B$ is the probability both A and B choose exchange, $(1 - p_A)p_B$ is the probability A chooses individual and B exchange, $p_A(1 - p_B)$ is the probability A chooses exchange and B chooses individual, and $(1 - p_A)(1 - p_B)$ is the probability both choose exchange. We imagine that subjects are engaged in tacit bargaining, the aim of which is to settle on values for p_A and p_B. Tacit agreement on a pair of values is this context's equivalent to agreement on a division of a resource pool. The amount player A earns from a particular "agreement" is given by the payoff to A from the four outcomes as weighted by the probability of their occurrence, viz., for A, $\text{Share}_A = p_A p_B(E_A) + (1 - p_A)p_B(I_A + E_A) + p_A(1 - p_B)(0) + (1 - p_A)(1 - p_B)(I_A) = (1 - p_A)I_A + p_B E_A$, and similarly for B.

In this tacit bargaining situation, the conflict point corresponds to the pair $p_A = p_B = 0$. At this point of strictly individual action, A earns I_A and B earns I_B. Identification of best hope agreements is not as straightforward. For B the best agreement would be $p_A = 1$ and $p_B = 0$, but this pair of values is not sustainable because A's payoff is zero, strictly less than the amount A gains from the individual response. Therefore B's best hope cannot be the point of agreement that gives B his or her maximum payoff. The same argument holds for player A, except in the three conditions where B's individual response carries a zero payoff. In those conditions, A's best hope outcome is the one that yields the maximum payoff. In general, though, a player's best hope is bounded by the requirement that the other player earn as much from that pair of p_A and p_B values as he or she could from the individual response alone. As Molm puts it, the upper limit of A's power use is set by the fact that "the average value that B receives from exchange with A must be greater than the value of B's individual alternative" (1987: 107).

Graphically depicted with A's earnings on the x-axis and B's on the y-axis, payoffs reachable by some combination of p_A and p_B, the "contract zone," is a quadrilateral bounded at the upper left by $(0, I_B + E_B)$, the upper right by (E_A, E_B), the lower right by $(I_A + E_A, 0)$ and the lower left by (I_A, I_B). Only those points up and to the right of (I_A, I_B) are sustainable agreements, and those on the boundary of the quadrilateral are where the total payoff is maximized. Graphically, B's best hope is the point on the boundary intersected by a vertical through the conflict point while A's best hope is the point intersected by a horizontal through the conflict point. The exact equations for these points can be derived in terms of the various payoff values. Further, to cover Molm's nine conditions, we must consider two cases that depend on whether $E_A < I_A$.

Once the best hopes are identified and resistances equated, the resulting equation can be solved to express the dependence of p_A on p_B as a function of the various payoffs. Two expressions result:

$$p_A = \begin{cases} p_B[(E_A I_B + E_A E_B)/(I_A E_B + E_A E_B)] \text{ if } I_A \le E_A \\ p_B[(I_A I_B + E_A E_B)/(2 I_A E_B)] \text{ if } I_A > E_A. \end{cases}$$

So there is a range of possible values for p_A and p_B consistent with the linear equiresistance formulation.

Because Molm's experiments are not explicit bargaining games, implications of this formulation should be briefly indicated. First, in these experiments, power use (PU) is defined as the difference between p_B and p_A. If $I_A \le E_A$ than $\partial PU/\partial I_A > 0$ while $\partial PU/\partial I_B < 0$, but a unit change in I_B has a larger impact on power use than a unit change in I_A. In Molm's terms, increasing the dependence of the more dependent actor has a greater impact on power use than increasing the dependence of the less dependent actor (Molm 1985: 818, Hypothesis 1). If, however, $I_A > E_A$, increasing the dependence of the more dependent actor may or may not have a greater impact than increasing the dependence of the less dependent actor. Additional consequences can be inferred from the partial derivatives of PU with respect to other payoff values. Second, the above analysis can be directly applied to the data when we find the value of p_B that maximizes the fit to the observed frequencies of the various choice pairs in each of the nine conditions (in effect, a total of thirty-six cells and nine estimated parameters). Preliminary results indicate that such a fitted model provides a significant improvement over a standard baseline model of independence. These two points indicate the empirical plausibility of the resistance analysis and offer encouragement to a fuller treatment that would try to make explicit the generativity involved in attaining the predicted outcomes.

Conciliation and Concessions

The research program of Lawler and colleagues also focuses on dyadic bargaining. Manipulated variables include the dependence of each party on the partner for quality outcomes and the extent to which each party can transmit negative sanctions to the other, such sanctions taking the form of acts which "destroy" the partner's resources. Dependence is typically manipulated by altering the probability of getting a favorable agreement from an alternative "supplier" (Lawler and Bacharach 1987). This "lottery" is held only if the dyad cannot reach agreement by the fifteenth round. On each round, a subject can repeat his or her last offer, accept other's last offer, or counteroffer but always in a direction giving themselves less than their last offer (this is a concession). In addition, a fine or a warning can be sent: a warning threatens a fine, a fine reduces other's point payoff from agreement by a fixed amount. No more than five fines can be sent, and the amount of reduction each is worth varies from a minimum of 2 percent to a maximum of 18 percent. Dependent variables include the proportion of times agreement is reached before bargaining ends, the amount of concessions made (distance between the maximum payoff index for a bargainer and his or her final offer), the proportion of trials where fines are levied, and the proportion of trials where warnings are sent.

As Lawler (1989) notes, the focus of this work is less on the terms of agreement and more on the process by which negotiation proceeds, whether or not agreement is reached. One conclusion Lawler and Bacharach (1987) reach is that high total dependence in the dyad leads to greater concessions. In their setup, bargainers in effect seek agreement on a division of $M = 40$ counters with the possibility if agreement is not reached of entering a lottery in which agreement "within a favorable range on the issue continuum" with a hypothetical other can occur. In the high dependence state, such agreement is not very likely for both parties (25 percent in the equal dependence condition and 40 percent and 10 percent in the unequal condition), whereas in the low dependence state, it is (75 percent in the equal condition and 90 percent and 60 percent in the unequal condition). Consider the two equal conditions and assume agreement "within a favorable range" translates into a payoff of $M/2$ (or some fixed quantity greater than this amount). In the high dependence condition, therefore, $u_{min} = .25(M/2)$ while in the low dependence condition $u_{min} = .75(M/2)$. Consider outcome $(x, M - x)$, then it is obvious that A's resistance to this alternative is higher in the low dependence condition than in the high dependence condition:

$$R_L = [M - x]/[M - .75(M/2)]$$
$$\geq [M - x]/[M - .25(M/2)] = R_H.$$

For instance, with $M = 40$ and $x = 20$, $R_L = .80$ while $R_H = .57$. For the same numerical example, the resistances to this alternative in the unequal cases are .91 and .71 in the low dependence case and .63 and .53 in the high dependence case. More important, the averages in the unequal conditions are nearly identical to resistances in the equal conditions, and thus the same concession behavior is predicted in the equal and unequal conditions when the concessions of the two parties are averaged (as is done in published reports). This fits well with the findings of Lawler and Bacharach.

In the matter of the coercive potential of fines, the reduction of point values reduces the payoff from all outcomes by a constant proportion. (It is unclear if a fine reduces the payoff from the lottery as well, and we assume it does not.) Let k be the proportionate reduction factor. The resistance equation becomes

$$R = [(1 - k)M - (1 - k)x]/[(1 - k)M - q(M/2)],$$

and differentiating with respect to k yields

$$dR/dk = [q(M/2)(M - x)]/[(1 - k)M - q(M/2)]^2,$$

which is positive. Therefore, fines increase resistance to a particular offer and thus should be negatively related to concessions. Again this fits with Lawler and Bacharach's findings. However, other aspects of their research require further study in terms of the rational action formulation.

Summary on Resistance Formulations

Key points of the dependence, power, bargaining, and concession research programs can be interpreted with a linear version of resistance theory. That version, though, must make a strong assumption in order that payoff point differences be interpretable as something more than idiosyncratic differences in utility evaluations. Of course, in the experimental setups, "control" groups can be used to assure the interpretability of exchange rate differences between conditions, but no matter how many results of this sort are amassed, an adequate, formal, and generative account cannot be produced without careful attention to the utility problem. At the same time, it would be desirable to derive, rather than simply postulate, the Equiresistance Principle from a fully generative understanding of the negotiation process. In the other research programs we examine, the specific ideas of resistance play no role, but the general rational action framework still applies.

Legitimation and Equity

In the research of Walker, Zelditch, and colleagues, the effects of legitimacy on collective action in the context of inequitable structures of reward are the principal focus of interest. The major finding is that "collective protest (and protest of all kinds) is reduced significantly when an inequitable structure is valid" (Walker, Rogers, and Zelditch 1988: 216). A valid structure is one legitimated by powerful others: the experimental context uses a wheel structure for problem solving—one central actor and four peripherals—and in the validity manipulation subjects are told that the wheel structure is important for scientific purposes. Inequity occurs because a bonus is given to the subject who first solves a problem requiring communication among all subjects each of whom has a piece of the puzzle. The central actor is in the position to always solve the puzzle first. Collective action takes the form of a proposal to add a communication link to the wheel structure, thus opening the possibility of someone other than the central actor solving the puzzle first. Adoption of the proposal requires a vote by team members. However, adding a link changes the communication structure from the wheel and in the validated condition violates the experimenter's legitimation of that structure as essential for scientific purposes.

The terminology suggests the applicability of collective action versions of the rational action model—in particular, the approach set out by Marwell, Oliver, and Prahl (1988). In their terms, each actor benefits from the collective action if it is successful. The size of the benefit to actor i is denoted by I_i. Each actor also has a level of resources that can be spent in pursuit of the collective action, denoted r_i and referring to the cost of pursuing the collective action. The likelihood that the action is successful is denoted by p. Marwell, Oliver, and Prahl (1988) assume that the likelihood of successful action depends on the amount of resources contributed to it. It is further assumed that a single individual cannot unilaterally provide the benefit. In present circumstances, the collective action is successful only if a majority of the five vote to add the link. A single individual can never provide the collective benefit by himself or herself. Let q_i denote the probability of a "yes" vote by person i on a change proposal. We assume that q_i is an inverse function of the (perceived) cost of attempting the change. That is, the more costly the "yes" vote is perceived to be, the less likely it is to be forthcoming. For the sake of definiteness, let $q_i = 1 - r_i$ and thereby assume that resource cost is scaled on a normalized 0-to-1 scale.

We can interpret the effects of legitimation as follows. To simplify, we assume that the benefits from and the costs of collective action do not differ from person to person. A subject is likely to propose a change only if the expected gain from attempting the change exceeds zero. The expected payoff is given by $p(I - r) - (1 - p)r$. The cost r is expended whether or not the action is successful and the benefit I gained only if it is successful. In other words, change is likely to be proposed only if pI exceeds the cost expended in the effort, r. The probability of a successful action is the probability that a majority vote in favor, that is, that 3 or more subjects vote in favor. Under independence, this probability p is given by

$$\binom{5}{5}q^5 + \binom{5}{4}q^4(1 - q) + \binom{5}{3}q^3(1 - q)^2$$

which reduces to

$$6q^5 - 15q^4 + 10q^3.$$

A protest action is more likely the greater the difference between pI and r. This difference is, substituting $1 - r$ for q,

$$\Delta = (6(1 - r)^5 - 15(1 - r)^4 + 10(1 - r)^3)I - r$$

and differentiating with respect to r yields

$$d\Delta/dr = -30(1 - r)^4 + 60(1 - r)^3 - 30(1 - r)^2 I - 1$$
$$= -30(1 - r)^2 r^2 I - 1,$$

which is less than zero for all values of I. In the legitimated condition, the protest action violates experimenter legitimation and thus incurs a "cost" that must be borne, a cost that can be avoided in the nonlegitimated structure. Each actor sees this cost as reducing the likelihood others will vote positively and thereby reduces the expected "profit" from the protest action and also the probability that the action is even initiated. In other words, validation reduces protest action by reducing the perceived probability that others will vote in favor of the protest action, a conclusion entirely consistent with the findings of Walker, Zelditch, and colleagues.

The connection to rational action and the problem of collective action suggests some additional areas for research. Oliver and Marwell (1988) examine how group size affects collective action, Marwell, Oliver, and Prahl (1988) how network structure influences collective action. Both extensions in the context of legitimation are worth pursuing, especially the latter, since it begins to forge the structuralism side to the generative structuralism approach to this research program. On the former topic, a comparison of simple examples suggests the relationship is not obvious. Consider 3- and 5-person groups and let $I = 10$. Then when $r = .8$, the expected payoff from protest, $pI - r$, is greater in the smaller group (.24 in the 3-person group versus $-.22$ in the 5-person group) and therefore the prediction is that legitimated structures are more likely to be the target of protest in the smaller group. But when $r = .2$, the expected payoff from protest is greater in the 5-person group than in the 3-person group (9.22 versus 8.76), and so the expectation is reversed: protest is more likely in larger groups. That is, *the lower the degree of legitimation, the more likely it becomes that protest increases with increasing group size.*

Distributive Justice

The work of Jasso (1988) on distributive justice clearly falls within the purview of adaptively rational action. Its distinctiveness arises from its identification of relevant payoffs to outcomes with the justice evaluations of those outcomes: choice of alternative is still governed by the maximization of payoff. For instance, consider her derivation that insider theft is preferred to outsider theft. Let x be the quantity of the good initially held, S the total amount of the good in the group, N the size of the group, and ϕ the individual specific parameter of proportionality. Then the initial justice evaluation is $ln[xN/\phi S]$. Let t be the amount stolen, so the thief's share is now $x + t$. If it is taken from an insider, then the total amount of the good does not change and so the new justice evaluation is $ln[(x + t)N/\phi S]$, whereas if it is taken from an outsider, then the total amount does change and the new justice evaluation is $ln[(x + t)N/\phi (S + t)]$. Clearly, the first is greater than the second and so "a person will prefer to steal from a fellow group member rather than from an outsider" (Jasso 1988: 14). Note that if one considers only the direct pay-offs, the two alternatives are not distinguishable, since they both increase the thief's holdings by the same amount.

Yet there remain unexploited opportunities in this formulation. The justice evaluation, in general, is given by

$$J = ln(A) - ln(C),$$

where A is actual holding and C is comparison holding. Having actors "choose" actions that lead to higher justice evaluations is to have them prefer an unjust situation (in their favor) to a just one. But if justice is valued, there should be a tendency to choose alternatives that move in the direction of $J = 0$. More conceptually, one element in an actor's to-tal utility function is a justice component. Then doing better for oneself in the sense of getting more A is one mechanism governing choice of action while attaining justice in terms of closing the distance to the com-parison holding is another. These two may pull in opposite directions or in the same direction, producing dynamic movement through utility space via the choice of actions, yielding an instantiation of the dynamic utility template.

The J function provides a self-oriented measure for each level of A but does not measure the actor's orientation to the entire distribution. One's position in the distribution may be evaluated as "just," yet the entire distribution may be viewed as unjust. One way to form such a summary judgment is to let the system justice evaluation be an average of the in-dividual justice evaluations, weighted by the concern that the actor feels for various others. The system pattern of concern can be summarized by a matrix. Action could be oriented to changes in system evaluation to-ward more overall just configurations. Patterns of network ties that re-strict concern for others could be proposed and their consequence for redistributive system level actions assessed.

Conclusions

We stressed at the outset that unification is a recursive process in which the outcome of any one integrative episode may enter into further such episodes. In the first part we discussed the key ideas of representation principle and of generativity. These ideas are combined when the representation principle defines a framework within which dynamic theoretical models can be constructed. In the second part we summarized two earlier integrative episodes in what we defined as the comprehensive mode: inter-program as contrasted with intra-program theoretical integration. The third part was the start of a novel integrative episode in the comprehensive mode. We tried to pull together key aspects of a number of theoretical research programs under a common framework defined by the representation principle that action is adaptively rational. But we do not intend to imply that we have simply subsumed them as totalities. This has been only one integrative episode and "more is to be done," as is quite obvious. We mention just one point: the issue of formally synthesizing the dynamic utility and the sanction response types of models has not been treated here (but see Cross 1983).

All research programs in group process that we examined give evidence of being consistent with a general rational action modeling strategy for the development of explicit theoretical models. Our treatments of the programs have, necessarily, been sketchy, given space and time limitations. Two general points emerge. Genuine theoretical integration of the programs depends on pushing beyond the intuitive logics that drive the research agendas and attaining formal models of the situation and of the capabilities of the actor, even if these models initially are quite simple. The current state of research in the programs we have examined, by and large, takes the relational structure in which a particular process is embedded as given and is content to work out how that structure influences outcomes. With a few exceptions (Markovsky 1988; Ridgeway 1991), work is missing on how outcomes might feed back and influence the formation and maintenance of structural configurations.

We close with one final reflection on a substantial difference between intra-program integration and inter-program or comprehensive integration that relates to the sociology of science. Let us recall that theorists acquire differential status and influence through their theory productions. Intellectual leaders of theory groups can get behind intra-program theory integrations and use their influence as the basis for moving the state of the program to the more integrated level. Especially in some fields, the value commitment to integration is very strong and leaders can appeal to it. In other fields, this value commitment may be weak and there may even be a kind of reverse commitment to sheer pluralism of fundamental orientations. Especially in such fields, comprehensive integrative efforts face a dual blockage to acceptance and diffusion. On the one hand, they tend to be produced in the interstices of research groups, so that their backing by intra-group intellectual leaders is structurally problematic. On the other hand, since the value commitment to integration is weak, this creates the tendency to simply regard the integrative work as another "approach." If we think of intellectual integration as "the many becoming one," we may highlight this difference in the following somber formula that describes a likely outcome of comprehensive integration efforts in sociology: The many become one and are increased by one. The various research groups continue to work their own territory, simply ignoring an intellectual framework that might require them to alter modes of thought built into their less comprehensive frameworks. In turn, this somber situation points to the need for another type of embodiment of the spirit of unification: more frequent interaction and genuine intellectual communication among members of distinct research groups. Indeed, the conference for which this paper was prepared illustrates this needed social element as well as the more diffuse or value sense of the spirit of unification. Thus, we can conclude on the hopeful note that with sufficient attention to the requisite social and cultural conditions, comprehensive integrative efforts may play a more important role in the future of theoretical sociology.

Reference Matter

References Cited

Berger and Zelditch: Introduction

Alexander, J. C. 1982. *Theoretical Logic in Sociology*. Vol. 1, *Positivism, Presuppositions and Current Controversies*. Berkeley: University of California Press.

Alexander, J. C., and P. Colomy. 1990. "Neofunctionalism Today: Reconstructing a Theoretical Tradition." In G. Ritzer, ed., *Frontiers of Social Theory*, pp. 33–67. New York: Columbia University Press.

Berger, J., D. G. Wagner, and M. Zelditch, Jr. 1989. "Theory Growth, Social Processes, and Metatheory." In J. H. Turner, eds., *Theory Building in Sociology: Assessing Theoretical Cumulation*, pp. 19–42. Newbury Park, Calif.: Sage.

———. 1992. "A Working Strategy for Constructing Theories: State Organizing Processes." In G. Ritzer, ed., *Studies in Metatheorizing in Sociology*, pp. 107–23. Newbury Park, Calif.: Sage.

Blau, P. M. 1977. *Inequality and Heterogeneity*. New York: Free Press.

Blumer, H. 1969. "The Methodological Position of Symbolic Interactionism." In H. Blumer, *Symbolic Interactionism*, pp. 1–59. Englewood Cliffs, N.J.: Prentice-Hall.

Fararo, T. J., and J. Skvoretz. 1984. "Institutions as Production Systems." *Journal of Mathematical Sociology* 10: 117–82.

———. 1987. "Unification Research Programs: Integrating Two Structural Theories." *American Journal of Sociology* 92: 1183–1209.

Granovetter, M. 1973. "The Strength of Weak Ties." *American Journal of Sociology* 83: 1420–43.

Heckathorn, D. D. 1984. "Mathematical Theory Construction in Sociology: Analytic Power, Scope, and Descriptive Accuracy as Trade-offs." *Journal of Mathematical Sociology* 10: 295–323.

Kuhn, T. S. 1970. *The Structure of Scientific Revolutions*. 2d ed. Chicago: University of Chicago Press.

Lakatos, I. 1968. "Criticism and the Methodology of Scientific Research Programmes." *Proceedings of the Aristotelian Society* 69: 149–86.

———. 1970. "Falsification and the Methodology of Scientific Research Programmes." In I. Lakatos and A. Musgrave, eds., *Criticism and the Growth of Knowledge*, pp. 91–195. Cambridge, Eng.: Cambridge University Press.

Laudan, L. 1977. *Progress and Its Problems: Towards a Theory of Scientific Growth*. Berkeley: University of California Press.

———. 1984. *Science and Values: The Aims of Science and Their Role in Scientific Debate*. Berkeley: University of California Press.

Maines, D. R., and M. J. Molseed. 1986. "The Obsessive Discoverer's Complex and the 'Discovery' of Growth in Sociological Theory." *American Journal of Sociology* 92: 158–64.

Merton, R. K. 1968 [1949]. "Manifest and Latent Functions." In *Social Theory and Social Structure*, pp. 73–138. New York: Free Press.

Ritzer, G. 1990. "Metatheorizing in Sociology." *Sociological Forum* 5: 3–15.

Toulmin, S. 1953. *The Philosophy of Science*. London: Hutchison.

Wagner, D., and J. Berger. 1985. "Do Sociological Theories Grow?" *American Journal of Sociology* 90: 697–728.

Wagner and Berger: Status Characteristics Theory

Adams, J. S. 1965. "Inequity in Social Exchange." In L. Berkowitz, ed., *Advances in Experimental Social Psychology*, vol. 2, pp. 267–99. New York: Academic Press.

Alves, W. M., and P. H. Rossi. 1978. "Who Should Get What? Fairness Judgments of the Distribution of Earnings." *American Journal of Sociology* 84: 541–64.

Anderson, B., J. Berger, M. P. Zelditch, Jr., and B. P. Cohen. 1969. "Reactions to Inequity." *Acta Sociologica* 12: 1–12.

Bales, R. F. 1950. *Interaction Process Analysis*. Reading, Mass.: Addison-Wesley.

———. 1953. "The Equilibrium Problem in Small Groups." In T. Parsons, R. F. Bales, and E. H. Shils, eds., *Working Papers in the Theory of Action*, pp. 111–61. Glencoe, Ill.: Free Press.

———. 1970. *Personality and Interpersonal Behavior*. New York: Holt, Rinehart and Winston.

Bales, R. F., and P. Slater. 1955. "Role Differentiation in Small Decision Making Groups." In T. Parsons and R. F. Bales, eds., *Family, Socialization, and Interaction Process*, pp. 259–306. Glencoe, Ill.: Free Press.

Bales, R. F., F. L. Strodtbeck, T. M. Mills, and M. E. Roseborough. 1951. "Channels of Communication in Small Groups." *American Sociological Review* 16: 461–68.

Balkwell, J. W. 1991a. "From Expectations to Behavior: A General Translation Function." *American Sociological Review* 56: 355–69.

———. 1991b. "Status Characteristics and Social Interaction: An Assessment of Theoretical Variants." In E. J. Lawler, B. Markovsky, C. L. Ridgeway, and H. A. Walker, eds., *Advances in Group Processes*, vol. 8, pp. 135–76. Greenwich, Conn.: JAI Press.

Balkwell, J. W., J. Berger, M. Webster, Jr., M. Nelson-Kilger, and J. Cashen. 1992. "Processing Status Information." In E. J. Lawler, B. Markovsky, C. L. Ridgeway, and H. A. Walker, eds., *Advances in Group Processes*, vol. 9, pp. 1–20. Greenwich, Conn.: JAI Press.

Berger, J. 1958. "Relations Between Performance, Rewards, and Action-Opportunities in Small Groups." Ph.D. diss., Harvard University.

———. 1960. "An Investigation of Processes of Role-Specialization in Small Problem-Solving Groups." Proposal funded by the National Science Foundation (July).

———. 1974. "Expectation States Theory: A Theoretical Research Program." In

J. Berger, T. L. Conner, and M. H. Fisek, eds., *Expectation States Theory: A Theoretical Research Program*, pp. 3–22. Cambridge, Mass.: Winthrop. Reprint. Lanham, Md.: University Press of America, 1982.

———. 1988. "Directions in Expectation States Research." In M. Webster, Jr., and M. Foschi, eds., *Status Generalization: New Theory and Research*, pp. 450–74. Stanford, Calif.: Stanford University Press.

Berger, J., B. P. Cohen, and M. Zelditch, Jr. 1966. "Status Characteristics and Expectation States." In J. Berger, M. Zelditch, Jr., and B. Anderson, eds., *Sociological Theories in Progress*, vol. 1, pp. 29–46. Boston: Houghton Mifflin.

———. 1972. "Status Characteristics and Social Interaction." *American Sociological Review* 37: 241–55.

Berger, J., and T. L. Conner. 1966. "Performance Expectations and Behavior in Small Groups." Technical Report No. 18, Laboratory for Social Research, Stanford University.

———. 1969. "Performance Expectations and Behavior in Small Groups." *Acta Sociologica* 12: 186–98.

———. 1974. "Performance Expectations and Behavior in Small Groups: A Revised Formulation." In J. Berger, T. L. Conner, and M. H. Fisek, eds., *Expectation States Theory: A Theoretical Research Program*, pp. 85–109. Cambridge, Mass.: Winthrop.

Berger, J., T. L. Conner, and W. L. McKeown. 1969. "Evaluations and the Formation and Maintenance of Performance Expectations." *Human Relations* 22: 481–502.

Berger, J., and M. H. Fisek. 1969. "The Structure of the Extended Theory of Status Characteristics and Expectation States." Paper presented at the annual meeting of the West Coast Small Groups Conference, Seattle, Wash., Apr. 23.

———. 1970. "Consistent and Inconsistent Status Characteristics and the Determination of Power and Prestige Orders." *Sociometry* 33: 287–304.

Berger, J., M. H. Fisek, and P. V. Crosbie. 1970. "Multi-Characteristic Status Situations and the Determinations of Power and Prestige Orders." Technical Report No. 35, Laboratory for Social Research, Stanford University.

Berger, J., M. H. Fisek, and L. Freese. 1976. "Paths of Relevance and the Determination of Power and Prestige Orders." *Pacific Sociological Review* 19: 45–62.

Berger, J., M. H. Fisek, and R. Z. Norman. 1989. "The Evolution of Status Expectations: A Theoretical Extension." In J. Berger, M. Zelditch, Jr., and B. Anderson, eds., *Sociological Theories in Progress: New Formulations*, pp. 100–130. Newbury Park, Calif.: Sage.

Berger, J., M. H. Fisek, R. Z. Norman, and D. G. Wagner. 1985. "The Formation of Reward Expectations in Status Situations." In J. Berger and M. Zelditch, Jr., *Status, Rewards, and Influence: How Expectations Organize Behavior*, pp. 215–16. San Francisco: Jossey-Bass.

Berger, J., M. H. Fisek, R. Z. Norman, and M. Zelditch, Jr. 1977. *Status Characteristics and Social Interaction: An Expectation States Approach*. New York: Elsevier.

Berger, J., R. Z. Norman, J. W. Balkwell, and L. F. Smith. 1992. "Status Inconsistency in Task Situations: A Test of Four Status Processing Principles." *American Sociological Review*, forthcoming.

Berger, J., S. J. Rosenholtz, and M. Zelditch, Jr. 1980. "Status Organizing Processes." *Annual Review of Sociology* 6: 479–508.

Berger, J., and J. L. Snell. 1961. "A Stochastic Theory for Self-Other Expectations." Technical Report No. 1, Laboratory for Social Research, Stanford University.

Berger, J., D. G. Wagner, and M. Zelditch, Jr. 1985. "Introduction: Expectation States Theory: Review and Assessment." In J. Berger and M. Zelditch, Jr., eds., *Status, Rewards, and Influence: How Expectations Organize Behavior*, pp. 1–72. San Francisco: Jossey-Bass.

———. 1992. "A Working Strategy for Constructing Theories: State Organizing Processes." In G. Ritzer, ed., *Studies in Metatheorizing in Sociology*, pp. 107–23. Newbury Park, Calif.: Sage.

Berger, J., M. Webster, Jr., C. L. Ridgeway, and S. J. Rosenholtz. 1986. "Status Cues, Expectations, and Behavior." In E. J. Lawler, ed., *Advances in Group Processes*, vol. 3, pp. 1–22. Greenwich, Conn.: JAI Press.

Berger, J., M. Zelditch, Jr., B. Anderson, and B. P. Cohen. 1968. "Distributive Justice: A Status Value Formulation." Technical Report No. 28, Laboratory for Social Research, Stanford University.

———. 1972. "Structural Aspects of Distributive Justice: A Status Value Formulation." In J. Berger, M. Zelditch, Jr., and B. Anderson, eds., *Sociological Theories in Progress*, vol. 2, pp. 119–46. Boston: Houghton Mifflin.

Bierhoff, H. W., E. Buck, and R. Klein. 1986. "Social Context and Perceived Justice." In H. W. Bierhoff, R. L. Cohen, and J. Greenberg, eds., *Justice in Social Relations*, pp. 165–85. New York: Plenum Press.

Caudill, W. 1958. *The Psychiatric Hospital as a Small Society*. Cambridge, Mass.: Harvard University Press.

Carli, L. L. 1991. "Gender, Status, and Influence." In E. J. Lawler, B. Markovsky, C. L. Ridgeway, and H. A. Walker, eds., *Advances in Group Processes*, vol. 8, pp. 89–114. Greenwich, Conn.: JAI Press.

Cohen, B. P., J. Berger, and M. Zelditch, Jr. 1972. "Status Conceptions and Interaction: A Case Study of the Problem of Developing Cumulative Knowledge." In C. G. McClintock, ed., *Experimental Social Psychology*, pp. 449–83. New York: Holt, Rinehart and Winston.

Cohen, B. P., and X. Zhou. 1991. "Status Processes in Enduring Work Groups." *American Sociological Review* 56: 179–88.

Cohen, E. G. 1972. "Interracial Interaction Disability." *Human Relations* 25: 9–24.

———. 1982. "Expectation States and Interracial Interaction in School Settings." *Annual Review of Sociology* 8: 209–35.

Cohen, E. G., M. Lohman, K. P. Hall, and D. Lucero. 1970. "Expectation Training I: Altering the Effects of Social Status Characteristics." Technical Report No. 3, Stanford University School of Education.

Cohen, E. G., and S. Roper. 1972. "Modification of Interracial Interaction Disability: An Application of Status Characteristics Theory." *American Sociological Review* 37: 643–55.

Cohen, E. G., and S. Sharan. 1980. "Modifying Status Relations in Israeli Youth." *Journal of Cross-Cultural Psychology* 11: 364–84.

Conner, T. L. 1966. "Continual Disagreement and the Assignment of Self-Other Performance Expectations." Ph.D. diss., Stanford University.

Cook, K. S. 1970. "Analysis of a Distributive Justice Experiment: Goal Objects and Task Performance Expectations." Master's degree apprenticeship paper, Stanford University.

———. 1975. "Expectations, Evaluations, and Equity." *American Sociological Review* 40: 372–88.

Cook, K. S., R. Cronkite, and D. G. Wagner. 1974. "Laboratory for Social Research Manual for Experiments in Expectation State Theory." Laboratory for Social Research, Stanford University.

Cook, T. 1974. "Producing Equal Status Interaction Between Indian and White Boys in British Columbia: An Application of Expectation Training." Ph.D. diss., Stanford University.

Crundall, I. A., and M. Foddy. 1981. "Vicarious Exposure to a Task as a Basis of Evaluative Competence." *Social Psychology Quarterly* 44: 331–38.

Dovidio, J. F., C. E. Brown, K. Heltmann, S. L. Ellyson, and C. F. Keating. 1988. "Power Displays Between Women and Men in Discussions of Gender-Linked Tasks: A Multichannel Study." *Journal of Personality and Social Psychology* 55: 580–87.

Driskell, J. E., Jr. 1982. "Personal Characteristics and Performance Expectations." *Social Psychology Quarterly* 45: 229–37.

Driskell, J. E., Jr., B. Olmstead, and E. Salas. 1992. "Task Cues, Dominance Cues, and Influence in Task Groups." *Journal of Applied Psychology*, forthcoming.

Eskilson, A., and M. G. Wiley. 1976. "Sex Composition and Leadership in Small Groups." *Sociometry* 39: 183–94.

Fararo, T. J. 1973. "An Expectation-States Process Model." In T. J. Fararo, *Mathematical Sociology*, pp. 229–37. New York: Wiley.

Fararo, T. J., and J. Skvoretz. 1986. "E-State Structuralism: A Theoretical Method." *American Sociological Review* 51: 591–602.

Fennell, M. L., P. Barchas, E. G. Cohen, A. M. McMahon, and P. Hildebrand. 1978. "An Alternative Perspective on Sex Differences in Organizational Settings: The Process of Legitimation." *Sex Roles* 4: 589–604.

Fisek, M. H. 1968. "The Evolution of Status Structures and Interaction in Task-Oriented Discussion Groups." Ph.D. diss., Stanford University.

———. 1974. "A Model for the Evolution of Status Structures in Task-Oriented Discussion Groups." In J. Berger, T. L. Conner, and M. H. Fisek, eds., *Expectation States Theory: A Theoretical Research Program*, pp. 55–83. Cambridge, Mass.: Winthrop.

Fisek, M. H., J. Berger, and R. Z. Norman. 1991. "Participation in Heterogeneous and Homogeneous Groups: A Theoretical Integration." *American Journal of Sociology* 97: 114–42.

Fisek, M. H., R. Z. Norman, and M. Nelson-Kilger. 1992. "Status Characteristics and Expectation States Theory: *A Priori* Model Parameters and Test." *Journal of Mathematical Sociology* 16: 285–303.

Foddy, M. 1988. "Paths of Relevance and Evaluative Competence." In M. Webster, Jr., and M. Foschi, eds., *Status Generalization: New Theory and Research*, pp. 232–47. Stanford, Calif.: Stanford University Press.

Foschi, M. 1968. "Imbalance Between Expectations and Evaluations." Paper presented at the meeting of the Canadian Sociology and Anthropology Association, Calgary.

———. 1970. "Contradiction of Specific Performance Expectations: An Experiment Study." Ph.D. diss., Stanford University.

———. 1971. "Contradiction and Change of Performance Expectations." *Canadian Review of Sociology and Anthropology* 8: 205–22.

———. 1972. "On the Concept of Expectations." *Acta Sociologica* 15: 124–31.

———. 1989. "Status Characteristics, Standards, and Attributions." In J. Berger,

M. Zelditch, Jr., and B. Anderson, eds., *Sociological Theories in Progress: New Formulations*, pp. 58–72. Newbury Park, Calif.: Sage.

Foschi, M., and M. Foddy. 1988. "Standards, Performances, and the Formation of Self-Other Expectations." In M. Webster, Jr., and M. Foschi, eds., *Status Generalization: New Theory and Research*, pp. 248–60. Stanford, Calif.: Stanford University Press.

Foschi, M., and R. Foschi. 1976. "Evaluations and Expectations: A Bayesian Model." *Journal of Mathematical Sociology* 4: 279–93.

———. 1979. "A Bayesian Model for Performance Expectations: Extension and Simulation." *Social Psychology Quarterly* 42: 232–41.

Foschi, M., G. K. Warriner, and S. D. Hart. 1985. "Standards, Expectations, and Interpersonal Influence." *Social Psychology Quarterly* 48: 108–17.

Fox, J., and J. C. Moore, Jr. 1979. "Status Characteristics and Expectation States: Fitting and Testing a Recent Model." *Social Psychology Quarterly* 42: 126–34.

Freese, L. 1970. "The Generalization of Specific Performance Expectations." Ph.D. diss., Stanford University.

———. 1974. "Conditions for Status Equality." *Sociometry* 37: 147–88.

Freese, L., and B. P. Cohen. 1973. "Eliminating Status Generalization." *Sociometry* 36: 177–93.

Gerber, G. L. 1989. "Women and Men in Policing: Leadership Roles and the Gender Stereotype Personality Traits." Grant proposal submitted to Rockefeller Foundation 1989 Research Grants Competition.

Greenstein, T. N., and J. D. Knottnerus. 1980. "The Evaluations on Status Generalization." *Social Psychology Quarterly* 43: 147–54.

Hall, K. E. P. 1972. "Sex Differences in Initiation and Influence in Decision-Making Among Prospective Teachers." Ph.D. diss., Stanford University.

Harrod, W. J. 1980. "Expectations from Unequal Rewards." *Social Psychology Quarterly* 43: 126–30.

Heinecke, C., and R. F. Bales. 1953. "Developmental Trends in the Structure of Small Groups." *Sociometry* 16: 7–38.

Hembroff, L. A. 1982. "Resolving Status Inconsistency: An Expectation States Theory and Test." *Social Forces* 61: 183–205.

Hembroff, L. A., M. W. Martin, and J. Sell. 1981. "Total Performance Inconsistency and Status Generalization: An Expectation States Formulation." *Sociological Quarterly* 22: 421–30.

Homans, G. C. 1953. "Status Among Clerical Workers." *Human Organization* 12: 5–10.

———. 1961. *Social Behavior: Its Elementary Forms*. New York: Harcourt, Brace and World.

———. 1974. *Social Behavior: Its Elementary Forms*. Rev. ed. New York: Harcourt Brace Jovanovich.

Humphreys, P., and J. Berger. 1981. "Theoretical Consequences of the Status Characteristics Formulation." *American Journal of Sociology* 86: 953–83.

Hurwitz, J. I., A. F. Zander, and B. Hymovitch. 1960. "Some Effects of Power on the Relations Among Group Members." In D. Cartwright and A. Zander, eds., *Group Dynamics*, pp. 448–56. New York: Harper and Row.

Jasso, G. 1978. "On the Justice of Earnings: A New Specification of the Justice Evaluation Function." *American Journal of Sociology* 83: 1398–1419.

———. 1980. "A New Theory of Distributive Justice." *American Sociological Review* 45: 3–32.

———. 1983. "Fairness of Individual Rewards and Fairness of the Reward Distribution: Specifying the Inconsistency Between the Micro and Macro Principles of Justice." *Social Psychology Quarterly* 46: 185–99.

———. 1989. "The Theory of the Distributive-Justice Force in Human Affairs: Analyzing the Three Central Questions." In J. Berger, M. Zelditch, Jr., and B. Anderson, eds., *Sociological Theories in Progress: New Formulations*, pp. 354–87. Newbury Park, Calif.: Sage.

Jasso, G., and P. H. Rossi. 1977. "Distributive Justice and Earned Income." *American Sociological Review* 42: 639–51.

Johnston, J. R. 1985. "How Personality Attributes Structure Interpersonal Relations." In J. Berger and M. Zelditch, Jr., eds., *Status, Rewards, and Influence: How Expectations Organize Behavior*, pp. 317–49. San Francisco: Jossey-Bass.

———. 1988. "The Structure of Ex-Spousal Relations: An Exercise in Theoretical Integration and Application." In M. Webster, Jr., and M. Foschi, eds., *Status Generalization: New Theory and Research*, pp. 309–26. Stanford, Calif.: Stanford University Press.

Johnston, J.R., and L.E.G. Campbell. 1988. *Impasses of Divorce*. New York: Free Press.

Katz, I. 1970. "Experimental Studies in Negro-White Relationships." In L. Berkowitz, ed., *Advances in Experimental Social Psychology*, vol. 5, pp. 71–117. New York: Academic Press.

Katz, I., and M. Cohen. 1962. "The Effects of Training Negroes upon Cooperative Problem Solving in Biracial Teams." *Journal of Abnormal and Social Psychology* 64: 319–25.

Kervin, J. B. 1972. "An Information Processing Model for the Formation of Performance Expectations in Small Groups." Ph.D. diss., Johns Hopkins University.

Knottnerus, J. D., and T. N. Greenstein. 1981. "Status and Performance Characteristics in Social Interaction: A Theory of Status Validation." *Social Psychology Quarterly* 44: 338–49.

Lee, M. T., and R. Ofshe. 1981. "The Impact of Behavioral Style and Status Characteristics on Social Influence: A Test of Two Competing Theories." *Social Psychology Quarterly* 44: 73–82.

Leik, R. K. 1963. "Instrumentality and Emotionality in Family Interaction." *Sociometry* 26: 131–45.

Lenski, G. 1966. *Power and Privilege*. New York: McGraw-Hill.

Lerner, M. 1965. "Evaluation of Performance as a Function of Performer's Reward and Attractiveness." *Journal of Personality and Social Psychology* 1: 355–60.

Lockheed, M. E. 1976. "Modification of Female Leadership Behavior in the Presence of Males." ETS-PR-76-28. Princeton, N.J.: Educational Testing Service.

———. 1985. "Sex and Social Influence: A Meta-Analysis Guided by Theory." In J. Berger and M. Zelditch, Jr., eds., *Status, Rewards, and Influence: How Expectations Organize Behavior*, pp. 406–29. San Francisco: Jossey-Bass.

Lockheed, M. E., and K. P. Hall. 1976. "Conceptualizing Sex as a Status Characteristic: Applications to Leadership Training Strategies." *Journal of Social Issues* 32: 111–24.

Lohman, M. R. 1970. "Changing a Racial Status Ordering by Means of Role Modeling." Ph.D. diss., Stanford University.

———. 1972. "Changing a Racial Status Ordering—Implications for Desegregation." *Journal of Education and Urban Society* 4: 383–402.

Markovsky, B. 1985. "Toward a Multilevel Distributive Justice Theory." *American Sociological Review* 50: 822–39.

———. 1988. "From Expectation States to Macro Processes." In M. Webster, Jr., and M. Foschi, eds., *Status Generalization: New Theory and Research*, pp. 351–65. Stanford, Calif.: Stanford University Press.

Markovsky, B., L. F. Smith, and J. Berger. 1984. "Do Status Interventions Persist?" *American Sociological Review* 49: 373–82.

Mazur, A. 1985. "A Biosocial Model of Status in Face-to-Face Primate Groups." *Social Forces* 64: 377–402.

Meeker, B. F., and P. A. Weitzel-O'Neill. 1977. "Sex Roles and Interpersonal Behavior in Task-Oriented Groups." *American Sociological Review* 42: 91–105.

Mohr, P. B. 1986. "Demeanor, Status Cue, or Performance?" *Social Psychology Quarterly* 49: 228–36.

Moore, J. C., Jr. 1968. "Status and Influence in Small Group Interactions." *Sociometry* 31: 47–63.

———. 1985. "Role Enactment and Self-Identity: An Expectation States Approach." In J. Berger and M. Zelditch, Jr., eds., *Status, Rewards, and Influence: How Expectations Organize Behavior*, pp. 262–316. Stanford, Calif.: Stanford University Press.

Morris, R. 1977. "A Normative Intervention To Equalize Participation in Task-Oriented Groups." Ph.D. diss., Stanford University.

Norman, R. Z., and F. S. Roberts. 1972. "A Measure of Relative Balance for Social Structures." In J. Berger, M. Zelditch, Jr., and B. Anderson, eds., *Sociological Theories in Progress*, vol. 2, pp. 358–91. Boston: Houghton Mifflin.

Norman, R. Z., L. F. Smith, and J. Berger. 1988. "The Processing of Inconsistent Status Information." In M. Webster, Jr., and M. Foschi, eds., *Status Generalization: New Theory and Research*, pp. 169–87. Stanford, Calif.: Stanford University Press.

Parcel, T. L., and K. S. Cook. 1977. "Status Characteristics, Reward Allocation, and Equity." *Sociometry* 40: 311–24.

Prescott, W. S. 1986. "Expectation States Theory: When Do Interventions Persist?" Manuscript, Dartmouth College.

Pugh, M. D., and R. Wahrman. 1983. "Neutralizing Sexism in Mixed-Sex Groups: Do Women Have To Be Better Than Men?" *American Journal of Sociology* 88: 746–62.

Rainwater, J. A. 1987. "Status Cues: A Test of an Extension of Status Characteristics Theory." Ph.D. diss., Stanford University.

Riches, P., and M. Foddy. 1989. "Ethnic Accent as Status Cue." *Social Psychology Quarterly* 52: 197–206.

Ridgeway, C. L. 1982. "Status in Groups: The Importance of Motivation." *American Sociological Review* 47: 76–88.

———. 1984. "Dominance, Performance, and Status in Groups: A Theoretical Analysis." In E. J. Lawler, ed., *Advances in Group Processes*, vol. 1, pp. 59–93. Greenwich, Conn.: JAI Press.

———. 1987. "Nonverbal Behavior, Dominance, and Status in Task Groups." *American Sociological Review* 52: 683–94.

———. 1988. "Gender Differences in Task Groups: A Status and Legitimacy Account." In M. Webster, Jr., and M. Foschi, eds., *Status Generalization: New Theory and Research*, pp. 188–206. Stanford, Calif.: Stanford University Press.

———. 1989. "Understanding Legitimation in Informal Status Orders." In J. Berger, M. Zelditch, Jr., and B. Anderson, eds., *Sociological Theories in Progress: New Formulations*, pp. 131–59. Newbury Park, Calif.: Sage.

———. 1991. "The Social Construction of Status Value: Gender and Other Nominal Characteristics." *Social Forces* 70: 367–86.

———. 1992. "Gender, Status, and Social Psychology." In P. England, ed., *Theory on Gender/Feminism in Theory*. Chicago: Aldine, forthcoming.

Ridgeway, C. L., and J. Berger. 1986. "Expectations, Legitimation, and Dominance Behavior in Task Groups." *American Sociological Review* 51: 603–17.

———. 1988. "The Legitimation of Power and Prestige Orders in Task Groups." In M. Webster, Jr., and M. Foschi, eds., *Status Generalization: New Theory and Research*, pp. 207–31. Stanford, Calif.: Stanford University Press.

Ridgeway, C. L., J. Berger, and L. F. Smith. 1985. "Nonverbal Cues and Status: An Expectation States Approach." *American Journal of Sociology* 90: 955–78.

Ridgeway, C. L., and C. Johnson. 1990. "What Is the Relationship Between Socioemotional Behavior and Status in Task Groups?" *American Journal of Sociology* 95: 1189–1212.

Rosenholtz, S. J. 1977. "The Multiple Ability Curriculum: An Intervention Against the Self-Fulfilling Prophecy." Ph.D. diss., Stanford University.

———. 1985. "Modifying Status Expectations in the Traditional Classroom." In J. Berger and M. Zelditch, Jr., eds., *Status, Rewards, and Influence: How Expectations Organize Behavior*, pp. 445–70. San Francisco: Jossey-Bass.

Rosenholtz, S. J., and E. G. Cohen. 1985. "Activating Ethnic Status." In J. Berger and M. Zelditch, Jr., eds., *Status, Rewards, and Influence: How Expectations Organize Behavior*, pp. 430–44. San Francisco: Jossey-Bass.

Sev'er, A. 1989. "Simultaneous Effects of Status and Task Cues: Combining, Eliminating, or Buffering?" *Social Psychology Quarterly* 52: 327–35.

Shelly, R. K. 1972. "Interpersonal Influence and Decision-Making: Monetary vs. Non-Monetary Rewards." Ph.D. diss., Michigan State University.

———. 1979. "Sentiment, Prestige, and Influence." Grant proposal to the National Science Foundation, Department of Sociology, University of Ohio.

———. 1988. "Social Differentiation and Social Integration." In M. Webster, Jr., and M. Foschi, eds., *Status Generalization: New Theory and Research*, pp. 366–76. Stanford, Calif.: Stanford University Press.

Shelly, R. K., M. Webster, Jr., and J. Berger. 1989. "Congruent Structures of Affect and Status." Paper presented at the annual meeting of the American Sociological Association, San Francisco (Aug.).

Skvoretz, J. 1988. "Models of Participation in Status Differentiated Groups." *Social Psychology Quarterly* 51: 43–57.

Sobieszek, B. I. 1970. "Multiple Sources and the Formation of Performance Expectations." Ph.D. diss., Stanford University.

Sobieszek, B. I., and M. Webster, Jr. 1973. "Conflicting Sources of Evaluation." *Sociometry* 36: 550–60.

Stewart, P., and J. C. Moore, Jr. 1992. "Wage Disparaties and Performance Expectations." *Social Psychology Quarterly* 55: 78–85.

Strodtbeck, F. L., R. M. James, and C. Hawkins. 1958. "Social Status in Jury Deliberations." In E. E. Maccoby, T. M. Newcomb, and E. L. Hartley, eds., *Readings in Social Psychology*, pp. 379–88. 3d ed. New York: Holt.

Talley, J., and J. Berger. 1983. "Social Control as a State Organizing Process." Manuscript, Stanford University.

Tammivaara, J. S. 1982. "The Effects of Task Structure on Beliefs About Competence and Participation in Small Groups." *Sociology of Education* 55: 212–22.

Torrance, E. P. 1954. "Some Consequences of Power Differences on Decision Making in Permanent and Temporary Three-Man Groups." *Research Studies* (State College of Washington, Pullman) 22: 130–40.

Tuzlak, A. 1988. "Boomerang Effects: Status and Demeanor over Time." In M. Webster, Jr., and M. Foschi, eds., *Status Generalization: New Theory and Research*, pp. 261–74. Stanford, Calif.: Stanford University Press.

Tuzlak, A., and J. C. Moore. 1984. "Status, Demeanor, and Influence: An Empirical Assessment." *Social Psychology Quarterly* 47: 178–83.

Wagner, D. G. 1988. "Status Violations: Toward an Expectation States Theory of the Social Control of Deviance." In M. Webster, Jr., and M. Foschi, eds., *Status Generalization: New Theory and Research*, pp. 110–22. Stanford, Calif.: Stanford University Press.

———. 1992a. "Gender Differences in Reward Preference: A Status-Based Account." Under review.

———. 1992b. "Status Inconsistency and Reward Preference." Under review.

Wagner, D. G., and J. Berger. 1974. "Paths of Consistent and Inconsistent Status Information and the Induction of Relevance." Technical Report No. 53, Laboratory for Social Research, Stanford University.

———. 1982. "Paths of Relevance and the Induction of Status-Task Expectancies: A Research Note." *Social Forces* 61: 575–86.

———. 1985. "Do Sociological Theories Grow?" *American Journal of Sociology* 90: 697–728.

Walker, H. A., and B. P. Cohen. 1985. "Scope Statements: Imperatives for Evaluating Theory." *American Sociological Review* 50: 288–301.

Walster, E., E. Berscheid, and G. W. Walster. 1973. "New Directions in Equity Research." *Journal of Personality and Social Psychology* 25: 151–76.

Wattendorf, J. F. 1979. "Interpersonal Similarity/Dissimilarity Bonds: An Expectation-States Approach." Ph.D. diss., Stanford University.

Webster, M. A., Jr. 1969. "Sources of Evaluations and Expectations for Performance." *Sociometry* 32: 243–58.

———. 1970. "Status Characteristics and Sources of Expectations." Report No. 82, Center for Social Organization of Schools, Johns Hopkins University.

———. 1980. "Integrating Social Processes." Research proposal funded by National Science Foundation.

Webster, M. A., Jr., and J. Berger. 1975. "Equating Characteristics and Social Interactions." Mimeograph, Department of Sociology, Stanford University.

Webster, M. A., Jr., and J. E. Driskell, Jr. 1979. "Status Generalization: A Review and Some New Data." *American Sociological Review* 43: 220–36.

———. 1983. "Beauty as Status." *American Journal of Sociology* 89: 140–65.

Webster, M. A., Jr., and D. R. Entwisle. 1974. "Raising Children's Expectations for Their Own Performance: A Classroom Application." In J. Berger, T. L. Conner, and M. H. Fisek, eds., *Expectation States Theory: A Theoretical Research Program*, pp. 211–43. Cambridge, Mass.: Winthrop.

Webster, M. A., Jr., L. Roberts, and B. Sobieszek. 1972. "Accepting Significant Others: Six Models." *American Journal of Sociology* 78: 576–98.

Webster, M. A., Jr., and R. Smith. 1978. "Justice and Revolutionary Coalitions: A Test of Two Theories." *American Journal of Sociology* 84: 267–92.

Webster, M. A., Jr., and B. I. Sobieszek. 1974. "Sources of Evaluations and

Expectation States." In J. Berger, T. L. Conner, and M. H. Fisek, eds., *Expectation States Theory: A Theoretical Research Program*, pp. 115–58. Cambridge, Mass.: Winthrop.

Wood, W., and S. J. Karten. 1986. "Sex Differences in Interaction Style as a Product of Perceived Sex Differences in Competence." *Journal of Personality and Social Psychology* 50: 341–47.

Yuchtmann-Yaar, E., and M. Semyonov. 1979. "Ethnic Inequality in Israeli Schools and Sports: An Expectation-States Approach." *American Journal of Sociology* 85: 576–90.

Yuchtmann-Yaar, E., and R. Shapira. 1981. "Sex as a Status Characteristic: An Examination of Sex Differences in Locus of Control." *Sex Roles* 7: 149–62.

Zelditch, M., Jr., and B. Anderson. 1966. "On the Balance of a Set of Ranks." In J. Berger, M. Zelditch, Jr., and B. Anderson, eds., *Sociological Theories in Progress*, vol. 1, pp. 244–68. Boston: Houghton Mifflin.

Zelditch, M., Jr., P. Lauderdale, and S. Stublarec. 1980. "How Are Inconsistencies Between Status and Ability Resolved?" *Social Forces* 58: 1025–43.

Zimmerman, D. H., and C. West. 1975. "Sex Roles, Interruptions, and Silences in Conversations." In B. Thorne and N. Henly, eds., *Language and Sex: Difference and Dominance*, pp. 105–29. Rawley, Mass.: Newbury House.

MacKinnon and Heise: Affect Control Theory

Abell, P. 1987. *The Syntax of Social Life: The Theory and Method of Comparative Narratives*. New York: Oxford University Press.

Anderson, N. H. 1981. *Foundations of Information Integration Theory*. New York: Academic Press.

†Averett, C., and D. Heise. 1987. "Modified Social Identities: Amalgamations, Attributions, and Emotions." *Journal of Mathematical Sociology* 13: 103–32.

Becker, H. S. 1982. *Art Worlds*. Berkeley: University of California Press.

*Britt, L., and D. Heise. 1992. "Impressions of Self-Directed Action." *Social Psychology Quarterly* 55: 335–50.

Corsaro, W., and D. Heise. 1990. "Event Structure Models from Ethnographic Data." In C. Clogg, ed., *Sociological Methodology: 1990*, pp. 1–57. Cambridge, Mass.: Basil Blackwell.

Fararo, T. J., and J. Skvoretz. 1984. "Institutions as Production Systems." *Journal of Mathematical Sociology* 10: 117–82.

Gergen, K. J. 1985. "The Social Constructionist Movement in Modern Psychology." *American Psychologist* 40: 266–75.

*Heise, D. 1979. *Understanding Events: Affect and the Construction of Social Action*. New York: Cambridge University Press.

*———. 1985. "Affect Control Theory: Respecification, Estimation, and Tests of the Formal Model." *Journal of Mathematical Sociology* 11: 191–222.

*———. 1986. "Modeling Symbolic Interaction." In S. Lindenberg, J. S. Coleman, and S. Nowak, eds., *Approaches to Social Theory*, pp. 291–309. New York: Russell Sage Foundation.

†———. 1987. "Affect Control Theory: Concepts and Model." *Journal of Mathematical Sociology* 13: 1–33.

---

*Asterisks mark key references in affect control theory. †Daggers mark articles reprinted in Smith-Lovin and Heise (1988).

————. 1988. "Computer Analysis of Cultural Structures." *Social Science Computer Review* 6: 183–96.

*————. 1989a. "Effects of Emotion Displays on Social Identification." *Social Psychology Quarterly* 52: 10–21.

————. 1989b. "Modeling Event Structures." *Journal of Mathematical Sociology* 14: 138–68.

————. 1990. "Careers, Career Trajectories, and the Self." In J. Rodin, C. Schooler, and K. W. Schaie, eds., *Self-Directedness: Cause and Effects Throughout the Life Course*, pp. 59–84. New York: Erlbaum.

————. 1991. "Event Structure Analysis: A Qualitative Model of Quantitative Research." In N. Fielding and R. Lee, eds., *Using Computers in Qualitative Research*, pp. 136–63. Newbury Park, Calif.: Sage.

*Heise, D., and E. Lewis. 1988. *Introduction to INTERACT*. (Program and documentation.) Durham, N.C.: National Collegiate Software Clearinghouse, Duke University Press.

†Heise, D., and N. MacKinnon. 1987. "Affective Bases of Likelihood Judgments." *Journal of Mathematical Sociology* 13: 133–51.

*Heise, D., and L. Thomas. 1989. "Predicting Impressions Created by Emotion-Identity Combinations." *Social Psychology Quarterly* 52: 141–48.

Kemper, T. D., and R. Collins. 1990. "Dimensions of Microinteraction." *American Journal of Sociology* 96: 32–68.

Latour, B. 1987. *Science in Action: How To Follow Scientists and Engineers Through Society*. Cambridge, Mass.: Harvard University Press.

*MacKinnon, N. 1985. "Affective Dynamics and Role Analysis." Final report, SSHRC Project 410-81-0089, Department of Sociology and Anthropology, University of Guelph, Ontario, Canada.

*————. Forthcoming. *Symbolic Interactionism as Affect Control*. Albany: SUNY Press.

*MacKinnon, N., and L. Keating. 1989. "The Structure of Emotion: A Review of the Problem and a Cross-Cultural Analysis." *Social Psychology Quarterly* 52: 70–83.

*Morgan, R., and D. Heise. 1988. "Structure of Emotions." *Social Psychology Quarterly* 51: 19–31.

Newell, A., and H. Simon. 1972. *Human Problem Solving*. Englewood Cliffs, N.J.: Prentice-Hall.

Osgood, C. E. 1962. "Studies of the Generality of Affective Meaning Systems." *American Psychologist* 17: 10–28.

*Robinson, D. T., and L. Smith-Lovin. 1992. "Selective Interaction as a Strategy for Identity Maintenance: An Affect Control Model." *Social Psychology Quarterly* 55: 12–28.

*Smith-Lovin, L. 1979. "Behavioral Settings and Impressions Formed from Social Scenarios." *Social Psychology Quarterly* 42: 31–42.

†————. 1987. "The Affective Control of Events Within Settings." *Journal of Mathematical Sociology* 13: 71–101.

*————. 1990. "Emotion as the Confirmation and Disconfirmation of Identity: An Affect Control Model." In T. D. Kemper, ed., *Research Agendas in the Sociology of Emotions*, pp. 238–70. Albany: SUNY Press.

*Smith-Lovin, L., and W. Douglas. 1992. "An Affect Control Analysis of Two Religious Groups." In V. Gecas and D. Frank, eds., *Social Perspectives in Emotions*, vol. 1, pp. 217–47. Greenwich, Conn.: JAI Press.

*Smith-Lovin, L., and D. Heise. 1988. *Analyzing Social Interaction: Advances in Affect Control Theory.* New York: Gordon and Breach. Reprinted from a special issue of the *Journal of Mathematical Sociology*, 13 (1987), numbers 1 and 2, edited by Smith-Lovin and Heise.

Stryker, S. 1980. *Symbolic Interactionism: A Social Structural Version.* Menlo Park, Calif.: Benjamin-Cummings.

Stryker, S., and A. Statham. 1985. "Symbolic Interaction and Role Theory." Chapter 6 in G. Lindzey and E. Aronson, eds., *Handbook of Social Psychology*, vol. 1. 3d ed. New York: Random House.

Swann, W. B., Jr., and C. A. Hill. 1982. "When Our Identities Are Mistaken: Reaffirming Self-Conceptions Through Social Interaction." *Journal of Personality and Social Psychology* 43: 59–66.

Thoits, P. A. 1989. "The Sociology of Emotions." *Annual Review of Sociology* 15: 317–42.

Wagner, D. G., and J. Berger. 1985. "Do Sociological Theories Grow?" *American Journal of Sociology* 90: 697–728.

†Wiggins, B., and D. Heise. 1987. "Expectations, Intentions, and Behavior: Some Tests of Affect Control Theory." *Journal of Mathematical Sociology* 13: 153–69.

Turner: A "Pure Theory" Research Program

Berger, J., D. Wagner, and M. Zelditch, Jr. 1989. "Theory Growth, Social Processes, and Metatheory." In J. H. Turner, ed., *Theory Building in Sociology: Assessing Theoretical Cumulation*, pp. 19–42. Newbury Park, Calif.: Sage.

Blau, P. M. 1964. *Exchange and Power in Social Life.* New York: Wiley.

Collins, R. 1975. *Conflict Sociology: Toward an Explanatory Science.* New York: Academic Press.

———. 1984. "The Role of Emotion in Social Structure." In K. R. Scherer and P. Ekman, eds., *Approaches to Emotion*, pp. 385–96. Hillsdale, N.J.: Erlbaum.

———. 1986. "Interaction Ritual Chains, Power and Property." In J. Alexander et al., eds., *The Micro-Macro Link*, pp. 177–92. Berkeley: University of California Press.

———. 1988. *Theoretical Sociology.* San Diego, Calif.: Harcourt Brace Jovanovich.

———. 1990. "Stratification, Emotional Energy and the Transient Emotions." In T. D. Kemper, ed., *Research Agendas in the Sociology of Emotions*, pp. 40–62. Albany: SUNY Press.

Durkheim, E. 1954 [1897]. *Suicide.* New York: Free Press.

———. 1965 [1912]. *The Elementary Forms of Religious Life.* New York: Free Press.

Erikson, E. 1950. *Childhood and Society.* New York: Norton.

Garfinkel, H. 1963. "A Conception of, and Experiments with, 'Trust' as a Condition of Stable Concerted Actions." In O. J. Harvey, eds., *Motivation and Social Interaction*, pp. 187–238. New York: Ronald Press.

———. 1967. *Studies in Ethnomethodology.* Englewood Cliffs, N.J.: Prentice-Hall.

Gecas, V. 1985. "Self-Concept." In *The Social Science Encyclopedia*, pp. 739–41. London: Routledge and Kegan Paul.

Giddens, A. 1984. *The Constitution of Society: Outline of the Theory of Structuration.* Berkeley: University of California Press.

Goffman, E. 1959. *The Presentation of Self in Everyday Life.* New York: Doubleday.

———. 1967. *Interaction Ritual*. Garden City, N.Y.: Doubleday.

———. 1974. *Frame Analysis*. New York: Harper and Row.

Habermas, J. 1970a. "On Systematically Distorted Communication." *Inquiry* 13: 205–18.

———. 1970b. "Toward a Theory of Communicative Competence." *Inquiry* 13: 360–75.

———. 1984. *The Theory of Communicative Action*, vol. 1. Boston: Beacon Press.

Kemper, T. D. 1978. *A Social Interactional Theory of Emotions*. New York: Wiley.

———. 1981. "Social Constructionist and Positivistic Approaches to the Sociology of Emotions." *American Journal of Sociology* 87: 336–62.

———. 1987. "How Many Emotions Are There? Wedding the Social and the Autonomic Components." *American Journal of Sociology* 93: 263–89.

Mead, G. H. 1934. *Mind, Self, and Society*. Chicago: University of Chicago Press.

———. 1938. *The Philosophy of the Act*. Chicago: University of Chicago Press.

Merton, R. K. 1968. *Social Theory and Social Structure*. New York: Free Press.

Parsons, T. 1951. *The Social System*. New York: Free Press.

Rosenberg, M. 1979. *Conceiving Self*. New York: Basic Books.

Scheff, T. J. 1988. "Shame and Conformity: The Deference/Emotion System." *American Sociological Review* 53: 395–406.

———. 1990. *Microsociology: Discourse and Social Structure*. Chicago: University of Chicago Press.

Schutz, A. 1967 [1932]. *The Phenomenology of the Social World*. Evanston, Ill.: Northwestern University Press.

Stinchcombe, A. 1968. *Constructing Social Theories*. New York: Harcourt, Brace and World.

Stryker, S. 1980. *Symbolic Interactionism: A Social Structural Version*. Menlo Park, Calif.: Benjamin-Cummings.

Turner, J. H. 1975a. "Marx and Simmel Revised." *Social Forces* 53: 619–27.

———. 1975b. "A Strategy for Reformulating the Dialectical and Functional Conflict Theories." *Social Forces* 53: 433–44.

———. 1979. "Toward a Social Physics." *Humbolt Journal of Social Relations* 7 (Fall/Winter): 123–39.

———. 1981a. "Emile Durkheim's Theory of Integration in Differentiated Social Systems." *Pacific Sociological Review* 24: 187–208.

———. 1981b. "A Note on George Herbert Mead's Behavioristic Theory of Social Structure." *Journal for the Theory of Social Behavior* 12: 213–22.

———. 1981c. "Returning to 'Social Physics': Illustrations for the Work of George Herbert Mead." *Current Perspectives in Social Theory* 2: 153–86.

———. 1983. "Theoretical Strategies for Linking Micro and Macro Processes: An Evaluation of Seven Approaches." *Western Sociological Review* 14: 4–15.

———. 1984a. "Durkheim's and Spencer's Principles of Social Organization." *Sociological Perspectives* 27: 21–32.

———. 1984b. *Societal Stratification: A Theoretical Analysis*. New York: Columbia University Press.

———. 1985a. *Herbert Spencer: A Renewed Appreciation*. Beverly Hills, Calif.: Sage.

———. 1985b. "In Defense of Positivism." *Sociological Theory* 3: 24–30.

———. 1986a. "The Mechanics of Social Interaction: Toward a Composite Model of Signaling and Interpreting." *Sociological Theory* 4: 95–105.

———. 1986b. *The Structure of Sociological Theory*. 4th ed. Chicago: Dorsey.

————. 1986c. "Toward a Unified Theory of Ethnic Antagonism." *Sociological Forum* 1: 403–27.

————. 1987a. "Analytical Theorizing." In A. Giddens and J. H. Turner, eds., *Social Theory Today*, pp. 156–94. Stanford, Calif.: Stanford University Press.

————. 1987b. "Toward a Sociological Theory of Motivation." *American Sociological Review* 52: 15–27.

————. 1988. *A Theory of Social Interaction*. Stanford, Calif.: Stanford University Press.

————. 1989a. "A Behavioral Theory of Social Structure." *Journal for the Theory of Social Behavior* 18: 354–72.

————. 1989b. "A Theory of Microdynamics." In *Advances in Group Processes*, vol. 7, pp. 1–26. Greenwich, Conn.: JAI Press.

————. 1990a. "Durkheim's Theory of Social Organization." *Social Forces* 68: 1–15.

————. 1990b. "The Misuse and Use of Metatheory." *Sociological Forum* 5: 37–54.

————. 1990c. "The Promise of Positivism." In D. G. Wagner and S. Seidman, eds., *General Theory and Its Critics*, pp. 85–102. New York: Basil Blackwell.

————. 1990d. "A Theory of Macrostructural Dynamics." In M. Zelditch, Jr., and J. Berger, eds., *Sociological Theories in Progress*, vol. 3, pp. 198–211. Newbury Park, Calif.: Sage.

————. 1991. *The Structure of Sociological Theory*. 5th ed., chapters 18–23. Belmont, Calif.: Wadsworth.

————. 1992. *A General Theory of Social Organization: Volume 1 on Macrodynamics*. Boston: Lexington.

Turner, J. H., L. Beeghley, and C. Powers. 1989. *The Emergence of Sociological Theory*. Belmont, Calif.: Wadsworth.

Turner, J. H., and E. Bonacich. 1980. "Toward a Composite Theory of Middleman Minorities." *Ethnicity* 10: 29–38.

Turner, J. H., and R. Collins. 1989. "Toward a Microtheory of Structuring." In J. H. Turner, ed., *Theory Building in Sociology: Assessing Theoretical Cumulation*, pp. 118–30. Newbury Park, Calif.: Sage.

Turner, J. H., and C. Powers. 1985. "Some Elementary Principles of Political Organization." *Research in Political Sociology* 2: 1–17.

Turner, J. H., and R. R. Singleton. 1978. "A Theory of Ethnic Opposition." *Social Forces* 56: 284–95.

Turner, R. H. 1962. "Role Taking: Process Versus Conformity." In A. Rose, ed., *Human Behavior and Social Processes*, pp. 20–40. Boston: Houghton Mifflin.

Wagner, D. G., and J. Berger. 1985. "Do Sociological Theories Grow?" *American Journal of Sociology* 90: 697–728.

Wilson, T. 1970. "Normative and Interpretative Paradigms in Sociology." In J. D. Douglas, ed., *Understanding Everyday Life*, pp. 64–83. London: Routledge and Kegan Paul.

Bueno de Mesquita: The Game of Conflict Interactions

Ahn, B. 1990. "Domestic Politics, Rational Actors, and Foreign War." Unpublished dissertation proposal, University of Rochester.

Altfeld, M., and B. Bueno de Mesquita. 1979. "Choosing Sides in Wars." *International Studies Quarterly* 23: 87–112.

Banks, J. 1990. "Equilibrium Behavior in Crisis Bargaining Games." *American Journal of Political Science* 34: 599–614.

Beck, D., and B. Bueno de Mesquita. 1985. "Forecasting Policy Decisions: An Expected Utility Approach." In S. Andriole, ed., *Corporate Crisis Management*, pp. 103–22. New York: Petrocelli Books.

Black, D. 1958. *The Theory of Committees and Elections*. Cambridge, Eng.: Cambridge University Press.

Blainey, G. 1973. *The Causes of War*. New York: Free Press.

Brodie, B. 1946. *The Absolute Weapon: Atomic Power and World Order*. New York: Harcourt, Brace.

Bueno de Mesquita, B. 1978. "Systemic Polarization and the Occurrence and Duration of War." *Journal of Conflict Resolution* 22: 241–66.

———. 1980. "Theories of International Conflict: An Analysis and an Appraisal." In T. R. Gurr, ed., *The Handbook of Political Conflict*, pp. 361–98. New York: Free Press.

———. 1981a. "Risk, Power Distributions, and the Likelihood of War." *International Studies Quarterly* 25: 541–68.

———. 1981b. *The War Trap*. New Haven, Conn.: Yale University Press.

———. 1982. "Conflict Forecasting Project: Iran and Soviet Union Analysis." Report to the Defense Advanced Research Projects Agency.

———. 1984. "Forecasting Policy Decisions: An Expected Utility Approach to Post-Khomeini Iran." *PS* 17: 226–36.

———. 1985a. "Toward a Scientific Understanding of International Conflict: A Personal View." *International Studies Quarterly* 29: 121–36.

———. 1985b. "*The War Trap* Revisited." *American Political Science Review* 79: 157–76.

Bueno de Mesquita, B., and G. Iusi-Scarborough. 1988. "Forecasting the Nature of Political Settlement in Nicaragua: An Expected Utility Approach." Paper prepared for the Conference on Nicaragua: Prospects for a Democratic Outcome, sponsored by the Orkand Corporation, Washington, D.C., Oct. 12–13.

———. 1989. "The Contribution of Expected Utility Theory to the Study of International Conflict." In M. Midlarsky, ed., *The Handbook of War Studies*, pp. 143–69. Winchester, Mass.: Unwin and Hyman.

———. 1990a. "Multilateral Negotiations: A Spatial Analysis of the Arab-Israeli Dispute." *International Organization* 44: 317–40.

———. 1990b. "Pride of Place: The Origins of German Hegemony." *World Politics* 43: 28–52.

———. 1991. "Big War, Little Wars: Avoiding Selection Bias." *International Interactions* 16: 159–69.

Bueno de Mesquita, B., and D. Lalman. 1986. "Reason and War." *American Political Science Review* 80: 1113–31.

———. 1987. "Modeling War and Peace." *American Political Science Review* 81: 227–30.

———. 1988a. "Arms Races and the Opportunity for Peace." *Synthese* 76: 263–83.

———. 1988b. "Systemic and Dyadic Explanations of War." *World Politics* 41: 1–20.

———. 1989a. "Dyadic Power, Expectations, and War." In R. J. Stoll and M. D. Ward, eds., *Power in World Politics*, pp. 177–91. Boulder, Colo.: Lynne Rienner.

———. 1989b. "The Road to War is Strewn with Peaceful Intentions." In P. Ordeshook, ed., *Models of Strategic Choice in Politics*, pp. 253–66. Ann Arbor: University of Michigan Press.

———. 1990. "Domestic Opposition and Foreign War." *American Political Science Review* 84: 747–65.

———. 1992. *War and Reason*. New Haven, Conn.: Yale University Press.

Bueno de Mesquita, B., D. Newman, and A. Rabushka. 1985. *Forecasting Political Events: Hong Kong's Future*. New Haven, Conn.: Yale University Press.

Bueno de Mesquita, B., R. Siverson, and G. Woller. 1992. "War and the Fate of Regimes." *American Political Science Review* 86: 638–46.

Bueno de Mesquita, B., and F. Stokman, eds. 1992. *Twelve into One: Models of Decision-Making in the European Community*. New Haven, Conn.: Yale University Press.

Decision Insights, Inc. 1989. "A Cambodian Strategy for the United States Department of State: Executive Summary." Manuscript, Reston, Va.

Deutsch, K. 1953. *Nationalism and Social Communication*. Cambridge, Mass.: MIT Press.

———. 1963. *The Nerves of Government*. New York: Free Press.

Deutsch, K., and J. D. Singer. 1964. "Multipolar Power Systems and International Stability." *World Politics* 16: 390–406.

Friedrich, C. 1977. *The Philosophy of Kant: Immanuel Kant's Moral and Political Writings*. New York: Modern Library.

George, A., and R. Smoke. 1974. *Deterrence in American Foreign Policy*. New York: Columbia University Press.

Gilpin, R. 1981. *War and Change in International Politics*. New York: Cambridge University Press.

Haas, E. 1957. *The Uniting of Europe*. Stanford, Calif.: Stanford University Press.

———. 1976. "Turbulent Fields and the Theory of Regional Integration." *International Organization* 30: 173–212.

Hussein, S. 1987. "Modeling War and Peace." *American Political Science Review* 81: 221–27.

Huth, P. 1988. "Extended Deterrence and the Outbreak of War." *American Political Science Review* 82: 423–42.

Huth, P., and B. Russett. 1984. "What Makes Deterrence Work? Cases from 1900 to 1980." *World Politics* 36: 496–526.

———. 1988. "Deterrence Failure and Crisis Escalation." *International Studies Quarterly* 32: 29–45.

Iusi-Scarborough, G., and B. Bueno de Mesquita. 1988. "Threat and Alignment Behavior." *International Interactions* 14: 85–93.

James, P., and J. Oneal. 1991. "The Influence of Domestic and International Politics on the President's Use of Force." *Journal of Conflict Resolution* 35: 307–32.

Jervis, R. 1976. *Perception and Misperception in International Politics*. Princeton, N.J.: Princeton University Press.

Kennedy, P. 1987. *The Rise and Fall of the Great Powers*. New York: Vintage.

Keohane, R., and J. Nye. 1977. *Power and Interdependence: World Politics in Transition*. Boston: Little, Brown.

Kim, C. 1991. "Third-Party Participation in Wars." *Journal of Conflict Resolution* 35: 659–77.

Kim, C., and B. Bueno de Mesquita. 1991. "Prospects for a New Regional Order in Northeast Asia." *Korean Journal of Defense Analysis* 3: 65–82.

Kim, W. 1989. "Power, Alliance, and Major Wars, 1816–1975." *Journal of Conflict Resolution* 33: 255–73.

Lalman, D. 1988. "Conflict Resolution and Peace." *American Journal of Political Science* 32: 590–615.

Lebow, R. N. 1981. *Between Peace and War: The Nature of International Crisis.* Baltimore, Md.: Johns Hopkins University Press.

Midlarsky, M. 1988. *The Onset of World War.* Winchester, Mass.: Unwin and Hyman.

Modelski, G. 1987. *Long Cycles in World Politics.* Seattle: University of Washington Press.

Morgan, T. C., and S. H. Campbell. 1991. "Domestic Structure, Decisional Constraints and War." *Journal of Conflict Resolution* 35: 187–211.

Morgenthau, H. 1973. *Politics Among Nations.* New York: Knopf.

Morrow, J. D. 1985. "A Continuous Outcome Expected Utility Theory of War." *Journal of Conflict Resolution* 29: 473–502.

———. 1987. "On the Theoretical Basis of a Measure of National Risk Attitudes." *International Studies Quarterly* 31: 423–38.

———. 1989. "Capabilities, Uncertainty, and Resolve: A Limited Information Model of Crisis Bargaining." *American Journal of Political Science* 33: 941–72.

———. 1991. "Electoral and Congressional Incentives and Arms Control." *Journal of Conflict Resolution* 35: 245–65.

Moul, W. 1987. "A Catch to *The War Trap.*" *International Interactions* 13: 171–76.

———. 1988. "Balances of Power and the Escalation to War of Serious Disputes Among the European Great Powers, 1815–1939: Some Evidence." *American Journal of Political Science* 32: 241–75.

Newman, D. 1982. "Security and Alliances: A Theoretical Study of Alliance Formation." Paper prepared for the annual meeting of the International Studies Association.

Nicholson, M. 1987. "The Conceptual Bases of *The War Trap.*" *Journal of Conflict Resolution* 31: 346–69.

Niou, E., P. Ordeshook, and G. Rose. 1989. *The Balance of Power: Stability and Instability in International Systems.* New York: Cambridge University Press.

Organski, K. 1958. *World Politics.* New York: Knopf.

Organski, K., and J. Kugler. 1980. *The War Ledger.* Chicago: University of Chicago Press.

———. 1986. "Hegemony and War." Paper presented at the annual meeting of the International Studies Association, Anaheim, Calif., Mar. 26–29.

Ostrom, C., and B. Job. 1986. "The President and the Political Use of Force." *American Political Science Review* 80: 541–66.

Powell, R. 1987. "Crisis Bargaining, Escalation, and MAD." *American Political Science Review* 81: 717–35.

Rubenstein, A. 1982. "Perfect Equilibrium in a Bargaining Model." *Econometrica* 50: 97–109.

Selten, R. 1975. "Reexamination of the Perfectness Concept for Equilibrium Points in Extensive Games." *International Journal of Game Theory* 4: 25–55.

Shepsle, K., and B. Weingast. 1981. "Structure-Induced Equilibrium and Legislative Choice." *Public Choice* 37: 503–19.

———. 1987. "The Institutional Foundations of Committee Power." *American Political Science Review* 81: 85–104.

Singer, J. D., S. Bremer, and J. Stuckey. 1972. "Capability Distribution, Uncertainty, and Major Power War, 1820–1965." In B. Russett, ed., *Peace, War, and Numbers*, pp. 19–48. Beverly Hills, Calif.: Sage.

Siverson, R., and J. King. 1980. "Attributes of National Alliance Membership and War Participation, 1815–1965." *American Journal of Political Science* 24: 1–15.

Stoessinger, J. 1974. *Why Nations Go to War*. New York: St. Martin's Press.

Wagner, R. H. 1984. "War and Expected Utility." *World Politics* 36: 407–23.

Waltz, K. 1964. "The Stability of a Bipolar World." *Daedalus* 93: 881–909.

———. 1979. *Theory of International Politics*. New York: Random House.

Wu, S. 1990. "To Attack or Not To Attack." *Journal of Conflict Resolution* 34: 531–52.

Zagare, F. 1982. "Review of *The War Trap*." *American Political Science Review* 76: 738–39.

Lawler and Ford: Metatheory and Friendly Competition

Bacharach, S. B., and E. J. Lawler. 1976. "The Perception of Power." *Social Forces* 55: 123–34.

———. 1980. *Power and Politics in Organizations: The Social Psychology of Conflict, Coalitions, and Bargaining*. San Francisco: Jossey-Bass.

———. 1981a. *Bargaining: Power, Tactics, and Outcomes*. San Francisco: Jossey-Bass.

———. 1981b. "Power and Tactics in Bargaining." *Industrial and Labor Relations Review* 34: 219–33.

Berger, J., D. G. Wagner, and M. Zelditch, Jr. 1989. "Theory Growth, Social Processes, and Metatheory." In J. H. Turner, ed., *Theory Building in Sociology: Assessing Theoretical Cumulation*, pp. 19–42. Newbury Park, Calif.: Sage.

Blalock, H. M., Jr. 1989. *Conflict and Power*. Beverly Hills, Calif.: Sage.

Blalock, H. M., Jr., and P. H. Wilken. 1979. *Intergroup Processes: A Micro-Macro Perspective*. New York: Free Press.

Blegen, M. A. 1987. "An Empirical Test of a Theory of Tactical Action." Ph.D. diss., University of Iowa.

Blegen, M. A., and E. J. Lawler. 1989. "Power and Bargaining in Authority-Client Relations." In R. Braungart and M. Braungart, eds., *Research in Political Sociology*, vol. 4, pp. 167–86. Greenwich, Conn.: JAI Press.

Boyle, E. E., and E. J. Lawler. 1991. "Resolving Conflict Through Explicit Bargaining." *Social Forces* 69: 1183–1204.

Chertkoff, J. M., and J. K. Esser. 1976. "A Review of Experiments in Explicit Bargaining." *Journal of Experimental Social Psychology* 12: 464–86.

Cohen, B. P. 1980. "The Conditional Nature of Scientific Knowledge." In L. Freese, ed., *Theoretical Methods in Sociology*, pp. 71–110. Pittsburgh: University of Pittsburgh Press.

Cohen, B. P., J. Berger, and M. Zelditch, Jr. 1972. "Status Conceptions and Interaction: A Case Study of the Problem of Developing Cumulative Knowledge." In C. G. McClintock, ed., *Experimental Social Psychology*, pp. 449–83. New York: Holt, Rinehart and Winston.

Cook, K. S., ed. 1987. *Social Exchange Theory*. Newbury Park, Calif.: Sage.

Cook, K. S., and R. M. Emerson. 1978. "Power, Equity, and Commitment in Exchange Networks." *American Sociological Review* 43: 721–39.

Cook, K. S., and R. M. Emerson, M. R. Gillmore, and T. Yamagishi. 1983.

"The Distribution of Power in Exchange Networks: Theory and Experimental Results." *American Journal of Sociology* 89: 275–305.

Cook, K. S., and M. R. Gillmore. 1984. "Power, Dependence, and Coalitions." In E. J. Lawler, ed., *Advances in Group Processes*, vol. 1, pp. 27–58. Greenwich, Conn.: JAI Press.

Dahrendorf, R. 1959. *Class and Class Conflict in Industrial Society.* Stanford, Calif.: Stanford University Press.

Deutsch, M. 1973. *The Resolution of Conflict.* New Haven, Conn.: Yale University Press.

Deutsch, M., and R. M. Krauss. 1962. "Studies of Interpersonal Bargaining." *Journal of Conflict Resolution* 6: 52–76.

Emerson, R. M. 1962. "Power Dependence Relations." *American Sociological Review* 27: 31–40.

———. 1972. "Exchange Theory, Part II: Exchange Relations, Exchange Networks, and Groups as Exchange Systems." In J. Berger, M. Zelditch, Jr., and B. Anderson, eds., *Sociological Theories in Progress*, vol. 2, pp. 58–87. Boston: Houghton Mifflin.

Gamson, W. A. 1968. *Power and Discontent.* Homewood, Ill.: Dorsey Press.

Gray, L., and I. Tallman. 1987. "Theories of Choice: Contingent Reward and Punishment Applications." *Social Psychology Quarterly* 50: 16–23.

Harsanyi, J. C. 1977. *Rational Behavior and Bargaining Equilibrium in Games and Social Situations.* New York: Cambridge University Press.

Heckathorn, D. 1985. "Power and Trust in Social Exchange." In E. J. Lawler, ed., *Advances in Group Processes*, vol. 2, pp. 148–68. Greenwich, Conn.: JAI Press.

Hegtvedt, K. A. 1988. "Social Determinants of Perception: Power, Equity, and Status Effects in an Exchange Situation." *Social Psychology Quarterly* 51: 141–53.

Hornstein, H. A. 1965. "The Effects of Different Magnitudes of Threat upon Interpersonal Bargaining." *Journal of Experimental Social Psychology* 1: 282–93.

Houweling, H., and J. G. Siccama. 1988. "Power Transitions as a Cause of War." *Journal of Conflict Resolution* 32: 87–102.

Kanter, R. M. 1977. *Men and Women of the Corporation.* New York: Basic Books.

Kipnis, D. 1976. *The Powerholders.* Chicago: University of Chicago Press.

Komorita, S. S., and M. Barnes. 1969. "Effects of Pressures To Reach Agreement in Bargaining." *Journal of Personality and Social Psychology* 13: 245–52.

Lawler, E. J. 1986. "Bilateral Deterrence and Conflict Spiral: A Theoretical Analysis." In E. J. Lawler, ed., *Advances in Group Processes*, vol. 3, pp. 107–30. Greenwich, Conn.: JAI Press.

———. 1992. "Power Processes in Bargaining." *Sociological Quarterly* 33: 17–34.

Lawler, E. J., and S. B. Bacharach. 1976. "Outcome Alternatives and Value as Criteria for Multistrategy Evaluations." *Journal of Personality and Social Psychology* 34: 885–94.

———. 1979. "Power Dependence in Individual Bargaining: The Expected Utility of Influence." *Industrial and Labor Relations Review* 32: 196–204.

———. 1986. "Power Dependence in Collective Bargaining." In D. Lipsky and D. Lewin, eds., *Advances in Industrial and Labor Relations*, vol. 3, pp. 191–212. Greenwich, Conn.: JAI Press.

———. 1987. "Comparison of Dependence and Punitive Forms of Power." *Social Forces* 66: 446–62.

Lawler, E. J., R. Ford, and M. A. Blegen. 1988. "Coercive Capability in Conflict: A Test of Bilateral Deterrence vs. Conflict Spiral Theory." *Social Psychology Quarterly* 51: 93–107.

Lawler, E. J., C. Ridgeway, and B. Markovsky. 1989. "Structural Social Psychology: An Approach to Micro-Macro Linkages." Unpublished manuscript.

Lawler, E. J., and J. Yoon. 1990. "Power and Ritual Behavior in Social Exchange." Paper presented at the meeting of the American Sociological Association, Washington, D.C.

Lindskold, S. 1978. "Trust Development, the Grit Proposal, and the Effects of Conciliatory Acts on Conflict and Cooperation." *Psychological Bulletin* 85: 772–93.

Markovsky, B., D. Willer, and T. Patton. 1988. "Power Relations in Exchange Networks." *American Sociological Review* 53: 220–36.

Michener, H. A., and E. D. Cohen. 1973. "Effects of Punishment Magnitude in the Bilateral Threat Situation: Evidence for the Deterrence Hypothesis." *Journal of Personality and Social Psychology* 26: 427–38.

Michener, H. A., and R. Suchner. 1972. "The Tactical Use of Social Power." In J. T. Tedeschi, ed., *Social Influence Processes*, pp. 239–86. Hawthorne, N.Y.: Aldine.

Molm, L. D. 1987. "Power-Dependence Theory: Power Processes and Negative Outcomes." In E. J. Lawler and B. Markovsky, eds., *Advances in Group Processes*, vol. 4, pp. 171–98. Greenwich, Conn.: JAI Press.

———. 1988. "The Structure and Use of Power: A Comparison of Reward and Punishment Power." *Social Psychology Quarterly* 51: 108–22.

———. 1989. "An Experimental Analysis of Imbalance in Punishment Power." *Social Forces* 68: 178–203.

———. 1990. "Structure, Action, and Outcomes: The Dynamics of Power in Social Exchange." *American Sociological Review* 55: 427–47.

Morgan, M. P. 1977. *Deterrence: A Conceptual Analysis*. Beverly Hills, Calif.: Sage.

Nemeth, C. 1972. "A Critical Analysis of Research Utilizing the Prisoner's Dilemma Paradigm for the Study of Bargaining." In L. Berkowitz, ed., *Advances in Experimental Social Psychology*. Vol. 6. New York: Academic Press.

Patchen, M. 1987. "Strategies for Eliciting Cooperation from an Adversary." *Journal of Conflict Resolution* 31: 164–85.

Pruitt, D. G. 1981. *Negotiation Behavior*. New York: Academic Press.

Rapoport, A. 1966. *Two-Person Game Theory*. Ann Arbor: University of Michigan Press.

Rubin, J. A., and B. R. Brown. 1975. *The Social Psychology of Bargaining and Negotiations*. New York: Academic Press.

Schellenberg, J. A. 1982. *The Science of Conflict*. Oxford, Eng.: Oxford University Press.

Schelling, T. C. 1960. *The Strategy of Conflict*. New York: Oxford University Press.

Siegel, S., and L. E. Fouraker. 1960. *Bargaining and Group Decision-making*. New York: McGraw-Hill.

Simmel, G. 1950. *The Sociology of Georg Simmel*. Trans. K. H. Wolff. Glencoe, Ill.: Free Press.

Strauss, A. 1978. *Negotiations: Varieties, Contexts, Processes, and Social Order*. San Francisco: Jossey-Bass.

Tedeschi, J. T., and T. V. Bonoma. 1972. "Power and Influence: An Introduction." In J. T. Tedeschi, ed., *Social Influence Processes*, pp. 1–49. Hawthorne, N.Y.: Aldine.

Tedeschi, J. T., B. R. Schlenker, and T. V. Bonoma. 1973. *Conflict, Power, and Games*. Hawthorne, N.Y.: Aldine.

Thibaut, J. W., and H. H. Kelley. 1959. *The Social Psychology of Groups*. New York: Wiley.

Thompson, W. R. 1986. "Polarity, the Long Cycle, and Global Power Warfare." *Journal of Conflict Resolution* 30: 587–615.

Tversky, A., and D. Kahneman. 1986. "Rational Choice and the Framing of Decisions." In R. M. Hogarth and M. W. Reder, eds., *Rational Choice: The Contrast Between Economics and Psychology*, pp. 67–94. Chicago: University of Chicago Press.

Wagner, D. G. 1984. *The Growth of Sociological Theories*. Beverly Hills, Calif.: Sage.

Wagner, D. G., and J. Berger. 1985. "Do Sociological Theories Grow?" *American Journal of Sociology* 90: 697–728.

Willer, D., B. Markovsky, and T. Patton. 1989. "Power Structures: Derivations and Applications of Elementary Theory." In J. Berger, M. Zelditch, Jr., and B. Anderson, eds., *Sociological Theories in Progress: New Formulations*, pp. 313–53. Newbury Park, Calif.: Sage.

Wright, E. O. 1985. *Classes*. London: New Left Books.

Yamagishi, T. 1986. "The Structural/Goal Expectation Theory of Cooperation in Social Dilemmas." In E. J. Lawler, ed., *Advances in Group Processes*, vol. 3, pp. 51–88. Greenwich, Conn.: JAI Press.

Yitzhak, S., and M. Zelditch, Jr. 1989. "Expectations, Shared Awareness, and Power." In J. Berger, M. Zelditch, Jr., and B. Anderson, eds., *Sociological Theories in Progress: New Formulations*, pp. 288–312. Newbury Park, Calif.: Sage.

Youngs, G. A., Jr. 1986. "Patterns of Threat and Punishment Reciprocity in Conflict Settings." *Journal of Personality and Social Psychology* 51: 541–46.

Zelditch, M., Jr., W. Harris, G. M. Thomas, and H. A. Walker. 1983. "Decisions, Nondecisions, and Metadecisions." In L. Kriesberg, ed., *Research in Social Movements, Conflict, and Change*, vol. 5, pp. 1–31. Greenwich, Conn.: JAI Press.

Jasso: Building the Theory of Comparison Processes

Alves, W. M. 1982. "Modeling Distributive Justice Judgments." In P. H. Rossi and S. L. Nock, eds., *Measuring Social Judgments: The Factorial Survey Approach*, pp. 205–34. Beverly Hills, Calif.: Sage.

Alves, W. M., and P. H. Rossi. 1978. "Who Should Get What? Fairness Judgments of the Distribution of Earnings." *American Journal of Sociology* 84: 541–64.

Alwin, D. F., N. J. Shepelak, L. S. Wolfarth, and D. L. Morgan. 1980. "Individual Responses to Inequity: Evaluating Normative Conceptions of Justice." Paper presented at the annual meeting of the American Sociological Association, New York (Aug.).

Atkinson, Anthony B. 1970. "On the Measurement of Inequality." *Journal of Economic Theory* 2: 244–63.

———. 1975. *The Economics of Inequality*. London: Oxford University Press.

Berelson, B., and G. A. Steiner. 1964. *Human Behavior: An Inventory of Scientific Findings*. New York: Harcourt, Brace and World.

Berger, J., M. Zelditch, Jr., B. Anderson, and B. P. Cohen. 1972. "Structural Aspects of Distributive Justice: A Status Value Formulation." In J. Berger, M. Zelditch, Jr., and B. Anderson, eds., *Sociological Theories in Progress*, vol. 2, pp. 119–46. Boston: Houghton Mifflin.

Blalock, H. M., Jr. 1967. "Status Inconsistency, Social Mobility, Status Integration and Structural Effects." *American Sociological Review* 32: 790–801.

Blau, P. M. 1960. "Structural Effects." *American Sociological Review* 25: 178–93.

———. 1964. *Exchange and Power in Social Life*. New York: Wiley.

———. 1977. "A Macrosociological Theory of Social Structure." *American Journal of Sociology* 82: 26–54.

Campbell, N. R. 1921. *What is Science?* New York: Dover.

Cervantes de Saavedra, Miguel. 1968 [1605, 1615]. *Don Quijote de la Mancha*. Ed. M. de Riquer. Barcelona: Juventud.

Coleman, J. S. 1973. *The Mathematics of Collective Action*. London: Heinemann.

Cook, K. S. 1975. "Expectations, Evaluations, and Equity." *American Sociological Review* 40: 372–88.

Cook, K. S., and D. M. Messick. 1983. "Psychological and Sociological Perspectives on Distributive Justice: Convergent, Divergent, and Parallel Lines." In D. M. Messick and K. S. Cook, eds., *Equity Theory: Psychological and Sociological Perspectives*, pp. 1–12. New York: Praeger.

Durkheim, E. 1964 [1893]. *The Division of Labor in Society*. Trans. G. Simpson. New York: Free Press.

———. 1951 [1897]. *Suicide*. Trans. J. A. Spaulding and G. Simpson. Ed. G. Simpson. New York: Free Press.

Emerson, R. M. 1972. "Exchange Theory, Part I: A Psychological Basis for Social Exchange." In J. Berger, M. Zelditch, Jr., and B. Anderson, eds., *Sociological Theories in Progress*, vol. 2, pp. 38–57. Boston: Houghton Mifflin.

Festinger, L. 1954. "A Theory of Social Comparison Processes." *Human Relations* 7: 117–40.

Gartrell, C. D. 1985. "Relational and Distributional Models of Collective Justice Sentiments." *Social Forces* 64: 64–83.

Goode, W. J. 1978. *The Celebration of Heroes: Prestige as a Control System*. Berkeley: University of California Press.

Harris, R. J. 1983. "Pinning Down the Equity Formula." In D. M. Messick and K. S. Cook, eds., *Equity Theory: Psychological and Sociological Perspectives*, pp. 207–41. New York: Praeger.

Homans, G. C. 1974 [1961]. *Social Behavior: Its Elementary Forms*. Rev. ed. New York: Harcourt Brace Jovanovich.

———. 1976. "Commentary." In L. Berkowitz and E. Walster, eds., *Advances in Experimental Social Psychology*, vol. 9, pp. 231–44. New York: Academic Press.

Hyman, H. H. 1968. "Reference Groups." In David L. Sills, ed., *International Encyclopedia of the Social Sciences*, vol. 13, pp. 353–61. New York: Macmillan.

James, William. 1952 [1891]. *The Principles of Psychology*. Chicago: Britannica.

Jasso, G. 1978. "On the Justice of Earnings: A New Specification of the Justice Evaluation Function." *American Journal of Sociology* 83: 1398–1419.

———. 1979. "On Gini's Mean Difference and Gini's Index of Concentration

(Comment on Allison, *ASR*, December 1978)." *American Sociological Review* 44: 867–70.

———. 1980. "A New Theory of Distributive Justice." *American Sociological Review* 45: 3–32.

———. 1981a. "Further Notes on the Theory of Distributive Justice (Reply to Sołtan)." *American Sociological Review* 46: 352–60.

———. 1981b. "Who Gains and Who Loses Under Alternative Income Distributional Regimes That Have Identical Magnitudes of the Gini Coefficient." *Proceedings of the 1981 Social Statistics Section of the American Statistical Association*, pp. 350–55.

———. 1982. "Measuring Inequality by the Ratio of the Geometric Mean to the Arithmetic Mean." *Sociological Methods and Research* 10: 303–26.

———. 1983a. "Fairness of Individual Rewards and Fairness of the Reward Distribution: Specifying the Inconsistency Between the Micro and Macro Principles of Justice." *Social Psychology Quarterly* 46: 185–99.

———. 1983b. "Social Consequences of the Sense of Distributive Justice: Small-Group Applications." In D. M. Messick and K. S. Cook, eds., *Theories of Equity: Psychological and Sociological Perspectives*, pp. 243–94. New York: Praeger.

———. 1983c. "Using the Inverse Distribution Function To Compare Income Distributions and Their Inequality." *Research in Social Stratification and Mobility* 2: 271–306.

———. 1985. "Marital Coital Frequency and the Passage of Time: Estimating the Separate Effects of Spouses' Ages and Marital Duration, Birth and Marriage Cohorts, and Period Influences." *American Sociological Review* 50: 224–41.

———. 1986a. "Is It Outlier Deletion or Is It Sample Truncation? Notes on Science and Sexuality (Reply to Kahn and Udry)." *American Sociological Review* 51: 738–42.

———. 1986b. "A New Representation of the Just Term in Distributive-Justice Theory: Its Properties and Operation in Theoretical Derivation and Empirical Estimation." *Journal of Mathematical Sociology* 12: 251–74.

———. 1987. "Choosing a Good: Models Based on the Theory of the Distributive-Justice Force." In E. J. Lawler and B. Markovsky, eds., *Advances in Group Processes*, vol. 4, pp. 67–108. Greenwich, Conn.: JAI Press.

———. 1988a. "Distributive-Justice Effects of Employment and Earnings on Marital Cohesiveness: An Empirical Test of Theoretical Predictions." In M. Webster, Jr., and M. Foschi, eds., *Status Generalization: New Theory and Research*, pp. 123–62. Stanford, Calif.: Stanford University Press.

———. 1988b. "Principles of Theoretical Analysis." *Sociological Theory* 6: 1–20.

———. 1989a. "Notes on the Advancement of Theoretical Sociology (Reply to Turner)." *Sociological Theory* 7: 135–44.

———. 1989b. "The Theory of the Distributive-Justice Force in Human Affairs: Analyzing the Three Central Questions." In J. Berger, M. Zelditch, Jr., and B. Anderson, eds., *Sociological Theories in Progress: New Formulations*, pp. 354–87. Newbury Park, Calif.: Sage.

———. 1990a. "Methods for the Theoretical and Empirical Analysis of Comparison Processes." In C. C. Clogg, ed., *Sociological Methodology 1990*, pp. 369–419. Washington, D.C.: American Sociological Association.

———. 1990b. "Predictions of Comparison Theory for Intergenerational Gifts and Bequests." Paper presented at the World Congress of Sociology, International Sociological Association, Madrid, Spain (July).

—. 1991a. "Cloister and Society: Analyzing the Public Benefit of Monastic and Mendicant Institutions." *Journal of Mathematical Sociology* 16: 109–36.

—. 1991b. "Distributive Justice and Social Welfare Institutions." In R. Vermunt and H. Steensma, eds., *Social Justice in Human Relations*, vol. 2, *Societal and Psychological Consequences of Justice and Injustice*, pp. 155–96. New York: Plenum Press. Revised version of paper presented at the International Conference on Social Justice in Human Relations, Leiden, the Netherlands, July 1986.

Jasso, G., and P. H. Rossi. 1977. "Distributive Justice and Earned Income." *American Sociological Review* 42: 639–51.

Judge, G. G., W. E. Griffiths, R. C. Hill, H. Lütkepohl, and T.-C. Lee. 1985. *The Theory and Practice of Econometrics*. 2d ed. New York: Wiley.

Kuhn, T. S. 1970 [1962]. *The Structure of Scientific Revolutions*. 2d ed., enlarged. Chicago: University of Chicago Press.

Lakatos, I. 1970. "Falsification and the Methodology of Scientific Research Programmes." In I. Lakatos and A. Musgrave, eds., *Criticism and the Growth of Knowledge*, pp. 91–195. Cambridge, Eng.: Cambridge University Press.

Lipset, S. M. 1968. "Stratification, Social: Social Class." In David L. Sills, ed., *International Encyclopedia of the Social Sciences*, vol. 15, pp. 296–316. New York: Macmillan.

Marx, Karl. 1968 [1849]. "Wage Labour and Capital." In *Karl Marx and Frederick Engels: Selected Works*, pp. 74–97. New York: International Publishers.

Merton, R. K. 1945. "Sociological Theory." *American Journal of Sociology* 50: 462–73.

—. 1957. "Continuities in the Theory of Reference Groups and Social Structure." In R. K. Merton, *Social Theory and Social Structure*, pp. 281–386. 2d ed. New York: Free Press.

—. 1967. *On Theoretical Sociology: Five Essays, Old and New*. New York: Free Press.

Merton, R. K., and A. S. Rossi. 1950. "Contributions to the Theory of Reference Group Behavior." In R. K. Merton and P. Lazarsfeld, eds., *Continuities in Social Research: Studies in the Scope and Method of "The American Soldier"*, pp. 40–105. New York: Free Press.

Popper, K. R. 1959 [1935]. *The Logic of Scientific Discovery*. New York: Basic Books.

—. 1963. *Conjectures and Refutations: The Growth of Scientific Knowledge*. New York: Basic Books.

Rossi, P. H. 1951. "The Application of Latent Structure Analysis to the Study of Social Stratification." Ph.D. diss., Columbia University.

—. 1979. "Vignette Analysis: Uncovering the Normative Structure of Complex Judgments." In R. K. Merton, J. S. Coleman, and P. H. Rossi, eds., *Qualitative and Quantitative Social Research: Papers in Honor of Paul F. Lazarsfeld*, pp. 176–86. New York: Free Press.

Rossi, P. H., and A. B. Anderson. 1982. "The Factorial Survey Approach: An Introduction." In P. H. Rossi and S. L. Nock, eds., *Measuring Social Judgments: The Factorial Survey Approach*, pp. 15–67. Beverly Hills, Calif.: Sage.

Runciman, W. G. 1961. "Problems of Research on Relative Deprivation." *Archives européennes de sociologie* 2: 315–23.

Sherif, M. 1968. "Self Concept." In David L. Sills, ed., *International Encyclopedia of the Social Sciences*, vol. 14, pp. 150–59. New York: Macmillan.

Simmel, G. 1950. *The Sociology of Georg Simmel*. Trans. and ed. K. H. Wolff. New York: Free Press.

Sołtan, K. E. 1981. "Jasso on Distributive Justice (Comment on Jasso, *ASR*, February 1980). " *American Sociological Review* 46: 348–52.

Sprague, H. T. 1977. "Happiness Is an Equation." *New York Times*, Jan. 16, sec. 10.

Stouffer, S. A., et al. 1949. *The American Soldier*. 2 vols. Studies in Social Psychology in World War II. Princeton, N.J.: Princeton University Press.

Thibaut, J. W., and H. H. Kelley. 1959. *The Social Psychology of Groups*. New York: Wiley.

Wagner, D. G., and J. Berger. 1985. "Do Sociological Theories Grow?" *American Journal of Sociology* 90: 697–728.

Wright, G. H. von. 1963. *The Varieties of Goodness*. London: Routledge and Kegan Paul.

Zelditch, M., Jr. 1968. "Status, Social." In David L. Sills, ed., *International Encyclopedia of the Social Sciences*, vol. 15, pp. 250–57. New York: Macmillan.

Gray: Small Group Power Structure

Adams, J. S., and A. K. Romney. 1959. "A Function Analysis of Authority." *Psychological Review* 66: 234–51.

Bales, R. F. 1950. *Interaction Process Analysis: A Method for the Study of Small Groups*. Cambridge, Mass.: Addison-Wesley.

———. 1955. "The Equilibrium Problem in Small Groups." In A. P. Hare, E. F. Borgatta, and R. F. Bales, eds., *Small Groups: Studies in Social Interaction*, pp. 449–90. New York: Knopf.

Baum, W. M. 1974. "On Two Types of Deviation from the Matching Law: Bias and Undermatching." *Journal of the Experimental Analysis of Behavior* 22: 231–42.

Berger, J., S. J. Rosenholtz, and M. Zelditch, Jr. 1980. "Status Organizing Processes." *Annual Review of Sociology* 6: 479–508.

Bolton, G. M., L. N. Gray, and B. H. Mayhew, Jr. 1970. "An Experimental Examination of a Stochastic Model of Dominance." *Social Forces* 48: 511–20.

Bush, R. R., and F. Mosteller. 1951. "A Mathematical Model for Simple Learning." *Psychological Review* 58: 313–23.

Cook, K. S., and R. M. Emerson. 1978. "Power, Equity, and Commitment in Exchange Networks." *American Sociological Review* 43: 721–39.

Cook, K. S., R. M. Emerson, M. R. Gillmore, and T. Yamagishi. 1983. "The Distribution of Power in Exchange Networks: Theory and Experimental Results." *American Journal of Sociology* 89: 275–305.

Doreian, P. 1978. "On the 'Social Law of Effect' for Task Oriented Groups." *Social Psychology Quarterly*

Elworth, J. T., and L. N. Gray. 1982. "Self-Reinforcement: Effects on Monads and Non-interactive Dyads." *Social Psychology Quarterly* 45: 129–35.

Estes, W. K. 1959. "Component and Pattern Models with Markovian Interpretations." In R. R. Bush and W. K. Estes, eds., *Studies in Mathematical Learning Theory*, pp. 9–52. Stanford, Calif.: Stanford University Press.

Gray, L. N., and W. I. Griffith. 1984. "On Differentiation in Small Group Power Relations." *Social Psychology Quarterly* 47: 391–96.

Gray, L. N., W. I. Griffith, M. J. Sullivan, and M. H. von Broembsen. 1982a. "Social Matching over Multiple Reinforcement Domains: An Explanation of Local Exchange Imbalance." *Social Forces* 61: 156–82.

Gray, L. N., W. I. Griffith, M. H. von Broembsen, and M. J. Sullivan. 1982b. "Group Differentiation: Temporal Effects of Reinforcement." *Social Psychology Quarterly* 45: 44–49.

Gray, L. N., and B. H. Mayhew, Jr. 1970. "Power Relations in Small Groups: A Regression Analysis." *Pacific Sociological Review* 13: 110–20.

———. 1972. "Proactive Differentiation, Communication Restraint, and Asymmetry of Social Power: A Multi-dimensional Analysis." *Human Relations* 25: 199–214.

Gray, L. N., B. H. Mayhew, Jr., and R. Campbell. 1974. "Communication and Three Dimensions of Power: An Experiment and a Simulation." *Small Group Behavior* 5: 289–320.

Gray, L. N., J. T. Richardson, and B. H. Mayhew, Jr. 1968. "Influence Attempts and Effective Power: A Re-examination of an Unsubstantiated Hypothesis." *Sociometry* 31: 245–58.

Gray, L. N., and M. C. Stafford. 1988. "On Choice Behavior in Individual and Social Situations." *Social Psychology Quarterly* 51: 58–65.

Gray, L. N., M. C. Stafford, and I. Tallman. 1991. "Rewards and Punishments in Complex Human Choices." *Social Psychology Quarterly* 54: 318–29.

Gray, L. N., and M. J. Sullivan. 1978. "Can You Create Structural Differentiation in Social Power Relations in the Laboratory?" *Social Psychology Quarterly* 41: 328–37.

Gray, L. N., and I. Tallman. 1984. "A Satisfaction Balance Model of Decision Making and Choice Behavior." *Social Psychology Quarterly* 47: 146–59.

———. 1986. "Predicting Choices in Asymptotic Decisions: A Comparison of Two Models." *Social Psychology Quarterly* 49: 201–6.

———. 1987. "Theories of Choice: Contingent Reward and Punishment Applications." *Social Psychology Quarterly* 50: 16–23.

Gray, L. N., and M. H. von Broembsen. 1974. "The Effect of Extraneous Mass Mediated Stimuli on the Structure of Interaction: Some Preliminary Findings." *Human Relations* 27: 793–812.

———. 1976. "On the Generalizability of the Law of Effect: Social Psychological Measurement of Group Structures and Process." *Sociometry* 39: 175–83.

Gray, L. N., M. H. von Broembsen, M. A. Kowalczyk, and J. S. Williams. 1976. "On the Social Law of Effect." *Journal of Social Psychology* 99: 221–31.

Graybill, F. A. 1961. *An Introduction to Linear Statistical Models*, vol. 1. New York: McGraw-Hill.

Griffith, W. I., and L. N. Gray. 1978. "The Effects of External Reinforcement on Power Structure in Task Oriented Groups." *Social Forces* 57: 222–35.

———. 1985. "A Note on the 'Social Law of Effect': Expanding the Model." *Social Forces* 63: 1030–37.

Hamblin, R. L. 1977. "Behavior and Reinforcement: A Generalization of the Matching Law." In R. L. Hamblin and J. H. Kunkel, eds., *Behavioral Theory in Sociology*, pp. 111–25. New Brunswick, N.J.: Transaction Books.

———. 1979. "Behavioral Choice and Social Reinforcement: Step Function Versus Matching." *Social Forces* 57: 1141–56.

Herrnstein, R. J. 1970. "On the Law of Effect." *Journal of the Experimental Analysis of Behavior* 13: 243–66.

Judson, D. H., and L. N. Gray. 1990. "Modifying Power Asymmetry in Dyads via Environmental Reinforcement Contingencies." *Small Group Research* 21: 492–506.

Killeen, P. 1972. "The Matching Law." *Journal of the Experimental Analysis of Behavior* 17: 489–95.

Mayhew, B. H., Jr., and L. N. Gray. 1969. "Internal Control Relations in Administrative Hierarchies: A Critique." *Administrative Science Quarterly* 14: 127–30.

———. 1971. "The Structure of Dominance in Triadic Interaction Systems: A Stochastic Process." *Comparative Group Studies* 2: 161–90.

———. 1972. "Growth and Decay of Structure in Interaction: Stochastic Models of Dominance and Related Asymmetric Structures." *Comparative Group Studies* 3: 131–60.

Mayhew, B. H., Jr., L. N. Gray, and M. L. Mayhew. 1971. "The Behavior of Interaction Systems: Mathematical Models of Structure in Interaction Sequences." *General Systems Yearbook* 16: 13–29.

Mayhew, B. H., Jr., L. N. Gray, and J. T. Richardson. 1969. "Behavioral Measurement of Operating Power Structures." *Sociometry* 32: 474–89.

Michaels, J. W., and J. A. Wiggins. 1976. "Effects of Mutual Dependency and Dependency Asymmetry on Social Exchange." *Sociometry* 39: 368–76.

Molm, L. D. 1981a. "The Conversion of Power Imbalance to Power Use." *Social Psychology Quarterly* 44: 151–63.

———. 1981b. "Power Use in the Dyad: The Effects of Structure, Knowledge and Interaction History." *Social Psychology Quarterly* 44: 42–48.

———. 1985. "Relative Effects of Individual Dependencies: Further Tests of the Relation Between Power Imbalance and Power Use." *Social Forces* 63: 810–37.

Murray, H. A. 1951. "Toward a Classification of Interactions." In T. Parsons and E. A. Shils, eds., *Toward a General Theory of Action*, pp. 434–64. Cambridge, Mass.: Harvard University Press.

Richardson, J. T., J. R. Dugan, L. N. Gray, and B. H. Mayhew, Jr. 1973. "Expert Power: A Behavioral Interpretation." *Sociometry* 36: 302–24.

Richardson, J. T., B. H. Mayhew, Jr., and L. N. Gray. 1969. "Differentiation, Restraint, and the Asymmetry of Power." *Human Relations* 22: 263–74.

Skinner, B. F. 1938. *The Behavior of Organisms*. New York: D. Appleton-Century.

Stevens, S. S. 1957. "On the Psychophysical Law." *Psychological Review* 64: 153–81.

Tallman, I., R. Marotz-Baden, and P. Pindas. 1983. *Adolescent Socialization in Cross-Cultural Perspective: Planning for Social Change*. New York: Academic Press.

Thibaut, J. W., and H. H. Kelley. 1959. *The Social Psychology of Groups*. New York: Wiley.

Thorndike, E. L. 1913. *Education Psychology*. Vol. 2, *The Psychology of Learning*. New York: Teachers' College, Columbia University.

Von Broembsen, M. H., and L. N. Gray. 1973. "Size and Ruling Elites: Effects of System Growth on Power Structures." *American Sociological Review* 38: 39–61.

Von Broembsen, M. H., B. H. Mayhew, Jr., and L. N. Gray. 1969. "The Stability of Power Structures in Short-Term Simulations." *Pacific Sociological Review* 12: 118–29.

Williams, J. S., L. N. Gray, and M. H. von Broembsen. 1976. "Proactivity and Reinforcement: The Contingency of Social Behavior." *Small Group Behavior* 7: 317–30.

Cook et al.: Exchange Relations and Exchange Networks

Anderson, B., and D. Willer. 1981. "Introduction." In D. Willer and B. Anderson, eds., *Networks, Exchange and Coercion*, pp. 1–21. New York: Elsevier.

Bacharach, S. B., and E. J. Lawler. 1981. *Bargaining: Power, Tactics, and Outcomes.* San Francisco: Jossey-Bass.

Berger, J., D. G. Wagner, and M. Zelditch, Jr. 1989. "Theory Growth, Social Processes, and Metatheory." In J. H. Turner, ed., *Theory Building in Sociology: Assessing Theoretical Cumulation*, pp. 19–42. Newbury Park, Calif.: Sage.

Blau, P. M. 1964. *Exchange and Power in Social Life.* New York: Wiley.

Bonacich, P. 1987. "Power and Centrality: A Family of Measures." *American Journal of Sociology* 92: 1170–82.

Breiger, R. L., S. A. Boorman, and P. Arabie. 1975. "An Algorithm for Clustering Relational Data with Applications to Social Network Analysis and Comparison with Multidimensional Scaling." *Journal of Mathematical Psychology* 12: 328–83.

Burgess, R. L., and D. Bushell, Jr., eds. 1969. *Behavioral Sociology: The Experimental Analysis of Social Process.* New York: Columbia University Press.

Burgess, R. L., and J. M. Nielsen. 1974. "An Experimental Analysis of Some Structural Determinants of Equitable and Inequitable Exchange Relations." *American Sociological Review* 39: 427–43.

Burt, R. S. 1976. "Positions in Networks." *Social Forces* 55: 93–122.

Cook, K. S. 1977. "Exchange and Power in Networks of Interorganizational Relations." *Sociological Quarterly* 18: 62–82.

———. 1982. "Network Structures from an Exchange Perspective." In P. V. Marsden and N. Lin, eds., *Social Structure and Network Analysis*, pp. 177–99. Beverly Hills, Calif.: Sage.

———. ed. 1987. *Social Exchange Theory.* Newbury Park, Calif.: Sage.

Cook, K. S., and R. M. Emerson. 1978. "Power, Equity, and Commitment in Exchange Networks." *American Sociological Review* 43: 721–39.

———. 1984. "Exchange Networks and the Analysis of Complex Organizations." In S. B. Bacharach and E. J. Lawler, eds., *Perspectives on Organizational Sociology: Theory and Research*, vol. 3, pp. 1–30. Greenwich, Conn.: JAI Press.

Cook, K. S., R. M. Emerson, M. R. Gillmore, and T. Yamagishi. 1983. "The Distribution of Power in Exchange Networks: Theory and Experimental Results." *American Journal of Sociology* 89: 275–305.

———. Forthcoming. *The Structure of Social Exchange: An Experimental Analysis.* Unpublished.

Cook, K. S., and M. R. Gillmore. 1984. "Power, Dependence, and Coalitions." In E. J. Lawler, ed., *Advances in Group Processes*, vol. 1, pp. 27–58. Greenwich, Conn.: JAI Press.

Cook, K. S., and K. A. Hegtvedt. 1986. "Justice and Power: An Exchange Analysis." In H. W. Bierhoff, R. L. Cohen, and J. Greenberg, eds., *Justice in Social Relations*, pp. 19–41. New York: Plenum Press.

Cook, K. S., K. A. Hegtvedt, and T. Yamagishi. 1988. "Structural Inequality, Legitimation, and Reactions to Inequity in Exchange Networks." In M. Webster, Jr., and M. Foschi, eds., *Status Generalization: New Theory and Research*, pp. 291–308. Stanford, Calif.: Stanford University Press.

Cook, K. S., J. O'Brien, and P. Kollock. 1990. "Exchange Theory: A Blueprint for Structure and Process." In G. Ritzer, ed., *Frontiers of Social Theory: The New Syntheses*, pp. 158–81. New York: Columbia University Press.

Emerson, R. M. 1972a. "Exchange Theory, Part I: A Psychological Basis for Social Exchange." In J. Berger, M. Zelditch, Jr., and B. Anderson, eds., *Sociological Theories in Progress*, vol. 2, pp. 38–57. Boston: Houghton Mifflin.

———. 1972b. "Exchange Theory, Part II: Exchange Relations and Networks." In J. Berger, M. Zelditch, Jr., and B. Anderson, eds., *Sociological Theories in Progress*, vol. 2, pp. 58–87. Boston: Houghton Mifflin.

———. 1976. "Social Exchange Theory." *Annual Review of Sociology* 2: 335–62.

———. 1981. "Social Exchange Theory." In M. Rosenberg and R. Turner, eds., *Social Psychology: Sociological Perspectives*, pp. 30–65. New York: Academic Press.

———. 1987. "Toward a Theory of Value in Social Exchange." In K. S. Cook, ed., *Social Exchange Theory*, pp. 11–58. Newbury Park, Calif.: Sage.

Emerson, R. M., K. S. Cook, M. R. Gillmore, and T. Yamagishi. 1983. "Valid Predictions from Invalid Comparisons: Response to Heckathorn." *Social Forces* 61: 1232–47.

Gillmore, M. R. 1983. "Sources of Solidarity and Coalition Formation in Exchange Networks." Ph.D. diss., University of Washington.

———. 1987. "Implications of General Versus Restricted Exchange." In K. S. Cook, ed., *Social Exchange Theory*, pp. 170–89. Newbury Park, Calif.: Sage.

Gray, L. N., and I. Tallman. 1987. "Theories of Choice: Contingent Reward and Punishment Applications." *Social Psychology Quarterly* 50: 16–23.

Heath, A. 1976. *Rational Choice and Social Exchange: A Critique of Exchange Theory*. Cambridge, Eng.: Cambridge University Press.

Heckathorn, D. D. 1983. "Extensions of Power-Dependence Theory: The Concept of Resistance." *Social Forces* 61: 1206–31.

Herrnstein, R. J. 1970. "On the Law of Effect." *Journal of the Experimental Analysis of Behavior* 13: 243–66.

Homans, G. C. 1961. *Social Behavior: Its Elementary Forms*. New York: Harcourt, Brace and World.

Kahneman, D., and A. Tversky. 1984. "Choices, Values, and Frames." *American Psychologist* 39: 341–50.

Kuhn, A. 1964. *The Study of Society: A Unified Approach*. Homewood, Ill.: Irwin-Dorsey.

Lawler, E. J., and S. B. Bacharach. 1987. "Comparison of Dependence and Punitive Forms of Power." *Social Forces* 66: 446–62.

Markovsky, B. 1987. "Toward Multilevel Sociological Theories: Simulations of Actors and Network Effects." *Sociological Theory* 5: 101–17.

Markovsky, B., D. Willer, and T. Patton. 1988. "Power Relations in Exchange Networks." *American Sociological Review* 53: 220–36.

Michaels, J. W., and J. A. Wiggins. 1976. "Effects of Mutual Dependency and Dependency Asymmetry on Social Exchange." *Sociometry* 39: 368–76.

Molm, L. D. 1981a. "A Contingency Change Analysis of the Disruption and Recovery of Social Exchange and Cooperation." *Social Forces* 59: 729–51.

———. 1981b. "The Conversion of Power Imbalance to Power Use." *Social Psychology Quarterly* 44: 151–63.

————. 1987. "Power-Dependence Theory: Power Processes and Negative Outcomes." In E. J. Lawler and B. Markovsky, eds., *Advances in Group Processes*, vol. 4, pp. 171–98. Greenwich, Conn.: JAI Press.

————. 1988. "The Structure and Use of Power: A Comparison of Reward and Punishment Power." *Social Psychology Quarterly* 51: 108–22.

————. 1989a. "An Experimental Analysis of Imbalance in Punishment Power." *Social Forces* 68: 178–203.

————. 1989b. "Punishment Power: A Balancing Process in Power-Dependence Relations." *American Journal of Sociology* 94: 1392–1418.

————. 1989c. "Structure, Action, and Outcomes: A Multilevel Analysis of Power." Paper presented at the meeting of the American Sociological Association, San Francisco, Aug. 8–12.

Molm, L. D., and J. A. Wiggins. 1979. "A Behavioral Analysis of the Dynamics of Social Exchange in the Dyad." *Social Forces* 57: 1157–79.

Stolte, J. F. 1987. "The Formation of Justice Norms." *American Sociological Review* 52: 774–84.

Stolte, J. F., and R. M. Emerson. 1977. "Structural Inequality: Position and Power in Network Structures." In R. L. Hamblin and J. H. Kunkel, eds., *Behavioral Theory in Sociology*, pp. 117–38. New Brunswick, N.J.: Transaction Books.

Thibaut, J. W., and H. H. Kelley. 1959. *The Social Psychology of Groups*. New York: Wiley.

Turner, J. H. 1986. *The Structure of Sociological Theory*. Chicago: Dorsey.

————. 1988. *A Theory of Social Interaction*. Stanford, Calif.: Stanford University Press.

Wagner, D. G., and J. Berger. 1985. "Do Sociological Theories Grow?" *American Journal of Sociology* 90: 697–728.

White, H. C., S. A. Boorman, and R. L. Breiger. 1976. "Social Structure from Multiple Networks, I: Blockmodels of Roles and Positions." *American Journal of Sociology* 81: 730–80.

White, H. C., and R. L. Breiger. 1975. "Patterns Across Networks." *Transaction* 12: 68–73.

Willer, D., and T. Patton. 1987. "The Development of Network Exchange Theory." In E. J. Lawler and B. Markovsky, eds. *Advances in Group Processes*, vol. 4, pp. 199–242. Greenwich, Conn.: JAI Press.

Yamagishi, T. 1987. "An Exchange Theoretical Approach to Network Positions." In K. S. Cook, ed., *Social Exchange Theory*, pp. 149–69. Newbury Park, Calif.: Sage.

Yamagishi, T., and K. S. Cook. 1990. "Power Relations in Exchange Networks: A Comment on 'Network Exchange Theory.'" *American Sociological Review* 55: 297–300.

Yamagishi, T., M. R. Gillmore, and K. S. Cook. 1988. "Network Connections and the Distribution of Power in Exchange Networks." *American Journal of Sociology* 93: 833–51.

Willer and Markovsky: Elementary Theory

Archimedes. 1897 [230 B.C.]. *The Works of Archimedes*. New York: Dover.

Berger, J., T. L. Conner, and M. H. Fisek. 1974. *Expectation States Theory: A Theoretical Research Program*. Cambridge, Mass.: Winthrop.

Bierstedt, R. 1976. "An Analysis of Social Power." In L. Coser and B. Rosenberg, eds., *Sociological Theory*, pp. 136–47. New York: Macmillan.

Blalock, H. M. 1969. *Theory Construction: From Verbal to Mathematical Formulations*. Englewood Cliffs, N.J.: Prentice-Hall.

Blau, P. M. 1964. *Exchange and Power in Social Life*. New York: Wiley.

Brennan, J. S. 1981. "Some Experimental Structures." In D. Willer and B. Anderson, eds., *Networks, Exchange and Coercion*, pp. 189–206. New York: Elsevier.

Carneiro, R. 1970. "A Theory of the Origin of the State." *Science* 169: 733–38.

Cook, K. S., and R. M. Emerson. 1978. "Power, Equity, and Commitment in Exchange Networks." *American Sociological Review* 43: 721–39.

Cook, K. S., M. R. Gillmore, and T. Yamagishi. 1986. "Power and Line Vulnerability as a Basis for Predicting the Distribution of Power in Exchange Networks." *American Journal of Sociology* 92: 445–48.

Cook, K. S., R. M. Emerson, M. R. Gillmore, and T. Yamagishi. 1983. "The Distribution of Power in Exchange Networks: Theory and Experimental Results." *American Journal of Sociology* 89: 275–305.

Dahl, R. 1957. "The Concept of Power." *Behavioral Science* 2: 201–18.

Edgeworth, F. Y. 1881. *Mathematical Psychics*. London: Kegan Paul.

Einstein, A. 1954 [1933]. *Ideas and Opinions*. New York: Crown.

Emerson, R. M. 1972a. "Exchange Theory, Part I: A Psychological Basis for Social Exchange." In J. Berger, M. Zelditch, Jr., and B. Anderson, eds., *Sociological Theories in Progress*, vol. 2, pp. 38–57. Boston: Houghton Mifflin.

———. 1972b. "Exchange Theory, Part II: Exchange Relations and Network Structures." In J. Berger, M. Zelditch, Jr., and B. Anderson, eds., *Sociological Theories in Progress*, vol. 2, pp. 58–87. Boston: Houghton Mifflin.

Fararo, T. J., and J. Skvoretz. 1989. "Theoretical Integration: Methods and Problems." Paper presented at the Stanford conference on Theory Growth and the Study of Group Process (Aug.).

Galileo. 1954 [1665]. *Dialogues Concerning Two New Sciences*. Trans. H. Crew and A. deSalvio. New York: Dover.

Gilham, S. A. 1981. "State, Law and Modern Economic Exchange." In D. Willer and B. Anderson, eds., *Networks, Exchange and Coercion*, pp. 129–52. New York: Elsevier.

Hansen, K. L. 1981. "'Black' Exchange and Its System of Social Control." In D. Willer and B. Anderson, eds., *Networks, Exchange and Coercion*, pp. 71–84. New York: Elsevier.

Homans, G. C. 1967. "Fundamental Social Processes." In N. J. Smelser, ed., *Sociology: An Introduction*, New York: Wiley.

Lakatos, I. 1970. "Falsification and the Methodology of Scientific Research Programmes." In I. Lakatos and A. Musgrave, eds., *Criticism and the Growth of Knowledge*, pp. 91–195. Cambridge, Eng.: Cambridge University Press.

Loukinen, M. 1981. "Social Exchange Networks." In D. Willer and B. Anderson, eds., *Networks, Exchange and Coercion*, pp. 45–94. New York: Elsevier.

Lukes, S. 1974. *Power: A Radical View*. London: Macmillan.

Markovsky, B. 1987. "Toward Multilevel Sociological Theories: Simulations of Actors and Network Effects." *Sociological Theory* 5: 101–17.

———. 1989. "How Simulation-Building Informs Theory-Building: The Case of Network Exchange Processes." Paper presented at the annual meeting of the Midwest Sociological Society, St. Louis (Mar.).

Markovsky, B., D. Willer, and T. Patton. 1988. "Power Relations in Exchange Networks." *American Sociological Review* 53: 220–36.

———. 1990. "Theory, Evidence, and Intuition." *American Sociological Review* 55: 300–305.

Markovsky, B., D. Willer, J. Skvoretz, M. Lovaglia, and J. Erger. 1991. "The Seeds of Weak Power: An Extension of Network Exchange Theory." Paper presented at the annual meeting of the American Sociological Association, Cincinnati (Aug.).

Marsden, P. V. 1983. "Restricted Access in Networks and Models of Power." *American Journal of Sociology* 88: 686–717.

Marx, K. 1967 [1867]. *Capital*. New York: International Publishers.

Nash, J. F. 1950. "The Bargaining Problem." *Econometrica* 18: 155–62.

———. 1953. "Two-Person Cooperative Games." *Econometrica* 21: 128–40.

Patton, T., and D. Willer. 1991. "Connection and Power in Centralized Networks." *Journal of Mathematical Sociology* 16: 31–49.

Sahlins, M. 1972. *Stone Age Economics*. New York: Aldine.

Simmel, G. 1964 [1917]. *The Sociology of Georg Simmel*. Trans. and ed. K. H. Wolff. New York: Free Press.

Stolte, J. F., and R. M. Emerson. 1977. "Structural Inequality: Position and Power in Network Structures." In R. L. Hamblin and J. H. Kunkel, eds., *Behavioral Theory in Sociology*, pp. 117–38. New Brunswick, N.J.: Transaction Books.

Toulmin, S. 1953. *The Philosophy of Science*. New York: Harper and Row.

Wagner, D. G. 1984. *The Growth of Sociological Theories*. Beverly Hills, Calif.: Sage.

Wagner, D. G., and J. Berger. 1985. "Do Sociological Theories Grow?" *American Journal of Sociology* 90: 697–728.

Weber, M. 1968 [1918]. *Economy and Society*. Berkeley: University of California Press.

———. 1964 [1918]. *From Max Weber: Essays in Sociology*. New York: Oxford University Press.

Willer, D. 1967. *Scientific Sociology*. Englewood Cliffs, N.J.: Prentice-Hall.

———. 1981. "Quantity and Network Structure." In D. Willer and B. Anderson, eds., *Networks, Exchange and Coercion*, pp. 109–27. New York: Elsevier.

———. 1984. "Analysis and Composition as Theoretic Procedures." *Journal of Mathematical Sociology* 10: 241–70.

———. 1986. "Vulnerability and the Location of Power Positions." *American Journal of Sociology* 92: 441–44.

———. 1987. *Theory and the Experimental Investigation of Social Structures*. New York: Gordon and Breach.

———. 1989. "An Investigation of Transitive Power." Paper presented at Sunbelt Social Network Conference, Tampa (Feb.).

Willer, D., and B. Anderson, eds., 1981. *Networks, Exchange and Coercion*. New York: Elsevier.

Willer, D., B. Markovsky, and T. Patton. 1989. "The Experimental Investigation of Social Structures." In J. Berger, M. Zelditch, Jr., and B. Anderson, eds., *Sociological Theories in Progress: New Formulations*, pp. 313–53. Newbury Park, Calif.: Sage.

Willer, D., and T. Patton. 1987. "The Development of Network Exchange

Theory." In E. J. Lawler and B. Markovsky, eds., *Advances in Group Processes*, vol. 4, pp. 199–242. Greenwich, Conn.: JAI Press.

Willer, D., and J. Skvoretz. 1989. "ExNet: Experimental and Electronic Network for the Study of Power Relations." Paper presented at the annual meeting of the American Sociological Association, San Francisco (Aug.).

Willer, D., and J. Szmatka. 1993. "Cross-National Experimental Investigations of Elementary Theory: Implications for the Generality of Theory and the Autonomy of Social Structure." In *Advances in Group Processes*, vol. 10, forthcoming. Greenwich, Conn.: JAI Press.

Willer, D., and J. Willer. 1973. *Systematic Empiricism*. Englewood Cliffs, N.J.: Prentice-Hall.

Windelband, W. 1958 [1901]. *A History of Philosophy*, vol. 2. New York: Harper and Row.

Yamagishi, T., M. R. Gillmore, and K. S. Cook. 1988. "Network Connections and the Distribution of Power in Exchange Networks." *American Journal of Sociology* 93: 833–51.

Walker and Zelditch: Power, Legitimacy, and Authority

Bachrach, P., and M. S. Baratz. 1962. "Two Faces of Power." *American Political Science Review* 56: 947–52.

———. 1963. "Decisions and Nondecisions: An Analytical Framework." *American Political Science Review* 57: 632–42.

———. 1970. *Power and Poverty*. Oxford: Oxford University Press.

Berger, J., M. Zelditch, Jr., B. Anderson, and B. P. Cohen. 1972. "Structural Aspects of Distributive Justice: A Status-Value Formulation." In J. Berger, M. Zelditch, Jr., and B. Anderson, eds., *Sociological Theories in Progress*, vol. 2, Boston: Houghton Mifflin.

Blumstein, P. W., K. G. Carssow, H. Hall, B. Hawkins, R. Hoffman, E. Ishem, C. P. Maurer, D. Spens, J. Taylor, and D. L. Zimmerman. 1974. "Honoring of Accounts." *American Sociological Review* 39: 551–66.

Cook, K. S., and K. A. Hegtvedt. 1983. "Distributive Justice, Equity, and Equality." *Annual Review of Sociology* 9: 217–41.

Dornbusch, S. M., and W. R. Scott. 1975. *Evaluation and the Exercise of Authority*. San Francisco: Jossey-Bass.

Erlin, H. C., and B. J. McLean. 1989. "Normalizing Illegitimate Acts." Senior honors thesis, Stanford University.

Ford, J. 1980. "The Effects of Covert Power on the Inhibition of Structural Change." Ph.D. diss., Stanford University.

Ford, J., and M. Zelditch, Jr. 1984. "Why Do Individuals Nondecide Under Uncertainty?" Working Paper No. 84-10, Center for Sociological Research, Stanford University.

———. 1988. "A Test of the Law of Anticipated Reactions." *Social Psychology Quarterly* 51: 164–71.

Lineweber, D. 1981. "Power, Opportunity Costs, and the Suppression of Dissent." Ph.D. diss., Stanford University.

Lineweber, D., D. Barr-Bryan, and M. Zelditch, Jr. 1982. "Effects of a Legitimate Authority's Justification of Inequality on the Mobilization of Revolutionary Coalitions." Technical Report No. 84, Laboratory for Social Research, Stanford University.

Lowi, T. 1964. "American Business, Public Policy, Case-Studies, and Political Theory." *World Politics* 16: 667–715.

Lunde, T. 1985. "Rethinking Accounts: Effects of Uncertainty About Norms on the Justification of Acts." Paper presented at the annual meeting of the American Sociological Association, New York City.

McCarthy, J. D., and M. N. Zald. 1977. "Resource Mobilization and Social Movements: A Partial Theory." *American Journal of Sociology* 82: 1212–41.

Moore, B. 1978. *Injustice: The Social Bases of Obedience and Revolt.* New York: M. E. Sharpe.

Oberschall, A. 1973. *Social Conflict and Social Movements.* Englewood Cliffs, N.J.: Prentice-Hall.

Olson, M. 1965. *The Logic of Collective Action.* Cambridge, Mass.: Harvard University Press.

Rawls, J. 1955. "Two Concepts of Rules." *Philosophical Review* 64: 3–32.

Samuel, Y., and M. Zelditch, Jr. 1989. "Expectations, Shared Awareness, and Power." In J. Berger, M. Zelditch, Jr., and B. Anderson, eds., *Sociological Theories in Progress: New Formulations*, pp. 288–312. Newbury Park, Calif.: Sage.

Scott, M. B., and S. Lyman. 1968. "Accounts." *American Sociological Review* 33: 46–82.

Shields, N. 1979. "Accounts and Other Interpersonal Strategies in a Credibility Detracting Context." *Pacific Sociological Review* 22: 255–72.

Thomas, G., J. Hooper, and M. Zelditch, Jr. 1981. "An Experimental Study of Pressure to Change when Change is Politically Impossible." Manuscript, Stanford University.

Thomas, G., H. Walker, and M. Zelditch, Jr. 1986. "Legitimacy and Collective Action." *Social Forces* 65: 378–404.

Tilly, C. 1978. *From Mobilization to Revolution.* Reading, Mass.: Addison-Wesley.

Wagner, D. G., and J. Berger. 1985. "Do Sociological Theories Grow?" *American Journal of Sociology* 90: 697–728.

Walker, H. A. 1979. "The Effects of Legitimacy on the Inhibition of Structural Change." Ph.D. diss., Stanford University.

———. 1985. "When Equality Is Inequitable: Validity, Propriety, and Third Party Allocations." Working Paper No. 85-3, Center for Sociological Research, Stanford University.

Walker, H. A., L. Rogers, K. Lyman, and M. Zelditch, Jr. 1989. "Legitimacy and the Support of Revolutionary Coalitions." Working Paper No. 89-3, Center for Sociological Research, Stanford University.

Walker, H. A., L. Rogers, and M. Zelditch, Jr. 1988. "Legitimacy and Collective Action: A Research Note." *Social Forces* 67: 216–28.

———. 1989. "All or Nothing: Response to the Illegitimacy of Acts, Persons, and Positions." Working Paper No. 89-4, Center for Sociological Research, Stanford University.

Walker, H. A., and L. Smith-Donals. 1985. "Gender or Status: The Effects of Differences in Sex on Behavior Under Certain Conditions of Disadvantage," Working Paper No. 85-2, Center for Sociological Research, Stanford University.

Walker, H. A., G. Thomas, and M. Zelditch, Jr. 1986. "Legitimation, Endorsement, and Stability." *Social Forces* 64: 620–43.

Walker, H. A., and M. Zelditch, Jr. 1985. "Legitimacy and the Exercise of Authority: Effects of Validity and Propriety." Working Paper No. 85-1, Center for Sociological Research, Stanford University.

Zelditch, M., Jr. 1978. "Outsider's Politics: A Review Essay." *American Journal of Sociology* 83: 1514–20.

———. 1984. "Meaning, Conformity, and Control." *Journal of Mathematical Sociology* 10: 183–90.

Zelditch, M., Jr., and J. Ford. 1984. "Uncertainty, Potential Power, and Nondecisions." Working Paper No. 84-3, Center for Sociological Research, Stanford University.

Zelditch, M., Jr., E. Gilliland, and G. Thomas. 1984. "Legitimacy of Redistributive Agendas." Working Paper No. 84-9, Center for Sociological Research, Stanford University.

Zelditch, M., Jr., W. Harris, G. Thomas, and H. A. Walker. 1983. "Decisions, Nondecisions, and Metadecisions." In L. Kriesberg, ed., *Research in Social Movements, Conflict, and Change*, vol. 5, pp. 1–32. Greenwich, Conn.: JAI Press.

Zelditch, M., Jr., and H. A. Walker. 1984. "Legitimacy and the Stability of Authority." In E. J. Lawler, ed., *Advances in Group Processes*, vol. 1, pp. 1–25. Greenwich, Conn.: JAI Press.

Cohen: From Theory to Practice

Allport, G. 1954. *The Nature of Prejudice*. Cambridge, Mass.: Addison-Wesley.

Bandura, A. 1969. *Principles of Behavior Modification*. New York: Holt, Rinehart and Winston.

Benton, J. 1992. "Treating Status Problems in the Classroom: Training Teachers To Assign Competence to Students Exhibiting Low-Status Behavior in the Classroom." Ph.D. diss., Stanford University.

Berger, J. 1958. "Relations Between Performance, Rewards, and Action-Opportunities in Small Groups." Ph.D. diss., Harvard University.

Berger, J., B. P. Cohen, and M. Zelditch, Jr. 1966. "Status Characteristics and Expectation States." In J. Berger, M. Zelditch, Jr., and B. Anderson, eds., *Sociological Theories in Progress*, vol. 1, pp. 29–46. Boston: Houghton Mifflin.

Berger, J., and T. L. Conner. 1969. "Performance Expectations and Behavior in Small Groups." *Acta Sociologica* 12: 186–98.

———. 1974. "Performance Expectations and Behavior in Small Groups: A Revised Formulation." In J. Berger, T. L. Conner, and M. H. Fisek, eds., *Expectation States Theory: A Theoretical Research Program*, pp. 85–110. Cambridge, Mass.: Winthrop.

Berger, J., and M. H. Fisek. 1970. "Consistent and Inconsistent Status Characteristics and the Determination of Power and Prestige Orders." *Sociometry* 33: 287–304.

———. 1974. "A Generalization of the Theory of Status Characteristics and Expectation States." In J. Berger, T. L. Conner, and M. H. Fisek, eds., *Expectation States Theory: A Theoretical Research Program*, pp. 163–205. Cambridge, Mass.: Winthrop.

Berger, J., M. H. Fisek, R. Z. Norman, and M. Zelditch, Jr. 1977. *Status Characteristics and Social Interaction: An Expectation-States Approach*. New York: Elsevier.

Bower, B. 1990. "The Effect of a Multiple Ability Treatment on Status and Learning in the Cooperative Social Studies Classroom." Ph.D. diss., Stanford University.

Cohen, B. P. 1989. *Developing Sociological Knowledge: Theory and Method*. 2d ed. Chicago: Nelson-Hall.

Cohen, E. G. 1972. "Interracial Interaction Disability." *Human Relations* 25: 9–24.

————. 1982. "Expectation States and Interracial Interaction in School Settings." *Annual Review of Sociology* 8: 209–35. Palo Alto, Calif.: Annual Reviews.

————. 1984a. "The Desegregated School: Problems in Status Power and Inter-ethnic Climate." In N. Miller and M. Brewer, eds., *Groups in Contact: The Psychology of Desegregation*, pp. 77–96. New York: Academic Press.

————. 1984b. "Talking and Working Together: Status, Interaction, and Learning." In P. Peterson and L. C. Wilkinson, eds., *The Social Context of Instruction: Group Organization and Processes*, pp. 171–87. New York: Academic Press.

————. 1986. *Designing Groupwork: Strategies for Heterogeneous Classrooms*. New York: Teachers College Press.

————. 1988. "Producing Equal Status Behavior in Cooperative Learning." Paper presented at the Conference of the International Association for the Study of Cooperation in Education, Kibbutz Shefayim, Israel. July 1–4, 1988.

Cohen, E. G., T. Deal, J. W. Meyer, and W. R. Scott. 1979. "Technology and Teaming in the Elementary School." *Sociology of Education* 52: 20–33.

Cohen, E. G., and E. DeAvila. 1983. "Learning To Think in Math and Science: Improving Local Education for Minority Children." Final report to the Johnson Foundation. Stanford University School of Education.

Cohen, E. G., and J. Intili. 1981. "Interdependence and Management in Bilingual Classrooms." Final report to NIE: Grant #G-80-0217. Stanford University School of Education.

————. 1982. "Interdependence and Management in Bilingual Classrooms." Final report, NIE Contract #NIE-G-81-0217. Center for Educational Research, Stanford University.

Cohen, E. G., M. Katz, and M. R. Lohman. 1976. "Center for Interracial Cooperation: A Field Experiment." *Sociology of Education* 48: 47–58.

Cohen, E. G., M. Lohmann, K. P. Hall, D. Lucero, and S. Roper. 1970. "Expectation Training I: Altering the Effects of a Racial Status Characteristic." Technical Report No. 2, Stanford University School of Education.

Cohen, E. G., and R. Lotan. 1990. "Beyond the Workshop: Conditions for First Year Implementation." Paper presented at the Conference of the International Association for the Study of Cooperation in Education, Baltimore, Md., July 10, 1990.

Cohen, E. G., R. Lotan, and L. Catanzarite. 1988. "Can Expectations for Competence Be Treated in the Classroom?" In M. Webster, Jr., and M. Foschi, eds., *Status Generalization: New Theory and Research*, pp. 27–54. Stanford, Calif.: Stanford University Press.

Cohen, E. G., R. Lotan, and C. Leechor. 1989. "Can Classrooms Learn?" *Sociology of Education* 62: 75–94.

Cohen, E. G., and S. Roper. 1972. "Modification of Interracial Interaction Disability: Application of Status Characteristics Theory." *American Sociological Review* 37: 643–55.

Cohen, E. G., and S. Sharan. 1980. "Modifying Status Relations in Israeli Youth." *Journal of Cross-Cultural Psychology* 11: 364–84.

Cook, T. 1974. "Producing Equal Status Interaction Between Indian and White Boys in British Columbia: An Application of Expectation Training." Ph.D. diss., Stanford University.

Dahl, R. F. 1989. "Organizational Characteristics and Conditions Affecting the Continuation of a Complex Instructional Technology." Ph.D. diss., Stanford University.

Dornbusch, S. M., and W. R. Scott. 1975. *Evaluation and the Exercise of Authority.* San Francisco: Jossey-Bass.

Ellis, N. 1987. "Collaborative Interaction and Logistical Support for Teacher Change." Ph.D. diss., Stanford University.

Freese, L. 1976. "The Generalization of Specific Performance Expectations." *Sociometry* 39: 194–200.

Galbraith, J. 1973. *Designing Complex Organizations.* Reading, Mass.: Addison-Wesley.

Gonzales, J. T. 1982. "Instructor Evaluations and Academic Effort: The Chicano in College." Ph.D. diss., Stanford University.

Hoffman, D., and E. G. Cohen. 1972. "An Exploratory Study To Determine the Effects of Generalized Performance Expectations upon Activity and Influence of Students Engaged in a Group Simulation Game." Paper presented at the meeting of the American Educational Research Association, Chicago.

Humphreys, P., and J. Berger. 1981. "Theoretical Consequences of the Status Characteristics Formulation." *American Journal of Sociology* 86: 953–83.

Katz, I., and L. Benjamin. 1960. "Effects of White Authoritarianism in Biracial Work Groups." *Journal of Abnormal and Social Psychology* 61: 448–556.

Katz, I., J. Goldston, and L. Benjamin. 1958. "Behavior and Productivity in Biracial Work Groups." *Human Relations* 11: 123–41.

Leechor, C. 1988. "How High and Low Achieving Students Differentially Benefit from Working Together in Cooperative Groups." Ph.D. diss., Stanford University.

Lotan, R. A. 1985. "Understanding the Theories: Training Teachers for Implementation of Complex Instructional Technology." Ph.D. diss., Stanford University.

―――. 1989. "Conditions for Effective Collegial Evaluation Systems." Paper presented at the annual meeting of the Sociology of Education Association, Asilomar, Calif., Feb. 12–13, 1989.

March, J. G., and H. A. Simon. 1958. *Organizations.* New York: Wiley.

Markovsky, B., R. Smith, and J. Berger. 1984. "Do Status Interventions Persist?" *American Sociological Review* 49: 373–82.

Meyer, J. W., and B. Rowan. 1977. "Institutionalized Organizations: Formal Structure as Myth and Ceremony." *American Journal of Sociology* 83: 340–63.

―――. 1978. "The Structure of Educational Organizations." In M. W. Meyer and Associates, eds., *Environments and Organizations,* pp. 199–215. San Francisco: Jossey-Bass.

Morris, R. 1979. "A Normative Intervention To Equalize Participation in Task-Oriented Groups." Ph.D. diss., Stanford University.

Parchment, C. 1989. "The Role of the Principal in the Implementation of a Complex Instructional Program." Ph.D. diss., Stanford University.

Perrow, C. 1967. "A Framework for the Comparative Analysis of Organizations." *American Sociological Review* 32: 194–208.

Pugh, M. D., and R. Wahrman. 1983. "Neutralizing Sexism in Mixed-Sex Groups: Do Women Have To Be Better Than Men?" *American Journal of Sociology* 88: 746–62.

Riordan, C., and J. Ruggiero. 1980. "Producing Equal-Status Interaction: A Replication." *Social Psychology Quarterly* 43: 131–36.

Robbins, A. 1977. "Fostering Equal Status Interaction Through the Establishment of Consistent Staff Behavior and Appropriate Situational Norms." Ph.D. diss., Stanford University.

Roper, S. S., and D. E. Hoffman. 1986. "Collegial Support for Professional Improvement: The Stanford Collegial Evaluation Program." *Oregon School Study Council Bulletin* 29: 1–25.

Rosenholtz, S. J. 1985. "Modifying Status Expectations in the Traditional Classroom." In J. Berger and M. Zelditch, Jr., eds., *Status, Rewards, and Influence: How Expectations Organize Behavior*, pp. 445–70. San Francisco: Jossey-Bass.

Rosenholtz, S. J., and E. G. Cohen. 1985. "Activating Ethnic Status." In J. Berger and M. Zelditch, Jr., eds., *Status, Rewards, and Influence: How Expectations Organize Behavior*, pp. 430–44. San Francisco: Jossey-Bass.

Tammivaara, J. S. 1982. "The Effects of Task Structure on Beliefs About Competence and Participation in Small Groups." *Sociology of Education* 55: 212–22.

Thompson, J. D. 1967. *Organizations in Action*. New York: McGraw-Hill.

Webster, M. A., Jr., and D. R. Entwisle. 1974. "Raising Children's Expectations for Their Own Performance: A Classroom Application." In J. Berger, T. L. Conner, and M. H. Fisek, eds., *Expectation States Theory: A Theoretical Research Program*, pp. 211–43. Cambridge, Mass.: Winthrop.

Webster, M. A., Jr., and B. I. Sobieszek. 1974. *Sources of Self-Evaluation: A Formal Theory of Significant Others and Social Influence*. New York: Wiley.

Fararo and Skvoretz: Methods and Problems

Alexander, J. C. 1982. *Theoretical Logic in Sociology*. Vol. 1, *Positivism, Presuppositions and Current Controversies*. Berkeley: University of California Press.

Alexander, J. C., B. Giesen, R. Munch, and N. J. Smelser, eds. 1987. *The Micro-Macro Link*. Berkeley: University of California Press.

Axelrod, R. 1984. *The Evolution of Cooperation*. New York: Basic Books.

Axten, N., and T. J. Fararo. 1977. "The Information Processing Representation of Institutionalized Social Action." In P. Krishnan, ed., *Mathematical Models of Sociology*, pp. 35–77. Keele, U.K.: Sociological Review Monograph 24. Reprint. Totowa, N.J.: Rowan and Littlefield, 1979.

Blau, P. M. 1977. *Inequality and Heterogeneity*. New York: Free Press.

———. 1988. "Structures of Social Positions and Structures of Social Relations." In J. H. Turner, ed., *Theory Building in Sociology: Assessing Theoretical Cumulation*, pp. 43–59. Newbury Park, Calif.: Sage.

Braithwaite, R. 1953. *Scientific Explanation*. Cambridge, Eng.: Cambridge University Press.

Bush, R., and F. Mosteller. 1955. *Stochastic Models for Learning*. New York: Wiley.

Cartwright, D., and F. Harary. 1956. "Structural Balance: A Generalization of Heider's Theory." *Psychological Review* 63: 277–93.

Cross, J. G. 1983. *A Theory of Adaptive Economic Behavior*. New York: Cambridge University Press.

Dewey, J. 1938. *Logic: The Theory of Inquiry*. New York: Holt.

Emerson, R. M. 1972. "Exchange Theory, Part I: A Psychological Basis for Social Exchange." In J. Berger, M. Zelditch, Jr., and B. Anderson, eds., *Sociological Theories in Progress*, vol. 2, pp. 38–57. Boston: Houghton Mifflin.

———. 1987. "Toward a Theory of Value in Social Exchange." In K. S. Cook, ed., *Social Exchange Theory*, pp. 11–46. Newbury Park, Calif.: Sage.

Emerson, R. M., K. S. Cook, M. R. Gillmore, and T. Yamagishi. 1983. "Valid Predictions from Invalid Comparisons: Response to Heckathorn." *Social Forces* 61: 1232–47.

England, J. L. 1973. "Mathematical Models of Two-Party Negotiations." *Behavioral Science* 18: 189–97.

Fararo, T. J. 1973. *Mathematical Sociology*. New York: Wiley.

———. 1978. "An Introduction to Catastrophes." *Behavioral Science* 23: 291–317.

———. 1987a. "Concrescence and Social Order: Process Philosophical Foundations of Sociological Theory." In J. Wilson, ed., *Current Perspectives in Social Theory*, vol. 8, pp. 77–121. Greenwich, Conn.: JAI Press.

———. 1987b. "Generativity in Theoretical Model-Building." In E. J. Lawler and B. Markovsky, eds. *Advances in Group Processes*, vol. 4, pp. 137–70. Greenwich, Conn.: JAI Press.

———. 1989a. *The Meaning of General Theoretical Sociology: Tradition and Formalization*. ASA Rose Monograph. New York: Cambridge University Press.

———. 1989b. "The Spirit of Unification in Sociological Theory." *Sociological Theory* 7: 175–90.

Fararo, T. J., and J. Skvoretz. 1984. "Institutions as Production Systems." *Journal of Mathematical Sociology* 10: 117–82.

———. 1986a. "Actions and Institution, Network and Function: The Cybernetic Concept of Social Structure." *Sociological Forum* 1: 219–50.

———. 1986b. "E-State Structuralism: A Theoretical Method." *American Sociological Review* 51: 591–602.

———. 1987. "Unification Research Programs: Integrating Two Structural Theories." *American Journal of Sociology* 92: 1183–1209.

Granovetter, M. 1973. "The Strength of Weak Ties." *American Journal of Sociology* 83: 1420–43.

Hacking, I. 1983. *Representing and Intervening*. New York: Cambridge University Press.

Harré, R., and P. Secord. 1973. *The Explanation of Social Behavior*. Totowa, N.J.: Littlefield.

Hechter, M. 1987. *Principles of Group Solidarity*. Berkeley: University of California Press.

———. 1989. "Rational Choice Foundations of Social Order." In J. H. Turner, ed., *Theory Building in Sociology: Assessing Theoretical Cumulation*, pp. 60–81. Newbury Park, Calif.: Sage.

Heckathorn, D. D. 1980. "A Unified Model for Bargaining and Conflict." *Behavioral Science* 25: 261–84.

———. 1983a. "Extensions of Power-Dependence Theory: The Concept of Resistance." *Social Forces* 61: 1206–31.

———. 1983b. "Valid and Invalid Interpersonal Utility Comparisons: Response to Emerson, Cook, Gillmore, and Yamagishi." *Social Forces* 61: 1248–59.

Heider, F. 1946. "Attitudes and Cognitive Organization." *Journal of Psychology* 21: 107–12.

Hempel, C. G. 1965. *Aspects of Scientific Explanation.* New York: Free Press.

Jasso, G. 1988. "Principles of Theoretical Analysis." *Sociological Theory* 6: 1–20.

Kaplan, A. 1964. *The Conduct of Inquiry.* San Francisco: Chandler.

Lawler, E. J. 1989. "Power Processes in Bargaining." Paper presented at the meeting of the Midwest Sociological Society, St. Louis.

Lawler, E. J., and S. B. Bacharach. 1987. "Comparison of Dependence and Punitive Forms of Power." *Social Forces* 66: 446–62.

Leinhardt, S., ed. 1977. *Social Networks: An Emerging Paradigm.* New York: Academic Press.

Leplin, J., ed. 1984. *Scientific Realism.* Berkeley: University of California Press.

Lorrain, F., and H. C. White. 1971. "Structural Equivalence of Individuals in Social Networks." *Journal of Mathematical Sociology* 1: 49–80.

March, J. G. 1986. "Bounded Rationality, Ambiguity, and the Engineering of Choice." In J. Elster, ed., *Rational Choice,* pp. 142–70. New York: New York University Press.

Markovsky, B. 1988. "From Expectation States to Macro Processes." In M. Webster, Jr., and M. Foschi, eds., *Status Generalization: New Theory and Research,* pp. 351–65. Stanford, Calif.: Stanford University Press.

Marsden, P. V., and E. O. Laumann. 1984. "Mathematical Ideas in Social Structural Analysis." In T. J. Fararo, ed., *Mathematical Ideas and Sociological Theory,* pp. 53–76. New York: Gordon and Breach.

Marwell, G., P. E. Oliver, and R. Prahl. 1988. "Social Networks and Collective Action: A Theory of the Critical Mass. III." *American Journal of Sociology* 94: 502–34.

Mayhew, B. H. 1980. "Structuralism Versus Individualism: Part I, Shadowboxing in the Dark." *Social Forces* 59: 335–75.

Merton, R. K. 1968 [1949]. *Social Theory and Social Structure.* New York: Free Press.

Molm, L. D. 1985. "Relative Effects of Individual Dependencies: Further Tests of the Relation Between Power Imbalance and Power Use." *Social Forces* 63: 810–37.

———. 1987. "Linking Power Structure and Power Use." In K. S. Cook, ed., *Social Exchange Theory,* pp. 101–29. Newbury Park, Calif.: Sage.

Nadel, S. F. 1951. *Foundations of Social Anthropology.* New York: Free Press.

———. 1957. *The Theory of Social Structure.* London: Cohen and West.

Newcomb, T. M. 1953. "An Approach to the Study of Communicative Acts." *Psychological Review* 60: 393–404.

Newell, A., and H. A. Simon. 1972. *Human Problem Solving.* Englewood Cliffs, N.J.: Prentice-Hall.

Oliver, P. E., and G. Marwell. 1988. "The Paradox of Group Size in Collective Action: A Theory of the Critical Mass. II." *American Sociological Review* 53: 1–8.

Rapoport, A. 1960. *Fights, Games, and Debates.* Ann Arbor: University of Michigan Press.

Ridgeway, C. L. 1991. "The Social Construction of Status Value: Gender and Other Nominal Characteristics." *Social Forces* 70: 367–86.

Skvoretz, J. 1984. "Languages and Grammars of Action and Interaction: Some Further Results." *Behavioral Science* 29: 81–97.

Skvoretz, J., and T. J. Fararo. 1989. "Action Structures and Sociological Action Theory." *Journal of Mathematical Sociology* 14: 111–37.

Skvoretz, J., D. Willer, and T. J. Fararo. 1993. "Towards Models of Power Development in Exchange Networks." *Sociological Perspectives* 36: 2.

Toulmin, S. 1953. *The Philosophy of Science.* London: Hutchison.

Von Neumann, J., and O. Morgenstern. 1947. *The Theory of Games and Economic Behavior.* 2d ed. Princeton, N.J.: Princeton University Press.

Wagner, D. G., and J. Berger. 1985. "Do Sociological Theories Grow?" *American Journal of Sociology* 90: 697–728.

Walker, H. A., L. Rogers, and M. Zelditch, Jr. 1988. "Legitimacy and Collective Action: A Research Note." *Social Forces* 67: 216–28.

Whitehead, A. N. 1978. *Process and Reality.* Corrected ed. New York: Free Press.

Willer, D. 1981. "Quantity and Network Structure." In D. Willer and B. Anderson, eds., *Networks, Exchange and Coercion,* pp. 109–27. New York: Elsevier.

———. 1984. "Analysis and Composition as Theoretic Procedures." *Journal of Mathematical Sociology* 10: 241–70.

———. 1987. *Theory and the Experimental Investigation of Social Structures.* New York: Gordon and Breach.

Index

In this index an "f" after a number indicates a separate reference on the next page, and an "ff" indicates separate references on the next two pages. A continuous discussion over two or more pages is indicated by a span of page numbers, e.g., "pp. 57–58." *Passim* is used for a cluster of references in close but not consecutive sequence.

Library of Congress Cataloging–in–Publication Data

Theoretical research programs: studies in the growth of theory/
edited by Joseph Berger and Morris Zelditch, Jr.
    p.   cm.
Includes bibliographical references and index.
ISBN 0-8047-2230-7 (cloth : acid-free paper) :
1. Sociology—Research. 2. Sociology—Philosophy.
I. Berger, Joseph, 1924–   . II. Zelditch, Morris.
HM48.T54 1993
301'.01'–dc20
93-12907
CIP

This book is printed on acid-free paper.